Norm Smith

X-198

An Introduction
to Quantitative Methods
for Decision Making

An Introduction to Quantitative Methods for Decision Making

SECOND EDITION

Richard E. Trueman
California State University, Northridge

HOLT, RINEHART AND WINSTON
New York Chicago San Francisco Atlanta
Dallas Montreal Toronto London Sydney

Library of Congress Cataloging in Publication Data
Trueman, Richard E
   An introduction to quantitative methods for
decision making.
   (Series in quantitative methods for decision making)
   1. Decision-making—Mathematical models.
2. Statistical decision.   I. Title.
HD69.D4T78   1977   658.4'03   76-55008
ISBN 0-03-018391-X

Printed in the United States of America
7890 032 1234567890

To my mother and the memory of my father

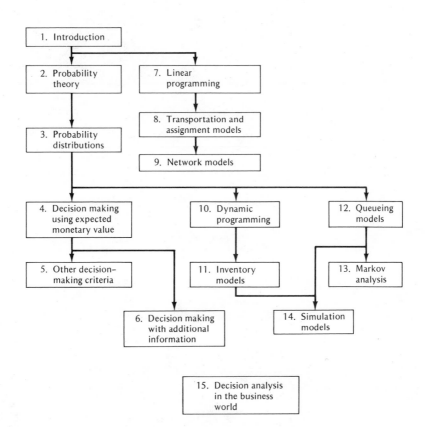

1. Introduction

2. Probability theory

7. Linear programming

8. Transportation and assignment models

3. Probability distributions

9. Network models

4. Decision making using expected monetary value

10. Dynamic programming

12. Queueing models

5. Other decision-making criteria

11. Inventory models

13. Markov analysis

6. Decision making with additional information

14. Simulation models

15. Decision analysis in the business world

TEXT ORGANIZATION

CONTENTS

PREFACE

In the second edition of this text, an overall effort has been made to further clarify a number of highly detailed topics, in many cases by incorporating simpler introductory examples. The introductory chapter has been considerably expanded, presenting a short history of decision analysis and an introduction to the primary emphasis in this text, the development and analysis of mathematical models for decision making. Two new chapters have been added, the first on Markov analysis and the second a final wrapup chapter presenting an overview of decision analysis in the business world. One chapter, on the very specialized topic of Bayesian decision analysis using continuous probability distributions, has been deleted, although an appreciable portion of this material was placed in the chapter introducing Bayesian decision analysis. In a number of the chapters, a section on practical applications has been added, generally detailing the successful implementation of a particular type of mathematical model in situations involving important business problems.

This book's primary objective is to introduce the reader to a number of the more important mathematical approaches and specialized techniques which can be used in the analysis of basic business problems requiring quantitative decisions. The aim is to develop an understanding of problem-solving methods, based upon a careful discussion of problem formulation, mathematical analysis, and solution procedures, utilizing numerous examples involving relatively believable business situations. Graphical presentations are frequently employed to clarify mathematical concepts and to simplify problem solving. For a number of the topics covered, sensitivity analysis is employed to determine the range over which a given solution is optimal and to explore the effect of errors or changes in input data values.

The first part of the text starts with the development of probability concepts and then covers in detail, discrete and continuous probability distributions, including subjective probability distributions. The next two chapters develop the approaches to decision making under uncertainty using expected value analysis, considering both monetary and utility values. This material lays the foundation for Bayesian statistical decision theory, the study of the economics of decision making when additional information is available.

The development and analysis of operations research models is the subject of the second part of the text. Topical coverage related to decision making under certainty includes linear programming, with problem formulation and post-optimality analysis of computer solutions stressed, transportation and assignment problems, network models, and deterministic dynamic programming and inventory models. Topics involving decision making under uncertainty include project scheduling, probabilistic dynamic programming and inventory models, queueing theory, Markov analysis, and simulation models.

The text contains enough material for a two-semester course in Quantitative Methods in Business at the upper-division undergraduate level or a one-semester MBA course, with some topics omitted. It could also be used for a one-quarter or one-semester course in Decision Theory or Decision Analysis (perhaps including linear programming), or a one-semester course in Operations Research. This text is designed to be essentially self-contained. Mathematical and probability concepts are introduced as needed, and, although mathematical rigor is retained, calculus is not required. A basic knowledge of algebra is assumed, and an introductory statistics course would undoubtedly be helpful, but it is by no means a prerequisite. Appendices at the end of the text include tables of the normal, cumulative binomial, and cumulative Poisson probability distributions, as well as a table of the normal loss integral and tables of random numbers and random variates.

I would like to express my appreciation to editor Rosalind Sackoff for her dedicated direction of this project, to consulting editor Robert Winkler for valued advice, and to reviewers of the second edition, in particular Professors Donald Aucamp, Southern Illinois University; Christopher Barry, University of Florida; Philip Carter, Michigan State University; Robert Clickner, Temple University; Mal Golden, University of Miami, Fla.; Paul Lerman, Fairleigh Dickinson University; Joe Moder, University of Miami, Fla.; William Roach, University of Kansas; Lloyd Rosenberg, Baruch College; Bruce Skalbeck, University of Wisconsin-Oshkosh; Richard Withycombe, University of Montana; Bruce Woodworth, Oregon State University. Thanks also go to my colleague Abe Feinberg, who contributed a substantial number of new chapter exercises for the second edition. I am most grateful for the encouragement, patience, and cooperation of my wife, Margaret, over the six-year period of this project.

R. E. T.

Woodland Hills, California
November 1976

An Introduction
to Quantitative Methods
for Decision Making

INTRODUCTION

1.1 NEED FOR QUANTITATIVE APPROACHES TO DECISION MAKING

The complexity of today's business operations, the high costs of technology, materials, and labor, as well as competitive pressures and the shortened time frame in which many important decisions must be made, all contribute to the difficulty of making effective decisions. For all these reasons, the need of the decision maker for every possible aid in the decision process has never been more apparent. The question as to what constitutes an "effective" decision is a difficult one to answer, because it depends on so many different economic, social, and political factors and viewpoints. Very few business decisions are made, however, which are not primarily based on quantitative measures of some nature. For example, a decision on the location of a new manufacturing plant would be primarily based on such economic factors as construction costs, prevailing labor rates, taxes, energy and pollution control costs, marketing transportation costs, and related factors. On the other hand, a decision as to the location of a new federal regional hospital may be heavily influenced by national, state, and local politics. Even in this case, quantitative measures, such as the number of voters expected to favor a given location (and who can thus be expected to be favorably inclined toward a politician promoting that location), may well play an important part in the final decision. An understanding of the applicability of quantitative methods to business decision making is, therefore, of fundamental importance to the business student.

In a very real sense, quantitative methods, along with their almost indispensable companion, the high-speed digital computer, represent a new form of applied science

1

technology. Decision analysis (also known as decision science, management science, operations research, and a few other names) can be viewed as a discipline that has evolved to aid the decision maker to better exploit this technology. (The author prefers "decision analysis" as a general term in preference to either "operations research" or "management science," because the types of problems encountered are always concerned with decisions, whereas these problems do not always involve research into operations or aspects of the science of management. For all practical purposes, these three terms can be used interchangeably.) As compared to business decision making done largely on a subjective basis in the past, relying heavily on the decision maker's previous experience and intuition, decision analysis facilitates the comparison of complicated alternatives, permits examination of the sensitivity of the solution to changes or errors in numerical values, and encourages rational decision making based on the best available approaches and techniques. It must be emphasized, however, that timely and competent decision analysis should be an aid to the decision maker's judgment, not a substitute for it.

1.2 SHORT HISTORY OF MODERN DECISION ANALYSIS

What we consider modern decision analysis really had its origins in the development of operations research during World War II. Research into wartime operations by multidisciplinary teams was initiated in Great Britain, with many important contributions also made by the United States. The "operations research" approach developed was to analyze the quantitative aspects of repetitive operational situations with a view to discerning the most important aspects, those having the most effect on these situations. Then, possible solutions would be proposed, analyzed, tested, evaluated, and modified when necessary as they were implemented. The techniques developed were generally tailored to the problem at hand, as illustrated by the following examples, taken from the first published book on operations research, by Morse and Kimball.[1]

1. Convoys versus submarines   During the years 1941 and 1942, the Germans introduced so-called wolf-pack tactics into their submarine operations against North Atlantic convoys. An analysis of the data available from wolf-pack U-boat attacks revealed two important facts: (1) the number of Allied ships lost per attack appeared to be independent of the convoy size, and (2) the exchange rate (the ratio of U-boats sunk to Allied merchant ships sunk) was approximately proportional to the square of the number of escort ships. As the number of escorts was increased, the squared effect was due to a decrease in the number of merchant ships lost and an increase in the number of U-boats sunk. Based on this analysis, the average size of convoys was increased, along with the average number of escorts per convoy. The actual benefit was even greater than anticipated, because the exchange rate increased to the point

[1]Philip M. Morse and George E. Kimball, *Methods of Operations Research*, The Technology Press of M.I.T. and John Wiley & Sons, Inc., New York, 1951.

where it became unprofitable for the Germans to attack North Atlantic convoys, so the U-boats went elsewhere. This was a turning point in the "Battle of the Atlantic."

2. Antiaircraft guns for merchant ships   In the Mediterranean, early in the war, a large number of British merchant ships were seriously damaged or sunk by low-level aircraft attacks. The obvious decision was to equip the ships with antiaircraft guns and crews. This was expensive, and antiaircraft guns were also in short supply, but a number of ships were so armed. After about a year, during which it was demonstrated that, with single guns and crews with little training, the enemy plane was shot down in only about 4 percent of the attacks, it appeared that the installations were not worth their cost. However, a more penetrating analysis discerned that the measure of effectiveness was not the number of attacking planes shot down, but the reduction in the attacking plane's effectiveness because of the antiaircraft fire. An analysis of attacks in which antiaircraft guns were fired and where they were not fired (or the ship was not armed) showed that 10 percent of the ships attacked were sunk in the former case, while 25 percent were sunk in the latter case. Clearly, the antiaircraft guns more than paid for themselves if they saved 15 percent of the ships attacked from being sunk.

After the war ended, an effort was made to apply the operations research approach, which had been so effective in a military context, to problems in business and industry. In 1947, George Dantzig was responsible for developing the simplex algorithm (computational technique) for solving linear programming problems. Over the past thirty years, linear programming has probably been the most valuable and widely used decision analysis techinque, thanks to the advent of the high-speed computer and sophisticated extensions of the original technique which facilitate the efficient solution of very large problems. During the 1950s, there was a steady growth in nonmilitary applications of operations research, along with a strong interest in professional development and education in this new field. Degree-granting college programs in operations research came into being, generally in schools of engineering or business administration. It was at this period that America's two major professional societies for decision analysis were formed. The Operations Research Society of America (ORSA) was founded in 1952, and its journal *Operations Research* began publication in 1953. In that year, The Institute of Management Sciences (TIMS) was founded, with its journal *Management Sciences* first appearing in 1954.

Much pioneering work was done at this time in developing new quantitative approaches to the solution of business and industrial problems. For example, in 1954, Leslie Edie published his detailed and innovative study relating to the efficient allocation of collectors to toll booths for the Port of New York Authority.[2] After establishing the fact that traffic arrivals over given time periods were essentially random in nature, Edie utilized queueing theory to determine the relationship between traffic volumes and mean waiting time as a function of the number and type (left hand or right hand) of toll booths. This was one of the first recognized applica-

---

[2]Leslie C. Edie, "Traffic Delays at Toll Booths," *Journal of the Operations Research Society of America*, Vol. 2, No. 2, May 1954, pp. 107–138.

tions of queueing theory to a problem area other than those involving the operation of telephone systems, whose analysis had been spurred by the publication in 1909 of *The Theory of Probabilities and Telephone Conversations* by the Danish mathematician A. K. Erlang. Implementation of the toll booth study's recommendations resulted in development of a systematic procedure to schedule toll booths and collectors so as to significantly decrease congestion delays.

In 1958, the project scheduling techniques of PERT (Project Evaluation and Review Technique) and CPM (Critical Path Method) were developed. It is interesting to note that the development of PERT and CPM occurred independently and almost concurrently, indicating the real need at that time for efficient methods of scheduling and monitoring lengthy, complex, and expensive projects. PERT, the better known of the two techniques, was the outgrowth of a United States Navy project for monitoring and controlling research and development (R and D) progress for the Polaris Fleet Ballistic Missile (FBM) program,[3] which was a very large program with many interrelated activities, some with a duration measured in years. The complexity of the interrelationships between the thousands of project activities made efficient overall coordination all but impossible. Implementation of PERT, which viewed the R and D program as a network of interrelated tasks to be completed according to a properly ordered sequence, gave FBM program management the capability to evaluate their progress at any point in time, to identify possible schedule slippages in future time periods, to take timely action to avoid or reduce such slippages, and to consider the effect of proposed or required changes on specified completion dates. By mid-1959, PERT was being used to cover some twenty-three networks, containing three thousand tasks, of the FBM weapons system. It is estimated that the use of PERT shortened the completion time of the FBM project by about two years, leading to savings of many millions of dollars. PERT became a standard management tool in the Navy and other service organizations, and improved versions of PERT and CMP quickly found their way into civilian use, in such areas as construction projects, installation of data-processing equipment, and shipbuilding.

By the 1960s, operations research groups were organized in a number of large companies, generally reporting at or near the highest level in the organization. National consulting firms specializing in the decision analysis area had been formed, and educational and professional development programs had expanded at all levels. In 1969, a third professional decision analysis society, the American Institute for Decision Sciences (AIDS), came into being and in 1970 started publishing the journal *Decision Sciences*.

Discussion of the current situation in the late 1970s is deferred until the final chapter, where we can build on material to be covered in the intervening chapters.

[3]D. G. Malcolm, J. H. Roseboom, C. E. Clark, and W. Fazar, "Application of a Technique for Research and Development Program Evaluation," *Operations Research*, Vol. 7, No. 5, September–October 1959, pp. 646–669.

1.3 BUILDING MATHEMATICAL MODELS

In this text, we will concentrate on the development and application of specific quantitative approaches to the determination of the optimal choice among alternative actions, including the evaluation of specific numerical values where required. In order to do this, we must construct what are called *mathematical models*.

A mathematical model of a business problem is analogous to a physical model of a physical system (for example, a miniature railroad layout or the representation of astronomical phenomena by a planetarium's projectors). Both types of models show the relationship of constituent parts and what occurs when certain factors change. However, the mathematical model is abstract, while the physical model is concrete. In addition, compared to physical models, mathematical models generally require more effort to understand but are easier to manipulate and to change.

The most common type of mathematical model is an equation or a set of equations and/or inequality relationships which express the interrelationships among the various factors of the particular problem under study. For example, suppose that we are told that the expense of making a certain customer marketing survey consists of a fixed cost of $50 to set up and administer the survey plus a cost of $5 for each customer contacted. A mathematical model of this situation would be constructed by first defining the variables in the problem by algebraic symbols. Suppose we use the following notation:

Let N = number of customers contacted
C = total survey cost, in dollars.

The mathematical model would then relate N and C as follows:

$$C = 50 + 5N.$$

At this point, we could make the model much more general by allowing for any combination of fixed cost and cost associated with each customer contacted. To do this,

let F = fixed cost of setting up and administering the survey, in dollars
E = cost for each customer contacted, in dollars,

The mathematical model now becomes

$$C = F + EN.$$

This is clearly a more flexible model than the previous one, because we are allowing for any cost values which may be supplied, not just the given values of $50 and $5.

With a little imagination, we can extend this model to any situation where we have a total cost which is a function of the quantity of an item and which consists of a fixed cost plus a variable cost directly proportional to the number of units of that item. For example, a manufacturer's cost to produce a new product could involve the fixed cost of purchasing new equipment plus a variable cost of materials and labor directly proportional to the number of units produced. With minor changes, this simple model could also be used for profit problems, breakeven analysis, and other applications.

We can now see some of the advantages of formulating a mathematical model.

1. Relationships between the various factors are more easily described and comprehended than by a verbal description.
2. The mathematical relationships may lead to insights into more general problems and even problems that appear on the surface to be unrelated.
3. The problem can be viewed in its entirety, with all the variables being considered simultaneously.
4. The model indicates the quantitative data needed to analyze the problem.
5. It may be possible to utilize powerful mathematical techniques which might appear unrelated to the problem at hand.
6. When considerable computational effort is necessary, such that a computer must be used, mathematical models are essential if a computer program must be written.

One of the major difficulties encountered by many students in their work with mathematical models is that of translating from the prose of a problem description to the proper mathematical formulation. For instance, inequality relationships often seem confusing, so a few examples may be helpful to show what such translations might look like.

Prose: "The fraction of defective items may not exceed 3 percent."
Translation: Let f = fraction of defective items.
Since f cannot exceed 0.03, it may be less than 0.03 or it may be equal to 0.03; in symbols,
$f \leq 0.03$. ("$\leq$" is verbalized as "less than or equal to.")
Prose: "The number of attendees at the meeting will be at least 30 but will not exceed 35."
Translation: Let n = number of attendees.
The value of n must fall between 30 and 35, inclusive.
$30 \leq n \leq 35$, *or* $29 < n < 36$, since n is an integer.
Prose: "More than 9 spares will be required."
Translation: Let s = number of spares required.
$s > 9$, *or*, since s must be an integer,
$s \geq 10$. ("$\geq$" means "greater than or equal to.")

In general, the first step is to read the given statement *very carefully;* the second step is to define the variable of interest; and the third step is to express the correct mathematical relationship. We will have more to say about the problem-solving process later in this chapter.

It is of considerable importance to separate conceptually the variables in a given problem into two broad classes, namely, controllable variables and uncontrollable variables. Controllable variables are, logically enough, those whose value is a matter of choice, often within prescribed limits. Uncontrollable variables are those over which one has no control. Thus, the number of copies of a certain monthly magazine stocked by a book store is certainly controllable, as is the magazine's selling price, within reasonable limits. On the other hand, the price the store pays for the magazine is not under its control, nor is the customer demand for the magazine (although demand might be stimulated by a price cut or inhibited by a noncompetitive price).

In solving mathematical models, we generally attempt to arrive at an optimal solution, based on some criterion or criteria for optimality. The major emphasis in this text is on quantitative measures of optimality (sometimes called measures of effectiveness) involving costs and/or profits, since most decisions will eventually be based upon economic considerations, like it or not, as graphically demonstrated by the financial trials and tribulations of many large cities.

The general approach to the development of mathematical models for decision making can be briefly stated as follows:

1. Formulate the problem. Determine the variables involved and categorize them into those over which you have no control and those over which you have control. The latter are often called decision variables. Specify all relevant constraints, such as financial limitations, production requirements, deadlines, and so forth.
2. Establish the criterion or criteria for optimality. This involves the definition of an appropriate goal or goals. In our work, optimal solutions will frequently involve either profit maximization or cost minimization.
3. Develop the model. Determine the specific mathematical relationships which exist among the different variables. These are usually stated in the form of an equation or a set of equations.
4. Perform the analysis. Substitute the values of the uncontrollable variables in the mathematical model and determine the values of the decision variables which lead to an optimal solution, according to the optimality criteria chosen. (The actual solution procedure will vary according to the type of model, as we will see throughout the book.) Furthermore, when the value of any uncontrollable variable is subject to change or is not known with any degree of accuracy, the solution can be reevaluated over a range of feasible changes in this variable. This type of analysis is called *sensitivity analysis*, and it is designed to explore the sensitivity of the solution to possible changes in a particular uncontrollable variable.

In practice, the development of a mathematical model should be strongly influenced by the objective for which the model is being constructed. As we have noted, our objective will be to aid a decision maker in choosing among several alternatives and/or in determining one or more specific numerical values. The model should be as simple as possible, consistent with a realistic approach to the problem, and should consider only those aspects which have major relevance to the required decision. For example, if we are trying to determine the optimal number of spare parts to stock for a particular item over a given time period, we will be interested in the number of failures which could conceivably occur in that time period, but not in the specific manner in which the failures occurred, unless certain types of failures were such that the item could be repaired, thus eliminating the need for a spare part when such failures occurred.

To avoid using mathematical models, on the basis that they contain uncertain factors, is to beg the issue. Decisions must be made, whether mathematical models are used or not. The rational approach is to employ appropriate mathematical models as an aid to the judgment of the decision maker, making sure that these models consider the relevant factors and are themselves economically feasible to develop and use.

1.4   ORGANIZATION AND COVERAGE OF TEXT

The second and third chapters of this text cover probability fundamentals and form the foundation for all later material relating to probabilistic models. Chapter 2, Probability Theory, discusses the basic concepts of probability, both objective and subjective, as well as the rules covering probability relationships. Chapter 3, Probability Distributions, is concerned with the general theory underlying both discrete and continuous probability distributions, with particular emphasis on the formulation and applicability of the binomial, Poisson, and normal distributions.

Chapter 4, Decision Making using Expected Monetary Value, introduces the concepts of what we call Bayesian decision theory, including opportunity loss and the value of information, and initiates the discussion of decision making under conditions of uncertainty, a vital consideration in business. For example, we may wish to know how many units of a particular product to stock when the demand for that product is uncertain. Or, we may attempt to select the most favorable investment in the face of uncertain economic factors. In such situations, we must define the possible so-called *states of nature* (events outside our control) and attempt to assign probability values to them. In the first example, the states of nature would be the possible demand levels; in the second example, the states of nature might be economic expansion, a stable economy, and economic recession. In many cases, the probability values will be subjective, representing judgmental estimates, and empirical, based on what has actually been observed in the past. (The calculation of subjective probabilities is covered in some detail in this text, since the judicious use of subjective probabilities is of considerable importance in business decision making.) Also in this chapter, the important topic of sensitivity analysis first appears. Through this approach, we can determine the range of data values over which a given solution is optimal, and this allows us to explore the effect on the solution of possible changes or errors in data values.

Chapter 5, Other Decision-Making Criteria, explores the problem of making decisions when the decision maker does not act solely on the basis of the dollar amounts involved, but rather on a subjective evaluation of the intrinsic value, or *utility* of such amounts. For example, a person might be unwilling to bid on a contract for which there appeared to be an equal chance of gaining $30,000 or of losing $10,000, simply because the effects of the possible loss of $10,000 would outweigh the possible gain of triple that amount. This could certainly not be considered unreasonable if a loss of $10,000 might result in demotion or even being fired!

Chapter 6, Decision Making with Additional Information, extends the Bayesian material of Chapter 4 by considering the situation where it is possible to purchase additional information before making a decision. This information could be a fixed amount, such as that obtained from a forecast, or a variable amount which depends on the size of a sample. For both these cases, the powerful technique of preposterior analysis will be used to demonstrate that the potential worth of such additional information can be determined before that information is actually purchased.

Chapter 7, Linear Programming, begins the study of a number of deterministic models, those which are considered to involve decisions under conditions of certainty. Compared with the obvious problems involved in making decisions under uncertainty, it seems as though decision making under certainty should be relatively easy. Unfortunately, this is quite rare. Generally, there are so many possible solutions that exhaustive enumeration of all possible solutions is completely impractical, even with high-speed computers, and we have to turn to sophisticated computational procedures to search efficiently for optimal solutions.

We will start by utilizing graphical solution techniques to illustrate basic linear programming concepts. Then, the necessary algebraic techniques will be developed. Later in the chapter, we will find that we are not entirely limited to the analysis of linear programming problems where complete certainty exists. Through the methods of postoptimality analysis, a form of sensitivity analysis, we will explore the effect on the optimal solution of limited changes or uncertainties in various problem factors.

The following chapter, Chapter 8, Transportation and Assignment Models, covers two specialized linear programming models which are more efficiently solved by specialized models than by the general linear programming model. As an example of the first model type, consider a situation where a company is attempting to determine the optimal distribution of a particular product from 5 manufacturing plants to 20 warehouses such that the overall shipping cost will be minimized. The per unit shipping costs for the 100 possible shipping routes are known and are constant. Considering all the possible combinations of routes and units shipped, the total number of possible solutions is enormous. Nevertheless, working out the optimal shipping pattern using the transportation method of linear programming, the number of routes actually used will not exceed 24, and the optimal solution can readily be worked out by hand in less than one hour or by computer in a few seconds, even with a small computer. In problems where, for example, we have m tasks and m individuals with different capabilities to perform those tasks, the assignment model can be used to allocate individuals to tasks in an optimal manner.

In Chapter 9, Network Models, models are studied whose analysis depends to a large extent on their actual representation as a network. Thus, we have a model to determine the shortest route through a network, such as a transportation network, and, for a system such as a network of communications sites, we have a model which will enable us to determine the shortest total connection length such that there is a communications path (not necessarily direct) from each site to every other site. There are also models which permit determination of the maximal flow through a network with capacity limits associated with its branches. Finally, network scheduling models such as CPM and PERT, mentioned earlier, are explored.

Chapter 10, Dynamic Programming, considers both deterministic and probabilistic situations which require (or can be formulated as) a series of sequential decisions. An example is the so-called cargo-loading or knapsack problem, in which several different items are to be shipped or carried together, subject to a total weight limit. Given the unit weight and unit profit (or value) of each item, it is desired to determine the number of units of each item such that the total profit (or value) is maximized. The dynamic programming approach is to consider each item in sequence, rather than all items at once, thereby breaking up the original problem into a series of smaller problems which can be solved more easily than the original problem.

Inventory Models, Chapter 11, begins with the study of deterministic models which involve the calculation of the optimal order quantity and frequency, considering such factors as demand per unit time, cost of placing orders, cost associated with goods held in inventory, and cost of running short. Comprehensive sensitivity analyses are performed on all factors of these models to show their relatively wide applicability in spite of some rather restrictive assumptions in the models. Next, probabilistic single-period models are examined, using an incremental (marginal) analysis approach. Such models are typified by the so-called newsboy problem, in which a newsboy wishes to find the most profitable number of newspapers to stock each day in the face of uncertain demand. Again, extensive sensitivity analyses are performed. The final topic involves the determination of the best ordering policy for multiple-period models for which there is a combination of random demand and random lead time (the time between placement of an order and its receipt). Some noneconomic measures of effectiveness are explored, such as the establishment of an upper limit for the fraction of order periods in which a shortage can be expected to occur.

Chapter 12, Queueing Models, is an introduction to the study of systems in which congestion can occur, resulting in the formation of waiting lines, or queues. After describing the nature and general characteristics of a number of different situations in which queues form, systems with a single server are analyzed to determine such so-called operating characteristics as mean waiting time and mean number in line, as a function of the arrival rate, the mean service time, and any system constraints. For example, we could model the situation of a bank with a single drive-up teller, where there is space for a maximum of, say, 4 cars, and customers arriving when 4 cars are in line must move on, either to return later (perhaps by circling the block) or to park and walk into the bank. Multiple-server models, applicable to situations such as the checkout operations in a supermarket with a number of checkstands, or to the failure and repair of machines in a factory where there are several repairmen, are examined next. The final section is concerned with the economics of queueing systems, the attempt to minimize the sum of the costs of providing service and the costs of obtaining service, primarily those associated with the value of the time wasted in queue. Sensitivity analysis is used to examine the effect of changing such factors as arrival rate, service rate, cost per server, and value of waiting time.

In Chapter 13, Markov Analysis, systems are considered in which the status of the system, called its state, can be defined by some descriptive measure or numerical value, and where the system moves from one state to another on a probabilistic basis. The so-called brand-switching model sometimes used in marketing studies is a classic example. Each state represents the use of a particular brand, and the customer switches from one brand to another with a certain probability. The model allows us to determine the long-run fraction of time each brand will be selected. In another situation, we will be interested in the probability of finally reaching some terminal state, called an absorbing state. As a simple illustration, a player in a tennis tournament can be considered to be in one of three states: in contention, eliminated, or the tournament winner. In each preliminary match, the player either wins and stays in contention, or loses and is eliminated. If the final match is reached, the player either wins the tournament or is eliminated. The states of being eliminated or being the tournament winner are clearly absorbing states, since they represent the end of the line for the player. This chapter also examines Markovian decision analysis, the economic comparison of alternatives in Markovian problems.

Simulation Models, Chapter 14, presents an in-depth examination of a general-purpose technique which can be applied to the analysis of an extremely broad range of problems. For the analytical mathematical models covered in previous chapters, once the appropriate model structure is chosen and the numerical values supplied, the identical solution would be obtained every time that particular model was solved. On the other hand, simulation models are, in essence, used to perform simulated experiments on a given system, so they yield statistical estimates, not optimal solutions. The primary advantage of simulation models, however, is that they can be much more realistic than analytical models, since the latter often contain assumptions which may represent oversimplifications. Indeed, in many business situations, there are just no analytical models which are even applicable.

Since simulation models generally require extensive calculations, this chapter is highly computer-oriented, discussing such topics as random number generation, computer simulation of queueing systems, and operational considerations for computerized models.

The final chapter, Chapter 15, Decision Analysis in the Business World, attempts to bridge the gap between learning about quantitative methods for decision making and actually applying that knowledge to the effective solution of practical problems. First, the decision analysis process is reviewed, starting from the point of recognition that a problem exists, and proceeding from the determination as to what kind of problem it is all the way through to successful implementation of the solution. Decision analysis in the different economic sectors—defense, private, and public—is then discussed. The last topic is an overview of decision analysis models, modeling, and modelers, considering practical methodology, communications problems, and future prospects.

1.5 BENEFITS FROM STUDYING QUANTITATIVE METHODS

In addition to learning about specific decision analysis models and techniques useful in business and industry, the business student can expect to gain several other benefits, such as development of the following capabilities.

Structured approach to problems. In developing and solving a number of different mathematical models, the student will, it is hoped, come to see that it saves time and effort to attack problems in a logical and consistent fashion. By carefully handling such necessary details as defining the problem variables (both decision variables and uncontrollable variables), specifying any constraints, establishing given mathematical relationships (using sketches where useful), and determining a suitable solution objective, problem-solving time will generally be minimized and the chances of arriving at the correct answer will be enhanced. Conceptual and computational errors will be measurably decreased, as compared to a relatively unstructured approach, and any errors made will be much easier to detect and correct.

Critical approach to problem solving. The perceptive student will learn to recognize common problem elements, thereby aiding evaluation of the applicability of particular mathematical models to a given problem, and will be alert to the explicit and implicit assumptions in such models, as well as their inherent limitations. Differences will be perceived between solution techniques valuable only for presenting concepts, such as the graphical method of linear programming, and practical solution techniques, such as the simplex method of linear programming (and its sophisticated variants), which are used to solve real business problems. Problem solutions will not be accepted uncritically; the effect of changes or possible errors in model data values will be examined through the techniques of sensitivity analysis. Moreoever, through such analyses, it will be seen that any apparent need to obtain more and/or better input data can be logically evaluated. Thus, crude estimates may suffice for data values to which the solution is relatively insensitive, while fairly refined estimates may be required for other data values. In all cases, the old saw about GIGO (garbage in, garbage out) must be clearly borne in mind. That is, if the required input data is unreliable or unavailable, the world's most sophisticated mathematical model cannot produce meaningful answers.

Preparation to be a producer, consumer, or interpreter of decision analysis studies. At some point in the student's career, association with some aspect of decision analysis studies is almost inevitable. Whether as a producer, consumer, or interpreter of such studies, a good background in quantitative methods will prove to be a solid asset. The ability to judge the applicability and limitations of solution techniques to a particular problem, as well as to critically analyze proposed solutions and the data on which they are based, is bound to be a valued skill in any business organization.

An individual's business education should be broad and comprehensive; an appreciation and basic understanding of what decision analysis can do and what it cannot do is vitally important in today's complex and ever-changing business world.

PROBABILITY THEORY

The concepts and applications of probability are extremely important to the decision maker, since almost every aspect of business is affected by uncertainty. For instance, how likely is it that a thirty-day supply of steel will be adequate if a strike occurs? What are the chances of getting a $500,000 contract involving $100,000 in bidding expenses? What are the odds that a newly developed product will sell well enough to make a profit within a year of its introduction? Clearly, the list of such situations is endless.

Probability has been termed the mathematical language of uncertainty. From this viewpoint, it represents a means to *measure and quantify uncertainty*. Thus, for example, if we make a random selection of a card from a bridge deck, we know that there is a "good chance" of drawing a red card. Since half the cards are red cards, we can actually quantify this judgment by stating that the probability of drawing a red card is 1/2, or 0.5, provided there is an equal opportunity to draw any card in the deck.

There are several different interpretations of probability which are of interest, but before discussing them, we need to establish certain definitions and relationships fundamental to a basic understanding of probability.

2.1 BASIC CONCEPTS OF PROBABILITY

In what is generally called a *statistical experiment*, a number of possible outcomes can be identified in advance, but there is no way of determining beforehand the exact outcome of any given so-called trial, or occurrence, of this experiment. The word "experiment" is used in the broadest possible sense and is not meant to designate, for example, some type of laboratory experiment. Thus, a statistical experiment could consist of submitting a bid on a contract, with the possible outcomes, as of the date of the bid award announcement, being "bid won," "bid lost," or "bid to be resubmitted." Another example of a statistical experiment would be to observe the number of days next month in which measurable rainfall is recorded at the San Francisco International Airport.

Any set or collection of experimental outcomes is called an *event*. A *compound event* can be divided into *elementary events*, which cannot be further subdivided. In the contract bid example, we could define an event "bid result determined," which would be a compound event consisting of the elementary events "bid won" and "bid lost." The definition as to what constitutes an elementary event is a function of the problem statement. Thus, in a different statistical experiment involving contract bidding, we might have defined such elementary events as "bid lost by less than $1000," "bid lost by $1000 to $2000," and "bid lost by over $2000."

If the outcome of a statistical experiment is a sequence of observations, then an elementary event can be represented by a specific sequence. Thus, if a statistical experiment consists of tossing a coin three times, then the sequence "heads, heads, tails" could represent an elementary event. Alternatively, the elementary event could be the number of heads appearing. We could also have thrown three coins at once and defined the number of heads as the elementary event.

Each elementary event is called a *sample point*, and the collection of all such sample points is known as the *sample space*, which we will denote by the letter S. The number of sample points need not be finite. For instance, we could consider as sample points all possible values for the amount of electrical energy used in our city tomorrow. (If we measure the energy value only to the nearest kilowatt-hour, the number of possible *measured* values will be finite; but the number of possible *actual* values, if there were no measurement limitation, would be infinite.)

Two or more events are *mutually exclusive* when only one of them can occur in any single trial (observation) of the given statistical experiment. Consider, for example, the statistical experiment whose outcome is the number of customers served by a bank teller in a given time period. The events "fewer than 10 customers served" and "exactly 12 customers served" are mutually exclusive. If one of them occurs, the other cannot possibly occur. Note that the first event is a compound event, consisting of the elementary events "0 customers served," "1 customer served," and so forth, while the second event is clearly an elementary event. The events "fewer than 10 customers served" and "exactly 8 customers served" are *not* mutually exclusive. If 8 customers are served, both events will occur.

Events are *collectively exhaustive* when they include, as a group, all sample points in the sample space. The events "fewer than 11 customers served," "11 to 20 customers served," and "more than 15 customers served" are collectively exhaustive, since they collectively include all possible sample points. Note, however, that the last two events are not mutually exclusive. For many applications, we will be interested in events which are both *mutually exclusive and collectively exhaustive*. In the bank teller example, such a collection of events would be, for example: "fewer than 5 customers served," "5 to 19 customers served," "20 to 40 customers served," and "more than 40 customers served."

If we denote a given event as E, its *complementary event* $\bar{E}$ (called "E bar" or "not E") contains all the sample points not in E. Thus, events E and $\bar{E}$ must be both mutually exclusive and collectively exhaustive. For the event "fewer than 5 customers served," the complementary event is "5 or more customers served," or, equivalently, "more than 4 customers served."

It is sometimes convenient to define a variable denoting the given event and to represent that event by enclosing its sample points in braces. If we define E_1 as the event "fewer than 4 customers served," we can write this as

$$E_1 = \{0, 1, 2, 3\}.$$

The sample space S, the certain event, would be represented as

$$S = \{0, 1, 2, 3, 4, \ldots\},$$

where the three dots (called an ellipsis) after the numeral 4 denote a continuing progression of similar values, in this case, 5, 6, 7, and so on. The complementary event to E_1 would be

$$\bar{E}_1 = \{4, 5, 6, \ldots\}.$$

An understanding of basic probability concepts is sometimes aided by a graphical presentation known as a *Venn diagram*, Figure 2.1. The rectangle represents the sample space S, which includes all the sample points. The irregular area represents event E_1, which, as defined, includes sample points 0, 1, 2, and 3. The complementary event $\bar{E}_1$ includes all the remaining sample points. We will find Venn diagrams quite useful in visualizing probability concepts and will make further use of them later.

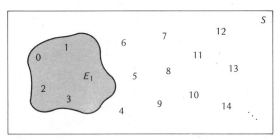

Figure 2.1

Let us now take an example to illustrate the ideas presented.

EXAMPLE 2.1

A small drive-in bank has room for a maximum of three cars (including the car being served) in the driveway leading to the bank teller's window. As a statistical experiment, we observe the number of cars in the driveway at random instants in time.

a) What is the sample space S?

The sample points consist of the possible number of cars in the driveway.

$$S = \{0, 1, 2, 3\}$$

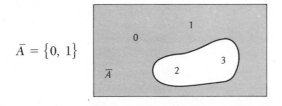

b) Define the event A, "more than 1 car."

$$A = \{2, 3\}$$

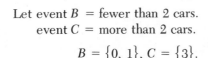

c) Interpret the event $\bar{A}$.

Event $\bar{A}$ is "one or fewer cars."

$$\bar{A} = \{0, 1\}$$

d) Are the events "fewer than 2 cars" and "more than 2 cars" mutually exclusive and collectively exhaustive?

Let event B = fewer than 2 cars.
event C = more than 2 cars.

$$B = \{0, 1\}, C = \{3\}.$$

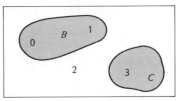

These events are mutually exclusive, since they have no sample points in common. They are not collectively exhaustive, however, because the sample point 2 is not included when the sample points of both events are combined. Had the event C been "more than 1 car," the two events would then have been both mutually exclusive and collectively exhaustive.

2.2 PROBABILITY AXIOMS

Once the sample space is clearly defined for any problem involving uncertainty, we can examine the probabilities of various events. To do this, we must first establish the accepted rules, or axioms, of probability.

Suppose we have a sample space S which contains a number of sample points. Let the event E_i be any collection of sample points within S and let $P(E_i)$ be the probability that event E_i occurs in any individual trial of the statistical experiment. Then, one way of stating the axioms of probability is:

1. The probability of event E_i is nonnegative:

$$P(E_i) \geq 0.$$

2. If the two events E_i and E_j, both in S (that is, containing only sample points in S), are mutually exclusive, then the probability that at least one of these events occurs, denoted as $P(E_i \text{ or } E_j)$, is

$$P(E_i \text{ or } E_j) = P(E_i) + P(E_j).$$

This axiom can be called the *additivity axiom*.

3. For the sample space S, which contains all the sample points:

$$P(S) = 1.$$

To illustrate the three probability axioms, look at the Venn diagram of Figure 2.2, where the areas represent probabilities of the included elementary events, rather than just the elementary events themselves. As stated in axiom 1, no probability area can be less than zero. The shaded area, which is the probability that E_i or E_j occurs, is seen to be just the sum of the individual probabilities of E_i and E_j, as given in axiom 2. Axiom 3 states that the entire area, denoted by S, has a probability of 1.

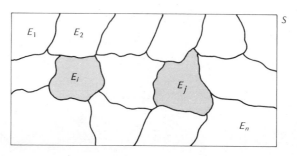

Figure 2.2

From the stated axioms, two basic rules of probability can be derived:

1. For any event E_i in S, since $P(S) = 1$, it must be true that $P(E_i) \leq 1$. Combining this relationship with that of axiom 1, we get:

$$0 \leq P(E_i) \leq 1. \tag{2.1}$$

2. For any set of mutually exclusive and collectively exhaustive events E_1, E_2, . . . , E_n in S, as shown in Figure 2.2, axioms 2 and 3 give

$$P(E_1 \text{ or } E_2 \text{ or } \cdots \text{ or } E_n) = P(E_1) + P(E_2) + \cdots + P(E_n)$$
$$= P(S) = 1. \tag{2.2}$$

Having presented the fundamental mathematical rules of probability, let us now discuss the various interpretations of probability.

2.3   OBJECTIVE PROBABILITY

Objective probabilities, as the name implies, are based on some type of objective, rather than subjective, basis (although we will observe that subjective elements are usually involved in the determination of probabilities). We generally classify objective probabilities into one of two types.

Classical, or *a priori* (before the fact), probabilities are frequently related to games of chance. As an example, consider the probability of drawing a winning lottery ticket when there are 10 winning tickets out of a total of 1000 tickets. With no further information, we would calculate the probability of winning as 10 chances in 1000, or 0.01. If we wished to know the probability of rolling a 3 on a die, the fact that a 3 shows on only one of the six faces of the die would lead us to believe that the probability of rolling a 3 would be 1/6. We have, however, introduced a subjective element here. We have assumed that the die is "fair," meaning that each side is equally likely to turn up when the die is rolled. Our probability estimate was based on a special case which arises frequently, especially in games of chance. This special case occurs when the elementary events in a statistical experiment are (or are assumed to be) equally likely.

When the elementary events are equally likely, then the probability that a given event E occurs will be equal to the ratio of the number of elementary events included in E to the number of elementary events in the sample space S. Stating this in a formula:

$$P(E) = \frac{\text{number of elementary events in } E}{\text{number of elementary events in } S}. \tag{2.3}$$

Thus, if the event A represented the drawing of a deuce from a bridge deck, we could readily calculate the probability of A by noting that there are 4 deuces out of 52 cards. Each card's suit and value constitutes an elementary event, so, assuming that each card has an equal chance of being selected, we have

$$P(A) = \frac{4}{52} = 0.077.$$

The second type of objective probability is called relative frequency, or *a posteriori* (after the fact). It is based on the concept that the probability of an observed event is equal to the relative frequency of the actual occurrence of that event in the long run. For example, suppose there are 2,000,000 male automobile drivers under the age of 20 in the Pacific Coast states. There is no way of determining the fraction of these drivers annually involved in injury accidents without actually gathering data on accidents. We must base our judgment on after-the-fact information. If these drivers were involved in 40,000 injury accidents last year, the probability that any randomly selected male driver, who was one of those 2,000,000 drivers, had an injury accident last year would be 40,000/2,000,000 or 0.02. If we wish to extrapolate this data and say that the probability of an injury accident for this class of drivers will be 0.02 this year, we are implicitly making a subjective assumption. We are assuming that the characteristics of the drivers and the factors responsible for such accidents will be, from a statistical standpoint, the same this year as last year. This may or may not be a reasonable assumption. If stiff penalties for drunk driving have been enacted recently or if the legal driving age has just been lowered, we might well feel that the injury accident probability will change significantly this year.

The relative frequency approach to probability, an approach based on empirical data, is very useful in many cases. It is, for instance, absolutely necessary in the setting of all types of insurance premiums, whether it be for life, fire, health, accident, or other type of insurance. It is a primary factor in statistical analyses which lead to the evaluation of probabilities, such as the probability of a customer switching from one consumer brand to another. But, as we observed in the injury accident example, the actual *use* of objective probabilities based on relative frequency data can, and frequently does, involve elements of subjectivity. Let us now consider the subjective interpretation of probability.

2.4 SUBJECTIVE PROBABILITY

There are many situations where the concept of probability based on relative frequency is meaningless. For instance, what is the probability that an expedition will land on Mars in the next decade? This is a unique event, one that has never occurred before. There is no way that we can interpret such a probability as a relative frequency. In addition, as we noted in the previous section, even when we have information whereby we can calculate an event probability based on relative frequency, that probability is generally not directly applicable to a similar event of interest. For instance, suppose that the congressional representation from Ohio had contained a majority of Democrats in 12 of the last 20 elections. In looking forward to the next election, it is certainly information worth considering, but it does not mean that the probability of an Ohio Democratic congressional majority is 12/20, or 0.60, in the next election. At that time, there will be a combination of issues, voter attitudes, candidates, and so forth, which surely has never occurred in the identical manner previously. The probability of an Ohio Democratic congressional majority in the next election will have to be judged in a subjective manner, taking into account all relevant information (again, a subjective judgment is required as to which information is, indeed, relevant).

Subjective probability can be interpreted as a measure of the *degree of belief* that a particular event will occur. Such a judgment is frequently made by an individual and sometimes by a group. If we believe that there is 0.60 probability that the Los Angeles Dodgers will defeat the New York Mets in their next meeting, we are looking only at the situation (pitchers, home team, and so forth) for that particular game (event), and we are not inferring that the Dodgers can expect to beat the Mets 60 times in their next 100 meetings. There is no relative frequency interpretation of this subjective probability value. If we stood by our judgment, we should be willing to bet on the Dodgers and give 3 to 2 odds. We will have more to say shortly on the association between betting odds and subjective probabilities.

An event need not be a one-time occurrence in order to apply subjective probability concepts. Consider a machinist about to begin the machining of an order of 100 parts requiring very close tolerances. He has machined similar, although not identical parts before. Based on past experience and his present confident attitude as he gets ready to produce the order, we might estimate the probability of producing a good part as 0.90 and intend this to imply a relative frequency, such that we would expect about 90 good parts out of the order of 100 parts.

Having now presented some of the considerations related to the concept of subjective probability, let us now discuss how such probability values can be "rationally" determined.

Assessment of Subjective Probabilities

Earlier we mentioned the situation where a business might wish to estimate the chances that a newly developed product will return a profit within a year of its initial marketing. How can we get its management to assess the desired subjective probability value in a reasonably "objective" manner? Several different approaches can be used to arrive at such subjective probabilities, and we will describe three of them.

Comparison of Fictitious Lotteries One approach is to set up two fictitious lotteries, which we would explain to management in the following manner.

> Lottery 1: You win $50 with probability 0.50.
>   You win $0 with probability 0.50.

(These probabilities are objective, based on, say, drawing a ball from an urn with 50 red balls and 50 white balls, randomly mixed. They are sometimes called *canonical probabilities*, or probabilities that everyone would agree upon.)

> Lottery 2: You win $50 if the new product becomes profitable in the first year.
>   You win $0 if the new product does not become profitable in the first year.

You are offered a choice between these two lotteries. Since both lotteries offer the same prizes, you should choose that lottery which offers the greatest chance of winning. (We will arrange for the outcome of lottery 1 to be determined at the same time that the outcome of lottery 2 is decided, so that there will be no time factor involved in the choice of lotteries.) If you choose lottery 1, you are expressing your feeling that there is less than 0.50 probability the product will be successful (show a profit in its first year). If you choose lottery 2, then you must feel that there is more than 0.50 probability of a successful product. Suppose you prefer lottery 2. Now we change the probabilities in lottery 1. We could set the probability of winning $50 to 0.75, so that the probability of winning $0 would be 0.25. If you now prefer lottery 1, your subjective probability of a successful product must then lie between 0.50 and 0.75. We could now change the probabilities in lottery 1 until you become indifferent to the two lotteries. At that point, your subjective probability of a successful product would be equal to the probability of winning $50 in lottery 1. Thus, if you were indifferent between lottery 2 and lottery 1 with a 0.60 probability of winning $50 and a 0.40 probability of winning $0, your subjective probability of a successful product would be pegged at 0.60.

In general, the lottery approach to the establishment of a subjective probability value for an event E involves setting up two hypothetical lotteries.

> Lottery 1: Win prize A with objective probability p.
>   Win prize B with objective probability $1 - p$.
> Lottery 2: Win prize A if event E occurs.
>   Win prize B if event E does not occur.

The desired subjective probability value $P(E)$ is equal to the value of p at which the decision maker is indifferent to the two lotteries. The so-called "prizes" can be anything, just as long as they are different and prize A is clearly preferable to prize B. They can even be losses, so prize A could be "lose $100" and prize B "lose $200."

To get a feeling for the probability value p in lottery 1, the person is asked to visualize an urn in which there are a total of 100 red and white balls. We could now ask how many red balls would have to be in the urn before there would be indifference to a choice between lottery 2 and a drawing from the urn (with the balls thoroughly mixed) whereby prize A is won if a red ball is drawn. Another way of looking at the probability value p is to draw a rectangle, labeling the left end 0 and the right end 1. Assume now the availability of a table of random numbers which are equally likely to fall anywhere in the interval between 0 and 1. Appendix E contains such a table. (These random numbers can be generated on a computer, as discussed in the chapter on Simulation Models.) The value of p would represent a division of the rectangle such that a fraction p of these random numbers could be expected to fall in the interval between 0 and p, as shown by the shaded region in Figure 2.3. The person making the judgment would be asked to locate p by judging the shaded area in relation to the total area (or, alternatively, in relation to the unshaded area) and equating this with the degree of belief in the probability that the event of interest would indeed occur.

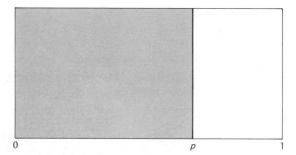

0 p 1

Figure 2.3

Establishing Betting Odds   A second method of assessing subjective probabilities is through the establishment of betting odds. Thus, if a union is taking a strike vote tomorrow, we might be willing to give 4 to 1 odds that there will be a vote in favor of a strike. If we think of this in terms of probability, we can then say that we believe there are 4 chances out of 5 that a strike will be favored. The subjective probability of a strike call would therefore be estimated as 0.80.

If a decision maker feels at home with the concept of betting odds, the subjective probability for any event on which odds are quoted can be readily converted to a probability value, as we just indicated. Thus, if odds of a to b are quoted on event E, this is the same as stating that the probability of event E is equal to $a/(a + b)$. If odds of 3 to 2 are given on event E, then $P(E) = 3/5 = 0.60$.

If we actually get to the point of considering a monetary bet between two individuals, at the given odds, we could look at it in a very straightforward fashion. Referring to the earlier example of the pending strike vote, we could set up the bets as follows:

Individual 1 bets \$4 that a strike will be called.
Individual 2 bets \$1 that a strike will not be called.

If we really believed that the odds favoring a strike call were 4 to 1, so that the probability of a strike call was 4/5, or 0.80, then we could consider this as a "fair" bet. By this, we mean that we would be indifferent to taking either side of the bet. If you are individual 1, you stand to win \$1 with probability 0.80 and to lose \$4 with probability 0.20. Since $(1)(0.80)$ and $(4)(0.20)$ are equal, the "expected value" of your winnings is zero. (We will have much more to say about expected values in the following chapter.) The situation is reversed if you are individual 2, but the net result is the same, since you stand to win \$4 with probability 0.20 and lose \$1 with probability 0.80.

In considering actual bets involving dollar amounts, we have a different situation than we do when using the lottery approach, where the prizes are identical for the two lotteries. In the latter case, the actual value of the prizes is not a factor; with the former, the actual amount bet can be important. Thus, we might be very willing to bet \$4 on a strike call in attempting to win \$1, but we might be most unwilling to risk

$4000 on the chance of winning $1000, or vice versa. When the monetary amounts involved become relatively large with respect to an individual's finances, then we have to take into account the attitude toward risk, or what we term the utility for money. We will discuss the subject of utility in some detail later, but, for now, we will consider that any monetary bets are relatively small, so that a "fair" bet can be readily determined.

Using a Reference Contract   A third approach to establishing subjective probability values is the reference contract method. To illustrate this concept, suppose you are offered $10 of a new bond issue is successful—all bonds sold at the time of the original bond offering. If you are willing to pay up to $7 for this contract, it is inferred that you believe the probability of a successful bond issue is 7/10, or 0.70. As with the monetary amounts in the betting situation, you would be looking at the "expected value" of the "$10 or nothing" gamble. If you are willing to pay a maximum of $7 to gain $10 with a probability p, then you are, in essence, equating $7 with $10p$, so that $p = 7/10 = 0.70$. Again, since monetary amounts are directly involved, we will assume that they are relatively small, so that we do not get into problems involving the individual's risk preferences.

It should be clear that the subjective nature of probability judgments means that the assessment of specific numerical values cannot be done with any great degree of precision. In many cases, it would not be meaningful to estimate probability values more closely than to the nearest 0.05. Even this degree of precision, however, can be most useful in the quantification of subjective judgments.

Employing a formal approach to the assessment of subjective probabilities forces us to quantify our judgment in a logical manner, rather than allowing us to specify probabilities "off the top of our head." By forcing us into making a decision (which lottery to take, which betting odds to specify, and so forth), instead of just stating a numerical probability value, we are hopefully impelled to make reasonably thoughtful judgments. Our probability values are then inferred from our decisions. Also, we see that we have demonstrated meaningful approaches to the evaluation of probabilities in situations that occur only once as well as in repetitive situations.

2.5   JOINT, MARGINAL, AND CONDITIONAL PROBABILITIES

Suppose a die is rolled and the resulting number observed. The sample space then consists of the numbers 1 through 6. Now, let event A be the appearance of an odd number and event B a number greater than 3. Since $A = \{1, 3, 5\}$ and $B = \{4, 5, 6\}$, the *joint event* $A \cap B$, representing the occurrence of both events A and B (with the symbol $\cap$ denoting "intersection") is $\{5\}$, since 5 is the only number common to both events. In other words, it is the only number in the sample space which is both odd and greater than 3. The relationships between events A, B, and $A \cap B$ are shown in Figure 2.4(a). The *joint probability* that events A and B will both occur at the same time is denoted as $P(A \cap B)$.

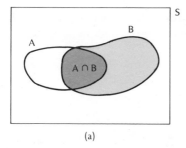
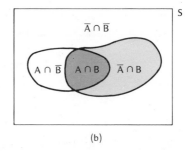

(a)   (b)

Figure 2.4

We term the *marginal probability* of an event the probability that the event occurs, without regard to any other events that occur simultaneously. $P(A)$ and $P(B)$ are both marginal probabilities. (The reason for the designation "marginal" probability will become apparent when we construct probability tables.) There is an important probability relationship for marginal probabilities which will now be illustrated. Referring to the die example, since event $\bar{B}$ represents the appearance of a number not exceeding 3, $\bar{B} = \{1, 2, 3\}$, so the joint event $A \cap \bar{B} = \{1, 3\}$, as seen in Figure 2.4(b). Thus $P(A)$, the probability an odd number appears, is equal to the sum of $P(A \cap B)$, the probability of an odd number whose value is at least 4, and $P(A \cap \bar{B})$, the probability of an odd number no greater than 3. The relationship $P(A) = P(A \cap B) + P(A \cap \bar{B})$ holds because event A must occur in conjunction with either event B or event $\bar{B}$, and events B and $\bar{B}$ are mutually exclusive and collectively exhaustive, since together they include all points in the sample space S. In the same fashion, since event $\bar{A} = \{2, 4, 6\}$, joint event $\bar{A} \cap B = \{4, 6\}$, again verified by referring to Figure 2.4(b), so that $P(B) = P(A \cap B) + P(\bar{A} \cap B)$. Observe that events A and $\bar{A}$, as required, are also mutually exclusive and collectively exhaustive. In general, when an event can occur jointly with another set of events which is mutually exclusive and collectively exhaustive, the marginal probability of the given event can be expressed as the sum of all the joint probabilities involving that event.

The *conditional probability* of the occurrence of event A, given that event B has occurred, is written $P(A|B)$ and verbalized as "the probability of A given B." Referring to Figure 2.4(a), visualize the areas A, B, and $A \cap B$ as probabilities. If we are told that a given sample point falls within area B, the probability that it also falls within A, $P(A|B)$, will be equal to the ratio of area $A \cap B$ to area B, so

$$P(A|B) = \frac{P(A \cap B)}{P(B)}, \qquad \text{provided that } P(B) > 0. \qquad \textbf{(2.4)}$$

Algebraically, for $P(A|B)$ to be defined, $P(B)$ must be greater than zero, because division by zero is meaningless. Conceptually, it would not be meaningful to talk about the probability that event A occurs, given that event B occurs, if it were the case that event B could never occur.

In a similar manner, if it is known that a sample point falls within A, the probability it also falls within B, $P(B|A)$, equals the ratio of area $A \cap B$ to area A, so

$$P(B|A) = \frac{P(A \cap B)}{P(A)}, \qquad \text{provided that } P(A) > 0. \qquad \textbf{(2.5)}$$

It should be noted that

$$P(A|B) + P(\bar{A}|B) = 1, \qquad \text{provided that } P(B) > 0, \qquad \textbf{(2.6)}$$

since we have, by Equation (2.4):

$$\frac{P(A \cap B)}{P(B)} + \frac{P(\bar{A} \cap B)}{P(B)} = \frac{1}{P(B)}[P(A \cap B) + P(\bar{A} \cap B)] = \frac{P(B)}{P(B)} = 1.$$

Similarly,

$$P(B|A) + P(\bar{B}|A) = 1, \qquad \text{provided that } P(A) > 0.$$

Conditional probabilities are very important in business decision making, since many probability values of interest are expressed in a natural way as conditional probabilities. For instance, we might require an estimate of the probability of a steel shortage should a strike occur; the probability of a successful nationwide marketing effort if a local test marketing has been successful; and so on.

Let us now take a numerical example to illustrate these probability concepts.

EXAMPLE 2.2

A certain Graduate School of Business Administration is attempting to determine the best allocation of courses and faculty for its two new MBA programs. One program, MBA I, is a comprehensive program, with no specialization. The other program, MBA II, allows some degree of specialization in one of several areas. Over the initial two years of the programs, the demand for each program has been tabulated for a three-way classification of students' undergraduate specialization—engineering, science (B.S. degree other than engineering), and "other" (B.A. degree). Suppose we define the five different events as follows:

M_1 = MBA I program objective,
M_2 = MBA II program objective,
U_1 = engineering undergraduate,
U_2 = science undergraduate,
U_3 = other undergraduate.

Observe that events M_1 and M_2 are mutually exclusive, as are events U_1, U_2, and U_3. The sample space S for the six joint events is

$$S = \{M_1 \cap U_1, M_1 \cap U_2, M_1 \cap U_3, M_2 \cap U_1, M_2 \cap U_2, M_2 \cap U_3\}.$$

The results of the evaluation appear in Table 2.1, which shows the number of observations (the frequency) in each of the six mutually exclusive categories (joint events) for the 150 students who entered the program.

Table 2.1   Frequency Table

Program	Event	Undergraduate Specialization Engineering Science Other Event U_1	U_2	U_3	
MBA I	M_1	42	12	36	90
MBA II	M_2	33	18	9	60
		75	30	45	150

It has been agreed that this data should form the basis for planning next year's course and faculty allocation. On this basis, a probability table can be constructed by dividing each of the given frequencies by 150, the total number of students. These probabilities, shown in Table 2.2, are primarily objective, derived from the given data. They are also subjective, since they are based on a belief that the preferences of future applicants will be similar to those of students who previously entered the program.

Table 2.2   Probability Table

Program	Event	Undergraduate Specialization Engineering Science Other Event U_1	U_2	U_3	Marginal Probability
MBA I	M_1	0.28	0.08	0.24	0.60
MBA II	M_2	0.22	0.12	0.06	0.40
Marginal Probability		0.50	0.20	0.30	1.00

In the following questions, we will consider only current undergraduate applicants to one of the two MBA programs.

a) What is the probability that an applicant is a science undergraduate wishing to enter the MBA II program?

The required probability is $P(M_2 \cap U_2)$, a joint probability whose value, from Table 2.2, is 0.12. Any of the other five joint probabilities is also readily obtainable from that table.

b) What is the probability that an applicant will be an engineering undergraduate?

This probability is the marginal, or unconditional, probability $P(U_1)$. Its value of 0.50 is found in the margin of Table 2.2, hence the designation "marginal" probability. We are interested only in the occurrence of the event U_1, without regard to whether it occurs with event M_1 or event M_2. The value of $P(U_1)$ is clearly equal to the sum of all the joint probabilities involving event U_1, namely, $P(M_1 \cap U_1)$ and $P(M_2 \cap U_1)$. This must be so because the events M_1 and M_2 are mutually exclusive. Thus we have

$$P(U_1) = P(M_1 \cap U_1) + P(M_2 \cap U_1) = 0.50.$$

c) What is the probability that an applicant's program objective will be MBA I?

Here again we have a marginal probability, $P(M_1)$. Since the events U_1, U_2, and U_3 are mutually exclusive, the value of $P(M_1)$ is the sum of the joint probabilities involving event M_1, so

$$P(M_1) = P(M_1 \cap U_1) + P(M_1 \cap U_2) + P(M_1 \cap U_3) = 0.60,$$

as we see from the first row of Table 2.2.

d) If it is known only that a particular applicant wishes to enter the MBA I program, what is the probability the applicant is an engineering undergraduate?

The required value is the conditional probability that event U_1 occurs given that event M_1 has occurred, or $P(U_1|M_1)$. From Equation (2.4), we have

$$P(U_1|M_1) = \frac{P(M_1 \cap U_1)}{P(M_1)} = \frac{0.28}{0.60} = 0.467.$$

In other words, about 47 percent of the MBA I program applicants can be expected to be engineering undergraduates.

e) If a certain applicant is known to be a science undergraduate, what is the probability the applicant will apply for the MBA I program?

The value desired is the probability that event M_1 occurs given that event U_2 has occurred, or the conditional probability $P(M_1|U_2)$. The relationship is

$$P(M_1|U_2) = \frac{P(M_1 \cap U_2)}{P(U_2)} = \frac{0.08}{0.20} = 0.40.$$

Thus, we expect 40 percent of the science undergraduates to apply for the MBA I program.

2.6   RULE OF ADDITION

We now develop a rule for the addition of the probabilities of events in a given sample space S. To develop this rule, we will utilize the Venn diagram in Figure 2.5.

The rectangle represents the sample space S. The irregular areas A and B represent events A and B. The shaded area A ∩ B represents the sample points common to both event A and event B.

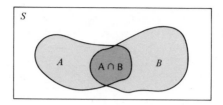

Figure 2.5

We wish to determine the probability that event A or event B (or both) will occur. We write this as $P(A \text{ or } B)$ or $P(A \cup B)$, where the symbol $\cup$ denotes "union". In probability usage, the term union always signifies what is called the "inclusive or," meaning that either one or both events occur.

If we now associate probabilities with the diagram of Figure 2.5, we wish to know the probability that a sample point lies within the region common to events A and B. Since events A and B both include the joint event $A \cap B$, we have

$$P(A \cup B) = P(A) + P(B) - P(A \cap B). \tag{2.7}$$

If we did not subtract the last term, we would be adding the probabilities of the sample points twice in the common region labeled $A \cap B$. Equation (2.7) is known as the *rule of addition*.

To illustrate the use of the rule of addition, consider again Example 2.2. Suppose we wish to know the probability that an applicant is an engineering undergraduate *or* will apply for the MBA I program.

The probability to be determined is $P(U_1 \cup M_1)$. By the rule of addition, we add the marginal probabilities of events U_1 and M_1 and subtract the joint probability of these two events:

$$\begin{aligned} P(U_1 \cup M_1) &= P(U_1) + P(M_1) - P(U_1 \cap M_1) \\ &= 0.50 + 0.60 - 0.28 \\ &= 0.82. \end{aligned}$$

If, in general, events A and B in sample space S contain no common sample points, as shown in the Venn diagram of Figure 2.6, then events A and B are *mutually exclusive*, so that if event A occurs, event B cannot occur, and vice versa. For this case, substituting $P(A \cap B) = 0$ in Equation (2.7), we have what is sometimes called the *special rule of addition*:

$$P(A \cup B) = P(A) + P(B) \tag{2.8}$$

when A and B are mutually exclusive events. This is just a restatement of probability axiom 2, stated in Section 2.2. Note the difference between Figure 2.6 and Figure 2.5.

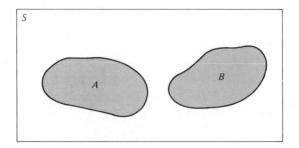

Figure 2.6

2.7 RULE OF MULTIPLICATION

If we take conditional probability Equations (2.4) and (2.5) and manipulate them slightly, we come up with an approach to the calculation of joint probabilities when marginal and conditional probabilities are known or readily obtained. Given events A and B in a sample space S, we know that

$$P(A\,|\,B) = \frac{P(A \cap B)}{P(B)}, \qquad \text{when } P(B) > 0.$$

Multiplying both sides by $P(B)$, we see that

$$P(A \cap B) = P(A\,|\,B)P(B). \tag{2.9}$$

Similarly, since

$$P(B\,|\,A) = \frac{P(A \cap B)}{P(A)}, \qquad \text{when } P(A) > 0,$$

we can multiply both sides by $P(A)$, obtaining

$$P(A \cap B) = P(B\,|\,A)P(A). \tag{2.10}$$

Equations (2.9) and (2.10) express the *rule of multiplication*, which we can illustrate graphically by what is called a "tree" diagram, as shown by Figure 2.7.

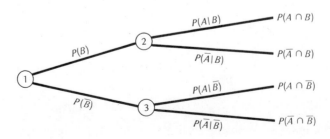

Figure 2.7

In a tree diagram, the nodes (circles) represent points where there are alternative possibilities (events), and the "branches" (arcs) the events. The probabilities for the events are given on the branches. At node 1, the alternatives are event B and event $\bar{B}$. At node 2, we know that event B has occurred, so the alternatives are events A and $\bar{A}$. The respective probabilities are conditional probabilities, $P(A|B)$ and $P(\bar{A}|B)$. Similarly, at node 3, event $\bar{B}$ has occurred, so the probabilities of the alternative events A and $\bar{A}$ are, respectively, $P(A|\bar{B})$ and $P(\bar{A}|\bar{B})$. The final column of joint probabilities is obtained by multiplying each conditional probability by its related marginal probability. For example, the joint probability $P(\bar{A} \cap \bar{B})$ at the bottom of the diagram is obtained by tracing a path back to the origin (node 1) and multiplying conditional probability $P(\bar{A}|\bar{B})$ by marginal probability $P(\bar{B})$.

Tree diagrams can be quite useful in the computation of joint probabilities, as we will show in the following example. Incidentally, Figure 2.7 illustrates, among other things, Equation (2.9). You should be able to easily sketch a similar figure to illustrate Equation (2.10), by starting with events A and $\bar{A}$ at node 1.

EXAMPLE 2.3

The Smith Company is interested in the possibility that a competitor, the Jones Company, will purchase new machinery. Smith is concerned about Jones' possible price cut, within the next six months, of a product that both companies manufacture. If the machinery is purchased, the president of Smith Company would be willing to give 3 to 1 odds that Jones will cut the price. If the machinery is not purchased, Smith feels that the odds would be 4 to 1 that Jones would not cut the price. Furthermore, Smith estimates the odds at 2 to 3 that the new machinery will be purchased. Smith wishes to estimate the overall probability of a price cut by Jones.

The first thing to do is to define the events of interest.

Let event M = new machinery purchased,
    event $\bar{M}$ = new machinery not purchased,
    event C = price is cut,
    event $\bar{C}$ = price is not cut.

Given the president's subjective betting odds, we can convert them to probabilities, as we showed earlier. We can also calculate their complementary event probabilities:

$$P(C|M) = 3/4 = 0.75, \quad \text{so that } P(\bar{C}|M) = 0.25,$$
$$P(\bar{C}|\bar{M}) = 4/5 = 0.80, \quad \text{so that } P(C|\bar{M}) = 0.20,$$
$$P(M) = 2/5 = 0.40, \quad \text{so that } P(\bar{M}) = 0.60.$$

The probability of interest to Smith is $P(C)$.

Since events M and $\bar{M}$ are mutually exclusive and the only events which occur jointly with event C,

$$P(C) = P(M \cap C) + P(\bar{M} \cap C).$$

We can solve for the joint probabilities $P(M \cap C)$ and $P(\bar{M} \cap C)$ by applying the rule of multiplication:

$$P(M \cap C) = P(C \,|\, M)P(M) = (0.75)(0.40) = 0.30,$$
$$P(\overline{M} \cap C) = P(C \,|\, \overline{M})P(\overline{M}) = (0.20)(0.60) = 0.12.$$

Then,

$$P(C) = 0.30 + 0.12 = 0.42.$$

The probability of a price cut would then be estimated as 0.42.

In the calculation of the required joint probability $P(M \cap C)$, for instance, the formula $P(M \cap C) = P(M \,|\, C)P(C)$ is also valid. However, the values of $P(M \,|\, C)$ and $P(C)$ are not given, so this formula is of no use to us in this example. This should become clear if we work out the joint probabilities using a tree diagram, as shown in Figure 2.8. If we had attempted to start at node 1 with events C and $\overline{C}$, with associated probabilities $P(C)$ and $P(\overline{C})$, we should have quickly realized that these probabilities were simply not available from the statement of the problem. As a matter of fact, we were trying to solve for $P(C)$.

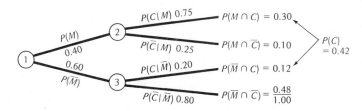

Figure 2.8

2.8   INDEPENDENT EVENTS

Consider two events A and B contained within a sample space S. Suppose that, if we know that event B has occurred, it gives us no information about the probability of occurrence of event A, and vice versa. If these conditions are met,

$$P(A \,|\, B) = P(A) \qquad \text{and} \qquad P(B \,|\, A) = P(B).$$

Then, according to the rule of multiplication, Equation (2.9),

$$P(A \cap B) = P(A \,|\, B)P(B) = P(A)P(B).$$

The same result is obtained using Equation (2.10):

$$P(A \cap B) = P(B \,|\, A)P(A) = P(A)P(B).$$

Therefore, A and B are *independent events* if and only if

$$P(A \cap B) = P(A)P(B). \tag{2.11}$$

Equation (2.11) is sometimes called the *special rule of multiplication*.

As an example of independent events, consider "rain tomorrow in Chicago" as event A and "rain tomorrow in Tokyo" as event B. If our subjective probability estimates were $P(A) = 0.2$ and $P(B) = 0.4$, then we could reasonably estimate the probability of the joint event $A \cap B$, "rain tomorrow in both Chicago and Tokyo," as $P(A \cap B) = P(A)P(B) = (0.2)(0.4) = 0.08$. It seems eminently reasonable to believe that weather conditions in Chicago and Tokyo are independent. If, however, we were considering weather conditions in Chicago and Detroit, say, our assumption of independence would be highly questionable.

Consider now a situation where we have a table of joint probabilities, such as that in Table 2.2 for the MBA example. In that example, we were interested in the two-way classification involving a student's choice of MBA program and his undergraduate specialization. In order for these classifications, or *attributes*, as they are sometimes called, to be independent, the probability of *each* joint event must be equal to the product of the probabilities of the corresponding marginal events. If this were the case, knowing a student's undergraduate specialization would give us no information as to which MBA program the student preferred, and vice versa.

If the value of *any* joint probability is not equal to the product of the corresponding marginal probabilities, then the two attributes are not independent. For instance, is $P(M_1 \cap U_2)$ equal to $P(M_1)P(U_2)$? The answer is in the negative, since, from Table 2.2,

$$P(M_1 \cap U_2) = 0.08 \quad \text{and} \quad P(M_1)P(U_2) = (0.60)(0.20) = 0.12.$$

Thus, the two attributes are not independent. If, for example, we knew that a student was an engineering undergraduate, we would get a different probability of preference for the MBA I program, say, than if the student were a science or "other" undergraduate. To see this, we can calculate the respective conditional probabilities:

$$P(M_1|U_1) = \frac{P(M_1 \cap U_1)}{P(U_1)} = \frac{0.28}{0.50} = 0.56,$$

$$P(M_1|U_2) = \frac{P(M_1 \cap U_2)}{P(U_2)} = \frac{0.08}{0.20} = 0.40,$$

$$P(M_1|U_3) = \frac{P(M_1 \cap U_3)}{P(U_3)} = \frac{0.24}{0.30} = 0.80.$$

If, on the other hand, our probability table had been as shown in Table 2.3, then the situation would have been quite different, as we will now demonstrate.

Table 2.3 Probability Table

| | | Undergraduate Specialization | | | |
| | | Engineering | Science | Other | |
Program	Event	U_1	Event U_2	U_3	Marginal Probability
MBA I	M_1	0.30	0.12	0.18	0.60
MBA II	M_2	0.20	0.08	0.12	0.40
Marginal Probability		0.50	0.20	0.30	1.00

In Table 2.3, you can easily verify that each joint probability is equal to the product of the corresponding marginal probabilities, so the two attributes are independent. Since this is the case, knowing a student's undergraduate specialization should give us no clue as to preference, say, for the MBA I program. This is confirmed by calculating the respective conditional probabilities:

$$P(M_1|U_1) = \frac{P(M_1 \cap U_1)}{P(U_1)} = \frac{0.30}{0.50} = 0.60 = P(M_1),$$

$$P(M_1|U_2) = \frac{P(M_1 \cap U_2)}{P(U_2)} = \frac{0.12}{0.20} = 0.60 = P(M_1),$$

$$P(M_1|U_3) = \frac{P(M_1 \cap U_3)}{P(U_3)} = \frac{0.18}{0.30} = 0.60 = P(M_1).$$

In Tables 2.2 and 2.3, the marginal probabilities are the same. The marginal probabilities can always be obtained by adding the appropriate joint probabilities. The joint probabilities uniquely determine the marginal probabilities, but the converse is obviously not true, as is clearly demonstrated by this example. Only if events are independent can we multiply marginal probabilities to get joint probabilities.

If we have a number of events $A_1, A_2, \ldots, A_n$ which are mutually independent (no event is affected by another event or combination of events), then the joint probability that all these mutually independent events occur together will be equal to the product of their individual event probabilities.

$$P(A_1 \cap A_2 \cap \cdots \cap A_n) = P(A_1)P(A_2)\cdots P(A_n), \tag{2.12}$$

for mutually independent events.

At this juncture, we should note that independent events and mutually exclusive events are two entirely different things. This is a point of confusion with many students, although it should not be. Independent events cannot be mutually exclusive, or they would not be independent, since the concept of mutual exclusivity means that if one event occurs, the other event cannot possibly occur. To give a simple example, suppose we flip a coin with distinguishable sides. The events "heads" and "tails" are clearly mutually exclusive. They cannot be independent, since if one occurs, the other cannot occur. On the other hand, if the coin is tossed twice, the events "heads on the first toss" and "tails on the second toss" are independent, since one is not influenced by the other. These two events, however, cannot possibly be mutually exclusive, since if one occurs, it in no way precludes the occurrence of the other.

2.9 BAYES' THEOREM

In the eighteenth century, the Reverend Thomas Bayes, an Englishman, discovered an interesting usage of the conditional probability relationship. Although the basic formula he developed can be applied to problems involving only objective probabilities, its most important applications have been those involving subjective probabilities. In some situations, Bayes interpreted probability as a degree of belief that a given outcome would occur. We explored this approach in some detail earlier in this chapter, and we will have much more to say about it later, when we delve into the topic of what is often called *Bayesian decision theory*.

In the type of situation where Bayes' approach is applicable, we are typically attempting to reason from effect to probable cause. That is, having observed the outcome of some type of statistical experiment (in the most general sense), we wish to evaluate the probability that the observed outcome was due to a particular event. Consider the following example.

EXAMPLE 2.4

Laboratory experiments have established that a test for a certain illegal drug gives a positive result 90 percent of the time when the drug has been used. When the drug has not been used, this test is negative 95 percent of the time. Of those suspected of using the drug, thorough tests on a random sample of these individuals showed that 10 percent were users of the drug. We wish to determine the probability that a suspected individual, whose test result is positive, is actually a user of the drug.

Let event A = individual uses the drug,
  event $\bar{A}$ = individual does not use the drug,
  event B = test result is positive (an outcome),
  event $\bar{B}$ = test result is negative (an outcome).

We are told that outcome B occurred, and we would like to know the probability that it could be attributed to event A, so the probability of interest is $P(A|B)$, the probability that event A occurs, given that event B has already occurred. The conditional probability relationship is

$$P(A|B) = \frac{P(A \cap B)}{P(B)}.$$

In the problem statement, we are given the following information:

$$P(B|A) = 0.90, \qquad P(\bar{B}|A) = 0.95, \qquad P(A) = 0.10.$$

The complementary probabilities are readily seen to be

$$P(\bar{B}|A) = 0.10, \qquad P(B|\bar{A}) = 0.05, \qquad P(\bar{A}) = 0.90.$$

By taking the problem data and structuring it in the form of a probability tree, as shown in Figure 2.9, the calculations of the joint probability $P(A \cap B)$ and the marginal probability $P(B)$ can be performed in a relatively straightforward fashion.

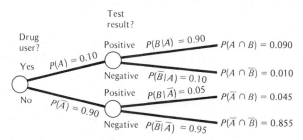

Figure 2.9

From Figure 2.9,

$$P(A \cap B) = 0.090,$$
$$P(B) = P(A \cap B) + P(\bar{A} \cap B) = 0.090 + 0.045 = 0.135.$$

Therefore,

$$P(A \mid B) = 0.090/0.135 = 0.667.$$

With a positive test result, the probability that the suspect uses the drug is 0.667.

This example illustrates the application of the Bayesian approach to statistical inference. Prior to making the test, the odds were 9 to 1 that the suspect *was not* a user of the drug, since only 10 percent of the individuals tested were users. After a positive test result, the odds changed to 2 to 1 that the suspect *was* a user of the drug. Thus the test evidence was used to modify, or revise, what is called the prior probability of the given event "individual uses the drug." This concept of probability revision, based on additional evidence, is very important in the study of statistical decision theory and will be discussed in depth in Chapters 6 and 7.

There is another way to show the calculation of revised probabilities which are based on the outcome of a statistical experiment. This involves a tabular presentation such as that shown in Table 2.4.

Table 2.4 Tabular Form for Calculating Revised Probabilities

(1) Event	(2) Prior Probability	(3) Outcome Probability	(4) Joint Probability	(5) Revised Probability
A	$P(A) = 0.10$	$P(B \mid A) = 0.90$	$P(A \cap B) = 0.090$	$P(A \mid B) = 0.667$
$\bar{A}$	$P(\bar{A}) = 0.90$	$P(B \mid \bar{A}) = 0.05$	$P(\bar{A} \cap B) = 0.045$	$P(\bar{A} \mid B) = 0.333$
	$\overline{1.00}$		$P(B) = \overline{0.135}$	$\overline{1.000}$

The construction of this table can be explained by considering what is contained in each column.

Column 1: The events, which must be mutually exclusive and collectively exhaustive.

Column 2: The prior (marginal) probabilities of the events. These probabilities must sum to 1.0.

Column 3: The conditional probabilities of the outcome (B, in this example). For each event, the conditional probability of the given outcome must be stated.

Column 4: The joint probability of each given event and the specified outcome. For a given event, each value in this column is the product of the prior and conditional probabilities associated with that event. The sum of all the joint probability values is the marginal probability that the specified outcome would occur.

Column 5: The revised (conditional) probability that each given event will occur, knowing that the specified outcome has occurred. For a given
event, the revised probability is obtained by dividing the associated
joint probability in column 4 by the marginal probability in column
4. This is just the standard conditional probability relationship. As
with prior probabilities, the revised probabilities must also sum to
1.0.

Again, of course, $P(A|B) = 0.667$. We also see that $P(\bar{A}|B) = 0.333$.

The tabular approach demonstrated here is not difficult to master. It spotlights
the probabilities required in the probability revision process, eliminates the need to
construct a probability tree, and introduces the student to some of the computations
required in Chapter 6, the study of decision making with additional information.

We are now ready for a formal development of Bayes' theorem. Suppose that a
number of events $A_1, A_2, \ldots, A_i, \ldots, A_n$ are mutually exclusive and collectively
exhaustive. Their prior marginal probabilities $P(A_1), P(A_2), \ldots, P(A_i), \ldots, P(A_n)$
are given. There is an experimental outcome B for which the conditional probabilities
$P(B|A_1), P(B|A_2), \ldots, P(B|A_i), \ldots, P(B|A_n)$ are also known. Given the information that outcome B has occurred, we wish to determine the revised probabilities
$P(A_i|B)$, for $i = 1, 2, \ldots, n$.

We begin with the fundamental conditional probability relationship,

$$P(A_i|B) = \frac{P(A_i \cap B)}{P(B)}.$$

The denominator can be formed as a sum of joint probabilities:

$$P(B) = P(A_1 \cap B) + \cdots + P(A_i \cap B) + \cdots + P(A_n \cap B).$$

Using the rule of multiplication, as in Equation (2.9), each required joint probability
can be expressed as the product of a known marginal and conditional probability. For
example, $P(A_i \cap B) = P(B|A_i)P(A_i)$. We thus arrive at the general form of Bayes'
theorem:

$$P(A_i|B) = \frac{P(B|A_i)P(A_i)}{P(B|A_1)P(A_1) + \cdots + P(B|A_i)P(A_i) + \cdots + P(B|A_n)P(A_n)}. \qquad \textbf{(2.13)}$$

As a further illustration of Bayes' theorem, consider the following example.

EXAMPLE 2.5

A certain company rates employee performance in three categories: excellent,
good, and fair. At the present time, the company's records show that 25 percent of its
employees are rated as excellent, 50 percent as good, and 25 percent as fair. The
company gives a test to each prospective employee who is otherwise fully qualified.
An applicant whose score exceeds 70 is hired. Past test results were broken into three
score ranges, 91 to 100, 81 to 90, and 71 to 80, and were correlated with employee
performance rating. The observed relationship between performance and score is
shown as a set of *conditional* probabilities in Table 2.5.

Table 2.5 Conditional Probabilities of Test Score
Given Performance Rating

Performance	Test Score		
	91–100	81–90	71–80
Excellent	0.70	0.20	0.10
Good	0.40	0.50	0.10
Fair	0.10	0.30	0.60

Since the test score categories are mutually exclusive and collectively exhaustive, the conditional probabilities in each *row* must sum to 1. Given a performance category, an employee's test score must fall in one of the three specified ranges. There is no such restriction on column probability totals, however, since each probability value in a particular column is conditional upon a different event.

Knowing only that an individual has passed the test, there would be a 25 percent chance the person would turn out to be an excellent employee, 50 percent chance a good employee, and 25 percent chance a fair employee. Now, suppose we are told that an employee scored between 91 and 100 on the test. Given this information, we wish to determine the revised probabilities that this person will turn out to be an excellent, good, or fair employee.

The first step is to define all events and outcomes, specify the required probabilities, and state all given probability values.

Let event E_1 = excellent employee performance,
   event E_2 = good employee performance,
   event E_3 = fair employee performance,
outcome B_1 = score between 91 and 100,
outcome B_2 = score between 81 and 90,
outcome B_3 = score between 71 and 80.

Table 2.6 Prior Event Probabilities and
Conditional Outcome Probabilities

Event E_i	Prior Probability $P(E_i)$	Conditional Outcome Probability $P(B_j\|E_i)$		
		B_1	B_2	B_3
E_1	0.25	0.70	0.20	0.10
E_2	0.50	0.40	0.50	0.10
E_3	0.25	0.10	0.30	0.60

The revised probabilities to be found are the conditional probabilities $P(E_1|B_1)$, $P(E_2|B_1)$, and $P(E_3|B_1)$. We are given data on the prior marginal probabilities $P(E_1)$, $P(E_2)$, and $P(E_3)$, as well as the entire set of conditional outcome probabilities of the form $P(B_j|E_i)$. These data are summarized in Table 2.6.

Now, utilizing the given prior probabilities and the conditional probabilities relating to outcome B_1 (third column, Table 2.6), Table 2.7 can be readily constructed. The procedure is just the same as for the previous example. Having three events, instead of two, adds no complications. We start by listing the events in

Table 2.7 Probability Revision Given Outcome B_1

(1) Event E_i	(2) Prior Probability $P(E_i)$	(3) Outcome Probability $P(B_1|E_i)$	(4) Joint Probability $P(E_i \cap B_1)$	(5) Revised Probability $P(E_i|B_1)$
E_1	0.25	0.70	0.175	0.438
E_2	0.50	0.40	0.200	0.500
E_3	0.25	0.10	0.025	0.062
	1.00		$P(B_1) = 0.400$	1.000

column 1 and their prior probabilities in column 2. The column 3 values are the conditional probability values for outcome B_1, taken from the first column of conditional probabilities in Table 2.6. The joint probabilities in column 4 are obtained from the product of the prior and conditional probabilities in the two preceding columns, and the marginal probability $P(B_1)$ is the sum of these joint probabilities. The revised probabilities in column 5 are calculated by dividing each joint probability in column 4 by the marginal probability $P(B_1)$ in that column.

Observe the direction of the change from the prior event probability values to the corresponding revised event probability values. Given a test score between 91 and 100, it is now much more likely that the person will be an excellent employee. This probability increased from 25 percent to about 44 percent. The probability of being a good employee just happened to remain unchanged, whereas the probability of being only a fair employee decreased sharply, as would be expected, from a value of 25 percent to just over 6 percent. It is always a good idea to compare the revised probabilities with the prior probabilities to verify that the changes appear to be intuitively reasonable.

If the test score had been, say, between 71 and 80 (outcome B_3), the results would have been quite different, as shown in Table 2.8. With a test score in the lowest range, there is now a 67 percent chance that the new employee will be rated fair, 22 percent chance rated good, and only 11 percent chance rated excellent.

Table 2.8 Probability Revision Given Outcome B_3

Event E_i	Prior Probability $P(E_i)$	Outcome Probability $P(B_3\|E_i)$	Joint Probability $P(E_i \cap B_3)$	Revised Probability $P(E_i\|B_3)$
E_1	0.25	0.10	0.025	0.111
E_2	0.50	0.10	0.050	0.222
E_3	0.25	0.60	0.150	0.667
	1.00		$P(B_3) = 0.225$	1.000

EXERCISES

2.1   For each of the areas specified below, identify a major decision which is strongly influenced by probability considerations, and state the nature of the probabilistic factor(s).
(a)   National government.
(b)   State government.
(c)   Law enforcement.
(d)   Professional sports.

2.2   In what sense can the process of registration for classes be considered a statistical experiment?

2.3   Suppose the Los Angeles Dodgers are playing a three-game series with the New York Mets. The overall outcome can be considered a statistical experiment. Define the elementary event as the sequence of Dodger wins in this series.
(a)   Define the sample space.
(b)   Is the event "Dodgers lose three games" an elementary event? Why?
(c)   Is the event "Mets win one game" an elementary event? Why?
(d)   Give at least one other way of defining the elementary event in this experiment. Be imaginative.

2.4   Give an example of a sample space which contains no sample points.

2.5   A company is considering the development of three products, A, B, and C. It may decide to develop all, any, or none of them.
(a)   What is the sample space for the products developed? (As an example of the notation to be used, sample point $\bar{A}B\bar{C}$ denotes development of product B only.)
(b)   Define the event F, the development of just one product.
(c)   Define the event G, development of more than one product.
(d)   Are events F and G mutually exclusive and collectively exhaustive? Explain briefly.

2.6   The sales personnel employed by the Acme Corporation, and their average monthly sales, are: Walker, $800; Hogan, $900; Teague, $1200; Kennedy, $850; Pace, $1000.

(a)   What is the sample space for sales personnel?

(b)   Employees whose sales exceed $800 per month are being considered for promotion. Define the event E, promotable employees.

(c)   Define the event X, employees whose average monthly sales are over $900.

(d)   Define the event Y, employees whose average monthly sales are less than $1000.

(e)   Are events X and Y mutually exclusive and collectively exhaustive? Explain briefly.

2.7 Are Equations (2.1) and (2.2), expressing two basic rules of probability, equally applicable to both objective and subjective probabilities? Explain.

2.8 Give examples, differing from those in the text, of both classical and relative frequency objective probabilities.

2.9 Suppose the weather forecast is for a 30 percent chance of rain tomorrow. How would you interpret the meaning of this as a probability value? What are some of the objective and subjective elements entering into this prediction?

2.10 Which of the following probabilities are primarily objective and which are primarily subjective? Explain each answer briefly. For those probabilities which can be considered primarily objective, what subjective elements can enter in?

(a)   The probability that the Dow-Jones Industrial Average will have increased by at least 5 percent one year from now.

(b)   The probability of drawing two consecutive aces from a deck of cards.

(c)   The probability that at least one hurricane will occur in Florida next October.

2.11 If the probability that the plans for a new shopping center will be approved is equal to p:

(a)   What are the odds against approval?

(b)   Determine the numerical odds against approval for p values of:

1.   0.30   2.   0.80   3.   0.10   4.   0.75

2.12 A gambler is offering odds on the game between football teams X and Y. His odds are as follows: 1 to 2 that team Y wins and 3 to 2 that team X wins.

(a)   Convert these odds into probabilities.

(b)   What probability is the gambler associating with a tie?

(c)   Convert the probability of a tie into odds.

2.13 Think about your degree of belief regarding an increase, by the close of the next business day, in the Dow-Jones average of thirty industrial stocks.

(a)   Consider a choice of two fictitious lotteries. The first pays $10 if the Dow-Jones average goes up and $0 if it does not. The second pays $10 if you select a red ball from an urn containing a combination of 200 red and white balls. How many red balls would you require to be in that urn before you would be indifferent to a choice between these two lotteries? On the basis of this, what is your subjective probability that the average will go up?

(b)   What odds would you give that the Dow-Jones average will go up? Are these odds consistent with the subjective probability you derived in (a)? If not, why not?

(c)   Suppose you were offered a reference contract worth $10 only if the Dow-Jones average went up. How much would you be willing to pay for this contract? What does this imply regarding your subjective probability that the average will go up? From a personal monetary viewpoint, why is this situation different than those in (a) and (b)?

2.14   Explain why a marginal probability can also be called an unconditional probability.

2.15   Given two events A and B which are not mutually exclusive, explain in words why the marginal probability of B is equal to the sum of the probabilities of the joint events $A \cap B$ and $\bar{A} \cap B$. Illustrate with a Venn diagram. Does this formula change if A and B are mutually exclusive? Explain.

2.16   An infamous insurance company had 100,000 life insurance policies written. Of these, only 60,000 were genuine, that is, were requested by the insured. Out of the total 70,000 policies were written on the lives of men. What is the probability that a policy selected at random is
(a)   fraudulent?
(b)   genuine and written on the life of a woman?

2.17   A manufacturing plant has 300 employees; 180 employees are men and 160 employees belong to the union. There are 60 women who are not members of the union. If an employee is chosen at random, what is the probability that the employee is:
(a)   a woman?
(b)   not a union member?
(c)   a woman who is a union member?
(d)   a man who is not a union member?

2.18   Two candidates for the office of mayor of Brokeville are Xactley and Youbett, otherwise known as X and Y. Each has been watching the polls to determine voter sentiments. A poll of 200 registered voters is taken by the Bullseye organization. The poll is devised to assess voter sentiments for X and Y, and also to see if sewage is the most important issue of the campaign. The results of the poll are:

	Voters for X	Voters for Y
Sewage most important issue	30	70
Other issue most important	60	40

(a)   What is the probability that a voter selected at random favors Xactley and does not believe that sewage is the most important issue?
(b)   What is the probability that a voter selected at random favors Youbett and believes that sewage is the most important issue?
(c)   What proportion of voters favor Xactley for mayor?
(d)   What proportion of voters believe that sewage is the most important issue?
(e)   A voter selected at random favors Xactley for mayor. What is the probability that this voter believes that sewage is the most important issue?

(f)   A voter selected at random believes that sewage is the most important issue in the campaign. What is the probability that this voter supports Youbett for mayor?

2.19   An exotic sports club has 750 members including 200 hang glider pilots and 600 scuba divers; 50 of the scuba divers are also hang glider pilots. If a member's name is selected at random, what is the probability that the member is
(a)   both a scuba diver and a hang glider pilot?
(b)   a scuba diver but not a hang glider pilot?
(c)   a hang glider pilot but not a scuba diver?

2.20   The members of a union were asked: "Would you favor a 4-day, 40-hour work week?" The responses, classified as to the number of years of union membership, were as follows

	Years of Union Membership			
Response	Under 1	1 to 3	4 to 10	Over 10
Yes	15	57	120	18
No	9	36	27	3
Don't know	6	3	6	0

Suppose that a union member is selected at random:
(a)   What is the probability he answered "yes?"
(b)   What is the probability that he answered "yes" and was in the union less than four years?
(c)   What is the probability he was in the union less than four years, if it is known that he answered "don't know?"
(d)   Because of the way in which the data are categorized, it is not possible to determine the probability that he has been a union member for at least two years, given that he answered "no." However, it is possible to bracket this probability. It must fall between two values. What are they?

2.21   It has been stated that, in some sense, all probabilities are conditional. Discuss this statement.

2.22   Given two events A and B, in a sample space S, explain in words why $P(A|\bar{B}) + P(\bar{A}|\bar{B}) = 1$. Illustrate, using a Venn diagram.

2.23   The Brinker Company is bidding on a study contract. The company estimates its probability of winning as 0.3. If it wins, there is a 0.8 probability of getting the follow-on production contract. If it does not win, the probability of obtaining the production contract is only 0.1.
(a)   Construct a probability table showing all joint and marginal probabilities.
(b)   What is the probability of winning the production contract?
(c)   What is the probability of getting the bid and not obtaining the production contract?

(d)   If it is known only that the production contract was not obtained, what is the probability the company's bid was successful?

2.24   Refer to the probability tree diagram in Figure 2.7. Start with the events A and $\bar{A}$ at node 1 and show all the marginal, conditional, and joint probabilities, just as was done in Figure 2.7 starting with events B and $\bar{B}$.

2.25   Precision Tool Company owns a five-year-old truck. After careful consideration, management has decided that there is one chance in five that the truck will need major repairs within the next year. The odds are 3 to 2 that it will require minor repairs. If major repairs are necessary, there is 0.75 probability the company will find purchase of a new truck more economical than repairing the present truck. If minor repairs are indicated, the odds are only 1 to 4 that the purchase of a new truck will prove to be justified. If no repairs are needed, Precision will keep the present truck at least through that year.
(a)   Use a probability tree to determine all joint probabilities.
(b)   What is the probability that a new truck will not be purchased within the next year?

2.26   A businessman feels that if he places a certain long distance business call station-to-station, he has a 0.40 chance of reaching his party the first time. If he is not successful, he can expect to get some information as to the best time to call, and he estimates that each subsequent call will have a probability of 0.7 of reaching his party.
(a)   What is the probability that it takes him exactly three calls to reach his party?
(b)   Suppose that a person-to-person call, on which he pays only when his party has been reached, costs $3.35. If a station-to-station call costs $1.20, what is the probability that it will be more expensive to call station-to-station than person-to-person, if the party must be reached?

2.27   In a survey of 500 married couples with at least one spouse employed, 300 of the families owned two or more cars. In 75 percent of the cases where more than one car was owned, both husband and wife were employed. In half the families, both spouses were employed.
(a)   What is the probability that a randomly selected family will own fewer than two cars?
(b)   What is the probability that a randomly selected family will own more than one car but only one spouse is employed?
(c)   Is the number of cars owned dependent on whether or not both spouses are employed? Explain the statistical evidence.

2.28   A firm has submitted bids on two jobs. It estimates the probability of getting contract A as 0.7, with that of getting contract B as 0.5. The probability of being unsuccessful on at least one of the bids is 0.6.
(a)   What is the probability that the firm will get at least one of the contracts?
(b)   With what probability would both bids be unsuccessful, assuming independence of the bid results?

2.29   An interplanetary spacecraft contains two independent radio communication systems. The probability that system A works throughout the mission is 0.98.

The probability that system B works throughout the mission is 0.99.
(a) What is the probability that exactly one of the radio systems fails during the mission?
(b) At least one of the radio systems must work throughout the mission. What is the probability that this is accomplished?

2.30 Officials of the Veterans' Administration are attempting to decide where to locate a large regional hospital. They are currently evaluating two possible sites and considering the next ten-year time period. Scientists say there is a 0.15 chance that an earthquake will occur in area B. Scientists estimate the earthquake probability in area A as 0.10. It is estimated that there is 0.80 probability that there will be no quake in either area.
(a) Construct a probability table showing all joint and marginal probabilities.
(b) What is the probability that there will be an earthquake in area A but not in area B?
(c) If there is a quake in area A, what is the probability of a quake in area B?
(d) Are the quake probabilities in the two areas independent? Explain.

2.31 The owner of a stereo equipment shop has kept careful records on sales. He has found that, once a woman enters the store and asks about stereo equipment, there is 0.15 probability she will purchase a receiver; 0.10 probability that she will purchase speakers; and 0.05 probability that she will purchase both. Considering only women inquiring about stereo equipment:
(a) What is the probability that a customer will purchase either a receiver or speakers?
(b) What is the probability that a customer will purchase either a receiver or speakers, but not both?
(c) If a customer purchases speakers, what is the probability she does not purchase a receiver?
(d) If a customer purchases a receiver, what is the probability she will purchase speakers?

2.32 One out of ten people employed by Company X is a college graduate, but the proportion is one out of four for Company Y. If one person from each company is chosen at random, what is the probability that
(a) both are college graduates?
(b) the Company X employee is not a college graduate?
(c) the Company X employee is a college graduate but the Company Y employee is not?
(d) at most one of the two is a college graduate?
(e) at least one of them is a college graduate?

2.33 An ardent horseracing enthusiast has been following a thoroughbred named Winning Ways III (or WW III for short). A survey of the current year's results shows that WW III wins 10 percent of the races when the track is dry and 20 percent of the races when the track is muddy. The track at which WW III is now running is muddy 30 percent of the time and dry otherwise.
(a) What proportion of his races has WW III been winning this year?
(b) On May 1, WW III won a major stakes race. What is the probability the track was muddy that day?

2.34   The two doctors at a clinic are known as Phil the Pill and Norm the Knife. According to clinic records, Phil prescribes medicine alone for 90 percent of his patients and surgery alone for the other 10 percent of his patients. By contrast Norm sends 40 percent of his patients to surgery and the other 60 percent to the hospital pharmacy for a prescription. Thirty percent of the clinic patients see Norm, the rest see Phil.
   (a)   What proportion of the clinic's patients are referred to surgery?
   (b)   What is the chance that a surgical patient selected at random was sent by Norm?

2.35   Two new ocean liners are christened AD and T to honor their famous predecessors, the Andrea Doria and the Titanic. The chance that the AD will cross the Atlantic Ocean and arrive on schedule is 0.75; the chance for the T is 0.65. The AD carries 1600 passengers; the T carries 1400 passengers. If a passenger's name is drawn at random from the combined list of 3000 passengers crossing the Atlantic Ocean, what is the probability that
   (a)   the passenger is on a ship that arrives on schedule?
   (b)   the passenger is on the AD, given that the passenger is on a ship that arrives on schedule?

2.36   In a certain assembly operation with two operators, the faster assembler builds 80 assemblies per hour, and the slower assembler builds only 50 assemblies per hour. However, the faster assembler produces, on the average, 2.5 percent defectives, compared to the slower assembler's defect rate of 1.2 percent.
   (a)   What is the overall probability of a defective assembly?
   (b)   An assembly is selected at random and found to be defective. What is the probability it was produced by the slower assembler?

2.37   A relatively inexpensive test will, 90 percent of the time, detect a flaw serious enough to make a manufactured casting unacceptable. If such a flaw does not exist, the test will be negative 80 percent of the time. In the past, 5 percent of the castings have been unacceptably flawed.
   (a)   Draw a probability tree for this problem. What is the probability of a negative test result?
   (b)   If the test results are positive on a randomly selected casting, what is the probability that it is unacceptable? Briefly explain your answer. (In other words, why is this probability so low?)

2.38   A company that manufactures electric blankets purchases its thermostats from three different suppliers in the following percentages: 20 percent from the Abel Company, 40 percent from the Bakewell Company, and 40 percent from the Cantfail Company. On the basis of past records, failures during final testing have been noted for 2.5 percent of the thermostats from the Abel Company, 1.5 percent from the Bakewell Company, and 1.0 percent from the Cantfail Company.
   (a)   What overall fraction of thermostats can be expected to fail during final testing? Illustrate with a probability tree.
   (b)   If a thermostat is observed to fail at final testing, what is the probability that it was supplied by the Abel Company?

(c) If a thermostat passes final testing, what is the probability that it was supplied by the Abel Company?

2.39 Refer to Example 2.5.

(a) If a new employee receives a test score between 81 and 90, what is the chance that employee will be rated fair, good, or excellent?

(b) Verify that the marginal probabilities of the three possible outcomes (B_1, B_2, or B_3) sum to 1.0. Briefly explain why this must be so.

CHAPTER 3

PROBABILITY DISTRIBUTIONS

In many business situations, a decision maker is faced with the problem of attempting to quantify judgment regarding probabilistic outcomes of an event. For instance, an automobile dealer placing an order for sports cars prior to the start of the new-car-selling season presumably bases the order on some estimate of the initial demand for these cars. If the (subjective) probability of each possible first-week demand for sports cars can be estimated, then, given a decision-making model, a considered judgment as to the best number of sports cars to order can be made. If the dealer assesses the probability that each possible value of the first-week demand for sports cars will occur, a *discrete probability distribution* has been specified, since the demand for sports cars can assume only a finite number of values. Consider another example. The Los Angeles Department of Water and Power (DWP) must plan far in advance for the peak summer-time daily demand for electricity. It is clear that the actual demand is unknown, because it depends on many diverse factors. DWP officials, however, must make reasonable judgments as to the peak demand in order to make the necessary decisions on construction, operation, and allocation of power sources. One way to make such judgments is to estimate, for a number of different demand values, the probability that the peak demand will exceed the given value. This information facilitates the construction of a *continuous probability distribution* of demand.

Following our study of basic probability theory, we now extend the discussion of probability by introducing the concepts of both discrete and continuous probability distributions and by examining in detail some of those distributions most frequently encountered. First, however, we must discuss the nature and attributes of random variables.

3.1   RANDOM VARIABLES

If any possible outcome of a statistical experiment can be represented by a unique numerical value, the function which defines the entire set of such values is called a *random variable*. As a very simple example, consider the toss of a fair die. The outcome of this statistical experiment is the number of spots showing, from 1 to 6. If we define a random variable X as the square of the number of spots showing, the possible values of X will be 1, 4, 9, 16, 25, and 36. Or, we could define a random variable Y in the following manner: if the number of spots is even, Y is equal to the number of spots; if the number of spots is odd, Y is equal to twice the number of spots. The possible values of Y are then 2, 4, 6, and 10. (Although there are six different outcomes, there are only four different values of Y. Observe carefully, however, that for each possible outcome, there is one and only one value of Y.) It should be apparent that, for any statistical experiment, the number of random variables which could be defined is unlimited.

Discrete random variables can assume only a finite or what is termed countably infinite number of values, usually, but not always, integers. The number of patrons in a movie theater, the number of different machines breaking down in a factory on a given day, and the fraction of phone booths occupied at a given instant in an airport are all discrete random variables with a finite number of values. The number of letters received by a post office during a certain time period would be a countably infinite discrete random variable, meaning that the number of possible values has no inherent limitation. Nonnumerical random outcomes can be assigned numerical values, thereby establishing random variables. Thus, if we are bidding on a contract, we could, if we so desired, assign the value 0 to losing the bid, 1 to winning the bid, and 0.5 to a request to resubmit a new bid. These numerical values are, of course, arbitrary.

Continuous random variables can take on any value within some particular interval or intervals. The amount of water used in a city in a given month, the daily tonnage produced by a steel blast furnace, and the noon atmospheric pressure at the Los Angeles International Airport are all continuous random variables. Frequently, we will find that discrete random variables, under certain conditions, can be closely and conveniently represented by continuous random variables. We will explore this point later.

In general, we will find that discrete random variables tend to involve counts, while continuous random variables usually involve measurements.

In future developments, we will represent a random variable by a capital letter and a specific value of that random variable by a lowercase letter. Thus, X could represent a random variable denoting the daily sales of a particular item, and x would be the actual sales recorded on a particular day.

We will first consider discrete probability distributions, particularly the binomial and Poisson. Then, we will take up the study of continuous probability distributions, with emphasis on the normal distribution.

3.2   DISCRETE PROBABILITY DISTRIBUTIONS

Probability Mass Functions and Cumulative Probability Functions

Any discrete probability distribution can be represented by what is termed a *probability mass function* (pmf). For any given random variable, the pmf is just an enumeration of each possible value which can occur and its associated probability. For a random variable X, assuming values $x_1, x_2, \ldots, x_n$ with associated probabilities $p_1, p_2, \ldots, p_n$, the pmf could be written as

$$P(x_i) = p_i, \qquad i = 1, 2, \ldots, n,$$

where the notation $P(x_i)$ is shorthand for $P(X = x_i)$, the probability that the random variable X assumes the specific value x_i. We will use this abbreviated notation whenever there is no possibility of confusion. A pmf must satisfy two conditions:

1. Each individual probability value must be nonnegative, or

$$P(x_i) \geq 0.$$

2. The individual probability values must sum to 1.0, so

$$\sum_i P(x_i) = 1,$$

where the symbol Σ is the Greek letter sigma, denoting a summation of all the terms in the given expression following the sigma, and the letter i beneath the sigma indicates that the summation is to be performed for all values of i, the so-called index of summation. Thus, for $i = 1, 2, \ldots, n,$

$$\sum_i P(x_i) = P(x_1) + /(x_2) + \cdots + P(x_n).$$

EXAMPLE 3.1

Data on mail orders for a certain lamp is shown in Table 3.1, where we let D denote the random variable "daily lamp orders," so that d represents a specific number of orders.

Table 3.1   Daily Lamp Orders over a Period of 100 Days

Orders, d	Frequency (number of days)	Relative Frequency
0	14	0.14
1	25	0.25
2	48	0.48
3	13	0.13
	100	

If we assume that the demand (see the first column) for this item will not change in the near future, we can utilize past experience as a guide. We can then use the third column of values in Table 3.1 as probabilities for the number of lamps ordered. The pmf would then be

$$P(0) = 0.14,$$
$$P(1) = 0.25,$$
$$P(2) = 0.48,$$
$$P(3) = 0.13.$$

When plotted, the abscissa represents the specific values of the random variable and the ordinate the associated probability values, as in Figure 3.1. Each probability value appears as a vertical line.

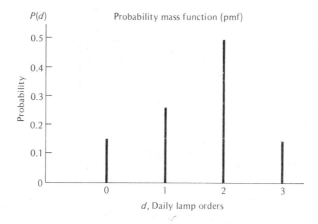

Figure 3.1

As we will see shortly, cumulative probability distributions are very useful when working with probability distributions. Given a random variable X, we define the *cumulative distribution function* (cdf) for a specific value x as the probability that X takes on a value less than or equal to x. (The cdf is probably the most used form of cumulative probability distribution.) The cdf would be denoted as $F(x)$. By definition, then,

$$F(x) \equiv P(X \leq x) = \sum_{x_i \leq x} P(x_i). \tag{3.1}$$

The summation on the right indicates that we are to add up all the probabilities for x_i values which do not exceed the specified x value.

From the data in Example 3.1, the values of $F(d)$ associated with the four possible values of the random variable D, daily lamp orders, are:

$$F(0) = P(D \leq 0) = P(0) = 0.14,$$
$$F(1) = P(D \leq 1) = P(0) + P(1) = 0.39,$$

$$F(2) = P(D \leqslant 2) = P(0) + P(1) + P(2) = 0.87,$$
$$F(3) = P(D \leqslant 3) = P(0) + P(1) + P(2) + P(3) = 1.00.$$

If these data are plotted in a manner similar to those for the pmf, the results will be as shown in Figure 3.2. In the figure the circles denote the fact that the higher $F(d)$ value applies at each point where the function takes a step. This follows from the "less than or equal to" inequality in the definition of a cdf, as stated in Equation (3.1).

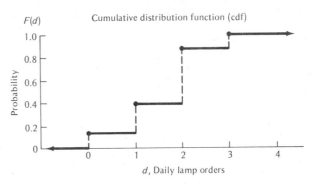

Figure 3.2

It should be noted that the cdf is actually a step function which is defined for any value of d, regardless of whether that value can be assumed by the random variable D. For example,

$$F(1.83) = P(D \leqslant 1.83) = P(0) + P(1) = 0.39,$$

as can be seen in Figure 3.2.

From the definition in Equation (3.1), the cdf can be stated algebraically as

$$F(d) = \begin{cases} 0.00 \text{ for } d < 0, \\ 0.14 \text{ for } 0 \leqslant d < 1, \\ 0.39 \text{ for } 1 \leqslant d < 2, \\ 0.87 \text{ for } 2 \leqslant d < 3, \\ 1.00 \text{ for } d \geqslant 3. \end{cases}$$

Returning now to the general case, the cdf must satisfy certain basic conditions. Given a random variable X:

1. $$0 \leqslant F(x) \leqslant 1,$$

which must be so because $F(x)$ is a probability.

2. $$F(a) \leqslant F(b), \qquad \text{if } a < b.$$

The cdf is a nondecreasing function. As the value of x increases from a to b, $F(x)$ must either increase (if X takes on a value in the interval between a and b) or remain the same (if X does not take on a value in that interval).

3. $F(-\infty) = 0,$ and $F(\infty) = 1.$

These limiting conditions follow naturally from the definition of a cdf in Equation (3.1). As we move to the left along the abscissa of a cdf graph, such as that in Figure 3.2, the probability must eventually go to zero. Similarly, as we move to the right, the probability must eventually become unity.

Assessment of Subjective Probability Distributions

Suppose we were attempting to estimate the demand for an item not stocked previously or for an item previously stocked but for which the probability distribution of demand appears to have changed. In such a situation, if the number of possible values of the random variable representing demand is relatively small, say approximately ten or less, a subjective discrete probability distribution can be structured, based on our degree of belief that each possible value of the random variable (demand) will occur. There are several ways of doing this, but we will illustrate only one, an approach which seems quite straightforward. To clarify the procedure, we will use a numerical example.

EXAMPLE 3.2

A tractor dealer is trying to decide how many of the new Model 007 tractors should be stocked. The initial stock will have to last a month, and during that period, on the basis of past experience, the dealer estimates that at least two, but no more than six, tractors will be sold. In order to determine the optimal number of tractors to stock, what is needed, in addition to knowledge of the economic factors of primary interest, is the probability distribution of demand.

The suggested method of estimating the desired distribution is based on the graphical construction of a probability mass function, such as that shown in Figure 3.1. To start, a horizontal axis is drawn and a scale constructed to show each value of the given random variable. For this example, the scale covers the range from 2 to 6 units. Then, as shown in Figure 3.3, a vertical line, of any convenient height, is drawn to represent the probability of occurrence of any one of the values of the random variable. This vertical line serves as a reference value. The probability of occurrence of each of the other possible values of the random variable is then compared to that of the reference value (or any subsequent value) and a vertical line of proportionate height is drawn. In this example, the reference value is the probability of a demand of 2 units (tractors).

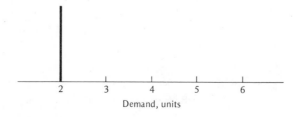

Figure 3.3

Suppose the tractor dealer then makes the following judgments:

a demand of 3 units is half again as likely (factor of 1.5);
a demand of 4 units is somewhat less likely (factor of, say, 0.8);
a demand of 5 units is half as likely (factor of 0.5);
a demand of 6 units is a quarter as likely (factor of 0.25).

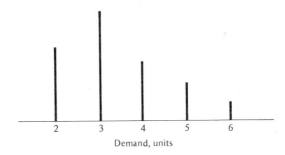

Figure 3.4

As the dealer makes each judgment, the appropriate line is drawn on the graph (Figure 3.4), adjusting its relative height until satisfied. (It is not always necessary to use the original reference line for comparative purposes. Any previously constructed line can be referenced. Thus, the demand for 4 units might have been expressed as half the demand for 3 units, and so on.) Since the vertical lines represent probabilities, their probability values must sum to 1.0. We can then establish any convenient vertical scale, measure the height of each line, and then divide its value by the sum of all these heights to get its individual probability value. This process of summing individual values and then dividing each such value by that sum is called a *normalizing process*. The sum of such normalized values must equal 1.0. In this example, if the height of the line representing the probability of a demand of 2 units is taken as 1.0, the sum of all five height values is $1.0 + 1.5 + 0.8 + 0.5 + 0.25 = 4.05$. The subjective probabilities are then, to the nearest 0.01:

$$P(2) = 1.0/4.05 = 0.25,$$
$$P(3) = 1.5/4.05 = 0.37,$$
$$P(4) = 0.8/4.05 = 0.20,$$
$$P(5) = 0.5/4.05 = 0.12,$$
$$P(6) = 0.25/4.05 = 0.06.$$

The resultant pmf is plotted in Figure 3.5.

As noted, this is only one of a number of possible approaches to the development of subjective discrete probability distributions. This particular approach appears to be intuitively appealing and conceptually straightforward.

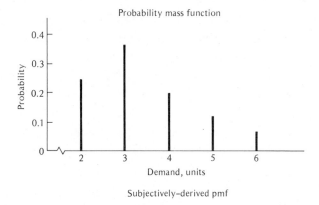

Figure 3.5

Expectation, Variance, and Standard Deviation

In Example 3.1, during the 100-day period covered by the data presented in Table 3.1, the total number of lamps ordered was $(0)(14) + (1)(25) + (2)(48) + (3)(13) = 160$. Now, suppose that the only information given us was that the random variable D, daily lamp orders, took on only the values 0, 1, 2, or 3, with probability values of 0.14, 0.25, 0.48, and 0.13, respectively. If we multiplied every possible value of the random variable D by the probability of that value's occurrence and then summed these products, we would get the expected value of D, written as $E(D)$. In this example, we have:

$$E(D) = (0)(0.14) + (1)(0.25) + (2)(0.48) + (3)(0.13)$$
$$= 0 + 0.25 + 0.96 + 0.39 = 1.60 \text{ orders per day.}$$

We can interpret this value as the mean number of daily orders over many many trials of the statistical experiment of recording the daily number of orders for the lamp.

For the general case, consider a random variable X which can assume n different values $x_1, x_2, \ldots, x_n$ with associated probabilities $P(x_1), P(x_2), \ldots, P(x_n)$. The expected value of X is denoted by $E(X)$. It is a weighted average of all the possible values of X and is expressed as

$$E(X) = \sum_i x_i P(x_i). \tag{3.2}$$

Thus, to get the expected value of a random variable, we take each possible value the random variable can assume, weight it by its probability of occurrence, and sum all these products.

Suppose we are offered a 50–50 chance at winning \$2 or losing \$1, and this opportunity is available to us 10,000 times. Then, since we could reasonably anticipate as many wins as losses, the total amount won would be very close to $(5000)(2) + (5000)(-1)$ or \$5000. With 10,000 "trials," if the total amount won were

$5000, the average amount won per "trial" would be 5000/10,000 = $0.50. We could have obtained this result by utilizing Equation (3.2), since the expected value of the random variable (profit, in this case) is equal to

$$(0.5)(2) + (0.5)(-1) = \$0.50.$$

Observe that $0.50 can never be won on any single trial, since we either win $2 or lose $1.

Even if the opportunity for this gamble occurs only once, and is not repeated, the expected value of the set of probabilistic outcomes is still meaningful. In this situation, if we had to pay $0.50 for each such wager, the wager would be considered "fair," since the long-term expectation of gain or loss would be zero. Thus, the expected value of a gamble (or risky venture) can be viewed as a measure of value of that gamble. As another example, visualize a situation where an investor has to decide between two possible investments. The first will yield a profit of $3000 with a probability of 0.75 or $0 with 0.25 probability. The second is equally likely to return a profit of either $1000 or $2000. The expected value of the first investment is $(0.75)(3000) + (0.25)(0) = \$2250$; the expected value of the second investment is $(0.5)(1000) + (0.5)(2000) = \$1500$. Most persons would prefer the first investment, since it has the higher expected value. (It should be noted, however, that those to whom $1000 meant a great deal would probably prefer the second investment, because it would assure them of at least $1000, win or lose. Such an outlook involves consideration of an individual's *utility* for money in risky situations, and this topic will be discussed in Chapter 5.)

The expected value of a random variable is a measure of the central tendency of that random variable. As we will see, it is a meaningful way to describe one characteristic of a random variable and to compare one random variable with another.

There are several rules, relating to expected values, which we will find to be important in subsequent derivations and developments.

1. If each value of a random variable is multiplied by a constant, the expected value of that product equals the constant times the expected value of the random variable. Given random variable X and constant a,

$$E(aX) = aE(X). \tag{3.3}$$

2. If a constant is added to a random variable, the expected value of the sum is equal to the expected value of the random variable plus the value of the constant. Give random variable X and constant a,

$$E(X + a) = E(X) + a. \tag{3.4}$$

3. If random variables $X_1, X_2, \ldots, X_n$ are added, the expected value of the sum of these random variables is equal to the sum of the expected values of the random variables.

$$E(X_1 + X_2 + \cdots + X_n) = E(X_1) + E(X_2) + \cdots + E(X_n). \tag{3.5}$$

We will make considerable use of this third rule a little later.

One measure of the dispersion, or spread, of a random variable about its expected value is called the *variance*. It is one of the fundamental measures by which we can conveniently describe certain probability distributions. The greater the dispersion of a random variable, the greater its variance. The variance $V(X)$ of a random variable X is defined as the expectation of the squared deviations of the individual values of X from the expected value of X.

$$V(X) = \sum_i \left[x_i - E(X)\right]^2 P(x_i). \tag{3.6}$$

By expanding the right-hand side of this equation, we can derive another expression for the variance:

$$\begin{aligned} V(X) &= \sum_i x_i^2 P(x_i) - 2E(X) \sum_i x_i P(x_i) + \left[E(X)\right]^2 \sum_i P(x_i) \\ &= E(X^2) - 2E(X)E(X) + \left[E(X)\right]^2 \\ &= E(X^2) - \left[E(X)\right]^2. \end{aligned} \tag{3.7}$$

As with expected values, there are several useful rules relating to variance.

1. If each value of a random variable is multiplied by a constant, the variance of that product equals the square of the constant times the variance of the random variable. Given random variable X and constant a,

$$V(aX) = a^2 V(X). \tag{3.8}$$

2. If a constant is added to a random variable, the variance of the sum is equal to the variance of the random variable. Given random variable X and constant a,

$$V(X + a) = V(X). \tag{3.9}$$

3. If we have a random variable X which represents the summation of *independent* random variables $X_1, X_2, \ldots, X_n$, the variance of the sum is equal to the sum of the individual variances, so that

$$V(X_1 + X_2 + \cdots + X_n) = V(X_1) + V(X_2) + \cdots + V(X_n). \tag{3.10}$$

As noted, Equation 3.10 is applicable only when the individual random variables are independent. The concept of independent random variables is very similar to the concept of independent events discussed in the previous chapter. Thus, given events A and B, we showed that these events are independent only if the probability of the joint event $A \cap B$ was equal to the product of the marginal probabilities, or $P(A \cap B) = P(A)P(B)$. If we have random variables X and Y, assuming specific values x_i and y_j, respectively, then X and Y are independent if $P(x_i \cap y_j) = P(x_i)P(y_j)$, for all i and j. The extension to the case of more than two independent random variables should be clear; it is entirely similar to the extension to more than two independent events, as given in Equation (2.12).

Although the variance is a good measure of the dispersion of a probability distribution, it has the disadvantage of being in squared units of measurement. Thus, if a random variable is measured in gallons, the variance will be measured in (gallons)^2. To avoid this inconvenience, we use the standard deviation as a measure of dispersion. The standard deviation is equal to the positive square root of the variance, so that the standard deviation will always be expressed in the same units of measurement as the random variable itself. For a random variable X, the standard deviation will be denoted as $S(X)$. By definition, then,

$$S(X) = \sqrt{V(X)}. \tag{3.11}$$

Let us now take an example to illustrate some of these concepts.

EXAMPLE 3.3

In the management of inventory, lead time is defined as the time between the placement of an order with a vendor and receipt of the actual goods. The Varoom Sales Company's best estimate of the lead time required for ordering a certain brand of television consoles from the Teevee Distribution Company is summarized in Table 3.2. A lead time of 3 days, for instance, means that the order will be received on the third day after the order is placed.

a) What is the expected lead time, in days?

Table 3.2 Data on Lead Time

Lead Time (days)	Probability
2	0.3
3	0.4
4	0.1
5	0.2

Let T be the random variable denoting lead time and t_i a specific value of T. The expected value of T is then, from Equation (3.2):

$$E(T) = \sum_i t_i P(t_i)$$

The required computations are shown in Table 3.3.

Table 3.3 Calculation of Expected Value $E(T)$

t_i	$P(t_i)$	$t_i P(t_i)$
2	0.3	0.6
3	0.4	1.2
4	0.1	0.4
5	0.2	1.0
		$E(T) = \overline{3.2}$ days

By our definition of lead time in this problem, an actual lead time value of 3.2 days can never occur, since the lead time will be 2, 3, 4, or 5 days. The value of 3.2 days is a weighted value which represents a measure of the central location of this probability distribution.

b) What is the standard deviation of the lead time?

To get the standard deviation $S(T)$, we first calculate the variance $V(T)$. This can be done by either of the two methods previously presented. Both methods are illustrated in Table 3.4.

Table 3.4 Calculation of Variance $V(T)$

t_i	$P(t_i)$	First Method (Equation 3.6)		Second Method (Equation 3.7)	
		$[t_i - E(T)]^2$	$[t_i - E(T)]^2 P(t_i)$	t_i^2	$t_i^2 P(t_i)$
2	0.3	$(-1.2)^2 = 1.44$	0.432	4	1.2
3	0.4	$(-0.2)^2 = 0.04$	0.016	9	3.6
4	0.1	$0.8^2 = 0.64$	0.064	16	1.6
5	0.2	$1.8^2 = 3.24$	0.648	25	5.0
			$V(T) = \overline{1.160}$ (days)^2		$E(T^2) = \overline{11.4}$ (days)^2

To complete the second method,

$$V(T) = E(T^2) - [E(T)]^2 = 11.4 - 3.2^2 = 1.16 \text{ (days)}^2.$$

The standard deviation of the lead time is $S(T) = \sqrt{V(T)} = \sqrt{1.16} = 1.08$ days.

At this point, we will take up the study of some of the more common discrete probability distributions. Our primary interest will be in their application later to decision analyses.

Binomial Distribution

Visualize a statistical experiment where there are only two possible outcomes of a given trial; success, with probability p, or failure, with probability $1 - p = q$. The designations "success" and "failure" are used only to differentiate the two outcomes, not to imply their degree of desirability. Thus, in a particular statistical experiment, finding a defective item could be designated as a success.

If we have a stationary process, whereby the probability p (and thus q) remains constant over a series of such trials, and if the result of each trial is independent of the result of any other trial, we have what is termed a *Bernoulli process*, or a sequence of Bernoulli trials (named after James Bernoulli, a seventeenth-century Swiss mathematician). As an example of a Bernoulli process, suppose we randomly selected some license plate numbers of automobiles registered in California and then checked the records to find out how many were station wagons. Each individual selection would represent a statistical trial, and each such trial would be independent if we sampled with replacement by allowing the (remote) possibility of selecting the same license number more than once. If we denoted success as selection of a station wagon, then the success probability would be equal to the proportion of automobiles registered as station wagons in California.

The distribution of the random variable R, denoting the number of successes in n Bernoulli trials, each with success probability p, is termed a binomial probability distribution with parameters n and p. The term *parameter* designates the type of information required to define a specific probability distribution from among a family of probability distributions. Thus, for the binomial distribution, the parameter n is the number of trials (a positive integer) and the parameter p is the individual trial success probability (any value between 0 and 1).

To show the form of the binomial distribution, consider the case where a random sample of four California automobile license numbers is taken and the type of vehicle determined. Let a success, event S, be the selection of a station wagon. A failure, event F, is the selection of any other type of car. What is the probability of selecting exactly one station wagon if the proportion of station wagons, among automobiles registered in California, is 0.20?

The probability of getting 1 success, followed by 3 failures, can be denoted as $P(S \cap F \cap F \cap F)$. Since each trial is independent, we have, by Equation (2.12):

$$P(S \cap F \cap F \cap F) = P(S)P(F)P(F)P(F) = pq^3 = (0.20)(0.80)^3 = 0.1024.$$

But, there are several possible orderings, or *permutations*, in which one success and three failures can occur. In this example, the possible permutations are: $SFFF$, $FSFF$, $FFSF$, $FFFS$. Each of these 4 permutations is equally likely to occur, since the trials are independent, so the probability of exactly 1 success is

$$P(R = 1) = P(1) = (4)(0.1024) = 0.4096.$$

For the general case, the probability of exactly r successes and $n - r$ failures in n Bernoulli trials, each with success probability p, is

$$P(r) = \binom{n}{r} p^r q^{n-r}, r = 0, 1, 2, \ldots, n, \tag{3.12}$$

where $\binom{n}{r} = \dfrac{n!}{r! \, (n - r)!}$ and $n!$ ("n factorial") $= (n)(n - 1)(n - 2) \ldots (1)$. (*Note:* $0! = 1$.) The term $\binom{n}{r}$ represents the number of distinguishable permutations (orderings) of r things of one kind and $n - r$ things of another kind. In the previous example, $n = 4$ and $p = 0.20$. Then, for $r = 1$,

$$P(1) = \binom{4}{1} (0.20)^1(0.80)^3 = \frac{4!}{1!3!}(0.20)(0.512) = (4)(0.1024) = 0.4096.$$

It is not difficult to show that Equation (3.12) represents a valid probability mass function (pmf). The so-called binomial theorem (see any basic algebra text or statistics handbook) can be used to expand the sum of any two terms raised to a power. If we perform this operation on $(p + q)^n$, we get

$$(p + q)^n = p^n + \binom{n}{n-1} p^{n-1}q + \binom{n}{n-2} p^{n-2}q^2 + \cdots + q^n.$$

Each of these terms is a binomial probability, as you can see by referring to Equation (3.12). Since $p + q = 1$, and $1^n = 1$, for any n, the sum of all the binomial probabilities must equal 1.0. Thus Equation (3.12) satisfies both the required conditions, as stated earlier, for a pmf.

Properties   Suppose we define a random variable R_j which takes the value 1 if trial j is a success, and the value 0 if it is a failure. With a success probability p, the expected value of R_j is

$$E(R_j) = (1)(p) + (0)(q) = p.$$

If the random variable R denotes the number of success in n trials, then

$$R = R_1 + R_2 + \cdots + R_j + \cdots + R_n.$$

From Equation (3.5), the expected value is

$$\begin{aligned} E(R) &= E(R_1) + E(R_2) + \cdots + E(R_j) + \cdots + E(R_n) \\ &= p + p + \cdots + p + \cdots + p \\ &= np. \end{aligned} \tag{3.13}$$

The standard deviation of the binomial distribution is also easily obtained. Utilizing equation (3.7), we first obtain the variance of R_j, which is the variance for a single Bernoulli trial:

$$\begin{aligned} V(R_j) &= E(R_j^2) - [E(R_j)]^2 = (1)^2 p + (0)^2 q - p^2 \\ &= p - p^2 = p(1 - p) = pq. \end{aligned}$$

Then, since the individual trials are independent (because we have stipulated a Bernoulli process), Equation (3.10) is applicable:

$$\begin{aligned} V(R) &= V(R_1) + V(R_2) + \cdots + V(R_j) + \cdots + V(R_n) \\ &= pq + pq + \cdots + pq + \cdots + pq = npq. \end{aligned}$$

The standard deviation is

$$S(R) = \sqrt{npq}. \tag{3.14}$$

Some examples of the binomial distribution are shown plotted as probability mass functions in Figure 3.6. When $p = 0.50$, the pmf is symmetrical, as shown in the middle graph of the figure. Also, for a given n, complementary p values result in pmf's which are mirror images, as shown by the first and third graphs in the figure. Thus, it is not necessary to tabulate p values greater than 0.50 in binomial probability tables.

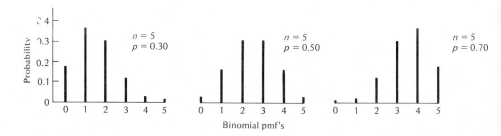

Figure 3.6

Use of Binomial Probability Tables　The binomial distribution is extremely useful in the solution of many types of problems, but it is unnecessary to compute each required probability value using Equation (3.12). Instead, we use readily available tables of the cumulative binomial distribution, such as those found in Appendix C. Cumulative probability tables are used because they simplify the computations of all types of binomial probabilities, as we will see.

　　It is important that the student be able to use binomial probability tables correctly with facility. We will now develop a simplified approach which is useful for any cumulative probability tables.

　　Letting the random variable R denote the number of successes, the cumulative binomial probability tables in Appendix C give values which we will designate as $P(R \geq r \,|\, B{:}n, p)$, the probability of r or more successes, given a binomial distribution with n Bernoulli trials, each with success probability p. This probability is shown in Figure 3.7, a diagram displaying the possible number of successes in n Bernoulli trials. If we visualize a pmf associated with a given distribution, as shown in the figure, we can see that each probability in the cumulative probability table represents a summation of individual probabilities $P(r)$, $P(r + 1)$, . . . , $P(n)$.

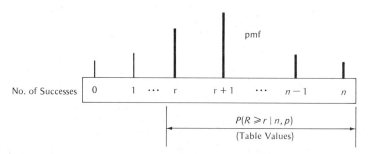

Figure 3.7

　　To illustrate the determination of binomial probabilities, we will take two problems. In working these problems, we will generally find that a sketch similar to that of Figure 3.7 will be most helpful.

EXAMPLE 3.4

A large company is currently evaluating 20 cost-reduction proposals voluntarily submitted by employees. None of these proposals are related. Past experience has been that 30 percent of such proposals are adopted.

a) What is the probability that fewer than 10 of these proposals will be adopted?

In this example, $n = 20$ and $p = 0.30$, and we wish to know $P(R < 10 | B{:}20, 0.30)$, where R is the random variable denoting the number of proposals adopted. The required binomial probabilities will be found in Appendix C. Our sketch, Figure 3.8, looks like this:

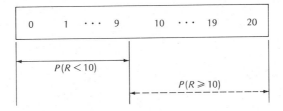

Figure 3.8

From this sketch, we see that $P(R < 10) = 1 - P(R \geqslant 10)$, so

$$P(R < 10 | B{:}20, 0.30) = 1 - P(R \geqslant 10 | B{:}20, 0.30)$$
$$= 1 - 0.0480 = 0.9520.$$

b) What is the probability that exactly 8 proposals will be adopted?

Here, the sketch shows that we must subtract $P(R \geqslant 9)$ from $P(R \geqslant 8)$.

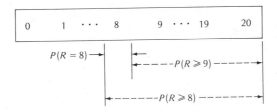

Figure 3.9

$$P(R = 8 | B{:}20, 0.30) = P(R \geqslant 8 | B{:}20, 0.30) - P(R \geqslant 9 | B{:}20, 0.30)$$
$$= 0.2277 - 0.1133 = 0.1144.$$

c) What is the probability that more than 5 proposals will be adopted?

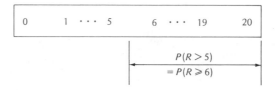

Figure 3.10

From the sketch:

$$P(R > 5 \,|\, B{:}20,\ 0.30) = P(R \geqslant 6 \,|\, B{:}20,\ 0.30) = 0.5836.$$

d) What is the probability that 4 or fewer proposals will be adopted?

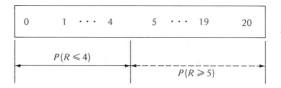

Figure 3.11

The sketch indicates that the desired probability is the complementary probability of $P(R \geqslant 5)$, so

$$P(R \leqslant 4 \,|\, B{:}20,\ 0.30) = 1 - P(R \geqslant 5 \,|\, B{:}20,\ 0.30)$$
$$= 1 - 0.7625 = 0.2375.$$

e) What is the probability that at least half the proposals will be adopted?

With 20 proposals we want $P(R \geqslant 10 \,|\, B{:}20,\ 0.30)$.

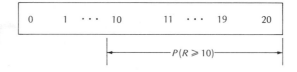

Figure 3.12

$$P(R \geqslant 10 \,|\, B{:}20,\ 0.30) = 0.0480.$$

f) What is the expected number of proposals adopted?

$$E(R) = np = (20)(0.30) = 6.0.$$

As we noted earlier, the symmetry of the binomial distribution eliminates the necessity for tables with p values exceeding 0.50. If we have a problem where the success probability is greater than 0.50, we must use a revised procedure.

Figure 3.13 shows how we utilize the symmetry of the binomial distribution. Suppose we label the two possible outcomes as event A and its complement, event $\bar{A}$. Initially we considered the occurrence of event A as a "success"; now we must consider the occurrence of event $\bar{A}$ as a success. We position event A successes in decreasing order, so that the count of event $\bar{A}$ successes is in increasing order. Then we examine the number of event $\bar{A}$ successes with success probability $1 - p < 0.50$.

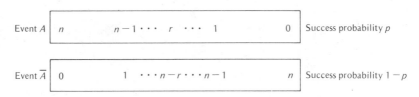

Figure 3.13

The actual procedure for $p > 0.50$ is as follows:

1. Substitute $n - r$ for r.
2. Substitute $1 - p$ for p.
3. Reverse any inequality ($\geqslant$ becomes $\leqslant$, $<$ becomes $>$, and so forth).

This procedure will now be illustrated with an example.

EXAMPLE 3.5

A part purchased from another company has been acceptable 95 percent of the time. A shipment of the parts has just been received. A decision has been made to take a random sample of 15 parts.

a) What is the probability that 13 or fewer parts will be acceptable?

We wish to know $P(R \leqslant 13 | B{:}15,\ 0.95)$. Thus, $n = 15$, $r = 13$, and $p = 0.95$. Since $n - r = 2$ and $1 - p = 0.05$, we have

$$P(R \leqslant 13 | B{:}15,\ 0.95) \equiv P(\bar{R} \geqslant 2 | B{:}15,\ 0.05)$$

where $\bar{R}$ is a random variable denoting the number of unacceptable parts. This relationship can be seen in Figure 3.14.

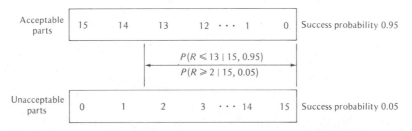

Figure 3.14

A success is now finding an unacceptable part, and we have:

$$P(\bar{R} \geqslant 2 | \text{B}:15, \ 0.05) = 0.1710.$$

Therefore, the probability of 13 or fewer acceptable parts = 0.1710 (the probability of 2 or more unacceptable parts).

b) What is the probability of more than 12 acceptable parts?

The required probability is $P(R > 12 | \text{B}:15, \ 0.95)$. Here, $n - r = 15 - 12 = 3$, so we must calculate $P(\bar{R} < 3 | \text{B}:15, \ 0.05)$, as shown in the accompanying sketch.

Figure 3.15

$$P(\bar{R} < 3 | \text{B}:15, \ 0.05) = 1 - P(\bar{R} \geqslant 3 | \text{B}:15, \ 0.05)$$
$$= 1 - 0.0362 = 0.9638.$$

There is a 0.9638 probability that more than 12 acceptable parts will be found.

c) What is the probability that exactly 14 parts will be acceptable?

According to our procedures,

$$P(R = 14 | \text{B}:15, \ 0.95) \equiv P(\bar{R} = 1 | \text{B}:15, \ 0.05).$$

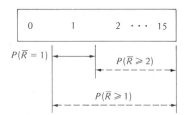

Figure 3.16

From the sketch:

$$P(\bar{R} = 1 | \text{B}:15, \ 0.05) = P(\bar{R} \geqslant 1 | \text{B}:15, \ 0.05) - P(\bar{R} \geqslant 2 | \text{B}:15, \ 0.05)$$
$$= 0.5367 - 0.1710 = 0.3657.$$

The probability of finding exactly 14 acceptable parts is 0.3657.

A systematic approach to the use of the cumulative binomial probability tables is detailed in Appendix 3A.

It should be noted that, for certain combinations of the parameters n and p not normally available in tables, the binomial distribution can be accurately approximated by other distributions, notably the Poisson distribution and the normal distribution. This will be discussed later in this chapter.

Applicability of the Binomial Distribution   From a theoretical standpoint, the binomial probability distribution is applicable only when sampling from an infinite statistical population or from a finite statistical population with replacement. The first case is illustrated by statistical events such as those related to games of chance where some type of physical process is, in essence, self-renewing after each trial—for example, throwing a die or spinning a roulette wheel. The other case is illustrated by the earlier example of the random selection of automobile license numbers, where the statistical population of license numbers is obviously finite, but we sampled with replacement, since we did not set aside those license numbers already selected. Thus, the success probability remained constant from trial to trial.

In practice, we find that the binomial distribution is an excellent approximation in many situations where it is theoretically not applicable. It is especially useful as a sampling distribution. For instance, as indicated by Example 3.5, many companies sample purchased or manufactured items to determine if they meet certain standards. This process is known as acceptance sampling. An entire lot is then accepted or rejected, depending on the number of unacceptable items in the sample. If the sample is a relatively small fraction (under 0.10, say) of the number in the lot, then the binomial distribution is a good approximation, although it is not exact, since we are sampling from a finite statistical population without replacement. (The exact probability distribution is hypergeometric, which will be discussed in the following section.) In the discussion of Bayesian decision analysis in Chapter 6, we will illustrate the use of the binomial distribution as a sampling distribution.

Hypergeometric Distribution

The binomial distribution is based on the assumption that each of the n statistical trials is independent and has the same success probability p. If we are sampling from a finite population, these conditions can be met only by sampling with replacement. This means that we would sample one item at a time and then mix it back in with the parent population before taking the next sample item. This is what we did, in effect, in the automobile license number example, since we did not exclude the possibility of the same number being selected more than once.

In the usual situation, when we sample from a finite population, we sample without replacement, because there is frequently no point to replacing each sample item. For instance, in acceptance sampling, it would make no sense to put back defective items. In some cases, sampling with replacement is impossible, such as when destructive testing of the sampled items is required.

If we have a lot of 1000 parts which contain 5 percent defective items, then there will be 50 defective items in that lot. If a random sample of 2 items is chosen from the lot, the probability of drawing a good item on the first drawing is 950/1000. However, the probability of drawing a good item on the second drawing is not 950/1000. If a good item was drawn the first time, the probability will be 949/999; if a defective item was drawn the first time, the probability will be 950/999. Thus, the probability changes from trial to trial, depending on the previous sampling results.

Suppose we have a finite population of size N with k elements of one kind, which we will call "successes," and $N - k$ elements of another kind, which we will call "failures." If R is a random variable representing the number of successes in n drawings from this finite population, then R has a hypergeometric distribution with parameters n, k, and N. We denote the probability of exactly r successes as $P(R = r \mid n, k, N)$.

To show the nature of the hypergeometric distribution, suppose we wish to know the probability of taking a sample of 3 items, from a lot of 5 items containing good items and 3 defective items, and obtaining 1 good item and 2 defective items. If we define a good item as a success, the desired hypergeometric probability is $P(R = 1 \mid 3, 2, 5)$. Going back to elementary probability theory, let us define a sample point as any feasible combination of 3 items drawn from the 5 items in the lot. The sample space then consists of all such feasible combinations. Suppose we designate the 2 good items as G_1 and G_2 and the 3 defective items as D_1, D_2, and D_3. The sample space S then consists of the 10 sample points $\{G_1D_1D_2, G_1D_1D_3, G_1D_2D_3, G_2D_1D_2, G_2D_1D_3, G_2D_2D_3, G_1G_2D_1, G_1G_2D_2, G_1G_2D_3, D_1D_2D_3\}$. If we assume that each item has an equal chance to be selected, each sample point is equally likely. Then, since the first 6 sample points in S are contained in the event "1 good item and 2 defective items," the probability of this event is 6/10 = 0.60. An enumeration of all the sample points is not required, however, to find the desired probability. The total number of sample points is the number of feasible combinations, which is the number of combinations of 5 things taken 3 at a time or $\binom{5}{3} = 10$. The number of sample points contained by the given event is equal to the number of combinations of 1 good item among the 2 good items in the lot, or $\binom{2}{1} = 2$, multiplied by the number of combinations of 2 defective items among the 3 defective items in the lot, or $\binom{3}{2} = 3$. The ratio of event sample points to total sample points is then (2)(3)/10 = 0.60, as before. In the general case, the hypergeometric probability of exactly r successes in n trials is

$$P(R = r \mid H\!:\! n, k, N) = \frac{\binom{k}{r} \binom{N - k}{n - r}}{\binom{N}{n}} \tag{3.15}$$

where r can take on integer values between 0 and the smaller of n and k. The expected value and variance of the hypergeometric distribution are

$$E(R) = n\left(\frac{k}{N}\right)$$

$$V(R) = \left(\frac{N-n}{N-1}\right) n \left(\frac{k}{N}\right)\left(\frac{N-k}{N}\right).$$

Since the hypergeometric distribution is a three-parameter distribution, even relatively limited hypergeometric probability tables rapidly become voluminous. It is well to know, then, that when the sample size n is a relatively small proportion (say 10 percent or less) of the population size N, a binomial distribution is a good approximation. Since the best estimate of the success probability p is the ratio of the number of successes k to the population size N, the parameters of the approximating binomial distribution are n and $p = k/N$. We implicitly utilized this relationship in Example 3.5, which involved the inspection of a purchased part. Although the number of parts involved in the shipment mentioned was not specified, it should now be clear that the number of acceptable parts in the sample must follow the hypergeometric distribution if the sampling was without replacement. We used the binomial approximation because it is easy to use and gives an accuracy which is more than adequate for practical applications. As a matter of interest, the hypergeometric distribution is the correct probability distribution in many applications for which the binomial distribution is actually used.

Poisson Distribution

Another discrete probability distribution of interest is the Poisson distribution, which we will find to be particularly important in the study of waiting lines in Chapter 12.

Visualize a situation where an event occurs at random points in time or space. Consider such examples as the arrival of customers at a service station, telephone calls to a mail order service, typographical errors in a book, and defects in woven material. Each of these situations represents what is called a *Poisson process* (named after the early nineteenth-century French mathematician S. D. Poisson), if the following conditions are met:

1. Over some time or space interval, the probability of the occurrence of the event is constant for any increment of time or space within that interval, regardless of when or where that increment starts. This is what is termed the stationarity assumption.
2. The occurrence of the event is completely independent of any other occurrence of that event.
3. In any small interval of time or space, such that the probability of the event is small (say under 0.1):

a) the probability that the event occurs is approximately proportional to the width of the interval. (If, for example, the probability of a customer arriving during a one-second interval were 0.01, the arrival probability over a two-second interval would be 0.02.)

b) the probability that two or more of these events occur is negligible.

The Poisson distribution gives the probability distribution of the number of events occurring in some interval of time or space when the expected number of events in that interval is known.

Let X = random variable denoting the number of events occurring in a given interval,

x = any specific number of events,

m = mean number of events occurring in the given interval.

The Poisson probability mass function is:

$$P(X = x \mid \text{Pn:}m) = \frac{m^x e^{-m}}{x!}, \qquad x = 0, 1, 2, \ldots \tag{3.16}$$

where e is the base of natural logarithms, with a value of approximately 2.71828, and Pn means Poisson.

The Poisson distribution is a one-parameter distribution, with the single parameter m denoting the mean number of events occurring in a given interval. The value of m is not constrained to be an integer but can take on any positive value.

By the nature of the events, there is no inherent upper limit to the value that the random variable may take. This is an example of a discrete probability distribution where the random variable assumes a countably infinite number of values. In practice, of course, we will be concerned only with values whose probability is greater than some minimum value, such as 0.001.

The binomial distribution, with the number of trials very large and the probability of success on any one trial very small, closely approaches the Poisson distribution. To demonstrate this, let us assume that customers arrive randomly at a small market at the average rate of 0.1 per minute. Over a ten-minute period, the probability distribution of arrivals would be Poisson, with a mean of 1.0 (0.1 per minute × 10 minutes). Suppose we now divide the ten-minute interval into tenths. The probability of exactly one arrival in any such time increment will be approximately 0.10 per 1.0 minute. Since the probability of more than one arrival in 1.0 minute is very small (0.10^2 for two arrivals, 0.10^3 for three arrivals, and so on), we will ignore it. We can then assume that each 1.0 minute increment represents a Bernoulli trial where a success occurs if there is an arrival in that interval. Then, over a ten-minute interval, we would have 10 such intervals, so the approximate probability distribution of arrivals would be binomial, with $n = 10$ and $p = 0.10$. Observe that the expected number of arrivals is $np = 1.0$. This distribution will give values fairly close to those for the Poisson distribution, but the approximation would be better if we made the time increments smaller. With time increments halved to 0.50 minutes, the probability of an arrival would also be halved, to 0.05, and the number of time increments in 10 minutes doubled, so the approximating binomial distribution would have parameters $n = 20$ and $p = 0.05$. If the time increments were 0.10 minute, the binomial parameters would be $n = 100$ and $p = 0.01$. Note that in each case the expected number of arrivals, np, remains constant at 1.0. These four distributions are compared in Table 3.5. You can see from this table that the binomial distribution with $n = 100$ and $p = 0.01$ is a very good approximation indeed. A binomial distribution with $n = 1000$ and $p = 0.001$ would be even better. In general, as n becomes very large and p very small, but with np always the same, the binomial distribution with parameters n and p approaches the Poisson distribution with parameter m equal to np.

Table 3.5 Binomial Approximations to the Poisson Distribution with Mean 1.0

	Probability			
	Binomial Distribution			
Number of Arrivals	$n = 10$ $p = 0.10$	$n = 20$ $p = 0.05$	$n = 100$ $p = 0.01$	Poisson Distribution $m = 1.0$
0	0.349	0.358	0.366	0.368
1	0.387	0.377	0.370	0.368
2	0.194	0.189	0.185	0.184
3	0.057	0.060	0.061	0.061
4	0.011	0.013	0.015	0.015
5	0.002	0.002	0.003	0.003
6	0.000	0.000	0.001	0.001

As noted earlier, the Poisson is a one-parameter distribution, whereas the binomial is a two-parameter distribution requiring extensive tables as the number of trials becomes large. When binomial tables are not available, we can use a Poisson distribution as an approximation to a binomial distribution having a large number of trials and a small success probability on each trial. We will illustrate this shortly.

Properties If X is a random variable denoting the number of events occurring in a given interval, and X has a Poisson distribution, the expected value and variance are:

$$E(X) = m, \qquad V(X) = m. \tag{3.17}$$

The standard deviation $S(X)$ is then equal to $\sqrt{m}$.

Some representative Poisson pmf's are shown in Figure 3.17. Observe that as m becomes relatively large with respect to the standard deviation (a multiple of 3 or more, say, or $m \geq 9$), the Poisson distribution tends to become quite symmetrical.

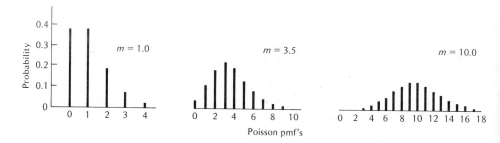

Poisson pmf's

Figure 3.17

Use of Poisson Probability Tables   We will now show an example of a situation where the Poisson distribution is applicable. As with the binomial distribution, we will not calculate individual Poisson probability terms, since the calculations, using equation (3.16), are quite tedious. We will use the cumulative Poisson probability tables in Appendix D in just the same way that we used the cumulative binomial probability tables earlier.

EXAMPLE 3.6

Customers arrive randomly at a bank at the average rate of 24 per hour during the time period between 1:30 PM and 2:00 PM on a Tuesday. What is the probability that exactly 5 customers arrive during a 12-minute segment of that time period?

This problem involves a Poisson distribution with mean of $(24)(12/60) = 4.8$ arrivals per 12 minutes. Figure 3.18 shows the required cumulative probability values.

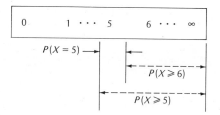

Figure 3.18

$$P(X = 5 \mid \text{Pn:}4.8) = P(X \geqslant 5 \mid \text{Pn:}4.8) - P(X \geqslant 6 \mid \text{Pn:}4.8)$$
$$= 0.5237 - 0.3490 = 0.1747.$$

There is a 0.1747 probability that exactly 5 customers will arrive during any 12-minute segment of the specified time period.

Poisson Approximation to the Binomial Distribution   As mentioned previously, the Poisson distribution can serve as an approximation to the binomial distribution when the number of trials is high and the success probability low. As a rough rule of thumb, the Poisson approximation is often used when $n \geqslant 20$, $p \leqslant 0.1$ and $np \leqslant 5$, or when $n \geqslant 20$, $1 - p \leqslant 0.1$ (so that $p \geqslant 0.9$) and $n(1 - p) \leqslant 5$. We will now show the use of this approximation.

EXAMPLE 3.7

A large mail order company's records show that it has properly filled 97 percent of customer orders during the past year. What is the probability that at least 98 of the next 100 orders will be filled correctly?

The proper distribution to use would be the binomial, with $n = 100$ trials and success probability $p = 0.97$. Then, if R is a random variable denoting the number of orders filled correctly, the desired probability is $P(R \geqslant 98 \mid B{:}100,\ 0.97)$. Since $n > 20$, $p > 0.9$ and $n(1 - p) = 100(0.03) = 3$, let us use the Poisson approximation, with mean $m = n(1 - p) = (100)(0.03) = 3.0$, which is the expected number of orders filled *incorrectly* in the next 100. The desired Poisson probability is then $P(\bar{R} \leqslant 1 \mid Pn{:}3.0)$, since filling at most 2 of 100 orders incorrectly is identical to filling at least 98 of 100 orders correctly.

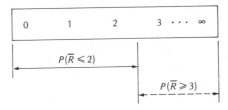

Figure 3.19

$$P(\bar{R} \leqslant 2 \mid Pn{:}3.0) = 1 - P(\bar{R} \geqslant 3 \mid Pn{:}3.0)$$
$$= 1 - 0.5768 = 0.4232.$$

The approximate probability of correctly filling at least 98 of the next 100 orders is 0.4232. From the binomial tables, the correct value is

$$P(\bar{R} \geqslant 98 \mid B{:}100,\ 0.97) = P(\bar{R} \leqslant 2 \mid B{:}100,\ 0.03)$$
$$= 1 - P(\bar{R} \geqslant 3 \mid B{:}100,\ 0.03) = 1 - 0.5802 = 0.4198.$$

The approximation is clearly quite good.

3.3 CONTINUOUS PROBABILITY DISTRIBUTIONS

Up to this point, we have discussed only discrete probability distributions, where a random variable can take on only a finite number of values (as with a binomial distribution) or a countably infinite number of values (as with a Poisson distribution). For any discrete probability distribution, it is relatively easy to visualize a probability associated with each possible value of the given discrete random variable. When we have a continuous random variable, such as the temperature at a certain location, the concept of associating a probability with each possible value of the random variable is no longer meaningful. Instead, we can only talk about the probability that the random variable falls within a given interval, such as a temperature range.

Probability Density Functions and Cumulative Distribution Functions

A continuous probability distribution can be viewed as a discrete probability distribution with a very large number of values very close to each other. For example, suppose that we have recorded 10,000 observations of the random variable X, monthly rainfall at selected locations, as shown in the first two columns of Table 3.6. We then convert the frequency values in the second column into probability values in the third column by dividing each frequency value by the total number of observations.

Table 3.6   Monthly Rainfall at Selected Locations

Rainfall, inches	Number of Observations	Probability
0 to under 2	553	0.0553
2 to under 4	1066	0.1066
4 to under 6	2090	0.2090
6 to under 8	3033	0.3033
8 to under 10	1885	0.1885
10 to under 12	1025	0.1025
12 to under 14	348	0.0348
	10,000	1.0000

This probability data is plotted in Figure 3.20, in what is called histogram form. In a histogram, the height of each rectangle is proportional to the number of observations included in the interval indicated by the rectangle's base, generally called the class interval. If the vertical axis is scaled in such a manner that the area of all these rectangles sums to 1.0, then the area of each individual rectangle will be equal to the probability that X falls within the given class interval. Thus the area of the rectangle covering the class interval from 4 to 6 represents the probability that X falls between 4 and 6. Suppose, now, that the class intervals are made very small, so that the rectangles become extremely narrow, as shown in Figure 3.21. The total area is still constrained to be 1.0, so that each rectangle still represents the probability that X falls in that class interval. If this process is continued until the class intervals become vanishingly small, but all the time keeping the total area 1.0, then, in the limit, we arrive at the continuous curve shown in Figure 3.22. This curve is called a *probability density function* (pdf), $f(x)$, for a continuous random variable X. The pdf is analogous to the pmf for a discrete probability distribution.

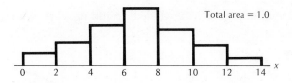

Figure 3.20

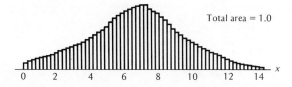

Figure 3.21

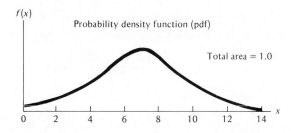

Figure 3.22

A pdf must satisfy two basic requirements:

1. $f(x)$ is always nonnegative.
2. The area under the curve $f(x)$ must equal 1.0.

These requirements are similar to those for a pmf for discrete probability distributions.

A very important concept should be made clear here. For any x, the value of $f(x)$ does *not* represent the probability that the value x occurs. For a continuous probability distribution, we can no longer refer to the probability of the random variable taking on an *exact* value, as we did for discrete probability distributions. A so-called point probability is meaningless for a continuous probability distribution, because there is no area under a point. We can only refer to the probability that the random variable falls within a given range.

Given the probability density function of a continuous random variable X, the *cumulative distribution function* (cdf) of X, denoted as $F(x)$, is defined as the probability that X is less than or equal to some specific value x. By definition, then,

$$F(x) = P(X \leq x). \tag{3.18}$$

For the pdf of Figure 3.22, the cdf would be as shown in Figure 3.23.

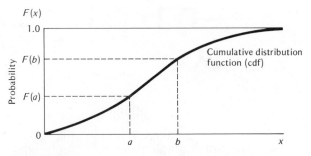

Figure 3.23

The cdf represents the accumulation of the area under the pdf with increasing x. (In calculus, this is called the process of integration.) For continuous probability distributions, the most useful property of the cdf is that it enables us to readily evaluate the probability that the random variable X lies within the interval (a, b), $b > a$. Specifically,

$$P(a \leqslant X \leqslant b) = F(b) - F(a) \qquad b > a. \tag{3.19}$$

This relationship, which we will use extensively, is shown in Figure 3.23. Incidentally, since the probability of the random variable assuming an exact value is zero, the use of the equals sign is immaterial in probability statements involving *continuous* random variables. (This is generally *not* true for discrete random variables.) Thus, we can use interchangeably the inequalities ">" and ">" and the inequalities "<" and "<." For instance,

$$P(a \leqslant X \leqslant b) \equiv P(a < X \leqslant b) \equiv P(a \leqslant X < b) \equiv P(a < X < b).$$

For continuous probability distributions, determination of the expected values and the variance generally requires the use of integral calculus. Since this text does not assume a knowledge of calculus, we will sometimes have to be content with merely stating the required values instead of deriving them.

Uniform Distribution

When a random variable X is equally likely to fall anywhere within an interval (a, b), $b > a$, we say that X has a uniform, or rectangular, probability distribution over that interval. The pdf is shown in Figure 3.24. Since the area under the function $f(x)$ forms a rectangle, the height of this rectangle must be such that its base times its height equals 1. Since the base equals $b - a$, the height must be $1/(b - a)$. The pdf is then

$$f(x) = \begin{cases} \dfrac{1}{b - a} & a \leqslant x \leqslant b \\ 0 & \text{elsewhere.} \end{cases} \tag{3.20}$$

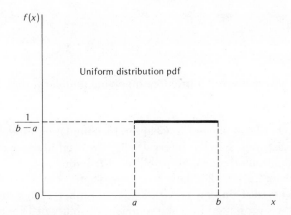

Figure 3.24

The cdf is readily determined by observing that, for any x within the interval (a, b), the area between a and x is the area of a rectangle with base $x - a$ and height $1/(b - a)$, so that $F(x) = (x - a)/(b - a)$ in this interval. The complete cdf for the uniform distribution is specified as follows:

$$F(x) = \begin{cases} 0 & x \leqslant a \\ \dfrac{x - a}{b - a} & a \leqslant x \leqslant b \\ 1 & x \geqslant b \end{cases} \qquad (3.21)$$

A graph of the cdf is displayed in Figure 3.25.

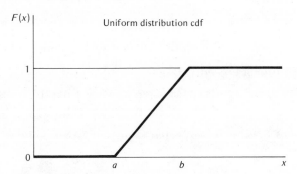

Figure 3.25

The expected value $E(X)$ for the uniform distribution is just the value halfway between a and b, since the distribution is symmetrical. Therefore,

$$E(X) = \frac{a + b}{2}.$$

The variance is

$$V(X) = \frac{(b-a)^2}{12}.$$

Let us now work a problem involving a uniform distribution.

EXAMPLE 3.8

As will be explained in Chapter 15, Simulation Models, random numbers uniformly distributed in the interval (0, 1) are used to generate random variables from many different types of probability distributions. If we have, say, an eight-digit number that is equally likely to fall anywhere between 0 and 1, we have a discrete probability distribution of 100,000,000 numbers. This distribution can be almost perfectly represented by a continuous probability distribution. Let us designate the random number as a random variable X. Referring to the pdf graphed in Figure 3.24, the limits a and b are then, respectively, 0 and 1. From Equation (3.21), the cdf, in the region of interest between 0 and 1, is

$$F(x) = \frac{x-a}{b-a} = \frac{x-0}{1-0} = x, \qquad 0 \leqslant x \leqslant 1.$$

a) What is the probability that such a random number falls between 0.2 and 0.8?

From Equation (3.19),

$$P(0.2 \leqslant X \leqslant 0.8 \,|\, U{:}0,\ 1) = F(0.8) - F(0.2),$$

for the uniform distribution over the interval (0, 1). Since $F(x) = x$, in the interval (0, 1), we have

$$F(0.8) - F(0.2) = 0.8 - 0.2 = 0.6.$$

b) What is the probability that such a random number exceeds 0.9?

Since X cannot exceed 1.0,

$$P(X > 0.9 \,|\, U{:}0,\ 1) = P(0.9 < X \leqslant 1.0 \,|\, U{:}0,\ 1) = F(1.0) - F(0.9)$$
$$= 1.0 - 0.9 = 0.1.$$

c) What is the expected value and variance of this random number?

$$E(X) = \frac{a+b}{2} = \frac{0+1}{2} = \frac{1}{2}.$$

$$V(X) = \frac{(b-a)^2}{12} = \frac{(1-0)^2}{12} = \frac{1}{12}.$$

Normal Distribution

The normal, or Gaussian, distribution is perhaps the most well known probability distribution. The chief reason for the extensive use of the normal distribution is that it has certain highly convenient mathematical properties and represents a reasonably good approximation to a number of different probability distributions which arise in practice. We will have more to say later about the rationale for using the normal distribution.

Properties The normal density function, the so-called "bell-shaped" curve, is a two-parameter symmetrical distribution. These parameters are μ, the mean or expected value, and σ, the standard deviation (the variance is then σ^2). If the random variable X has a normal probability distribution, its pdf is

$$f(x) = \frac{1}{\sigma\sqrt{2\pi}}e^{-(x-\mu)^2/2\sigma^2}, \qquad -\infty < x < \infty. \tag{3.23}$$

This function is not in a mathematical form which would enable us to determine the cdf analytically. Therefore, we must use tables to determine the area (probability) under any portion of the normal curve. In order to avoid the overwhelming task of preparing tables for each required value of μ and σ, we utilize a special form of the normal distribution by making a very simple transformation.

If we have a normally distributed random variable Z which has a mean of 0 and a standard deviation of 1, the pdf of Z is, from Equation (3.23),

$$f(z) = \frac{1}{\sqrt{2\pi}}\,e^{-z^2/2}, \qquad -\infty < z < \infty. \tag{3.24}$$

The random variable Z is usually called a *standardized normal variable*, and it requires only a single probability table, since the values of both the mean and standard deviations are fixed. Any random variable X can be converted to a standardized random variable Z by subtracting its mean and dividing by its standard deviation. This gives the number of standard deviations from the mean. The required transformation is then

$$Z = \frac{X - \mu}{\sigma}. \tag{3.24}$$

The relationship between the pdf's of X and Z is shown in Figure 3.26. Note that the vertical scale is different for $f(x)$ and $f(z)$, since the coefficients of these pdf's differ by a factor of σ, as can be seen from Equations (3.22) and (3.23). The maximum value of $f(z)$ occurs at $z = 0$ and equals $1/\sqrt{2\pi}$, or 0.3989. The maximum value of $f(x)$ occurs at $x = \mu$ and equals $1/(\sigma\sqrt{2\pi})$, or $0.3989/\sigma$. Remember that these are density values, *not* probability values.

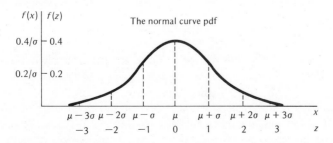

Figure 3.26

Cumulative probability values of the standardized normal distribution are tabulated in Appendix A. In this table, values of the cdf $F(z)$ are given for z values from -3 to $+3$. The table coverage is indicated graphically in Figure 3.27. Incidentally, z is often called the standard normal deviate.

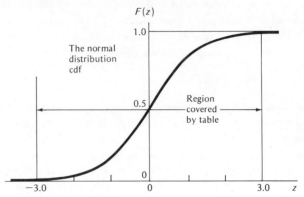

Figure 3.27

In Figure 3.28 is shown a sketch of the standardized normal probability distribution. The value z_a may be positive or negative.

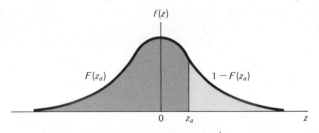

Figure 3.28

To find the probability that Z falls in any interval (z_a, z_b), or, in other words, $P(z_a \leq Z \leq z_b)$, we utilize the fundamental property of the cdf given in Equation (3.20), namely:

$$P(z_a \leq Z \leq z_b) = F(z_b) - F(z_a), \qquad z_b > z_a. \tag{3.25}$$

Tables of the normal probability distribution have been structured in several different ways, generally giving values of $F(z)$ or $F(z) - 0.5$ for positive z values only. The student should be able to use any kind of normal probability table if he performs a logical analysis, utilizing the symmetry of the normal probability distribution and complementary probabilities. For example, suppose the normal probability table gives values of $F(z)$ for positive values of z only. To find $F(z)$ when z is negative, a straightforward relationship can be determined, utilizing Figure 3.29.

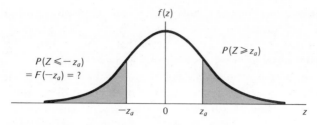

Figure 3.29

By the symmetry of the normal pdf,

$$P(Z \leq -z_a) = P(Z \geq z_a),$$

as indicated by the shaded areas in Figure 3.29. Since

$$P(Z \leq -z_a) = F(-z_a)$$

and

$$P(Z \geq z_a) = 1 - P(Z \leq z_a) = 1 - F(z_a),$$
$$F(-z_a) = 1 - F(z_a).$$

Applicability of the Normal Distribution   Before presenting an example showing how the normal probability distribution is handled, it seems worthwhile to elaborate somewhat on the usefulness of the normal probability distribution.

To begin with, any number of empirical (actual, rather than theoretical) probability distributions tend toward a bell-shaped density function. We can think of such physical characteristics as the height of adult females, the intelligence quotient of children, and so on. There is no evidence, however, that any kind of physical *law* exists whereby certain characteristics will follow a normal distribution, although a number of people believed this in the nineteenth century. The name "normal" actually came from early efforts to associate this distribution with all continuous random variables.

The normal distribution was originally discovered in the eighteenth century by De Moivre, who found it to be a limiting form of the binomial distribution. When certain conditions are met, the normal distribution can serve as a satisfactory approximation to other probability distributions, among which are the binomial distribution and the Poisson distribution. The great utility of the normal curve, when applicable as an approximation to other distributions, lies in the fact that only the standard probability table of the normal distribution is required, regardless of the value of the mean and standard deviation. Contrast this with the need for a separate table for each value of the mean for a Poisson distribution and for each combination of the success probability and number of trials for a binomial distribution. Later in this chapter we will discuss the use of the normal curve as an approximation to the binomial distribution.

In theoretical statistics, the assumption of a normal distribution is the only way that certain types of problems can be solved, because the normal distribution has certain mathematical properties possessed by no other theoretical probability distribution. Also, in applied statistics, the assumption of a normal distribution in many cases gives acceptable results even when the given probability distribution is known to be nonnormal.

Finally, we state without proof that if a number n of identical and independent random variables, each with mean μ and variance σ^2, are sampled, then the distribution of sample means approaches a normal distribution with mean μ and variance σ^2/n as n becomes large, regardless of the form of the probability distribution from which the random variables are drawn. This result is known as the *central limit theorem*, and is extremely useful in the area of statistical inference.

Now, let us work a problem using the normal distribution. By always drawing a simple sketch to determine the required probabilities, we will avoid the need to memorize formulas for different cases.

Use of Normal Probability Tables   For clarity, we will use the notation $P(X > x \mid N{:}\mu, \sigma)$ to designate the probability that the random variable X exceeds a specific value x when X is normally distributed with mean μ and standard deviation σ. The notation $P(Z > z)$ is a convenient shorthand for the standardized normal distribution probability $P(Z > z \mid N{:}0, 1)$.

EXAMPLE 3.9

A manufacturing company anticipates that its maximum daily demand for electric power during the next few months will fluctuate randomly around a mean of 100 kilowatts. The demand distribution would appear to be reasonably well represented by a normal probability distribution with a standard deviation of 10 kilowatts.

a) What is the probability that maximum demand will exceed 120 kilowatts on a given day?

The parameters of this normal distribution are $\mu = 100$, $\sigma = 10$. If X is the random variable denoting daily demand, then $Z = (X - 100)/10$, so, for any specific value x, the standardized normal deviate $z = (x - 100)/10$. We wish to know $P(X > 120 \mid N{:}100, 10)$. For $x = 120$, $z = (120 - 100)/10 = 2.0$. Thus, $P(X > 120 \mid N{:}100, 10) \equiv P(Z > 2.0)$. At this point, a sketch is always a good idea. The shaded area represents the desired probability.

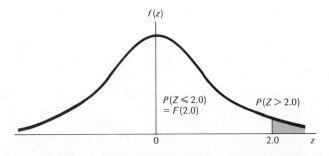

Figure 3.30

Using the values of $F(z)$ in Appendix A:

$$P(Z > 2.0) = 1 - P(Z < 2.0)$$
$$= 1 - F(2.0) = 1 - 0.9772$$
$$= 0.0228 = P(X > 120 | N{:}100, \ 10).$$

b) What is the probability, on a given day, that the maximum demand is less than 85 kilowatts?

The required probability is $P(X < 85 | N{:}100, \ 10)$. For $x = 85$, $z = (85 - 100)/10 = -1.5$, so find $P(Z < -1.5)$.

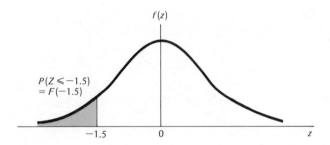

$f(z)$

$P(Z \leqslant -1.5)$
$= F(-1.5)$

-1.5 0 z

Figure 3.31

$$P(Z < -1.5) = F(-1.5)$$
$$= 0.0668 = P(X < 85 | N{:}100, \ 10).$$

c) What is the probability that a given day's maximum demand will exceed 95 kilowatts?

The probability of interest is $P(X > 95 | N{:}100, 10)$. Then, for $x = 95$, $z = (95 - 100)/10 = -0.5$, and we must calculate $P(Z > -0.5)$.

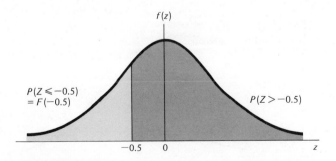

$f(z)$

$P(Z \leqslant -0.5)$
$= F(-0.5)$

$P(Z > -0.5)$

-0.5 0 z

Figure 3.32

Based on complementarity,

$$P(Z > -0.5) = 1 - P(Z < -0.5)$$
$$= 1 - F(-0.5) = 1 - 0.3085$$
$$= 0.6915 = P(X > 95 \,|\, N{:}100,\ 10).$$

d) What is the probability that the maximum demand on a given day will fall between 90 and 125 kilowatts?

The probability of interest is $P(90 \leqslant X \leqslant 125 \,|\, N{:}100,\ 10)$. We convert this to the form $P(z_1 \leqslant Z \leqslant z_2)$, where $z_1 = (90 - 100)/10 = -1.0$, and $z_2 = (125 - 100)/10 = 2.5$.

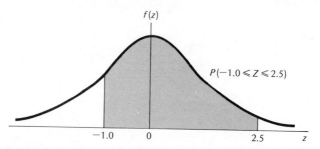

Figure 3.33

From Figure 3.33 and Equation (3.19),

$$P(-1.0 \leqslant Z \leqslant 2.5) = F(2.5) - F(-1.0)$$
$$= 0.9938 - 0.1587$$
$$= 0.8351 = P(90 \leqslant X \leqslant 125 \,|\, N{:}100,\ 10).$$

e) What value of maximum demand will be exceeded only 20 percent of the time?

Here, we are faced with a different type of problem. We are given that $P(X > x_a \,|\, N{:}100,\ 10) = 0.20$ and must find the value of x_a. The related normalized probability is $P(Z > z_a) = 0.20$.

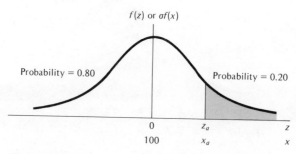

Figure 3.34

From Figure 3.34:

$$P(Z < z_a) = 0.80,$$

so

$$F(z_a) = 0.80.$$

In Appendix A, we now look for the value of $F(z_a)$ closest to the required value. The closest value is 0.7995, associated with a z_a value of 0.84. Thus $z_a \cong 0.84$. (To get one more decimal place for the value of z_a, we would have to interpolate, as explained in Appendix 3B.) This process, involving determination of the standard normal deviate, given the probability, is called *inverse interpolation*.

The z_a value of 0.84 is not the required answer, because we need to find x_a. Since, by definition, $z = (x - \mu)/\sigma$, the value of x associated with a given z value is:

$$x = \mu + z\sigma. \tag{3.26}$$

Therefore,

$$x_a = \mu + z_a\sigma$$
$$= 100 + (0.84)(10) = 108.4 \text{ kilowatts.}$$

    f) At what value of maximum demand is there a probability of 0.35 that demand will be less than this value?

The desired value is x_a, where $P(X < x_a | N:100, 10) = 0.35$. We must first solve for z_a, where $P(Z < z_a) = 0.35$.

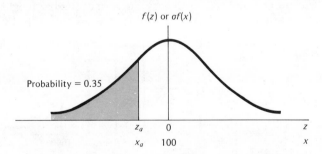

f(z) or σf(x)

Probability = 0.35

z_a 0   z

x_a 100   x

Figure 3.35

Then, $P(Z < z_a) = F(z_a) = 0.35.$

From Appendix A, the table value closest to 0.35 is 0.3483, so $z_a \cong -0.39$. To complete the solution,

$$x_a = \mu + z_a\sigma$$
$$= 100 + (-0.39)(10) = 96.1 \text{ kilowatts.}$$

Assessment of Subjective Probability Distributions

    For a continuous random variable (or a discrete random variable with enough values to warrant its approximation by a continuous random variable), the methods of establishing a subjective probability distribution tend to be somewhat different than those for a discrete random variable, discussed earlier. Our goal is the establishment of a cumulative distribution function, from which we can obtain any desired probability values. There are a number of possible approaches, and we will show two of them. To illustrate these approaches, we will consider the situation where a sales manager is required to estimate the weekly demand for heating oil in a certain locality. The sales manager believes there is a very small chance (1 percent, say) that weekly demand will be less than 1000 gallons or more than 1800 gallons. We will let D be the random variable denoting this weekly demand.

The first approach is analogous to that shown previously for a discrete probability distribution, where we constructed a probability mass function, step by step. Now, however, we construct a bar chart, or histogram, by asking the sales manager to estimate the probability that demand falls within a given range. By arbitrarily selecting the bar height for any one interval and then drawing the relative bar heights for each other interval, in proportion to the probability that demand falls in that interval, a diagram such as that of Figure 3.36 can be developed.

To convert the graph in Figure 3.36 to a probability density function, let us assume that the probability of a demand less than 1000 gallons and the probability of a demand greater than 1800 gallons are both 0.01, so that the probability of a demand between 1000 and 1800 gallons is 0.98. Since, as shown in Figure 3.36, the interval widths are the same (not an absolute requirement, but a convenience), the probability represented by each bar is proportionate to its height. If the individual heights (using any convenient scale) are divided by the sum of the bar heights and then multiplied by 0.98, we then arrive at the probability values shown in Figure 3.37.

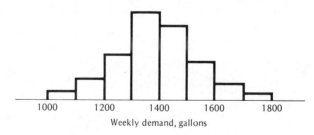

Weekly demand, gallons

Figure 3.36

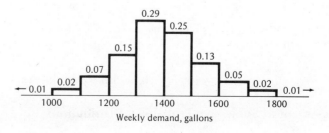

Weekly demand, gallons

Figure 3.37

Now, by cumulating the probability values, starting at the left of Figure 3.37, we can readily determine the cdf values for the interval endpoints. This information is plotted in Figure 3.38, and a smooth curve has been drawn through the data points.

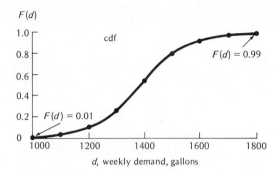

Figure 3.38

The second approach involves the direct construction of the cdf. This can be done in several different ways, among which are the following.

1. Ask the sales manager to assess the subjective probability that demand will not exceed each of a set of specified values, using either the lottery or betting-odds approach, as described in the previous chapter.
2. Specify a set of probability values, or odds, and then ask the sales manager to associate these with cumulative demand values.

In either case, the cdf can be readily developed from the data points thus obtained, and the results would be plotted just as in Figure 3.38. If odds are used, they would be converted to probabilities, of course.

As we will see later, certain types of problems in Bayesian decision analysis become tractable only if we can assume that the random variable of interest has a normal probability distribution. Any given cdf, whether objective or subjective, can be tested for normality by plotting it on what is called normal probability graph paper. The probability scale spacing on this special graph paper is so designed that any cumulative normal probability distribution can be plotted as a straight line.

The subjective probability distribution for heating oil demand has been plotted on normal probability graph paper in Figure 3.39. Although the curve-fit to a straight line is by no means perfect, it appears to be reasonably good in the range between $F(d) = 0.02$ and $F(d) = 0.98$. If we were to approximate this cdf by the normal distribution represented by the straight line shown, the mean would be the value of d for which $F(d) = 0.50$, so the mean would be about 1392 gallons. The standard deviation could be determined by noting that, from Appendix A, $F(z) = 0.84$ when $z = 1.0$, so that $F(d) = 0.84$ when d is 1.0 standard deviations above the mean. From Figure 3.39, $F(1548) = 0.84$, so the standard deviation is approximately equal to $1548 - 1392 = 156$ gallons.

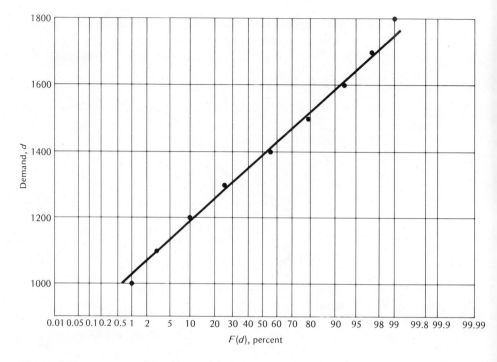

Figure 3.39

Exponential Distribution

As we noted earlier, the Poisson distribution is a discrete probability distribution of the number of events occurring in some interval. Let us now consider a Poisson process involving the number of occurrences of an event over a time period t. We define the intensity λ (Greek lambda) of a Poisson process as the expected number of occurrences per unit time. The expected number of occurrences in a time interval t will be λt. Then, if we substitute λt for m in Equation (3.16), we get

$$P(X = x \mid \text{Pn:}\lambda t) = \frac{(\lambda t)^x e^{-\lambda t}}{x!}, \qquad x = 0, 1, 2, \ldots \quad \textbf{(3.27)}$$

Now, suppose that we are interested in the probability distribution of the interarrival time, the time between occurrences of the given event. To derive this, we first determine, from Equation (3.27), the probability of no occurrence of the event in time t.

$$P(X = 0 \mid \text{Pn:}\lambda t) = \frac{(\lambda t)^0 e^{-\lambda t}}{0!} = e^{-\lambda t}.$$

Let us now define the random variable T as the time between occurrences of the given event. Since the event can occur at any time, T must be a continuous random variable. The probability of no occurrence of the event in time t will be equal to the probability that T exceeds t, so we have

$$P(T > t) = P(X = 0 \,|\, \text{Pn}{:}\lambda t) = e^{-\lambda t}.$$

The cdf of T, is, by definition, $F(t) = P(T \leq t)$. Therefore,

$$F(t) = \begin{cases} P(T \leq t) = 1 - P(T > t) = 1 - e^{-\lambda t}, & t \geq 0 \\ 0, & t < 0 \end{cases} \qquad \textbf{(3.28)}$$

The distribution of the random variable T is called the *exponential distribution.* Using calculus, the pdf can be determined as

$$f(t) = \begin{cases} \lambda e^{-\lambda t}, & t \geq 0 \\ 0, & t < 0 \end{cases}$$

The expected value and variance of the exponential distribution are

$$E(T) = \frac{1}{\lambda}, \qquad V(T) = \frac{1}{\lambda^2}. \qquad \textbf{(3.29)}$$

Values of $F(t)$ can be obtained directly from the cumulative Poisson tables. Observe that

$$F(T) = 1 - e^{-\lambda t} = 1 - P(X = 0 \,|\, \text{Pn}{:}\lambda t) = P(X \geq 1 \,|\, \text{Pn}{:}\lambda t).$$

Thus, given λ, $F(t)$ is equal to the cumulative Poisson probability of the occurrence of one or more events when the mean number of events in a given interval is λt. As an example, if $\lambda = 3$ and $t = 1.5$, $\lambda t = 4.5$, so

$$F(1.5) = P(T \leq 1.5) = P(X \geq 1 \,|\, \text{Pn}{:}4.5) = 0.9889.$$

Representative curves of the exponential pdf are shown in Figure 3.40.

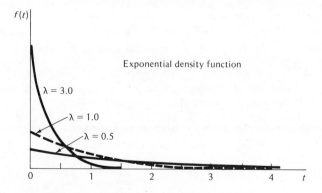

Figure 3.40

We will use the exponential distribution extensively in the chapter on Queueing Models.

Approximation of Discrete Probability Distributions

When a random variable can take on any one of many possible discrete values (say at least 20) which are relatively evenly spaced, it is often much more convenient to approximate this discrete probability distribution with a continuous probability distribution. For instance, consider the distribution of the number of new cars sold daily in a large city. The distribution of the actual number sold is obviously a discrete probability distribution, with perhaps hundreds of possible values, each pair of consecutive values one unit apart. For computational convenience, a continuous probability distribution would generally be employed for any analysis of discrete probability distribution.

As an example of the representation of a discrete probability distribution by a continuous probability distribution, consider the use of the normal distribution as an approximation to the binomial distribution. The normal approximation will be satisfactory only when the binomial probabilities form a reasonably symmetrical distribution about the mean. If the binomial parameters are n, the number of trials, and p, the success probability on each trial, a rough rule of thumb is that, for a good normal approximation, the smaller of the mean number of successes, np, and the mean number of failures, $n(1 - p)$, should be a minimum of about three times the standard deviation, $\sqrt{np(1 - p)}$. The normal distribution parameters are: mean $\mu = np$ and standard deviation $\sigma = \sqrt{np(1 - p)}$. As the number of trials n becomes large, the binomial distribution approaches the normal distribution, as we noted earlier. Therefore, the normal approximation improves as n increases.

Approximating a binomial distribution by a normal distribution is most helpful when the binomial parameters are such that binomial tables are not readily available for the given values. Nevertheless, we will, for comparative purposes, take an example where a binomial table is available.

EXAMPLE 3.10

In a residential area of a city, the fraction of families with no TV set is 0.10. A random sample is to be taken of 100 families in this area.

a) Is it reasonable to represent the sample probability distribution of the number of families with no TV set by a normal distribution? If so, what are the parameters of this normal distribution?

The sample should have a binomial distribution with parameters $n = 100$ and $p = 0.10$. To check the validity of a normal approximation, note that

$$np = (100)(0.10) = 10.0,$$
$$n(1 - p) = (100)(0.90) = 90.0,$$
$$\sqrt{np(1 - p)} = \sqrt{(100)(0.10)(0.90)} = 3.0.$$

Now, $np < n(1 - p)$, and $np/\sqrt{np(1 - p)} > 3$, so the normal approximation should be satisfactory. The parameters will be

$$\mu = np = 10.0, \qquad \sigma = \sqrt{np(1 - p)} = 3.0.$$

The given binomial distribution, plotted as a histogram, and the normal distribution, used as an approximation, are both plotted in Figure 3.41. Visually, the fit of the normal approximation is quite good.

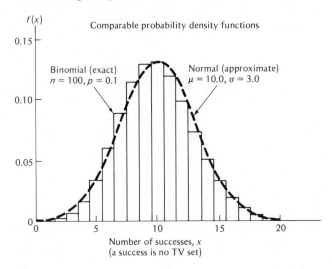

Figure 3.41

b) What is the probability that exactly 12 families in the sample have no TV set?

Let X be the random variable describing the number of families in the sample that have no TV set. Now, since the normal distribution is continuous, we know that the probability that a continuous random variable assumes a particular value is zero. However, we are using a continuous distribution to represent a discrete distribution, so we must make what is termed a "continuity correction." As shown by the histogram in Figure 3.41, we assume that each discrete value actually extends halfway to the adjoining value on either side. Then, in general, for the normal approximation to the binomial probability $P(X = x \mid B{:}n, p)$, we use the relationship

$$P(X = x \mid B{:}n, p) \cong P\big[x - 0.5 \leqslant X \leqslant x + 0.5 \mid N{:}np, \sqrt{np(1 - p)}\,\big].$$

In this example:

$$P(X = 12 \mid B{:}100,\ 0.1) \cong P(11.5 \leqslant X \leqslant 12.5 \mid N{:}10.0,\ 3.0).$$

Now, we convert to a standardized normal distribution. For $x = 11.5$, $z = (x - \mu)/\sigma = (11.5 - 10.0)/3.0 = 0.50$. For $x = 12.5$, $z = (12.5 - 10.0)/3.0 = 0.83$. Then, the required probability is:

$$
\begin{aligned}
P(0.50 \leqslant Z \leqslant 0.83) &= F(0.83) - F(0.50) \\
&= 0.7967 - 0.6915 \\
&= 0.1052 = P(11.5 \leqslant X \leqslant 12.5 \mid N{:}10.0,\ 3.0).
\end{aligned}
$$

The exact binomial probability is:

$$P(X = 12 | B:100, 0.1) = 0.0988.$$

c) What is the probability that 10 or more families in the sample will have no TV set?

The binomial probability is $P(X \geq 10 | B:100, 0.1)$. The normal approximation, with continuity correction, is $P(X \geq 9.5 | N:10.0, 3.0)$. For $x = 9.5$, $z = (9.5 - 10.0)/3.0 = -0.17$. We then evaluate $P(Z \geq -0.17)$.

$$
\begin{aligned}
P(Z \geq -0.17) &= 1 - P(Z \leq -0.17) \\
&= 1 - F(-0.17) = 1 - 0.4325 \\
&= 0.5675 = P(X \geq 9.5 | N:10.0, 3.0).
\end{aligned}
$$

The exact binomial probability is $P(X \geq 10 | B:100, 0.1) = 0.5487$.

As you can see from a close inspection of Figure 3.41, the normal approximation will not be very good for estimating probabilities in the tails of the binomial distribution. Also, if the value of p or $1 - p$ is quite small, the Poisson approximation (discussed earlier) to the binomial distribution may be better than the normal approximation.

3.4 MIXED PROBABILITY DISTRIBUTIONS

Suppose the weekly demand for a certain product can be approximated by a normal distribution with a mean of 300 units and a standard deviation of 50 units. This product must be stocked at the beginning of each week and cannot be reordered during the week. Assume that a decision has been made to stock 350 units each week. (The optimal number of units to stock will be determined by the costs of overordering and underordering, as will be explained in Chapter 11, Inventory Models.) What is the form of the probability distribution of *sales*?

As long as demand does not exceed 350 units, the number stocked, the number of units sold will equal the number of units demanded. However, if demand exceeds 350 units, the number of units sold will be limited to 350, all the units on hand. The probability of selling 350 units is then equal to the probability that demand is 350 units or more. Therefore, if demand is represented by the random variable D and sales by the random variable S:

$$
\begin{aligned}
P(S < 350) &= P(D < 350 | N:300, 50) \\
&= P(Z < 1.0) = F(1.0) = 0.8413. \\
P(S = 350) &= P(D \geq 350 | N:300, 50) \\
&= P(Z \geq 1.0) = 1 - F(1.0) = 0.1587.
\end{aligned}
$$

Thus, the distribution of S is both continuous and discrete, as shown in the plot of its cdf in Figure 3.42. Observe that, at $S = 350$, the cdf takes an instantaneous jump from 0.8413 to 1.0.

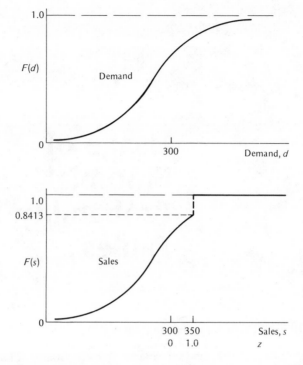

Figure 3.42

If we wished to find a probability such as $P(S > 325)$, which involved both the continuous and the discrete portions of this distribution, we would break the required probability into two parts:

$$P(S > 325) = P(325 < S < 350 \,|\, \text{N:300, 50}) + P(S = 350)$$
$$= F(1.0) - F(0.5) + 0.1587$$
$$= 0.8413 - 0.6915 + 0.1587 = 0.3085.$$

A little thought should convince you that $P(S > 325) = P(D > 325)$, since we stock more than 325 units. Any time there is a demand for more than 325 units, we will sell more than 325 units. Therefore, we could state:

$$P(S > 325) = P(D > 325) = P(Z > 0.5) = 1 - P(Z < 0.5)$$
$$= 1 - F(0.5) = 1 - 0.6915 = 0.3085.$$

A probability distribution which has both continuous and discrete elements is termed a *mixed probability distribution*. It should be clear that mixed probability distributions can arise naturally in the context of practical problems. We will discuss such distributions in more detail in Chapter 11, Inventory Models.

Usage of Binomial Probability Tables

Let p = probability of success on an individual Bernoulli trial
n = number of trials,
r = actual number of successes,
R = random variable denoting number of successes,
$P(R \geq r|n, p)$ = probability of r or more successes, given n and p.
(The Appendix C values are of this form.)

Case I: $p \leq 0.50$

1. Numerical example: $n = 20$, $p = 0.3$

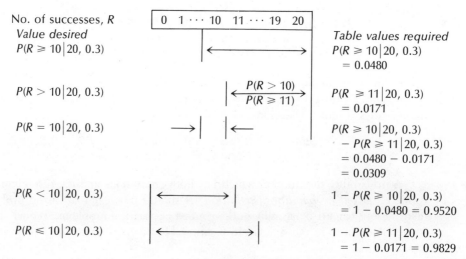

No. of successes, R	0 1 ⋯ 10 11 ⋯ 19 20	
Value desired		*Table values required*
$P(R \geq 10|20, 0.3)$		$P(R \geq 10|20, 0.3)$ = 0.0480
$P(R > 10|20, 0.3)$	$P(R > 10)$ / $P(R \geq 11)$	$P(R \geq 11|20, 0.3)$ = 0.0171
$P(R = 10|20, 0.3)$		$P(R \geq 10|20, 0.3)$ − $P(R \geq 11|20, 0.3)$ = 0.0480 − 0.0171 = 0.0309
$P(R < 10|20, 0.3)$		$1 − P(R \geq 10|20, 0.3)$ = 1 − 0.0480 = 0.9520
$P(R \leq 10|20, 0.3)$		$1 − P(R \geq 11|20, 0.3)$ = 1 − 0.0171 = 0.9829

2. General case

No. of successes, R	$0\ \ 1\ \cdots\ r\ \ r+1\ \cdots\ n-1\ \ n$	Table values required
Value desired $P(R \geqslant r\vert n,\ p)$		$P(R \geqslant r\vert n,\ p)$
$P(R > r\vert n,\ p)$	$\dfrac{P(R>r)}{P(R\geqslant r+1)}$	$P(R \geqslant r+1\vert n,p)$
$P(R = r\vert n,\ p)$		$P(R \geqslant r\vert n,\ p)$ $-\ P(R \geqslant r+1\vert n,\ p)$
$P(R < r\vert n,\ p)$		$1 - P(R \geqslant r\vert n,\ p)$
$P(R \leqslant r\vert n,\ p)$		$1 - P(R \geqslant r+1\vert n,\ p)$

Case II: $p > 0.50$

No. of successes, R	$n\ \ n-1\ \cdots\ r\ \ \cdots\ \ 1\ \ \ 0$	with success probability p

No of failures, $\bar{R}$	$0\ \ \ \ 1\ \cdots\ n-r\ \cdots\ n-1\ \ n$	with failure probability $1-p$

When $p > 0.50$:

1. Substitute $n - r$ for r.
2. Substitute $1 - p$ for p.
3. Reverse any inequality ($\geqslant$ becomes $\leqslant$, $<$ becomes $>$, and so forth).
4. Use Case I procedures.

Numerical Examples

$$P(R < 4\vert 10,\ 0.8) = P(\bar{R} > 6\vert 10,\ 0.2) = P(\bar{R} \geqslant 7\vert 10,\ 0.2) = 0.0009.$$

$$P(R > 4\vert 10,\ 0.8) = P(\bar{R} < 6\vert 10,\ 0.2) = 1 - P(\bar{R} \geqslant 6\vert 10,\ 0.2)$$
$$= 1 - 0.0064 = 0.9936.$$

$$P(R \geqslant 4\vert 10,\ 0.8) = P(\bar{R} \leqslant 6\vert 10,\ 0.2) = 1 - P(\bar{R} \geqslant 7\vert 10,\ 0.2)$$
$$= 1 - 0.0009 = 0.9991.$$

$$P(R = 4\vert 10,\ 0.8) = P(\bar{R} = 6\vert 10,\ 0.2)$$
$$= P(\bar{R} \geqslant 6\vert 10,\ 0.2) - P(\bar{R} \geqslant 7\vert 10,\ 0.2)$$
$$= 0.0064 - 0.0009 = 0.0055.$$

$$P(R \leqslant 4\vert 10,\ 0.8) = P(\bar{R} \geqslant 6\vert 10,\ 0.2) = 0.0064.$$

Endpoint Values (not in the tables)

1. $P(R \geq 0 | n, p) = 1$, so $P(R = 0 | n, p) = 1 - P(R \geq 1 | n, p)$.
2. $P(R \geq n + 1 | n, p) = 0$, so $P(R = n | n, p) = P(R \geq n | n, p) - 0 = P(R \geq n | n, p)$.

Numerical Examples

$$P(R = 6 | 6, 0.5) = P(R \geq 6 | 6, 0.5) = 0.0156$$
$$P(R = 6 | 6, 0.9) = P(\bar{R} = 0 | 6, 0.1) = 1 - P(\bar{R} \geq 1 | 6, 0.1)$$
$$= 1 - 0.4686 = 0.5314$$

Linear Interpolation In Normal Probability Tables

Suppose we are given a z_a value, such as 0.724, that falls between two values in the table. How do we get the associated value of $F(z_a)$, in this case $F(0.724)$? The graph of Figure 3.43 shows an expanded diagram of the two table values bracketing the desired value.

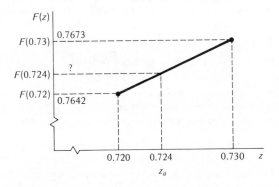

Figure 3.43

Since 0.724 is 0.4 of the way between 0.720 and 0.730, we approximate the desired value of $F(0.724)$ by a value 0.4 of the way between $F(0.72)$ and $F(0.73)$. Therefore,

$$F(0.724) = F(0.72) + (0.4)\big[F(0.73) - F(0.72)\big]$$
$$= 0.7642 + (0.4)(0.7673 - 0.7642)$$
$$= 0.7642 + (0.4)(.0031) = 0.7642 + .0012$$
$$= 0.7654.$$

If the situation is reversed, so that the given value is $F(z_a)$, then we must bracket that value by the two nearest values within the body of the table and perform what is termed inverse interpolation. To illustrate, let us find the value of z_a for which $F(z_a) = 0.85$. An expanded diagram, showing the values of interest, is presented in Figure 3.44. Since, as shown, 0.8500 is a fraction 15/23 of the way between 0.8485 and 0.8508, the value of z_a is approximately 15/23, or 0.7 of the way between 1.030 and 1.040, so that

$$z_a = 1.030 + (0.7)(0.010) = 1.037.$$

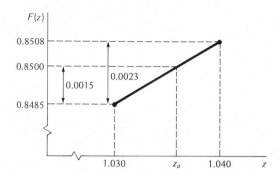

Figure 3.44

EXERCISES

3.1   Describe the basic characteristics of a random variable in your own words, without using such terms as "sample point," "sample space," or "statistical experiment."

3.2   Give at least one real-world example of each of the following.
     (a)   A discrete random variable with a countably infinite number of values.
     (b)   A discrete random variable which assumes only fractional values (plus, possibly, the integers 0 and 1).
     (c)   A continuous random variable assuming only negative values.

3.3   Why is the concept of *random* sampling important? Cite at least one example where sampling must be performed, but random sampling is infeasible. Do you think it can be said that true random sampling is, for many applications, an idealization? Discuss.

3.4   A set of values constitutes a pmf only if what conditions are met?

3.5   An agricultural researcher has developed an improved hybrid variety of corn. A planting of 100 stalks of the new variety produces the following yields:

Number of Ears	Number of Plants Yielding That Number of Ears
20	8
21	16
22	32
23	24
24	16
25	4
	100

Let Y be a random variable denoting the number of ears of corn yielded by a plant.

(a) Graph the probability mass function and cumulative distribution function of Y.

(b) Calculate the mean value of Y.

(c) Calculate the standard deviation of Y.

3.6 In a certain college class, there are twenty students. Their ages are distributed as follows.

Age	Number
18	5
19	6
20	4
21	4
24	1

Let X be a random variable denoting the age of a student selected at random from this class.

(a) Plot the pmf and cdf of X.

(b) Find $P(X > 20)$.

(c) Find $P(X \leq 21)$.

(d) Find $P(X = 19)$.

(e) Find $P(19 < X \leq 22)$.

(f) What is the mean age of the students in this class?

(g) What is the standard deviation of the students' ages?

3.7 A contractor is constructing an addition to a home. He estimates that it will take between 8 and 12 working days. He feels that 10 days is the most likely time, and that 11 days is only half as likely. He estimates a time of 9 days as two-thirds as likely as that of 10 days. A time of 8 or 12 days is only half as likely as a time of 11 days.

(a)   Specify his subjective probability distribution (to the nearest 0.01 for each probability value).

(b)   On the basis of his subjective probability distribution, what is the expected time to completion? What is the standard deviation?

(c)   Plot the pmf and cdf for this distribution.

3.8   The cdf of the random variable X is as follows.

$$F(x) = \begin{cases} 0 \text{ for } x < -1, \\ 0.5 \text{ for } -1 \leqslant x < 0, \\ 0.8 \text{ for } 0 \leqslant x < 2, \\ 1.0 \text{ for } x \geqslant 2. \end{cases}$$

(a)   Specify the pmf and plot it.

(b)   Determine the expected value and variance of X.

3.9   Working from the basic definition of the cdf of a random variable X, as $F(x) = P(X \leqslant x)$, state in your own words why the value of $F(x)$, for all x, must lie between 0 and 1, inclusively.

3.10 Inspection of a manufactured assembly consists of taking a sample of four items and classifying each item as good or defective. Define a random variable G which represents the number of good items in the sample. Suppose, on the basis of past experience, the probability distribution of the number of defectives is

Defectives	0	1	2	3	4
Probability	0.80	0.09	0.05	0.03	0.03

(a)   Find the expected value $E(G)$.

(b)   Find the variance $V(G)$.

(c)   Let the random variable $H = G + 5$. Find $E(H)$ and $V(H)$.

(d)   Let the random variable $L = 5G$. Find $E(L)$ and $V(L)$.

3.11 In order for a series of statistical trials to form a Bernoulli process, what basic conditions must be met? Describe in your own words.

3.12 If R is a random variable denoting the number of successes in n Bernoulli trials, each with success probability p, and $\bar{R}$ is a random variable denoting the number of failures, show that

$$P(R \geqslant r | n, p) = P(\bar{R} \leqslant n - r | n, 1 - p),$$

using the basic Equation (3.12) and demonstrating term-by-term equality of the above expressions.

3.13 In a particular telephone poll, useful information has been obtained on 40 percent of the calls. A pollster makes ten calls. What is the probability that

(a)   at least four calls are productive?

(b)   exactly four calls are productive?

(c)   six or more calls are unproductive?

3.14 An infamous insurance company had 100,000 life insurance policies written. Of these, only 60,000 were genuine, that is, were requested by the insured. Out of

the total, 70,000 policies were written on the lives of men. If a random sample of eight policies is chosen, what is the probability that
(a)   exactly four are fraudulent?
(b)   at least four are written on the life of a woman?
(c)   at least two are genuine?

3.15   The Quantitative Methods Department of Pragmatic University has three graduate assistantships to offer. From the list of candidates, it decides to make four offers. In the past, 30 percent of the offers have been turned down.
(a)   What is the probability that there will be at least three acceptances?
(b)   What is the probability that there will be too many acceptances?
(c)   If the university wishes to be at least 90 percent certain of getting a minimum of three acceptances, what is the minimum number of offers it should make?
       Hint: This is a trial and error process.

3.16   The Small Business Administration arranges loans to entrepreneurs of small businesses. In a certain type of business enterprise, 25 percent of the loans go to businesses which fail within a two-year period after the loan is made. If twenty such loans are made, what is the probability that, within a two-year period after the loan is made:
(a)   At least half of the enterprises will not fail?
(b)   Fewer than three of the enterprises will fail?
(c)   Exactly six of the enterprises will fail?
(d)   At least six, but no more than ten, of the enterprises will fail?

3.17   A purchased part is inspected by taking a sample of ten items from each lot of 500 items received. On the basis of economic considerations, the fraction defective in each lot should not exceed 10 percent. It has been decided to accept the remainder of the lot if there is no more than one defective in the sample; this criterion is sometimes called the *decision rule*. If the lot is rejected, it must be completely inspected.
(a)   The number of defectives in the sample will be distributed according to what kind of probability distribution? What are the parameters of this distribution?
       Using the binomial distribution as an approximation to the true probability distribution, what is the probability that
(b)   A lot with a fraction defective of 0.10 is rejected? (Since this lot fraction defective is acceptable, this decision would be in error. This type of error is called the producer's risk.)
(c)   A lot with a fraction defective of 0.15 is accepted? (Since this lot fraction defective is not acceptable, this decision would also be in error. This type of error is called the consumer's risk.)
(d)   How would the magnitude of the answers in (b) and (c) change if it were decided to accept only lots with no defectives in the sample?
(d)   From the standpoint of producer's and consumer's risk, comment briefly on the choice of the maximum number of defectives allowed for acceptance of a lot.

3.18 How does the hypergeometric distribution differ from the binomial distribution? What is the primary motivation for approximating a hypergeometric distribution by a binomial distribution whenever this is feasible? In general, when is this feasible?

3.19 Of six available political speakers, four are Democrats and two are Republicans. If two speakers are chosen at random, what is the probability that
   (a) both a Democrat and a Republican are selected?
   (b) both speakers are from the same party?

3.20 Out of twelve customer accounts, four are delinquent and eight are paid up. If four accounts are selected at random from these twelve accounts, what is the probability that
   (a) all four are paid up?
   (b) three are paid up?
   (c) all four are delinquent?

3.21 Give at least two examples, differing from those in the text, of real-world situations in which a random variable could be expected to follow a probability distribution quite close to a Poisson distribution.

3.22 Why is the Poisson approximation to the binomial distribution particularly useful when it is applicable? For each of the following binomial distributions, determine if the Poisson approximation is valid. If it is, state the mean of the appropriate Poisson distribution.
   (a) $n = 150, p = 0.06$.
   (b) $n = 40, p = 0.90$.
   (c) $n = 60, p = 0.05$.

3.23 A manufacturer of large electrical equipment produces a certain type of transformer. Orders for this transformer appear to arrive in a purely random fashion at the average rate of 1.5 per week. Over an eight-week period, what is the probability that
   (a) exactly 18 orders will be received?
   (b) over 15 orders will be received?
   (c) no more than 10 orders will be received?
   (d) between 9 and 16 orders will be received?

3.24 In a certain scientific spacecraft, there are 200 electronic components of a particular type. During the mission time of the spacecraft, the individual failure probability for these components is believed to be 0.001. Assuming that failures of these components are independent,
   (a) the number of failures during the mission would follow what type of probability distribution? What are the values of the parameters of this distribution?
   Utilize an approximation to the true probability distribution to find the probability that, during the mission,
   (b) there are no failures.
   (c) there are fewer than three failures.
   (d) one or two failures occur.

3.25   For a continuous random variable, why do we have to work with a probability density function rather than individual probability values, as with a probability mass function?

3.26   A random variable X has a triangular probability density function as shown in the graph below. Plot the cumulative distribution function of X. [*Hint:* Calculate the area under the pdf at several points. Recall that the area of a triangle equals ½ times the base times the height.]

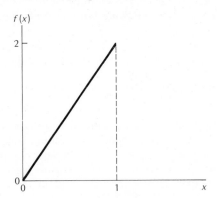

3.27   As shown in Figure 3.25, the cdf for a uniform distribution is a linear function in the interval $a \leq x \leq b$. In this region, let $F(x) = c_1 x + c_2$. Knowing the values of $F(x)$ at the endpoints $x = a$ and $x = b$, solve for the values of c_1 and c_2, and verify the complete cdf, as given in Equation (3.21).

3.28   The Fail-Anytime Flashlight Battery Company advertises that all its batteries last at least six months from the time of sale, and that its batteries are equally likely to fail at any time between six and eighteen months. Presumably, none last more than eighteen months. Assuming that battery lifetimes are uniformly distributed between six and eighteen months, what proportion of their batteries last
(a)   at least fifteen months?
(b)   no more than ten months?
(c)   between eight months and sixteen months?

3.29   A small company estimates that its net profit for the year will be between $100,000 and $120,000. It believes that the actual value is equally likely to fall anywhere within that range. What is the probability that the annual net profit will be
(a)   over $114,000?
(b)   in the range between $109,500 and $112,000?
(c)   less than $103,000 or greater than $118,000?

3.30   It has been stated that, in effect, there never has been nor will there ever be a normal probability distribution. Discuss this statement.

3.31 What is the relationship between a normally distributed random variable X, with mean μ and standard deviation σ, and the standardized random variable Z? What is the advantage of utilizing this relationship in problem solving?

3.32 Under what conditions is it necessary to perform inverse interpolation in the normal probability table? Why is this process termed "inverse" interpolation? (You may find Appendix 3B helpful.)

3.33 Suppose you are given a random variable X, which is normally distributed, with mean μ and standard deviation σ. Utilizing the standardized normal probability table:
(a) Given two values x_a and x_b, $x_b > x_a$, state the steps required to solve for the probability that X lies in the interval between x_a and x_b.
(b) Given the probability p that X exceeds some value x_a, state the steps required to solve for the value of x_a.

3.34 Many standardized normal probability tables differ from that in Appendix A by giving, for positive z values only, the probability that the standardized random variable Z falls between 0 and some value z, rather than the probability that Z is less than a given z value. For such tables, and denoting the probability value associated with a given z as $P(z)$, explain clearly how to determine the probability that the standardized random variable Z lies between the values z_a and z_b, $z_b > z_a$, for the following cases:
(a) z_a and z_b both positive.
(b) z_a negative and z_b positive.
(c) z_a and z_b both negative.

3.35 East-West Airlines has a policy of hiring only American stewardesses whose height is between 5 feet 2 inches and 5 feet 10 inches. If the height of American women is approximately normally distributed with a mean of 5 feet 5 inches and a standard deviation of 3 inches, what is the probability that a potential applicant would be
(a) too tall?
(b) too short?
(c) of acceptable height?
(d) between 5 feet 4 inches and 5 feet 8 inches?

3.36 The best information regarding the cost of a research project is that it is normally distributed with a mean of $50,000 and a standard deviation of $5000. The available funds are limited to $60,000. What is the probability that the project cost
(a) will not exceed the available funds?
(b) will be between $40,000 and $55,000?
(c) will be less than $45,000?
What is the cost which
(d) will not be exceeded more than 15 percent of the time?
(e) will be exceeded 95 percent of the time?

3.37 Losers' International, an organization of dieters, advertises a special Losers' Weekend. In the advertisement, it is stated that average weight loss during this three-day weekend averages ten pounds with a standard deviation of two pounds. Assuming that the weight lost during the weekend is approximately normally distributed, what proportion of dieters lose

(a)   at least 5.2 pounds?
(b)   less than 8.0 pounds?
(c)   more than 13.5 pounds?
(d)   4.5 to 15.5 pounds?
(e)   90 percent of the dieters will lose at least how many pounds?

3.38   A 46-ounce can of fruit juice is filled in a production line by automatic equipment. The actual liquid measure varies and tends to be normally distributed with a standard deviation of 0.2 ounces. Since state regulations require that no more than one can in twenty have under 46 ounces of liquid, the average liquid measure has been set at 46.5 ounces.

(a)   Is the state regulation being met?
(b)   What is the probability that there will be between 46.3 and 46.6 ounces in a given can?
(c)   What is the probability that there will be over 46.8 ounces in a given can?
(d)   To the nearest 0.01 ounce, what should the average liquid measure be to just meet the state standard?

3.39   A steel shaft, with a specified diameter of 1.000 inch, must be manufactured to rather close tolerances. The maximum allowable diameter is 1.003 inches, and the minimum allowable diameter is 0.998 inch. If the shaft diameter is approximately normally distributed, with a mean diameter of 1.000 inch and a standard deviation of 0.0015 inch:

(a)   What fraction of the shafts produced will be acceptable?
(b)   What fraction of the unacceptable shafts will be oversized?
(c)   How would the fraction of unacceptable shafts change if the mean diameter could be increased to 1.0005 inches, while maintaining the same standard deviation?

3.40   In midsummer, the weekly demand for water from a suburban reservoir tends to be normally distributed with a mean of 50,000 gallons and a standard deviation of 10,000 gallons.

(a)   What demand level will be exceeded 80 percent of the time?
(b)   What demand level will be exceeded only 10 percent of the time?
(c)   Between what demand levels will 25 percent of the demands fall below the mean and 20 percent of the demands above the mean?

3.41   Suppose you were asked to construct an approximate cdf for the probability distribution of the number of meals served daily by a certain restaurant. Assuming no such records are kept, you would presumably question those in the organization who are in a position to make such an estimate, such as the chef, waitresses, and hostesses. In developing the cdf for such a subjective probability distribution, which of the two methods discussed in the text would you prefer to use? Why?

3.42   The Handy-Dandy Company has developed a new household gadget. The sales
       manager has made the following probability estimates for the demand for this
       item.

> At least 10,000 units: Odds of 9 to 1.
> At least 20,000 units: Odds of 3 to 1.
> At least 30,000 units: A 50–50 chance.
> At least 50,000 units: Odds of 1 to 4.
> At least 70,000 units: Only 1 chance in 20.

(a)   Convert these figures to probabilities and sketch a smooth curve, in the
      form of a cdf, representing the sales manager's subjective probability
      distribution for demand. (Since it cannot be expected that the probability
      estimates of the sales manager will be completely consistent, some of the
      data points may not lie on the curve.)
(b)   From your graph, estimate the probability of a demand
      1.   less than 60,000 units.
      2.   greater than 25,000 units.
      3.   between 20,000 and 40,000 units.

3.43   Briefly discuss the nature of the relationship between the exponential
       distribution and the Poisson distribution. Why is the exponential distribution
       continuous, since the Poisson distribution is discrete?

3.44   The lifetime of an electronic component in a citizen's band radio has an
       exponential distribution with a mean of two years. What is the probability that the
       component lasts at least
       (a)   one year?
       (b)   two years?
       (c)   three years?
       [Hint: Utilize the cumulative Poisson tables, as explained in the text.]

3.45   The Motley Makeup Company tells its prospective sales people that one potential
       customer out of four will buy its glamourizing products. Assuming this to be true,
       you contact 48 potential customers. Using the normal approximation to the
       binomial distribution, what is the probability that
       (a)   at least 14 customers buy?
       (b)   not more than 11 customers buy?
       (c)   exactly 12 customers buy?
       [Hint: Don't forget to make a continuity correction.]

3.46   It is believed that a special school bond issue is favored by 65 percent of those
       who will vote on it. It takes a two-thirds majority of those voting to pass the bond
       issue. Using the normal approximation to the binomial distribution, if there are
       6000 voters:
       (a)   What is the probability that the bond issue passes?
       (b)   What is the probability that the number of favorable votes falls between 3880
             and 3930?
       (c)   What is the number of favorable votes which can be expected to be
             exceeded 75 percent of the time in a comparable situation?

3.47 Why is it often advantageous to approximate a discrete probability distribution by a continuous probability distribution? What do you think might characterize a continuous probability distribution for which a discrete probability distribution could be a useful and, perhaps, necessary approximation?

3.48 A small part is purchased in lots of 2500. In the past, 2 percent of these parts have proved to be defective. Using the normal approximation to the binomial distribution, what is the probability that, in a given lot, there will be
   (a) No more than 60 defectives?
   (b) Between 40 and 60 defectives?
   (c) Exactly 40 defectives?

3.49 In the state of Euphoria, partial election returns in the gubernatorial race are as follows: Windbag—501,000; Cornpone—499,000. These votes are believed to be a random sample of all votes cast in this election.
   (a) The total vote for the two candidates is 5,000,000. Based on the results after the first 1,000,000 votes, what are Cornpone's chances of winning the election?
   (b) What is the probability that Cornpone would get no more than 499,000 votes out of the 1,000,000 votes cast if the voters had no preference between the two candidates?

3.50 The food concessionaire at the local baseball stadium has refrigerator capacity for up to 25,000 hot dogs. Hot dog demand for a night game is estimated to be normally distributed with a mean of 20,000 and a standard deviation of 5,000.
   (a) What is the probability that 25,000 hot dogs will be sold?
   (b) Sketch the cdf for the probability distribution of sales.

3.51 In the spring, a retail store receives a shipment of 100 men's summer suits, with no opportunity to reorder. The best estimate of the seasonal demand for these suits appears to be in the range of 80 to 120, with any quantity in that range being equally likely. Approximating the discrete demand distribution by a uniform distribution over the given range:
   (a) Sketch the cdf for the (mixed) probability distribution of sales.
   (b) What is the expected number of suits sold?

CHAPTER 4

DECISION MAKING USING EXPECTED MONETARY VALUE

In this chapter, we present some of the fundamental concepts involved in making decisions under conditions of uncertainty. The primary emphasis will be on problems where a single optimal decision is required, although we will also discuss problems where a sequence of optimal decisions is to be determined. We will concentrate on the analysis of situations involving discrete probability distributions. The final section, however, includes a discussion of certain topics relating to decision making with continuous probability distributions. We will start by defining the terms commonly used in the analysis of decisions under uncertainty.

4.1 BASIC CONCEPTS

An *event*, as described in Chapter 2, is a collection of experimental outcomes. As discussed in that chapter, an event can have a numerical description (demand for 12 units of a particular item) or a nonnumerical description (an employee strike). We have no direct control over the occurrence of an event. On the other hand, an *act*, sometimes called an action, alternative, decision, or strategy, represents the choice of a particular action from some specified set of alternative actions. Just as with an event, the description of an act may be essentially numerical or it may be nonnumerical. Thus, an act could be the stocking of 15 units of an item, or it could represent a decision to build a stockpile in anticipation of a possible strike.

A *conditional profit* (CP) is the profit associated with a particular combination of an act and an event. Thus, we might have a conditional profit of $10 associated with the act of stocking 15 units of an item when the event is a demand for 12 units of that item. Costs can be handled as negative profits.

For a given problem, a *payoff table* lists the events (mutually exclusive and collectively exhaustive) and a set of mutually exclusive acts. For each combination of act and event, the conditional profit is specified or calculated. The weighted profit associated with a given combination of act and event is obtained by multiplying the conditional profit for that act and event combination by the probability of occurrence of the given event. The *expected monetary value* (EMV) of an act is the summation of all the weighted profits associated with that act.

We will illustrate these basic concepts with a highly simplified example.

EXAMPLE 4.1

An investor has decided to invest a certain sum in one of two stocks, either Washington Ornamental Works (ticker symbol WOW), which is somewhat specula-tive, or Tennessee Underwear Factories (ticker symbol TUF), which is fairly conser-vative. Over the six-month period of interest to this investor, she feels that the economy will either advance or stagnate, with about a 40 percent chance it will advance. If the economy advances, the investor anticipates a $2000 profit if she invests in WOW stock or a $1400 profit with TUF stock. However, if the economy stagnates, she expects WOW stock to lose $300, while TUF stock would gain $200. If this investor wishes to maximize her expected monetary value, which stock should she purchase?

We start by defining the events (over which the investor has no control) and the acts (possible decisions).

Let event E_1 = economy advances,
    event E_2 = economy stagnates,
      act A_1 = buy WOW stock,
      act A_2 = buy TUF stock.

Table 4.1 is the payoff table, showing the conditional profit for each of the four possible act and event combinations.

Table 4.1 Investor's Payoff Table

	Conditional Profit ($)	
	Act	
Event, E_i	A_1 (Buy WOW)	A_2 (Buy TUF)
E_1 (Economy advances)	2000	1400
E_2 (Economy stagnates)	−300	200

We will first calculate the EMV for both acts and then indicate how the quantities involved in these calculations can be conveniently presented in a tabular format.

Since the probability that the economy advances (event E_1) is estimated as 0.40, the probability that it stagnates (event E_2) must be 0.60, because these are the only two events in this problem and they are mutually exclusive and collectively exhaustive. The calculations of the EMVs for act A_1 (buy WOW) and for act A_2 (buy TUF) then easily follow according to the rules for calculating any expected value.

$$EMV(A_1) = (0.40)(2000) + (0.60)(-300) = 800 - 180 = \$620,$$

$$EMV(A_2) = (0.40)(1400) + (0.60)(200) \quad = 560 + 120 = \$680.$$

To maximize EMV, the investor's choice should be act A_2, buy TUF. The EMV of the optimal act is generally denoted as EMV* (EMV "star"), so

$$EMV* = EMV(A_2) = \$680.$$

Table 4.2 Investor's EMV Calculations

Event E_i	Probability $P(E_i)$	Conditional Profit ($) Act A_1	Act A_2	Weighted Profit ($) Act A_1	Act A_2
E_1	0.40	2000	1400	800	560
E_2	0.60	-300	200	-180	120
				EMV 620	680

The preceding calculations can be more clearly and compactly shown by organizing them as in Table 4.2. The optimal act is A_2, and EMV* = $680, as before. We can interpret the $680 value in the following manner: if the investor had a very large number of such investment opportunities, all identical, she would expect to obtain a $1400 profit 40 percent of the time and a $200 profit 60 percent of the time. On a long-term average basis, her expected profit per investment opportunity would be $680.

4.2 OPPORTUNITY LOSS

Another very meaningful way of viewing such problems as those just discussed involves the analysis of relative, rather than absolute, values. This is a particularly useful approach for certain types of problems, as we will see later.

Given that a certain event occurs, the *conditional opportunity loss* (COL) of a particular act is equal to the difference between the conditional profit for that act and the conditional profit of the most favorable act for that event. The COL values are calculated separately for each *event* by first finding the most favorable act for that event and then taking the difference between that conditional profit value, and, in turn, each conditional profit value for that event. Continuing with Example 4.1, this procedure is illustrated in Table 4.3, where the investor's COL values are calculated.

Table 4.3 Investor's Conditional Opportunity Losses

	Conditional Profit ($)		Conditional Opportunity Loss ($)	
Event	Act		Act	
E_i	A_1	A_2	A_1	A_2
E_1	2000	1400	0	600
E_2	−300	200	500	0

The COL values in Table 4.3 may be explained as follows: If event E_1 occurred, the maximum profit of $2000 (underscored) would be achieved by selecting act A_1. Therefore, the selection of act A_1 would result in zero opportunity loss, since it is the best decision that can be made if event E_1 occurs. If act A_2 were chosen, with a conditional profit of $1400, this selection would result in a conditional opportunity loss of $2000 − 1400 = \$600$. If event E_2 occurred, the best act would be A_2, with a conditional profit of $200 (underscored). Thus, no opportunity loss would be associated with the selection of A_2. However, if act A_1 were selected, the conditional opportunity loss would be $200 − (−300) = \$500$. The investor would have been $500 worse off in that situation if she had chosen act A_1.

A mistake sometimes made is to calculate opportunity losses for each act, instead of for each event. An opportunity loss arises from making the "wrong" choice of an act (with the benefit of hindsight). We have no choice among events; they are outside our control.

It should be clear that there must be at least one zero COL value associated with each event and that there can never be a negative opportunity loss. Observe that, for a given event, an act can be profitable and still incur an opportunity loss, provided there is another act with a higher profit.

The weighted opportunity loss for an act-event combination is the COL value for that combination multiplied by the probability that the given event occurs. The *expected opportunity loss* (EOL) of a given act equals the summation of all the weighted opportunity losses associated with that act. Whether the objective be one of maximizing expected profit or minimizing expected cost, the optimal act will always be the act that has the smallest EOL value, denoted as EOL*. This act will always be the same as the act associated with EMV*. The expected opportunity loss and expected monetary value approaches are completely consistent and will always give identical answers as to the optimal act or acts.

Table 4.4 Investor's EOL Calculations

Event E_i	Probability $P(E_i)$	Conditional Opportunity Loss ($) Act A_1	Conditional Opportunity Loss ($) Act A_2	Weighted Opportunity Loss ($) Act A_1	Weighted Opportunity Loss ($) Act A_2
E_1	0.40	0	600	0	240
E_2	0.60	500	0	300	0
				EOL 300	240

The EOL calculations for the investor's problem are shown in Table 4.4. From the results of Table 4.4, the optimal act is act A_2, which has the lowest EOL. Thus, EOL* = $240. The selection of act A_2 as the optimal act comes, of course, as no surprise, since we found it to be optimal when the EMV calculations were performed.

4.3 VALUE OF INFORMATION

In situations of the nature discussed, the occurrence of a specific event is probabilistic in nature. That is, it is assumed we have no control over the occurrence of a given event. However, what if we had information as to exactly which event would occur? For example, suppose we are contemplating raising the price on a certain product we manufacture, and we have a single large competitor. Our decision to implement this price increase depends, say, on our degree of belief that our competitor will match our price increase or will leave his price unchanged. In this situation, the events are our competitor's anticipated responses to a price increase, and these events, for which we can establish subjective probabilities, are clearly outside our control. The acts under consideration are an increase in the product price or an unchanged product price. If we had a spy in our competitor's organization who could tell us exactly what their response would be to such a price increase on our part, then this spy would be able to supply us with perfect information as to which event would occur if we acted to raise the price of our product. Given such perfect information, we would be able to choose the optimal act with certainty. We will have more to say about the meaningfulness of perfect information a little later.

The *expected profit with perfect information* (EPPI) is the expected profit based on perfect information as to which event will occur. We choose the optimal act for each event, multiply its conditional profit by the given event probability to get the weighted profit, and then we sum these weighted profits to get EPPI.

For Example 4.1, the calculation of EPPI is developed in Table 4.5. Realizing that the investor has no control over the probability distribution of events, if she faced this situation a number of times, so that the individual event occurrences were distributed according to the given event probabilities, perfect information would allow her to select act A_1 every time event E_1 would occur and act A_2 every time event E_2 would occur. The average profit obtained would then be $920.

Table 4.5 Investor's EPPI Calculations

Event E_i	Probability $P(E_i)$	Optimal Act	Profit of Optimal Act ($) Conditional Value	Profit of Optimal Act ($) Weighted Value
E_1	0.40	A_1	2000	800
E_2	0.60	A_2	200	120
				EPPI 920

EPPI is the expected profit with perfect information, as calculated before the perfect information is obtained. We can call it a prior expectation. (After the perfect information is obtained, EPPI is a meaningless concept.)

The EOL for any act is equal to EPPI less the EMV for that act. If you think about it, this really is not too surprising, considering the way we define opportunity loss as, in essence, being the difference between "what we have" and "what we would like to have." Table 4.6 shows these relationships for Example 4.1.

Table 4.6 Relationship between EOL, EMV, and EPPI—Investor's Problem

	Value ($) Act A_1	Value ($) Act A_2
EPPI	920	920
− EMV	−620	−680
= EOL	300	240

At this point, we introduce a very important concept. We define the *expected value of perfect information* (EVPI) as the maximum amount one would be willing to pay to obtain perfect information as to which event would occur. EPPI represents the maximum obtainable expected monetary value with perfect information as to which event will actually occur (as calculated before perfect information is received) and EMV* represents the maximum obtainable expected monetary value, given only the prior event probabilities, with no information as to which event will actually occur. Therefore, perfect information would increase expected profit from EMV* up to the value of EPPI, so the amount of that increase would be equal to the expected value of perfect information. We then have

$$EVPI = EPPI - EMV^*.$$

Since, as noted earlier, EOL^* is also equal to $EPPI - EMV^*$,

$$EVPI \equiv EOL^*.$$

Thus, the expected value of perfect information is identical to the expected opportunity loss of the optimal act. Another way of looking at this relationship is to observe that perfect information reduces the expected opportunity loss from EOL^* to zero, so $EVPI \equiv EOL^*$.

In this example, $EVPI = EOL^* = \$240$. If the investor could get a perfect forecast of the movement of the economy (advancing or stagnating), she should consider paying up to \$240 for such a forecast. At a payment of exactly \$240, she should be indifferent to the alternatives of paying \$240 for perfect information and paying nothing and receiving no information. At a payment exceeding \$240, the investor would be financially better off by not purchasing a perfect forecast, even if it were available. (If a perfect forecast could be obtained, note that the investor would be considering parting with an actual monetary amount in order to obtain a more favorable *gamble* with an *expected* additional payoff of \$240.)

Consideration of the expected value of perfect information is an important concept in the analysis of business problems. The EVPI value, in a given problem, gives us an absolute upper bound on the amount that we should spend to get additional information on which to base a given decision. Actually, since it is generally impossible or, at least, impractical to obtain perfect information, the value of EVPI tends to be appreciably more than should be spent getting additional information. In the study of Bayesian decision theory, we will find the concepts of EVPI and EOL quite important in the determination of optimal sampling procedures.

4.4 PROBLEM SOLVING

In solving problems such as the one just discussed, involving one or more decisions, it is quite useful to develop a general approach to problem formulation and solution. This helps to delineate the common structure of all such problems and to set up an orderly procedure for the efficient determination of the optimal decision(s). A suggested procedure follows.

1. Symbolically define the events (mutually exclusive and collectively exhaustive) and the acts (mutually exclusive).
2. State or calculate the conditional profit or cost (or opportunity loss) associated with each possible combination of act and event.
3. Specify the probability of each event.

4. Specify the criterion (or criteria) for the decision as to the optimal act. (We will discuss criteria other than EMV* or EOL* in the following chapter.)
5. Weight the conditional profits, costs, or losses by the associated event probabilities, and sum these weighted values for each act.
6. On the basis of the specified decision criterion, determine the optimal act.

We will continue to follow this general procedure in the solution of the example problems in this chapter.

4.5   COST MINIMIZATION PROBLEM

Suppose we now tie together the material presented thus far in this chapter by considering a problem which differs from Example 4.1 in two important respects. First, it involves cost minimization, rather than profit maximization; and second, the events are essentially numeric.

EXAMPLE 4.2

A certain piece of equipment is to be purchased for a construction project at a remote location. This equipment contains an expensive part which is subject to random failure. Spares of this part can be purchased at the same time the equipment is purchased. Their unit cost is $1000, and they have no scrap value. If the part fails on the job and no spare is available, the part will have to be manufactured on a special-order basis and flown in. If this is required, the total cost, including down time of the equipment, is estimated as $8000 for each such occurrence. Based on previous experience with similar parts, the following probability estimates of the number of failures expected over the duration of the project are provided: $P(0$ failures$) = 0.80$, $P(1$ failure$) = 0.15$, $P(2$ failures$) = 0.05$. The probability of more than two failures is considered to be negligible.

a) Based on the criterion of maximizing EMV, determine EMV* and the optimal number of spares to purchase initially.

In this problem, the possible events are the number of part failures that may occur, or, in more directly useful terms, the number of spares that will actually be required. The acts are the number of spares initially purchased. Clearly, there would be no point in purchasing more than two spares.

Let event E_0 = 0 spares required (no failures),
event E_1 = 1 spare required (1 failure),
event E_2 = 2 spares required (2 failures),
act A_0 = 0 spares purchased,
act A_1 = 1 spare purchased,
act A_2 = 2 spares purchased.

Now, we must calculate the conditional cost for each possible combination of number of spares required and number of spares initially purchased. This is done in Table 4.7.

Table 4.7   Calculation of Conditional Costs

Spares Required	Spares Purchased	Purchase Cost ($)	Emergency Cost ($)	Total Cost ($)
0	0	0	0	0
0	1	1000	0	1,000
0	2	2000	0	2,000
1	0	0	8,000	8,000
1	1	1000	0	1,000
1	2	2000	0	2,000
2	0	0	16,000	16,000
2	1	1000	8,000	9,000
2	2	2000	0	2,000

Using the conditional cost values from Table 4.7 and the given event probability values, the expected cost can now be calculated for each of the three possible acts. The computations are shown in Table 4.8.

Table 4.8   Calculation of Expected Costs

Event E_i	Probability $P(E_i)$	Conditional Cost ($)			Weighted Cost ($)		
		A_0	A_1	A_2	A_0	A_1	A_2
E_0	0.80	0	1000	2000	0	800	1600
E_1	0.15	8,000	1000	2000	1200	150	300
E_2	0.05	16,000	9000	2000	800	450	100
					2000	1400	2000

The optimal act is clearly A_1, purchase one spare. Since the values here are costs, but EMV is expressed in terms of profit,

$$\text{EMV*} = \text{EMV}(A_1) = -\$1400.$$

b) Based on opportunity losses, determine the optimal act and EOL*.

The conditional opportunity loss values can be readily found by constructing Table 4.9, which is similar to Table 4.3. We must keep in mind, however, that we are now working with conditional costs, rather than conditional profits. Thus, the under--

lined value for each event is the lowest conditional cost, whereas in Table 4.3 it was the highest conditional profit.

Table 4.9   Opportunity Loss Calculations

Event	Conditional Cost ($)			Conditional Opportunity Loss ($)		
		Act			Act	
E_i	A_0	A_1	A_2	A_0	A_1	A_2
E_0	0	1000	2000	0	1000	2000
E_1	8,000	1000	2000	7,000	0	1000
E_2	16,000	9000	2000	14,000	7000	0

As an illustration of the COL calculations in Table 4.9, if event E_1 occurs, the optimal choice is act A_1, with a cost of $1000. The COL of act A_1 is, therefore, zero. Act A_0, with a cost of $8000, would be $7000 less favorable than act A_1. Act A_2, with a cost of $2000, is clearly $1000 worse than act A_1.

We are now ready to calculate the EOL values, and this is done in Table 4.10.

Table 4.10   EOL Calculations

Event	Probability	Conditional Opportunity Loss ($)			Weighted Opportunity Loss ($)		
			Act			Act	
E_i	$P(E_i)$	A_0	A_1	A_2	A_0	A_1	A_2
E_0	0.80	0	1000	2000	0	800	1600
E_1	0.15	7,000	0	1000	1050	0	150
E_2	0.05	14,000	7000	0	700	350	0
					EOL 1750	1150	1750

The optimal act is again seen to be A_1, purchase one spare, and

$$EOL^* = EOL(A_1) = \$1150.$$

Observe that act A_1 is preferred by $600 to both acts A_0 and A_2, just as was true when the expected costs were computed, referring back to Table 4.8.

c) Find the expected profit with perfect information and the expected value of perfect information.

To find EPPI, we must determine the optimal act for each event and weight its conditional value by the event probability. In this example, it should be obvious, without any numerical calculations, that the optimal act, for a given event, is to purchase exactly as many spares as there are failures. The required calculations are shown in Table 4.11.

Table 4.11   EPPI Calculations

			Cost of Optimal Act ($)	
Event E_i	Probability $P(E_i)$	Optimal Act	Conditional Value	Weighted Value
E_0	0.80	A_0	0	0
E_1	0.15	A_1	1000	150
E_2	0.05	A_2	2000	100
				250

If we had perfect information, our expected cost would be $250, so

$$\text{EPPI} = -\$250.$$

EVPI, as demonstrated earlier, is identical to EOL*; therefore,

$$\text{EVPI} = \text{EOL*} = \$1150.$$

As a check, recall that EMV* was $-\$1400$. Thus,

$$\text{EVPI} = \text{EPPI} - \text{EMV*} = -250 - (-1400) = \$1150.$$

If we could in some way get perfect information beforehand specifying the exact number of failures that would occur during the project time period, we should be willing to pay up to $1150 for this information. In a practical situation, it is impossible to obtain information pinpointing the exact number of random failures to be expected in a given time period, but it would certainly be worth some amount if, for instance, a method of detecting impending failure could be devised. With adequate warning of an impending failure and no available spare, a spare could be special-ordered in time to avoid the heavy down-time penalty cost for the equipment, perhaps $6000 of the $8000 total cost of a breakdown when no spare was available. Since such a failure detector would not give perfect information (the exact number of failures during the project time period), its cost would have to be quite a bit less than $1150, the limiting value of additional information, or it would not be worth considering. If it could be used on more than one such project, however, its allowable cost could be considerably higher.

4.6   SENSITIVITY ANALYSIS

Having performed an analysis and selected the optimal act, it is frequently important to examine the impact on that decision of a change or an error in the input data. In many actual business problems for which mathematical models are used, some of the required numerical values which are known, such as material costs, may change with little or no notice, whereas other values, particularly subjective probabilities, cannot be specified with any real degree of confidence. The process of examining the impact of changes or errors is called *sensitivity analysis*.

In the elementary sensitivity analyses to be performed in this chapter, we will allow only one input data item to be a variable. We will then examine that data item from two different standpoints. For all possible values of the input data item, we will determine (1) the optimal act, which permits us to evaluate the effect of a data value change on the selection of the optimal act, and (2) the economic effect of an error in the assumed value of the data item. Knowing the optimal act given the assumed value, the decrease in EMV can be calculated for data values for which that act is no longer optimal.

The procedures to be followed will be illustrated by sensitivity analyses of the two decision problems previously worked out. We will find that the first step is to determine indifference points between alternative acts, because the required decision in problems of this nature is the selection of a particular act.

EXAMPLE 4.3

We will perform sensitivity analyses of the investor's problem presented in Example 4.1. The information given in that problem is summarized in Table 4.12.

Table 4.12 Basic Information for Investor's Problem

| | | Conditional Profit ($) | |
| | | Act | |
Event E_i	Probability $P(E_i)$	A_1 (Buy WOW stock)	A_2 (Buy TUF stock)
E_1 (Economy advances)	0.40	2000	1400
E_2 (Economy stagnates)	0.60	−300	200

There are five independent input data items, the four conditional profit figures and the probability of *either* E_1 or E_2 (because $P(E_1) + P(E_2) = 1$).

    a) Since the probabilities in this example are certainly highly subjective, examine the sensitivity to the value of $P(E_1)$.

Let $x = P(E_1)$, so that $P(E_2) = 1 - x$. The EMVs of the two acts are then

$$\text{EMV}(A_1) = 2000x + (-300)(1 - x) = 2300x - 300,$$
$$\text{EMV}(A_2) = 1400x + (200)(1 - x) \quad = 1200x + 200.$$

Now, let x' be the value of x for indifference between acts A_1 and A_2. Equating their EMVs, we get

$$2300x' - 300 = 1200x' + 200,$$
$$1100x' = 500,$$
$$x' = 0.455.$$

To verify that this is correct, the EMVs can be calculated for $P(E_1) = 0.455$.

$$\text{EMV}(A_1) = (0.455)(2000) + (0.545)(-300) = 910 - 164 = \$746,$$
$$\text{EMV}(A_2) = (0.455)(1400) + (0.545)(200) \quad = 637 + 109 = \$746.$$

Since the EMVs are the same, the indifference probability value must be correct.

The relationship between the EMVs of the two acts, as a function of the value of $P(E_1)$, is shown in Figure 4.1.

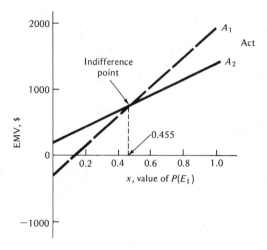

Figure 4.1

If the true value of $P(E_1)$ is 0.455 or less, act A_2 is optimal, and there will be no economic loss because of that choice. If $P(E_1)$ is greater than 0.455, act A_1 is optimal, and the decrease in EMV because of choosing act A_2 is equal to the difference between EMV(A_1) and EMV(A_2), or $2300x - 300 - (1200x + 200) = \$(1100x - 500)$. This information is summarized in Table 4.13.

Table 4.13 Investor's Problem—Sensitivity Analysis of x (Probability of Event E_1)

	Decision Effect	Economic Effect of an Error
Actual Value of x	Optimal Act	Decrease in EMV When Act A_2 Chosen (\$)
0 to 0.455	A_2	0
0.455 to 1.0	A_1	$1100x - 500$

Having performed this sensitivity analysis, we now know the optimal act for any value of $P(E_1)$ and the associated economic consequences if the optimal act turns out not to be the one selected on the basis of the assumed value of $P(E_1)$. If, for example, the actual value of $P(E_1)$ were 0.60, act A_1 would be optimal, and the choice of act A_2 (which was based on the assumed value of 0.40) would result in a decrease in EMV of $(1100)(0.60) - 500 = \$160$.

As a check on this figure,

$$EMV(A_1) = (2300)(0.60) - 300 = \$1080,$$
$$EMV(A_2) = (1200)(0.60) + 200 = \$920,$$

so

$$EMV(A_1) - EMV(A_2) = \$160.$$

b) Perform a sensitivity analysis on the value of the conditional profit of buying WOW stock, given that the economy advances.

Let v, instead of \$2000, be the conditional profit of act A_1, given event E_1. Then,

$$EMV(A_1) = 0.40v + (0.60)(-300) = 0.40v - 180.$$

Since the factors determining $EMV(A_2)$ are unchanged, $EMV(A_2) = \$680$, as before. If v' is the value of v for indifference between the two acts,

$$0.40v' - 180 = 680,$$
$$0.40v' = 860,$$
$$v' = \$2150.$$

If the conditional profit of act A_1, given event E_1, is less than \$2150, act A_2 is optimal, since it was optimal with a value of \$2000. Above a value of \$2150, act A_1 will be optimal. This is illustrated in Figure 4.2.

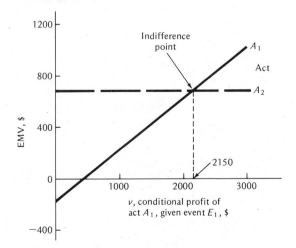

Figure 4.2

If the actual value of v is \$2150 or less, act A_2 is optimal. If v exceeds \$2150, act A_1 is optimal, and the decrease in EMV from selecting act A_2 is equal to $EMV(A_1) - EMV(A_2) = 0.40v - 180 - 680 = \$(0.40v - 860)$. Table 4.14 shows the results of this analysis.

Table 4.14 Investor's Problem—Sensitivity Analysis of v (Conditional Profit of Act A_1 Given Event E_1)

	Decision Effect	Economic Effect of an Error
Actual Value of v (\$)	Optimal Act	Decrease in EMV When Act A_2 Chosen (\$)
0 to 2150	A_2	0
$\geqslant$ 2150	A_1	$0.40v - 860$

As an example of the use of this information, if v were actually \$2500, act A_1 would be optimal, and the selection of act A_2 (based on an assumed value of \$2000) would lead to a decrease in EMV of $(0.40)(2500) - 860 = \$140$.

EXAMPLE 4.4

For the spare parts problem, Example 4.2, the problem information is summarized in Table 4.15. For convenience in calculating the conditional costs, the two cost factors have been expressed in notational form, as follows:

Let i = cost of initially purchased spare (given value of \$1000),
  e = emergency cost if no spare available (given value of \$8000).

Table 4.15 Information for Spare Parts Problem

		Conditional Cost (\$)		
			Act	
		A_0	A_1	A_2
	Probability	(Purchase	(Purchase	(Purchase
Event, E_i	$P(E_i)$	0 spares)	1 spare)	2 spares)
E_0 (0 spares required)	0.80	0	i	$2i$
E_1 (1 spare required)	0.15	e	i	$2i$
E_2 (2 spares required)	0.05	$2e$	$e + i$	$2i$

In this problem, i, the cost of an initially purchased spare, should be accurately known, but e, the emergency cost when a spare is unavailable, might well be quite different from its estimated value of $8000. Therefore, a sensitivity analysis will be performed on the value of the emergency cost.

The calculation of the expected cost values is shown in Table 4.16, working from Table 4.15, with $i = \$1000$.

Table 4.16 Calculation of Expected Costs—Emergency Cost a Variable

Event E_i	Probability $P(E_i)$	Conditional Cost ($) Act A_0	A_1	A_2	Weighted Cost ($) Act A_0	A_1	A_2
E_0	0.80	0	1000	2000	0	800	1600
E_1	0.15	e	1000	2000	$0.15e$	150	300
E_2	0.05	$2e$	$e + 1000$	2000	$0.10e$	$0.05e + 50$	100
					$0.25e$	$0.05e + 1000$	2000

First, we will find the value of e for which we would be indifferent to purchasing 0 or 1 spare. Then, we will find the value of e for indifference between 1 and 2 spares. From the calculations of Table 4.16, we have

$$\text{expected cost of act } A_0 = 0.25e,$$
$$\text{expected cost of act } A_1 = 0.05e + 1000,$$
$$\text{expected cost of act } A_2 = 2000.$$

Let e_1 be the value of e for indifference between acts A_0 and A_1, and e_2 the value for indifference between acts A_1 and A_2. Solving for e_1,

$$0.25e_1 = 0.05e_1 + 1000,$$
$$0.20e_1 = 1000,$$
$$e_1 = \$5000.$$

Solving for e_2,

$$0.05e_2 + 1000 = 2000,$$
$$0.05e_2 = 1000,$$
$$e_2 = \$20,000.$$

With the assumed value of $8000 for e, act A_1 is optimal. If the actual value of e is under $5000, act A_0 is optimal, and the additional cost of act A_1 is equal to the expected cost of act A_1 less the expected cost of act A_0, or $0.05e + 1000 - 0.25e = 1000 - 0.20e$. Similarly, if the value of e is more than $20,000, act A_2 is optimal, so the additional cost of act A_1 is $0.05e + 1000 - 2000 = 0.05e - 1000$, the difference between the expected cost of act A_1 and that of act A_2. These results are summarized in Table 4.17.

Table 4.17 Sensitivity Analysis of e (Emergency Cost)

Actual Value of e, $	Decision Effect Optimal Act	Economic Effect of an Error Increase in Expected Cost When Act A_1 Chosen ($)
$\leqslant 5000$	A_0	$1000 - 0.20e$
5000 to 20,000	A_1	0
$\geqslant 20,000$	A_2	$0.05e - 1000$

Figure 4.3, a plot of the three expected cost functions, gives a good overall picture of this sensitivity analysis. Only two of the three indifference points are meaningful, as noted on the graph. At the third indifference point, for acts A_0 and A_2, act A_1 would obviously be preferred, since it has the lowest expected cost.

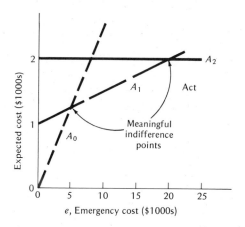

Figure 4.3

The optimal decision to purchase 1 spare, based on the assumed emergency cost of $8000, would remain optimal for any emergency cost between $5000 and $20,000, so it is clear that it would take a considerable change in the emergency cost to change the optimal number of spares.

The sensitivity analysis procedure developed in this section can be basically summarized as follows.

1. Choose an appropriate input data item as a variable and define it notationally. Consider all other input data items to be fixed at their given values specified in the problem.
2. If there are only two acts in the problem, develop algebraic expressions for the EMV (or expected cost or EOL) of both. If there are more than two acts,

choose two that can be meaningfully compared. This will generally be clear in the context of the problem, as was illustrated in Example 4.4. If not, several different pairs may have to be tried.

3. Equate the two expressions and solve for the indifference value(s) of the selected input data item.
4. Determine the range of values of the data item for which each act under consideration is optimal.
5. For each such range, develop an equation for calculating the economic effect of erroneously choosing the act which is optimal for the assumed value of the data item. This is done by differencing the appropriate equations developed in step 2.

4.7   DECISION TREE ANALYSIS

The earlier material in this chapter has been concerned with the problem of making a single optimal decision, involving probabilistic outcomes, at a given point in time. Suppose we are now faced with the problem of making a sequence of decisions, perhaps over a period of time. Each such decision may depend on previous decisions and may lead to a set of probabilistic outcomes. We wish to specify an optimal comprehensive decision-making policy which will cover all contingencies. A graphically oriented approach to the solution of such multistage decision problems is called *decision tree analysis*. This approach can best be illustrated with an example.

EXAMPLE 4.5

Fadco Manufacturing Company is involved in the development of a new regional product. This product is of such a nature that it will tend to be either quite successful or quite unsuccessful. If the product is successful, it is expected to gross $100,000; if unsuccessful, only $20,000. Fadco is faced with an immediate decision as to one of three possible choices:

1. Test market the product, at a cost of $10,000.
2. Immediately market the product regionally, at a cost of $50,000.
3. Drop the product.

If the product is test marketed, the results will be classified as favorable or unfavorable, and then a decision must be made whether to market the product regionally or to drop it. If the test-marketing results are favorable, management estimates that the probability of success in the regional market is 0.80; if unfavorable, the estimated success probability is only 0.30. From past experience, Fadco estimates that there is a 50–50 chance of a favorable test-marketing result. Without the experience derived from a test marketing, the probability of a successful direct regional marketing effort is believed to be slightly less than 0.5, and management has settled on a probability of 0.45. What course of action should Fadco pursue?

Since this type of problem involves the consideration of sequential decisions, we will structure our problem-solving approach somewhat differently from that used previously. We will utilize a graphical construction, called a decision tree, to show the relationship between events, acts, probabilities, and profits or losses.

Our objective in this problem is to determine the sequence of marketing decisions which will maximize the expected profit.

In defining events and acts, we will differentiate between those which take place at different points in time. There are then six different events, which we label

E_1 = favorable test-marketing result,
E_2 = unfavorable test-marketing result,
E_3 = successful immediate regional marketing,
E_4 = unsuccessful immediate regional marketing,
E_5 = regional marketing successful after test marketing,
E_6 = regional marketing unsuccessful after test marketing.

The five acts to be considered are

A_1 = test market,
A_2 = market regionally immediately,
A_3 = drop product immediately,
A_4 = market regionally after test marketing,
A_5 = drop product after test marketing.

Acts A_1, A_2, and A_3 represent the first decision stage, the earliest point in time; acts A_4 and A_5, which cannot come until after a test marketing, represent the second (and final) decision stage in this problem.

To get some idea of what the eventual decision tree will look like, a preliminary table can be constructed as follows: for each decision stage, provide two columns, the first labeled "Acts" and the second "Events." In the first column, identify the acts and allow ample vertical space between them. (The reason for this will become clear.) In the second column, separately identify the possible events associated with the acts in the preceding column. Space out these events vertically also, consistent with their relationship to the acts, as shown in Table 4.18(a). Draw lines connecting related acts and events. Continue this process of connecting the appropriate events to acts to events . . . , as in Table 4.18(b), until the relationships are completely developed in Table 4.18.

Now, we are ready to draw the decision tree itself. Each set of acts at a given stage is preceded by a numbered square called a *decision fork*. Each individual act is represented by a branch to the right of that decision fork. Each set of events is preceded by a circle called a *chance fork*. Each individual event is represented by a branch to the right of that chance fork. At the decision forks, a choice is available to Fadco; at the chance forks, Fadco has no control over the outcome. From Table 4.18, it appears that most of the tree emanates from act A_1, so allowance should be made for this in allocating drawing space. The net result (after one or two trials) should look something like the layout of Figure 4.4, initially without all the numbers.

Table 4.18 Layout Preparatory to Constructing Decision Tree

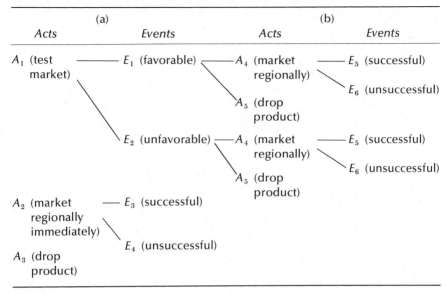

	(a)		(b)
Acts	*Events*	*Acts*	*Events*
A_1 (test market)	E_1 (favorable)	A_4 (market regionally)	E_5 (successful)
			E_6 (unsuccessful)
		A_5 (drop product)	
	E_2 (unfavorable)	A_4 (market regionally)	E_5 (successful)
			E_6 (unsuccessful)
		A_5 (drop product)	
A_2 (market regionally immediately)	E_3 (successful)		
	E_4 (unsuccessful)		
A_3 (drop product)			

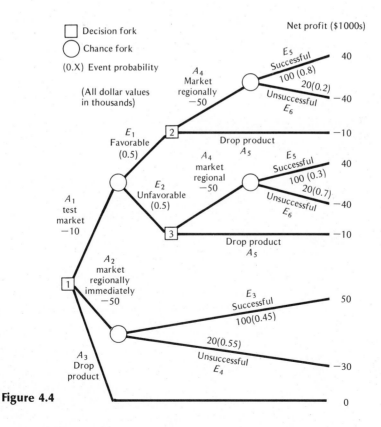

Figure 4.4

After the basic tree has been drawn, the required numerical values are added. Profits are placed on the event branches, and costs (expressed as negative profits) on the act branches. (For convenience in this problem, dollar amounts have been expressed in thousands.) Numbers in parentheses are used to indicate event probabilities.

The net profits in the column at the right are readily obtained by summing the monetary values along the branches. Thus, following along the four branches at the top of the figure, test marketing costs $10,000, regional marketing costs $50,000, and a successful product earns $100,000, with a resulting (conditional) net profit of $40,000. The other values are calculated in a similar fashion. Once the net figures at the right have been calculated, the conditional values on the branches are no longer of interest and should be ignored.

Now, we apply what is sometimes called the "rollback" principle, by starting with the calculations for the decision forks nearest the terminal branches at the right-hand side of the tree.

At decision fork 2, if we market regionally, act A_4, the expected net profit is $(0.8)(40) + (0.2)(-40) = 24$ ($24,000). This is the preferred decision, as shown by an asterisk in the "pruned" tree of Figure 4.5, since the alternative decision, dropping the product, act A_5, has an expected value of $-$10,000. We then place the value 24 above decision fork 2, to indicate the expected value of the optimal decision at that point. A double bar can be placed on the other branches to delete nonoptimal acts at that decision fork.

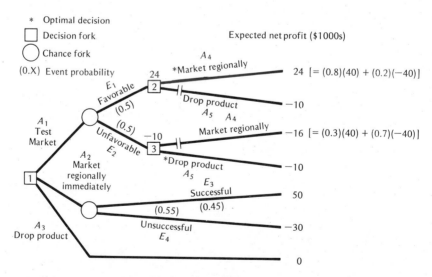

Figure 4.5

At decision fork 3, act A_4 has an expected net profit of $(0.3)(40) + (0.7)(-40) = -16$ ($-$16,000). The preferred alternative here is to drop the product, act A_5, at an expected profit of $-\$10,000$. The value -10 is placed above decision fork 3, and act A_4 is deleted.

The rollback process is now performed again, using expected values based on the preferred alternatives found at decision forks 2 and 3 and the original alternative of directly marketing regionally. These results are shown in Figure 4.6.

Figure 4.6

At this point, the problem has been solved. Fadco should test market, with an expected profit of $7000. Now, we must specify the entire sequence of optimal decisions, by noting the preferred alternatives after the test-marketing results become known. From Figure 4.5, Fadco's optimal sequence of decisions is

Test market: If results favorable, market regionally.
            If results unfavorable, drop product.

In our problem notation, the optimal solution is to choose act A_1. Then, if event E_1 occurs, choose act A_4. If event E_2 occurs, choose act A_5.

Suppose we now look back and ask what it would be worth to have perfect information in this problem. Perfect information on the success (event E_3) or failure (event E_4) of a direct regional marketing effort would certainly be of value. If Fadco knew that immediate regional marketing would be successful, it should choose act A_2, market regionally immediately. On the other hand, if it had information that immediate regional marketing would be unsuccessful, it should drop the product, act A_3. (This assumes that an unfavorable marketing report would decrease the probability of a favorable test marketing, making test marketing uneconomical. This assumption is conservative, since it tends to minimize the value of EVPI.) Assuming no control over the probability of a successful or unsuccessful regional marketing, but perfect information as to which would occur, the expected profit with perfect information would be calculated as in Table 4.19. From the results of these calculations, the expected value of perfect information can now be determined:

$$\text{EVPI} = \text{EPPI} - \text{EMV}^* = 22{,}500 - 7{,}000 = \$15{,}500.$$

Table 4.19 Expected Profit with Perfect Information

Event	$P(E_i)$	Optimal Act	Conditional Profit ($1000s)	Weighted Profit ($1000s)
E_3 (Immediate regional marketing would be successful)	0.45	A_2 (Market regionally)	50	22.5
E_4 (Immediate regional marketing would be unsuccessful)	0.55	A_3 (Drop product)	0	0
				EPPI = $\overline{22.5}$

Fadco could afford to pay up to $15,500 if, in some manner, the company could get perfect information beforehand as to whether immediate regional marketing would be successful.

Now let us explore the rationale behind the decision tree solution process. Examining Figure 4.4, if we attempt to structure this problem as we did earlier problems, we would be initially faced with the optimal choice of one of three decisions, namely, act A_1, A_2, or A_3. The EMV of acts A_2 and A_3 can be readily determined. Two events, E_3 and E_4, are associated with act A_2, and the conditional profits and probabilities associated with these events are known, so the calculation of EMV is straightforward. If act A_3 is chosen, the EMV of this act is zero, with probability 1.0. On the other hand, when we attempt to evaluate the EMV of act A_1, we must know the conditional profits associated with the two events E_1 and E_2, *but*, these conditional profits cannot be determined without finding, for both of these events, the preferred alternative between acts A_4 and A_5. It should now be clear that we cannot solve the problem in this manner without considerable difficulty.

The rollback process, by working backward in time, so to speak, allows us to determine the optimal decision at each decision fork *where there are no subsequent decisions remaining to be evaluated.* Thus, the optimal acts can initially be determined at decision forks 2 and 3, since no additional decisions are required after those decision forks have been reached. Then, when the optimal acts have been chosen at decision forks 2 and 3, so that the EMV of act A_1 can be calculated, the optimal act at decision fork 1 can be selected.

In this example problem, decisions had to be evaluated at two points in time, so that we had two decision stages. Decision fork 1 comprised one decision stage and decision forks 2 and 3 the other. As you can readily visualize, the pictorial representation of a decision tree gets rather cluttered with more than about three decision stages and perhaps a dozen or so decision forks. For larger problems, a computer solution is almost mandatory.

Let us now outline a general procedure for manually solving problems involving sequential decisions.

1. Determine the number of decision stages. Define all acts and events.
2. If it is found to be helpful in drawing a decision tree, develop a rough

preliminary table to establish the entire sequence of acts and events, decision stage by decision stage.

3. Make a rough sketch of the way the tree should look, and then draw the branches of the tree showing all the decision forks and chance forks. Leave adequate room for all descriptive information and numbers.

4. Label all acts and events. Supply the conditional profits (or opportunity losses) associated with each branch, as well as the event probabilities on the event branches.

5. Tracing through each sequence of branches connected from left to right, add the conditional profits (or opportunity losses) on those branches and place the sum next to the rightmost branch.

6. Starting at the right of the decision tree, work backward, using the rollback process. Determine the optimal act(s) at each successive decision stage, based on maximum EMV or minimum EOL, as appropriate for the problem. At each decision fork, place the expected value of the optimal act above that decision fork and delete branches indicating nonoptimal decisions. (As each decision stage is evaluated, it may be helpful to redraw the decision tree, as in Figures 4.5 and 4.6.)

7. When the optimal act at decision fork 1 is finally determined, trace the optimal sequence of decisions starting with that act and specify the overall optimal strategy.

Decision tree analysis is actually a form of what is known as probabilistic dynamic programming. Another decision tree problem, similar to this one, has been worked out in the chapter on Dynamic Programming and may be helpful to gain additional insight.

Sensitivity Analysis

As demonstrated earlier, sensitivity analyses of optimal solutions are important when the actual values of input data items could vary from their stated values. This is certainly the case when subjective probabilities are involved, as in decision tree problems.

At decision fork 1, we will perform separate sensitivity analyses of $P(E_1)$, the probability of a favorable test-marketing result, and $P(E_3)$, the probability of a successful immediate regional marketing effort. Then, we will relate these two analyses.

If only $P(E_1)$ is to be allowed to vary, then only $EMV(A_1)$ will be affected, as can be seen from Figure 4.5. From Figure 4.6, $EMV(A_2) = \$6000$ and $EMV(A_3) = \$0$. Therefore, it makes sense to find the value of $P(E_1)$ for indifference between acts A_1 and A_2, since we would never choose act A_3 if A_2 were available.

Let $t = P(E_1)$, so that $P(E_2) = 1 - t$. Then, knowing the optimal decisions at decision forks 2 and 3, from Figure 4.5,

$$EMV(A_1) = 24t + (-10)(1 - t) = 34t - 10.$$

Equating the EMVs of acts A_1 and A_2, and solving for t', the indifference value of t,

$$34t' - 10 = 6,$$
$$34t' = 16,$$
$$t' = 0.471.$$

The decision to test market, act A_1, would be preferred for any value of t exceeding 0.471. If act A_1 had been chosen, based on the stated value of $t = 0.5$, but the actual value of t made immediate regional marketing, act A_2, optimal, the decrease in EMV would be $EMV(A_2) - EMV(A_1) = 6 - (34t - 10) = 16 - 34t$ (in $1000s). This information is shown in Table 4.20.

Table 4.20 Sensitivity Analysis of t (Probability of Event E_1)

	Decision Effect	Economic Effect of an Error
Actual Value of t	Optimal Act	Decrease in EMV When Act A_1 Chosen ($1000s)
0 to 0.471	A_2	$16 - 34t$
0.471 to 1.0	A_1	0

Again at decision fork 1, if we let r be the probability of a successful immediate regional marketing, event E_3, then we would be indifferent to the alternatives test market, act A_1, or market regionally immediately, act A_2, if their EMVs were equal. The EMV of act A_1 is $7000, from Figure 4.6. For act A_2, we now have, from Figure 4.5,

$$EMV(A_2) = 50r + (-30)(1 - r) = 80r - 30.$$

The indifference value r' can be found by equating $EMV(A_1)$ and $EMV(A_2)$.

$$80r' - 30 = 7,$$
$$80r' = 37,$$
$$r' = 0.462.$$

Act A_1 would be optimal for $r < 0.462$. Having chosen act A_1, based on the stated value of $r = 0.45$, if the actual value of r made act A_2 optimal, the decrease in EMV would be $EMV(A_2) - EMV(A_1) = 80r - 30 - 7 = 80r - 37$ (in $1000s). Table 4.21 shows this analysis.

Table 4.21 Sensitivity Analysis of r (Probability of Event E_3)

	Decision Effect	Economic Effect of an Error
Actual value of r	Optimal Act	Decrease in EMV When Act A_1 Chosen ($1000s)
0 to 0.462	A_1	0
0.462 to 1.0	A_2	$80r - 37$

Since t and r are both probabilities whose values directly influence the choice between the same set of acts, A_1 and A_2, their sensitivity to errors can be directly compared. Table 4.22 shows, for both t and r, the difference between the stated value and the indifference value, and the expected decrease in EMV if an error is made.

Table 4.22 Comparative Sensitivity Analysis of Probability Values $P(E_1)$ and $P(E_3)$

				Decrease in EMV If Error Made ($1000s)	
Variable	Stated Value	Indifference Value	Difference	Equation	Decrease per 0.01 Probability Change
$t = P(E_1)$	0.5	0.471	0.029	$16 - 34t$	$(34)(0.01) = 0.34$
$r = P(E_3)$	0.45	0.462	0.012	$80r - 37$	$(80)(0.01) = 0.80$

From the information in Table 4.22, if an error in a data value would change a previously optimal act, an error in the value of $P(E_3)$ would have more of an effect on the solution than a comparable error in the value of $P(E_1)$. This is so because of two factors: the stated value of $P(E_3)$ is closer to its indifference value, and EMV decreases at a faster rate when the optimal act would change because of an error in $P(E_3)$. (From a sensitivity analysis viewpoint, we are not interested in the situation where an error in a data value would move that value *away* from the indifference value. In that case, the original optimal solution would become even more favorable.) The results of this analysis are illustrated graphically in Figure 4.7.

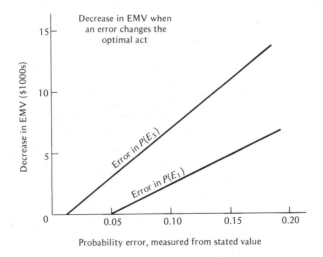

Figure 4.7

From Figure 4.7, an error in $P(E_3)$ of 0.05 in the "wrong" direction would decrease EMV by \$3000, while a comparable error in $P(E_1)$ would decrease EMV by only \$700. For every additional 0.01 of error, the decrease in EMV would be \$800 for $P(E_3)$, but only \$340 for $P(E_1)$. Fadco now knows how sensitive the solution is to its estimates of the values of $P(E_1)$, the probability of a favorable test marketing, and $P(E_3)$, the probability of a successful immediate regional marketing. If the company wishes to refine these estimates, it should direct most of its efforts toward the estimate of $P(E_3)$.

Sensitivity analysis has an important role in the analysis of practical decision-making problems. It is an extremely general approach which allows us to explore the effect on the optimal decision(s) of possible changes or errors in any of the problem variables. The sensitivity to probability values, as worked out in the preceding example, is clearly of interest because of the inherent subjective nature of most probabilities. However, we could have also explored the sensitivity of the solution to profit or cost values, such as the cost of test marketing, the profitability of successful regional marketing, and so forth.

4.8   DECISION MAKING WITH CONTINUOUS PROBABILITY DISTRIBUTIONS

When the probability distribution of events is continuous, rather than discrete, decision analysis generally becomes considerably more complicated, except for certain special cases. In this section, we will look at two such cases for which the conditional profit, conditional cost, or COL values are a linear function of the random variable of interest. The first case involves problems where the probability distribution of events can be of any form, either continuous or discrete, and the optimal act is to be determined. The second case is concerned with the calculations of expected profit, expected cost, or EOL values when there is a normal probability distribution of events.

Linear Payoff and Loss Functions

In Example 4.2, we had only three different events, each of which represented a given number of part failures. We determined the conditional costs for all nine combinations of these three events and the three alternative acts, and we then calculated the associated COL values. In the more general case, the events often represent a particular value of a random variable, such as the fraction of items defective in a given lot, the proportion of customers who would buy a new product, the average dollar sales per customer for a given item, and so forth. If, for each act, the payoff is a linear function of the random variable of interest, it becomes a straightforward process to develop an expression for the act's COL as a function of the random variable. The general term for such an expression, whether it be linear or not, is loss function.

We will consider situations where there are two possible acts and where the payoffs associated with these acts are linear functions of the random variable, whatever it may be. With linear payoffs, the loss functions are also linear, as we will demonstrate.

We will first discuss the concepts and mathematical developments relating to generalized linear payoff and loss functions and then will illustrate them with an example problem.

If X is the random variable of interest and $R_i(x)$ is the payoff or reward associated with act i and a specific value $X = x$, we can write the expression for a linear payoff as:

$$R_i(x) = a_i + b_i x,$$

where a_i and b_i are constants known as the intercept and slope, respectively. If we have just two acts, or what is often called a *two-action problem*, the linear payoff functions are:

$$R_1(x) = a_1 + b_1 x \qquad \text{(payoff of act 1)},$$
$$R_2(x) = a_2 + b_2 x \qquad \text{(payoff of act 2)}.$$

Suppose these functions resemble those shown in Figure 4.8. Now, let x' be the value of x for indifference between the two acts. Equating their payoffs and solving for x'.

$$a_1 + b_1 x' = a_2 + b_2 x',$$

$$x' = \frac{a_1 - a_2}{b_2 - b_1} \qquad \text{for } b_1 \neq b_2.$$

The values of a_1, a_2, b_1, and b_2 may be positive, negative, or zero, except that b_1 and b_2 cannot be equal, since the payoff functions would then be parallel and one of them would always be preferred for all values of x.

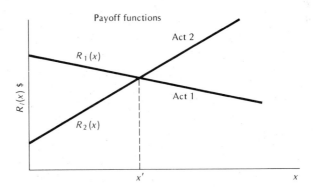

Figure 4.8

The *loss function* for a given act is just the COL of that act as a function of the value of the random variable. To determine the loss functions for the two acts, consider first the result if act 1 is chosen. Observe, from Figure 4.8, that act 1 is the preferred act for $x < x'$, since $R_1(x) > R_2(x)$. Thus, the COL of act 1 is zero in this region. For $x > x'$, however, act 2 is preferred, so the selection of act 1 would result in a COL equal to the difference between the payoff which could have been obtained from act 2 and that actually obtained by choosing act 1. This difference is just $R_2(x) - R_1(x)$. The situation is essentially reversed if act 2 is chosen. For $x < x'$, the COL will be $R_1(x) - R_2(x)$, while for $x > x'$, when act 2 is preferred, the COL will be zero.

Now, let $L_i(x)$ = loss function (COL) for act i, given any specific value x of the random variable X. Examining Figure 4.8, the loss function $L_1(x)$ for act 1, in the region above the indifference point x', will be directly proportional to the difference, $b_2 - b_1$, between the slopes of the two acts, and to the distance, $x - x'$, from the indifference point. Similarly, for act 2, if x is less than x', $L_2(x)$ will again be directly proportional to the difference in slopes, $b_2 - b_1$, and the distance, now $x' - x$, from the indifference point.

The complete loss functions for the two acts can, therefore, be stated as follows.

$$L_1(x) = \begin{cases} 0 & \text{if } x \leq x' \\ (b_2 - b_1)(x - x') & \text{if } x > x'. \end{cases}$$

$$L_2(x) = \begin{cases} (b_2 - b_1)(x' - x) & \text{if } x < x' \\ 0 & \text{if } x \geq x'. \end{cases}$$

The loss functions are plotted in Figure 4.9.

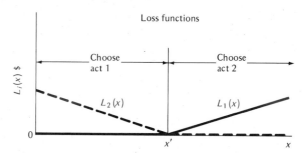

Figure 4.9

Selection of Optimal Act   With a linear payoff function, the optimal act can be readily determined. The expected value of payoff function R_i is

$$E(R_i) = E(a_i + b_i X).$$

As shown in Equations (3.4) and (3.5) in Chapter 3,

$$E(R_i) = E(a_i + b_i X) = a_i + b_i E(X).$$

Thus, with linear payoff functions, we need know only the expected value of the random variable in order to determine the expected value of the payoff. Nothing need be known about the form of the probability distribution of X. Knowing $E(X)$, the preferred act can be readily selected. It will be that act with the highest payoff for the value $x = E(X)$. This will also be the act whose COL is zero when $x = E(X)$. For the payoff functions shown in Figure 4.8, resulting in the loss functions of Figure 4.9, act 1 would be chosen if $E(X) < x'$, and act 2 if $E(X) > x'$. For $E(X) = x'$, we would be indifferent to our choice of these two acts.

Let us take an example to illustrate the analysis of a two-action problem with linear payoffs.

EXAMPLE 4.6

The Groovy Gadget company is about to begin production of a new gadget which it hopes will be a big seller during the coming Christmas season. The company will be distributing this item to the 2000 variety stores which are the company's retail outlets. The wholesale selling price of the gadget is $1.50 per unit, while the total variable costs per unit are $1.30. One of Groovy Gadget's design engineers has just come up with an idea for a special modification of existing production equipment which would cut the variable unit costs for the gadget to $1.20. The estimated cost for the modification is $11,000. The company's financial policy is that a capital expenditure of this nature must pay for itself over a single Christmas season, since the market for gadgets is so volatile.

   a) As a function of the mean number of units ordered per store, develop and plot the payoff functions for:

   Act 1: Retain the present production process.
   Act 2: Use the modified production process.
Let $\bar{X}$ = random variable denoting *mean* order size per store,
       (The bar over the X is standard statistical notation for a mean value and serves as a reminder that the random variable represents a mean order size and not the size of an individual order.)
$R_i(\bar{x})$ = total payoff associated with act i and mean order size $\bar{x}$.
For all 2000 stores, the total payoffs are
$$R_1(\bar{x}) = (2000)(1.50 - 1.30)\,\bar{x} \qquad\quad = 400\,\bar{x},$$
$$R_2(\bar{x}) = (2000)(1.50 - 1.20)\,\bar{x} - 11,000 = 600\,\bar{x} - 11,000.$$

The payoff functions for the two acts are shown in Figure 4.10.

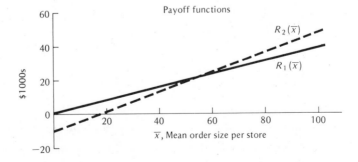

Figure 4.10

b) Determine the mean order size per store for indifference between the two acts.

Let $\bar{x}' =$ value of $\bar{x}$ for indifference.
Equating the two payoffs,

$$600\,\bar{x}' - 11{,}000 = 400\,\bar{x}',$$
$$200\,\bar{x}' = 11{,}000,$$
$$\bar{x}' = 55 \text{ units.}$$

c) Develop the loss functions for the two acts and plot them.

Clearly, from Figure 4.10, act 1 would be preferred for $\bar{x} < \bar{x}'\,(= 55)$, and act 2 would be favored for $\bar{x} > \bar{x}'$. Thus,

$$L_1(\bar{x}) = 0 \qquad \text{if } \bar{x} \leqslant 55.$$
$$L_2(\bar{x}) = 0 \qquad \text{if } \bar{x} \geqslant 55.$$

The difference in slopes, $b_2 - b_1$, of the payoff functions is just the difference between the coefficients of the random variable in those functions, or $600 - 400 = 200$, in this example. With this information, the complete loss function can now be stated:

$$L_1(\bar{x}) = \begin{cases} 0 & \text{if } \bar{x} \leqslant 55, \\ 200(\bar{x} - 55) & \text{if } \bar{x} > 55. \end{cases}$$

$$L_2(\bar{x}) = \begin{cases} 200(55 - \bar{x}) & \text{if } \bar{x} < 55, \\ 0 & \text{if } \bar{x} \geqslant 55. \end{cases}$$

Table 4.23 shows a tabular presentation of this information, which is plotted in Figure 4.11. For two-action problems with linear payoff functions, the loss functions will always be symmetrical about a vertical line through the indifference value (55, in this example).

Table 4.23   Loss Functions

| | $L_1(\bar{x})$, \$ | $L_2(\bar{x})$, \$ |
| | | Act |
Event	1	2
$\bar{x} \leqslant 55$ (act 1 best)	0	$200(55 - \bar{x})$
$\bar{x} \geqslant 55$ (act 2 best)	$200(\bar{x} - 55)$	0

d) If Groovy Gadget's best estimate of the mean order size per store is 40 units, should the company modify the production process?

Since act 1 is preferable if $\bar{x} < 55$, as has been shown in several different ways, the production process should not be modified.

The expected payoffs would be

$$E(R_1) = (400)(40) \qquad\qquad = \$16,000,$$
$$E(R_2) = (600)(40) - 11,000 = \$13,000.$$

The present production process is favored by an expected difference of $3000.

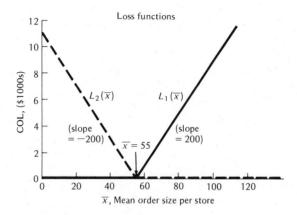

Figure 4.11

Normal Loss Integral

If the random variable can be represented by a normal probability distribution, and we have a linear loss function, there is a relatively straightforward way to calculate EOL* ($\equiv$ EVPI) and thereby determine how much perfect information would be worth.

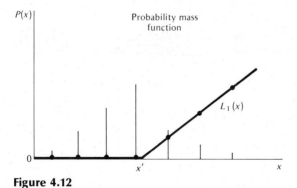

Figure 4.12

To determine EOL*, the expected opportunity loss of the optimal act, let us make the assumption that, for any given random variable X, $E(X) < x'$, so act 1 is preferred and the applicable loss function is $L_1(x)$. (Later, we will show what happens when $E(X) > x'$.) If we were working with a discrete probability distribution of X, the relationship between this probability distribution and the loss function $L_1(x)$ would be similar to that of Figure 4.12. To calculate EOL*, we would, for each distinct value x_i, weight the associated COL value, $L_1(x_i)$, by $P(x_i)$, and then we would sum all these products. The only COL values used would be those shown as dots on the graph of $L_1(x)$.

With a continuous probability distribution, the situation is much different, since there are an infinite number of COL values. For a normal probability distribution, the picture is as shown in Figure 4.13, where a normal density function is shown together with the loss function $L_1(x)$. For convenience, we denote the mean, $E(X)$, of the given normal probability distribution as x_0 and its standard deviation as σ_0.

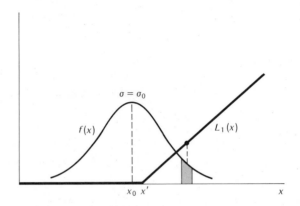

Figure 4.13

If we divided the area under the normal curve into segments, such as the one shown shaded in Figure 4.13, each segment would represent a probability. If this probability were multiplied by the COL value at the segment midpoint, as indicated by the dot, we would have a weighted COL value. If the normal curve were divided into such segments over the interval where the loss function was nonzero, we could then sum the product of each probability and its associated COL value to get EOL*. The smaller the segment width (and thus the greater the number of segments), the more accurate would be the EOL* value. This process is tedious indeed and fortunately unnecessary.

Through the use of calculus, we can in effect calculate the EOL* value using infinitesimally thin segments. It can be shown that

$$EOL^* = C\sigma_0 N(D_0),   \tag{4.1}$$

where
$$C = |b_2 - b_1|,$$

$$D_0 = \left| \frac{x' - x_0}{\sigma_0} \right|,$$

$$N(D_0) = \text{normal loss integral.}$$

C is the absolute value of the slope of the nonzero portion of the loss function, while D_o is the absolute value of the number of standard deviations from the mean at which the loss function first becomes positive. The *normal loss integral* is defined as the product of a standardized normal density function (mean 0 and standard deviation 1) and a loss function with a slope of unity, which we can call a standardized loss function. Values of the normal loss integral are tabulated in Appendix B.

Letting $z' = (x' - x_o)/\sigma_o$, for convenience, we can now show the relationship between the standardized loss function and the standardized normal curve, as in Figure 4.14.

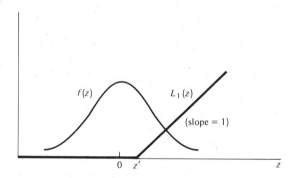

Figure 4.14

Some points are worth noting about the value of EOL*, or EVPI. If x' were closer to x_o, so that z' moved toward 0 in Figure 4.14, thereby moving the loss function toward the center of the normal curve, the COL values would be more heavily weighted, thus increasing $N(D_o)$ and EOL*. The maximum value of $N(D_o)$, and thus EOL*, occurs when $D_o = 0$. The closer x' is to x_o, the more the uncertainty about which act to choose; thus perfect information is worth more. If σ_o increased, we would have a compounded increase in EOL*, since, in addition to the linear increase from the σ_o multiplier, z' would decrease, thereby increasing $N(D_o)$. A higher value of σ_o is associated with a greater degree of uncertainty in the value of x_o, and the value of perfect information is thereby increased.

When the normal loss integral is used in two-action problems, the algebraic sign of z' is ignored, since $D_o = |z'|$. To see why this is so, consider what would have happened if x_o had exceeded x'. Then, z' would have been negative. With $x_o > x'$, the optimal decision would have been to choose act 2, so the loss function would be reversed. This is why the loss function always rises toward the near tail (the tail closest to the z' value) of the normal curve in this type of problem. The standardized curves would then be as shown in Figure 4.15. If the z' value in that figure were identical in magnitude to that in Figure 4.14, then Figure 4.15 would be a mirror image of Figure 4.14 with respect to a vertical line at $z = 0$, and the EOL* values would be identical.

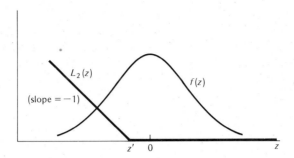

Figure 4.15

As an illustration of the use of the normal loss integral, consider the following extension of the previous example.

EXAMPLE 4.7

The Groovy Gadget Company is about to begin production of a new gadget which it hopes will be a big seller during the coming Christmas season. This item will be distributed to the 2000 variety stores which are the company's retail outlets. The total variable costs per unit are $1.30, and the wholesale selling price of the gadget is $1.50 per unit. Although there is a considerable difference in the number of units of this item that individual stores will order, Groovy's best estimate of the mean order size per store is 40 units. The uncertainty as to this amount, however, is reflected in its estimate that there is only a 50–50 chance the mean order size will fall between 30 and 50 units. Management is willing to assume a normal probability distribution for the subjective estimate of the *mean* number of units ordered per store.

The subjective assumption that the *mean* number of units ordered per store is normally distributed in no way implies that there is a normal probability distribution of the individual quantities ordered by each store. This distribution will tend to resemble that shown in Figure 4.16, an essentially continuous distribution skewed to the right, reflecting the large order quantities of a relatively few large stores.

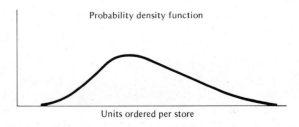

Figure 4.16

One of Groovy Gadget's design engineers has just come up with an idea for a special modification of existing production equipment which would cut the variable unit costs for the gadget to $1.20. The estimated cost for the modification is $11,000. The company wishes to determine if this modification can be economically justified. Their financial policy is that a capital expenditure of this nature must pay for itself over a single Christmas season, since the market for gadgets is so volatile.

As we found earlier, the optimal act, with no additional information, is for the company to choose act 1, retaining the present production process. To calculate EOL*, the expected opportunity loss of the optimal act, we need to combine the loss function $L_1(\bar{x})$ with the normal probability distribution of $\bar{X}$, with standard deviation as yet undetermined.

When the company estimated a 50–50 chance of the value of the mean order size falling between 30 and 50 units per store, it was making the equivalent probability statement that $P(30 < \bar{X} < 50) = 0.5$. When management was shown the normal curve of Figure 4.17, with the values of 30, 40, and 50 properly located, it agreed that this was at least a reasonable distribution for the value of $\bar{X}$, since management believed that the distribution was symmetrical and that the value of $\bar{X}$ was unlikely to be less than 30 or more than 50 units.

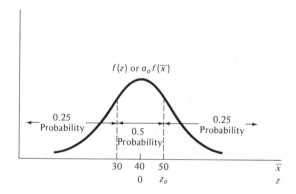

Figure 4.17

Since $P(\bar{X} < 50) = F(50) = 0.75$, the equivalent standard normal deviate z_a, as indicated in Figure 4.17, is found by inverse interpolation in Appendix A. Since the value of z_a is 0.67, an $\bar{x}$ value of 50 is 0.67 standard deviations above the mean. If we designate the standard deviation of this distribution as σ_o, we have

$$0.67\sigma_o = 50 - 40 = 10.$$

Since 0.67 is very nearly ⅔, and the subjective estimate leading to the value of 10 is obviously imprecise, we will make the approximation:

$$\tfrac{2}{3}\, \sigma_o \cong 10,$$
$$\sigma_o \cong 15.$$

Examining Equation (4.1), to calculate EOL* we need, in addition to the value of σ_o just determined, the values of C and D_o. From the loss functions determined earlier in Example 4.6, the loss function coefficient C is 200. With $\sigma_o = 15$,

$$D_o = |z'| = \left| \frac{\bar{x}' - \bar{x}_o}{\sigma_o} \right| = \left| \frac{55 - 40}{15} \right| = 1.00,$$

$$N(D_o) = 0.0833.$$

The standardized curves for this example are shown in Figure 4.18.

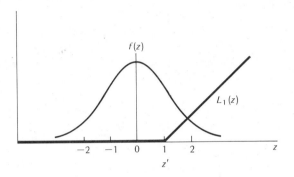

Figure 4.18

Then,
$$\text{EOL*} = C\sigma_o N(D_o)$$
$$= (200)(15)(0.0833) = \$250.$$

Groovy Gadget could afford to pay no more than $250 for perfect information that the mean order size per store would or would not exceed the indifference value of 55 units.

Given a normal probability distribution of the random variable, the normal loss integral can also be used to evaluate expected profit or expected cost if the profit or cost function is of the same general form as a loss function. This is illustrated by Example 4.8.

EXAMPLE 4.8

A manufacturing company has received a production contract from the government. It has 100 days to complete the contract. For each day or fraction of a day past the deadline, there is a penalty cost of $1000. The production manager feels that the company does not have much leeway, but its best estimate is 90 days for completion of the contract. Because of possible delays in getting material, production problems, and so forth, the manager's uncertainty regarding this estimate is reflected by his belief that the time to contract completion can be represented by a normal probability distribution with a mean of 90 days and a standard deviation of 10 days.

a) What is the expected penalty cost?

Suppose we let the random variable X represent the number of days to completion of the contract. Since the penalty cost changes by $1000 per day in discrete steps, the penalty function will be zero for $X \leq 100$, and for $X > 100$ will form what is generally called a staircase function or step function, as shown in Figure 4.19.

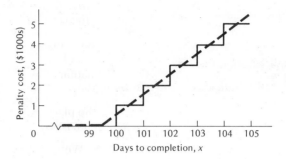

Figure 4.19

If we now approximate the step function by constructing a linear function through the midpoints of the steps, as shown by the dotted line, and then display the probability distribution of the time to completion, we get the graph of Figure 4.20. The positive portion of the penalty cost function, which is clearly in the form of a loss function, starts at 99.5 days, as can be seen from Figure 4.19.

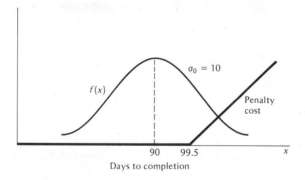

Figure 4.20

We can now determine the expected penalty cost by using the formula for EOL* and substituting the proper values. The loss function coefficient C is just the $1000 per day penalty cost, the slope of the loss function for x values exceeding 99.5 days. The standard deviation σ_o was estimated as 10 days. Now we need only $N(D_o)$. As shown following Equation (4.1), $D_o = |(x' - x_o)/\sigma_o|$. In this problem, the value equivalent to x' would be 99.5 days. Therefore,

$$D_o = \left| \frac{99.5 - 90}{10} \right| = 0.95.$$

From Appendix B, $N(0.95) = 0.0916$.

$$\text{Expected penalty cost} = C\sigma_o N(D_o)$$
$$= (1000)(10)(0.0916) = \$916.$$

(Using the actual step loss function shown in Figure 4.19 and obtaining the probabilities from the normal probability table for each discrete loss value, the expected penalty cost is $912. The approximation using the linear loss function is very close, well within 1 percent.)

 b) By a judicious use of overtime, the plant manager feels that he can cut the standard deviation to 5 days, at a cost of $800. Is it worth it?

With a change in σ_o, D_o also changes. We now have

$$D_o = \left| \frac{99.5 - 90}{5} \right| = 1.90,$$
$$N(D_o) = 0.011.$$
$$\text{Expected penalty cost} = (1000)(5)(0.011) = \$55.$$

The reduction in expected penalty cost is $916 - 55 = \$861$, which exceeds the $800 cost to achieve the reduction. Therefore, the use of overtime is economically justifiable.

 c) How much would it be worth if the expected time to complete the contract could be reduced to 85 days, given the original standard deviation of 10 days?

With $x_o = 85$ and $\sigma_o = 10$,

$$D_o = \left| \frac{99.5 - 85}{10} \right| = 1.45,$$
$$N(D_o) = 0.0328.$$
$$\text{Expected penalty cost} = (1000)(10)(0.0328) = \$328.$$

The value of reducing the expected completion time would be $916 - 328 = \$588$.

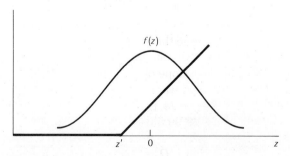

Figure 4.21

In the discussion of the normal loss integral, we have limited our analyses to the case where the loss function rises toward the near tail of the normal curve, as illustrated in Figures 4.14 and 4.15. This condition always applies for the COL values in a two-action problem with linear payoffs, as explained earlier. However, for the case when conditional profits or costs follow the general form of a linear loss function, as in Example 4.8, it is entirely possible for this linear function to rise toward the *far* tail of the normal curve, as illustrated in Figures 4.21 and 4.22.

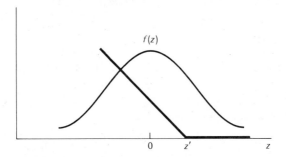

Figure 4.22

Now, if we let D' be the value of D when the loss function rises toward the *far* tail of the normal curve, it is not difficult to show that the normal loss integral for D' is related to the normal loss integral for D as follows:

$$N(D') = D + N(D). \qquad (4.2)$$

To illustrate the use of Equation (4.2), suppose that the estimated time to contract completion in Example 4.8 had been 102 days, resulting in the situation shown in Figure 4.23.

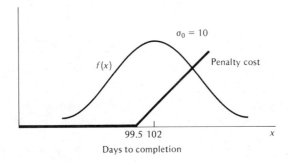

Figure 4.23

Since the penalty cost function rises toward the far tail of the normal curve, we have

$$D_o' = \left| \frac{102 - 99.5}{10} \right| = 0.25.$$

Then,

$$N(D_o') = 0.25 + N(0.25) = 0.25 + 0.2863 = 0.5363.$$
$$\text{Expected penalty cost} = C\sigma_o N(D_o') = (1000)(10)(0.5363) = \$5363.$$

As would be anticipated, the expected penalty cost would be greatly increased if the mean completion time were changed from 90 days to 102 days.

EXERCISES

4.1 (a) Explain clearly the distinction between an act and an event.
     (b) In a given problem, why must the events be mutually exclusive?

4.2 Given the complete set of events in a given situation, how is the expected monetary value determined for a given act? Explain in your own words.

4.3 Bernie's of Berlin insures commercial aircraft against loss and damage. For a Hopdup 797 class aircraft, replacement cost is $4 million and the average damage in accidents, excluding those involving total loss, is $20,000. From past data for this class of aircraft, the annual probability of a total loss is 0.0005 and that of other accidents is 0.02. If Bernie's wishes to cover its operating costs and profits by charging 20 percent more than its expected payments, what should its annual premium be for aircraft insurance for each Hopdup 797?

4.4 Cutrate Construction Company is attempting to decide on its bid amount on a building construction project requiring sealed bids. The bidding expense incurred has been $10,000 and the estimated construction costs would be $140,000. Cutrate is considering four possible bids. As shown in the accompanying table, the company estimated its probability of being low bidder, based on previous experience.

Bid amount, $1000s	170	180	190	200
Probability of being low bidder	0.95	0.75	0.50	0.20

     (a) What is the optimal bid and its expected profit? [*Hint:* Calculate the EMV for each bid.]
     (b) How does the bidding expense affect the selection of the optimal bid? Explain.

4.5 An oil wildcatter has five promising drilling sites. The chances of striking oil at each one of these sites is believed to be 0.25. The cost of drilling is $100,000 per site. The estimated value of an oil strike is $1 million. All five sites will be drilled.
     (a) Using the binomial distribution, find the probabilities of zero, one, two, three, four and five oil strikes. Determine the conditional profit for each of these six possible outcomes and calculate the expected monetary value for this wildcatter.
     (b) Calculate the EMV directly by determining first the expected number of successful strikes and then the expected gross profit.

4.6 (a) Discuss the concept of conditional opportunity loss.
     (b) Can a conditional opportunity loss ever be negative? Explain.

4.7 A speculator in Superbowl tickets can buy up to four of these valuable ducats for $15 each. He intends to hold out for $40 no matter what happens. On the basis of previous speculations, his demand probabilities at the $40 price are:

Number of tickets demanded	0	1	2	3	4
Probability	0.4	0.1	0.3	0.1	0.1

For the actions of purchasing zero, one, two, three, or four tickets:
(a) Prepare a table of conditional profits.
(b) Construct an opportunity loss table.
(c) Calculate the expected opportunity loss. How many tickets should the speculator buy?

4.8 State, in your own words, the meaning of the expected value of perfect information and the expected profit with perfect information. What is their relationship to each other?

4.9 You are one of two manufacturers with a no-calorie cola. You consider a $2 million advertising campaign or a $1 million campaign. Your competitor considers the same two alternatives. If each of you spends $1 million, net profits on the new cola will be $500,000 each. If one of you spends $2 million and the other $1 million, the one spending more nets $2 million and the other nets nothing. If each of you spends $2 million, you each sustain a net loss of $2 million, because of consumer reaction to excessive advertising. Chances of your competitor spending $1 million on advertising are estimated to be 0.5.
(a) Construct your conditional profit table for this situation.
(b) Calculate your expected monetary value for each of the two actions.
(c) On the basis of the criteria of maximizing expected monetary value, which action should you take?
(d) Calculate your expected profit with perfect information.
(e) What is your minimum expected opportunity loss?
(f) What is the most you should pay an informant for perfect information on your competitor's action?

4.10 For the advertising problem of Exercise 4.9, perform and interpret separate sensitivity analyses, similar to those of Example 4.1, for
(a) the probability that your competitor spends $1 million on advertising.
(b) the amount that one competitor nets when spending $2 million when the other spends only $1 million (and nets zero).

4.11 Police Lieutenant Shark receives a tip of a narcotics sale to take place in a senator's office the following night. This tipster has been correct 40 percent of the time. If the lieutenant does not raid that office at the time of the supposed sale, he neither gains nor loses career progress points. If he leads a raid and the tip is false, he loses 50 career progress points; if the tip is correct, he earns 100 points.
(a) If the lieutenant wishes to maximize his expected career progress points, what should he do?
(b) If a career progress point is worth $10 to the lieutenant, what is the most he would pay for a perfect tip?

4.12 For the problem of Exercise 4.11, perform and interpret separate sensitivity analyses for
      (a) the career progress points gained by a correct tip.
      (b) the probability of a correct tip.

4.13 The Triumph Toy Company is bringing out a new type of animated doll. Triumph is attempting to decide whether to bring out a full, partial, or minimal product line. The company has categorized three possible levels of product acceptance and has estimated their probability of occurrence. Management will make its decision on the basis of maximizing the expected profit from the first year of production. The relevant data is shown in the accompanying table.

First-Year Profit ($1000s)

Product Acceptance	Probability	Product Line		
		Full	Partial	Minimal
Good	0.2	80	70	50
Fair	0.4	50	45	40
Poor	0.4	−25	−10	0

      (a) What is the optimal product line and its expected profit?
      (b) Develop an opportunity loss table and calculate the EOL values. What is EOL* and the optimal act?
      (c) How much would it be worth to know the product acceptance level before making the product line decision?
      (d) An advertising campaign, costing $15,000, could be expected to raise the probabilities of both "good" and "fair" acceptance by 0.1. Would it be worth spending the money?

must equal 100% ✗

4.14 Vokia and Mania are neighboring countries. Their present trade relationship is rather cool, and very little trade goes on between them. Within the next few months, a high-level meeting between trade officials of the two countries will set policy for the next several years. "Informed" estimates are that there is 0.5 probability that the status quo will be maintained, 0.4 probability that trade relationships will be normalized, and 0.1 probability that reciprocal trade agreements will be enacted to develop a "warm" trade relationship.
      The Vokian Company is just about to make a production decision on three new products it has been developing. Production and marketing capabilities limit the company to the introduction of just one of these three products. Each product has been designed for a different market. Product A is primarily designed to sell in Vokia and a better trade relationship with Mania would hurt its sales by bringing in competitive Manian products. Product C, on the other hand, would be a good seller in Mania, if trade regulations permitted, but its sales potential is somewhat limited in Vokia. Product B, in terms of sales appeal, is somewhere between products A and C. The estimated annual profit for each

product, as affected by the two countries' trade relationship, is shown in the accompanying table.

Annual Profit ($1000s)

Trade Relationship	Product		
	A	B	C
Cool	100	80	60
Normal	80	90	100
Warm	40	100	150

(a) Which product should be developed and what is its expected profit?
(b) Develop an opportunity loss table and calculate the EOL for each product. What is EOL*?
(c) What is the expected profit with perfect information and the expected value of perfect information?

4.15 A newsstand receives its weekly order of Glimpse magazine on Monday and cannot reorder. Each copy costs $0.15 and sells for $0.25. Unsold copies may be returned the following week for a $0.10 rebate. When the newsstand runs out of copies and cannot supply a customer, it estimates its "goodwill" loss as $0.20 in future profits, figuring that the customer will take her business elsewhere for a couple of weeks, on the average. Demand has been remarkably constant, ranging between 7 and 10 copies, as shown in the accompanying table.

Demand, copies	7	8	9	10
Fraction of time	0.30	0.40	0.20	0.10

(a) Construct a payoff table and use it to determine the optimal number of copies to stock and the expected profit.
(b) Construct an opportunity loss table and find the optimal number of copies to stock and EOL*.
(c) How much would it be worth to know the exact demand each week? What would be the expected profit if this were possible?

4.16 In the preceding newsstand problem, let s = number of units stocked and d = number of units demanded. Develop equations for the profit as a function of s and d, depending on which is larger.

4.17 In the newsstand problem in Exercise 4.15, suppose that none of the customers were regular customers, so that a lost sale resulted only in a profit foregone, with no additional goodwill cost.
(a) Intuitively, would you expect the optimal number to stock to tend to increase or decrease? Why?
(b) What would be the optimal number to stock and the expected profit?

4.18 In the newsstand problem in Exercise 4.15, suppose it were now possible to reorder, at a unit cost of $0.20, and a would-be purchaser would return the following day to purchase the magazine.

(a)   Intuitively, would you expect the optimal number to stock to tend to increase or decrease? Why?

(b)   What would be the optimal number to stock and the expected profit?

4.19   Your local auto insurance company offers two different collision deductibles, $100 or $250 per occurrence. The annual premium for the lower deductible amount costs an additional $25. You consider yourself to be an excellent driver with a negligible chance of two or more accidents in the coming year, a 10 percent chance of one accident, and a 90 percent chance of no accidents. With the high cost of repairs, any accident you may be involved in will cost at least $250 in collision repairs. You wish to minimize your expected insurance plus collision repair costs. Construct an appropriate table of conditional costs (or negative conditional profits). Which deductible should you buy to minimize expected conditional costs?

4.20   For the insurance problem of Exercise 4.19, perform and interpret separate sensitivity analysis for

(a)   the additional annual premium for $100 deductible insurance.

(b)   the probability of no accidents.

4.21   A company manufacturing large electrical equipment is anticipating the possibility of a total or a partial copper strike in the near future. It is attempting to decide whether to stockpile a large amount of copper, at an additional cost of $50,000; a small amount, costing an additional $20,000; or to stockpile no additional copper at all. (The stockpiling costs, consisting of excess storage, holding, and handling costs, and so forth, are over and above the actual material costs.)

     If there is a partial strike, the company estimates that an additional cost of $50,000 for delayed orders will be incurred only if there is no stockpile at all. If a total strike occurs, the cost of delayed orders is estimated at $100,000 if there is only a small stockpile and $200,000 with no stockpile. The company estimates the probability of a total strike as 0.1 and that of a partial strike as 0.3.

(a)   Develop a conditional cost table showing the cost for all act-event combinations.

(b)   Determine the preferred act and its cost. What is EPPI?

(c)   Develop a conditional opportunity loss table.

(d)   Without calculating EOL*, find EVPI.

4.22   Suppose, in Example 4.2, the problem involving the optimal number of spares, that a failure detector had been developed which would warn of incipient failures. With such a device, there would be time to special-order a spare if one were about to be needed and no spare was on hand. The cost of downtime would thus be avoided.

(a)   Determine the optimal number of spares.

(b)   How much would the failure detector be worth in this situation?

4.23   Joe Gladhand sells used cars for Cool Cars, Inc. He has been offered a choice of three commission plans. Plan 1 would pay him $100 per car sold. Plan 2 specifies payment of $50 per car for the first two cars sold and $200 for each additional sale. Plan 3 would pay a flat $100 plus $50 for each car sold. From recent sales figures, the number of cars sold by Gladhand each week appears to vary in a

completely random fashion, with a mean of 2.9. Extracting the required Poisson probabilities to only *two* decimal places:
(a)   Construct Joe's payoff table.
(b)   Which plan appears to be most profitable for Joe? What would be his expected weekly income with that plan?
(c)   Which plan minimizes Cool Cars' cost? What is its expected cost?
(d)   Construct Joe's COL table.
(e)   Construct Cool Cars' COL table, considering only payments to Joe.

4.24 The Hi-Bounce Company manufactures guaranteed tennis balls. At the present time, approximately 10 percent of the tennis balls are defective. A defective ball leaving the factory costs the company 50 cents to honor its guarantee. At a cost of 10 cents per ball, the company can conduct a test, which always correctly identifies both good and bad tennis balls.
(a)   Draw a decision tree and determine the optimal strategy and its expected cost.
(b)   At what test cost should the company be indifferent to testing?

4.25 The Hi-Bounce Company, referred to in Exercise 4.24, has developed a new test that costs only 4 cents per tennis ball tested. The test, however, is only 95 percent accurate, so it correctly identifies either a good ball or a bad ball with probability 0.95.
(a)   If 10 percent of all tennis balls are defective, what is the probability that the test will give a favorable result for a randomly chosen tennis ball?
(b)   Shipping a defective ball costs 50 cents; discarding a good ball results in a loss of 25 cents. Construct a decision tree to compare the desirability of this test versus no test at all. Determine the optimal strategy and its expected cost.
(c)   At what test cost would you be indifferent to testing?

4.26 The Good Earth Company is developing a new soil nutrient. If the product is successful, it is anticipated to yield a $500,000 profit. If unsuccessful, it is estimated that the costs and adverse publicity would result in a loss of $1 million. In the past, similar products have been successful 60 percent of the time. At a cost of $50,000, the new nutrient can be tested on a special strain of wheat. Successful nutrients test favorably on this wheat strain 80 percent of the time; unsuccessful nutrients test favorably only 30 percent of the time.
     Good Earth must make a decision as to whether to conduct a test, market the product without a test, or drop the product. If it conducts the test, it would then have to decide whether to market or to drop the product, depending on the test results.
(a)   By using basic probability relationships, show that the probability of a favorable test is 0.60.
(b)   Develop a decision tree. Specify the optimal strategy and its EMV.
(c)   Suppose that a more expensive testing process were available which gave perfect information, so that a successful product or an unsuccessful product would always be correctly identified. Assuming no change in the probability of a favorable test (or in the probability of a successful product without testing), how much could the company afford to pay for this testing process?

4.27 The Jensun Company has been offered a study contract to refine a device for reducing automobile exhaust emissions. Following the study contract, there will be awards for prototype production contracts for a few preliminary models and then awards for production contracts. All contracts are for fixed dollar amounts; the study contract is for $10,000, the prototype contract for $10,000, and the production contract for $50,000.

Jensun has decided to consider two levels of effort, high and low, on the study contract. A high level of effort will cost more, but it will increase the company's chances of getting the prototype contract. The probability of getting the production contract depends on the level of effort on the study contract and also on the level of effort (again high or low) on the prototype contract, if one is received. If Jensun receives a production contract, it will incur additional production expenses unless a high level of effort was employed on the prototype contract. All this information, with probability and cost figures, is summarized in the accompanying table.

				Cost ($1000s)		
Study Contract Level of Effort	Probability of Winning Prototype Contract	Prototype Contract Level of Effort	Probability of Winning Production Contract	Study Contract	Prototype Contract	Additional Production Expense
High	0.7	High	0.8	15	10	0
		Low	0.6	15	6	5
		None*	0.2	15	0	10
Low	0.4	High	0.7	5	10	0
		Low	0.5	5	6	5
		None*	0.1	5	0	15

*Prototype contract not received.

(a) Develop a decision tree and use it to determine the optimal strategy. Specify this strategy completely.

(b) What is the expected value of the optimal strategy?

4.28 Given the data of Exercise 4.27, perform a sensitivity analysis on the probability p of winning the prototype contract if a high level of effort is used on the study contract.

(a) Determine the value of p for indifference between a high study contract effort and a low study contract effort (assuming subsequent optimal decisions in each case, as worked out in Exercise 4.27).

(b) Assuming that a high level of effort is optimal on the study contract, prepare a table to show, as a function of the value of p, the optimal act and the economic effect of an error (decrease in EMV) if an error is made.

(c) Plot the decrease in EMV as a function of the deviation of p from its stated value of 0.7, when this deviation would be such as to change the optimal act.

4.29   In the Triumph Toy Company problem (Exercise 4.13), the odds of "good" product acceptance are thought to be quite close to 1 to 4, so the probability of 0.2 seems reasonably firm for "good" product acceptance. Suppose, however, that uncertainty exists as to the probabilities of "fair" or "poor" product acceptance. Thus, a sensitivity analysis of these subjective probabilities is in order.

If p is the probability of "fair" product acceptance:
(a)   Express the EMV of each act as a function of p.
(b)   On a single graph, plot, for each act, EMV versus p, over the entire allowable range of p. (Since the EMVs are linear functions of p, it is necessary to calculate only two data points in order to construct each line.)
(c)   From your graph, specify the optimal act for each possible value of p.
(d)   Which one act should be chosen if it is desired to minimize the maximum expected opportunity loss which can occur over the entire range of p values? What is the value of this maximum expected opportunity loss?

4.30   Fadco Manufacturing Company (Example 4.5) is uncertain as to how much it will gross if its new product is successful. Let x be the gross profit if the product is successful.
(a)   If test marketing is performed, over what range of values for x will the optimal decision be to market regionally if the test marketing result is favorable, and to drop the product if the test marketing result is unfavorable?
(b)   Working from the results in part (a), for what value of x would Fadco be indifferent to test marketing or to marketing regionally immediately?

4.31   Explain the relationship between loss functions and linear payoff functions for a two-action problem. Illustrate with sketches.

4.32   Why does the assumption of a linear payoff function simplify the determination of the optimal act prior to sampling?

4.33   The Zippee Company manufactures a certain special part which it sells for $4 a unit. The special-purpose machine on which these parts are made must be replaced, and Zippee is considering two possible replacement candidates, the Model 901 and Model 909. Both of these machines have the same purchase cost, but the Model 909 is a little more complicated, so its maintenance cost is $1500 per year, whereas that of the Model 901 is $1000 per year. However, to balance this, the unit production cost is $3 for the Model 901 but only $2.75 for the Model 909, which has certain labor-saving features. Because of production commitments, one of these machines must be purchased, so the purchase cost is not a factor in their selection.
(a)   Determine the payoff functions, based on annual net profit, for the two machines. At what annual sales level would Zippee be indifferent as to which machine they purchased?
(b)   State the algebraic form of the loss functions associated with the payoff functions in part (a).
(c)   Sketch the payoff and loss functions, specifying numerical values on both axes.

4.34 A toy manufacturer is considering production of a highly topical game which can be expected to have a very short sales life. The estimated unit cost would be $2.95 and the selling price $4.95. The manufacturer has a fixed cost of production of $10,000.
(a) Write the profit equation and determine the breakeven point.
(b) Sketch the loss functions, labeling both axes numerically, for the actions:
1. Produce the new game.
2. Do not produce the new game.
(c) State algebraically the two opportunity loss functions in (b).
(d) The Sales Department estimates that there is a 50–50 chance of selling 5000 units. If 5000 units are not sold, it believes the number of units sold will be either 4000 or 6000 units, with the latter number favored by 3 to 2 odds. Determine whether the game should be produced.

4.35 The Biggs Company is planning to continue the long-term production of a certain part in very large quantities. To produce this part, the company has a special machine which has now reached the point where it is no longer economical to use. There are two models of this type of machine on the market and both have the same estimated life of ten years. The purchase price and operating costs, expressed as an annual cost in the ten-year period, are $10,000 for Model 1 and $12,000 for Model 2. The variable cost of production, however, is $0.14 per unit for Model 1 and $0.12 per unit for Model 2.
(a) Write the payoff functions for purchase of each of the models.
(b) What is the annual number of units produced at which Biggs would be indifferent as to which model it purchased?
(c) State algebraically and graph the appropriate opportunity loss functions.

4.36 Given a normal probability distribution of sales and a linear payoff function, explain and illustrate with a sketch how the expected opportunity loss of the optimal act will be affected by
(a) a decrease in the variance of the prior estimate of the mean sales quantity.
(b) a decrease in the difference between the expected mean value of sales and the breakeven value.

4.37 The food concessionaire at the local baseball stadium makes 30 cents on each hot dog sold. His refrigerator holds at most 25,000 hot dogs. Hot dog demand for a night game is estimated to be normally distributed with a mean of 20,000 and a standard deviation of 5,000. Unsold hot dogs can be kept or returned without any loss. No resupply is possible at night. What is the expected cost due to the lack of unlimited refrigeration space for hot dogs?

4.38 A local electric power utility generates up to 240,000 kilowatt-hours of electricity each day. If power demand exceeds that level, the utility buys surplus energy from another utility at 20 cents per kilowatt-hour above its own cost. What is the excess cost of buying such surplus electricity if daily demand is normally distributed.
(a) with a mean of 230,000 and a standard deviation of 20,000 kilowatt-hours?
(b) with a mean of 240,000 and a standard deviation of 20,000 kilowatt-hours?
(c) with a mean of 250,000 and a standard deviation of 20,000 kilowatt-hours?
(d) with a mean of 250,000 and a standard deviation of 40,000 kilowatt-hours?

4.39 A company stocks 500 units of a certain product at the beginning of each month and cannot reorder during the month. For every unit that is demanded but which it is unable to supply, the company attaches a shortage cost of $5, which is its estimate of the goodwill loss associated with a dissatisfied customer. Demand tends to be normally distributed with mean μ and standard deviation σ.

(a) Explain, with the aid of equations and diagrams, how the normal loss integral can be utilized in the evaluation of the expected monthly shortage cost.

(b) Calculate the monthly shortage cost for the following normal distributions of demand.

    1. $\mu = 500$, $\sigma = 50$.
    2. $\mu = 500$, $\sigma = 100$.
    3. $\mu = 450$, $\sigma = 50$.
    4. $\mu = 450$, $\sigma = 100$.

(c) Briefly discuss the numerical differences between the answers in part (b).

4.40 A movie producer is considering investing $1 million in a new film. The paid audience needed to recoup the cost of the film is 2,000,000 viewers, since each viewer yields a profit of 50 cents. The producer estimates the potential audience for this film at a mean of 2,200,000, with a standard deviation of 160,000.

(a) Algebraically, state the payoff functions for the producer and plot them.
(b) Do the same for the loss functions for the producer.
(c) Should he finance this film? Why?
(d) What is EVPI for the producer? State clearly what perfect information refers to in this problem.

4.41 The Ree Store is considering issuing its own credit card to its 12,000 customers. The estimated annual cost to run a credit card operation would be $150,000. Ree believes that the credit card will increase profit per customer by an average of $15 per year, but this figure could, with equal likelihood, be within the range of $13 to $17 or could be outside that range.

(a) Develop the loss functions for the acts:
    1. Issue a credit card.
    2. Do not issue a credit card.
(b) Determine the optimal act and its expected opportunity loss, assuming a normal probability distribution for the mean annual profit increase per customer.

4.42 A well-established insurance agent has a clientele of 200 customers. His company has just brought out a new type of term life insurance policy. He has been offered a choice of two compensation plans. Plan 1 would pay him a fixed amount of $5000 and 20 percent of the total first-year premiums. Plan 2 is a straight 30 percent commission of the total first-year premiums. His decision will commit him for a one-year period. In going over the new policy and considering his clientele's probable needs, the agent estimates that, for each customer, he should be able to average a $200 annual premium for the new term insurance. His uncertainty as to this amount, however, is reflected in his estimate that there is only a 50–50 chance the average amount will fall between $150 and $250. He is willing to assume a normal probability distribution for his subjective estimate of the average annual premium spent on the new insurance.

(a)   Develop and plot the payoff functions for both plans.

(b)   Develop and plot the loss functions for both plans.

(c)   Determine the optimal act and its expected opportunity loss.

OTHER
DECISION-MAKING
CRITERIA

In the previous chapter, when we analyzed a problem with probabilistic outcomes, our choice of the optimal act was based on the criterion of expected monetary value (EMV). Now we will consider another measure of value, called utility, as an alternative to monetary values. We will also consider the situation where event probabilities are not given, so that decisions cannot be based on expected values, either monetary or utility. For this situation, several possible decision criteria will be discussed.

5.1 UTILITY

In many situations, both personal and business, where monetary values are the prime consideration, decisions are faced which may involve both relatively large monetary amounts and commensurate high risks. If the monetary amounts are sufficiently high, compared to the assets of the decision maker, the choice of the preferred alternative will frequently involve strong consideration of the current asset position. Consider, for instance, the following situations.

1. A reliable friend offers you the opportunity to participate in a high-risk oil-drilling venture. He requires an investment of $1000 and, based on similar drilling situations, he estimates that the odds are 3 to 2 in favor of bringing the well in, in which case your share would be $5000. In case of a dry hole, you lose your $1000. What would you do?

On an EMV basis, we have

$$\text{EMV} = \frac{3}{5}(5000 - 1000) + \frac{2}{5}(0 - 1000) = 2400 - 400 = \$2000.$$

Since this amount is double the required investment, the deal seems to be a good one. Consider, however, that you will actually either gain $4000 or lose $1000. If a loss of $1000 will practically bankrupt you, then you may be well advised to pass up this opportunity, since you would stand a high probability (40 percent) of losing that $1000.

2. A business faces a possible loss amounting to $500,000. It is estimated that the probability of sustaining this loss is 0.001 annually. Should the firm pay $1000 per year to avoid this risk completely?

   The EMV of the annual loss is $(500,000)(0.001) = \$500$. Why should the firm pay $1000 to avoid this loss? It certainly would not if it based its decision on the EMV criterion. But, although this loss might never occur, the possibility exists that the firm might incur a very substantial loss. It would certainly consider paying some amount greater than $500 per year to be protected against such a loss. This is the whole idea of insurance protection.

3. You have just won $5000 on a quiz show. You have one last opportunity to compete on the show. You can either take your winnings or you can return the $5000 and choose one of two envelopes. One envelope contains a list of grand and glorious prizes totaling $20,000; the other envelope contains a message saying: "Thanks for being on the show." The prizes are yours if you pick the right envelope. What would you do?

   Calculating expected values, the EMV of choosing one of the envelopes is $(0.5)(20,000) + (0.5)(0) = \$10,000$, or twice the value of the $5000 you have already won. But would you really give up a sure $5000 for a 50–50 chance on $20,000 or nothing? Many people would not, because they would think of all the things they could do with $5000 and how they would regret it for the rest of their lives if they wound up with nothing.

As we have shown with these three examples, the choice between two (or more) acts may very logically result in the selection of an act which does not have the most favorable EMV. In such cases, the decision maker has indicated that the act with the most favorable EMV is simply too risky, so it is entirely rational to prefer an act which has a less favorable EMV. In the language of decision theory, we say that the preferred act has the highest expected utility. The question now is how to define and measure this utility.

5.2 MEASURING UTILITY

We will define *utility* as a subjective numerical measure of the value of an act to a decision maker when a particular event occurs. Utility is therefore a conditional measure, just as are conditional profit, conditional cost, and conditional opportunity loss. Being subjective, the utility of a given combination of an act and event will differ from individual to individual and even for the same individual as circumstances change. Since a specific utility value is associated with an act and an event, we might refer to the utility of the combination of act A_i and event E_j as the utility of A_iE_j. However, to be consistent with the terminology that has developed in the area of utility theory, we will refer to a combination of act and event as an *outcome*. This simplifies the notation, but the conditional nature of a utility value should be remembered.

Utility can be measured in several different ways, but we will be interested in what is termed *cardinal utility*, whereby numerical values are assigned to different outcomes. The general concept (somewhat oversimplified) of cardinal utility theory is that each individual attempts to optimize the expected value of something defined as utility, and that, for each individual, a relationship between utility and outcome (generally dollars) can be found in a particular set of circumstances.

Utility is measured on an interval scale, which means that we *arbitrarily* select both a zero point and the size of the unit interval. The unit of utility is sometimes called the *utile*. Temperature is a good example of a property measured on an interval scale. On an interval scale, we can make only relative, rather than absolute, comparisons. A temperature of 60°F is obviously warmer than a temperature of 20°F, but we cannot say that it is three times as warm. An interval measure is appropriate for decision-making purposes because our requirement is for comparative, not absolute, judgments.

The basic postulates of cardinal utility are as follows.

1. If outcome A is preferred to outcome B, then the utility of outcome A, $U(A)$, is greater than the utility of outcome B, $U(B)$. If outcome B is preferred to outcome C, then $U(B) > U(C)$. Then, if we make the assumption that preferences are transitive, outcome A would be preferred to outcome C, since $U(A) > U(B) > U(C)$.

2. If the decision maker is indifferent between outcome B for certain and a lottery in which he receives outcome A with probability p and outcome C with probability $1 - p$, then we can state that $U(B) = pU(A) + (1 - p)U(C)$.

In any decision involving uncertainty, a basic assumption of cardinal utility theory is that a rational individual will choose that alternative which maximizes expected utility. Once we know the utility function, the probability assigned to events in a decision-making situation and the consequences of each possible outcome, we should be able to predict the person's choice in that situation, since he or she will attempt to maximize expected utility. The argument here is that if the utility values in a given situation are a valid measure of the individual's preferences, then maximizing expected utility is conceptually the same as maximizing EMV when monetary amounts are indicative of relative preferences.

By suitable questioning, we can find the relationship between utility and dollars for a decision maker. Determination of an individual's utility function is usually done by either the *certainty equivalent* or the *standard gamble* technique.

5.3   CERTAINTY EQUIVALENT TECHNIQUE

Suppose we ask a person to choose between two possible alternatives involving outcomes (payoffs) A, B, and C. There is a choice of

1. B or
2. a lottery between A and C, with probabilities of p and $1 - p$, respectively.

We will assume that, given a direct choice, A is preferred to B, which, in turn, is preferred to C.

Let us now ask the person to express a preference between the first alternative and the second alternative. We wish to do this with p, A, and C fixed, while B is allowed to vary. Since, on a preference scale, B is constrained to fall between A and C, there will be some value of B for which he will be indifferent to the choice between B for certain and the uncertain outcome of A or C. At that point, we say that the expected utilities of the two alternatives are equal, so that, as in postulate 2,

$$U(B) = pU(A) + (1 - p)U(C).$$

If we arbitrarily fix $U(C)$ and $U(A)$, the utility values for the least favorable and most favorable outcomes, respectively, we can then specify a value of p and ask the individual at what value of B he will be indifferent to the two alternatives. This will enable us to solve for $U(B)$, the utility of outcome B, which is equal to the utility of alternative 1. This procedure can then be repeated for different values of p to get additional utility values for other outcomes in the interval between C and A. Another way, which is often preferable, is to use a calculated utility value to establish other values. Thus, suppose that outcomes C and A represented gains of $0 and $1000, respectively, and that the individual was indifferent to $400 for certain and a lottery with an even chance of getting A or C. Given the specified utility values of A and C, we could then calculate the utility of $400. If we now wished to determine the utility of an amount between $0 and $400, we could repeat the specified procedure, using $400 as outcome A. Similarly, if we wanted to find the utility of an amount between $400 and $1000, we could use $400 as outcome C. The advantage of this approach is that it allows us to keep the values of p somewhere near 0.5, which is generally desirable, since it appears that the use of probabilities much below 0.25 or much above 0.75 makes judgmental estimates more difficult for some persons.

As we have noted, since utility is measured on an interval scale, there is no natural origin for a utility scale, so one is free to assign arbitrary utility values to any two monetary amounts. Having done this, however, there will be for each individual a unique value for the utility assignable to any other monetary amount. Let us now take an example to illustrate the process of constructing a utility curve using the certainty equivalent technique.

EXAMPLE 5.1

We are trying to determine the utility function of the entrepreneur of a small business. Our primary interest lies in the range of monetary value she is most accustomed to dealing with, namely, $0 to $20,000.

We start by arbitrarily establishing two points on her utility curve. Suppose we let $U(\$0) = 0$ utiles and $U(\$20,000) = 100$ utiles. Now, by a procedure whereby we pose hypothetical, but hopefully credible, situations to our entrepreneur, we will derive additional points on her utility curve.

1. We tell her that she has a 50–50 chance of getting a special lot of merchandise on which she can make a $20,000 profit. We then ask her how much cash she would want to let someone else take over this opportunity. She says she would be happy to get $10,000, but at $8000 she would be indifferent. At any lesser amount, she would prefer the gamble. Knowing that she is indifferent to the utility of $8000 and the utility of an even chance of $20,000 or nothing, we can now solve for $U(\$8000)$:

$$U(\$8000) = (0.5)U(\$20,000) + (0.05)U(\$0)$$
$$= (0.5)(100) + (0.5)(0)$$
$$= 50 \text{ utiles.}$$

Thus, on the entrepreneur's utility scale, the distance corresponding to the interval from $0 to $8000 is the same as the distance corresponding to the interval from $8000 to $20,000. Does this mean that her utility for $20,000 is twice her utility for $8000? If you think so, think again. Remember that utility scales are not *absolute*. If, for instance, $U(\$0)$ had been set at 980 utiles and $U(\$20,000)$ at 990 utiles, $U(\$8000)$ would have been 985 utiles.

2. We now ask the entrepreneur to visualize a situation where another company has offered to purchase some special-purpose equipment she owns. There is an even chance of getting a production contract, worth a profit of $8000, which requires this equipment. Otherwise, the equipment will be essentially worthless, since it was purchased years ago for a particular production contract and never used since. We ask her how much she would sell the equipment for, and, after a good deal of thought, she states that she would be indifferent at an offer of $3000.

Now we can determine the utility to her of $3000:

$$U(\$3000) = (0.5)U(\$8000) + (0.5)U(\$0)$$
$$= (0.5)(50) + (0.5)(0)$$
$$= 25 \text{ utiles.}$$

Here, we utilized the previously determined value for $U(\$8000)$, by using $8000 as the preferred alternative in the lottery.

3. Let us now locate a utility value outside the specified range of $0 to $20,000. We will do this by modifying the certainty equivalent technique so that we solve for $U(C)$, given $U(A)$, $U(B)$, and p. To get the utility for a negative

monetary amount, we ask the entrepreneur how high a bidding expense she would be willing to risk on a bid for a contract worth a profit of $8000. (Bidding expenses are reimbursable if the contract is obtained.) We tell her that there is an equal chance of winning or losing the bid. After thinking it over, she says that she would be indifferent to submitting a bid at a bidding expense of $2000.

The utility of −$2000 can now be calculated:

$$U(\$0) = (0.5)U(\$8000) + (0.5)U(-\$2000)$$
$$0 = (0.5)(50) + (0.5)U(-\$2000)$$

so that,

$$U(-\$2000) = -50 \text{ utiles.}$$

The entrepreneur's utility curve is plotted as Figure 5.1. Incidentally, it should be pointed out that the decision-maker's utility function, when plotted, may show inconsistencies, with some points lying appreciably above or below what would seem to be a reasonable curve, based on the derived data. If this should be the case, it may be desirable to go back and reevaluate one or more of the utility values and/or to derive additional utility values.

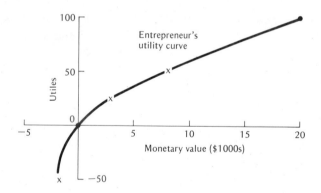

Figure 5.1

Now that we have her utility curve plotted, we can make a reasonable estimate of her behavior when faced with monetary choices. We can solve for a single unknown, which can be a monetary value, the utility of a monetary value, or the probability of a given lottery. As one example, suppose the entrepreneur is offered $5000 for some seasonal merchandise which she estimates will sell for $10,000 if it turns out to be popular and only $3000 if it does not. With what probability would it have to be popular in order that she would be indifferent to the offer?

Let p = probability that merchandise will be popular.

Then, for the utilities of the two alternatives to be equal,

$$U(\$5000) = pU(\$10,000) + (1 - p)U(\$3000),$$
$$36 = 58p + 25(1 - p)$$
$$= 33p + 25,$$

so, $$p = 11/33 = 1/3.$$

Now let us discuss the standard gamble technique for constructing a utility function.

5.4 STANDARD GAMBLE TECHNIQUE

The standard gamble technique is set up in precisely the same manner as the certainty equivalent technique. That is, we have three outcomes, A, B, and C, which are preferred in that order. The individual then has, again, the choice of

1. B or
2. a lottery between A and C, with probabilities of p and $1 - p$, respectively.

As before, we ask the person to express her preference between the first and second alternatives. Now, however, we fix A, B, and C, while allowing p to vary. If $p = 1$, her choice is between B and A, and she would naturally choose alternative 2. If, on the other hand, $p = 0$, the choice is between B and C, and she would now choose alternative 1. Thus, as p decreases from 1 to 0, her decision, at some point, will change from alternative 2 to alternative 1. There will be a value of p at which she will be indifferent to the choice of alternative 1 or alternative 2, so at this point we say that the utility of alternative 1 is equal to the expected utility of alternative 2, or

$$U(B) = pU(A) + (1 - p)U(C).$$

If we arbitrarily fix $U(C)$ and $U(A)$, the utility values for the least favorable and most favorable outcomes, C and A, respectively, we can then specify a value of B and ask the person at what value of p she will be indifferent to the two alternatives. This will enable us to solve for $U(B)$, the utility of outcome B, which is equal to the utility of alternative 1. This procedure can then be repeated for different values of B to get additional utility values for other outcomes in the interval between C and A. As we have shown previously, using the certainty equivalent technique, we can also use a derived utility value to obtain additional values and can even determine utility values for monetary outcomes outside the range between outcomes C and A.

Suppose we now rework Example 5.1, showing how the same utility values could have been developed using the standard gamble technique. The primary point of interest is in the way we restructure each decision situation from the way in which it was presented when the certainty equivalent technique was used. We will again start with $U(\$0) = 0$ utiles and $U(\$20,000) = 100$ utiles, and we will derive the same three points on the utility curve.

1. We tell the entrepreneur that she has a chance to purchase a special lot of merchandise at a price which would net a profit of $20,000. We then ask what

the probability of getting the lot would have to be before she would be indifferent to selling this opportunity for $8000. She replies that, at a probability of 0.4 (where the gamble has an EMV of $8000), she would prefer the sure $8000. When the probability is raised to 0.5, however, she says that she would be indifferent to the two alternatives. We then have

$$U(\$8000) = (0.5) \ U(\$20,000) + (0.5) \ U(\$0)$$
$$= (0.5)(100) + (0.5)(0) = 50 \text{ utiles.}$$

2. The entrepreneur has been offered $3000 for some special-purpose equipment she owns. It has not been used for years, but there is a possibility that a production contract, requiring the use of this equipment, will be received. What would the probability of receiving this contract, worth a net profit of $8000, have to be before she would be indifferent to selling or keeping the equipment? She is somewhat reluctant to take a chance on $8000 or nothing, versus a sure $3000, but she says that she would be indifferent if the chances were 50–50 of getting the contract. Thus, in her judgment,

$$U(\$3000) = (0.5) \ U(\$8000) + (0.5) \ U(\$0)$$
$$= (0.5)(50) + (0.5)(0) = 25 \text{ utiles.}$$

If she is consistent in her utility preferences, she should then be indifferent to $3000 for certain and one chance in four of getting a similar contract worth a net profit of $20,000, since

$$(0.25) \ U(\$20,000) + (0.75) \ U(\$0) = (0.25)(100) + (0.75)(0)$$
$$= 25 \text{ utiles.}$$

3. We now evaluate her utility for a monetary amount outside the given range of $0 to $20,000. We offer her the opportunity to bid, at a bidding expense of $2000, on a contract with a net profit of $10,000, less bidding expenses. She stands to gain $8000 or lose $2000 if she bids, and she has the option of not bidding. At what probability of winning the bid will she be indifferent as to whether or not she submits a bid? Since $2000 would be a substantial loss to her, she is quite conservative, insisting on at least an even chance of winning the bid before she will make the decision to bid. On this basis,

$$U(\$0) = (0.5) \ U(\$8000) + (0.5) \ U(-\$2000),$$
$$0 = (0.5)(50) + (0.5) \ U(-\$2000),$$

and $U(-\$2000) = -50$ utiles.

As we have noted, these utility values are the same as those calculated earlier, using the certainty equivalent technique and plotted in Figure 5.1. Let us now take a different example of the use of the calculated utility curve. Suppose an entrepreneur has a business opportunity with the following probability distribution of estimated net returns: $10,000 profit with 0.5 probability, $5000 profit with 0.25 probability, and $1500 loss with 0.25 probability. How much would such a business opportunity be worth to him?

Let x = monetary value of the business opportunity.

The utility of x will be equal to the expected utility of the risky business opportunity, so,

$$U(x) = (0.5) U(\$10,000) + (0.25) U(\$5000) + (0.25) U(-\$1500)$$
$$= (0.5)(58) + (0.25)(36) + (0.25)(-30)$$
$$= 29 + 9 - 7.5 = 30.5.$$

Then, from the utility curve, $x \cong \$4000$. Since the EMV of the business opportunity is $5875, as you can readily calculate, he would prefer, in this instance, any certain amount exceeding $4000 to a gamble with an EMV of $5875.

5.5 DECISION MAKING WITH NONMONETARY OUTCOMES

Cardinal utility theory is also applicable to situations involving nonmonetary outcomes. To illustrate this, we will present an example which shows how utilities can be assigned to nonnumerical outcomes and then utilized in decision making.

EXAMPLE 5.2

A nationally known politician is pondering his chances for the presidential nomination of his party. He must make a decision whether or not he will enter the primary "popularity contest" in a particular state. He considers four possible outcomes, which he ranks in order of decreasing utility.

A = he enters and makes a good showing.
B = he enters and makes a fair showing.
C = he does not enter.
D = he enters and makes a poor showing.

We can get a clearer picture of this situation if we separate decisions and events and draw a very simple decision tree, as shown in Figure 5.2. There is only one decision fork, with two alternatives or acts, and one chance fork, with three events.

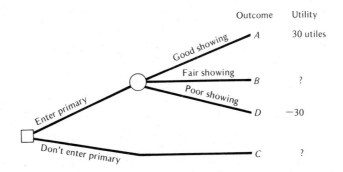

Figure 5.2

In the assignment of utilities to these outcomes, the politician's personal decision analyst first arbitrarily sets $U(A) = 30$ utiles and $U(D) = -30$ utiles, as indicated in Figure 5.2. Then, since the outcomes are fixed, he utilizes the standard gamble technique to assess the utilities of outcomes B and C. He asks the politician to consider two alternatives.

1—outcome B for certain.
2—outcome A with probability p or outcome D with probability $1 - p$.

The politician says that he would prefer outcome B if outcomes A and D were equally likely, but if the odds favoring outcome A rise to 3 to 1, he would be indifferent to the two alternatives. Then,

$$U(B) = (0.75)\, U(A) + (0.25)\, U(D)$$
$$= (0.75)(30) + (0.25)(-30)$$
$$= 22.5 - 7.5 = 15 \text{ utiles.}$$

In attempting to assign a utility value to outcome C, the analyst again asks the politician to think about two alternatives:

1—outcome C for certain.
2—outcome A with probability p or outcome D with probability $1 - p$.

If outcomes A and D were equally likely, the politician would prefer outcome C. He would be indifferent to the two alternatives, however, if the odds favoring outcome A were 2 to 1. Thus,

$$U(C) = (2/3)\, U(A) + (1/3)\, U(D)$$
$$= (2/3)(30) + (1/3)(-30)$$
$$= 20 - 10 = 10 \text{ utiles.}$$

According to his best judgment, if the politician enters the primary, there is a 50–50 chance that he will make a good showing. However, if he does not make a good showing, he feels the odds are 3 to 2 that he will make a poor showing, rather than a fair showing. Based on these estimates, the analyst calculates the following probabilities.

$$P(\text{good showing}) = 0.5,$$
$$P(\text{fair showing}) = (0.4)(1.0 - 0.5) = 0.2,$$
$$P(\text{poor showing}) = (0.6)(1.0 - 0.5) = 0.3.$$

Should the politician enter the primary?

Let us define the act E as "enter the primary." The expected utility of this act will be the sum of the weighted utilities of the three possible outcomes, A, B, and D. Therefore,

$$U(E) = (0.5)(30) + (0.2)(15) + (0.3)(-30)$$
$$= 15 + 3 - 9 = 9 \text{ utiles.}$$

Since the complementary act $\bar{E}$, "do not enter the primary," is identical to outcome C, which has a utility of 10 utiles, act $\bar{E}$ would be preferred. His decision should then be to refrain from entering the primary. His campaign manager could well assign different utility values, based on his own assessment of the utility of each act to the politician, and thereby come up with the opposite decision.

5.6   GENERAL TYPES OF UTILITY CURVES

In Example 5.2, the outcomes were not associated with monetary values. Most applications of utility theory, however, *are* associated with monetary outcomes, and we will now discuss the general appearance of utility curves when utility is a function of monetary value. To illustrate the shape of such curves, consider three hypothetical managers, each accustomed to responsibility for monetary amounts ranging from a loss of $150,000 up to a profit of $150,000. The utility curves for these three, whom we will call manager 1, manager 2, and manager 3, are shown as similarly labeled curves in Figure 5.3.

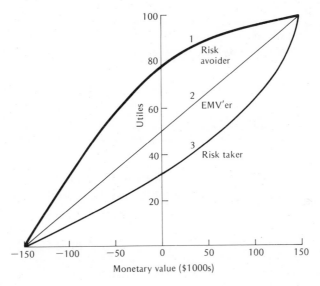

Figure 5.3

Manager 1 has the utility curve of what is often termed a "risk avoider." From a financial standpoint, he is quite conservative. For example, suppose he had an opportunity to bid on a project with a bidding cost of $50,000 and an expected net profit of $100,000 if the bid were successful. Would he bid if his chances of success were 50–50? Let us find out. The utility of an unsuccessful bid is $U(-\$50,000) = 57$ utiles, whereas that of a successful bid is $U(\$100,000) = 96$ utiles. His utility for bidding is

$$U(\text{bid}) = (0.5)(57) + (0.5)(96) = 76.5 \text{ utiles.}$$

The utility of not bidding is $U(\$0) = 78$ utiles, so manager 1 would not bid in this situation, even though the expected profit from bidding is $25,000, as you can readily calculate. A risk avoider will have a utility curve which increases at a slower and slower rate with increasing monetary value.

The next utility curve, that of manager 2, is a linear function. He is what is sometimes referred to as an "EMV'er." That is, he makes his decisions strictly on the basis of expected monetary values. Facing the same situation as manager 1, his utility for −$50,000 is 33 utiles and his utility for $100,000 is 83 utiles. His utility for bidding would be

$$U(\text{bid}) = (0.5)(33) + (0.5)(83) = 58 \text{ utiles},$$

which is precisely his utility for a gain of $25,000, the EMV of bidding.

The utility curve of manager 3 shows that he is a "risk taker," since his utility function increases at a faster and faster rate with increasing monetary value. He may be willing to take a gamble even when its expected value is less than that of a sure thing. Suppose, for example, his company is in the process of suing another company for $150,000. His company's lawyers believe they have a probability of 0.6 of winning the suit and 0.4 probability of getting nothing. The other company has offered to settle out of court for $100,000. Manager 3 would not favor this, because, in his subjective judgment, the utility of the settlement, 63 utiles, is less than the utility of the suit:

$$U(\text{suit}) = (0.6)\, U(\$150,000) + (0.4)\, U(\$0)$$
$$= (0.6)(100) + (0.4)(30.5) = 72.2.$$

On an expected value basis, however,

$$E(\text{suit}) = (0.6)(150,000) + (0.4)(0) = \$90,000,$$

so the value of the settlement is greater than the expected value of the suit. Risk avoiders would tend to favor the settlement. As a matter of interest, manager 3 would not favor a settlement until it exceeded $120,000, which has a utility just over 72 utiles.

There is no intent to imply that every individual will have, in a particular situation, a utility curve similar to one of the three curves in Figure 5.3. In many cases, a utility function will be a combination of these curves. An individual may be a risk taker for small amounts and a risk avoider for large amounts. Thus, he or she may be willing to risk $100 or so gambling at Las Vegas, knowing that the odds favor the "house," and at the same time pay insurance premiums which are larger than expected losses, in order to avoid the possibility of large losses.

5.7   IMPLICATIONS OF UTILITY

Some years ago, the results were reported from a study of some 100 businessmen in decision-making positions at a large company.[1] Each man was asked

[1]R. O. Swalm, "Utility Theory—Insights into Risk Taking," *Harvard Business Review*, vol. 44 (1966): pp. 123–136.

to state the maximum single amount he might recommend spending in any one year. His "planning horizon" was defined as twice this amount. Using the standard gamble technique, his utility function was then defined over a range from a positive amount equal to his planning horizon down to a negative amount equal to about one-half his planning horizon.

Although it was found that there were marked differences in attitudes toward risk, ranging from extremely conservative to highly speculative, most managers tended to be risk avoiders. In addition, many of the utility functions were quite similar in their general shape, even though the planning horizons ranged from $50,000 to $24,000,000. There was also a rather consistent pattern of high aversion to losses. Thus, as a fairly typical example, a manager with a planning horizon of $100,000 might have the same number of positive utiles for a gain of $100,000 as negative utiles for a loss of, say, $30,000, with $0 having a utility of 0 utiles. If this were so, he would not recommend a proposal with an even chance of $100,000 profit or $50,000 loss, since that would have a lower utility than doing nothing.

It seems clear that most individual managers, judging from the shapes of their utility functions, are strongly motivated by self-preservation, because large losses tend to look bad on the manager's record, even when balanced by even larger gains. If, however, a company had a number of opportunities with an even chance of gaining $100,000 or losing $50,000, it would be well advised to take as many opportunities as it could possibly get, assuming that these monetary amounts were relatively small by company standards. The larger the number of independent profitable (based on EMV) risky ventures, the smaller the chance of incurring a net loss.

The utility of money, as a concept, appears to become important whenever the monetary amounts become significant in terms of what the individual (or company) possesses in the way of discretionary funds or compared to the funds generally handled over the customary planning period. If these conditions do not apply, then decisions should be based on EMV. As stated earlier, decisions based on expected monetary value indicate that, knowingly or unknowingly, the decision maker is simply employing a linear utility function.

5.8   DECISION TREE ANALYSIS

In the previous chapter, we showed the decision tree approach to the analysis of multistage decision problems. In Example 4.5, we determined the optimal marketing strategy for Fadco Manufacturing Company based on maximizing EMV. As we now know, we had therefore tacitly assumed that Fadco's utility function was linear. Suppose we rework that example with a nonlinear utility function. For convenience, we will restate the problem.

EXAMPLE 5.3

Fadco Manufacturing Company is involved in the development of a new regional product. This product is of such a nature that it will tend to be either quite successful or quite unsuccessful. If the product is successful, it is expected to gross $100,000; if unsuccessful, only $20,000. Fadco is faced with an immediate decision as to one of three possible choices.

1. Test market the product, at a cost of $10,000.
2. Immediately market the product regionally, at a cost of $50,000.
3. Drop the product.

If the product is test marketed, the results will be classified as favorable or unfavorable, and then a decision must be made whether to market the product regionally or drop it. If the test marketing results are favorable, management estimates that the probability of success in the regional market is 0.80; if unfavorable, the estimated success probability is only 0.30. From past experience, Fadco estimates that there is a 50–50 chance of a favorable test marketing result and a probability of 0.45 of a successful direct regional marketing, if test marketing is bypassed. If Fadco's current utility function for money is as shown in Figure 5.4, what course of action should Fadco pursue?

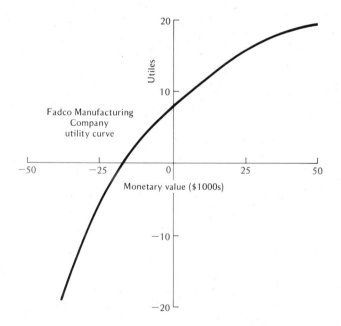

Figure 5.4

The first step is to construct a decision tree, as shown in Figure 5.5, to relate the decision forks, chance forks, and associated monetary values. (To review the details involved in the construction of this decision tree, see Example 4.5.) Figure 5.5 is a copy of Figure 4.4 (minus the formal labeling of acts and events), with an additional column at the right showing the conversion of the net profit values into their corresponding utility values. From this point on, we consider only utiles, rather than dollars, but we handle the reduction of the decision tree in exactly the same way as we did before.

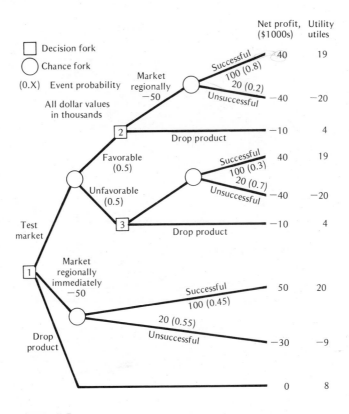

Figure 5.5

In Figure 5.6 is shown the initial reduction of the original decision tree of Figure 5.5. The decisions at decision forks 2 and 3 are unchanged from those of the original problem, based on EMV. If Fadco test markets, it should market regionally if the test market results are favorable; it should drop the product if the test market results are unfavorable.

In the completely reduced tree of Figure 5.7, observe that the most favorable strategy is now to drop the product. On an EMV basis, Fadco had found that test marketing was preferable. Why the change in strategy? The answer is not difficult. With Fadco's present utility function, the firm would be unwilling to incur the expense of test marketing when faced with an even chance of getting an unfavorable result and then dropping the product. From the standpoint of utility, an unfavorable result is more heavily weighted than a favorable result, even though the favorable result has a higher EMV.

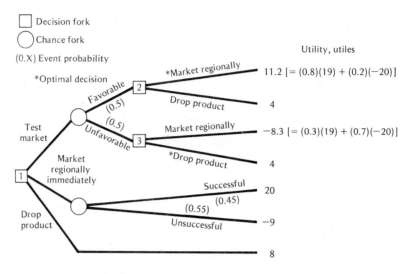

Figure 5.6

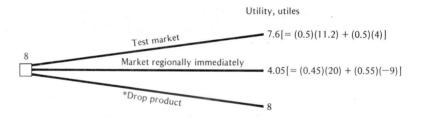

Figure 5.7

At this point, a sensitivity analysis could be performed, just as in Chapter 4, to test the sensitivity of the decision to changes in the subjective probability values or changes in the value of other problem variables.

5.9   DECISION MAKING WITH MINIMAL INFORMATION

In many situations, any one of a set of mutually exclusive and collectively exhaustive events may occur, and a choice must be made between several alternative acts. If we have no knowledge of event probabilities, we cannot make a decision based on either EMV or expected utility. In this situation, we would have to turn to other decision criteria, and we will now discuss briefly some of the decision criteria which have been suggested. First, however, we must put forth a strong disclaimer for the use of such criteria.

It is difficult to visualize a situation where the event probabilities are completely unknown. Some information, however slight, is almost always available from which a set of subjective event probabilities can be developed, perhaps using a method similar to that detailed in Chapter 3. Interestingly enough, Halter and Dean have demonstrated that each of the criteria to be discussed is, in some sense, logically inconsistent. Furthermore, they show that each is equivalent to assuming a subjective probability distribution of the events.[2] If we then allow the usage of subjective probabilities, we can optimize on the basis of expected value, whether it be profit, opportunity loss, or utility.

Coverage of these decision criteria is solely from the standpoint of familiarization with some of the approaches that have been used. These criteria are best illustrated with examples.

EXAMPLE 5.4

A farmer is attempting to decide which of three crops he should plant on his one-hundred-acre farm. The profit from each is dependent on the rainfall during the growing season. He has categorized the amount of rainfall as substantial, moderate, or light. He estimates his profit for each crop as shown in the table. He wishes to plant only one crop, the "best" one.

	Average Profit ($)		
Rainfall	Crop A	Crop B	Crop C
Substantial	7000	2500	4000
Moderate	3500	3500	4000
Light	1000	4000	3000

In the absence of any event probabilities, the farmer can make his choice based on any of several possible decision criteria. We will now discuss four of the better known decision criteria which have been proposed for such a situation.

1. Maximax—choose the act which maximizes the maximum profit or minimizes the minimum loss for any one event. In this example, the farmer would plant crop A, which has the maximum profit of $7000 *if* rainfall should be substantial. This criterion is very optimistic (the "best of all possible worlds" approach) and represents a dangerously narrow viewpoint.
2. Maximin—choose the act which maximizes the minimum achievable profit or

[2]A. N. Halter and G. W. Dean, *Decisions under Uncertainty with Research Applications* (Cincinnati: South-Western Publishing Company, 1971), pp. 82–93.

minimizes the maximum possible loss. Using this criterion, the farmer would note that the minimum profit from crop A is $1000, from crop B is $2500, and from crop C is $3000. He would therefore choose crop C, with the maximum of these minimum values, since he would then expect no less than $3000 profit regardless of the amount of rainfall, whether it be substantial, moderate, or light. This criterion is a rather conservative and pessimistic one, as it involves protection against the worst that can happen. (Incidentally, this criterion is frequently referred to as minimax, even for a profit problem, but it should not be confused with the criterion of minimax regret, to be discussed shortly.)

3. Equal likelihood, or Laplace—if there is no reason to consider any one event more likely than another, all events should be considered equally likely. With n events, each event thus has a probability of $1/n$. Using these probabilities, we then choose the act with the highest expected profit or the lowest expected loss. Since all events are equally weighted, we can simply add for each act the profits or losses for all the events and then divide by the number of events. Thus, the expected profit, in dollars, of crop A would be 11,500/3, that of crop B, 10,000/3, and that of crop C, 11,000/3. The farmer would then choose crop A, with an expected profit of $3833.

4. Minimax regret—for each conditional profit or cost value, we define a regret value equal to the difference between that value and the most favorable value we could have obtained if we had known that particular event would actually occur. We then select that act which minimizes the maximum regret. As you may already have perceived, "regret" is, in this context, just the same as conditional opportunity loss. We construct a regret table, as shown below, find the maximum regret for each act, and then choose that act with the minimum of the maximum regret values.

	Regret ($)		
Rainfall	Crop A	Crop B	Crop C
Substantial	0	4500	3000
Moderate	500	500	0
Light	3000	0	1000

The maximum regret if crop A or crop C is planted would be $3000; that for crop B would be $4500. Using the minimax regret criterion, the farmer would be indifferent to planting crop A or crop C, since, regardless of the rainfall, he could never do worse than make $3000 less profit than if he had perfect information. With crop B, however, he would make $4500 less profit than the maximum possible, if substantial rainfall were to occur.

Suppose we now take a cost problem with unknown probabilities and evaluate the choice of the best act under the different decision criteria just presented.

EXAMPLE 5.5

A manufacturing company is concerned with the possibility of a steel strike. It will cost an extra $10,000 to acquire an adequate stockpile. If there is a strike and the company has not stockpiled, management estimates an additional expense of $50,000 in lost sales, late order charges, and so forth. Should the company stockpile or not?

Let us set up a conditional cost table and then apply the previous decision criteria.

	Conditional Costs	
	Act	
Event	A_1 (Stockpile)	A_2 (Don't stockpile)
E_1 (Strike)	$10,000	$50,000
E_2 (No strike)	10,000	0

1. Maximax—in a cost problem, the maximax criterion really means "minimin." We take the minimum of the minimum costs of all acts. Here, the minimum cost of A_1 is $10,000 and the minimum cost of act A_2 is $0. Therefore, the company would choose not to stockpile, with a cost of $0.
2. Minimax—the minimum of the maximum costs would be taken. The maximum cost for act A_1 is $10,000, but the maximum cost for act A_2 is $50,000. The company should stockpile, at a cost of $10,000, since this is preferable to the maximum possible cost of $50,000 if it does not stockpile.
3. Equal likelihood—if both events were equally likely, the expected cost of act A_1 would obviously be $10,000, and the expected cost of act A_2 would be $25,000. The company would choose to stockpile if it believed there was a 50–50 chance of a strike.
4. Minimax regret—considering each event in turn and recalling that the act with minimum cost has zero regret, the regret table is shown here.

	Regret Values	
	Act	
Event	A_1 (Stockpile)	A_2 (Don't stockpile)
E_1 (Strike)	$ 0	$40,000
E_2 (No strike)	10,000	0

The maximum regret for act A_1 is $10,000, and for act A_2 $40,000. The company would minimize the maximum regret by stockpiling, with a maximum regret of $10,000.

In this problem, since there are only two events, we can readily solve for the preferred act, based on EMV, as a function of the event probabilities. This is the logical approach to the analysis of this problem. Thus, if the costs are expressed as negative profits and p is the probability of a strike,

$$E(A_1) = -10,000p + (-10,000)(1 - p) = -\$10,000,$$
$$E(A_2) = -50,000p + (0)(1 - p) = -\$50,000p.$$

Thus, the company's decision should be:

$$\text{For } p \leqslant 0.2, \text{ choose act 2,}$$
$$p > 0.2, \text{ choose act 1.}$$

It boils down to this, using sensitivity analysis: if the company feels that the odds against a strike are at least 4 to 1, it should not stockpile; otherwise, it should stockpile.

EXERCISES

5.1   Describe a business situation where a decision maker faces a decision under uncertainty and where a decision based on maximizing the expected monetary value cannot be made. How do you think the decision maker would make the required decision?

5.2   In a situation involving a probabilistic distribution of events, where the monetary value of each event is a known value for each of several possible decisions, why is it not always reasonable to choose that decision which maximizes EMV?

5.3   A classified advertisement offers for sale a letter supposedly written by a famous aviator. If the letter is authentic, it could easily be sold for $500; if it is not, its value is zero. After a careful inspection of the letter, you believe it to be authentic with probability 0.8. If your utility function for money is linear, what should your highest offer for the letter be?

5.4   Suppose you are offered a choice between lotteries A and B.

Lottery A: You win $10,000 (with probability 1.0).
Lottery B: You win $50,000 with probability 0.10.
                You win $10,000 with probability 0.89.
                You win $0 with probability 0.01.

Which lottery would you choose? Now make a choice between lotteries C and D.

Lottery C: You win $10,000 with probability 0.11.
                You win $0 with probability 0.89

Lottery D: You win $50,000 with probability 0.10.
             You win $0 with probability 0.90.

Prove that, if you chose lottery A, then you should have chosen lottery C, and if you chose lottery B, then you should have chosen lottery D. If you selected A and D or B and C, explain your choices. In light of the proof, would you change your choices? If not, why not?

5.5   Explain how a value is established for the utility of a single monetary amount
      (a)   using the certainty equivalent technique.
      (b)   using the standard gamble technique.
      If you actually were attempting to determine the utility function of a business executive, which technique would you prefer to use? Why?

5.6   A young entrepreneuer, E, has a utility of 0.5 for the status quo (no loss, no gain). E's net worth is $50,000, and her utility for complete bankruptcy is zero. An opportunity arises for E to gain $100,000 which has a utility, for her, of 1.0.
      (a)   Plot three points of E's utility function on a graph. Connect the three points to form E's utility curve, as in Figure 5.1.
      (b)   E assesses the chances of the $100,000 gain to be 0.4 and chances of a $50,000 loss to be 0.6. Using E's utility curve drawn in part (a), will she take this investment opportunity? Why or why not?

5.7   A parcel of land is offered for sale. The land is presently zoned for agriculture, but rumors have been circulating that this parcel will be rezoned for commercial use, that is, for a shopping center. As agricultural land, the parcel is worth $50,000; as commercial land its value is $250,000. What is the smallest probability of commercial rezoning that you would require to offer $100,000 for the parcel if your utility for $150,000 is 10 utiles, for $0 is 0 utiles, and for −$50,000 is −10 utiles?

5.8   A promoter of world championship prize fights has the following utilities.

	No Fight	Fight in Bad Location	Fight in Good Location
Cash value	0	−$1,000,000	+$5,000,000
Utility	100	0	1000

Unfortunately, the promoter's best fighter likes unusual locations and insists on choice of location.
      (a)   What is the highest probability of this fighter's choosing a bad location that would allow the promoter to sign a contract with him? [*Hint:* Use the standard gamble technique.]
      (b)   For the maximum probability value in (a), what would be the EMV of this contract?
      (c)   How would you categorize the promoter's attitude toward risk?
      (d)   If the promoter's utility for money were linear, at what probability would he be indifferent to signing the contract?

5.9   The Triumph Toy Company is bringing out a new type of animated doll.

Triumph is attempting to decide as to whether to bring out a full, partial, or minimum product line. The company has categorized three possible levels of product acceptance and has estimated its probability of occurrence. Management will make its decision on the basis of maximizing the expected utility of the anticipated profit from the first year of production. The relevant product data is shown in the accompanying table.

Product Acceptance	Probability	Anticipated First-Year Profit, ($1000s) Product Line		
		Full	Partial	Minimal
Good	0.2	80	70	50
Fair	0.4	50	45	40
Poor	0.4	−25	−10	0

Triumph has evaluated its utility function, in terms of the first-year profit, as follows.

Profit, $1000s	80	70	60	50	40	30	20	10	0	−10	−20	−30
Utility, utiles	40	37	34	30	25	20	14	7	0	−10	−25	−45

(a) Plot Triumph's utility function for first-year profit values.
(b) Determine the optimal product line. What is its expected utility? What is the dollar amount associated with this utility value? How can this dollar amount be interpreted?
(c) On the basis of maximizing EMV, the optimal decision (as calculated in Exercise 4.13) was to bring out a partial product line, and EMV* was $28,000. Compare your decision in (b), and discuss the reason for any difference.

5.10 For the problem in Exercise 5.9, suppose an advertising campaign could be expected to raise both the probabilities of "good" and "fair" product acceptance by 0.1. Explain how you could determine how much Triumph could spend for this campaign before the company would be indifferent to conducting or not conducting it. Do not perform these calculations. [*Hint:* This is a trial and error process, since all profit values are changed and the utility function is nonlinear.]

5.11 An old comedian's joke refers to a contest with a first prize of a one week-trip to a famous American city and a second prize of a two-week trip to that same city. What does this tell you of the comedian's preferences regarding time spent in that famous city? Can you tell whether the comedian would rather stay at home or travel to that famous city? Discuss.

5.12 The Gnu Products Company has a fairly tight research budget at the moment. The company is considering funding a research project in an area which is rather new to it. Although it is unable to attach meaningful monetary values to the success of this project, it has agreed to characterize the possible outcomes of this project as "successful," "partially successful," or "unsuccessful." If the company does not fund this project, it can use the required funds elsewhere and would prefer to do this, unless the project is successful.

In the evaluation of feelings about the different possible outcomes, the board of directors decides that it would be indifferent to funding the project if the odds were 4 to 1 for the project being successful, rather than unsuccessful. Furthermore, it would also be indifferent to funding the project if there were a 50–50 chance that it would be successful or partially successful.

(a)   Establish a notation for the four possible outcomes and rank them. Arbitrarily assign two utility values and calculate the remaining two values.

(b)   The board of directors believes that, if the project is funded, the probability of it being successful is 0.3, of being partially successful is 0.5, and of being unsuccessful is 0.2. What is their optimal course of action?

(c)   Assign a different set of utility values to two of the outcomes, one of which was not used for the initial assignment in part (a). Recalculate the other two utility values and show that the optimal decision is again the same as that worked out in part (b).

(d)   Assuming that the probability of being unsuccessful remains at 0.2, over what range for the probability of being successful will the board favor funding the project?

5.13   In Example 5.2, involving the politician considering whether to enter the primary:

(a)   His utility for outcome B (he enters and makes a fair showing) is somewhat uncertain. Perform a sensitivity analysis to determine his optimal decision for all feasible values of $U(B)$.

(b)   The utility values are all as given and derived, but all that is known about the probabilities of outcomes A, B, and D is that the odds are 3 to 2 that, if the politician enters and does not make a good showing, he will make a poor showing rather than a fair showing. If p is the probability of making a good showing, over what range of p values should he choose to enter the primary?

5.14   Consider some monetary costs associated with the following risks that you are very possibly insured against:

1.   flood, fire, or wind damage to automobile—$200 loss.
2.   theft of household goods—$1000 loss.
3.   hospitalization due to an accident—$4000 expense.

(a)   On an annual basis, how much would it be worth to you to protect against these specific dollar risks by obtaining annual insurance which would pay for the entire amount of loss or cost?

(b)   What is the approximate estimate of the annual probability with which you face each of these risks?

(c)   For each of these risks, how does the amount you would be willing to pay annually for insurance compare with the expected value of the loss? Discuss the implications from the standpoint of your utility for losses.

5.15   Comment on this statement in the text: "An individual may be a risk taker for small amounts and a risk avoider for large amounts." Can you explain this phenomena? Sketch a utility function consistent with such a utility preference, and assign arbitrary numerical values for utilities and dollars. Show two sample calculations, one demonstrating risk taking and the other risk avoidance, and explain why they illustrate these characteristics.

5.16   By means of an experiment, we have obtained utility values for selected dollar amounts for Dr. Zero (a well-known professor nicknamed for the usual amount of change she brings to the coffee machine). These values are:

Dollar Amount	Utility
+100,000	1.0
+ 80,000	0.8
+ 60,000	0.5
+ 40,000	0.25
− 20,000	0.0

(a)   Draw a graph of Dr. Zero's utility function.
(b)   From this graph, what is her utility for $50,000?
(c)   Is Dr. Zero a risk lover or a a risk avoider? Explain.
(d)   Use the graph drawn in part (a) to determine if Dr. Zero would use $35,000 of her present funds for an investment with a 0.5 chance of returning $60,000 and a 0.5 chance of losing her entire investment.

5.17   An automobile owner faces the decision as to which deductible amount of comprehensive insurance coverage to select. Comprehensive coverage includes losses due to fire, vehicle theft, vandalism, and the forces of nature. The possible choices are zero deductible coverage for $60 per year or $50 deductible coverage for $45 per year. (The owner pays the first $50 of any loss of at least $50). Considering incidents covered by the comprehensive portion of the policy, the owner feels that the annual chances of more than one such incident are negligible. The probability of no loss is estimated as 0.85. If there is a loss, the owner believes that it will be at least $50.

Some of the owner's utility values are tabulated below.

Amount	− $95	− $60	− $50	− $45	$0
Utility	0.2	0.4	0.45	0.47	0.5

(a)   Sketch the owner's utility curve. Is the owner a risk avoider, an EMV'er, or a risk taker?
(b)   On the basis of the utility curve drawn in part (a), should the owner take the zero deductible or the $50 deductible comprehensive coverage?

5.18   Suppose a small entrepreneur's utility function for *total* assets is

$$U(A) = 18A - 0.08A^2 \quad \text{for} \quad 0 \leq A \leq 100,$$

where A represents his total assets in $1000s.

(a) Plot the entrepreneur's utility function. How would you classify his attitude toward risk?

(b) Suppose his total assets are currently $20,000. Should he accept a business opportunity which has a probability of 0.6 of netting a profit of $20,000 and a probability of 0.4 of resulting in a $20,000 loss?

(c) Should he accept this opportunity if his current assets are $80,000?

(d) Compare your answers to parts (b) and (c). Does this entrepreneur's behavior seem reasonable? Explain.

5.19 Suppose a company has several independent investment opportunities, each of which has an equal chance of gaining $100,000 or losing $60,000. What is the probability that the company will lose money on two such investments? on three such investments? on four such investments?

If a company has a number of independent investment opportunities, in each of which the financial risk is relatively small, compared to its overall asset position, why should the company try to maximize EMV, rather than expected utility? What frequently happens, however, to thwart this in actual practice?

5.20 The Jensun Company has been offered a study contract to refine a device for reducing automobile exhaust emissions. Following the study contract, there will be awards for prototype production contracts for a few preliminary models and then awards for production contracts. All contracts are for fixed dollar amounts; the study contract is for $10,000, the prototype contract for $10,000, and the production contract for $50,000.

Jensun has decided to consider two levels of effort, high and low, on the study contract. A high level of effort will cost more, but it will increase the company's chances of getting the prototype contract. The probability of getting the production contract depends on the level of effort on the study contract and also on the level of effort (again high or low) on the prototype contract, if one is received. If Jensun receives a production contract, it will incur additional production expenses unless a high level of effort was employed on the prototype contract. All this information, with probability and cost figures, is summarized in the accompanying table.

Study Contract Level of Effort	Probability of Winning Prototype Contract	Prototype Contract Level of Effort	Probability of Winning Production Contract	Cost ($1000s)		
				Study Contract	Prototype Contract	Additional Production Expense
High	0.7	High	0.8	15	10	0
		Low	0.6	15	6	5
		None*	0.2	15	0	10
Low	0.4	High	0.7	5	10	0
		Low	0.5	5	6	5
		None*	0.1	5	0	15

*Prototype contract not received.

Jensun has decided to maximize expected utility, based on its utility function, as tabulated below, for changes in its current asset position.

Profit, $1000s	60	50	40	30	20	10	0	-5
Utility, utiles	10	9.7	9.1	8.0	6.4	4.0	0	-4.0

Plot a utility curve in order to be able to determine the required utility values. Develop a decision tree and use it to find the optimal strategy. Specify this strategy completely.

5.21 Given the following payoff or profit matrix,

		Acts	
Events	1	2	3
1	20	60	40
2	30	10	40
3	80	50	40

For each of the following decision criteria, state the preferred action and specify the values leading to its selection.
(a) Maximin.
(b) Maximax.
(c) Equal likelihood.
(d) Minimax regret.

5.22 Redo the preceding problem, assuming that the table entries are costs instead of profits.

5.23 In the Triumph Toy Company problem, Exercise 5.9, suppose that the product acceptance probabilities are not known, so that the available information is as shown below.

	Anticipated First-year Profit ($1000s)		
	Product Line		
Product Acceptance	Full	Partial	Minimal
Good	80	70	50
Fair	50	45	40
Poor	-25	-10	0

Determine the optimal decision under each of the following decision criteria and show how you arrived at it.
(a) Maximax.
(b) Maximin.
(c) Equal likelihood.
(d) Minimax regret.

Discuss the difference between these results. What decision would you make? Why?

5.24   A company manufacturing large electrical equipment is anticipating the
possibility of a total or a partial copper strike in the near future. It is attempting
to decide whether to stockpile a large amount of copper, at an additional cost of
$50,000; a small amount, costing an additional $20,000; or to stockpile no
additional copper at all. (The stockpiling costs, consisting of excess storage,
holding, and handling costs and so forth, are over and above the actual material
costs.)

   If there is a partial strike, the company estimates that an additional cost of
$50,000 for delayed orders will be incurred only if there is no stockpile at all. If a
total strike occurs, the cost of delayed orders is estimated at $100,000 if there is
only a small stockpile and $200,000 with no stockpile.

   The company has no real feeling for the probability of either a total or
partial strike. What decision would they make under each of the following
decision criteria? State how your decision was determined.

(a)   Maximax.
(b)   Maximin.
(c)   Equal likelihood.
(d)   Minimax regret.

What do you feel is the "best" decision in this situation? Explain.

CHAPTER 6

DECISION MAKING WITH ADDITIONAL INFORMATION

In decision-making situations discussed earlier, we were generally faced with making a single optimal decision based on some measure of value, either EMV or expected utility. Now, we will consider situations where it is possible to obtain additional information on which to base a decision. Since such information almost always has a cost associated with it, we will be interested in determining, before making the required expenditure, whether this information is worth its cost. Also, if there is flexibility in the choice of the amount of additional information, we wish to determine the optimal amount of such information. We refer to the process of obtaining additional information as sampling, regardless of the actual form it takes.

If we do decide to obtain additional information, we will be interested in incorporating this information into the decision process. This will be done by revising the event probabilities through the use of Bayes' theorem and then using these revised probabilities to recalculate the expected value of each possible act. Then, at this point, we can again evaluate the worth of yet additional information (if such information is available) and make the decision whether or not its cost is justified. This process continues until additional information is either not available or no longer economically justifiable. At that point, we make what is called a *terminal decision*, choosing the act which is optimal, based on all the information previously incorporated into the analysis.

In this chapter, we will investigate the Bayesian approach to the analysis of decisions involving discrete probability distributions of events. An adequate treatment of Bayesian decision making when the events are represented by continuous probability distributions is beyond the scope of this text.

6.1 SAMPLING WITH A FIXED AMOUNT OF INFORMATION

We will start by taking an example problem considered earlier and will first find the optimal solution to the problem as originally presented. Then, we will incorporate a fixed amount of additional information and solve the problem again. Next, we will show that, prior to obtaining this information, we could have analyzed the possible results and calculated what is called the expected value of sample information, thus enabling us to compare the actual cost of the information with its expected worth.

EXAMPLE 6.1

An investor has decided to invest a certain sum in one of two stocks, either Washington Ornamental Works (ticker symbol WOW), which is somewhat speculative, or Tennessee Underwear Factories (ticker symbol TUF), which is fairly conservative. Over the six-month period of interest to this investor, she feels that the economy will either advance or stagnate, with about a 40 percent chance it will advance. If the economy advances, the investor anticipates a $2000 profit if she invests in WOW stock or a $1400 profit with TUF stock. However, if the economy stagnates, she expects WOW stock to lose $300 and TUF stock to gain only $200. The investor wishes to maximize her expected monetary value.

Optimal Decision without Additional Information

This problem is the same as Example 4.1, so we label the events and acts just as we did in Table 4.1, which is repeated here as Table 6.1.

Table 6.1 Investor's Payoff Table

	Conditional Profit ($)	
	Act	
Event, E_i	A_1 (Buy WOW)	A_2 (Buy TUF)
E_1 (Economy advances)	2000	1400
E_2 (Economy stagnates)	−300	200

We can determine the optimal act by either finding the act with maximum expected monetary value (EMV*) or minimum expected opportunity loss (EOL*), but in the type of Bayesian analyses to be performed, we will find that the concept of opportunity losses is particularly meaningful. We will therefore work almost exclusively with opportunity losses rather than profits or costs. It should be pointed out, however, that these analyses could be performed without using opportunity losses.

The opportunity losses in this problem can be determined directly from the data of Table 6.1 and are shown as Table 6.2 (which is a copy of Table 4.4). Note that we refer to the probabilities given or estimated at the start of an analysis as *prior probabilities*, just as we did in the discussion of Bayes' theorem in Chapter 2.

Table 6.2   Investor's EOL Calculations

Event E_i	Prior Probability $P(E_i)$	Conditional Opportunity Loss ($)		Weighted Opportunity Loss ($)	
		Act		Act	
		A_1	A_2	A_1	A_2
E_1	0.40	0	600	0	240
E_2	0.60	500	0	300	0
				EOL 300	240

With no additional information, the investor should choose act A_2, buy TUF stock. EOL* = \$240 = EVPI, so she would not be willing to pay more than that amount if she could in some way get perfect information whether the economy will advance or stagnate in the next six months.

Optimal Decision with Additional Information

Before making her decision as to which stock to purchase, the investor notices an advertisement extolling the advisory services of the Astounding Investment Company. Calling the toll-free number, she is informed that, for a fee of \$100, AIC will supply her with its prediction of the movement of the economy in the next six months. AIC claims that, when the economy was at a similar point in the past, it correctly predicted the trend 80 percent of the time when the economy advanced and 70 percent of the time when the economy stagnated.

A prediction by AIC can be considered as the outcome of the statistical experiment in which it evaluates the state of the economy. To denote the possible outcomes of this experiment,

let B_1 = prediction that economy advances,
   B_2 = prediction that economy stagnates.

The probability information supplied by AIC is in the form of conditional probabilities often called "likelihoods" in statistical terminology. The given likelihoods, along with their complementary values, are displayed in Table 6.3.

If we know that event E_i has occurred, then one and only one of the outcomes B_1 and B_2 must occur, since these outcomes are mutually exclusive and, by definition in this problem, collectively exhaustive. Thus, in Table 6.3, observe that the sum of the probabilities in each *row* equals 1.0. [We demonstrated this relationship in Equation

(2.6).] The probabilities in a given *column* are unrelated, because each is conditional upon the occurrence of a different event.

Table 6.3 AIC Prediction Likelihoods

	Prediction	
Event, E_i	B_1—Economy advances $P(B_1 \mid E_i)$	B_2—Economy stagnates $P(B_2 \mid E_i)$
E_1 (Economy advances)	0.80	0.20
E_2 (Economy stagnates)	0.30	0.70

Impressed with AIC's apparent expertise, the investor decides to pay the fee. A few days later, AIC informs her that, in its considered judgment, the economy will stagnate in the next six months. With this additional information, the investor can now revise the prior event probabilities to get what we now refer to as *posterior probabilities*. These posterior probabilities can then be used to recalculate the EOLs and determine the optimal act, given the additional information (the prediction).

Table 6.4 shows the calculation of the revised probabilities, given a prediction that the economy will stagnate, outcome B_2. The calculations are entirely similar to those performed in Table 2.4, the tabular construction illustrating Bayes' theorem in Chapter 2.

Table 6.4 Probability Revision with Outcome B_2 (Prediction Economy Stagnates)

(1) Event E_i	(2) Prior Probability $P(E_i)$	(3) Likelihood $P(B_2 \mid E_i)$	(4) Joint Probability $P(B_2 \cap E_i)$	(5) Posterior Probability $P(E_i \mid B_2)$
E_1	0.40	0.20	0.08	0.16
E_2	0.60	0.70	0.42	0.84
			$P(B_2) = 0.50$	1.00

In Table 6.4, the first two columns are self-explanatory. The likelihoods in column (3) came from Table 6.3. They are the conditional probabilities that the outcome representing the result of additional information would have occurred, given, in turn, each of the possible events. Column (4) joint probabilities are obtained by multiplying the probabilities in columns (2) and (3), since, by the rule of multiplication, $P(B_2 \cap E_i) = P(B_2 \mid E_i) P(E_i)$. Since the events E_1 and E_2 are mutually exclusive and collectively exhaustive, the sum of the probabilities of the joint events $B_2 \cap E_1$ and $B_2 \cap E_2$ must be equal to the marginal probability of B_2, $P(B_2)$. $P(B_2)$ is the probability that the particular sample result, namely outcome B_2, would occur, given the combination of the prior probabilities and the likelihoods of the sample result, as presented in Table 6.3. Finally, in column (5), the posterior (revised) probabilities are calculated according to Bayes' theorem, by dividing the column (4) values by the marginal probability $P(B_2)$. (This process of dividing each number in a column of numbers by the sum of all such numbers is known as a normalizing process. The sum of these normalized values must always be 1.0, and thus these values constitute a probability distribution of the events E_1 and E_2.)

With AIC's prediction of a stagnant economy, observe that the odds favoring a stagnant economy have jumped from 3 to 2 (0.60 to 0.40) to more than 5 to 1 (0.84 to 0.16). This certainly seems reasonable, since AIC's predictions have proved correct most of the time.

Now, having calculated the posterior event probabilities, we use these revised probabilities to recalculate the EOLs of the permissible acts. As shown in Table 6.5, we do this in exactly the same way as for the prior probabilities, with the expected values now being based on the posterior probabilities. When the posterior probabilities are used to recalculate EOL or EMV values, we consider them new marginal probabilities which replace the prior marginal probabilities. Therefore, the notation used for these revised probabilities is again $P(E_i)$, rather than $P(E_i|B_j)$.

Table 6.5 EOL Values Based on Revised Event Probabilities, Given Outcome B_2 (Prediction Economy Stagnates)

Event E_i	Revised Probability $P(E_i)$	Conditional Opportunity Loss ($) Act A_1	Conditional Opportunity Loss ($) Act A_2	Weighted Opportunity Loss ($) Act A_1	Weighted Opportunity Loss ($) Act A_2
E_1	0.16	0	600	0	96
E_2	0.84	500	0	420	0
			EOL	420	96

From the results of the calculations with the revised probabilities, act A_2 is optimal, and the investor should buy TUF stock, just as she was about to do before she saw AIC's advertisement. Now she wonders, naturally enough, if she just threw her money away when she did business with AIC. After all, she would have made the same decision without its advice.

The investor's point is well taken. The "sample" information she received did, indeed, turn out to be worthless. But, the actual outcome, the prediction of a stagnant economy, was only one of two possibilities. If the other outcome had occurred, the prediction of an advancing economy, the information she purchased might well have turned out to be worthwhile. We will now show, through what is called *prepos-*

terior analysis, that the investor could have determined, before buying the advisory service, whether it was economically sound to do so.

Preposterior Analysis

Before paying AIC, the investor could have evaluated what would have happened if each possible outcome (prediction) had occurred. Since there were only two possible outcomes, and one of them has already been evaluated, only the other one remains to be analyzed. The probability revision for outcome B_1 is developed in Table 6.6.

Table 6.6 Probability Revision with Outcome B_1 (Prediction Economy Advances)

Event E_i	Prior Probability $P(E_i)$	Likelihood $P(B_1 \mid E_i)$	Joint Probability $P(B_1 \cap E_i)$	Posterior Probability $P(E_i \mid B_1)$
E_1	0.40	0.80	0.32	0.64
E_2	0.60	0.30	0.18	0.36
			$P(B_1) = \overline{0.50}$	$\overline{1.00}$

As would be expected, the prediction of an advancing economy changes the event probabilities considerably. The odds on an advancing economy change from 2 to 3 to nearly 2 to 1. Now, using these posterior probabilities, the EOLs are recalculated in Table 6.7.

Table 6.7 EOL Values Based on Revised Event Probabilities, Given Outcome B_1 (Prediction Economy Advances)

Event E_i	Revised Probability $P(E_i)$	Conditional Opportunity Loss ($) Act A_1	A_2	Weighted Opportunity Loss ($) Act A_1	A_2
E_1	0.64	0	600	0	384
E_2	0.36	500	0	180	0
				EOL $\overline{180}$	$\overline{384}$

The prediction of an advancing economy, outcome B_1, would change the optimal act from A_2 to A_1, buy WOW stock. This certainly seems reasonable, since WOW is clearly preferred over TUF if the economy advances.

At this point in the analysis, we are ready to determine the expected value of the information obtainable from AIC.

For each possible outcome, we take the posterior EOL of the optimal act, given that outcome, and weight it by the probability the outcome occurs. The sum of these weighted values is EOL'*, the *preposterior EOL after sampling*. (The "prime" symbol in EOL'* is used to indicate a value obtained after sampling.) *The preposterior EOL after sampling is the expected opportunity loss after sampling, as calculated before actually taking the sample.* The determination of EOL'* takes into account each possible sample outcome and its probability of occurrence. The calculation of EOL'* for this problem is shown in Table 6.8. The outcome probabilities for B_1 and B_2 come, respectively, from the probability revision calculations of Tables 6.6 and 6.4; the optimal EOL' values are from Tables 6.7 and 6.5. It is purely coincidental that the outcome probabilities are both 0.5.

Table 6.8 Preposterior EOL Incorporating Information from AIC

Outcome B_i	Outcome Probability $P(B_i)$	Optimal Act	Optimal EOL' ($)	Weighted EOL' ($)
B_1	0.50	A_1	180	90
B_2	0.50	A_2	96	48
			EOL'*	138

Preposterior analysis permits measurement of the economic value of additional information prior to purchasing that information. Knowing the preposterior opportunity loss after incorporating the additional information (the prediction), we can now calculate, before sampling, the *expected value of sample information*. EVSI is just the expected reduction in opportunity loss through sampling.

$$\text{EVSI} = \text{EOL*} - \text{EOL'*}.$$

(Some texts use EVII, the expected value of imperfect information, since sampling is not always involved. This example is a case in point. However, we will use EVSI because it is the most common designation.)

In this example,

$$\text{EVSI} = 240 - 138 = \$102.$$

Given the sampling cost, denoted as SC, we can finally determine whether the information was worth the price paid for it, on an expected value basis. ENGS, the *expected net gain from sampling*, is expressed as

$$\text{ENGS} = \text{EVSI} - \text{SC}.$$

If AIC's services are purchased,

$$\text{ENGS} = 102 - 100 = \$2.$$

For the investor, the price of the investment service was, indeed, reasonable, although hardly a bargain. For her \$100 investment, the expected return is \$102, the expected reduction in opportunity loss (and also the expected increase in profit) contributed by the additional information supplied by AIC.

To summarize the approach, the investor should have performed the preposterior analysis before buying the investment service. Since the preposterior analysis showed that sampling was economically justified, she should have purchased the service. Then, with outcome B_2, the investor would have selected act A_2, buy TUF stock, based on the results of the preposterior analysis.

In this type of problem, where the amount of additional information obtainable by sampling is fixed and only one sample is feasible, only two decisions are required. The first decision is whether or not to sample and the second is the choice of the optimal act.

Given the events, the prior probabilities associated with those events, the acts, the conditional opportunity loss of each act and event combination, the possible sample outcomes, and the likelihood associated with each combination of event and sample outcome, the procedure is basically as follows.

1. Determine EOL*, the expected opportunity loss of the optimal act prior to sampling.
2. Perform a preposterior analysis to determine EOL'*, the weighted preposterior EOL after sampling, considering all possible sample outcomes and the optimal EOL value associated with each of them.
3. Calculate the expected value of sample information, EVSI (= EOL* − EOL'*). Note that EVSI can never be negative; it must be positive or zero.
   a) If EVSI does not exceed SC, the sampling cost, the expected net gain from sampling, ENGS (= EVSI − SC), is nonpositive, so sampling is not worthwhile. Select the optimal act determined in step 1.
   b) If EVSI exceeds SC, so that ENGS is positive, sampling is worthwhile, so take the sample. Given the particular sample outcome, choose the optimal act, based on the calculations already performed during the analysis.

The entire decision process can be represented by a decision tree. All the basic information in the problem is summarized in the decision tree of Figure 6.1. What a decision tree does not show is the probability revision process itself.

If the initial decision is not to buy the investment service, the choice is between the two possible acts, and A_2, with EOL* = \$240, would be chosen. If the initial decision is to purchase the forecast, the remaining choice depends on which of the two probabilistic outcomes, B_1 or B_2, occurs. In each case, the optimal act is selected as indicated. In the right-hand column of probability values, note that the probabilities associated with purchasing the service are the revised or posterior probabilities. The weighted opportunity loss of the forecast, EOL'*, is $138, so that the expected value of the service (EVSI) is 240 − 138 = $102, as determined previously.

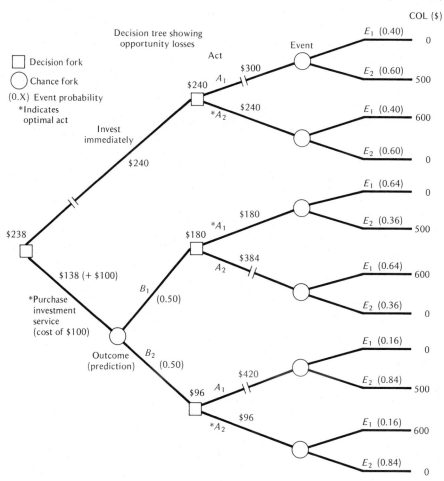

Figure 6.1 Investor's decision tree.

Now, we will consider a second example of a situation where a fixed amount of information is available.

EXAMPLE 6.2

A farmer is attempting to decide which of three crops he should plant on his one-hundred-acre farm. The profit from each crop is strongly dependent on the rainfall during the growing season. He has categorized the amount of rainfall as substantial, moderate, or light. He estimates his profit for each crop as shown in the table.

	Estimated Profit ($)		
Rainfall	Crop A	Crop B	Crop C
Substantial	7000	2500	4000
Moderate	3500	3500	4000
Light	1000	4000	3000

Over the range of dollars involved, the farmer's utility for money is linear, so he wishes to maximize expected profit. Based on the weather in previous seasons and the current projection for the coming season, he estimates the probability of substantial rainfall as 0.2, that of moderate rainfall as 0.3, and that of light rainfall as 0.5.

    a)   From the available data, determine the optimal decision as to which crop to plant.

Let event E_1 = substantial rainfall,
     event E_2 = moderate rainfall,
     event E_3 = light rainfall,
       act A_1 = plant crop A,
       act A_2 = plant crop B,
       act A_3 = plant crop C.

The calculation of EMVs is shown in Table 6.9.

Table 6.9 Farmer's EMV Calculations

Event, E_i	Prior Probability $P(E_i)$	Conditional Profit ($)			Weighted Profit ($)		
		A_1	Act A_2	A_3	A_1	Act A_2	A_3
E_1	0.2	7000	2500	4000	1400	500	800
E_2	0.3	3500	3500	4000	1050	1050	1200
E_3	0.5	1000	4000	3000	500	2000	1500
				EMV	2950	3550	3500

The EMVs in the bottom row of Table 6.9 represent the expected profit in dollars for each act. The maximum EMV, EMV*, is $3550, and the optimal act is A_2, plant crop B. Observe that it would make no sense to plant more than one kind of crop, since the maximum expected profit is clearly obtained by planting all 100 acres with crop B. If crop B were planted each year for a long enough period that event E_1 (substantial rainfall) occurred 20 percent of the time, event E_2 (moderate rainfall) occurred 30 percent of the time, and event E_3 (light rainfall) occurred 50 percent of the time, then we would expect an average profit of $3550. The other two EMVs can be interpreted in a similar fashion.

As discussed earlier, there are advantages to working with opportunity losses, rather than with profits, so Table 6.10 has been developed. The conditional opportunity losses were determined from the conditional profit values in Table 6.9, where the maximum conditional profit for each event has been underlined. The optimal act is again A_2, with EOL* = EOL(A_2) = $1050.

Table 6.10   Farmer's EOL Calculations

		Conditional Opportunity Loss ($)				Weighted Opportunity Loss ($)		
Event E_i	Prior Probability $P(E_i)$	Act A_1	A_2	A_3		Act A_1	A_2	A_3
E_1	0.2	0	4500	3000		0	900	600
E_2	0.3	500	500	0		150	150	0
E_3	0.5	3000	0	1000		1500	0	500
					EOL	1650	1050	1100

Before making his decision about which crop to plant, suppose the farmer finds that Zeta Forecasters, Inc., will make a detailed survey of his current rainfall prospects using its proprietary and highly sophisticated computer program. It will, for a fee of $500, predict whether the rainfall will be substantial, moderate, or light. Furthermore, the company supplies the farmer with information on its prediction accuracy in the past, as shown in Table 6.11.

Table 6.11   Forecast Accuracy of Zeta Forecasters, Inc.

	Rainfall Prediction		
Actual rainfall	Substantial	Moderate	Light
Substantial	0.70	0.25	0.05
Moderate	0.30	0.60	0.10
Light	0.10	0.20	0.70

The probabilities in Table 6.11 are conditional probabilities, namely P(rainfall prediction | actual rainfall). Thus, for example, given that the rainfall actually turned out to be substantial, Zeta had predicted this correctly 70 percent of the time, while 25 percent of the time they had predicted moderate rainfall, and only 5 percent of the time light rainfall. These conditional probabilities, related to the outcome of a statistical experiment, are called likelihoods, as we have noted. To denote the outcomes of the experiment,

let B_1 = forecast of substantial rainfall,
   B_2 = forecast of moderate rainfall,
   B_3 = forecast of light rainfall.

Using the notation established, a table of the likelihood values appears as Table 6.12.

Table 6.12 Likelihood Values, Zeta Fore casters, Inc.

Event, E_i	Forecast Likelihood		
	$P(B_1\|E_i)$	$P(B_2\|E_i)$	$P(B_3\|E_i)$
E_1	0.70	0.25	0.05
E_2	0.30	0.60	0.10
E_3	0.10	0.20	0.70

   b) Perform a complete preposterior analysis and determine whether it would be economical for the farmer to purchase a forecast from Zeta.

Initially, it should be observed that EOL* = $1050 = EVPI, so even a perfect forecast would be worth no more than $1050. As can be seen and as would be expected, Zeta's track record is hardly perfect, but its $500 fee is definitely worth consideration.

For each of the three possible outcomes (forecast results), we will first revise the prior probabilities. Then, using the resultant posterior probabilities, we will calculate the revised EOL values for each outcome. Finally, we will determine the expected value of sample information and the expected net gain from sampling.

Employing the same tabular approach as previously used, the probability revision calculations are performed in Tables 6.13, 6.14, and 6.15. For each outcome, you should compare the posterior and prior probabilities and mentally verify that the shift in probability values seems reasonable. Also note that the marginal outcome probabilities, $P(B_1)$, $P(B_2)$, and $P(B_3)$, sum to 1.0.

Table 6.13   Probability Revision Based on Outcome B_1
(Forecast of Substantial Rainfall)

Event E_i	Prior Probability $P(E_i)$	Likelihood $P(B_1\|E_i)$	Joint Probability $P(B_1 \cap E_i)$	Posterior Probability $P(E_i\|B_1)$
E_1	0.2	0.70	0.14	0.500
E_2	0.3	0.30	0.09	0.321
E_3	0.5	0.10	0.05	0.179
			$P(B_1) = \overline{0.28}$	$\overline{1.000}$

Table 6.14   Probability Revision Based on Outcome B_2
(Forecast of Moderate Rainfall)

Event E_i	Prior Probability $P(E_i)$	Likelihood $P(B_2\|E_i)$	Joint Probability $P(B_2 \cap E_i)$	Posterior Probability $P(E_i\|B_2)$
E_1	0.2	0.25	0.05	0.151
E_2	0.3	0.60	0.18	0.546
E_3	0.5	0.20	0.10	0.303
			$P(B_2) = \overline{0.33}$	$\overline{1.000}$

Table 6.15   Probability Revision Based on Outcome B_3
(Forecast of Light Rainfall)

E_i	Prior Probability $P(E_i)$	Likelihood $P(B_3\|E_i)$	Joint Probability $P(B_3 \cap E_i)$	Posterior Probability $P(E_i\|B_3)$
E_1	0.2	0.05	0.01	0.026
E_2	0.3	0.10	0.03	0.077
E_3	0.5	0.70	0.35	0.897
			$P(B_3) = \overline{0.39}$	$\overline{1.000}$

For each outcome, the revised probabilities are now used to recalculate the EOL values, given the additional information supplied by that outcome. Tables 6.16, 6.17, and 6.18 show these calculations.

Table 6.16   EOL Values Based on Revised Event Probabilities, Given Outcome B_1

Event E_i	Revised Probability $P(E_i)$	Conditional Opportunity Loss ($) Act A_1	A_2	A_3	Weighted Opportunity Loss ($) Act A_1	A_2	A_3
E_1	0.500	0	4500	3000	0	2250	1500
E_2	0.321	500	500	0	160	160	0
E_3	0.179	3000	0	1000	537	0	179
				EOL	697	2410	1679

Table 6.17   EOL Values Based on Revised Event Probabilities, Given Outcome B_2

Event E_i	Revised Probability $P(E_i)$	Conditional Opportunity Loss ($) Act A_1	A_2	A_3	Weighted Opportunity Loss ($) Act A_1	A_2	A_3
E_1	0.151	0	4500	3000	0	680	453
E_2	0.546	500	500	0	273	273	0
E_3	0.303	3000	0	1000	909	0	303
				EOL	1182	953	756

Table 6.18   EOL Values Based on Revised Event Probabilities, Given Outcome B_3

Event E_i	Revised Probability $P(E_i)$	Conditional Opportunity Loss ($) Act A_1	A_2	A_3	Weighted Opportunity Loss ($) Act A_1	A_2	A_3
E_1	0.026	0	4500	3000	0	117	78
E_2	0.077	500	500	0	38	38	0
E_3	0.897	3000	0	1000	2691	0	897
				EOL	2729	155	975

Based on the marginal outcome probabilities from Tables 6.13, 6.14, and 6.15 and on the revised EOL values just determined, the preposterior EOL after sampling, EOL'*, is calculated in Table 6.19.

Table 6.19 Farmer's Preposterior EOL of Forecast

Outcome B_i	Outcome Probability $P(B_i)$	Optimal Act	Optimal EOL' ($)	Weighted EOL' ($)
B_1	0.28	A_1	697	195
B_2	0.33	A_3	756	249
B_3	0.39	A_2	155	60
	1.00		EOL'*	504

From all these results,

$$EVSI = EOL^* - EOL'^*,$$
$$= 1050 - 504 = \$546.$$

Utilizing the calculations already performed, there is another way to find EVSI. The *conditional value of sample information*, CVSI, is the value of sample information conditional upon a particular sample outcome. For a given sample outcome, CVSI is equal to the value *after sampling* of the EOL of the optimal act prior to sampling less the EOL of the optimal act after sampling. The CVSI values are then weighted by the respective outcome probabilities, and the sum of these products is EVSI. Table 6.20 illustrates these computations.

Table 6.20 Calculation of EVSI Using CVSI Values

			EOL after Sampling ($)			
(1) Outcome B_i	(2) Outcome Probability $P(B_i)$	(3) Optimal Act After Sampling	(4) Prior Optimal Act (A_2)	(5) Posterior Optimal Act	(6) CVSI ($) (4) − (5)	(7) Weighted CVSI ($) (2) × (6)
B_1	0.28	A_1	2410	697	1713	481
B_2	0.33	A_3	953	756	197	65
B_3	0.39	A_2	155	155	0	0
	1.00				EVSI	546

The first three columns are the same as those in the preceding table, Table 6.19. For each outcome, column (4) contains the EOL after sampling of act A_2, the prior optimal act, and column (5) contains the EOL of the optimal act after sampling. Starting with the first row, the data in columns (3), (4), and (5) come from Tables 6.16, 6.17, and 6.18, respectively. Each CVSI value in column (6) is the difference between the values in columns (4) and (5). Column (7) values are the CVSI values weighted by the outcome probabilities in column (2).

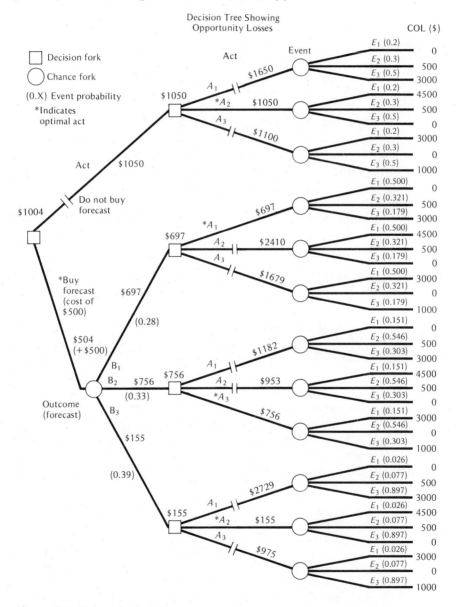

Figure 6.2 Farmer's decision tree.

EVSI, of course, is again $546, but the concept of CVSI gives us some additional insights. Outcome B_1 has the highest CVSI, because, given outcome B_1, a high penalty would be paid by not changing from act A_2 to act A_1, which is far superior for that outcome. On the other hand, if outcome B_3 occurs, the CVSI value would be zero, since the optimal act would not change.

With the EVSI determined and the sampling (forecast) cost, SC, known, the farmer can now calculate his expected net gain from sampling.

$$\text{ENGS} = \text{EVSI} - \text{SC},$$
$$= 546 - 500 = \$46.$$

The price of Zeta's forecast can be economically justified, and the farmer should be willing to buy it.

The decision tree for this problem is shown in Figure 6.2. With three events and three sample outcomes, it has more than twice as many branches as the decision tree in Figure 6.1. Nevertheless, it is still quite readable, and it does furnish a rather complete picture of the structure of the problem as a whole. The final figure of $1004 appearing above the initial decision fork is the sum of the preposterior EOL after sampling, $504, and the $500 sampling cost. The expected net gain from sampling is the difference of $46 between the $1004 and the $1050 value of EOL* without sampling.

6.2 SAMPLING WITH A CHOICE OF THE AMOUNT OF INFORMATION

In general, the process of sampling involves the selection of items from what we term a statistical population for the purpose of classifying or recording a numerical measure of some characteristic of these items. When we are sampling from a shipment of parts, for example, determining whether each part sampled is good or defective is a process of classification. On the other hand, if we are recording a city's maximum demand for electrical power on a certain set of days, this process certainly involves a numerical measure. In the first example, the statistical population would be the entire shipment of parts. In the second example, the population would be the city's daily records of maximum power demand over the time period of interest.

Sampling would not be necessary if it were practicable to examine every item in the statistical population of interest. Generally, 100 percent sampling is uneconomical, because its cost usually is greater than the value of the information obtained. In some cases, sampling is destructive, as, for example, when the breaking strength of steel bars is measured. Here, 100 percent sampling would give us complete information about a totally destroyed product! As another example, we might wish to determine whether a certain production process required an adjustment to maintain production tolerances. With 100 percent sampling, the entire production quantity would have to be completed before we could make a judgment as to the need for the adjustment, and this is obviously nonsensical.

In this text, references to sampling, unless otherwise noted, denote *simple random sampling.* By this we mean that, in the given statistical population, each possible sample of size *n* has an equal chance of being selected. For example, take the case of a statistics class of 30 students. Suppose we wished to take a random sample of five students and measure their individual heights. We would have simple random sampling if every possible combination of five students had an equal chance of being selected. One way to accomplish this would be to assign a unique number to each student, write this number on a slip of paper, deposit the slips in a bowl, and then draw five slips to identify the five students chosen.

The process of sampling gives us information about the statistical population from which we are sampling. This information is generally used to draw some kind of statistical inference and may be used to make a decision. Thus, when inspecting a random sample of 50 units from a large quantity of transistors, finding 5 defective units would lead us to believe that around 10 percent of the transistors were defective. Depending on the economics of the situation and possibly other factors, we might or might not decide to reject the entire lot of transistors.

Now, suppose that additional information is available in a decision-making situation and the amount of such information is no longer fixed but is open to choice. As the amount of information is increased, as, for example, by increasing the size of the sample, the expected value of sample information increases, but so does the sampling cost. If for any given amount of information, the expected net gain from sampling, ENGS, is positive, then that information is worthwhile obtaining. By using preposterior analysis, we can determine the optimal amount of information, the amount which maximizes ENGS. If ENGS is always negative, regardless of the amount of information, it will not pay to sample, and the currently optimal act should be selected.

If sampling is worthwhile, we take the sample and then calculate the posterior event probabilities, just as we have done previously. These posterior probabilities then become prior probabilities for the next evaluation, which proceeds in just the same way as described in the previous paragraph. This process ends when it no longer pays to obtain additional information. At that point, we make a terminal decision.

As an example of the type of decision-making situation just described, there is an inspection problem, called acceptance sampling, which is of considerable importance in many companies. Consider the usual alternatives when a lot consisting of purchased or manufactured items has just been received. If the lot is accepted without inspection, defective items will show up sometime later and will require replacement or rework, generally at a relatively high cost. The other basic choice is to inspect each item and to immediately replace or repair each defective item found, generally at a relatively low cost, but incurring an inspection cost for every item in the lot. If in a given lot the fraction defective is relatively low, it will cost less to accept all the items without inspection than to inspect them all. Should the fraction defective be relatively high, then the reverse will be true.

In this situation, the possibility of obtaining additional information on a given lot should be investigated. Such information can be obtained by taking a sample of the items in that lot and performing a preposterior analysis, in a manner similar to those presented earlier. Based on the number of defective items actually found, a decision can then be made to accept the remainder of the lot without further inspection or to inspect it 100 percent. The possibility of taking another sample, before making it a terminal decision, may also be considered.

In general, if there are no more than c defectives in a sample of size n, the decision will be to accept the remainder of the lot (unless further sampling turns out to be preferable). This combination of n and c is called a decision rule. The determination of the optimal sample size and decision rule is quite involved, both from a conceptual and from a computational standpoint. The interested reader is referred to more advanced texts such as those by Schlaifer and by Dyckman, Smidt, and McAdams. (See the references at the end of the text under the heading Probability and Decision Making.)

6.3   PRACTICAL APPLICATIONS

There have been a number of important and productive projects in the general area of Bayesian decision analysis with discrete probability distributions, but not very much appears to have been published in this area. In a number of instances, this appears to have been due to the reluctance of firms to release what they consider confidential company information. Nevertheless, there are some interesting applications, of which two are discussed here.

A very interesting decision analysis on the desirability of seeding hurricanes was performed by Stanford Research Institute in 1970 for the Environmental Science Service Administration.[1] Prior to this study, government experiments in seeding hurricanes with silver iodide gave some promise of reducing peak sustained surface wind speeds, the major factor (directly and indirectly, through tidal action) in property destruction by hurricanes. It is entirely possible, however, that seeding may have no effect or may even worsen the hurricane, in which case the government would bear legal and social responsibility for any excessive damages resulting from the effects of seeding. Hurricanes are extremely complex and unpredictable, and the consequences of seeding a particular hurricane can never be known with certainty. In the decision analysis, a set of discrete values was chosen to represent a reasonable range of the possible changes in maximum sustained wind speed, and the property damage associated with each such change was estimated. For the actions of seeding and of not seeding, probabilities were assigned, on the basis of available data, to each postulated change in wind speed. Estimated government responsibility costs were also included for the action of seeding when the result would turn out to be an increase in wind speed. The value of additional information came into the analysis in the form of information which could be obtained by further cloud-seeding experi-

---

[1] R. A. Howard, J. E. Matheson, and D. W. North, "The Decision to Seed Hurricanes," *Science*, Vol. 176, June 16, 1972, pp. 1191–1202.

ments. The general conclusion from the analysis, backed up by sensitivity analyses, was that it was desirable, where tactically feasible (depending on a hurricane's actual path), to seed, given the known seeding costs and estimated damage and government responsibility costs. At the time the paper was written, the government had not made a policy decision on hurricane seeding, and the authors made the point that the decision not to seed, if made, should represent a conscious policy decision rather than a "do nothing" policy.

The Decision Analysis Group (DAG) of the Stanford Research Institute performed an analysis of a major facilities expansion decision and described this study in a 1971 report,[2] although the original problem has been disguised. The firm for whom the study was conducted had to decide whether (1) to abandon the project and lose the investment in a pilot plant, (2) to build a production plant, considering expansion if production were successful, or (3) to postpone the decision while gathering additional technical and economic information. The study was conducted in three phases, in the manner in which the DAG structures their decision analyses. In the first, or deterministic, phase, the decision variables and state (uncontrolled) variables were defined, relationships established, and numerical values assigned. The present value of the investment was used as the measure of profitability, and many combinations of decision and state variable values were evaluated. In the second, or probabilistic, phase, probabilities were assigned to values of the important variables, leading to associated probability distributions of values, and risk preferences were assessed. Further sensitivity analyses were also performed. The third, or informational, phase determined the value of additional information by determining how much it would be worth to eliminate uncertainty in each of the problem's important variables. The outcome of the analysis indicated that construction of the production plant was definitely preferred to abandoning the project, but there were large uncertainties in two major technical factors, leading to a recommendation to postpone the decision until better information could be obtained.

A number of very interesting potential practical applications of decision analysis, primarily in the field of agricultural economics, are explored in considerable detail in a book by Halter and Dean.[3] Some of the applications discussed are the following: selecting an optimal stocking rate for cattle on California rangeland, where feed supplies are highly variable from year to year; production planning by turkey growers who must make a choice between various kinds of contract production and independent production; and the problem of determining whether or not to drill an oil well. There is also an application in forest management, where a vertically integrated firm in the pulp and paper industry must decide whether to buy and develop its own timberland or to purchase raw material in the open market.

[2]Carl S. Spetzler and Ramon M. Zamora, "Decision Analysis of a Facilities Investment and Expansion Problem," Stanford Research Institute publication DAG-46, August 1971.

[3]Albert N. Halter and Gerald W. Dean, *Decisions Under Uncertainty with Research Applications*, South-Western Publishing Company, Cincinnati, Ohio, 1971.

EXERCISES

6.1   What is a terminal decision? When is it made?

6.2   Explain why the process of incorporating additional information is known as *Bayesian* revision.

6.3   What is the relationship between likelihoods, events, and sample outcomes? How are likelihood values used in the probability revision process?

6.4   A company purchases a particular subassembly in lots of 100 units. In the last 50 lots, the number of defectives found is shown below.

Number of lots	10	18	16	6
Number of defectives	0	1	2	3

   (a)   If these lots are considered to be representative of current supplier performance, establish a set of prior probabilities for the fraction defective in a given lot.
   (b)   Suppose a sample of size 10 is taken from a lot just received and no defectives are found. Using the appropriate binomial probabilities, revise the prior probabilities. Assume that the manufacture of the subassemblies is a Bernoulli process.
   (c)   Briefly explain the change between the revised and prior probabilities.

6.5   Customers appear to arrive randomly (that is, according to a Poisson process) at a certain small bank during the opening hour. The manager, who is interested in scheduling the proper number of bank tellers, believes that there is 0.2 probability that the arrival rate will be 20 customers/hour, 0.4 probability that it will be 30 customers/hour, and 0.4 probability that there will be 40 customers/hour.
   (a)   Calculate the revised probabilities of these arrival rates if the manager observes six customers arriving during the first 15 minutes.
   (b)   Compare the revised and prior probabilities, explaining in general the direction and magnitude of the changes in the revised probabilities.

6.6   Explain clearly the concept of the conditional value of sample information. Under what conditions will the CVSI be zero?

6.7   Explain clearly what constitutes a preposterior analysis. What is the significance of the word "preposterior"?

6.8   Comment on the following statement: "If additional information was purchased and incorporated into the decision analysis and the optimal decision at that point was unchanged from the optimal decision without the information, then the information was worthless and should never have been purchased."

6.9   When performing a probability revision, how is the probability of a particular outcome determined? How are the outcome probabilities used in the calculation of EVSI?

6.10   Describe in your own words two different methods of calculating the expected value of sample information.

6.11   What is the meaning of the expected value of sample information? What are the maximum and the minimum possible values of EVSI? Under what conditions could the maximum value of EVSI be attained? The minimum value?

6.12   For a decision-making problem involving discrete event probabilities, explain clearly the method of incorporating a fixed amount of additional information into the decision-making process.

6.13   You inherit 50 acres of essentially worthless swampland about 25 miles from a large city. You ignore an offer for $100 per acre. The next day you read in the newspaper that a new airport is planned adjacent to your 50 acres provided that all government agencies approve and a bond issue is passed. The bonds pass all agencies except the Environmental Protection Agency (EPA) have approved the new airport. You are now offered $5000 cash per acre for your land. The EPA is scheduled to consider the new airport next month. If they approve it, your land will be worth $10,000 per acre; if they turn it down, your land would bring about $100 per acre. You estimate chances of EPA approval to be about 0.3. For $40,000 a well-placed government source will provide you with information regarding the intended EPA action. Two-thirds of the time, this source has provided correct information in advance of EPA approval. In 85 percent of the cases where the EPA has turned down new projects, the source was right.
(a)   Prepare a conditional profit table for your possible actions and results of the possible EPA decisions.
(b)   Prepare the corresponding opportunity loss table.
(c)   Perform a preposterior analysis for the two possible outcomes.
(d)   Calculate EVSI and ENGS.
(e)   Determine your optimal strategy.
(f)   If $40,000 is too high a price for the information, what is it worth?

6.14   A manufacturer of industrial chemicals produces a certain chemical in batches of 100 gallons. On the average, 75 percent of the batches are of acceptable quality. Selling a good batch earns a profit of $500, but selling a batch of poor quality results in a loss of $1000, owing to replacement costs and potential loss of customer goodwill. At a cost of $75, a test can be performed which is 80 percent accurate in its prediction. That is, a good batch tests good 80 percent of the time, and a poor batch tests poor 80 percent of the time.
(a)   Perform a preposterior analysis and determine whether the test should be made.
(b)   How much should the company be willing to pay for a test which would always make a perfect identification of a good or a poor batch?

6.15   In the chemical manufacturing problem of Exercise 6.14, the expected net gain from sampling is $50.00 for the test. Suppose an improved test can be performed which is 95 percent accurate in its prediction. Perform a preposterior analysis and determine how much the company could afford to pay for this test before it would be indifferent to a choice between the improved test and the original test.

6.16   A system analyst, eager for advancement to senior systems analyst, estimates her chances of immediate promotion with her present employer to be 0.4. The promotion would bring with it a $2000 annual raise. Another company offers her the desired senior position with the $2000 salary increase, but the company is located quite a bit farther from her home. She estimates additional commuting costs to be $1000 per year. Considering only a one-year period:

(a) Determine whether or not the analyst should take the position with the other company.

For a fee of $150, a management insider at her present company offers to obtain an improved assessment of her chances for promotion. In the past, when promotions were given, his prediction was correct 85 percent of the time; when they were not given, his prediction was correct 75 percent of the time.

(b) Perform a preposterior analysis. Calculate EVSI and ENGS. Should the analyst pay for the insider's information?

(c) Determine the CVSI values for both the possible predictions of the insider. Use these CVSI values to check the EVSI calculation in (b).

6.17 A certain production part, which is machined in lots of 100 units, requires a very difficult setup on an automatic screw machine. When the setup has been properly made, the fraction defective has averaged 0.10. With an improper setup, the fraction defective has averaged 0.40. In the past, the proper setup has been made 80 percent of the time.

At a cost of $40, a skilled mechanic can be brought in to guarantee a proper setup for a given lot, thereby resulting in a fraction defective of 0.10. It costs $6 to repair each defective unit in a lot.

(a) Should the mechanic be brought in to adjust the setup on all lots or none of them?

While the production process is going on, checking a unit to determine if it is defective costs $3 in lost production time and inspection time.

(b) Perform a preposterior analysis and determine if it would be worthwhile to take a sample of one unit before making the decision whether or not to bring in the mechanic.

6.18 The Triumph Toy Company is bringing out a new type of animated doll. Triumph is attempting to decide as to whether to bring out a full, partial, or minimal product line. The company categorized three possible levels of product acceptance and has estimated its probability of occurrence. Management makes its decision on the basis of maximizing the expected profit from the first year of production. The relevant data are shown in the accompanying table.

| | | Anticipated First-Year Profit ($1000s) | | |
| | | Product Line | | |
Product Acceptance	Probability	Full	Partial	Minimal
Good	0.2	80	70	50
Fair	0.4	50	45	40
Poor	0.4	−25	−10	0

(a)   Develop an opportunity loss table and determine the optimal act and EOL*.

(b)   The company's Marketing Department recommends a test marketing program, at a cost of $3000, whereby it will determine if the reaction is favorable or unfavorable. An analysis of the results of similar test marketings on other new products yields the following information.

Product Acceptance	Probability of Favorable Test Marketing Reaction
Good	0.08 ∘ ∘
Fair	0.60
Poor	0.25

Perform a preposterior analysis and determine if test marketing is worthwhile.

(c)   Construct a decision tree showing all opportunity losses and probability values, as in Figure 6.1.

6.19   The Jyant Electrical Company, a manufacturer of large electrical equipment, is anticipating the possibility of a total or a partial copper strike in the near future. The company is attempting to decide whether to stockpile a large amount of copper, at an additional cost of $50,000; a small amount, costing an additional $20,000; or to stockpile no additional copper at all. (The stockpiling costs, consisting of excess storage, holding, and handling costs, and so forth, are over and above the actual material costs.)

 If there is a partial strike, it is estimated that an additional cost of $50,000 for delayed orders will be incurred only if there is no stockpile at all. If a total strike occurs, the cost of delayed orders is estimated at $100,000 if there is only a small stockpile, and at $200,000 with no stockpile. The company estimates the probability of a total strike as 0.1, that of a partial strike as 0.3, and that of no strike as 0.6.

(a)   Develop an opportunity loss table and determine the optimal act and EOL*.

A management consulting firm, ESP, Ltd., can be hired to conduct an in-depth study of all factors relevant to the strike. It will then predict either that a strike is improbable, a partial strike is likely, or a total strike is likely. On the basis of past performance, Jyant estimates ESP's prediction accuracy as shown here.

Strike Situation	Prediction Probability		
	No Strike	Partial Strike	Total Strike
No strike	0.75	0.15	0.10
Partial strike	0.15	0.60	0.25
Total strike	0.05	0.05	0.90

The following results are available from a computer program for Bayesian revision.

	Revised Event Probability Based on Given Outcome		
	Prediction		
Event	No Strike	Partial Strike	Total Strike
No strike	0.900	0.327	0.267
Partial strike	0.090	0.655	0.333
Total strike	0.010	0.018	0.400

The marginal probabilities of the possible outcomes are: P(No Strike) = 0.500, P(Partial Strike) = 0.275, and P(Total Strike) = 0.225.

(b) Perform a preposterior analysis and determine how much Jyant could afford to pay ESP for the in-depth study.

6.20 Explain the statement: "The terms *prior* and *posterior,* when applied to probabilities, are relative terms, relative to a given sample." Is it possible for a set of probabilities to be both prior and posterior probabilities? Explain.

6.21 Suppose that, in a certain problem, the set of prior event probabilities is, respectively, 0.2, 0.3, 0.1, 0.25, and 0.15. For what set of likelihood values will the set of posterior probabilities be identical to that of the prior probabilities? Perform the actual calculations and demonstrate this. Generalize this result for the case of any number of events and any set of prior probabilities, and explain, in your own words, why the set of prior probabilities is not changed by the information from the sample.

6.22 A quality control inspector has prepared a table of EOLs after sampling for acceptance or rejection of a 10,000 unit batch. The sample size is 100.

Number of Defectives in the Sample	EOL After Sampling	
	Acceptance	Rejection
0	$ 6.25	$36.00
1	9.00	27.00
2	12.25	18.75
3	16.00	11.00
4	25.00	5.25
5	56.25	2.25

If the decision rule without sampling is to accept each batch, what is the conditional value of sample information for each possible outcome?

6.23 A field known to contain oil is to be explored by drilling proving wells to determine the extent of the oil pool. The first proving well costs $2,000,000, but each additional well only costs $250,000. On the basis of previous experience, the expected value of sample information is $1,600,000 from the first well. Each additional proving well drilled beyond the first one increases the expected value of sample information by half the increase in value of the previous well. In other words, the EVSI of two wells is $2,400,000, or $1,600,000 from the first well plus $800,000 from the second well. If it is desired to maximize the expected net gain from sampling, how many proving wells should be drilled?

6.24 The Testem Company is considering the manufacture of a precision test unit for the checkout of numerically controlled machine tools. The development cost of this test unit would be $50,000 and the variable cost per unit $500. The selling price would be $700 per unit. The possible acts are:
(1) Manufacture the test unit.
(2) Do not manufacture the test unit.
    In Testem's marketing area, 2500 companies own numerically controlled machine tools for which the test unit would be suitable. On the basis of past experience with this type of market, Testem estimates that the fraction of companies which would buy the test unit is as given below.

Fraction of Customers Buying Unit	Probability
0.08	0.4
0.10	0.4
0.12	0.2

(a) Express the cost and COL values in terms of the fraction of customers who would buy.
(b) Determine the expected opportunity loss of each act. Should Testem manufacture the test unit?
(c) Suppose that a sample of 10 customers is chosen, and 2 of the 10 customers state that they would buy the test unit. What should the decision be after this sample is taken and the results analyzed?

CHAPTER 7

LINEAR
PROGRAMMING

In this chapter, we will attempt to lay the foundation for a fundamental understanding of the formulation and solution of linear programming models. Of all the well-known operations research models, linear programming and related techniques have been by far the most productive, as measured by their effective application to the solution of a great variety of large-scale problems in business and industry. The advent of the high-speed digital computer has made it practical to solve with incredible speed problems involving hundreds or even thousands of decision variables.

Since virtually all real-world linear programming problems are solved by computer, the emphasis will be placed on learning the basic concepts of linear programming, rather than on the attainment of any particular expertise in the manual solution of small linear programming problems. The interpretation of a computer solution will be discussed and the results of such a solution will be extended through the technique of sensitivity analysis. The preparation of linear programming problems for computer solution will also be covered.

Basically, linear programming is a deterministic mathematical technique which involves the allocation of scarce resources in an optimal manner on the basis of a given criterion of optimality. Frequently, the criterion of optimality is either maximum profit or minimum cost, depending on the type of problem. The following are but a few examples of some types of problems that have been tackled and solved utilizing linear programming techniques.

Product-mix Selection A company can manufacture several different products, each of which requires the use of limited production resources, such as machine time, process time, and labor time. What quantity of each product should be produced in order to maximize profit?

Minimum-Cost Diet A hospital wishes to provide its patients with meals which are balanced, varied, and meet certain minimum nutritional requirements. What is the minimum-cost selection of food items which will meet these constraints?

Blending Problems A chemical product can be made from a variety of available raw materials, each of which has a particular composition and price. Subject to availability of the raw materials and to minimum and maximum constraints on certain product constituents, what is the minimum-cost blend?

Production Planning A company faces a certain expected demand each month for a manufactured product. Considering the initial number of units in inventory, the available production capacity, constraints on production, employment, and inventory levels, and all relevant cost factors, what is the minimum-cost production plan over the planning horizon of n months?

7.1 GRAPHICAL APPROACH

The basic concepts of linear programming can best be illustrated and explored by a simple example. For the case of two decision variables (often called activity variables), a graphical solution can be readily developed, and this pictorial representation can yield very valuable insights. (For three decision variables, a graphical solution is possible but rather unwieldy; beyond three decision variables, a graphical solution is no longer possible.)

It should be clearly pointed out that the graphical approach to solving linear programming problems is a completely impractical method of solution for realistic problems. Nevertheless, it is extremely useful in explaining the basic concepts and techniques of linear programming, and that alone justifies its use.

EXAMPLE 7.1

Consider the production planning decision of the Valvton Company, which makes valves and pistons. Both valves and pistons must be machined on a lathe and processed on a grinder. The pistons must also be polished. Each valve and each piston requires a certain amount of steel. Table 7.1 summarizes the amount of each resource (machine time and steel, in this case) used in the manufacture of one valve

Table 7.1 Resource Requirements

	Grinder Time (hr)	Lathe Time (hr)	Polishing Time (hr)	Steel (lb)		Unit Profit ($)
Each valve requires	0.3	1.0	0	1.0	and yields	3
Each piston requires	0.5	1.5	0.5	1.0	and yields	4
Available resources	300	750	200	600		

and one piston. The table also presents the unit profit for both valves and pistons and the amount of each resource available weekly. Valvton wishes to determine the values of the decision variables, the number of valves and pistons to be produced, which maximize profit, subject to the constraints on available machine time and steel.

Restrictions Imposed by Limited Resources

In the problem formulation phase of a linear programming problem, we investigate the effect of only one resource at a time, so let us take them in order, as presented in Table 7.1.

1. *Grinder time.* With 300 hours of grinder time available, suppose only valves were to be produced:

$$\text{Maximum valve production} = \frac{300 \text{ hr}}{0.3 \text{ hr/valve}} = 1000 \text{ valves.}$$

On the other hand, if only pistons were to be produced:

$$\text{Maximum piston production} = \frac{300 \text{ hr}}{0.5 \text{ hr/piston}} = 600 \text{ pistons.}$$

Or, we could produce any combination of valves and pistons which did not require more than 300 hours of grinder time.

The two data points developed (1000 valves, 0 pistons; and 0 valves, 600 pistons) define the endpoints of the line representing the grinder time restriction, as plotted in Figure 7.1.

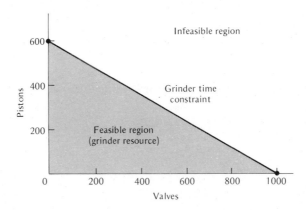

Figure 7.1

Within the triangle formed by the two axes and the linear function representing the grinder time restriction, any combination of valves and pistons is feasible, *considering only grinder resources* and, of course, the obvious restriction that the quantity of valves and pistons must be nonnegative. The region above and to the right of this triangle represents combinations which are infeasible because of grinder time limitations. For any combination of valves and pistons lying on the line representing the grinder time restriction, the grinder resource will be fully utilized. For any such combination lying within the shaded area, which we call the *feasible region*, there will be excess grinder time.

At this point, we might look at the data of Table 7.1 and observe that it will clearly be impossible to produce 1000 valves, since the limited amount of steel available will permit a maximum of 600 valves to be manufactured. This is absolutely true, but each constraint must be considered separately during the problem formulation phase. During the solution phase, the interaction of the different constraints will be taken care of "automatically" by the computational algorithm, which is what we call the computing procedure.

2. *Lathe time.* Examining next the availability of lathe time, we could apply all 750 hours to the production of 750 valves, to the production of 500 pistons, or to any combination of valves and pistons not using more than 750 hours of lathe time. These data are graphed in Figure 7.2, along with the restrictions due to grinder time.

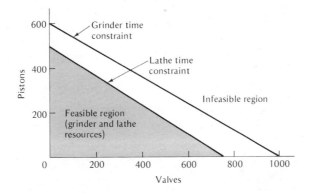

Figure 7.2

From the graph, it is apparent that the constraint on lathe time availability is more restrictive than that of grinder time availability. As a consequence, the feasible region, for both grinder and lathe resources, is the region defined by the latter resource alone. We say that the lathe time constraint dominates the grinder time constraint, and the grinder time constraint is, therefore, *redundant.*

3. *Polishing time.* Since valves require no polishing, their production is not limited by the amount of polishing time available. Maximum piston production would be 400, with 200 hours available and 0.5 hour polishing time per piston. The resultant constraint line will be parallel to the horizontal axis, at a value of 400 pistons.

4. *Steel.* With valves and pistons both taking 1.0 pound of steel per unit, maximum valve *or* piston production would be 600 units. This constraint is represented by a line connecting the points (600 valves, 0 pistons; and 0 valves, 600 pistons).

In Figure 7.3, the steel and polisher constraints have been added, but the redundant grinder time constraint is not shown. The feasible region is now a polygon, instead of a triangle. The arrows on each given constraint line indicate the direction of the feasible region, which is determined by the sign of the constraint inequality. If that sign were reversed, the feasible region would be on the opposite side of the line.

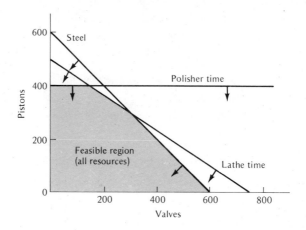

Figure 7.3

Graphical Determination of Optimality

Having determined the feasible region, considering all resources, we can now work toward an optimal solution. To do this, we will set up a system of linear inequalities. For those needing a brief review of linear equations, this material will be found in Appendix 7A.

The first thing to do is to introduce a suitable notation for this problem.

Let v = number of valves produced,
p = number of pistons produced,
z = total profit in dollars.

The constraints, which define the limitations placed on the decision variables, may now be written as follows:

Grinder time constraint	$0.3v + 0.5p \leq 300$
Lathe time constraint	$1.0v + 1.5p \leq 750$
Polishing time constraint	$0.5p \leq 200$
Steel constraint	$1.0v + 1.0p \leq 600$
Nonnegativity constraints	$v \geq 0, p \geq 0$

The first four constraints, which involve the limitation of scarce resources, are called *restrictions*, and they are written as $\leq$ inequalities. The final nonnegativity constraints are necessary because we cannot produce a negative quantity of valves or pistons.

As we observed earlier, the constraint on grinder time is not a factor in the analysis, since at least one constraint is more restrictive; thus, we do not have to consider the first constraint. (Actually, in this particular example, both the lathe time and the steel constraints are more restrictive than the grinder time constraint.)

The function to be optimized (maximized or minimized) is called the *objective function*. In this profit maximization problem, the objective function represents the total profit obtained from any specified combination of valves and pistons. Since each valve earns \$3 profit and each piston \$4 profit, the objective function is:

$$\text{maximize } z = 3v + 4p.$$

For any value of z, the objective function represents a line with constant slope. The value of the slope will always be equal to the negative of the ratio of the coefficient of the variable plotted on the horizontal axis to the coefficient of the variable plotted on the vertical axis. In this example, v is on the horizontal axis and p on the vertical axis, so the slope is $-3/4$, or -0.75. As the value of z increases, we can visualize a line moving parallel to itself and away from the origin. We can easily plot several such lines by specifying a value for z, setting v to zero, and solving for p to get one point on the line, and then setting p to zero and solving for v to get a second point. We used this same general procedure to plot the constraint lines. The table below gives values which establish three lines (with arbitrary z values).

	Point 1		Point 2	
z	v	p	v	p
600	0	150	200	0
1200	0	300	400	0
1800	0	450	600	0

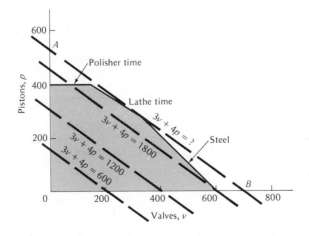

Figure 7.4

These three lines are shown in Figure 7.4 superimposed on the feasible region. It should be apparent that we can achieve a higher profit than $1800 by moving as far as possible in the direction of increasing profit, which in this case is away from the origin. The line representing maximum profit is that line which just touches the edge of the feasible region. In the figure this line is shown as line AB, which touches the edge of the feasible region at the point where the lathe time and steel constraint lines intersect. The optimal product mix can be determined by simultaneously solving these two constraint equations:

$$
\begin{aligned}
1.0v + 1.5p &= 750 \\
-(1.0v + 1.0p &= 600) \\
\hline
0.5p &= 150, \\
p &= 300.
\end{aligned}
$$

Substituting this value of p in either of the two constraint equations, we get

$$v = 300.$$

Therefore, the maximum achievable profit is

$$z = (3)(300) + (4)(300) = \$2100.$$

The equation of the objective function line yielding the maximum profit is thus $3v + 4p = 2100$.

Observe carefully that the optimal solution point can never be an interior point of the feasible region. This is always true, since any solution at an interior point can always be bettered by moving in the direction of increasing profit, perpendicular to the objective function line. If there is a single (unique) optimal solution, the optimal solution point must be at a vertex of the feasible region. (We will discuss multiple optimal solutions in the next section.)

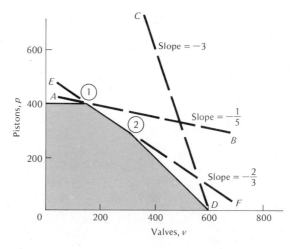

Figure 7.5

Changes in the Objective Function

Referring to Figure 7.5, we might consider briefly how the solution would change if the objective function coefficients were different. The slope of the objective function line is equal to the negative of the coefficient of v divided by the coefficient of p. Thus, a slope only slightly negative, such as $-1/5$, would lead to an optimal solution point at the intersection of the polisher time and lathe time constraint lines, as shown by line AB in Figure 7.5. Such a slope would occur if pistons were five times as profitable as valves; for example, if the objective function involved maximizing $2v + 10p$. The most profitable product mix would be 400 pistons, the maximum number which can be produced, and 150 valves. On the other hand, if we were trying to maximize $30v + 10p$, we would have a highly negative slope of -3, with valves three times as profitable as pistons. In this case, shown by line CD in Figure 7.5, we would find the optimal solution point at the intersection of the steel constraint line and the v-axis. Clearly, this would mean producing 600 valves and no pistons. An objective function with a slope identical to that of one of the constraints bounding the feasible region will result in a theoretically infinite number of optimal solutions. Suppose, for example, that the objective function requires maximizing $2v + 3p$. This function has the same slope $(-2/3)$ as that of the lathe time constraint and is illustrated by line EF. When the optimal solution occurs at an edge, rather than at a vertex, of the feasible region, we will have multiple (nonunique) optimal solutions. The solutions at the endpoints of line EF are: $v = 150$, $p = 400$ and $v = 300$, $p = 300$, denoted as points 1 and 2, respectively, in Figure 7.5. The remaining solutions include all points on the line connecting these two solutions. Since this line, which represents the lathe time constraint, has the equation $1.0v + 1.5p = 750$, we can determine any allowable pair of v and p values by either choosing a value of v between 150 and 300 and then solving for p, or by choosing a value of p between 300 and 400 and then solving for v. For example, if $v = 210$, $(1.0)(210) + 1.5p = 750$, so $p = 360$. Or, if $p = 320$, $1.0v + (1.5)(320) = 750$, and $v = 270$.

Effect of Additional Constraints

Additional constraints can be readily shown graphically. Suppose, for example, available storage space limited the weekly production of valves to no more than 400, and a minimum quantity of 100 pistons was required to meet prior commitments. These additional constraints on production are shown in Figure 7.6. The feasible region would be noticeably decreased, compared to the case without such additional constraints. Any time a constraint is added that reduces the size of the feasible region, the value of the objective function will either be unaffected or be worsened. For the original objective function, the two additional constraints would not affect the optimal value of the objective function, since the optimal solution point would still be at the vertex where the steel and lathe time constraint lines intersect, as can be visualized in Figure 7.6. However, if the objective function to be maximized had been, for example, $30v + 10p$ (slope $= -3$), the original optimal solution would have been at $v = 600$, as can be seen in Figure 7.5, with a profit of

(600)(30) = \$18,000. Then, the additional limitation on valve production would have eliminated this solution. From Figure 7.6, you should convince yourself that the new optimal solution would be $v = 400$, $p = 200$, with a profit of (30)(400) + (10)(200) = \$14,000, a substantial reduction.

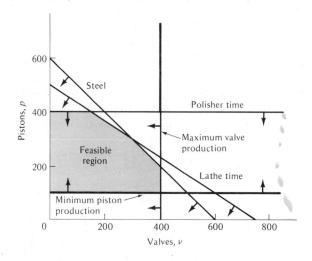

Figure 7.6

7.2 PROBLEM FORMULATION

Let us consider now the general process of formulating linear programming problems. We will consider several different examples and will be concerned primarily with formulating the system of constraints and the objective function to be optimized.

It is generally an excellent idea to develop a systematic approach to a particular class of problems. In the formulation of linear programming problems, the following steps are recommended.

1. Define all decision variables and specify units.
2. Determine whether the objective function is to be maximized or minimized.
3. Specify the objective function.
4. Specify each constraint.

EXAMPLE 7.2 (Diet Problem)

A farmer wishes to determine the lowest cost daily feed mixture for his cattle. To meet minimum nutritional requirements, the mixture must contain at least 10,000 units of nutrient A, 20,000 units of nutrient B, and 15,000 units of nutrient C. Two commercial feeds are available. Each pound of the first costs \$0.15 and contains 100 units of nutrient A, 400 units of nutrient B, and 200 units of nutrient C. Each pound of the second costs $0.20 and contains 200 units of nutrient A, 250 units of nutrient B, and 200 units of nutrient C. Formulate this as a linear programming problem.

The data are summarized in the accompanying table.

	Units /lb		
Nutrient	Feed 1	Feed 2	Required Units
A	100	200	10,000
B	400	250	20,000
C	200	200	15,000
Cost/lb	$0.15	$0.20	

The decision variables are the daily amounts of both feeds.

Let x_1 = daily amount of first commercial feed, in pounds,
   x_2 = daily amount of second commercial feed, in pounds,

and
   z = daily cost of feed mixture, in dollars.

The objective is clearly to minimize the daily cost of the feed mixture, and there will be three constraints, one for each nutrient, to insure that the sum of the individual nutrient contributions will be at least as great as the minimum required amount in each case. For example, considering nutrient A, the contribution of x_1 pounds of the first commercial feed, supplying 100 units per pound, will be $100x_1$ units, while the contribution of x_2 pounds of the second commercial feed will be $200x_2$ units. The sum of these two contributions of nutrient A must be at least 10,000 units. The nutrient B and C requirements must also be satisfied by adding the individual contributions supplied by each feed. The problem can then be stated as

$$\text{minimize } z = 0.15x_1 + 0.20x_2$$

subject to
$$100x_1 + 200x_2 \geqslant 10,000 \text{ (nutrient A requirement)}$$
$$400x_1 + 250x_2 \geqslant 20,000 \text{ (nutrient B requirement)}$$
$$200x_1 + 200x_2 \geqslant 15,000 \text{ (nutrient C requirement)}$$

and
$$x_1, x_2 \text{ both} \geqslant 0.$$

These constraints, which are in the form of $\geqslant$ inequalities, are generally called *requirements*. Such constraints usually represent a minimum requirement of some nature, rather than a restriction on the use of a scarce resource, as with $\leqslant$ inequalities.

Since this problem has only two decision variables, it is of some interest to show the graphical solution to such a minimization problem. This solution is shown in

Figure 7.7. Because the constraints involve minimum requirements, the feasible region lies above the lines representing the constraint equation. For any point below these lines, one or more of the minimum requirements would not be met, so such a solution would be infeasible. Note that the feasible region is unbounded, since there is no inherent limitation on the amounts by which the minimum requirements can be exceeded.

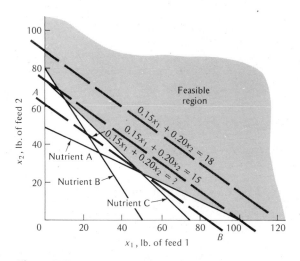

Figure 7.7

From the statement of the objective function, its slope is $-0.15/0.20$, or -0.75. Since the objective function represents cost, which we are trying to minimize, it should be clear, from Figure 7.7, that the minimum cost will be achieved at a point where the objective function is closest to the origin and just touches the feasible region. Visualize starting with an objective function with a relatively high cost and then moving the objective function line in the direction of decreasing cost. The objective function which minimizes the cost is shown by line AB, which passes through the point where the nutrient A and nutrient C constraint lines intersect. Simultaneously solving those two constraint equations, we find that the optimal solution is to buy 50 pounds of the first commercial feed and 25 pounds of the second commercial feed, with a daily cost of $12.50. At the optimal solution point, observe that we will exactly meet the minimum requirements for nutrients A and C and will have an excess of 6250 units of nutrient B. Verify this latter value for yourself.

EXAMPLE 7.3 (Product Mix Problem)

A manufacturer has five precision lathes, each available 80 hours per week. He manufactures three different products on these lathes. Each unit of product 1 takes 2 hours to machine, requires 1 pound of copper and 2 pounds of steel, and sells for $15. Each unit of product 2 takes 1 hour to machine, requires 2 pounds of copper and 3 pounds of steel, and sells for $10. Each unit of product 3 takes 2 hours to machine, requires 1 pound of steel, and sells for $14. An adequate amount of copper is available, but the weekly amount of steel available is 1000 pounds. Contract commitments require that at least 100 units of product 1 be produced each week. The Sales Department estimates that no more than 400 units of product 3 can be sold each week. Copper costs $0.20 per pound, steel costs $0.50 per pound, and the cost of machining is $5 per hour. Formulate a linear programming model to determine the optimal product mix.

The given data are as shown in the table.

Product	Machining, hr	Copper, lb	Steel, lb	Selling Price, $
1	2	1	2	15
2	1	2	3	10
3	2	0	1	14
Availability	400	No limit	1000	
Cost	$5/hr	$0.20/lb	$0.50/lb	

Here, the decision variables involve the weekly production of each product.

Let x_1 = weekly production of product 1, in units,
  x_2 = weekly production of product 2, in units,
  x_3 = weekly production of product 3, in units,

and

  z = total weekly profit, in dollars.

We would like to maximize the total weekly profit, but the unit profit from each product is not given, so we must calculate it before we can set up the objective function. For a unit of each product, in turn, we must subtract the cost of copper, steel, and machining from the selling price. Each unit of product 1, for instance, sells for $15 but has associated costs of $0.20 for 1 pound of copper, $1 for 2 pounds of steel and $10 for 2 hours of machining, leaving a profit of $3.80. The unit profit for all three products is

$$\text{Unit profit on product } 1 = 15 - (1)(0.20) - (2)(0.50) - (2)(5)$$
$$= 15 - 11.20 = \$3.80.$$
$$\text{Unit profit on product } 2 = 10 - (2)(0.20) - (3)(0.50) - (1)(5)$$
$$= 10 - 6.90 = \$3.10.$$
$$\text{Unit profit on product } 3 = 14 - (1)(0.50) - (2)(5)$$
$$= 14 - 10.50 = \$3.50$$

The constraints involve limited steel and machining time resources and limited sales of product 3, as well as a minimum requirement for product 1. Consider, for example, the limited availability of machining time. With x_1 units of product 1 and 2 hours machining required per unit, the total machining time on product 1 is $2x_1$ hours. For products 2 and 3, the total machining time is $1x_2 + 2x_3$, since product 2 requires 1 hour per unit and product 3 requires 2 hours per unit. The sum of the machining times for all three products must not exceed 400 hours, the available time from all 5 lathes. The other constraints can be determined in a similar fashion. We can then state the objective function and the constraints:

$$\text{maximize } z = 3.80x_1 + 3.10x_2 + 3.50x_3,$$

subject to
$$2x_1 + x_2 + 2x_3 \leq 400 \text{ (machining time limitation)}$$
$$2x_1 + 3x_2 + x_3 \leq 1000 \text{ (steel limitation)}$$
$$x_1 \geq 100 \text{ (minimum product 1 production)}$$
$$x_3 \leq 400 \text{ (maximum product 3 sales)}$$

and
$$x_1, x_2, x_3 \geq 0.$$

EXAMPLE 7.4 (Investment Policy (blending) Problem)

An insurance company has an investment limit of $1,000,000. The board of directors has decreed that no more than $100,000 may be invested in common stocks and no more than $200,000 in first mortgage trust deeds. State regulations require that at least 60 percent of the total investment be in government bonds, yielding 4 percent annually. Any amount may be invested in 6 percent municipal bonds. The board has narrowed its choice to two common stocks, S_1 and S_2, currently yielding 10 percent and 8 percent, respectively. It has specified that at least 70 percent of the investment in common stocks must be in S_2, considered to be a safer investment than S_1. As for first mortgage trust deeds, two candidates have been selected, T_1 and T_2, offering returns of 8 percent and 7 percent, respectively. No more than 35 percent of the investment in trust deeds may be in T_1, which is not as secure an investment as T_2. Formulate a suitable linear programming model.

Let s_1 = dollars invested in S_1 stock,
s_2 = dollars invested in S_2 stock,
t_1 = dollars invested in T_1 trust deeds,
t_2 = dollars invested in T_2 trust deeds,
g = dollars invested in government bonds,
m = dollars invested in municipal bonds,
and
z = total annual profit, dollars.

Our objective appears to be the maximization of the total profit per unit time. The most convenient time unit is one year, since the percentage return figures are all given on an annual basis. Therefore, the objective function involves maximizing the sum of the six possible individual investments:

$$\text{maximize } z = 0.10s_1 + 0.08s_2 + 0.08t_1 + 0.07t_2 + 0.04g + 0.06m.$$

Let us now consider each individual constraint in turn.

a) No more than $100,000 may be invested in common stocks.

$$s_1 + s_2 \leq 100,000.$$

b) No more than $200,000 may be invested in trust deeds.

$$t_1 + t_2 \leqslant 200,000.$$

c) At least 60 percent of the investment must be in government bonds.

$$g \geqslant 0.60(s_1 + s_2 + t_1 + t_2 + g + m).$$

A common mistake made here is to specify that g must be at least 60 percent of $1,000,000 or $600,000. This is not correct, since there is no stipulation that exactly $1,000,000 be invested. We must set a minimum of 60 percent of the *actual* amount invested, rather than 60 percent of the maximum amount which *could* be invested.

d) At least 70 percent of the investment in common stocks must be in S_2 stock.

$$s_2 \geqslant 0.70(s_1 + s_2).$$

Again, note that s_2 must be at least 70 percent of the actual investment in common stocks, not 70 percent of the maximum possible investment of $100,000, since there is no requirement that this amount be invested in common stocks. If, for example, the optimal solution required an investment of $50,000 in common stocks, s_2 would have to exceed $35,000, not $70,000.

e) No more than 35 percent of the investment in trust deeds may be in T_1 trust deeds.

$$t_1 \leqslant 0.35(t_1 + t_2).$$

f) No more than $1,000,000 may be invested.

$$s_1 + s_2 + t_1 + t_2 + g + m \leqslant 1,000,000.$$

The inequality is appropriate, because all the available funds may not be invested.

Placing all decision variables on the left-hand side and all constants on the right-hand side of the constraints, we can now state the problem as follows:

maximize $z = 0.10s_1 + 0.08s_2 + 0.08t_1 + 0.07t_2 + 0.04g + 0.06m$

subject to

$$
\begin{array}{llllll}
s_1 + & s_2 & & & & \leqslant 100,000 \\
& & t_1 + & t_2 & & \leqslant 200,000 \\
-0.60s_1 - & 0.60s_2 - & 0.60t_1 - & 0.60t_2 + & 0.40g - & 0.60m \geqslant 0 \\
-0.70s_1 + & 0.30s_2 & & & & \geqslant 0 \\
& & 0.65t_1 - & 0.35t_2 & & \leqslant 0 \\
s_1 + & s_2 + & t_1 + & t_2 + & g + & m \leqslant 1,000,000
\end{array}
$$

and s_1, s_2, t_1, t_2, g, m all $\geqslant 0.$

7.3   ASSUMPTIONS IN LINEAR PROGRAMMING MODELS

Although it has not been stated explicitly up to this point, in all linear programming models there are three basic assumptions which must be met in order for such models to be applicable.

Proportionality   The amount of each resource used (or requirement supplied) and the associated contribution to profit (or cost) must be exactly proportional to the value of each decision variable, often called its activity level. For example, if the number of valves produced were halved, the total amount of each resource required in the manufacture of valves would also be halved, as would the total profit contribution from valves.

Divisibility   The decision variables must be allowed to assume a continuous range of values. (In such problems as that of the Valvton Company, where we wished to determine the optimal production quantity of individual items, it is clear that we cannot produce a fractional piston or valve. However, we assume that with the given optimal resource allocation, any fractional items to be produced will be partially completed during a given time period and then finished during the next time period.) If any of the variables can assume only integer values or are limited to a discrete number of values, we no longer have a linear programming model but a discrete programming model. Such models tend to be much more complex than linear programming models and will not be covered in this text.

Additivity   The total amount of each resource utilized (or requirement supplied) and the total profit (or cost) are equal to the sum of the respective individual amounts. Thus, in the feed blending example, the total amount of nutrient A is exactly equal to the sum of the amount of nutrient A contributed by the first commercial feed and that contributed by the second commercial feed. The total cost of the feed mixture equals the cost for the given amount of the first commercial feed plus the cost for the given amount of the second commercial feed.

These three postulates mean that all constraints and the objective function must be characterized by linear relationships. In addition, we have assumed that the linear programming model is completely deterministic, having no stochastic elements. Stochastic linear programming models will not be considered in this text.

7.4   SIMPLEX METHOD

As we have indicated, the graphical approach to linear programming is useful only to illustrate basic concepts and not to solve practical problems, which typically have many decision variables, not two or three. We will now discuss in some detail the simplex method, an algebraic approach to the solution of any linear programming problem. Although more efficient computational techniques have been developed for the solution of large problems (some having thousands of variables and equations), the version of the simplex algorithm presented here illustrates the principles involved in solving linear programming problems. We will study it, not as an end in itself, but primarily to provide a foundation for the later study of post-optimality analysis of computer solutions. As a matter of interest, many of the specialized computational techniques for large linear programming problems are actually variants of the simplex method.

Let us work with Example 8.1, the product mix problem previously solved graphically. Before actually getting into the simplex algorithm, we will need to set up the problem algebraically and define some fundamental concepts. The set of governing constraints, which are inequalities, can be converted to equations by the addition of what are called *slack variables*.

$$v + 1.5p + S_1 \qquad\qquad\qquad = 750 \text{ (lathe time constraint)} \qquad\qquad \textbf{(7.1)}$$

$$0.5p \quad + S_2 \qquad\qquad = 200 \text{ (polishing time constraint)} \qquad \textbf{(7.2)}$$

$$v + \quad p \qquad\quad + S_3 \qquad = 600 \text{ (steel constraint)} \qquad\qquad\qquad \textbf{(7.3)}$$

$$-3v - \quad 4p \qquad\qquad\quad + z = \quad 0 \text{ (objective function)} \qquad\qquad \textbf{(7.4)}$$

where $S_1 =$ lathe time slack (unused resource), in hours,

$S_2 =$ polisher time slack (unused resource), in hours,

$S_3 =$ steel slack (unused resource), in pounds,

$z =$ value of the objective function—to be maximized,

and $v, p, S_1, S_2, S_3 \geqslant 0.$

The slack variables, as noted in their definitions, represent unused resources. For example, since it takes 1.0 hour of lathe time per valve and 1.5 hours of lathe time per piston, a product mix consisting of 100 valves and 120 pistons would require a lathe time totaling $(1.0)(100) + (1.5)(120) = 280$ hours. With 750 hours of lathe time available, the unused amount of this resource would be $750 - 280 = 470$ hours. This would be the value of the lathe time slack, S_1. This value could have been determined directly from Equation (7.1) by substituting the values $v = 100$ and $p = 120$ and solving for S_1.

Excluding the value z of the objective function, there are five variables in the problem. Only two of them are decision variables, or what are frequently called activity variables. The other three variables are slack variables, representing unused resources. The variable z is not a decision variable, since its value depends on the value of those variables appearing in the objective function. Incidentally, although the objective function looks different than before, it has not changed. All we have done is to place all the variables on the left-hand side of the equation.

At this point, we introduce some terminology which has become commonly accepted in the analysis of linear programming models. Any solution of the problem satisfying all the constraints is called a *feasible solution*. As we observed earlier, we will be interested only in a feasible solution which occurs at an extreme point, or vertex. Such a solution is called a *basic feasible solution*. In general, with n decision variables and m inequality constraints (restrictions) requiring m slack variables, any basic feasible solution will have at most m variables with nonzero values. These "nonzero" variables are called *basic variables*, and the set of basic variables is often called the *basis*. The "zero" variables are termed *nonbasic variables*. The term "basic" comes from the condition that, using the simplex algorithm, we always solve a system of m equations in $m + n$ unknowns by setting n variables to zero and then solving the resulting system of m equations in m unknowns, giving a unique *basic solution*. A basic solution will be infeasible if it contains any variables with negative values, but we will always work with a basic feasible solution. We will find that the simplex algorithm starts with an initial basic feasible solution, moving to successive basic feasible solutions and terminating when the optimal basic feasible solution has been reached. (When a solution contains basic variables which are so-called artificial variables, to be discussed later, a basic solution will not be feasible.)

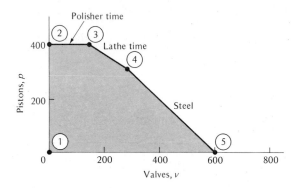

Figure 7.8

In Figure 7.8, we show again the feasible region, this time with each vertex numbered. At each vertex, two of the five variables must be zero, since there are three constraint equations and there must be one and only one basic (nonzero) variable for every constraint equation. The graph shows only the values of the two decision variables, but by noting which two of the five variables are zero at each vertex, we can readily solve for the values of the other three variables. Table 7.4 shows the value of all variables and the associated profit z.

Table 7.4   Basic Feasible Solutions

Vertex Number	"Zero" Variables	Valves v	Pistons p	Lathe Time (hr) S_1	Polisher Time (hr) S_2	Steel (lb) S_3	Profit ($) z
		Variables			Slack Variables		
1	v, p	0	0	750	200	600	0
2	v, S_2	0	400	150	0	200	1600
3	S_1, S_2	150	400	0	0	50	2050
4	S_1, S_3	300	300	0	50	0	2100
5	p, S_3	600	0	150	200	0	1800

A brief discussion of Table 7.4 may be helpful. To show how the numbers are derived, consider vertex 3, for example. Since vertex 3 is on both the polisher time and the lathe time constraint lines, all available polisher time and lathe time is being used. The slack variables S_1 and S_2 associated with these resources must therefore be zero. From Equation (7.2), p must then be 400. Substituting this value of p in Equation (7.1), v must equal 150, since S_1 is zero. Going to Equation (7.3), we now find that S_3 must be 50, since $v + p = 550$. From the objective function, Equation (7.4), z equals \$2050. Note that at vertex 4, where S_1 and S_3 are zero, we have to solve Equations (7.1) and (7.3) simultaneously to get the values of v and p.

Although it is theoretically possible to enumerate all basic feasible solution points, it is computationally quite impractical to do so, since the number of such solutions could be as large as $(m + n)!/(m!n!)$. The simplex algorithm provides us with an efficient algebraic technique for moving from one basic feasible solution to another basic feasible solution until the optimal solution is reached. (We will discuss later what happens if there is no optimal solution or the solution is unbounded.) The steps of the procedure are listed below for problems where the constraints are all in the form of restrictions.

1. Choose an initial basic feasible solution.
2. Examine the objective function and determine whether there is at least one nonbasic variable which would improve the solution if its value were increased from its current value of zero. If so, choose the nonbasic variable which, for each unit increase in its value, yields the greatest increase in the value of the objective function. (We call this nonbasic variable the "entering variable.") If no such improvement is possible, stop—the optimal solution has been reached.
3. For the entering variable, increase its value until a current basic variable is forced down to a value of zero. We call this current basic variable the "departing variable."
4. With the exception of the constraint equation where the departing variable has been forced to zero, eliminate the entering variable from all other equations, including the objective function. Go back to step 2.

In Table 7.4, as the solution moved from one vertex to an adjacent vertex, the second column shows that it was always true that one of the two nonbasic ("zero") variables went into the solution as a basic variable (the entering variable) and was replaced by a previously basic variable (the departing variable).

The development of each new basic feasible solution, always moving toward an optimal solution, is called an *iteration*. (A flow chart of the simplex algorithm is shown later, in Figure 7.9, after the computational procedure has been explained in some detail.)

Example Problem Solved by the Simplex Algorithm

The initial basic feasible solution is obtained in a very straightforward manner.

We start at the origin by setting all activity variables (v and p) to zero. From Equations (7.1) to (7.3), we can immediately see that $S_1 = 750$, $S_2 = 200$, and $S_3 = 600$. The profit z is zero, from Equation (7.4). Obviously, we can do better, since we produce nothing and utilize none of the available resources. Clearly, the solution can be improved by increasing either v or p. As a general rule, the entering variable will be that variable with the highest per unit profit contribution. In this example, each unit of v contributes \$3, and each unit of p contributes \$4. Therefore, we want to bring in as many units of p as possible. (We could select as the entering variable that variable which yields the greatest *total* profit, but this involves considerably more computational effort. Such effort has not, in general, paid off by reducing the overall computational time to arrive at an optimal solution.) Note that we make only one interchange of variables at a time, in order to make certain that we move from one basic feasible solution to another.

The required calculations will turn out to be quite straightforward because of the particular form of the equations involved. An examination of Equations (7.1) to (7.4) will show that they meet two primary conditions: (1) each constraint equation contains exactly one basic variable, and that variable has a coefficient of one; (2) each basic variable appears in one and only one constraint equation and does not appear in the objective function. A set of equations meeting these conditions is said to be in *canonical form*. In the simplex algorithm, the equations will always be in canonical form. We will first state the simplex procedure and then illustrate it completely, using the Valvton problem, Example 7.1.

Always working from a canonical set of equations, the procedure is basically as follows.

1. The variable with the most negative coefficient in the z (objective function) equation is selected as the entering variable. In case of a tie, an arbitrary selection may be made. If none of the z equation coefficients are negative, stop—the optimal solution has been reached.
2. In each constraint equation, if the coefficient of the entering variable is positive, divide that coefficient into the RHS (right-hand side) value, to get what we can call a *test ratio*. (If the coefficient of the entering variable is zero or negative, ignore this equation, since this constraint cannot limit the value of the entering variable.) Choose, as the so-called *pivot equation*, that equation which has the smallest test ratio. The departing variable will be the current basic variable in the pivot equation. The coefficient of the entering variable in the pivot equation is called the *pivot element*.
3. All coefficients in the pivot equation are divided by the pivot element, and the entering variable now becomes the basic variable in that equation. We call this equation the new pivot equation, and it becomes the initial constraint equation in the next canonical set, although its row position need not change.
4. In the new pivot equation, solve for the value of the entering variable. Use the resultant expression to replace (and thus eliminate) the entering variable in all equations other than the pivot equation, including the z equation.

5. Multiply out and combine terms to form the new set of canonical equations, including the pivot equation. Specify the solution. Go to step 1.

This procedure will now be followed for the problem of Example 7.1.

First iteration

Starting equations:
$$
\begin{aligned}
(7.1) \quad & v + 1.5p + S_1 && = 750 \\
(7.2) \quad & 0.5p + S_2 && = 200 \\
(7.3) \quad & v + p + S_3 && = 600 \\
(7.4) \quad & -3v - 4p + z && = 0
\end{aligned}
$$

1. Entering variable is p (-4 is most negative coefficient in z equation). *Comment:* For each unit of p brought into the solution, profit will increase by $4.

2.

Equation	Test Ratio	Basic Variable Which Would Be Forced Out
(7.1)	$750/1.5 = 500$	S_1
(7.2)	$200/0.5 = 400$	S_2 (departing variable)
(7.3)	$600/1 = 600$	S_3

Comment: We want to bring in as many units of p as possible. When the number of units of p reaches 400, basic variable S_2, in Equation (7.2), will be forced to zero. A greater value of p would force S_2 negative, indicating a requirement for more polisher time than is available. Thus, Equation (7.2) represents the pivot equation, S_2 is the departing variable, and 0.5 is the pivot element.

3. Divide Equation (7.2) by 0.5, giving $p + 2S_2 = 400$, the new pivot equation. *Comment:* To be in canonical form, the basic variable in each equation must have a coefficient of 1, and this was accomplished by dividing the equation containing the new basic variable by the pivot element.

4. Pivot equation is $p + 2S_2 = 400$, so $p = -2S_2 + 400$. Wherever p appears in the other equations, replace it by $-2S_2 + 400$, its algebraic equivalent.

Previous Equation	New Equation
(7.1)	$v + 1.5(-2S_2 + 400) + S_1 = 750$
(7.2)	$p + 2S_2 = 400$ (pivot equation)
(7.3)	$v + (-2S_2 + 400) + S_3 = 600$
(7.4)	$-3v - 4(-2S_2 + 400) + z = 0$

Comment: The new basic variable can be in only one equation, so it must be eliminated from all other equations.

5. Multiplying out and combining terms, the new equations and corresponding solution are

Equation			Solution
$v + S_1 - 3S_2$	$= 150$	(7.5)	$S_1 = 150$
$p + 2S_2$	$= 400$	(7.6)	$p = 400$
$v - 2S_2 + S_3$	$= 200$	(7.7)	$S_3 = 200$
$-3v + 8S_2$	$+ z = 1600$	(7.8)	$z = 1600$

Comment: In each constraint equation, every variable is nonbasic (has a value of zero) except the basic variable in that equation. Since the basic variable always has a coefficient of 1, its value must be equal to the RHS value. Except for z, the objective function contains only nonbasic variables, so z equals the RHS value.

Since there is a negative coefficient in the z equation, this solution cannot be optimal, so we proceed to the next iteration.

Second iteration

Starting equations:
(7.5) $v + S_1 - 3S_2 = 150$
(7.6) $p + 2S_2 = 400$
(7.7) $v - 2S_2 + S_3 = 200$
(7.8) $-3v + 8S_2 + z = 1600.$

1. Entering variable is v (only negative coefficient in z equation).

2.

Equation	Test Ratio	Basic Variable Which Would Be Forced Out
(7.5)	$150/1 = 150$	S_1 (departing variable)
(7.6)	—	p cannot be forced out
(7.7)	$200/1 = 200$	S_3

Comment: Since v does not appear in Equation (7.6), its value cannot affect the basic variable in that equation. S_1 is the departing variable. Equation (7.5) is the pivot equation, whose pivot element (coefficient of v) is 1.

3. Divide Equation (7.5) by 1, giving $v + S_1 - 3S_2 = 150$, the new pivot equation.

4. From the new pivot equation, $v = -S_1 + 3S_2 + 150$.

Previous Equation	New Equation
(7.5)	$v + S_1 - 3S_2 = 150$ (pivot equation)
(7.6)	$p + 2S_2 = 400$
(7.7)	$(-S_1 + 3S_2 + 150) - 2S_2 + S_3 = 200$
(7.8)	$-3(-S_1 + 3S_2 + 150) + 8S_2 + z = 1600$

5. New equations and solution are:

Equation			Solution	
$v + S_1 - 3S_2$	$= 150$	(7.9)	$v =$	150
$p \quad\;\; + 2S_2$	$= 400$	(7.10)	$p =$	400
$-S_1 + S_2 + S_3$	$= 50$	(7.11)	$S_3 =$	50
$3S_1 - S_2 \quad\;\; + z = 2050$		(7.12)	$z =$	2050

A glance at the coefficients in the objective function tells us that the solution is still not optimal, since the coefficient of S_2 is -1. Bringing S_2 into the solution will therefore increase the profit z. As before, the maximum amount of S_2 must be calculated. Incidentally, note that S_2 was in the initial solution, was later forced out, and now is reentering the solution. This phenomenon is quite common in linear programming solutions.

The fact that each unit of S_2 brought in will yield a profit of $1 can be readily verified by examining the effect of such a change in each constraint equation. In Equation (7.9), each unit of S_2 forces v to increase by 3 units, increasing profit by $(3)(3) = \$9$. In Equation (7.10), each unit of S_2 must decrease p by 2 units, thereby reducing profit by $(2)(4) = \$8$. In Equation (7.11), each unit of S_2 will decrease S_3 by 1 unit, but there is no cost associated with S_3, which is just the unused amount of steel. The net result, then, is a $1 increase in profit for each unit of S_2 brought into the solution.

Third iteration

Starting equations:
$$(7.9) \quad v + S_1 - 3S_2 \qquad\qquad\;\; = 150$$
$$(7.10) \quad p \qquad + 2S_2 \qquad\qquad = 400$$
$$(7.11) \qquad\;\; -S_1 + S_2 + S_3 \qquad = 50$$
$$(7.12) \qquad\;\;\; 3S_1 - S_2 \qquad + z = 2050$$

1. Entering variable is S_2 (only negative coefficient in z equation).

2. Equation	Test Ratio	Basic Variable Which Would Be Forced Out
(7.9)	Negative	v cannot be forced out
(7.10)	$400/2 = 200$	p
(7.11)	$50/1 = 50$	S_3 (departing variable)

Comment: Introducing units of S_2 into Equation (7.9) will actually increase the value of v. S_3 is the departing variable, and Equation (7.11) is the pivot equation, with pivot element 1 (coefficient of S_2).

3. Divide Equation (7.11) by 1, giving $-S_1 + S_2 + S_3 = 50$, the new pivot equation.

4. From the new pivot equation, $S_2 = S_1 - S_3 + 50$.

Previous Equation	New Equation
(7.9)	$v + S_1 - 3(S_1 - S_3 + 50) = 150$
(7.10)	$p + 2(S_1 - S_3 + 50) = 400$
(7.11)	$-S_1 + S_2 + S_3 = 50$ (pivot equation)
(7.12)	$3S_1 - (S_1 - S_3 + 50) + z = 2050$

5. New equations and solution are

Equation		Solution
$v - 2S_1 + 3S_3 = 300$	(7.13)	$v = 300$
$p + 2S_1 - 2S_3 = 300$	(7.14)	$p = 300$
$-S_1 + S_2 + S_3 = 50$	(7.15)	$S_2 = 50$
$2S_1 + S_3 + z = 2100$	(7.16)	$z = 2100$

Observe that there are no variables with negative coefficients in the objective function equation. Therefore, this must be an optimal solution. Thus, adding units of S_1 or S_3 would serve only to decrease the profit, z.

At this point, we can recap the concept behind the simplex algorithm. We start the process at an extreme point of the feasible region (in this case, the origin), so that we have an initial basic feasible solution. We then move to an adjacent extreme point by bringing in a previously nonbasic variable and removing a previously basic variable. The algorithm guarantees that each iteration will result in an improvement in the value of the objective function (except in the case of degeneracy, to be discussed later, when the objective function value can remain unchanged). The algorithm terminates when an optimal basic feasible solution has been achieved.

In practice, the calculations of the simplex algorithm can be performed without writing out the variables in each equation. Although we will stress the importance of computer solution of linear programming problems, we will now show, for completeness, how the computational procedures of the simplex algorithm can be mechanized.

Computational Procedure of the Simplex Algorithm

The linear system of equations in the linear programming model can be conveniently represented in tabular form. By "detaching" the variable symbols from their coefficients, leaving an array of numbers representing the coefficients and constant terms, we now have what is called a *tableau*, in linear programming jargon. For the example problem just presented, the initial tableau is shown in Table 7.5. (The data on grinder time have been eliminated, because the grinder time constraint is redundant, being dominated by at least one other constraint. This redundant constraint would be handled properly, but its inclusion would only complicate the calculations.)

Table 7.5 Initial Tableau

Basis	v	p	S_1	S_2	S_3	RHS
S_1	1	1.5	1	0	0	750
S_2	0	0.5	0	1	0	200
S_3	1	1	0	0	1	600
z	-3	-4	0	0	0	0

The symbol for each variable appears at the head of the column of its detached coefficients, and RHS stands for right-hand side value, as mentioned earlier. Note that the variable z does not appear as a column entry. This is customary, since the detached coefficients for the variable representing the value of the objective function will always be the same—a one in the final (objective function) row and zeroes in all other rows. Adding this column would therefore contribute no useful information. From the data of Table 7.5, the variables constituting the basis are readily identified. As we have noted, the basic variable in a given constraint equation will have a coefficient of one in that equation and a coefficient of zero in all the other equations, including the objective function.

In the following discussion of the simplex algorithm, you should relate the computations back to the earlier calculations performed without using the detached coefficients. This will help you to see why these computations are performed and will enable you to check the numerical values.

The computational procedures here are almost identical with those just explained, but take advantage of the column alignment of coefficients and also generally use the term "row" in place of "equation."

1. Select the column containing the nonbasic variable with the most negative coefficient in the z (objective function) row. The variable in that column, frequently called the *pivot column*, will be the entering variable. If none of the z row coefficients are negative, stop—the optimal solution has been reached.

From the tableau in Table 7.6, which is a "working copy" of Table 7.5, the pivot column is marked by an arrow below -4, the most negative value for a nonbasic variable in the z row. The entering variable is p.

2. In each constraint row, if the coefficient of the entering variable is positive, divide that coefficient into the RHS value, to get the test ratio. (If the coefficient of the entering variable is zero or negative, ignore this row, since this constraint cannot limit the value of the entering variable.) Choose, as the *pivot row*, that row which has the smallest test ratio. The departing variable will be the current basic variable in the pivot row. The coefficient of the entering variable in the pivot row is called the pivot element.

Table 7.6 Tableau I (initial tableau)

Basis	v	p	S_1	S_2	S_3	RHS	Test Ratio
S_1	.1	1.5	1	0	0	750	$750/1.5 = 500$
$\rightarrow S_2$	0	*0.5	0	1	0	200	$200/0.5 = 400$
S_3	1	1	0	0	1	600	$600/1 = 600$
z	-3	-4 $\uparrow$	0	0	0	0	

In the tableau of Table 7.6, all coefficients of the entering variable are positive in the constraint equations, and the resulting test ratios are shown in the last column of that table. Since the smallest test ratio appears in row 2, that becomes the pivot row, and it is marked by an arrow. The departing variable is the current basic variable in that row, S_2. The pivot element, the coefficient in both the pivot row and the pivot column, is 0.5, which is asterisked in the table.

3. *All* coefficients in the pivot row are divided by the pivot element, and the entering variable now becomes the basic variable in that row. We call this equation the new pivot equation, and it becomes the initial constraint equation in the next tableau, although its row position does not change. (Preserving the order of the constraint equations will be useful in later analyses, but it is not a requirement of the solution process.)

Dividing the pivot row, row 2, by the pivot element, 0.5, we get the initial constraint equation of the next tableau, as shown in row 2 of Table 7.7 (see page 238). The basic variable in this new pivot equation is now p, the entering variable.

4. In all rows other than the pivot row, including the z row, eliminate the coefficient of the entering variable by substituting for the entering variable its algebraic equivalent, using the new pivot equation. (As will be shown, this can be done by multiplying the pivot equation coefficients by the coefficient of the entering variable and subtracting.) These equations become the new constraint equations and the new objective function.

For the first constraint equation in Table 7.6, the coefficient in the pivot column is 1.5, so we subtract 1.5 times the new pivot equation (the second constraint equation in Table 7.7), thereby eliminating the coefficient of p in the new equation. The result, in coefficient form, is shown on the next page.

v	p	S_1	S_2	S_3	RHS
1	1.5	1	0	0	750
$-(0$	1.5	0	3	0	600)
1	0	1	-3	0	150

The resulting coefficients are the coefficients of the first constraint equation in Table 7.7. That equation is the detached coefficient representation of Equation (7.5).

Since the second constraint equation in Table 7.6 became the new pivot equation, we move on to the third constraint equation in Table 7.6. Its coefficient in the pivot column is 1.0, so we subtract 1.0 times the new pivot equation. This becomes the third constraint equation in Table 7.7.

v	p	S_1	S_2	S_3	RHS
1	1	0	0	1	600
$-(0$	1	0	2	0	400)
1	0	0	-2	1	200

Finally, to calculate the new objective function, the required multiplier of the new pivot equation is -4.

v	p	S_1	S_2	S_3	RHS
-3	-4	0	0	0	0
$-(0$	-4	0	-8	0	$-1600)$
-3	0	0	8	0	1600

This is the z row in Table 7.7. Now we would return to step 1.

Check that Tableau II, Table 7.7, represents the detached coefficients of Equations (7.5) to (7.8).

Starting with Tableau II in Table 7.7 and following the four-step procedure just detailed, the computations of the simplex algorithm were carried out for the next two iterations, producing Table 7.8 and Table 7.9, where the optimal solution is indicated

Table 7.7 Tableau II

Basis	v	p	S_1	S_2	S_3	RHS	Test Ratio
→ S_1	*1	0	1	−3	0	150	150/1 = 150
p	0	1	0	2	0	400	—
S_3	1	0	0	−2	1	200	200/1 = 200
z	−3	0	0	8	0	1600	
	↑						

by the absence of any negative coefficients of the nonbasic variables in the z row. The computations for these two tables are not difficult, and you can readily perform them to verify that you understand the simplex algorithm.

Table 7.8 Tableau III

Basis	v	p	S_1	S_2	S_3	RHS	Test Ratio
v	1	0	1	−3	0	150	—
p	0	1	0	2	0	400	400/2 = 200
→ S_3	0	0	−1	*1	1	50	50/1 = 50
z	0	0	3	−1	0	2050	
				↑			

Table 7.9 Tableau IV (optimal solution)

Basis	v	p	S_1	S_2	S_3	RHS
v	1	0	−2	0	3	300
p	0	1	2	0	−2	300
S_2	0	0	−1	1	1	50
z	0	0	2	0	1	2100

A flow chart of the simplex algorithm is shown as Figure 7.9. (A discussion of nonunique and unbounded solutions, referred to in that flow chart, will be found in the following section.)

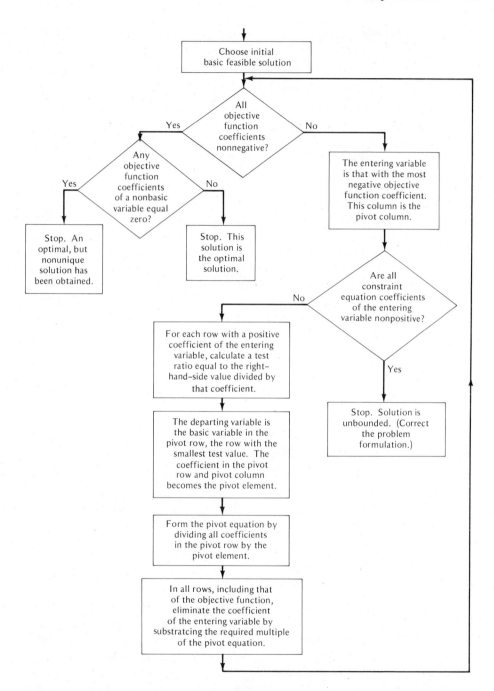

Figure 7.9 Flow chart of the simplex algorithm

7.5 ALTERNATIVE SOLUTION POSSIBILITIES

In most real-world linear programming problems, a unique optimal solution will be obtained. There are, however, several other possibilities.

Alternative Optimal Solutions   If, in the final solution, one of the nonbasic variables has a zero coefficient in the objective function row, that variable can be brought into the solution in any amount (up to its limiting value) without changing the objective function value. Theoretically, there are an infinite possible number of solutions in this case.

As an example, if the slope of the objective function in the Valvton problem had been the same as that of the lathe time constraint, as shown in Figure 7.10, the final z row coefficient of S_3, as shown in Table 7.9, would have been 0 instead of 1. In that case, as you can easily check by calculating the test ratios in Table 7.9, up to 50 units of S_3 could be brought into the solution without changing the value of z. The values of S_2, v, and p, the basic variables in the optimal basis, would be different for each distinct value of S_3, since S_3 appears in each of the constraint equations with a nonzero coefficient. Graphically, as shown in Figure 7.10, the optimal solution could comprise any combination of the activity variables v and p falling on the line connecting vertex 3 and vertex 4.

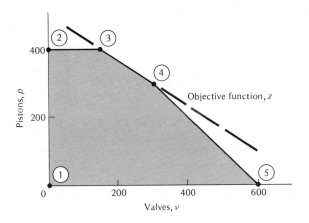

Figure 7.10

Unbounded Solution   Suppose that, at some point in the optimal solution process of a maximization problem, we have obtained a nonoptimal solution, with at least one nonbasic variable having a negative coefficient in the objective function row. If the coefficients of any such nonbasic variable are zero or negative in all the constraint equations, that variable can be introduced in unlimited quantity, since none of the current basic variables will be driven to zero. The objective function value, therefore, can be made as large as desired. Graphically, the situation might appear as shown in Figure 7.11, where the feasible region is unbounded to the right and from above. Then, if we are attempting to maximize an objective function whose slope is indicated by the dashed line, there is no limit to the value of the objective function, and we say that the solution is unbounded. This is clearly an impossible situation for any real problem and indicates that an error has been made in the formulation of the problem. One such error to look for is the reversal of the inequality sign for one or more constraints.

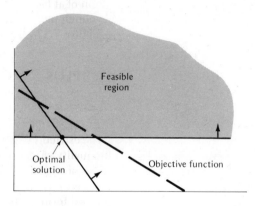

Figure 7.11

Note that an unbounded feasible region does not necessarily imply an unbounded solution. If, in Figure 7.11, we were attempting to minimize the objective function, the optimal solution would be achieved at the point of intersection of the two constraint equation lines.

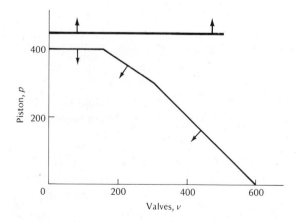

Figure 7.12

No Feasible Solution   It is possible that the problem constraints are such that no feasible solution can be achieved. Such a situation generally points to an error in problem formulation. Another possibility is that of conflicting management policies, such as specifying a minimum production quantity of a certain product but limiting the quantity of a resource required to produce it, thereby making it impossible to produce the required minimum quantity of the product. In the Valvton example, for instance, a requirement for the production of at least 450 pistons would mean that no solution could be obtained, since only enough polisher time is available to produce a maximum of 400 pistons. As shown in Figure 7.12 on the previous page, there is no feasible region.

7.6 CONSTRAINT RELATIONSHIPS—SURPLUS AND ARTIFICIAL VARIABLES

In the previous problem solved by the simplex method, we considered only constraints involving what we have called restrictions, where a given limitation could not be exceeded, as indicated by a $\leq$ inequality. As we saw, a restriction inequality is converted to an equation by the addition of a slack variable, which represents the unused or unallocated portion of the limited resource.

Constraint equations involving what we term requirements often indicate that a minimum quantity of a particular item is required, as specified by a $\geq$ inequality. As an example, in the diet problem of Example 7.2, the minimum daily requirement of 10,000 units of nutrient A led to the inequality constraint

$$100x_1 + 200x_2 \geq 10,000,$$

where x_1 = pounds of feed 1 and x_2 = pounds of feed 2. Suppose we introduce a variable, S, to form the equation

$$100x_1 + 200x_2 - S = 10,000.$$

Because it is not in the required canonical form, this relationship is not satisfactory for the simplex algorithm. Recall that each equation must have a variable which appears only in that equation and has a coefficient of 1. True, the variable S would appear only in this equation, but its coefficient is -1. If we multiplied both sides of the equation by -1, the coefficient of S would become 1, but the constant term on the right-hand side of the equality would then become negative. This is not permissible, since it would make the value of the basic variable in that equation negative. S now represents what is called a *surplus variable*, rather than a slack variable.

The way out of the difficulty is to add an additional variable with a coefficient of 1. We call this type of variable an *artificial variable* (for reasons which will become clear) and designate it as A. Our equation then finally becomes

$$100x_1 + 200x_2 - S + A = 10,000.$$

Since we already had an equation and included the artificial variable only because of the particular computational algorithm, we must make sure that the artificial variable will have a value of zero in the optimal solution. We can do this by assigning to the artificial variable an *arbitrarily large penalty* in the objective function. The value of this penalty is frequently expressed as $-M$ for maximization problems and $+M$ for minimization problems, where M is a number so large that it dominates everything else in the problem. This method (often called the "big M" method) makes the initial solution highly nonoptimal, but insures that all artificial variables will be zero in the optimal solution. Artificial variables have no economic significance; they are, as their name implies, unrelated to the real problem. They are used only to obtain an initial basic feasible solution. *If all the artificial variables cannot be driven out, then there is no feasible solution.*

If one of the constraints in a problem must be satisfied as a strict equality, it can be easily handled by adding an artificial variable to get the initial solution going. As before, the value of the artificial variable coefficient in the objective function will represent a penalty of M. An equality constraint requires neither a slack variable nor a surplus variable.

There is another solution technique, called the two-phase method, which is frequently used for computer solutions of linear programming problems involving artificial variables. This technique avoids the use of the arbitrarily large value M, which is somewhat awkward to handle from a computer programming standpoint. Phase I involves the replacement of the original objective function by a modified objective function, which is just the sum of the artificial variables. When this objective function is minimized, phase I is completed. If the value of the objective function is positive, there is no feasible solution, since the artificial variables are not all zero. If the objective function value is zero, all artificial variables are then zero, and the second phase begins. The *original objective function* now is substituted for the modified objective function, and the initial phase II solution is the optimal basic feasible solution from phase I. The computations then proceed in the customary simplex fashion.

7.7 SIMPLEX ALGORITHM APPLIED TO MINIMIZATION PROBLEMS

Minimization problems in linear programming can be handled in one of two ways. The first is to reverse the sign of the coefficients of the objective function to be minimized and then handle the problem as a maximization problem. Thus, if the objective were to

$$\text{minimize } 8x_1 + 5x_2 - 2x_3,$$

the objective could be equivalently stated as

$$\text{maximize } -8x_1 - 5x_2 + 2x_3.$$

The second way is to modify the simplex algorithm so that the entering variable is now the nonbasic variable whose coefficient in the objective function row has the greatest *positive* value, instead of the greatest negative value, as in a maximization problem. An optimal solution is then reached when the coefficients of all the non-basic variables in the objective function row are *nonpositive*.

We will now solve a very simple linear programming problem where the objective function is to be minimized. We choose to handle this directly as a minimization problem, to show how the simplex algorithm functions in such a case. This example will also illustrate the use of surplus and artificial variables.

EXAMPLE 7.5

$$\text{Minimize } z = x_1 + 3x_2$$

subject to
$$x_1 + x_2 \geqslant 4$$
$$2x_1 + x_2 \leqslant 6$$
$$x_2 = 3$$

and
$$x_1, x_2 \geqslant 0.$$

We will solve this problem by the "big M" method and then indicate the differences if the two-phase method had been used. Finally, since there are only two activity variables, a graphical interpretation of the solution process will be shown.

"Big M" Method

To get this problem into the proper form for solution, the first constraint, with a $\geqslant$ inequality, requires both a surplus and an artificial variable. The second constraint requires a slack variable, and the third constraint, an equation, requires an artificial variable. Finally, the objective function must be modified to include the artificial variables. (This problem is so simple that the solution can be quickly found by trial and error. Our interest, of course, is not in the solution, per se, but in the problem-solving approach.) We can then state the problem as:

$$\text{minimize } z = x_1 + 3x_2 + MA_1 + MA_2$$

subject to
$$x_1 + x_2 - S_1 \qquad + A_1 \qquad = 4$$
$$2x_1 + x_2 \qquad + S_2 \qquad = 6$$
$$x_2 \qquad\qquad + A_2 = 3$$

and
$$x_1, x_2, S_1, S_2, A_1, A_2 \geqslant 0.$$

The initial basic variables are then the slack variable S_2 and the artificial variables A_1 and A_2. S_1 is a surplus variable, and initially a nonbasic variable, along with x_1 and x_2. The value M is a very large number.

Before we can begin the simplex algorithm, we must first get rid of the coefficients of the artificial variables in the z row, since all basic variables must have zero coefficients in the objective function equation. We can do this by solving for A_1 and A_2 in the constraint equations and then substituting the resulting expressions back into the objective function. From the first and third constraint equations:

$$A_1 = 4 - x_1 - x_2 + S_1$$
$$A_2 = 3 - x_2.$$

Then,

$$z = x_1 + 3x_2 + M(4 - x_1 - x_2 + S_1) + M(3 - x_2)$$
$$= (1 - M)x_1 + (3 - 2M)x_2 + MS_1 + 7M.$$

Placing all the variables on the left side of the objective function, as we did in Example 7.1, we now get a canonical equation set:

$$x_1 + \qquad x_2 - \quad S_1 \qquad + A_1 \qquad\qquad = 4 \qquad \textbf{(7.17)}$$
$$2x_1 + \qquad x_2 \qquad\quad + S_2 \qquad\qquad\qquad = 6 \qquad \textbf{(7.18)}$$
$$x_2 \qquad\qquad\qquad + A_2 \quad = 3 \qquad \textbf{(7.19)}$$
$$(M - 1)x_1 + (2M - 3)x_2 - MS_1 \qquad\qquad\qquad + z = 7M \qquad \textbf{(7.20)}$$

with $\qquad\qquad x_1, x_2, S_1, S_2, A_1, A_2 \geqslant 0,$

and z is to be minimized.

The initial basic solution is

$$x_1 = 0, \qquad x_2 = 0, \qquad S_1 = 0, \qquad S_2 = 6, \qquad A_1 = 4, \qquad A_2 = 3, \qquad z = 7M.$$

This is not a feasible solution, because there are artificial variables with positive values. It is a basic solution because the number of variables with positive values does not exceed the number of constraints. The initial tableau is shown in Table 7.10. Since M is very large, the most *positive* value for a nonbasic variable in the z row is $2M - 3$. The entering variable is then x_2. Calculating the test ratios, the smallest is 3, in the third row, so that row becomes the pivot row. Since the pivot element is 1, in the third row and second column, the new pivot equation is the same as the equation in the pivot row. This becomes the initial constraint equation in Tableau II, Table 7.11.

Table 7.10 Tableau I

Basis	x_1	x_2	S_1	S_2	A_1	A_2	RHS	Test Ratio
A_1	1	1	−1	0	1	0	4	4/1 = 4
S_2	2	1	0	1	0	0	6	6/1 = 6
→ A_2	0	*1	0	0	0	1	3	3/1 = 3
z	$M - 1$	$2M - 3$	$-M$	0	0	0	7M	
		↑						

In Tableau II, the other two constraint equations and the objective function are calculated in just the same way as in the earlier maximization example, by subtracting the required multiple of the new pivot equation to get rid of the pivot row coefficients of the entering variable. The calculations of the z row of Tableau II are on the next page. The required multiple of the new pivot equation is $2M - 3$.

x_1	x_2	S_1	S_2	A_1	A_2		RHS
$M - 1$	$2M - 3$	$-M$	0	0	0		$7M$
$-($ 0	$2M - 3$	0	0	0	$2M - 3$		$6M - 9)$
$M - 1$	0	$-M$	0	0	$-2M + 3$		$M + 9$

Table 7.11 Tableau II

Basis	x_1	x_2	S_1	S_2	A_1	A_2	RHS	Test Ratio
→ A_1	*1	0	-1	0	1	-1	1	$1/1 = 1$
S_2	2	0	0	1	0	-1	3	$3/2 = 1.5$
x_2	0	1	0	0	0	1	3	$3/0 = \infty$
z	$M - 1$	0	$-M$	0	0	$-2M + 3$	$M + 9$	

↑ (under x_1)

After this first iteration, the solution is

$$x_1 = 0, \qquad x_2 = 3, \qquad S_1 = 0, \qquad S_2 = 3, \qquad A_1 = 1, \qquad A_2 = 0, \qquad z = M + 9$$

We still do not have a feasible solution, since there is an artificial variable with a positive value.

In Tableau II, x_1 is the only nonbasic variable with a positive value in the z row, so x_1 is the new entering variable. From the test ratios, row 1 is the pivot row, so that A_1 is the departing variable.

Continuing in the same fashion, the third tableau, Table 7.12, now shows a basic feasible solution, since both artificial variables are now nonbasic. Furthermore, we have now arrived at the optimal solution. How do we know? We observe that none of the nonbasic variables have positive coefficients in the z row.

Table 7.12 Tableau III (optional solution)

Basis	x_1	x_2	S_1	S_2	A_1	A_2	RHS
x_1	1	0	-1	0	1	-1	1
S_2	0	0	2	1	-2	1	1
x_2	0	1	0	0	0	1	3
z	0	0	-1	0	$-M + 1$	$-M + 2$	10

The optimal solution is

$$x_1 = 1, \qquad x_2 = 3, \qquad S_1 = 0, \qquad S_2 = 1, \qquad A_1 = A_2 = 0, \qquad z = 10.$$

In this highly simplified example, it turned out that the first basic feasible solution was the optimal solution. In general, of course, this will not be true.

Two-Phase Method

The two-phase method is really almost the same conceptually as the big M method, with the artificial variables driven out first and the standard simplex procedure following from that point.

If we had used the two-phase method in this problem, the objective function would have been

$$\text{minimize } z = A_1 + A_2.$$

Since these artificial variables will be basic in the first iteration, we must substitute for them their equivalent expressions in terms of nonbasic variables, just as we did in the big M method. As shown earlier,

$$A_1 = 4 - x_1 - x_2 + S_1$$
$$A_2 = 3 - x_2.$$

The objective function then becomes

$$\text{minimize } z = -x_1 - 2x_2 + S_1 + 7.$$

In the simplex solution for this modified problem, the first tableau will be as shown in Table 7.10, except that the coefficients in the objective function row are now 1, 2, -1, 0, 0, 0, and 7, respectively, as determined from the objective function just stated. Observe that these values are simply the coefficients of the values of M in the z row of Table 7.10.

In the second tableau, showing the results of the first iteration, the results will be as shown in Table 7.11, except for the z row, where the coefficients now become 1, 0, -1, 0, 0, -2, and 1, as you can readily calculate. After the second iteration, the results would be given by Table 7.12, except for the z row coefficients, which are 0, 0, 0, 0, -1, -1, and 0. Note again that these are just the coefficients, in Table 7.12, of the values of M in the z row. Phase I has now been successfully completed, since the objective function value has been reduced to zero.

At this point, we start the set of subsequent iterations with the final phase I tableau, but with the original objective function replacing the final phase I objective function. We must, however, modify the original objective function, if necessary, to eliminate any variables which are basic in the final phase I solution. The original objective function was

$$\text{minimize } z = x_1 + 3x_2.$$

Since x_1 and x_2 are both basic variables at this point in the solution process, we must express them in terms of nonbasic variables, using the equations represented by the detached coefficients in the final phase I tableau. From Table 7.12, the required equations are taken from the coefficients in row 1, where x_1 is the basic variable, and row 3, where x_2 is the basic variable. The artificial variables, which have been driven out, can be ignored. Then,

$$x_1 = S_1 + 1$$
$$x_2 = 3,$$

and the objective function is

$$\text{minimize } z = x_1 + 3x_2 = S_1 + 10.$$

The objective function coefficients would then be 0, 0, -1, and 0 for x_1, x_2, S_1, and S_2, respectively, and the RHS value would be 10, just as shown in Table 7.12. This, of course, is the optimal solution, since there is no objective function coefficient (other than that for an artificial variable) with a positive value.

Graphical Interpretation

With only two activity variables, x_1 and x_2, in this problem, it is straightforward to show the graphical solution, which is presented in Figure 7.13. A circled number indicates the solution point corresponding to each iteration.

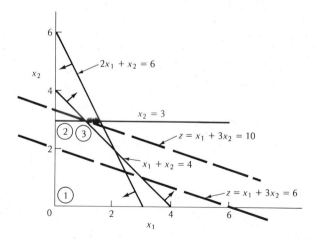

Figure 7.13

With 6 variables in the problem and 3 constraint equations, each basic (but not necessary feasible) solution must have $6 - 3 = 3$ nonbasic variables. We know that the initial basic solution was at the origin, vertex 1, and that the simplex algorithm then directed the solution along the x_2 axis to vertex 2 and then across to vertex 3. At each numbered vertex, let us now solve for the values of all basic variables and the objective function, as was done earlier in Table 7.4 for the Valvton problem. We will work directly with Equations (7.17) to (7.20), always listing first the nonbasic variables.

Vertex 1

$x_1 = 0$

$x_2 = 0$

$S_1 = 0$ [the sum of x_1 and x_2 provides no surplus in Equation (7.17)].

Equation (7.17): $0 + 0 - 0 + A_1 = 4, A_1 = 4$.

Equation (7.18): $0 + 0 + S_2 = 6, S_2 = 6$.

Equation (7.19): $0 + A_2 = 3, A_2 = 3$.

Equation (7.20): $0 + 0 - 0 + z = 7M, z = 7M$.

Vertex 2

$x_1 = 0$

$S_1 = 0$

$A_2 = 0$ [Equation (7.19) is now feasible].

Equation (7.19): $x_2 + 0 = 3, x_2 = 3$.

Equation (7.17): $0 + 3 - 0 + A_1 = 4, A_1 = 1$.

Equation (7.18): $0 + 3 + S_2 = 6, S_2 = 3$.

Equation (7.20): $0 + (2M - 3)(3) - 0 + z = 7M, z = M + 9$.

Vertex 3

$S_1 = 0$

$A_2 = 0$

$A_1 = 0$ [Equation (7.17) is now feasible].

Equation (7.19): $x_2 + 0 = 3, x_2 = 3$.

Equation (7.17): $x_1 + 3 - 0 + 0 = 4, x_1 = 1$.

Equation (7.18): $(2)(1) + 3 + S_2 = 6, S_2 = 1$.

Equation (7.20): $(M - 1)(1) + (2M - 3)(3) - 0 + z = 7M, z = 10$.

Several points are worth noting about the graph in Figure 7.13.

1. Because of the equality constraint, $x_2 = 3$, the feasible "region" actually consists only of the marked line between the other two constraints. Equality constraints should be avoided if at all possible, because they severely limit the range of possible solutions (and can preclude any feasible solution).
2. The initial solution point is at the origin, vertex 1, and the next solution point is at vertex 2. Both these solutions are clearly outside the feasible "region" and are therefore infeasible.
3. The third solution point is at vertex 3. This represents the first feasible solution. Looking at the slope of the objective function, this solution is also the optimal solution, since we are trying to minimize the value of the objective function.

7.8 ALTERNATIVE OBJECTIVE FUNCTIONS

In the Valvton problem, we assumed that no cost was attached to idle equipment or facilities. This is not necessarily true, since there may be standby power costs, maintenance, and so forth. Any *incremental* costs incurred by an idle machine, department, or other productive unit should be included, provided that they are not costs which are incurred regardless of whether the equipment or facilities are in use or are idle.

Idle equipment costs appear in the objective function and are represented by negative coefficients of the slack variables. Suppose that the cost of idle lathe capacity was $10 per hour and the cost of idle polisher capacity was $5 per hour. The lathe and polisher slack variables were S_1 and S_2, respectively. Unit profit per valve (v) was $3 and unit profit per piston (p) was $4. The revised objective function would be

$$\text{maximize } z = 3v + 4p - 10S_1 - 5S_2.$$

Perhaps an emergency order could result in a situation where we wanted to maximize the time the equipment was in use, temporarily disregarding economic considerations. For this case, we would then attempt to minimize the appropriate slack variables. This objective function would be

$$\text{minimize } z = S_1 + S_2.$$

Note that we are weighting these slacks equally.

7.9   DEGENERACY

Earlier, in the Valvton problem, we saw that with n decision variables and m inequality constraints, exactly m nonzero variables and n zero variables were present in any basic feasible solution. If, at some point in the simplex algorithm, we have a basic feasible solution with more than n zero variables and thus fewer than m nonzero variables, we have a condition known as *degeneracy*.

In a graphical solution, degeneracy is indicated when, at some extreme point, more than two constraint equation lines intersect. Suppose, for example, in the Valvton problem, that only 150 hours of polisher time had been available. Then, looking at the vertex yielding the optimal solution (see Figure 7.4), the polisher time constraint line would have also passed through that vertex. There would have been zero polisher slack, instead of the 50 hours in the original problem, and three variables, instead of the normal two, would be zero.

In the simplex algorithm, degeneracy can be easily recognized. Remember that, after selecting the entering variable, we calculated test ratios for each constraint equation to find the smallest positive value of that variable which would just drive out one of the current basic variables. If there is a tie for the lowest test ratio, more than one basic variable is driven out, and we then have a degenerate solution at the start of the next iteration.

When degeneracy occurs at an extreme point which is not the optimal solution point, it is possible in some cases for the solution to "cycle," or to return to the same basis, thereby precluding attainment of the optimal solution. Computational procedures have been developed to cope with such cycling, but a discussion of them is beyond the scope of this introductory text.

7.10 DUALITY

We will show that, for every linear programming problem, there is a closely related problem called its *dual*. The relationship between these two problems is of considerable practical interest, as we will see.

Let us now formally state the general mathematical form of a linear programming problem where the objective function is to be maximized and where the constraints are all $\leq$ inequalities. We call this the *primal* linear programming problem.

$$\text{Maximize } z = c_1x_1 + c_2x_2 + \cdots + c_nx_n$$

subject to
$$a_{11}x_1 + a_{12}x_2 + \cdots + a_{1n}x_n \leq b_1$$
$$a_{21}x_1 + a_{22}x_2 + \cdots + a_{2n}x_n \leq b_2$$
$$\vdots$$
$$a_{m1}x_1 + a_{m2}x_2 + \cdots + a_{mn}x_n \leq b_m$$

and
$$x_1 \geq 0, x_2 \geq 0, \ldots, x_n \geq 0$$

or, in more succinct mathematical form:

$$\text{maximize } z = \sum_{j=1}^{n} c_jx_j$$

subject to
$$\sum_{j=1}^{n} a_{ij}x_j \leq b_i, \quad i = 1, 2, \ldots, m$$

and
$$x_j \geq 0, \quad j = 1, 2, \ldots, n,$$

where a_{ij}, b_i, and c_j are constants (unrestricted in sign) dependent on the particular problem, and the x_j are activity levels, or decision variables.

It should be noted that any linear programming problem can be structured into the mathematical form shown by straightforward transformations. These transformations are discussed below.

1. A minimization problem can be transformed into a maximization problem by multiplying the objective function by -1. Thus, the objective function

$$\text{minimize } c_1x_1 + c_2x_2$$

is equivalent to

$$\text{maximize } -c_1x_1 - c_2x_2.$$

2. A requirements constraint, involving a $\geq$ inequality, can be changed to a $\leq$ inequality by multiplying the given constraint equation through by -1. Thus,

$$a_{21}x_1 + a_{22}x_2 \geq b_2$$

is equivalent to

$$-a_{21}x_1 - a_{22}x_2 \leq -b_2.$$

3. An equality can be replaced by two inequalities which force the equality condition. If

$$a_{31}x_1 + a_{32}x_2 = b_3,$$

then the pair of equations

$$a_{31}x_1 + a_{32}x_2 \leqslant b_3$$
and
$$-a_{31}x_1 - a_{32}x_2 \leqslant -b_3$$

specifies the required equivalence.

4. Since all decision variables in a linear programming problem must be nonnegative, to meet the requirements of the simplex algorithm, a variable which is unrestricted in sign can be replaced by the difference between two nonnegative variables. Thus, x_j (unrestricted in sign) $= x_j^+ - x_j^-$, where $x_j^+ \geqslant 0$ and $x_j^- \geqslant 0$.

Having shown that any linear programming problem can be structured in this primal form, we can state the corresponding dual problem.

$$\text{Minimize } w = b_1y_1 + b_2y_2 + \cdots + b_my_m$$

subject to
$$a_{11}y_1 + a_{21}y_2 + \cdots + a_{m1}y_m \geqslant c_1$$
$$a_{12}y_1 + a_{22}y_2 + \cdots + a_{m2}y_m \geqslant c_2$$
$$\vdots$$
$$a_{1n}y_1 + a_{2n}y_2 + \cdots + a_{mn}y_m \geqslant c_n$$
and
$$y_1 \geqslant 0, y_2 \geqslant 0, \ldots, y_m \geqslant 0,$$

where the y_i's represent the dual variables.

The dual problem is then

$$\text{minimize } \sum_{i=1}^{m} b_iy_i$$

subject to
$$\sum_{i=1}^{m} a_{ij}y_i \geqslant c_j, \quad j = 1, 2, \ldots, n$$

and
$$y_i \geqslant 0, \quad i = 1, 2, \ldots, m.$$

The dual and primal problems are related in the following manner.

1. A *dual variable* is associated with each constraint in the primal problem (excluding the nonnegativity constraints), and there is a dual constraint for each primal variable.
2. The objective function coefficients in the dual are the right-hand side coefficients in the primal. Similarly, the right-hand side coefficients in the dual are the objective function coefficients in the primal.

3. The coefficients in the dual constraints are the same as those in the primal constraints, but with row and column coefficients interchanged. That is, the coefficients in row i of the primal problem are the same as the coefficients in column i of the dual problem.
4. The objective function is minimized instead of maximized.

By converting the dual problem into primal form, using the transformations discussed, taking its dual and then again expressing the result in primal form, it can be readily demonstrated that the dual of the dual is the primal.

We will now take an earlier example, the Valvton problem, which is already in primal form, and formulate and solve its dual problem. We will then discuss some important primal-dual properties revealed by the results.

The primal problem is

$$\text{maximize } z = 3v + 4p,$$

subject to
$$v + 1.5p \leqslant 750 \text{ (lathe time constraint)}$$
$$0.5p \leqslant 200 \text{ (grinder time constraint)}$$
$$v + \quad p \leqslant 600 \text{ (steel constraint)}$$

and
$$v, p \geqslant 0.$$

Since there are three constraints, there must be three dual variables, which we will label as y_1, y_2, and y_3. Then, according to the rules for constructing the dual, the dual problem is:

$$\text{minimize } w = 750y_1 + 200y_2 + 600y_3$$

subject to
$$y_1 \qquad + y_3 \geqslant 3$$
$$1.5y_1 + 0.5y_2 + y_3 \geqslant 4$$

and
$$y_1, y_2, y_3 \geqslant 0.$$

Before solving the dual problem, let us discuss the economic interpretation of the dual variables. In this example, the variables y_1, y_2, and y_3 represent, respectively, the marginal value associated with one additional unit (hour) of lathe time, one additional unit (hour) of grinder time, and one additional unit (pound) of steel. In the dual problem, the objective is to minimize the total marginal value of all resources, subject to the constraints that the marginal value of the required resource for each product must be not less than that product's profit. Thus, in the first dual constraint, the sum of the marginal values of the 1 hour of lathe time and 1 pound of steel required for each valve must at least equal the $3 unit profit on valves. In the second dual constraint, the sum of the marginal values of the 1.5 hours of lathe time, 0.5 hour of grinder time, and 1 pound of steel required for each piston must be not less than the $4 unit profit on pistons. (These resource requirements for the production of each valve and piston came originally from Table 7.1.)

To solve the dual problem, we must add the required surplus and artificial variables. Using the "big M" approach, we restate the problem as

$$\text{minimize } w = 750y_1 + 200y_2 + 600y_3 + MA_1 + MA_2$$

subject to

$$y_1 \qquad + y_3 - T_1 \qquad + A_1 \qquad = 3$$

$$1.5y_1 + 0.5y_2 + y_3 \qquad - T_2 \qquad + A_2 = 4$$

and

$$y_1, y_2, y_3, T_1, T_2 \geq 0$$

where T_1 and T_2 are surplus variables and A_1 and A_2 are artificial variables.

Just as we did in Example 7.5, we must eliminate the nonzero coefficients of the artificial variables from the objective function, since these artificial variables are basic variables in the initial solution. When we do this, the initial tableau is as shown in Table 7.13, as you should verify.

Table 7.13 Initial Solution

Basis	y_1	y_2	y_3	T_1	T_2	A_1	A_2	RHS	Test ratio
A_1	1	0	1	-1	0	1	0	3	$3/1 = 3$
$\rightarrow A_2$	*1.5	0.5	1	0	-1	0	1	4	$4/1.5 = 8/3$
w	$2.5M - 750$	$0.5M - 200$	$2M - 600$	$-M$	$-M$	0	0	$7M$	

After two iterations, the artificial variables are driven out, and we have the first basic *feasible* solution (not shown), with a value of $2250. After the third iteration, the optimal solution has been reached, as indicated by the fact that the coefficients of the nonbasic variables in the objective function are all nonpositive, as shown in Table 7.14.

Table 7.14 Optimal Solution

Basis	y_1	y_2	y_3	T_1	T_2	A_1	A_2	RHS
y_3	0	-1	1	-3	2	3	-2	1
y_1	1	1	0	2	-2	-2	2	2
w	0	-50	0	-300	-300	$-M + 300$	$-M + 300$	2100

The optimal solution is

$$y_1 = 2, \qquad y_2 = 0, \qquad y_3 = 1, \qquad T_1 = 0, \qquad T_2 = 0, \qquad A_1 = A_2 = 0, \qquad w = 2100.$$

We generally call the optimal values of the dual variables *shadow prices*.

If we now compare the values in Table 7.14, the optimal tableau for the dual problem, with those in Table 7.9, the optimal tableau for the primal problem, we can observe a number of interesting points.

1. The optimal value of the objective function is the same for both primal and dual, $2100.
2. The simplex algorithm solves both the primal and the dual problems simultaneously. The shadow prices, the optimal values of the dual variables, are the coefficients of the slack variables in the objective function equation in the optimal solution of the primal problem.

Dual variable	y_1	y_2	y_3
Shadow price	2	0	1
Slack variable	S_1	S_2	S_3
z-row coefficient	2	0	1

3. If a dual variable is basic in the optimal solution, the corresponding primal constraint is binding, so that the associated slack variable is zero. Conversely, if a primal constraint has a slack variable with a positive value, the corresponding dual variable is zero.

Primal solution	Dual solution
$v = 300$	$T_1 = 0$
$p = 300$	$T_2 = 0$
$S_1 = 0$	$y_1 = 2$
$S_2 = 50$	$y_2 = 0$
$S_3 = 0$	$y_3 = 1$

The economic relationships are as follows.

Primal Activity Variables and Dual Surplus Variables   Since the surplus variable T_1 is zero, the marginal value of the resources going into production of valves is exactly equal to the unit profit of valves. The same holds true for the production of pistons. If a surplus variable, say T_2, were positive, it would mean that the marginal value of the resources going into the production of pistons would exceed the unit profit, so it would not pay to produce pistons, and the value of p would then be zero.

Primal Slack Variables and Dual Shadow Prices   When a slack variable is zero, it shows that the corresponding resource is completely utilized. The associated shadow price is the increase in the value of the objective function if an additional unit of that resource becomes available. Thus, in the optimal solution, $S_1 = 0$, so all 750 hours of lathe time is being utilized. Since $y_1 = 2$, an additional hour of lathe time would increase the total profit by $2. When a slack variable is positive, the corresponding resource is not being completely utilized, so its marginal value is zero. Since $S_2 = 50$, 50 hours of grinder time are unused, and an additional hour of grinder time has zero value. As we will see in the section on Sensitivity Analysis, the numerical values of the shadow prices hold only so long as the optimal basis remains feasible.

Having illustrated some of the important properties of duality with a numerical example, we now state, for the general case, two important theorems relating to duality.

Theorem 1—If either the primal or the dual problem has a feasible solution such that the optimal objective function value is finite, then the other problem has a feasible solution with the same optimal objective function value.

Theorem 2—If, in an optimal solution, a dual variable is basic, the corresponding slack variable in the primal problem will be zero; if a variable in the primal problem is basic, the corresponding dual slack variable is zero. This is sometimes called the "theorem of complementary slackness," and it enables us to solve the dual problem, given the primal solution, and vice versa.

There are several reasons for our interest in duality. For one, we will make particular use of the shadow prices in performing sensitivity analyses. From a computational standpoint, since the number of basic variables cannot exceed the number of constraints, it may be worthwhile to solve the dual problem if the number of dual constraints is appreciably less than the number of primal constraints. Also, the dual problem plays an important role in the solution of a number of related problems, notably the transportation problem, to be considered in the following chapter.

7.11   COMPUTER SOLUTION OF LINEAR PROGRAMMING PROBLEMS

In the real world, practical linear programming problems are always solved by computer. Hand computations are completely impractical for problems other than very small ones, and even the manual solution of small problems is generally avoided because of the high probability of making arithmetic errors. Thus, after learning the fundamental concepts associated with the simplex method, it appears desirable to become acquainted with the general preparation of input data for a linear programming computer program and the analysis of the output data printed out when the optimal solution is reached.

For computer solution, the linear system of equations can be conveniently represented in tableau form, as we have demonstrated. The initial tableau for the Valvton problem is shown in Table 7.5.

Let us now go through the steps necessary to set up this problem for computer solution. Although a large number of linear programming computer programs are available, we will not discuss any one particular program but will illustrate the general principles involved. We will discuss the preparation of the required input data and the analysis of the most unsophisticated type of output, consisting solely of the coefficients in the final optimal tableau. This output is readily available and, although minimal, is sufficient to give us a good deal of information if we know how to analyze it.

The following numerical data must be input (in one form or another) to the program in an order dependent on the design of the particular program.

1. Number of constraint equations of each type
    a) Restrictions ("less-than" inequalities)
    b) Equalities
    c) Requirements ("greater than" inequalities)
2. Number of activity variables
3. Table of constraint equations coefficients, with the rows arranged in a given order, such as restrictions first, equalities, and then requirements
4. Column of RHS initial values
5. Objective function coefficients
6. Information as to whether this is a minimization or maximization problem

After the input data has been read in, the computer program usually supplies all required surplus, slack, and artificial variables "automatically." The program then performs the required iterations until the optimal solution is reached. At that point, as shown in Table 7.15, the optimal tableau is printed out. (This tableau contains the same information as that of Table 7.9.) Although it is admittedly not in a very handy form, the tableau contains a good deal of useful information, as we will see.

Table 7.15 Optimal Tableau

v	p	S_1	S_2	S_3	RHS
1	0	−2	0	3	300
0	1	2	0	−2	300
0	0	−1	1	1	50
0	0	2	0	1	2100

To make the interpretation a little more straightforward, the dotted lines have been drawn to set off the column of right-hand side values and the objective function row. We can now derive the following information, some of which has been discussed previously.

1. The RHS column gives solution values for the basic variables, which are identified as those with a coefficient of 1 in just one constraint equation and a coefficient of 0 in all other equations. Thus, v, p, and S_2 are basic variables. For each of these variables, the value of that basic variable is then equal to the RHS value in the row in which its coefficient of 1 appears. Thus, in the first row, we see that $v = 300$; in the second row, that $p = 300$; and in the third row, that $S_2 = 50$.
2. The profit z is found in the lower right-hand corner, in the objective function row and the RHS column, and is equal to $2100.
3. In the *optimal tableau*, the values in the objective function row (excluding, obviously, the RHS value) are called "shadow prices," as we noted in the

section on Duality. These represent the rate of decrease (increase) in the value of the objective function for each unit increase (decrease) in the value of the associated nonbasic variable. Thus the total profit would decrease by \$2 for every unit of S_1 in the solution. Since S_1 represents lathe time slack and the available lathe time is completely utilized, a unit increase in S_1 has the identical effect as a unit decrease in the amount of lathe time available. Similarly, a unit increase in S_3, steel slack, is the same as a unit decrease in steel availability, and would decrease total profit by \$1. *The shadow prices are applicable so long as the optimal basis remains feasible.*

4. The coefficients above and to the left of the dotted lines represent substitution rates for basic variables. If there is a change in the level of any nonbasic variable, its effect may be calculated, in turn, on each constraint equation by subtracting algebraically, from the RHS value, the amount of the change times the substitution rate for that variable. This is a very important feature and will be discussed in detail in the following section.

7.12 SENSITIVITY ANALYSIS

In actual practice, it is often not enough simply to obtain the optimal solution and consider the problem solved. Frequently, we would like to know the effect on the optimal solution if constraints or objective function coefficients change. Working from the previous optimal solution tableau, it is usually possible to evaluate numerically the effect of such changes without solving the problem again from scratch. In the analyses that follow, we will consider only changes in one variable at a time.

In the final tableau (and any other tableau, for that matter), the substitution rates represented by the various coefficients are applicable only as long as the basis does not change. Therefore, one of the first things we would like to do is to determine the range over which some of the more important factors can change without changing the basis.

Changes in Right-Hand Side Values in Original Tableau

After having obtained an optimal solution, suppose we were informed that the available amount of resource k had changed, either up or down. If the change in this resource is such that the optimal basis remains *feasible*, it will be unnecessary to calculate a new solution to determine the change in total profit. For each unit increase (decrease) in this resource, the total profit will increase (decrease) by the value of the shadow price associated with the slack variable S_k for this resource. We wish to find the permissible range for the amount of this resource such that the shadow price is applicable.

We will let Δ^+ be the maximum allowable increase and Δ^- be the maximum allowable decrease in the available amount of a given resource. There are two cases to be considered.

Case 1: Resource k is not fully utilized, so that its associated slack variable S_k has a positive value. In this situation, the shadow price will always be zero, since additional units of the resource have no value. This shadow price applies for an unlimited increase in the amount of this resource, so that $\Delta^+ = \infty$. On the other hand, we could decrease this resource only until the slack vanishes, so that $\Delta^- = S_k$.

Case 2: Resource k is fully utilized, so that its associated slack variable $S_k = 0$. The procedure for determining the value of Δ^- is the same as that for determining, in the simplex algorithm, how many units of the entering variable should come into the solution. In the column in which slack variable S_k appears, calculate the test ratio for each row. The smallest positive test ratio is the value of Δ^-. If there is no positive test ratio, Δ^- is unlimited. For Δ^+, the process is entirely similar, except that we consider only negative test ratios. The smallest absolute value of all negative test ratios is Δ^+. An absence of negative test ratios means that Δ^+ is unlimited.

Table 7.16 Sensitivity Analysis of RHS Values

Resource	Original Value	Slack Variable and its Optimal Value	Test Ratios	Maximum Allowable Change Δ^-	Δ^+	Allowable Range
Lathe time	750 hr	$S_1 = 0$	$\dfrac{300}{-2} = -150$			(750 − 150 to 750 + 50)
			$\dfrac{300}{2} = 150$	150		600 to 800 hr
			$\dfrac{50}{-1} = -50$		50	
Polisher time	200 hr	$S_2 = 50$	—	50	∞	(200 − 50 to 200 + ∞)
						≥ 150 hr
Steel	600 lb	$S_3 = 0$	$\dfrac{300}{3} = 100$			(600 − 50 to 600 + 150)
			$\dfrac{300}{-2} = -150$		150	550 to 750 lb
			$\dfrac{50}{1} = 50$	50		

In Table 7.16 are shown the calculations involved in determining the allowable range over which each of the three resource amounts can vary without changing the basis. The original values of the resource amounts are taken from Table 7.1, while the values of the slack variables and their associated test ratios are derived from the data of Table 7.15.

To explain the rationale behind this sensitivity analysis, consider the first Δ^- value of 150 in Table 7.16. If the lathe time resource were reduced from 750 to 600 hours, this would be equivalent to having the original 750 hours, but with 150 hours of lathe time slack, S_1. In the second row of Table 7.15, the basic variable $p = 300$. With an S_1 value of 150, p would be driven to zero. (Remember that S_3 is nonbasic, so its value is already zero.) If the lathe time resource were reduced by more than 150 hours, p would be forced out of the basis and it would be necessary to perform another iteration to determine the new optimal solution. The Δ^+ value of 50 is derived from the third row equation. If the lathe time resource were increased from 750 to 800 hours, this would be equivalent to having the original 750 hours, but with -50 hours of lathe time slack S_1. With an S_1 value of -50, the basic variable, S_2, in the third row, would be driven to zero. If S_1 were more negative, S_2 would be driven out of the basis, and the shadow price would no longer be applicable.

The polisher time resource is not fully utilized in the optimal solution, since its slack variable $S_2 = 50$. Thus, $\Delta^- = 50$, and Δ^+ is unlimited, so that the shadow price of zero applies over a range of $(200 - 50)$ to $(200 + \infty)$, or for polisher time ≥ 150 hours.

For the steel resource, the associated slack variable, S_3, is zero, so that the available steel is completely utilized. We then follow the same procedure as for the lathe time resource. The maximum allowable positive value is 50, so $\Delta^- = 50$, and the maximum allowable negative value is -150, so $\Delta^+ = 150$. Since the original constraint value was 600 pounds, the amount of steel could range between $600 - 50$ and $600 + 150$, or from 550 to 750 pounds, without changing the basis.

A comment on negative slack variables (used in the calculation of Δ^+ values) is in order. Earlier, we said that none of the variables in a basic feasible solution could be negative. This is still true. The concept of a negative slack variable is an artificiality, introduced after the solution process has been completed, to represent the effect of an increase in a resource. Note that our analysis of RHS value changes arrived at a range of values for the amount of each resource, and this range can never include negative values.

Having gone through all these computations, we now know the range of applicability for the shadow prices shown in the final tableau. For example, the basis would still be optimal if the lathe time were reduced by 150 hours, and, since the lathe time shadow price is \$2 per hour, the resultant profit would be $2100 - (150)(2.00) = \$1800$. Lathe time could be increased by 50 hours, with an additional profit of $(50)(2.00)$, for a total profit of \$2200. The first 50 hours of polisher time removed will have no effect on the solution, since we have an excess supply of this resource. Additional polisher time, in any amount, is, of course, worthless. In either case, any such change will not affect the total profit, since the shadow price of polisher time is zero. If we attempted to remove more than 50 hours of polisher time, the basis would change and we would have to perform a new iteration. As for steel, a

50 pound decrease in the available amount will drop the profit to $2100 - (50)(1)$ or $2050, whereas an additional 150 pounds would raise the profit to $2250.

Calculating the Effect on Basic Variables   Now that we know how to calculate the new profit value for permissible one-at-a-time changes in our resources, we would also like to determine the associated changes in the values of the basic variables. This is easily done. In each row, the new value of the basic variable will be equal to the RHS value in the optimal tableau minus the amount of the resource change multiplied by the coefficient of its slack variable (the substitution rate) in that equation, carefully observing its algebraic sign. For example, suppose that lathe time availability is decreased by 100 hours. This represents a positive slack of 100 hours. Remembering that S_3 is zero, the first constraint equation could be written as

$$v - (2)(100) = 300,$$

so,

$$v = 300 + 200 = 500.$$

In the second equation,

$$p = 300 - (2)(100) = 100.$$

In the third equation,

$$S_2 = 50 - (-1)(100) = 150.$$

If lathe time were to be increased by 100 hours, equivalent to a negative slack of 100, this would be outside the range of applicability and the basis would have to change, invalidating the existing shadow prices and substitution rates.

The analysis here has considered only changes in the RHS values of constraints involving restrictions, or $\leq$ inequalities. Similar analyses can be performed for changes in the RHS values for requirements constraints, which have $\geq$ inequalities.

Changes in Original Objective Function Coefficients

If the original objective function coefficients, the unit profits, of the basic decision variables change, the optimal profit will change. For each of these coefficients, we can determine the range over which they can change *without changing the basis*. Over that range, the change in profit will be equal to the change in the particular coefficient multiplied by the number of units of that variable in the optimal solution. Unlike the case when RHS values change, changes in the original objective function coefficients do not affect the values of the basic variables, so long as the basis is not changed.

Suppose we let Δ^+ be the maximum allowable increase, and Δ^- the maximum allowable decrease, in the value of the objective function coefficient for a given decision variable. The analysis depends on whether the decision variable is nonbasic or basic in the optimal solution.

Nonbasic Variable   The shadow price of a nonbasic variable is the amount by which it is unprofitable, so Δ^+ is equal to the shadow price. A greater increase would require the nonbasic variable to come into the solution. Since a decrease in the objective function coefficient would just make units of that decision variable even more unprofitable, Δ^- is unlimited. (For a minimization problem, Δ^- would equal the magnitude of the shadow price, while the value of Δ^+ would be unlimited.)

Basic Variable   Before going through the somewhat complicated explanation of the effect of a change in the objective function coefficient of a basic variable, we will show that it is not difficult to mechanize the required computations in a manner quite similar to that shown for the evaluation of resource changes. For each nonzero coefficient in the objective function row, we calculate a test ratio equal to that coefficient divided by the coefficient which is the same column and in the row in which the variable of interest is basic. The smallest positive test ratio becomes Δ^-. If there is no positive test ratio, Δ^- is unlimited. The smallest absolute value of all negative test ratios is Δ^+. Δ^+ is unlimited if there is no negative test ratio.

Table 7.17 shows, for the Valvton problem data of Table 7.15, the analysis of the changes in the objective function coefficients of the two activity variables such that the optimal solution basis will not change.

Table 7.17   Sensitivity Analysis of Objective Function Coefficients

Decision Variable	Basic in Row	Original Objective Function Value*	Test Ratios	Maximum Allowable Change Δ^-	Δ^+	Allowable Range
v	1	$3.00	$\dfrac{2}{-2} = -1$		1	(3.00 − 0.33 to 3.00 + 1.00)
			$\dfrac{1}{3} = 0.33$	0.33		$2.67 to $4.00
p	2	$4.00	$\dfrac{2}{2} = 1$	1		(4.00 − 1.00 to 4.00 − 0.50)
			$\dfrac{1}{-2} = -0.5$		0.5	$3.00 to $4.50

From Table 7.1.

When a decision variable is basic in the optimal solution, we go through a procedure generally similar in nature to that involved in analyzing the effect of a change in the amount of a resource already fully utilized in the optimal solution. Now, however, the test ratio involves the objective function coefficients rather than the RHS values. As an example of the rationale behind the calculations in Table 7.17, consider decision variable v, which is basic in the optimal solution. Suppose its objective function coefficient is *decreased* by an amount d. Thus, an amount dv is added to the objective function equation, which now becomes

$$dv + 2S_1 + S_3 + z = 2100.$$

Since v is a basic variable, it must be eliminated from the objective function equation, just as though v were an entering variable in a simplex iteration. (Remember that a basic variable cannot have a nonzero coefficient in the objective function.) As a basic variable, v appears only in the first constraint equation, where

$$v - 2S_1 + 3S_3 = 300,$$

so $$v = 300 + 2S_1 - 3S_3.$$

Substituting this expression in the objective function equation, we get

$$d(300 + 2S_1 - 3S_3) + 2S_1 + S_3 + z = 2100,$$

so that

$$(2 + 2d)S_1 + (1 - 3d)S_3 + z = 2100 - 300d.$$

We set, in turn, each of the coefficients of the nonbasic variables (S_1 and S_3, in this case) to zero. We can then determine the maximum allowable change in d before a nonbasic variable would come into the solution, thus changing the basis.

For S_1: $2 + 2d = 0$,   so $d = 2/(-2) = -1$.
For S_3: $1 - 3d = 0$,   so $d = 1/3$.

With only one positive and one negative test ratio, $\Delta^- = \frac{1}{3}$ and $\Delta^+ = 1$. Thus, the original objective function coefficient of v can be increased by 1 or decreased by 0.33. With a given value of \$3, the unit profit of valves can therefore range from \$2.67 to \$4 without changing the basis. Within this range, a decrease (increase) of \$d would decrease (increase) z by \$300d, since $v = 300$ in the optimal solution.

The analysis for activity variable p, which is basic in row 2 of the optimal solution, is performed in the same fashion. The unit profit for pistons could drop by as much as \$1 or increase by \$0.50 without changing the basis. Since there are 300 pistons in the optimal solution, a change of \$d in the unit profit would result in a \$300d change in z.

In this small-scale example, there were no nonbasic activity variables. Suppose, however, that the optimal solution had included no valves, so $v = 0$, and that the associated shadow price for v was \$1.25. Then, since the original unit profit of valves was \$3, the shadow price for v would indicate that valves were unprofitable by \$1.25. Their profit would have to be increased to more than \$4.25 before they would come into the solution. On the other hand, their original unit profit could be decreased by any amount without affecting the solution, since they would just become more unprofitable.

With only two activity variables in this problem, the change in the objective function coefficients of these variables can be interpreted graphically. If the unit profit of p is held at \$4, varying the unit profit of v from \$2.67 to \$4 causes the slope the objective function to range between $-2.67/4 = -2/3$ and $-4/4 = -1$. Referrir back to Figure 7.4, these are precisely the slopes of the lathe time and steel cor straints, respectively, as can be verified by checking Equations (7.1) and (7.3). Fr any objective function whose slope falls between those limiting values, the current optimal solution point at the intersection of the lathe time and steel constraints wi remain optimal. In a similar fashion, holding the unit profit of v at \$3 and varying th unit profit of p from \$3 to \$4.50 results in a change in the objective function slo$\text{}$ over a range of $-3/3 = -1$ to $-3/4.50 = -2/3$. This is again the range in slopes f$\text{}$ which the current optimal solution remains optimal.

It is also worth noting that, since it is the *ratio* of the coefficients of v and p whic determines the slope, any value of that ratio falling between 2/3 and 1 will not chang the existing optimal solution basis. Thus, if the unit profit of v dropped to \$2 and th unit profit of p fell anywhere within the range of \$2 to \$3, the current solution woul remain optimal.

Sensitivity analyses can also be performed on the constraint equatio coefficients, but this becomes considerably more complicated. Since this type $\text{}$ analysis almost mandates the use of matrix arithmetic, which has not been discusse$\text{}$ it will not be covered. There is also another technique, called *parametric program ming*, which extends the techniques of sensitivity analysis. A meaningful discussion $\text{}$ this topic is beyond the level of this text.

The following example is presented to tie together the material on optim$\text{}$ solutions and sensitivity analyses.

EXAMPLE 7.6

A company manufactures three products, A, B, and C. Each product must b machine-processed in three departments, as shown in the following table.

Table 7.18 Problem Data

Product	Machine Time Required (hr)			Per Unit Profit Contribution
	Dept. 1	Dept. 2	Dept. 3	
A	1	1	2	\$30
B	2	1	1	25
C	1	2	1	35
Hours available per month	800	1000	2000	

A computer LP program, after two iterations, gives the optimal tableau as in th$\text{}$ accompanying table.

Table 7.19 Optimal Solution

Product			Slack			
A	B	C	Dept. 1	Dept. 2	Dept. 3	RHS
1	3	0	2	−1	0	600
0	−1	1	−1	1	0	200
0	−4	0	−3	1	1	600
0	30	0	25	5	0	25,000

a) What is the optimal product mix?

Let x_1 = units of product A

x_2 = units of product B

x_3 = units of product C

S_1 = Dept. 1 slack, in hours

S_2 = Dept. 2 slack, in hours

S_3 = Dept. 3 slack, in hours

Basic variables — row 1: $x_1 = 600$

— row 2: $x_3 = 200$

— row 3: $S_3 = 600$.

Optimal product mix: 600 units of product A, 200 units of product C.

b) What is the total profit? Check this value by totaling the profit from the individual products.

From the z row, $z = 25,000$. Total profit $= \$25,000$.

Individual profit contributions — product A: $(600)(30) = \$18,000$

— product B: $(0)(25)\ \ =\ \ \ \ \ \ \ 0$

— product C: $(200)(35) =\ \ \ \ 7,000$

$\$25,000$

c) How many processing hours are being used in each department?

The easy way to answer this question is to utilize the values of the slacks.

Dept. 1: 800 hours available. $S_1 =$ 0. 800 hours used.

Dept. 2: 1000 hours available. $S_2 =$ 0. 1000 hours used.

Dept. 3: 2000 hours available. $S_3 = 600$. 1400 hours used.

Check by totaling machine time requirements for each product. Working from the per unit values in Table 7.18:

Dept. 1: $(1)(600) + (2)(0) + (1)(200) =$ 800 hours

Dept. 2: $(1)(600) + (1)(0) + (2)(200) = 1000$ hours

Dept. 3: $(2)(600) + (1)(0) + (1)(200) = 1400$ hours

d) For each department, determine the range over which the basis would remain unchanged.

Dept.	Original Value (hr)	Slack	Test Ratios			Δ^-	Δ^+	Allowable Range
1	800	$S_1 = 0$	600/2	=	300	300		$(800 - 300$
			200/-1	=	-200		200	to $800 + 200)$
			600/-3	=	-200		200	500 to 1000 hr
2	1000	$S_2 = 0$	600/-1	=	-600		600	$(1000 - 200$
			200/1	=	200	200		to $1000 + 600)$
			600/1	=	600			800 to 1600 hr
3	2000	$S_3 = 600$	—			600	∞	$\geqslant 1400$ hr

e) An additional 10 hours in each department would be worth how much? Consider one department at a time.

Observe that, for all three departments, the value of 10 hours is well within the allowable range for the optimal basis to remain unchanged, so that all that has to be done is to multiply the 10 hours by the appropriate shadow price.

$$\text{Dept. 1: } (10)(25) = \$250.$$
$$\text{Dept. 2: } (10)(5) \ = \$ \ 50.$$
$$\text{Dept. 3: } (10)(0) \ = \$ \ \ 0.$$

(Since machine time in Department 3 is already in oversupply, additional time in that department is clearly worthless.)

f) If the availability of processing time in Department 1 were increased to 900 hours, how would the solution change? (Work this out directly from the optimal tableau.) Evaluate the new profit directly and then check it by summing the individual product profits.

The value of 900 hours, which is within the allowable range for Department 1 machine time, must be expressed in terms of the slack which it represents. Since 900 hours is 100 hours more than is currently available in Department 1, this is equivalent to a negative slack, so $S_1 = -100$. The product of the value of S_1 and, in turn, each of the coefficients (substitution rates) in the column for Department 1 slack, will determine the change in the basis variables. (Remember that nonbasic variables x_2 and S_2 have a value of zero.)

$$\text{Row 1: } x_1 + \ \ (2)(-100) = \ \ \ 600, \ x_1 = 800 \text{ units.}$$
$$\text{Row 2: } x_3 + (-1)(-100) = \ \ \ 200, \ x_3 = 100 \text{ units.}$$
$$\text{Row 3: } S_3 + (-3)(-100) = \ \ \ 600, \ S_3 = 300 \text{ hours.}$$
$$z \text{ row: } \ \ \ z + \ (25)(-100) = 25{,}000, \ \ z = \$27{,}500.$$

New solution: 800 units of product A, 100 units of product C.

Total profit = $27,500.

Check: Total profit = (800)(30) + (0)(25) + (100)(35) = $27,500.

g) Over what range could the unit profits of the three products change, one at a time, without changing the product mix?

Product	Basic in Row	Original Profit ($)	Column Test Ratios		Δ^-	Δ^+	Allowable Range
A	1	30	30/3 =	10	10		(30 − 10
			25/2 =	12.5			to 30 + 5)
			5/−1 =	−5		5	$20 to $35
B	Nonbasic	25	—		∞	30	(25 − ∞
(Product B is currently unprofitable							to 25 + 30)
by the shadow price of $30.)							⩽$55
C	2	35	30/−1 = −30				(35 − 5
			25/−1 = −25			25	to 35 + 25)
			5/1 = 5		5		$30 to $60

h) If the profit on each product, considered individually, were to drop by $2, what would be the effect on total profit?

Verify first that the $2 change is within the allowable range for all three products.

Product	Units in Optimal Solution	Profit Change ($) Per Unit	Total	New Total Profit
A	600	−2	−1200	25,000 − 1200 = $23,800
B	0	−2	0	25,000
C	200	−2	−400	25,000 − 400 = 24,600

7.13   PRACTICAL APPLICATIONS

The following two examples are meant to illustrate the very substantial payoffs that have been achieved through the effective use of linear programming models.

1. Phosphate Mining and Blending[1]   The Swift Chemical Company operates a large phosphate mine in Florida. The phosphate rock is stored in inventory piles by granule size and grade in BPL (bone phosphate of lime) units. Customers are fertilizer plants, each generally designed for rock within a certain narrow BPL range. In early 1973, Swift found itself in a depressed market, with over one million tons of low-grade phosphate rock which could not be sold. The Operations Research Department of an affiliated company was then called in as a management consultant. Working very closely with Swift personnel, the group developed a linear programming model to maximize net revenue received plus the value of the ending inventory. This model typically contains about 1700 constraints and 4000 variables. Utilizing data on mining forecasts and sales contracts, the model provides suggested schedules for monthly shipments for the current year, anticipated revenues, intermediate inventory positions, and outside purchase requirements. Monthly runs are performed with updated data. Over the first eighteen months of usage, the model was credited with increasing annual profits by several million dollars. Interestingly, the model indicated that the optimal sales strategy was to generally recommend shipping the lowest allowable BPL grade to a customer, a strategy which was in opposition to previous practice and cast doubt on the model's validity. After several months of parallel runs using both strategies, however, it was found that the new strategy consistently generated significantly higher profits. By selling more rock in the apparently less profitable lower grades, it turned out that a better match was obtained between sales and supplies, thereby increasing sales and reducing the need for outside purchases. The model has also been used very effectively to plan both short-range and long-range sales strategies. In late 1973, the model demonstrated the ability to handle, with no change in structure, a tremendous change in the phosphate market, when both demand and phosphate rock prices skyrocketed. Revamping of the company's sales strategy, in response to such a sudden change in the market, would undoubtedly have been much less effective had they not possessed the linear programming model.

2. Facilities Expansion[2]   The Tubular Products Division (TPD) of the Babcock and Wilcox Company (BW) manufactures specialty steel products, particularly specialty tubing for power generation and conversion equipment. With the increasing energy demand, TPD predicted as early as 1971 that it would need additional capacity by 1976. Several different designs were identified for the required new hot mill, and the capital investment cost was estimated as about $49 million. At this point, BW's Operations Research Department was called in to assist in evaluating the performance of alternative new hot mill designs and their compatability with existing facilities. A linear programming model was developed to determine the least-cost allocation of products to mills. The model incorporated constraints on approximately

[1]James M. Reddy, "A Model to Schedule Sales Optimally Blended from Scarce Resources," *Interfaces*, Vol. 6, No. 1, Pt. 2, November 1975, pp. 97–107.
[2]Wayne Drayer and Steve Seabury, "Facilities Expansion Model," *Interfaces*, Vol. 5, No. 2, Pt. 2, February 1975, pp. 104–109.

600 different products and contained about 1600 variables. Eighteen different mill designs were evaluated under multiple product demand operating conditions. The model was also used to evaluate the phaseout of older facilities, different facility locations, and different start-up dates for the new facilities. The mill ultimately selected was originally estimated to have a capacity of 100,000 tons/year; however, model results, later verified by plant engineers, indicated that its capacity would be over 140,000 tons/year. This difference had a significant impact on both manufacturing and financial considerations. The new equipment was purchased and was scheduled for operation in 1976. Management felt that the new facilities would substantially improve the company's competitive position and would reduce its annual operating costs by several million dollars.

A third example illustrates the use of a linear programming model to attempt to optimally allocate resources in a situation where the payoff cannot be expressed in direct economic terms.

3. *Planning Political Campaign Strategies*[3]   The extremely high expenditure of funds over the relatively short period of a political campaign frequently results in the inefficient uses of resources, both manpower and financial. In the 1970 campaign of Democrat John V. Tunney for the United States Senate seat in California, operations research techniques were applied to the task of developing a method to target important precincts for registration and "get-out-the-vote" efforts in the campaign, as well as to identify "swing" precincts for media and candidate attention. An unconventional linear programming model was developed to estimate the number of loyalists (voters who vote for their own party) and defectors (voters who vote for the other party) in each of a series of geographical units. In some of these units, a single objective function, such as maximization of Republican loyalty or of Democratic loyalty, was deemed appropriate. In other units, it appeared desirable to solve for both objective functions and to average the results. On the basis of the model results, Tunney was able to concentrate his campaign resources and efforts on those districts with the greatest potential for additional votes. He did win the election, carrying a number of districts lost by the Democratic candidate in the gubernatorial election won two years earlier by the Republican candidate.

SUMMARY

You should now have a basic understanding of the approach to the formulation of linear programming models and the assumptions inherent in such model formulations. Although you will probably never have to work out a real linear programming problem by hand, what has been learned about the simplex method should give an appreciation of the mathematical approach to such models, especially the use of computational

[3]Joel D. Barkan and James E. Bruno, "Operations Research in Planning Political Campaign Strategies," *Operations Research*, Vol. 20, No. 5, September-October 1972, pp. 925–941.

algorithms. In particular, the idea of iterative solutions which progress toward a final optimal solution (if one exists) is an extremely important concept, one that is embodied in the solution of a number of different types of mathematical models, not only linear programming models. In combination with an understanding of the simplex method, the discussion of duality laid the groundwork for sensitivity analysis of the optimal solution. Such postoptimality analysis allows us to examine the effect of certain limited changes in the original problem without solving the entire problem again.

Linear programming models are just one class of a broader categorization of optimization models known as mathematical programming models. These include, but are not limited to, integer, geometric, nonlinear, and dynamic programming models. Of these, only dynamic programming models, both deterministic and stochastic, will be covered in this text. We will, however, discuss some specialized linear programming models, known as the transportation and assignment problems, in the following chapter. In this book, the discussion of linear programming covers only the fundamental aspects of deterministic linear programming. For more coverage, the reader is referred to the many excellent texts devoted entirely to the subject of linear programming.

Linear Equations

The general form for a linear equation can be written as $y = mx + b$, where

y = dependent variable,
x = independent variable,
m = numerical constant called the slope,
b = numerical constant called the intercept.

The slope, m, is the rate of change of y for a one-unit change in x. Thus, if x increases by one unit, y increases by m units. The intercept, b, is the value of y when x equals zero. The values of m or b may be positive, negative, or zero. The equation is said to be linear because, for any change in x, the change in y is strictly proportional.

Determination of the Equation of a Line

If the coordinates are known for two points on a given line, the equation of that line can be readily determined. Suppose that the coordinates of the first point are x_1, y_1 and the coordinates of the second point are x_2, y_2, as shown in Figure 7.14. The change in y from point 1 to point 2 is $y_2 - y_1$ and the corresponding change in x is $x_2 - x_1$. Dividing the total change in y by the total change in x will then give us the change in y per unit change in x, so that the slope of the line is

$$m = \frac{(y_2 - y_1)}{(x_2 - x_1)}.$$

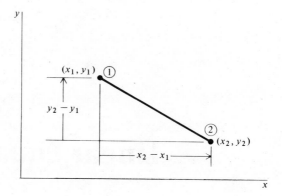

Figure 7.14

Example

For a certain linear function:

$$\text{At point 1,} \qquad x_1 = 1 \qquad \text{and} \qquad y_1 = 5.$$
$$\text{At point 2,} \qquad x_2 = 3 \qquad \text{and} \qquad y_2 = 2.$$
$$m = (2 - 5)/(3 - 1) = -3/2 = -1.5.$$

Perhaps the easiest way to find the intercept is to substitute, in the basic equation $(y = mx + b)$, the values of x and y at one of the known points and the value just determined for the slope. Suppose we use the coordinates at point 1:

$$b = y_1 - mx_1 = 5 - (-1.5)(1) = 5 + 1.5 = 6.5.$$

Thus the equation for the line is

$$y = -1.5x + 6.5.$$

As a check, it is a good idea to substitute the x value of the other point to make sure the calculated value of y is correct. Thus, for $x_2 = 3$,

$$y_2 = (-1.5)(3) + 6.5 = -4.5 + 6.5 = 2, \text{ which checks.}$$

Determination of Intersection Points

For a given pair of lines, we will sometimes need to know the particular coordinates at their point of intersection. (Two straight lines, unless parallel, must intersect. Two lines are parallel only if their slopes are equal.)

Suppose we are given two lines with the following equations, which are in a more general form than the slope-intercept form (where y always has a unit coefficient):

$$a_1x + b_1y = c_1.$$
$$a_2x + b_2y = c_2.$$

We wish to solve for that value of x and y which satisfies both equations.

Incidentally, to get the preceding equations into slope-intercept form, we divide through by the coefficient of y and then isolate y on the left-hand side of the equation. For these two equations, the result is

$$y = -\frac{a_1}{b_1}x + \frac{c_1}{b_1}; \qquad \text{slope} = -\frac{a_1}{b_1}, \qquad \text{intercept} = \frac{c_1}{b_1}.$$

$$y = -\frac{a_2}{b_2}x + \frac{c_2}{b_2}; \qquad \text{slope} = -\frac{a_2}{b_2}, \qquad \text{intercept} = \frac{c_2}{b_2}.$$

Example

Determine the intersection of the two lines, graphed in Figure 7.15, whose equations are

(1) $2x + 3y = 12.$
(2) $2x + y = 8.$

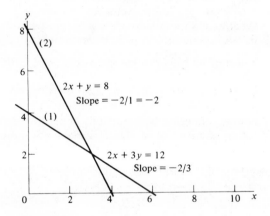

Figure 7.15

We can solve for y by subtracting Equation (2) from Equation (1), giving us

$$2y = 4, \qquad y = 2.$$

Substituting in Equation (2), we find that

$$2x + 2 = 8, \qquad 2x = 6, \qquad x = 3.$$

If we had wished to solve for x first, we could have multiplied Equation (2) by -3 and then added it to Equation (1).

$$\begin{array}{rl} (1) & 2x + 3y = 12 \\ -3 \times (2) & -6x - 3y = -24 \\ \hline & -4x = -12, \quad x = 3. \end{array}$$

Substituting in Equation (1),

$$(2)(3) + 3y = 12, \quad 3y = 12 - 6 = 6, \quad y = 2.$$

EXERCISES

7.1   A manufacturing shop has four departments, each with some temporary surplus capacity. Management is considering utilizing this available capacity for the manufacture of two products. Each unit of product 1 requires 2 hours in department A, 3 hours in department C, and 1 hour in department D. Each unit of product 2 requires 2 hours in department A, 3 hours in department B, 1 hour in department C, and 30 minutes in department D. The profit contribution is $3 per unit for product 1 and $3.60 per unit for product 2. The available capacities are:

Department	A	B	C	D
Time available, hr	8	9	7.5	3

   (a)   Formulate as a linear programming problem. Define the variables, specify the objective function, and specify the constraints as inequalities.
   (b)   Solve graphically for the optimal product mix and its associated profit.
   (c)   Which constraint is redundant? Explain.
   (d)   What would the relationship between the unit profits of products 1 and 2 have to be before it would become best to produce only product 1?

7.2   (a)   Reformulate the problem in Exercise 7.1 by adding slack variables to form constraint equations.
   (b)   Number each basic feasible solution point on your graph. For each such point, knowing which activity variables and/or slack variables must be zero and utilizing the equations in part (a), determine algebraically the values of all activity and slack variables and the value of the objective function. Tabulate these values as in Table 7.4.

7.3   A bicycle manufacturer makes four different styles of bicycles. Pertinent information is shown in the table below.

Style	Profit Contribution per Bike	Assembly Time per Bike	Brake Type
Sportster	$12	30 min	Hand
Jetset	25	1 hr	Hand
Speedster	12	45 min	Coaster
Runabout	16	45 min	Hand

There are 32 hours of assembly time available per day. 48 Sportster tires are in stock. The other three styles use a different type of tire, of which 144 are in stock. Minimum demand is forecast at 6 Sportsters and 6 Jetsets per day. There are 30 coaster brakes and 55 sets (front and rear) of hand brakes.

     Formulate a linear programming model to optimize daily production. Do not solve.

7.4   A drapery manufacturer is making up specifications for a new fabric. She has decided to use cotton because of its sun resistance and ease of care, acetate for its shrink resistance and drapability, polyester for its strength and ability to take a dye, and rayon for its economy and durability. The fabric must be washable, so it must be no more than half acetate. It should contain at least as much cotton as rayon and acetate combined. Since the drapery manufacturer wants to guarantee the drapes for five years, she has decided the fabric should be at least 5 percent polyester. The cost per pound of fiber is $0.79 for rayon, $0.89 for acetate, $1.49 for cotton, and $2.29 for polyester.

Formulate a linear programming model for determination of the optimal blend. Do not solve. [*Hint:* Be sure you have a constraint such that the optimal solution is *not* that of producing nothing!]

7.5   A jewelry maker wants to clear inventory of raw material to raise cash. He wishes to use the material to produce his three most popular items, brooches, rings, and necklaces. These items require various combinations of diamonds, silver, gold, and platinum, as shown in the accompanying table.

Item	Unit Selling Price	Diamonds	Silver, grains	Gold, grains	Platinum, grains
Brooch	$1100	3	0	0	40
Ring	450	1	0	60	20
Necklace	475	1	400	80	0

Diamonds cost $300 each; silver costs $4.20 per ounce; gold costs $120 per ounce; and platinum costs $110 per ounce. The jeweler has 75 diamonds in stock, 2000 grains of silver, 600 grains of gold, and 360 grains of platinum. Assume that 440 grains equal 1 ounce.

Formulate a linear programming model. Do not solve.

7.6   A large business firm would like to allocate next year's advertising budget among the various media to maximize the return to the firm. The year's expenditures for advertising are not to exceed $2.0 million, with not more than $1.1 million spent during the first six months. The media used are newspapers, magazines, radio, and television. Spending on the different media is restricted by the following company policies.

1. At least $200,000 is to be spent on newspapers and magazines combined in each half of the year.
2. At most, 80 percent of the advertising expenditures is to be spent on television in each six-month period.
3. At least $50,000 is to be spent on radio for the year.
4. At least 25 percent of the advertising expenditures on television is to be spent in the second six-month period.

Returns from a dollar spent on advertising in each medium are as follows.

Medium	Returns
Radio	$ 5.00
Television	20.00
Newspapers	10.00
Magazine	15.00

Construct a linear programming model for this firm's advertising budget allocation problem. Do not solve.

7.7   A manufacturer makes three products, toasters, irons, and waffle irons. The company is able to obtain all the raw material it needs. The available production capacity during the 80-hour production work week is as follows.

	Weekly Capacity, in Units		
Operation	Toasters	Irons	Waffle Irons
Stamping	400	800	1000
Casting	—	400	320
Wiring	500	500	640
Assembly and testing	800	1000	800

The contribution to profit per toaster sold is $1.50; for irons it is $2.25, and for waffle irons it is $2.70.

Formulate as a linear programming problem with inequality constraints. Do not solve. [Hint: Convert capacity values to hours of production capacity required per unit.]

7.8   A park wishes to maximize the fees collected from visitors for use of its campsites, trailer facilities, and lodges. Each visitor to the park pays $1.50 per night. Campsites cost $5 per night, trailer facilities cost $7 per night, and a room in the lodge costs $15 per night. The park has 200 campsites, 50 trailer facilities, and 80 rooms in the lodge. Entry to the park is by vehicle only. Only one vehicle is permitted for each campsite, each trailer facility, and each room at the lodge.

The park roads are such that no more than 300 vehicles can be in the park at any one time. Each campsite holds a maximum of six persons; each trailer site, four persons; each room in the lodge is limited to two persons. Because of water and sewage facilities, not more than 1000 people can be in the park on any one night.

(a)   List the assumptions necessary to formulate this fee maximization problem as a linear programming problem.

(b)   Carefully define the variables.

(c)   Specify the objective function and constraints. Do not solve.

7.9   In every 100 pounds of bite-size dry cat food, the requirements are for at least 30 pounds of crude protein and 7 pounds of crude fat, and at most 5 pounds of crude fiber, 10 pounds of ash, and 10 pounds of moisture. Two ingredients are available.

	Ingredient 1	Ingredient 2
Crude Protein	25 percent	40 percent
Crude fat	10	6
Crude fiber	4	5
Ash	8	10
Moisture	10	8
Cost per lb	$0.25	$0.30

(a)   Formulate as a linear programming problem, based on a 100-pound mixture (which forces an equality constraint). Graphically determine the optimal product mix and its cost. By calculating the weight of each constituent, show that all the constraints are met.

(b)   At what ratio of ingredient 1 cost to ingredient 2 cost will there be a multiplicity of possible solutions?

(c)   What would happen to the solution if ingredient 1 contained only 7 percent crude fat? Explain why.

(d)   Reformulate the objective function and determine graphically the least *weight* mixture that meets the dietary requirements (in pounds). Why has the cost decreased, as compared to that in the original problem?

7.10 A toy company manufacturers walking, talking dolls in two factories and ships them, six to a carton, to three warehouses. Excess production must be stored at the warehouses, subject to their available storage capacity. The pertinent data for this week are shown in the accompanying table.

	Distribution Costs, $ per Carton			Weekly Production Capacity
		To:		
From	Warehouse 1	Warehouse 2	Warehouse 3	
Newcastle	0.75	1.20	1.50	50 cartons
Fernwood	1.20	0.90	1.40	120
Warehouse demand, cartons	30	75	35	
Warehouse capacity, cartons	60	100	50	
Weekly storage cost per carton	$0.25	$0.30	$0.27	

Formulate, but do not solve, a linear programming model to optimize distribution, using the following notation.

Let x_1 = units shipped from Newcastle to Warehouse 1,
x_2 = units shipped from Newcastle to Warehouse 2,
x_3 = units shipped from Newcastle to Warehouse 3,
x_4 = units shipped from Fernwood to Warehouse 1,
x_5 = units shipped from Fernwood to Warehouse 2,
x_6 = units shipped from Fernwood to Warehouse 3.

[*Hint:* Units stored at a warehouse are equal to the units received less those demanded.] Assume that the weekly storage cost per carton applies to all cartons which are stored.

7.11 A manufacturer of purses makes three basic styles—a three-compartment bag, which takes 1.0 hour to assemble, a shoulder-strap bag, taking 1.5 hours to assemble, and a tote bag, taking 0.8 hour to assemble. 100 man-hours are available to assemble the bags. The profit is $5 on the sale of a three-compartment bag, $10 on the sale of a shoulder-strap bag, and $3 on the sale of a tote bag. The firm has order commitments for 15 three-compartment bags, 15 shoulder-strap bags, and 20 tote bags. Enough material is available for 25 three-compartment bags, 30 shoulder-strap bags, and 50 tote bags.

(a) Formulate a linear programming model, specifying the constraints as inequalities.

(b) Reformulate an alternative linear programming model by defining each required activity variable as the number of units in excess of the minimum order commitment. Make all the necessary changes from the formulation in part (a).

(c) What is the advantage of the formulation in part (b)? Given the solution to this modified problem, how would you determine the solution to the original problem?

7.12 Considering the type of examples discussed in this chapter, give at least one example of a situation where the proportionality assumption does not hold, and one example of a situation where the additivity assumption is not valid.

7.13 Explain clearly the difference between a feasible solution, a basic solution, and a basic feasible solution.

7.14 What conditions must be met for a set of equations to be in canonical form?

7.15 In the simplex algorithm, how are the pivot column and pivot row chosen? Distinguish between maximization and minimization problems.

7.16 Under what conditions are artificial variables required in constraint equations? What is their function?

7.17 Joe owns a used-furniture store. He has 500 square feet of floor space available for new purchases. The following pieces of furniture are available to him.

Type	Square Feet per Item	Selling Price	Cost
Sofa	35	$90	$50
Bed	50	40	20
Dining set	70	90	40
Chest	10	11	6
Patio set	100	45	20

Joe does not want to stock more sofas than beds. For each patio set stocked, he wants to have at least one of everything else. He has $450 allocated for these purchases.

(a) Formulate a linear programming model to optimize his purchases. Specify the constraints as inequalities. Do not solve.

(b) Formulate the constraints as equations, by adding only slack variables. Do not solve.

7.18 Solve the following linear programming problem (a) graphically, (b) by the simplex method.

$$\text{Maximize} \quad 3x_1 + 2x_2$$

subject to
$$x_1 + x_2 \leq 10$$
$$x_1 + 4x_2 \leq 12$$

and
$$x_1, x_2 \geq 0.$$

7.19 Solve the following linear programming problem by the simplex method in one iteration. If there are alternative optimal solutions, identify them.

$$\text{Maximize} \quad 9x_1 + 6x_2 + 5x_3$$

subject to
$$18x_1 + 12x_2 + 15x_3 \leq 72$$
$$x_1 + x_2 + x_3 \leq 10$$

and
$$x_1, x_2, x_3 \geq 0.$$

7.20 Solve the following linear programming problem by the simplex method in one iteration.

$$\text{Maximize} \quad 6x_1 + 10x_2 + 8x_3 + 3x_4$$

subject to
$$x_1 + x_2 + x_3 + x_4 \leq 10$$
$$2x_1 + 6x_2 + 8x_3 + 3x_4 \leq 48$$
$$5x_1 + x_2 + 7x_3 + x_4 \leq 35$$
$$2x_1 + x_2 + 3x_3 + 4x_4 \leq 2$$

and
$$x_1, x_2, x_3, x_4 \geq 0.$$

7.21 Verify that the following linear programming problem has an unbounded optimal solution (a) graphically, (b) using the simplex method.

$$\text{Maximize} \quad 11x_1 + 7x_2$$

subject to
$$5x_1 + 2x_2 \geq 20$$
$$3x_1 - 4x_2 \leq 12$$

and
$$x_1, x_2 \geq 0.$$

7.22 Solve the following degenerate linear programming problem in one iteration.

$$\text{Maximize} \quad 10x_1 + 15x_2 + 3x_3$$

subject to
$$x_1 + 3x_2 + 11x_3 \leq 6$$
$$4x_1 + 5x_2 + 14x_3 \leq 10$$

and
$$x_1, x_2, x_3 \geq 0.$$

7.23 Solve the following linear programming problem using the "big M" method.

$$\text{Minimize} \quad 10y_1 + 12y_2$$

subject to
$$y_1 + y_2 \leq 3$$
$$y_1 + 4y_2 \geq 2$$

and
$$y_1, y_2 \geq 0.$$

7.24 A manufacturer produces a standard and a deluxe model of a certain product. Both models must be processed in three departments. The sales department estimates that no more than 75 deluxe models can be sold monthly. Production information is shown here.

Department	Required Hours per Unit		Hours Available Monthly
	Standard Model	Deluxe Model	
Layout	3	6	1020
Wiring	4	15	1500
Assembly	4	10	1200
Profit contribution per unit	$10	$30	

(a) Formulate as a linear programming problem and solve graphically for the best combination of models.
(b) How much excess capacity does each department have?
(c) Is any constraint redundant? If so, state which one and why it is redundant.
(d) How would the solution change if the profitability of the deluxe model were increased $5 per unit?
(e) How would the solution change if the profitability of the deluxe model were decreased $5 per unit?
(f) Solve for the optimal solution by the simplex method. From your graphical solution in part (a), you should observe that the optimal solution can be obtained in two iterations if production of the standard model appears in the first iteration, rather than production of the deluxe model, which would be selected by the conventional simplex algorithm. (Remember that the simplex algorithm always moves from one extreme point solution to another.)

7.25 A roofing material company makes two kinds of shingles, wood and slate. Based on labor availability, it can make 200 pounds of wood shingles per hour or 100 pounds of slate shingles per hour. The plant works an 8-hour day, and daily processing capacity is limited to 1000 pounds of shingles. There is a daily requirement for 400 pounds of slate shingles for a large construction project. The company can sell all the shingles it can produce, and it makes a profit of $20 per 100 pounds for wood shingles and $30 per 100 pounds for slate shingles.

(a) Formulate this problem as a linear programming model to optimize daily production. Use inequality constraints. [*Hint:* Convert production of each item to hours per 100 pounds.]

(b) Solve graphically for the optimal daily product mix. What is the maximum achievable daily profit?

(c) From your graph, how would the solution change if the daily processing capacity limitation were removed? Specify the product mix and associated profit.

(d) What is the minimum daily processing capacity required to allow the optimal solution determined in part (c)? Show this constraint as a dotted line on your graph.

(e) Solve the problem in part (a) by the simplex algorithm using the "big M" method.

7.26 A manufacturer has available 20 hours of hand labor per week and 15 hours of machine time per week. He is considering the manufacture of other products to use this excess capacity. Product 1 requires 30 minutes of labor and 18 minutes of machine time per unit, and contributes a profit of $4. Product 2 requires 18 minutes of labor and 24 minutes of machine time per unit, and its profit contribution is $3. Product 3 takes 30 minutes of machine time and 30 minutes of labor per unit, with a profit contribution of $5. Demand for product 1 will not exceed 10 units per week, but demand for product 3 will be at least 5 units per week.

(a) Formulate a linear programming model. Set up constraint equations using the notation to be specified. Let x_i be the number of units of product i produced. Arrange the equations in the following order: first, all "less-than" inequalities; then, any equations; finally, all "greater-than" inequalities. In order of increasing subscript for x_i, and proceeding row by row, first assign surplus variables, then, slack variables, and lastly, artificial variables. (The initial solution basis will then consist of the last m variables assigned, where m is the number of constraints.)

(b) Solve this problem using the simplex alogorithm with the "big M" method.

(c) Solve this problem through phase I, using the two-phase method. Specify the complete tableau at the start of phase II.

[*Note:* In setting up the objective functions in parts (b) and (c), do not forget that the objective function coefficient for any basic variable must be zero. Therefore, any basic variable appearing in the objective function must be eliminated by substituting its equivalent expression, in terms of nonbasic variables, as was illustrated in Example 7.5.]

7.27 Jane Petrole owns a chain of service stations, some of which stay open all night. She has determined her need for attendants as shown in the accompanying table.

Period	Time of Day	Minimum Number Required
1	4 PM– 8 PM	40
2	8 PM–12 AM	20
3	12 AM– 4 AM	10
4	4 AM– 8 AM	25
5	8 AM–12 PM	35
6	12 PM– 4 PM	30

Each attendant works eight consecutive hours. Petrole wishes to minimize the total number of employees.

(a) Formulate a linear programming model with inequality constraints. Do not solve. [*Hint:* The number of employees in each period consists of those who start in that period plus those who started in the previous period.] Let x_i equal the number of employees starting work in period i.

(b) Set up the constraints as equations. Let s_i equal the number of surplus employees in period i. Include any necessary artificial variables.

(c) The optimal tableau is as shown below, omitting the artificial variables. Specify the complete optimal solution.

Basis	x_1	x_2	x_3	x_4	x_5	x_6	s_1	s_2	s_3	s_4	s_5	s_6	RHS
x_5	0	0	−1	0	1	0	0	0	0	1	−1	0	10
x_2	0	1	1	0	0	0	0	0	−1	0	0	0	10
x_4	0	0	1	1	0	0	0	0	0	−1	0	0	25
s_6	0	0	0	0	0	0	−1	1	−1	1	−1	1	10
x_6	0	0	1	0	0	1	−1	1	−1	0	0	0	30
x_1	1	0	−1	0	0	0	0	−1	1	0	0	0	10
z	0	0	0	0	0	0	−1	0	−1	0	−1	0	85

(d) The optimal solution given by the tableau in part (c) is nonunique. Why? Which currently nonbasic activity variable can enter the solution without destroying optimality, and what is the maximum number of units of that variable which can be brought in without changing the optimal total number of employees? Bring into the solution this maximum number of units and find the complete revised optimal solution.

(e) Determine an additional optimal solution somewhere between the two optimal solutions obtained previously.

(f) Are there any nonbasic surplus variables which could enter the solution without destroying optimality? If so, bring into the solution the maximum possible number of units of the first one (lowest subscript) and determine the complete optimal solution.

[*Note:* In parts (d), (e), and (f), only the solution values are required, not the complete tableau.]

7.28 A certain product must weigh 100 pounds. Any of three available raw materials can be used in its manufacture, subject to certain restrictions. The product must contain at least 60 pounds of material A and no more than 50 pounds of materials B and C combined. There are 80 pounds of material A and 40 pounds each of materials B and C. Material A costs $1.50 per pound, material B costs $1.20 per pound, and material C costs $1.00 per pound.

(a) Formulate a linear programming model using inequality constraints.

(b) One of the constraints is redundant. Specify which one and state why.

(c) Solve the problem by *common sense* alone. Specify the optimal product mix and its cost.

(d) Specify the constraint equations (including the redundant one), using the variable x_i and the following notation for the subscript i.

   Subscripts 1, 2, and 3 — units of materials A, B, and C, respectively

   Subscript 4 — excess units of material A (over requirement)

   Subscripts 5, 6, and 7 — slack units of materials A, B, and C, respectively

   Subscript 8 — slack units of materials B and C combined

   Subscript 9 — artificial variable for total weight equation

   Subscript 10 — artificial variable for material A requirement

(e) Solve this problem in two iterations, using the "big M" method. After the first iteration, choose x_9 as the departing variable.

The optimal tableau is as shown below.

Basis	x_1	x_2	x_3	x_4	x_5	x_6	x_7	x_8	x_9	x_{10}	RHS
x_5	0	0	0	1	1	0	0	0	0	-1	20
x_6	0	1	0	0	0	1	0	0	0	0	40
x_7	0	-1	0	-1	0	0	1	0	-1	1	0
x_8	0	0	0	-1	0	0	0	1	-1	1	10
x_3	0	1	1	1	0	0	0	0	1	-1	40
x_1	1	0	0	-1	0	0	0	0	0	1	60
z	0	-0.2	0	-0.5	0	0	0	0	$-M+1$	$-M+0.5$	130

(f) What is the optimal product mix and associated cost?

(g) The optimal solution is degenerate. Why?

(h) How many additional pounds of material A could be added without changing the basis?

(i) Working from the optimal tableau, determine the complete solution obtained if an additional 1 pound of material A must be used. Calculate the total cost by two different methods.

7.29 (a) Formulate the dual of the service station problem in Exercise 7.27.
[*Hint:* Note that the model in Exercise 7.27 is a minimization problem with

"greater-than" inequality constraints, which is the so-called standard dual form. If you take the dual of this problem, you will end up with a maximization problem with "less-than" inequality constraints, which is the so-called standard primal form.]

(b) What is the advantage of this particular dual formulation in this example?

(c) From the optimal tableau for the problem in Exercise 7.27, determine the optimal solution to the dual problem. Verify that the objective function value is the same for the dual problem as it was for the original primal problem.

7.30 Construct the dual of the following primal linear programming problem.

$$\text{Minimize } 3x_1 + 2x_2 - x_3$$

subject to

$$x_1 + 6x_2 \leqslant 24$$
$$3x_2 + 4x_3 \leqslant 27$$
$$2x_1 + 7x_3 = 36$$
$$x_1 + x_2 + x_3 \geqslant 10$$

and

$$x_1, x_2, x_3 \geqslant 0.$$

7.31 Consider the following primal problem.

$$\text{Maximize } = 2x_1 + 3x_2 + 5x_3$$

subject to

$$x_1 + 5x_2 + 2x_3 \leqslant 100$$
$$2x_1 + 2x_2 + 8x_3 \leqslant 250$$

and

$$\text{all } x_i \geqslant 0.$$

(a) Construct the dual formulation of this problem.

(b) Solve the dual problem graphically.

(c) From your solution to the dual problem and utilizing the relationship between the primal and the dual solutions, as well as the algebraic form of the primal, determine the complete solution to the primal problem. Verify that the objective function value for the primal problem is identical to that for the dual problem.

7.32 Consider the following problem (Example 7.5).

$$\text{Minimize } = x_1 + 3x_2$$

subject to

$$x_1 + x_2 \geqslant 4$$
$$2x_1 + x_2 \leqslant 6$$
$$x_2 = 3$$

and

$$x_1, x_2 \geqslant 0.$$

(a) Convert this problem to standard primal form.

(b) Construct the dual to this problem. Use two dual nonnegative variables to represent the primal equality constraint, and then convert them into a single dual variable unrestricted in sign.

(c) From the primal solution to Example 7.5, construct the complete dual solution and verify that the objective function value is the same as that for the primal problem.

7.33 Sensitivity analysis of optimal solutions is an important concept. State at least two reasons why and discuss briefly.

7.34 Of what value are the shadow prices in the optimal solution tableau? What condition must hold in order for them to be applicable?

7.35 Explain the function of the substitution ratios in the optimal tableau:
(a)   in sensitivity analysis.
(b)   in determining new solution values when a nonbasic variable is brought into the solution, assuming that the number of units brought in do not change the basis.

7.36 In the context of sensitivity analysis, what is the interpretation of a negative slack variable? How is it used?

7.37 For a nonbasic activity variable in the optimal solution, by how much and in which direction would its objective function coefficient have to change in order for it to come into the solution? Explain. Consider both maximization and minimization problems.

7.38 The following linear programming problem is given.

$$\text{Maximize} \quad 9x_1 + 11x_2 + 13x_3$$

subject to
$$x_1 + x_2 + x_3 \leq 17$$
$$7x_1 + 5x_2 + 3x_3 \leq 29$$

and
$$x_1, x_2, x_3 \geq 0.$$

The simplex method yields the following optimal solution tableau.

x_1	x_2	x_3	S_1	S_2	RHS
$-1\frac{1}{3}$	$-\frac{2}{3}$	0	1	$-\frac{1}{3}$	$7\frac{1}{3}$
$2\frac{1}{3}$	$1\frac{2}{3}$	1	0	$\frac{1}{3}$	$9\frac{2}{3}$
$21\frac{1}{3}$	$10\frac{2}{3}$	0	0	$4\frac{1}{3}$	$125\frac{2}{3}$

(a)   Specify the optimal solution and the value of the objective function.
(b)   By how much would the value of the objective function change if the RHS value of the first constraint equation were 18 instead of 17?
(c)   What would the value of the objective function become if the RHS value of the second constraint were 28 instead of 29?
(d)   How large would its objective function coefficient have to be in order for x_1 to come into the optimal solution?
(e)   Repeat part (d) for x_2.

7.39 A roofing material company makes both wood and slate shingles, as indicated in the accompanying table.

Product	Production Time per Pound	Daily Requirement	Profit per Pound
Wood shingles	0.005 hr.	Not specified	$0.20
Slate shingles	0.010	At least 400 lb	0.30

Daily production time is limited to 8 hours, and the daily processing capacity is a maximum of 1000 pounds of shingles.

After three iterations of a linear programming model designed to optimize production, the optimal tableau is as shown below.

Production		Slack			
Wood Shingles	Slate Shingles	Surplus Slate Shingles	Production Time	Production Capacity	RHS
0	0	1	200	−1	200
1	0	0	−200	2	400
0	1	0	200	−1	600
0	0	0	20	0.1	260

(a) What is the optimal solution and associated profit?
(b) For both production time and production capacity, over what range for their values will the shadow prices remain applicable?
(c) Suppose that an additional half-hour of production time becomes available, but the production capacity remains unchanged. What is the new optimal solution and associated profit?
(d) If production capacity were decreased to 960 pounds of shingles, by how much would the profit change? Verify this by calculating the new optimal solution and summing the profit contributions.
(e) For both wood and slate shingles, considered separately, over what range could their profit values vary without changing the optimal basis?
(f) What would the new profit value become if the profit on slate shingles increased by $0.05 per pound.

7.40 In Exercise 7.24, the optimal solution tableau is as shown below.

Production		Slack				
Standard	Deluxe	Layout	Wiring	Assembly	Monthly Sales	RHS
0	0	1	0.3	−1.05	0	210
0	1	0	0.2	−0.2	0	60
1	0	0	−0.5	0.75	0	150
0	0	0	−0.2	0.2	1	15
0	0	0	1	1.5	0	3300

(a) Find the optimal solution and profit.
(b) In which of the three departments, Layout, Wiring, and Assembly, are the resources being fully utilized? How did you determine this?

(c) Verify your answer in (b) by determining the allocation of these resources to the individual products, based on the optimal product mix.

(d) Determine the range over which each one of the departmental resources could change, one at a time, without changing the basis.

(e) By how much could the monthly sales limit on deluxe models change without changing the basis? How much would the profit change over this range?

(f) Suppose 1550 hours were available in the Wiring Department. What would the new solution and profit become?

(g) If 60 hours less time were available in the Assembly Department, how would the production of standard and deluxe models be affected? What would the profit become?

(h) Over what range could the profit on deluxe models change without changing the product mix?

7.41 The optimal solution tableau for Exercise 7.9 is shown here.

Ingredients		Surplus		Slack			
Number 1	Number 2	Protein	Fat	Fiber	Ash	Moisture	RHS
0	0	0.067	0	1	0	0	0.667
0	0	-0.133	0	0	1	0	0.667
0	0	0.133	0	0	0	1	1.333
0	0	0.267	1	0	0	0	1.667
0	1	-6.667	0	0	0	0	33.333
1	0	6.667	0	0	0	0	66.667
0	0	-0.333	0	0	0	0	26.667

(a) What is the optimal solution and its associated cost?

(b) From the optimal tableau, only the protein requirement is being met exactly. How do you know that this is so?

(c) Determine the range over which the amount of protein can vary without changing the basis. [Note: Since we are working here with a surplus variable rather than a slack variable, the direction of the allowable changes from the original target value of 30 pounds will be reversed. That is, the minimum positive test ratio will determine the upper limit of the range for a requirement, rather than the lower limit, as it would for a restriction.]

(d) Suppose the minimum required value of protein had been set at 27 pounds. What would the new solution and associated cost become?

(e) For both of the ingredients, in turn, over what range could their costs vary without changing the basis? Since this is a minimization problem, the direction of the changes determined by the test ratios will be reversed from that which would be calculated for a maximization problem.

(f) What would the new cost be if the cost per pound of ingredient 1 dropped by $0.02?

CHAPTER 8

TRANSPORTATION AND ASSIGNMENT MODELS

The models to be studied in this chapter represent linear programming problems of a specialized nature. The constraints are generally in the form of equations, rather than inequalities, and the coefficients in the constraint equations are always 0 or 1. These models have particularly useful applications in the efficient allocation of the flow of units through some type of distribution network.

For transportation problems, we will first study techniques for obtaining an initial solution. Then, we will show how to employ an iterative solution procedure to reach the optimal solution. In this procedure, each successive solution will be a basic feasible solution and will be at least as good as the previous solution. For assignment problems, the solution technique to be used is also of an iterative nature, but no feasible solution is actually obtained until the final optimal solution is achieved. We will discuss both minimization and maximization problems.

For the small problems we will study, the manual solution techniques are readily mastered and generally provide considerable insight into the techniques of problem formulation and solution. For larger problems, different techniques are generally employed. These techniques are computer-oriented and, from a conceptual viewpoint, tend to be quite sophisticated. They are beyond the scope of this text.

8.1 THE TRANSPORTATION PROBLEM

Consider a situation where a single product is to be distributed from several manufacturing plants (sources) to several warehouses (destinations). Associated with each possible shipping route is a transportation cost, and the objective is to minimize the total shipping cost by selecting the optimal shipping pattern. This problem, and others of a similar nature, form a special class of linear programming problems known as transportation or distribution problems. Although these problems can be solved by standard linear programming techniques, their mathematical structure allows us to use specialized, more efficient techniques in their solution.

The algebraic formulation of the transportation problem is as follows:

Let x_{ij} = units shipped from source i to destination j,
c_{ij} = unit cost of shipping from source i to destination j,
a_i = units available from source i,
b_j = units required at destination j,
z = total shipping cost.

Then, if there are m sources and n destinations, this problem can be formulated in the following manner.

$$\text{minimize } z = \sum_{i=1}^{m} \sum_{j=1}^{n} c_{ij} x_{ij}$$

subject to
$$\sum_{j=1}^{n} x_{ij} = a_i \qquad \text{for } i = 1, 2, \ldots, m$$

$$\sum_{i=1}^{m} x_{ij} = b_j \qquad \text{for } j = 1, 2, \ldots, n$$

and
$$x_{ij} \geq 0 \qquad \text{for all } i \text{ and } j.$$

Now, we assume that the total demand must equal the total supply,

so
$$\sum_{i=1}^{m} a_i = \sum_{j=1}^{n} b_j.$$

Because of this equality, one of the constraint equations is redundant, and any one constraint equation may be eliminated. As we learned earlier, in any linear programming problem the number of basic variables in a basic feasible solution is equal to the number of constraint equations. In transportation problems, then, the number of basic variables in any basic feasible solution will equal $m + n - 1$, the number of nonredundant constraints. The number of activity variables is mn, the number of possible shipping routes. If, as sometimes occurs, the sum of the units available differs from the sum of units required, we need only add a "dummy" source or destination to meet the requirement that total demand equals total supply. This will be clearly illustrated later. (If, however, the total demand exceeds the total supply, and there is no alternative source of supply available, then there is no feasible solution.)

For ease in presentation and solution, transportation problems are generally presented in the form of a rectangular array. The format we will use is shown in Table 8.1. By exploiting the special structure of transportation problems, we are able to solve these problems using an $m \times n$ tableau rather than the $(m + n - 1) \times (mn)$ tableau that would be required if the simplex method were used.

Table 8.1   The Generalized Transportation Tableau

Destination j

		1	2	. . .	n	Supply
	1	c_{11} x_{11}	c_{12} x_{12}	. . .	c_{1n} x_{1n}	a_1
Source i	2	c_{21} x_{21}	c_{22} x_{22}	. . .	c_{2n} x_{2n}	a_2
	$\vdots$	$\vdots$	$\vdots$		$\vdots$	$\vdots$
	m	c_{m1} x_{m1}	c_{m2} x_{m2}	. . .	c_{mn} x_{mn}	a_m
Demand		b_1	b_2	. . .	b_n	

Although only minimization problems have been discussed thus far, the transportation model is equally applicable to maximization problems of a similar nature, as will be shown later.

The solution procedure to be illustrated involves the selection of an initial feasible solution and a determination as to the optimality of this solution. If it is nonoptimal, then an iterative solution process will be employed to reach an optimal solution. We will illustrate the entire solution procedure with a simple numerical example.

EXAMPLE 8.1

An electronics company, with four different manufacturing facilities (sources), supplies a complex component to a company which requires this component at its three assembly plants (destinations). The weekly production quantity (supply) of this component at each manufacturing facility and the weekly requirement (demand) at each assembly plant, along with the shipping cost per unit for each possible route from manufacturing facility to assembly plant, are shown in Table 8.2. The numbers at the upper right-hand corner of each cell represent the cost, in dollars, of transporting one unit from the given source to the given destination. The electronics company wishes to determine how many units to ship from each manufacturing facility to each assembly plant such that all requirements will be met, all production quantities will be used, and the overall shipping cost will be minimized.

Generating an Initial Solution

We will show two methods for establishing an initial basic feasible solution. The first, sometimes called the method of mutually preferred flows, is very quick but generally not too close to the optimal solution. The other method, called VAM (Vogel's Approximation Method), is more time-consuming, but it tends to give a solution nearer the optimal solution, and it frequently gives the optimal solution for small problems.

Table 8.2

		Destination			
		1	2	3	Supply
Source	1	4	3	7	70
	2	5	2	10	50
	3	13	8	17	30
	4	9	3	11	20
Demand		60	10	100	

Mutually Preferred Flows Method   Each route chosen represents the most favorable (lowest cost, in a cost-minimization problem; highest profit, in a profit-maximization problem, and so forth) route of those still available. The term *mutually preferred* refers to the fact that the route selected is the preferred route in both row and column. The procedure for a minimization problem is contained in the following steps.

1. Find the lowest cost cell in the array. If there is a tie, make an arbitrary choice.
2. Compare the available units in that row with the required units in that column.
   a) If the available units are fewer than the required units, assign the available units to the chosen cell and delete the row. Change the required units to the previous value minus the number of units just allocated.
   b) If the required units are fewer than the available units, assign the required units to the chosen cell and delete the column. Change the available units to the previous value minus the number of units just allocated.
   c) If these values are equal and this is *not* the last cell chosen, follow the procedure of either step (a) or (b), except that the remaining number of

required *or* available units is set, not to zero, but to an infinitesimally small positive value, commonly denoted as ϵ (epsilon). (This situation indicates a degenerate solution; the subject of degeneracy will be discussed later in this section.) However, if it is the last cell chosen, assign the remaining units to this cell. Stop—this solution is complete.

3. Return to step 1, considering only the remaining rows and columns of the array.

In a maximization problem, the highest profit (or whatever) cell would be chosen in step 1.

For the example problem, the initial basic feasible solution is shown in Table 8.3. The circled numbers represent the assignments and the numbers in the upper left-hand corner represent the order of selection, for handy reference.

Table 8.3

		Destination			
		1	2	3	Supply
Source	1	[2] 4 (60)	[ ] 3 ✕	[3] 7 (10)	7̶0̶ 1̶0̶ 0
	2	[ ] 5 ✕	[1] 2 (10)	[3] 10 (40)	5̶0̶ 4̶0̶ 0
	3	[ ] 13 ✕	[ ] 8 ✕	[3] 17 (30)	3̶0̶ 0
	4	[ ] 9 ✕	[ ] 3 ✕	[3] 11 (20)	2̶0̶ 0
Demand		6̶0̶ 0	1̶0̶ 0	1̶0̶0̶ 0	

In this example, the first choice (denoted by a 1 in the upper left-hand corner of the cell) is $x_{22} = 10$, which eliminates column 2, leaving 40 units still available from source 2. The second choice is $x_{11} = 60$, which eliminates column 1 and leaves 10 units still available from source 1. The last four choices are then completely "locked in," so their order is immaterial, and they have all been labeled as third choices. The total cost is

$$(60)(4) + (10)(2) + (10)(7) + (40)(10) + (30)(17) + (20)(11) = \$1460.$$

Note that we have a basic feasible solution, since we have 4 rows and 3 columns, so that $m + n - 1 = 4 + 3 - 1 = 6$, and there are 6 nonzero variables in the solution.

VAM (Vogel's Approximation Method) From a conceptual viewpoint this technique is rather interesting. It involves chosing the route that, by its selection, avoids the greatest penalty which would be incurred if that route had not been selected. For a minimization problem, the selection procedure is as follows.

1. For each row, calculate the penalty value as the difference between the lowest cost cell and the next lowest cost cell in that row.
2. Calculate the column penalties in the same way.
3. For the highest penalty value, find the lowest cost cell associated with that penalty.
4. Allocate the maximum possible number of units to that cell and adjust the values for the associated available and required units.
5. If a row has been eliminated, the column penalty values are reevaluated, and vice versa.

This process continues, just as in the mutually preferred flows method, until all allocations have been made. For a maximization problem, we work with the highest valued and next highest valued cells.

The VAM initial solution to the example problem starts with the calculation of row and column penalties, as in Table 8.4. The highest penalty is in row 4, so the first allocation is $x_{42} = 10$ units, which satisfies the demand in column 2. If we had not made an allocation to cell (4, 2), we would have had to suffer a penalty of at least $6 per unit, since the 10 units would have to be assigned (eventually) either to cell (4, 1) ($6 penalty per unit) or cell (4, 3) ($8 penalty per unit). The number 1 in the upper left-hand corner of cell (4, 2) in Table 8.5 indicates that this is the first allocation made. We now update the row penalties.

Table 8.4

Destination

		1	2	3	Supply	Penalty
	1	4	3	7	70	1
	2	5	2	10	50	3
Source	3	13	8	17	30	5
	4	9	3	11	20	6
Demand		60	10	100	170	
Penalty		1	1	3		

Table 8.5

Destination

	1	2	3	Supply	Penalty
Source 1	4	✕ 3	7	70	~~1~~ 3
Source 2	5	✕ 2	10	50	~~3~~ 5
Source 3	13	✕ 8	17	30	~~5~~ 4
Source 4	9 ① ⑩ 3		11	~~20~~ 10	~~6~~ 2
Demand	60	~~10~~ 0	100		
Penalty	1	1	3		

The next allocation, shown in Table 8.6, is 50 units to route (2, 1), which uses up all units supplied by source 2. The column penalties are now updated.

Table 8.6

Destination

	1	2	3	Supply	Penalty
Source 1	4	✕ 3	7	70	~~1~~ 3
Source 2	② ㊿ 5	✕ 2	✕ 10	~~50~~ 0	~~3~~ 5
Source 3	13	✕ 8	17	30	~~5~~ 4
Source 4	9 ① ⑩ 3		11	~~20~~ 10	~~6~~ 2
Demand	~~60~~ 10	~~10~~ 0	100		
Penalty	~~1~~ 5	~~1~~	~~3~~ 4		

The remainder of the allocations are shown in Table 8.7, along with all the numbers involved. The cost of this solution is $1360, which is considerably better than the initial solution using the mutually preferred flows method.

Table 8.7

Destination

Source	1	2	3	Supply	Penalty
1	③ ⑩ 4	✕ 3	④ ㉠ 7 (⑥⓪)	~~70~~ ~~60~~ 0	~~1~~ ~~3~~
2	② ㊿ 5	✕ 2	✕ 10	~~50~~ 0	~~3~~ ~~3~~
3	✕ 13	✕ 8	④ ㉚ 17	~~30~~ 0	~~3~~ ~~4~~
4	✕ 9	① ⑩ 3	④ ⑩ 11	~~20~~ ~~10~~ 0	~~6~~ ~~2~~
Demand	~~60~~ ~~10~~ 0	~~10~~ 0	~~100~~ ~~40~~ ~~10~~ 0		
Penalty	~~1~~ ~~5~~	~~1~~	~~3~~ ~~4~~		

Now we must find out if this is the optimal solution. If it is not, we need a technique for developing an optimal solution.

Working toward an Optimal Solution

In the VAM solution shown in Table 8.7, the ✕'s indicate nonbasic variables, those not in the current solution. If we have arrived at an optimal solution, introducing any one of those nonbasic variables into the solution would increase the total cost. What we must do, then, is to examine, in turn, the effect of bringing each one of these nonbasic variables into the solution. If we find one or more nonbasic variables which, if introduced, would result in a lower cost solution, we select that nonbasic variable which would give the greatest per-unit improvement and bring in as many units of it as possible. We then reevaluate all nonbasic variables in the same manner, continuing this process until we arrive at the optimal solution. We will show two procedures for working toward optimality, using Example 8.1 for illustrative purposes.

Stepping-stone Method   In Table 8.8, the circled numbers represent the values of the basic variables. Consider now the analysis of shipping route (1, 2). The value of x_{12} is currently zero, and we would like to know if it would be worthwhile to ship from source 1 to destination 2. If one unit of x_{12} is brought in, this will have to be balanced by a reduction of one unit for a basic variable in row 1 and a reduction of one unit for a basic variable in column 2. These changes, in turn, will trigger at least one additional change. If we think of the circled numbers (values of the basic variables) as "stepping-stones," we must find a path from the cell being evaluated such that the one-unit increase will be balanced out by other one-unit decreases and increases associated only with cells containing stepping-stones.

Table 8.8

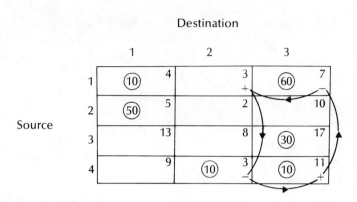

The evaluation proceeds as follows: In cell $(1, 2)$ we place a plus sign, denoting an increase of one unit. In cell $(4, 2)$, which is the only stepping-stone in that column, we place a minus sign, denoting a balancing one-unit decrease. The decrease of one unit in row 4 must now be balanced by an increase in another row 4 basic variable, and the only one available is x_{43}. We therefore place a plus sign in cell $(4, 3)$. This now forces a decrease in a column 3 basic variable. If the decrease is associated with cell $(1, 3)$, this completes a "loop" by balancing both column 3 and row 1, where we initiated the one-unit increase. In general, the procedure involves the development of a closed loop by moving from stepping-stone to stepping-stone until we have a complete row-column balance. For any nonbasic variable, such a closed loop can always be obtained, provided we have a nondegenerate basic feasible solution, one with exactly $m + n - 1$ basic variables. As we will show, we can always satisfy this condition.

The additional cost of adding one unit of x_{12} is calculated by adding the unit costs $(c_{ij}\text{'s})$ associated with plus signs and subtracting the unit costs associated with minus signs. Thus we have:

$$\text{Cost of adding one unit of } x_{12} = 3 - 3 + 11 - 7 = \$4.$$

Each unit shipped by route $(1, 2)$ would change the overall shipping pattern in such a way as to increase the total cost by $4. This value can be called the *change value* for nonbasic variable x_{12}. The change value for a given nonbasic variable is just the change in total cost if one unit of that variable is brought into the solution. Evaluation of the change values for the six nonbasic variables is shown in Table 8.9. Observe, in particular, the more complicated route to complete the loop for cell $(2, 2)$.

Having completed the evaluation of the six nonbasic variables, we find that either x_{31} or x_{32} could profitably be introduced into the solution. Either one would decrease the total cost by $1 for every unit introduced. Suppose we arbitrarily select

Table 8.9

Cell	Stepping-stone Cells					Change Value (Cost of Adding One Unit)
	−	+	−	+	−	
(1, 2)	(4, 2)	(4, 3)	(1, 3)			$3 - 3 + 11 - 7 = +4$
(2, 2)	(4, 2)	(4, 3)	(1, 3)	(1, 1)	(2, 1)	$2 - 3 + 11 - 7 + 4 - 5 = +2$
(2, 3)	(1, 3)	(1, 1)	(2, 1)			$10 - 7 + 4 - 5 = +2$
(3, 1)	(1, 1)	(1, 3)	(3, 3)			$13 - 4 + 7 - 17 = -1$
(3, 2)	(4, 2)	(4, 3)	(3, 3)			$8 - 3 + 11 - 17 = -1$
(4, 1)	(1, 1)	(1, 3)	(4, 3)			$9 - 4 + 7 - 11 = +1$

x_{31} as the new entering variable. Now we must determine which of the current basic variables will leave the solution. We increase the value of x_{31} until one of the basic variables in its negatively labeled stepping-stone cells is driven to zero. This will occur when x_{31} equals the smallest value of the basic variables in negatively labeled stepping-stone cells. For the nonbasic variable x_{31}, the two candidate basic variables are x_{11}, with a value of 10, and x_{33}, with a value of 30. Thus we can, in the next solution, set $x_{31} = 10$, and x_{11} will be driven out of the solution. If we attempted to introduce more than 10 units of x_{31}, we would drive x_{11} negative, and that is not allowed. The value of x_{13} increases by 10, thus becoming 70, and x_{33} is reduced from 30 to 20. The new basic feasible solution is shown in Table 8.10. The number in the lower left-hand corner of each cell containing a nonbasic variable represents the change value, the effect on total cost of adding one unit of that variable to the solution. These numbers were evaluated in exactly the same manner as shown in Table 8.9.

Table 8.10

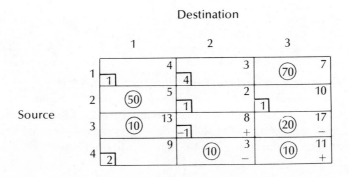

This solution is still not the optimal solution, since we have a negative change value, that in cell (3, 2). The loop for that cell clearly requires cells (4, 2), (4, 3), and (3, 3), as shown by the plus and minus signs. The maximum allowable value of x_{32}

will be the smaller of the values x_{42} and x_{33}, or 10 units. Thus, x_{42} will be driven out of the solution. The new solution, including the change values, is shown in Table 8.11. Since there are no negative change values, this is the optimal solution, and the change values are now the shadow prices, referring back to the terminology introduced in connection with the simplex method. It is interesting to note that the four lowest cost routes (1–1, 1–2, 2–2, and 4–2) are not used. As shown in Table 8.12, the total cost of this solution is $1340, $20 less than the initial solution using VAM. We will discuss various aspects of the optimal solution after presenting the second solution procedure.

Table 8.11

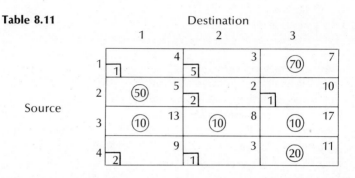

Table 8.12   Optimal Solution

Source	Destination	Unit Cost	Units Shipped	Shipping Cost
1	3	$ 7	70	$ 490
2	1	5	50	250
3	1	13	10	130
3	2	8	10	80
3	3	17	10	170
4	3	11	20	220
				$1340

MODI (Modified Distribution) Method   In this method, which is based on the simplex method, we will take advantage of duality to simplify the computation of the change values. Let u_i be the dual variable corresponding to source availability constraint i, and let v_j be the dual variable corresponding to destination requirement constraint j. Then, as noted in the appendix to this chapter, for all basic variables x_{ij},

$$u_i + v_j = c_{ij},$$

where u_i and v_j are unrestricted in sign. For the nonbasic variables, the change values are equal to $c_{ij} - (u_i + v_j)$. Thus, given the values of the dual variables, all the required change values can be calculated directly.

To illustrate the procedure, we start again with the VAM solution. Since variables x_{11}, x_{13}, x_{21}, x_{33}, x_{42}, and x_{43} are basic variables, we can write the following equations:

$$
\begin{aligned}
u_1 && + v_1 && && = c_{11} = && 4 \\
u_1 && && + v_3 && = c_{13} = && 7 \\
u_2 && + v_1 && && = c_{21} = && 5 \\
u_3 && && + v_3 && = c_{33} = && 17 \\
u_4 && + v_2 && && = c_{42} = && 3 \\
u_4 && && + v_3 && = c_{43} = && 11.
\end{aligned}
$$

Because of the redundancy in the original transportation linear programming problem, this is an underdetermined system of equations, with six equations in seven unknowns. However, we can arbitrarily set one of the dual variables to any value and solve for the remaining values. The most convenient thing to do is to find the dual variable which appears most often in these equations and set its value to zero. If we do this in this example, we will set $v_3 = 0$. This has the effect of dropping the constraint on the requirements at destination 3, thereby removing the redundancy in the system of equations. Then, we can easily solve for the remaining variables, since we now have

$$
\begin{aligned}
u_1 && + v_1 && && = && 4 \\
u_1 && && + 0 && = && 7 \\
u_2 && + v_1 && && = && 5 \\
u_3 && && + 0 && = && 17 \\
u_4 && + v_2 && && = && 3 \\
u_4 && && + 0 && = && 11.
\end{aligned}
$$

Thus, in turn, we find first that $u_1 = 7$, $u_3 = 17$, and $u_4 = 11$. Then, $v_1 = -3$, $u_2 = 8$, and $v_2 = -8$. Using these values, we can now solve directly for the change values. Since the coefficients of the dual variables are always 0 or 1 in this type of problem, observe that the change values can be calculated without performing any multiplications or divisions.

At this point, rather than use equations, let us go to a more convenient tabular representation. We show in Table 8.13 the u_i's with sign reversed, as row factors at the right, and the v_j's, with sign reversed, as column factors at the bottom. Since the change value for a nonbasic cell equals $c_{ij} - (u_i + v_j) = c_{ij} + (-u_i) + (-v_j)$, it can now be calculated by simply adding the cost coefficient in that cell to the row and column factors. In each cell, the change value is the value in the lower left-hand corner. The change value determination for cell (2, 2), for example, is just $-8 + 2 + 8 = 2$, a much easier calculation than the comparable computation with the stepping-stone method, where we first had to find a loop and then had to perform the calculations for five stepping-stones.

Table 8.13

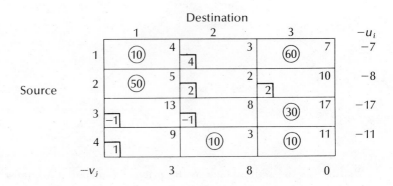

Since we have negative change values, the solution is nonoptimal. For comparative purposes, with respect to the stepping-stone method calculations, suppose we again choose to bring x_{31} into the solution, although x_{32} is just as good a candidate. We can use the stepping-stone method to find the required set of basic variables which will be changed by the introduction of x_{31}. When this is done, we find that we should ship 10 units from source 3 to destination 1, so $x_{31} = 10$, $x_{33} = 20$, $x_{13} = 70$, and x_{11} drops out of the solution.

Now let us evaluate the row and column factors for the next table, Table 8.14. This time we will do it directly in the table, recalling that, for every basic variable x_{ij}, the sum of the row factor, the column factor, and the c_{ij} must equal zero.

Table 8.14

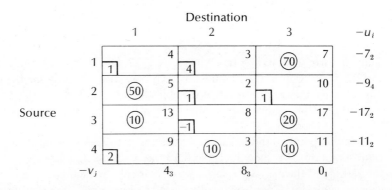

First we set a v_j or u_i value to zero. Suppose we again choose $v_3 = 0$, since there are three basic variables in the third column. The associated row factors are then $-u_1 = -7$, $-u_3 = -17$, and $-u_4 = -11$. Next we use these row factors to evaluate as many column factors as possible. The column 2 factor can be determined at this point, using basic variable x_{42}. Since $-11 + 3 + (-v_2) = 0$, $-v_2 = 8$. Also, using basic variable x_{31}, $-17 + 13 + (-v_1) = 0$, so $-v_1 = 4$. With $-v_1$ determined, basic variable x_{21} permits $-u_2$ to be calculated, as $-u_2 + 5 + 4 = 0$, and $-u_2 = -9$. (The subscripts attached to the row and column factors serve only to indicate, for later reference, the order in which these factors were obtained, that is, on the first, second, third, or fourth labeling "pass.") Now, for the remaining nonbasic variables, it is a simple matter to add up the $c_{ij} - u_i - v_j$ values to get all the change values, as shown. Thus, for example, the change value for cell $(1, 2)$ is $-7 + 3 + 8 = 4$. We find that the solution is nonoptimal, since we have a change value of -1 for x_{32}. It should be clear that 10 units of x_{32} should be brought into the solution, dropping out x_{43}. The basic feasible solution, along with the MODI evaluation for optimality, is shown in Table 8.15. Here, the initial zero is the row 3 factor, $-u_3$, and only two additional labeling passes are required. All change values are nonnegative, so the optimal solution has been reached.

Table 8.15

	Destination			
	1	2	3	$-u_i$
Source 1	[1] 4	[5] 3	⑦⓪ 7	10_3
Source 2	㊿ 5	[2] 2	[1] 10	8_3
Source 3	⑩ 13	⑩ 8	⑩ 17	0_1
Source 4	[2] 9	[1] 3	⑳ 11	6_3
$-v_j$	-13_2	-8_2	-17_2	

Incidentally, we could add a constant k, unrestricted in sign, to the c_{ij}'s for any row or column without affecting the change values. This is so because all required allocations must be satisfied exactly, so that we are interested only in relative rather than absolute comparisons. If, for example, a value k were added to *all* c_{13} in the third column, so that $c_{13} = 7 + k$, and so forth, we would find that $-v_3 = -(17 + k)$, and the other row and column factors would be unchanged. The change values would not be affected at all, as you should prove to yourself.

Sensitivity Analysis

A change value in the optimal solution (in other words, a shadow price) represents the amount by which a given nonbasic variable would increase the cost for every unit brought into the solution. It also indicates the amount of reduction required in the c_{ij} value of a nonbasic variable x_{ij} before it would become desirable for that variable to be in the solution. Thus, if c_{41} were reduced from 9 to 6, the change value of cell $(4, 1)$ would also be reduced by 3 units, becoming -1, and x_{41} would enter the solution. If c_{41} were 7, the change value would be zero, and we could introduce any amount of x_{41} (up to its limit of 10 units) without changing the total cost. If any of the shadow prices are zero, it means that there are alternative optimal solutions, rather than a unique optimal solution.

A sensitivity analysis of the c_{ij}'s of the basic variables can also be performed. As in the previous chapter, we will evaluate the range over which the original objective function coefficients can change without changing the basis.

First of all, we know, from the optimal solution array, that the basis consists of variables x_{13}, x_{21}, x_{31}, x_{32}, x_{33}, and x_{43}, with values, respectively, of 70, 50, 10, 10, 10, and 20. The objective function coefficients of interest are then c_{13}, c_{21}, c_{31}, c_{32}, c_{33}, and c_{43}.

For each basic variable, we must identify the nonbasic variables whose shadow prices would be affected by a change in the c_{ij} of that basic variable. This process is facilitated by first making a table showing, for each nonbasic variable, its stepping-stone cells and their signs, as was done in Table 8.9. Table 8.16 is developed from the optimal solution in Table 8.15 and also includes the shadow prices from that table.

Table 8.16 Stepping-stones and Shadow Prices of Nonbasic Variables

Nonbasic Variable	Stepping-stones (Basic Variables) −	+	−	Shadow Price ($)
(1, 1)	(1, 3)	(3, 3)	(3, 1)	1
(1, 2)	(1, 3)	(3, 3)	(3, 2)	5
(2, 2)	(2, 1)	(3, 1)	(3, 2)	2
(2, 3)	(2, 1)	(3, 1)	(3, 3)	1
(4, 1)	(3, 1)	(3, 3)	(4, 3)	2
(4, 2)	(3, 2)	(3, 3)	(4, 3)	1

From the information presented in Table 8.16, a complete sensitivity analysis can be performed as follows: for each basic variable x_{ij}, list those nonbasic variables whose shadow prices are affected by c_{ij}. For each such nonbasic variable, indicate the signed amount by which c_{ij} can change before the shadow price of the nonbasic variable will be driven to zero. The smallest absolute values of these individual changes, considering positive and negative changes separately, determine, respectively, the limiting changes Δ^- (the maximum allowable decrease) and Δ^+ (the maximum allowable increase). Then, as shown in Table 8.17, the range of allowable change can be determined for each basic variable.

As an example of the calculations, four shadow prices of nonbasic variables would be affected by a change in c_{31} as can be determined from Table 8.16. Decreases in c_{31}

Table 8.17   Sensitivity Analysis of Basic Variables

Basic Variable x_{ij}	Original Coefficient c_{ij}	Nonbasic Variables Affected	Allowable Individual Change*	Maximum Allowable Change Δ^-	Δ^+	Allowable Range
(1, 3)	7	(1, 1)	−1		1	⩽$8
		(1, 2)	−5			(7 − ∞
						to 7 + 1)
(2, 1)	5	(2, 2)	−2			⩽$6
		(2, 3)	−1		1	(5 − ∞
						to 5 + 1)
(3, 1)	13	(1, 1)	−1		1	$12 to $14
		(2, 2)	2			(13 − 1
		(2, 3)	1	1		to 13 + 1)
		(4, 1)	−2			
(3, 2)	8	(1, 2)	−5			⩽$9
		(2, 2)	−2			(8 − ∞
		(4, 2)	−1		1	to 8 + 1)
(3, 3)	17	(1, 1)	1	1		$16 to $18
		(1, 2)	5			(17 − 1
		(2, 3)	−1		1	to 17 + 1)
		(4, 1)	2			
		(4, 2)	1	1		
(4, 3)	11	(4, 1)	−2			⩽$12
		(4, 2)	−1		1	(11 − ∞
						to 11 + 1)

A positive value represents a decrease.

of \$2 and \$1, respectively, would drive to zero the shadow prices in cells (2, 2) and (2, 3), so Δ^-, the maximum allowable decrease in c_{31}, is \$1. Increases in c_{31} of \$1 and \$2, respectively, would force to zero the shadow prices in cells (1, 1) and (4, 1). Thus, Δ^+, the maximum allowable increase in c_{31}, is \$1. In the case of basic variables for which the direction of change for the affected nonbasic variables is always negative, the Δ^- value is unlimited, and there is no lower limit for the allowable change in the objective function value.

If we were interested in the sensitivity analysis of just one basic variable, it would not be necessary to form complete tables such as Tables 8.16 and 8.17. Suppose, for example, that we wish to determine the allowable change in the objective function coefficient of cell (3, 3) only. Working from the optimal solution, we can add a cost k to c_{33} and then recalculate the MODI factors and perform a MODI evaluation as in Table 8.18.

Table 8.18

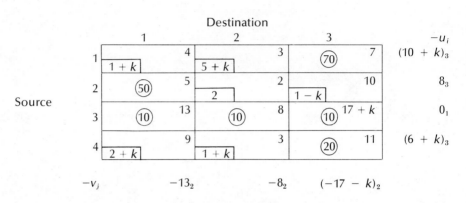

From Table 8.18, it should be apparent that the maximum positive value of k is 1, limited by the shadow price in cell (2, 3), and the maximum negative value of k is also 1, limited by the shadow prices in cells (1, 1) and (4, 2). Thus, c_{33} can range between $17 - 1$ and $17 + 1$, or 16 to 18, without changing the basis. Since 10 units are being shipped from source 3 to destination 3, each unit increase of $1 in c_{33} (within the allowable range, of course) would increase the cost by $10.

Degeneracy

Suppose the transportation example problem is modified slightly, by changing the demand at destinations 1 and 3 from 60 and 100 to 50 and 110, respectively. The initial problem array is then as shown in Table 8.19. Using VAM, the first two assignments are shown in Table 8.20. Upon making the second assignment of 50 units to cell (2, 1), both row 2 availability and column 1 requirements are reduced to zero. When the remaining three assignments are made in column 3, we will have only five basic variables instead of the required six (rows + columns − 1). We will not have a basic feasible solution at that point and will not, therefore, be able to work toward an optimal solution using MODI or the stepping-stone method.

When degeneracy is encountered, it can be readily handled by eliminating either a row or a column, but not both. The one not eliminated retains an infinitesimally small amount, ϵ, to be assigned just as any other amount. To illustrate, suppose, after the second assignment, we reduce the column requirement to zero but

Table 8.19

	Destination			Supply
	1	2	3	
1	4	3	7	70
2	5	2	10	50
Source 3	13	8	17	30
4	9	3	11	20
Demand	50	10	110	170

Table 8.20

	Destination			Supply	Penalty
	1	2	3		
1	✕ 4	✕ 3	7	70	7̶ 3
2	②(50) 5	✕ 2	✕ 10	5̶0̶ 0	3̶ 5
Source 3	✕ 13	✕ 8	17	30	3̶ 4
4	✕ 9 ① (10) 3		11	2̶0̶ 10	6̶ 2
Demand	5̶0̶ 0	1̶0̶ 0	110	170	
Penalty	1̶	1̶	3		

Table 8.21

	Destination			Supply	Penalty
	1	2	3		
1	✕ 4	✕ 3	③ (70) 7	7̶0̶ 0	1̶ 3̶
2	②(50) 5	✕ 2	③ (ε) 10	5̶0̶ ε̶ 0	3̶ 3̶
Source 3	✕ 13	✕ 8	③ (30) 17	3̶0̶ 0	3̶ 4̶
4	✕ 9 ① (10) 3		③ (10) 11	2̶0̶ 1̶0̶ 0	6̶ 2̶
Demand	5̶0̶ 0	1̶0̶ 0	1̶1̶0̶ 4̶0̶ 1̶0̶ 0		
Penalty	1̶	1̶	3̶		

reduce the row availability to ϵ. The remaining four assignments will all be in column 3, as shown in Table 8.21.

We can now proceed to use MODI, as in Table 8.22, since we have a nondegenerate basic feasible solution. This solution is nonoptimal, so we bring in x_{32} and drop out x_{42}, as shown in Table 8.23. This is the optimal solution. Once we have reached optimality, we simply ignore the ϵ cell, so that $x_{23} = 0$. This solution is optimal, but it is degenerate. This does not concern us, since we have reached the optimal solution.

Table 8.22

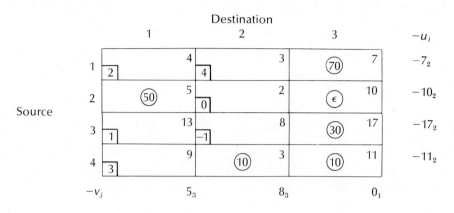

In general, we handle the ϵ cell (or cells) just as we would any other basic variable. When adding or subtracting ϵ in any basic change, ϵ is treated as zero (except when subtracted from another ϵ). For instance, if the shadow price in cell $(2, 2)$ were negative, x_{22} would come into the solution. The maximum amount would be the minimum of $x_{32} = 10$ and $x_{23} = \epsilon$, so we could bring in ϵ units. After this had been done, we would have $x_{32} = 10 - \epsilon = 10$, $x_{33} = 20 + \epsilon = 20$, $x_{23} = 0$, and $x_{22} = \epsilon$. This turns out to be the optimal solution, so $x_{22} = 0$. The cost would be identical to that of the previous solution, since the cost decrease was a multiple of ϵ, which is zero. If, during any MODI or stepping-stone iteration, the entering variable forces more than one basic variable to drop out of the solution, a degenerate solution will result. To avoid this, let only one basic variable go to zero, and assign a value ϵ to the other basic variable(s) which would have been driven out. The choice of which basic variable to set to zero is arbitrary.

Other Facets of Transportation Problems

Unequal Supply and Demand   Since total supply and demand must be equal, in order that we may solve a transportation problem by the methods shown, we must artificially create such an equality when it does not exist in the original problem. We can easily do this by adding a dummy row or column, as required. The procedure will be illustrated in the following example. The cost associated with each dummy cell can be set to zero or to a very high or a very low value (say M or $-M$) if this aids the solution process. For example, if a dummy demand point is added to absorb excess supply in a cost minimization problem, the shipping cost for the dummy cells should be set to a high value, rather than to zero, to avoid a possibly inefficient initial solution. Once the initial solution has been obtained, the cost for each dummy cell should be set to zero. As noted earlier, if demand exceeds supply, and there is no alternative supply source, no feasible solution can be obtained. However, if shortages are unavoidable, demands should be adjusted to meet the available supply, using some reasonable criteria established by the firm's management. The reduced problem can then be solved by the transportation algorithm. The resulting solution will provide the most effective allocation of available resources.

Maximization Problems   If we have a profit maximization problem which is a transportation problem, we can convert it to a minimization problem by reversing the coefficients in the objective function and minimizing the objective function, just as we have done up to this point. Alternatively, we can make some minor changes in the procedures and treat the problem directly as a maximization problem. The required changes are as follows.

1. In the initial solution, we work toward a maximization solution.
   a) If the method of mutually preferred flows is used, we select, for each successive assignment, the highest valued cell, rather than the lowest valued cell.
   b) Using VAM, the penalty values now represent the difference between the two highest valued cells in each row and column. Each new assignment is to the highest valued cell in the row or column with the maximum penalty value.
2. When working toward optimality, using either the stepping-stone method or

MODI, the only difference involves the analysis of the change values. In an optimal maximization solution, all the change values must be nonpositive, rather than nonnegative. A positive change value would indicate a cell where an allocation would increase the total profit. As before, a zero change value in the optimal solution shows that the optimal solution is not unique.

Let us now work an example maximization transportation problem which involves problem formulation and unequal supply and demand.

EXAMPLE 8.2

A company manufactures a certain product at two factories and distributes it to three warehouses. Each factory runs both a regular shift and, when necessary, an overtime shift for any remaining production requirements. Production costs differ between factories, and the selling price of the product varies at the different warehouse locations. The pertinent information is given in Table 8.24.

Table 8.24

Factory	Weekly Production Capability (units)		Unit Production Cost	
	Regular	Overtime	Regular	Overtime
1	100	40	$17	$24
2	150	30	18	23

Warehouse	Weekly Requirements (units)	Unit Selling Price
1	80	$35
2	120	37
3	70	34

Transportation Cost ($ Per Unit)

Warehouse

		1	2	3
Factory	1	6	7	6
	2	4	2	8

From an examination of the problem data, it should be clear that our objective is to select that combination of regular and overtime production which, when allocated to shipping routes in an optimal fashion, will maximize profit. First of all we observe that the regular production of 250 units is inadequate to meet the total demand of 270 units. However, when the total possible overtime production of 70 units is included, we actually have a potential surplus of 50 units. In order to balance supply and demand, this surplus must be absorbed by a dummy warehouse. The number of units allocated to the dummy warehouse represents the amount of unused production capacity. Now, since the profit for overtime production is different than that for regular production, we must handle the overtime production at each factory by considering each factory's overtime production as a separate source. Then, for each possible production and shipping combination, we must calculate the associated profit, which is equal to the unit selling price less the unit production cost and the unit shipping cost. These calculations are shown in Table 8.25.

Table 8.25 Calculation of Net Profits

Factory	Warehouse	Unit Selling Price ($)	Per Unit Cost ($) Production	Per Unit Cost ($) Transportation	Net Profit ($)
1 (R) (Regular)	1	35	17	6	12
	2	37	17	7	13
	3	34	17	6	11
2 (R)	1	35	18	4	13
	2	37	18	2	17
	3	34	18	8	8
1 (O) (Overtime)	1	35	24	6	5
	2	37	24	7	6
	3	34	24	6	4
2 (O)	1	35	23	4	8
	2	37	23	2	12
	3	34	23	8	3

We can now set up the transportation array for an initial solution. For convenience, the profits associated with the dummy warehouse are set to zero, as shown in Table 8.26. They could be any value, so long as all are set to the same value. Setting them to zero is a good idea, because, in the initial solution, assignments to the dummy warehouse will tend to be made last, and this is as it should be. (For the same reason, in a cost minimization problem, the unit costs of dummy destinations should *not* be set to zero, but to a cost which is high compared to the cost of routes to all other destinations.) As we indicated earlier, however, the addition of an arbitrary constant to all c_{ij}'s in a given row or column will not affect the *optimal allocation*, although the total profit or cost will obviously be affected.

The initial solution in Table 8.26 was obtained using VAM. As usual, the numbers in the upper left-hand corner show the order of route selection. It might be noted that there was a three-way tie for the initial penalty cost. The first allocation, to cell (2, 2), was made because that cell was tied for maximum penalty in both row and column. A penalty tie in the second allocation was resolved in the same way, although an arbitrary selection would have been completely acceptable.

Table 8.26

		Warehouse					
	1	2	3	4	Supply	Penalty
1 (R)	4 (30) 12	✕ 13	3 (70) 11	✕ 0	~~100~~ ~~30~~ 0	~~7~~ ~~7~~ ~~12~~
2 (R)	2 (30) 13	1 (120) 17	✕ 8	✕ 0	~~150~~ ~~30~~ 0	4 5
Factory Production 1 (O)	✕ 5	✕ 6	✕ 4	6 (40) 0	~~40~~ 0	~~7~~ ~~7~~ 5
2 (O)	5 (20) 8	✕ 12	✕ 3	6 (10) 0	~~30~~ ~~10~~ 0	4 5 8
Demand	~~80~~ ~~50~~ ~~20~~ 0	~~120~~ 0	~~70~~ 0	~~50~~ ~~10~~ 0		
Penalty	~~7~~ 4 3	4	~~3~~ 7	~~0~~		

Now we employ the MODI method to determine if this is the optimal solution. In Table 8.27, we start with a column 1 factor of zero, since there are three basic variables in that column. This is not *the* optimal solution, but it is *an* optimal solution, since there are no *positive* change values. The one change value of zero, in the bottom row, tells us that the solution is nonunique. We could ship up to 20 units by that route (revising the shipping pattern as required) without changing the total profit. The two extreme-point optimal solutions are tabulated in Table 8.28. The

Table 8.27

		Warehouse				$-u_i$
	1	2	3	4	
1 (R)	(30) 12	13 $\boxed{-3}$	(70) 11	0 $\boxed{-4}$	-12_2
2 (R)	(30) 13	(120) 17	8 $\boxed{-4}$	0 $\boxed{-5}$	-13_2
Factory Production 1 (O)	5 $\boxed{-3}$	6 $\boxed{-6}$	4 $\boxed{-3}$	(40) 0	-8_4
2 (O)	(20) 8	12 $\boxed{0}$	3 $\boxed{-4}$	(10) 0	-8_2
$-v_j$	0_1	-4_3	1_3	8_3	

shipments to warehouse 4, the dummy warehouse, are ignored, since they merely represent unused capacity. If we assume that the number of units shipped by any route must be an integer, there will be 19 additional optimal solutions. (If the commodity is divisible into fractional units, there will be an infinite number of additional optimal solutions. However, if the optimal solution is unique, and the supply and demand values are all integers, then the solution values will all be integers, since no fractional allocations will ever be made at any point in the solution process.)

Table 8.28 Two Optimal Solutions

Factory	Production	Warehouse	Unit Profit	Units Shipped	Profit
1	Regular	1	$12	30	$ 360
1	Regular	3	11	70	770
2	Regular	1	13	30	390
2	Regular	2	17	120	2040
2	Overtime	1	8	20	160
					$3720
1	Regular	1	$12	30	$ 360
1	Regular	3	11	70	770
2	Regular	1	13	50	650
2	Regular	2	17	100	1700
2	Overtime	2	12	20	240
					$3720

Transshipment

As an alternative to direct shipments to major cities, a nationwide distributor may ship to several regional locations, each in turn supplying cities within its territory, or it may route shipments to a particular city through one or more intermediate cities. When a source or destination can act as an intermediate point for shipment, we have a *transshipment* problem.

Although the transshipment problem appears to be of a more general nature than the transportation problem, with a relatively small effort the transshipment problem can be solved using the transportation model. In the general case, each location in the transportation network must be considered as both a potential source and a potential destination. (Any location which cannot function as a transshipment point can be assigned an arbitrarily high cost or an arbitrarily low profit, as appropriate.) In order to permit complete flexibility in transshipments, a large quantity must be added at every location. This quantity has to be large enough to permit the maximum possible transshipment, so it need be no greater than the total amount shipped from all sources to all destinations in the original problem. We assign zero cost to a shipment from a location to itself, so it will always be desirable for a location to ship a fictitious quantity to itself at zero cost if it cannot transship units in such a manner as to decrease total costs.

The actual procedure is as follows: if there are m sources and n destinations, we set up a transportation array which is of size $m + n$ by $m + n$ rather than m by n, as in the customary case. If the total number of units shipped from all sources to all destinations is T, the given supply at each source and the given demand at each destination are each increased by an amount T. The *demand* at each source and the *supply* at each destination are set at the value T, instead of zero. The problem is then solved by one of the standard transportation methods. In the final solution, we simply disregard any quantity shipped from a point to itself.

As an illustration of a transshipment problem, we will rework an earlier problem with additional data.

EXAMPLE 8.3

Consider the electronics company problem in Example 8.1. In addition to the data presented in Table 8.2 showing the available supply at each source, the demand at each destination, and the unit shipping costs for all routes, suppose that transshipments between manufacturing facilities and between assembly plants are now allowed, with shipping costs as shown in Table 8.29.

Table 8.29 Transshipment Transportation Costs ($) per Unit

Sources   Destinations

	1	2	3	4			1	2	3
1	—	2	9	5		1	—	6	5
2	2	—	8	5		2	6	—	8
3	9	8	—	6		3	5	8	—
4	5	5	6	—					

Combining the supply, demand, and cost data from Tables 8.2 and 8.29, we get the array shown in Table 8.30, where the total supply of 170 units has been added to the demand and supply at all locations. Having previously obtained an optimal solution to the original problem, as shown in Table 8.12, we can use that solution as an initial solution, instead of expending the effort to obtain an initial solution using VAM, say. We need only add 170 units to each route on the diagonal. The initial solution is also shown in Table 8.30.

Table 8.30 Transshipment Data and Initial Solution

		Source 1	Source 2	Source 3	Source 4	Destination 1	Destination 2	Destination 3	Supply
Source	1	0 (170)	2	9	5	4	3	7 (70)	240
	2	2	0 (170)	8	5	5 (50)	2	10	220
	3	9	8	0 (170)	6	13 (10)	8 (10)	17 (10)	200
	4	5	5	6	0 (170)	9	3	11 (20)	190
Destination	1	4	5	13	9	0 (170)	6	5	170
	2	3	2	8	3	6	0 (170)	8	170
	3	7	10	17	11	5	8	0 (170)	170
Demand		170	170	170	170	230	180	270	

The optimal solution, which is nonunique, can be obtained in two iterations. One of the optimal solutions is shown in Figure 8.1, along with the optimal solution to the original problem.

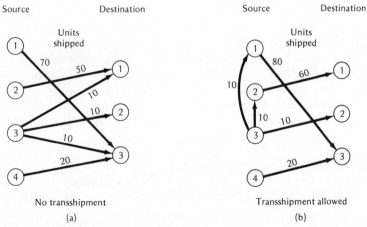

Figure 8.1 Optimal solutions

In the transshipment solution shown in Figure 8.1b, observe that there are, in essence, two changes from the solution in Figure 8.1a. The 10 units previously shipped directly from source 3 to destination 1 are now routed through source 2, and the 10 units shipped directly from source 3 to destination 3 are now routed through source 1. The new optimal cost is $1330, a decrease of $10 from the optimal solution without transshipment. It should be apparent that the optimal cost with transshipment can be lower than the optimal cost without transshipment, but can never be higher.

8.2 PRACTICAL APPLICATIONS OF TRANSPORTATION MODELS

A transportation linear programming model has been developed to analyze multicommodity purchasing-allocation networks, primarily those where grain and ore processors have the privilege of "milling-in-transit."[1] Under milling-in-transit, a manufacturer can ship raw material from its source to a plant, manufacture it into finished or intermediate goods, and then ship these products to a final destination, paying for freight costs as though the company had shipped only raw material from the source to the final destination without intermediate processing. The model can be used to determine the most economical raw material sources and associated purchasing requirements, and has been implemented by a major food processor, supplanting an existing inefficient manual system based almost entirely on experience and judgment. Use of the computerized model has provided the company with a standardized analytical tool for all manufacturing facilities, has permitted it to explore many more purchasing-allocation alternatives, and has greatly reduced the time required for a typical analysis.

A second application is a most unusual one. A cooperative association of the electrical power companies of Norway is using the transportation method of linear programming to allocate transmission costs.[2] These costs are calculated as the product of the power in megawatts times the distance in kilometers for each company in the highly interconnected grid system. Because of the complexities of the interconnections, the companies have agreed to allocate costs on the basis of that overall power allocation which minimizes the total megawatt-kilometer value for the system. The transportation algorithm is well suited for this purpose. It allows the companies to shorten the calculation of the cost allocation from weeks, as it formerly took by manual methods, to a matter of less than a minute, using a very efficient transportation computer code.

---

[1]Robert E. Markland, "Analyzing Multi-Commodity Distribution Networks Having Milling-in-Transit Features," *Management Science*, Vol. 21, No. 12, August 1975, pp. 1405–1416.

[2]Oddmund Aarvik and Paul Randolph, "The Application of Linear Programming to the Determination of Transmission Fees in an Electrical Power Network," *Interfaces*, Vol. 6, No. 1, November 1975, pp. 47–49.

8.3 THE ASSIGNMENT PROBLEM

Just as the transportation problem is a special case of the general linear programming problem, the assignment problem is a special case of the transportation problem. The assignment problem arises when we have m facilities and m tasks and must assign exactly one facility to each task. Thus we have a transportation problem with an equal number of origins and destinations, where each origin has a capacity of one unit and each destination has a requirement of one unit. Given the cost of making each possible assignment, we wish to minimize the total cost of all assignments. (By modifying the approach slightly, we can also handle maximization problems.) Such problems arise in the assignment of men to tasks, tractors to trailers, and so forth.

In tabular form, the solution of a four-man, four-task problem might look as shown in Table 8.31.

Table 8.31

		Task j				
		1	2	3	4	Capacity
Man i	1			1		1
	2	1				1
	3		1			1
	4				1	1
	Requirement	1	1	1	1	

Mathematically, we can state the problem as follows.

Let c_{ij} = cost of assigning man i to task j,

x_{ij} = 1 if man i assigned to task j,

= 0 otherwise.

$$\text{Minimize} \sum_{i=1}^{m} \sum_{j=1}^{m} x_{ij} c_{ij}$$

subject to

$$\sum_{i=1}^{m} x_{ij} = 1, \quad j = 1, 2, \ldots, m$$

$$\sum_{j=1}^{m} x_{ij} = 1, \quad i = 1, 2, \ldots, m.$$

We could solve this problem as a transportation problem, with all row and column sums equal to one unit, so that an ϵ value would have to be introduced at each allocation because of the degeneracy of the solution. There is, however, a more efficient procedure, which takes advantage of the special nature of this mathematical model. We will show a solution procedure, called the Hungarian method, which is based on the fact that any constant can be added to or subtracted from each element of a row or a column without changing the nature of the problem, as we indicated earlier for transportation problems.

EXAMPLE 8.3

A trucking concern has five trailers awaiting pickup at different locations in a city. In a nearby city, it has five tractors, each one capable of handling any of the trailers. Given the distance, in miles, between each tractor and each trailer, as shown in Table 8.32, what is the selection of tractor-trailer allocations which will minimize the total distance traveled to pick up the trailers?

Table 8.32   Original Data

Trailer

		1	2	3	4	5
	A	18	16	23	19	14
	B	25	21	19	23	17
Tractor	C	16	17	20	18	22
	D	19	17	25	22	21
	E	14	13	17	17	16

The first thing to do is to find the minimum element in each row and subtract it from all elements in that row, as in Table 8.33. (Alternatively, we could have started with columns.) A little thought should convince you that, on a *comparative* basis, nothing has really changed. Since tractor A, for instance, must be assigned to one of the five trailers, we have simply reduced the distance by 14 units (miles) for *each* assignment. The optimal assignment for this partially reduced array will be exactly the same as for the original distance array, but the total distance will be decreased by 77 units, the sum of the row element reductions. The next step is to subtract the minimum element in each column from all elements in that column. (See Table 8.34.)

At this point, with what is sometimes called a fully reduced array (at least one zero in every row and column), we look for a set of zeroes with which to make the assignments. If we can make an assignment of all tractors and trailers, using only zero distance values, then this must be an optimal assignment, with a total distance equal to the amount of row and column element reductions, as we can readily verify.

We look first for all rows and columns with a single zero, since such a condition

Table 8.33 First Reduction

	1	2	3	4	5	Minimum element
A	4	2	9	5	0	14
B	8	4	2	6	0	17
C	0	1	4	2	6	16
D	2	0	8	5	4	17
E	1	0	4	4	3	13
						77

Table 8.34 Second Reduction

	1	2	3	4	5
A	4	2	7	3	0
B	8	4	0	4	0
C	0	1	2	0	6
D	2	0	6	3	4
E	1	0	2	2	3
Minimum element	0	0	2	2	0	4 (total)

forces a given assignment, unless one has already been made in that row or column. If we look first at the rows, we find that assignment A–5 is required in row A, as indicated in Table 8.35. This assignment then eliminates both row A and column 5, so that the zero in cell (B, 5) is eliminated. Thus B–3 can be assigned in row B. In row C, no assignment is possible, yet. In row D, the assignment must be D–2, and that eliminates the zero in cell (E, 2). Looking at the remaining columns, we can assign C–1, eliminating the zero in cell (C, 4). We now find that we have no assignment, using a zero element, for tractor E or trailer 4. (The numbers in the upper left-hand corner of the assigned cells are used only to reference the order, which is nonunique, in which the assignments were made.)

Since only four of the required five assignments can be made using zero elements, we need to create more zero elements. This can be done by a rather ingenious procedure involving adding and subtracting a constant from certain rows and col-

Table 8.35

	1	2	3	4	5
A					① 0
B			② 0		✗
C	④ 0			✗	
D		③ 0			
E		✗			

umns. We first "cover" all zeroes by the minimum possible number of lines drawn through rows and/or columns. This process of drawing covering lines has a dual purpose: if a *minimum* of m (in this example, five) lines is required to cover all zeroes, then we say that we have a set of independent zeroes, and an optimal solution, possibly nonunique, can then be determined. If fewer than m lines will cover all zeroes, the covering lines will indicate how we should proceed toward an optimal solution.

At this point in the solution process, as shown in Table 8.36, all zeroes can be covered by just four lines (and, incidentally, there is more than one such combination of lines). Therefore, we do not have an optimal solution. We now locate the minimum element value, V, not crossed out and subtract it from every element in the matrix. Since this will force all zero values to become $-V$, we must add V to each row and column with a line through it. As you can prove to yourself, the actual process can be performed by simply subtracting V from each element not covered by a line and adding V to every element at the intersection of two lines. The resultant ele-

Table 8.36

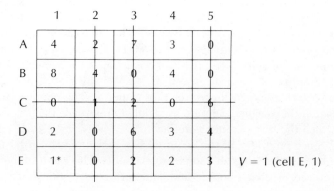

	1	2	3	4	5
A	4	2	7	3	0
B	8	4	0	4	0
C	0	1	2	0	6
D	2	0	6	3	4
E	1*	0	2	2	3

$V = 1$ (cell E, 1)

Table 8.37

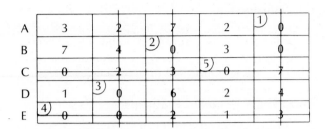

ments are shown in Table 8.37. This time, we find that it takes five lines to cover all the zeroes, so we must have five independent zeroes. Now, as shown in Table 8.37, an optimal solution can be determined by the process of elimination described earlier. The optimal assignments, and their distances, referring back to the original distance array, are shown in the accompanying table. (In Table 8.37, both the covering lines and the order in which the assignments are made are nonunique.)

Tractor	Trailer	Distance (mi)
A	5	14
B	3	19
C	4	18
D	2	17
E	1	14
		82

For an array of size $m \times m$, the Hungarian method for solving the assignment problem can be summarized as follows.

1. Subtract the minimum element in each row from all elements in that row. Subtract the minimum element in each column from all elements in that column. (Either row or column subtractions can be performed first.)
2. Cover all zeroes by the minimum possible number of lines drawn through rows and/or columns. If the number of covering lines is less than m, go to step 3. If the number of covering lines is equal to m, the solution is optimal. Go to step 4.
3. Find the minimum element value, V, not crossed out. Subtract V from each element not covered by a line and add V to every element at the intersection of two lines. Go to step 2.
4. Determine the optimal assignments. A single zero in a row or column im-

mediately identifies an optimal assignment. By crossing off rows and columns for which assignments have been determined, the remaining assignments will be found by a process of elimination. There may be more than one optimal solution.

If we have an array where the number of rows and the number of columns are unequal, we simply add a dummy row or column as required, with the cell values set to zero. This will be illustrated in the following section.

Maximization Assignment Problems

The Hungarian method for solving the assignment problem is in the form of a minimization technique, but it can be easily adapted to the solution of maximization problems. We simply reverse the relationship of the array elements by subtracting all elements in each row from the largest element in that row. (This could also be done using columns.) Then we continue with the customary solution procedure. An example will illustrate the method.

EXAMPLE 8.4

You have three employees, each of whom must be assigned to one of four possible tasks. The employees are of unequal ability, however, and you want to fill each task with the best employee available, leaving one task unassigned. The numbers in Table 8.38a indicate each employee's relative ability. The higher the number, the greater the ability. What arrangement do you recommend to maximize overall efficiency, assuming that a valid measure is the total efficiency "score" of all employees?

First, we must add a dummy row (employee) with zero cell value, to balance the array. Then we subtract each cell value from the maximum value in its row, as in Table 8.38b. Observe that this process preserves the proper relationships. For instance, the "cost" of assigning employee B to task 1 is 30 units less (and therefore more desirable) than that of an assignment to task 2. A glance at the original "ef-

Table 8.38

Original Array		Task					Task				Reversed Array
		1	2	3	4		1	2	3	4	
	A	80	30	20	60	A	0	50	60	20	
Employee	B	100	70	0	50	B	0	30	100	50	
	C	60	90	80	90	C	30	0	10	0	
(Dummy) D		0	0	0	0	D	0	0	0	0	
			(a)					(b)			

ficiency" array reveals the same relative relationship, with a 30-unit difference in favor of assigning employee B to task 1. We can now proceed with the standard technique. Since the dummy row gives us a zero in every column, there is no need for a column reduction step. The initial evaluation is in Table 8.39a, and the last array, Table 8.39b, gives the optimal solution, since four lines are required to cover all the zeroes.

Table 8.39

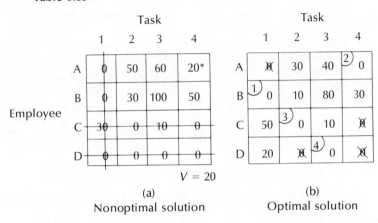

(a)
Nonoptimal solution

(b)
Optimal solution

The optimal set of assignments is indicated in the accompanying table.

Assignment	"Efficiency"
A–4	60
B–1	100
C–2	90
	250

SUMMARY

Although transportation and assignment linear programming models could be solved by the simplex method explained in the previous chapter, we have taken advantage of their special structure to utilize a tabular approach which greatly simplifies the computational procedures.

For transportation models, an initial basic feasible solution can be developed, using procedures such as the method of mutually preferred flows or VAM (Vogel's Approximation Method). Then, the stepping-stone method or the MODI (Modified Distribution) method can be employed to work toward the optimal solution, that which minimizes the objective function value. Utilizing the information in the tabular presentation of the optimal solution, sensitivity analysis of the transportation costs can be readily performed. Degeneracy, which can occur relatively frequently in a transportation model, as compared to a general linear programming model (since all activity variables in a transportation model generally assume integer values), can be easily handled. Procedures are straightforward for handling the case of unequal supply and demand, as well as maximization, rather than minimization, of an objective function. The transshipment problem, in which shipments can be routed through intermediate points, can be solved by the transportation model after introducing certain artificialities into that model.

The assignment problem, a special case of the transportation problem, could be solved by a transportation algorithm, but the solution would be degenerate at every iteration. Instead, a procedure called the Hungarian method is frequently used. This algorithm, while iterative, develops a feasible solution only at the final iteration. With only a minor change, the algorithm can handle maximization problems as well as minimization problems.

Transportation and assignment models really are network-oriented, since they can be visualized as approaches to the efficient allocation of resources within some type of distribution network. In the discussion on the transshipment problem, for instance, Figure 8.1 illustrated a network presentation of optimal solution. In the following chapter, we will study more explicit network models.

The Dual Transportation Problem

Suppose we take a transportation problem with two sources and three destinations. Using the notation shown in Table 8.40, where the c_{ij}'s represent costs and the x_{ij}'s represent units shipped, the problem statement is

$$\text{minimize } c_{11}x_{11} + c_{12}x_{12} + c_{13}x_{13} + c_{21}x_{21} + c_{22}x_{22} + c_{23}x_{23}$$

$$\text{subject to} \quad
\begin{aligned}
x_{11} + x_{12} + x_{13} &= a_1 \\
x_{21} + x_{22} + x_{23} &= a_2 \\
x_{11} \quad\quad\quad + x_{21} \quad\quad\quad &= b_1 \\
x_{12} \quad\quad\quad + x_{22} \quad\quad &= b_2 \\
x_{13} \quad\quad\quad + x_{23} &= b_3
\end{aligned}$$

and

$$x_{ij} \geq 0, \text{ for all } i \text{ and } j.$$

Observe that all coefficients of the x_{ij}'s are either 0 or 1.

Table 8.40

		Destination			
		1	2	3	Supply
Source	1	c_{11} x_{11}	c_{12} x_{12}	c_{13} x_{13}	a_1
	2	c_{21} x_{21}	c_{22} x_{22}	c_{23} x_{23}	a_2
Demand		b_1	b_2	b_3	

Let us now replace each constraint equation by two inequalities, where one is the negative of the other but both have the same inequality relationship. The resultant problem then can be expressed in the conventional primal form as:

$$\text{maximize } -c_{11}x_{11} - c_{12}x_{12} - c_{13}x_{13} - c_{21}x_{21} - c_{22}x_{22} - c_{23}x_{23}$$

subject to

$$
\begin{aligned}
x_{11} + x_{12} + x_{13} &\leq a_1 \\
-x_{11} - x_{12} - x_{13} &\leq -a_1 \\
x_{21} + x_{22} + x_{23} &\leq a_2 \\
-x_{21} - x_{22} - x_{23} &\leq -a_2 \\
x_{11} \qquad\qquad + x_{21} &\leq b_1 \\
-x_{11} \qquad\qquad - x_{21} &\leq -b_1 \\
x_{12} \qquad\qquad + x_{22} &\leq b_2 \\
-x_{12} \qquad\qquad + x_{22} &\leq -b_2 \\
x_{13} \qquad\qquad + x_{23} &\leq b_3 \\
-x_{13} \qquad\qquad - x_{23} &\leq -b_3
\end{aligned}
$$

and

$$x_{ij} \geq 0, \text{ for all } i \text{ and } j.$$

Let the dual variables be

u_i^- for the original i^{th} supply constraint
u_i^+ for the added i^{th} supply constraint
v_j^- for the original j^{th} demand constraint
v_j^+ for the added j^{th} demand constraint.

Then the dual problem is:

$$
\begin{aligned}
\text{minimize } a_1 u_1^- &- a_1 u_1^+ + a_2 u_2^- - a_2 u_2^+ + b_1 v_1^- \\
&- b_1 v_1^+ + b_2 v_2^- - b_2 v_2^+ + b_3 v_3^- - b_3 v_3^+
\end{aligned}
$$

subject to

$$
\begin{aligned}
u_1^- - u_1^+ + v_1^- - v_1^+ &\geq -c_{11} \\
u_1^- - u_1^+ + v_2^- - v_2^+ &\geq -c_{12} \\
u_1^- - u_1^+ + v_3^- - v_3^+ &\geq -c_{13} \\
u_2^- - u_2^+ + v_1^- - v_1^+ &\geq -c_{21} \\
u_2^- - u_2^+ + v_2^- - v_2^+ &\geq -c_{22} \\
u_2^- - u_2^+ + v_3^- - v_3^+ &\geq -c_{23}
\end{aligned}
$$

and all

$$u_i^-, u_i^+, v_j^-, v_j^+ \geq 0.$$

If we replace $u_i^+ - u_i^-$ by u_i and $v_j^+ - v_j^-$ by v_j, where u_i and v_j are now unrestricted in sign; and if, at the same time, we reverse the sign of the constraint inequalities and multiply through by -1, we get:

$$\text{minimize } -a_1 u_1 - a_2 u_2 - b_1 v_1 - b_2 v_2 - b_3 v_3$$

subject to

$$
\begin{aligned}
u_1 + v_1 &\leq c_{11} \\
u_1 + v_2 &\leq c_{12} \\
u_1 + v_3 &\leq c_{13} \\
u_2 + v_1 &\leq c_{21} \\
u_2 + v_2 &\leq c_{22} \\
u_2 + v_3 &\leq c_{23}
\end{aligned}
$$

where all u_i and v_j are unrestricted in sign. By changing the signs of the objective function coefficients, this becomes a maximization problem.

In general, if the primal problem is

$$\text{minimize} \sum_{i=1}^{m} \sum_{j=1}^{n} c_{ij} x_{ij}$$

subject to

$$\sum_{j=1}^{n} x_{ij} = a_i \quad i = 1, 2, \ldots, m$$

$$\sum_{i=1}^{m} x_{ij} = b_j \quad j = 1, 2, \ldots, n$$

and

$$x_{ij} \geq 0,$$

the dual problem is then

$$\text{maximize} \sum_{i=1}^{m} a_i u_i + \sum_{j=1}^{n} b_j v_j$$

subject to

$$u_i + v_j \leq c_{ij} \quad \text{for all } i \text{ and } j$$

where u_i and v_j are unrestricted in sign.

As we noted in the section on Duality in the previous chapter, for each primal basic variable in any basic feasible solution, the corresponding dual constraint must be met as an equality (according to the so-called theorem of complementary slackness), so that

$$u_i + v_j = c_{ij}, \quad \text{for all basic } x_{ij} \ (x_{ij} > 0).$$

The remaining dual constraints will all be inequalities of the form

$$u_i + v_j \leq c_{ij}, \quad \text{for all nonbasic } x_{ij} \ (x_{ij} = 0).$$

The value of $c_{ij} - (u_i + v_j)$ represents the amount by which each unit of x_{ij} would increase the objective function value. This, then, is just the change value for variable x_{ij}. In a primal minimization (maximization) problem, the optimal solution has been reached when all change values are nonnegative (nonpositive).

EXERCISES

8.1 Conceptually, how does the transportation model differ from the general linear programming model studied in the previous chapter? Be specific.

8.2 (a) Using the notation shown in Table 8.1, write out the general form for the objective function and each constraint equation for a transportation problem with three sources and two destinations when the objective is to minimize distribution costs.

(b) Choose any one constraint equation and demonstrate that this equation can be formed from a linear combination of all the other constraint equations, thereby making it redundant.

8.3 Briefly discuss the *rationale* of Vogel's Approximation Method.

8.4   Why would you expect Vogel's Approximation Method to usually result in a better initial solution than the method of mutually preferred flows?

8.5   Suppose that a transportation problem solution has been found to be nonoptimal.
(a)   How is the new entering variable selected?
(b)   How does one determine the maximum number of units to be brought in?

8.6   Water is to be pumped from three wells to meet demands in five towns in such a way as to minimize the surcharge costs. In the accompanying table, well capacities and town demands are expressed in gallons per hour (gph). Determine an initial solution for the distribution of water from wells to towns.

		Surcharge (cents per 100 gallons) Town					Capacity (gph)
		1	2	3	4	5	
	A	10	19	2	4	16	400
Well	B	3	15	9	18	7	600
	C	11	6	22	13	8	700
Demand (gph)		300	200	500	350	350	

(a)   Use mutually preferred flows. Calculate the hourly surcharge cost.
(b)   Use VAM. Calculate the hourly surcharge cost.
(c)   Compare your results for parts (a) and (b) and discuss any difference.

8.7   In the above water distribution problem, determine the allocation of well water that minimizes the total surcharge cost. Use for your initial solution the solution obtained by the mutually preferred flows method; then find the optimal solution using the MODI method. What is the hourly surcharge cost?

8.8   An oil producer wishes to determine the most profitable allocation from its four fields to three different customers. The table below contains monthly production capacities and demands in thousands of barrels (bbl), along with the profit for each well and customer combination. How much production from each well should go to each customer?

Profit per 1000 bbl ($)
Customer

		R	S	T	Capacity (1000s bbl)
	A	400	600	800	160
Well	B	500	1200	1000	180
	C	200	1800	1100	220
	D	900	500	1300	240
Demand (1000s bbl)		100	320	370	

8.9   In the preceding problem, there are alternative optimal solutions. From your solution to the problem, identify these alternative optimal solutions.

8.10 A company has factories in Denver, Detroit, and Houston and outlets in Portland, Atlanta, Waco, and Newark. The costs of transportation between cities for one of its specialized products is shown in the accompanying table, along with weekly production and demand figures.

Plant	Transportation Costs in $ Per Unit				Weekly Production, Units
	Outlet				
	Portland	Atlanta	Waco	Newark	
Denver	38	30	30	45	17
Detroit	60	25	50	32	20
Houston	42	20	16	70	30
Weekly demand, units	10	14	15	28	

(a) Establish initial feasible shipping patterns using both VAM and the mutually preferred flows method. Compare the costs of these solutions.

(b) Using the initial solution determined by the mutually preferred flows method, find the optimal solution using the MODI method.

8.11 The optimal distribution of empty railroad cars has been a major problem to the railroads. Suppose that there are surplus cars at locations 1, 2, and 3, while additional cars are required at locations 4, 5, 6, and 7, as tabulated below.

	Location						
	1	2	3	4	5	6	7
Surplus cars	2	5	6				
Required cars				1	3	7	2

The costs associated with distributing cars are shown here.

From	Cost per Car ($) To			
	4	5	6	7
1	8	15	12	12
2	10	11	7	12
3	12	8	6	7

Determine how the surplus cars should be distributed so as to minimize the distribution costs:

(a) by using VAM for the initial solution and then the stepping-stone method. Calculate the total cost at each iteration.

(b) by starting with the method of mutually preferred flows and then using the MODI method. Calculate the total cost at each iteration.

8.12 In transportation problems, why is the sensitivity analysis of a nonbasic variable so much easier than that of a basic variable?

8.13 In Exercise 8.11, the optimal solution is as follows.

From location	1	1	2	3	3	3
To location	4	7	6	5	6	7
Number of cars	1	1	5	3	2	1

(a) Using the MODI method, determine the shadow prices for all nonbasic variables. How low would the per-unit cost for route (2, 5) have to become before we would be indifferent to using that route? At this cost, what would be the maximum number of cars which could be shifted to that route?

(b) By how much could the cost of moving a car from location 2 to location 6 change, in either direction, without changing the basis? For the upper limit on this cost, substitute this cost value in the optimal array and reevaluate the shadow prices. For the route which now has a zero shadow price, what is the maximum number of cars which could be shipped by that route?

(c) By how much could the cost of moving a car from location 3 to location 7 change, in either direction, without changing the basis? For the lower limit on this cost, what is the first new route that would come into the solution if this limit were violated? Repeat for the upper limit.

8.14 For the oil-producer problem in Exercise 8.8:

(a) What would have to be the increase in profit for shipping from well C to customer T before that route would come into the solution? How many units could now be shipped by the new route, and which old route would drop out?

(b) By how much could the profit for shipping from well A to customer T change, in either direction, before the basis would have to change? If these limits were exceeded, in either direction, which new route(s) would come into the solution?

(c) Repeat the calculations of part (b) for the route from well B to customer S.

8.15 Solve the following initially degenerate transportation problem using the method of mutually preferred flows for the initial solution and MODI for the optimal solution.

Shipping Cost ($) per Unit
Warehouse

	D	E	F	G	Supply
A	1	3	5	7	100
Factory B	5	6	4	9	200
C	2	10	6	8	350
Demand	100	150	250	150	

8.16 Perform a complete sensitivity analysis for all basic variables in Exercise 8.15.

8.17 (a) In the process of solving a transportation problem, how do you recognize when degeneracy has occurred?
(b) What must be done in the solution process at this point? Why is it necessary to do this?

8.18 The Goode Company has two plants in which a product is manufactured. This product is delivered to four warehouses. Overtime can be used to increase production capacity. If overtime is used, it increases the unit delivered cost by 50 percent. Through the use of overtime, capacity can be increased to 550 units total at plant A and 650 units total at plant B. Costs, capacities, and requirements are given in the table. Find the optimal distribution pattern and its cost.

	Unit Delivered Cost ($)				Basic Capacity,
	Warehouse				
Plant	1	2	3	4	Units
A	30	22	30	18	400
B	20	16	24	28	400
Units required	200	250	350	300	

8.19 Hifreeq, Inc. manufactures microwave ovens in two factories and ships them to three warehouses. The pertinent information is summarized below.

	Shipping Costs per Oven ($)			Maximum
	Warehouse			
	1	2	3	Capacity
Factory 1	7.50	8.00	8.90	200 units
Factory 2	8.80	6.90	7.75	140
Demand, units	120	80	100	

Only enough units are to be manufactured to meet demand. Determine the number of units to be produced at each factory and the distribution pattern which minimizes shipping costs. Calculate the total shipping cost.

8.20 In Exercise 8.13, suppose that Hifreeq has just lost 80 units of factory 1 capacity, so all the demand cannot be satisfied. For every unit not shipped to the warehouses, there is a penalty cost. This cost is $5 for warehouse 1, $5 for warehouse 2, and $6 for warehouse 3.
   (a) Rework the problem and determine the optimal number of units to be shipped to each warehouse and the total cost.
   (b) If warehouse 2 must be supplied all 80 units demanded, what distribution pattern will now minimize the total cost under this additional constraint? [Hint: Work from the optimal tableau of part (a).] What is the total cost penalty for eliminating the possibility of a shortage at warehouse 2?

8.21 After studying market conditions, the Ring Away Company has drawn up a one-year sales program for its new bath salts. According to the program, estimated sales of this product in each quarter of the year is as follows.

Quarter	1	2	3	4
Expected sales (thousands of pounds)	700	500	800	1200

For the coming year the company is planning that total production be equal to expected sales, with beginning and ending inventories assumed to be zero. It is also stipulated that, in each quarter, production and inventory must be sufficient to meet sales (that is, no backordering is allowed).

The factory operates in two shifts with capacity limits of 600 and 500, respectively (in thousands of pounds per quarter). The cost of producing 1000 pounds is $60 in shift 1 and $70 in shift 2. The cost of storing 1000 pounds for one quarter is $20.

The company would like to schedule production in each quarter so as to minimize total costs of production and storage.
   (a) Formulate this problem as a transportation problem in tabular form. [Hint: Let the supply points be each shift in each quarter, and let the demand points be the expected sales in each quarter. For example, the cost of producing on the second shift in the first quarter for delivery in the third quarter is $110 ($70 + 2 \cdot 20$) for one thousand pounds of bath salts. Note that you cannot produce in the future for delivery in the past; for example, you cannot produce in the second quarter for delivery in the first quarter.]
   (b) Determine the optimal solution by a common sense approach.
   (c) Verify that your solution in (b) is optimal by using MODI.

8.22 Ace Gadget Company is attempting to determine the most economical allocation over the next four months for its production of handigadgets. Ace has 1000 units on hand at the start of the first month and can produce 3000 units per month. The monthly demands to be supplied are, respectively, 3200, 3400, 2800, and 3600 units, a total of 13,000 units. Thus, at the end of the four months, the company will have supplied all the demand and have zero inventory on hand.

Any unit which is produced in a given month incurs no inventory charge if it is supplied during that month. If it is to be placed into inventory, however, there is a charge of $2 per unit for storage preparation. In addition, there is a monthly charge of $2 per unit for every month a unit is held in inventory. Thus, a unit produced in period 2 and supplied in period 2 incurs no inventory cost. If it is held over into period 3 and supplied then, there will be a cost of $4. If not supplied until period 4, the cost will be $6 per unit. (The units in inventory at the start of period 1 incur no additional cost if used during the first month, $2 if used during the second month, and so forth.)

Set up a transportation model where the sources consist of the initial units in inventory (for which the $2 preparation cost has already been absorbed) and the four monthly production quantities, and the destinations are the monthly demands. Since a unit cannot be supplied before it is produced, any "route" involving production in a given period and requirements in an earlier period is infeasible and can be assigned an infinite cost.

Determine the optimal allocation, between current demand and demand in future months, of the initial inventory and of each month's production, considering only the inventory costs involved. Use the method of mutually preferred flows to obtain an initial solution.

8.23   Case Manufacturing Company has decided to add a new manufacturing facility to meet increased demand. The new plant will have a production capacity of 18,000 units per week. The marketing department has recommended that the plant be built in either St. Louis or Knoxville. The product is shipped in cases of *10 units* to Kansas City, Cincinnati, Chicago, and Pittsburgh. Production and distribution costs, as well as production and demand values, are as shown below.

Plant Location	Per Unit Production Cost	Capacity (units/wk)	Distribution Center	Demand (units/wk)
Kansas City	$1.55	14,000	Kansas City	16,000
Toledo	1.57	20,000	Cincinnati	12,000
Proposed			Chicago	10,000
St. Louis	1.50	18,000	Pittsburgh	14,000
Knoxville	1.48	18,000		

Distribution Costs per Case ($)

From	To			
	Kansas City	Cincinnati	Chicago	Pittsburgh
Kansas City	1.20	1.50	1.40	1.70
Toledo	1.50	1.30	1.30	1.35
St. Louis	1.40	1.35	1.40	1.60
Knoxville	1.70	1.35	1.50	1.40

Where should the new plant be located to minimize total costs? Set this up as a transportation problem, showing all numerical values. Do *not* solve, but explain briefly how you would determine which of the proposed plants to select.

8.24 In a minimization transportation problem, how can we determine when the optimal solution has been reached? in a maximization transportation problem?

8.25 In a maximization transportation problem, suppose that the unit profit associated with a variable in cell (i, j) is r_{ij}.

(a) If that variable is nonbasic and its shadow price is $-s_{ij}$, over what range of profit values would that nonbasic variable remain out of the basis?

(b) If that variable is basic and is the only basic variable in its row, how would you determine the range of profit values for which it would remain in the basis?

8.26 A company has three plants, each of which manufactures the same product. Production costs differ among these plants, as do the raw material costs. The product's sales price is also different at each of the four warehouses supplied by these plants.

Plant	Production Cost per Unit	Raw Material Cost per Unit	Capacity, Units
1	$14	$12	1600
2	18	10	1200
3	13	10	1400

Transportation Cost ($) per Unit

| | Plant | | | | Requirement, |
Warehouse	1	2	3	Sales Price ($)	Units
1	4	6	5	32	1300
2	1	6	4	33	1000
3	5	7	3	31	1000
4	7	2	9	34	900

Determine the optimal shipping pattern. Use VAM to obtain the initial solution.

8.27 The National Diversified Company is producing widgets at two plants, both of which have a capacity of 80 units per month. It has orders from three customers for next month. Smith has contracted to purchase 70 units, and Jones has a contract for 40 units. The third customer, Young, as well as Jones, wishes to purchase as many of the remaining units as possible. Net contributions to profit, including shipping costs, are as shown here.

	Profit Contribution ($) per Unit		
	Jones	Smith	Young
Plant 1	11	10	9
Plant 2	5	6	8

What is the optimal allocation of widgets to customers to maximize profits? [*Hint:* By setting up a dummy destination for the additional units wanted by Jones, make it possible for both Jones and Young to purchase all or any of the units not contracted for. A dummy plant will also be required to balance the problem, but this dummy plant must not supply any of the *contracted* demands.]

8.28   In Exercise 8.11, the railroad car distribution problem, suppose that it became possible to transship cars through both source and destination locations, with the following costs.

Cost per Car ($)

Source	1	2	3	Destination	4	5	6	7
1	—	8	4	4	—	4	5	11
2	8	—	14	5	4	—	10	14
3	4	14	—	6	5	10	—	9
				7	11	14	9	—

(a)   Construct a tabular presentation of this problem as a transshipment problem.

(b)   For your initial solution, start with the optimal solution to Exercise 8.11 (as given in Exercise 8.13) and add 13 units to all the cells on the diagonal. Then, determine the optimal solution using MODI.

(c)   Specify the assignments which changed, as compared to the optimal solution without transshipment.

8.29   Transshipment has now been allowed in the problem of Exercise 8.15, with the cost data as shown.

Shipping Cost ($) per Unit

Factory	A	B	C	Warehouse	D	E	F	G
A	—	5	6	D	—	3	6	9
B	5	—	4	E	3	—	7	8
C	6	4	—	F	6	7	—	4
				G	9	8	4	—

(a)   Set up the resulting transshipment problem in tabular form.

(b)   Form an initial solution by first assigning 650 units to all the cells on the diagonal. Then use VAM to get the remaining assignments.

(c)   Determine the optimal solution using MODI. Which routes represent transshipment in the optimal solution?

8.30   From a conceptual standpoint, how does an assignment problem differ from a transportation problem?

8.31   In solving transportation models, each solution is a basic feasible solution. How does this compare with the Hungarian method for solving assignment problems?

8.32   The Farmout Company has four unrelated computer programs to be written. It wishes to have each of these programs done by a separate independent software firm, in order to judge their capabilities firsthand. Bids have been submitted on these programming tasks as follows, where all amounts are costs in thousands of dollars and × denotes that a company has failed to bid on a particular program.

	Bid Amounts ($1000s)			
	Program			
Company	1	2	3	4
A	10.3	18.2	15.9	8.6
B	12.0	17.4	×	6.4
C	11.1	20.1	16.8	9.1
D	×	19.6	17.5	8.2

(a)   Determine the optimal assignment of programs to companies using the Hungarian method. Find the total cost.

(b)   From the final array values, by how much would company D have to reduce its bid on Program 2 for there to be an additional optimal solution? What would be the assignments for this additional solution? Verify that it gives the same total cost as the solution in (a).

8.33   Solve for the optimal assignment in Exercise 8.32 by the transportation method, using the method of mutually preferred flows and then MODI. (Each supply and demand value will be 1, and the solution will be degenerate at each assignment, so there must be three basic variables with a value of ϵ.)

8.34   Suppose that, in Exercise 8.32, a fifth company, company E, also submitted bids on the four programs, as follows.

Program   1   2   3   4
Bid, $1000s   11.7 19.0 15.7 7.8

(a)   Determine the optimal assignment of programs and the total cost.

(b)   Why is this solution guaranteed to be at least as good as the solution to the original problem in Exercise 8.32?

8.35   Five quality control inspectors, U, V, W, X, and Y, are to be assigned to inspect products P, Q, R, S, and T, on the basis of one inspector for each product. It is desired to minimize the overall fraction defective after inspection. In the following table of data indicating inspector performance, an asterisk indicates that the inspector is not capable of inspecting that product.

Fraction Defective After Inspection
(in tenths of a percent)

		Product				
		P	Q	R	S	T
	U	1	2	3	4	4
	V	*	6	8	*	7
Inspector	W	12	2	*	5	11
	X	6	15	7	9	16
	Y	5	7	6	8	6

(a)   Find the allowable assignment that minimizes the overall fraction defective after inspection.

(b)   What assumption is inherent in your solution when you minimize the sum of the fraction defective values? What is the mean fraction defective for your solution in part (a)?

8.36   Four sorority sisters have agreed that they will each take a different college major. Their best estimate of their grade point average in each major is shown in the accompanying table.

Expected Grade Point Average

		Major			
		A	B	C	D
	Jones	2.4	2.6	2.8	3.0
Student	Green	4.0	3.7	3.6	3.5
	Smith	3.1	2.8	3.4	3.2
	Adams	3.2	3.6	3.7	2.9

(a)   Which student should take which major if the sorority sisters wish to maximize their overall grade point average? What is the resultant overall grade point average?

(b)   Repeat part (a) if there is no requirement to take different majors. [*Hint:* Use common sense.]

8.37   Four operators, A, B, C, and D, are to be assigned to tasks I, II, III, and IV (on the basis of one operator per task) to minimize the overall time required to perform the tasks. Given the table of estimated times below, find an assignment that minimizes the overall time required. Specify the estimated total time to complete all tasks.

Estimated Time (hours)
Tasks

		I	II	III	IV
	A	6	2	4	10
	B	7	3	5	11
Operator	C	8	1	5	12
	D	5	2	3	15

8.38 A company has three job orders. This company operates on a project basis and has three project teams available. Each team must be assigned one job order, and they have proposed different approaches to the three jobs. The following estimates of man-days of development and engineering time required under each approach have been made.

	Development Time, Man-Days			Engineering Time, Man-Days		
	Job			Job		
Team	A	B	C	A	B	C
1	8	6	9	3	3	5
2	6	3	7	5	9	8
3	5	2	6	6	9	10

Development expense is $120 per man-day, and engineering expense is $100 per man-day.

(a) Find the assignment of teams to jobs which minimizes costs.

(b) The company will receive $2000 for job A, $1800 for job B, and $2100 for job C. Which teams should be assigned to which jobs in order to maximize profit?

(c) Explain why your solutions are identical in parts (a) and (b).

8.39 Mystic Airlines has flights in both directions between Houston and Los Angeles, as shown in the accompanying table. If a flight crew is based in Los Angeles and flies to Houston, it must return to Los Angeles on a later flight, and vice versa if it is based in Houston. To meet flight regulations, crews must have at least a four-hour layover between flights. There is a two-hour time differential between Houston and Los Angeles.

Specify which crews (by flight number) should be based in Los Angeles and which in Houston in order to minimize the total time spent on the ground away from home base. Find this total time.

[Hint: Form two tables, with Los Angeles flights as rows and Houston flights as columns. The first table applies to crews based in Los Angeles and the second to crews based in Houston. The table elements are the minimum required layover times for each combination of flights. For example, the combination of flights 4 and 25 would require a twenty-seven-hour layover for a Los Angeles-based crew (because of the four-hour minimum layover) and a seventeen-hour layover for a Houston-based crew. Then, form a third table consisting of the minimum elements for each flight combination. Now solve as an assignment problem.]

Flight Number	Los Angeles to Houston		Flight Number	Houston to Los Angeles	
	Depart (L.A. Time)	Arrive (Houston Time)		Depart (Houston Time)	Arrive (L.A. Time)
1	6:00 AM	10:00 AM	21	7:00 AM	7:00 AM
2	8:00 AM	12:00 Noon	22	8:00 AM	8:00 AM
3	9:00 AM	1:00 PM	23	10:00 AM	10:00 AM
4	12:00 Noon	4:00 PM	24	4:00 PM	4:00 PM
5	5:00 PM	9:00 PM	25	7:00 PM	7:00 PM
6	11:00 PM	3:00 AM	26	9:00 PM	9:00 PM

NETWORK MODELS

The transportation and assignment models studied in the previous chapter have a strong network orientation, but an understanding of network concepts is not a requirement for their solution. This chapter will be concerned with the analysis of models whose structure is strongly dependent upon their actual representation as a network. We will study models relating to the shortest route through a network, to the shortest route which connects all locations in a network, to maximal flows in a network, and to project scheduling, which involves the analysis of the longest route through a network.

Although most of the required concepts will be explained as needed, it is desirable to introduce some of the basic terminology of network analysis. A typical network, as drawn in Figure 9.1, consists of nodes and arcs.

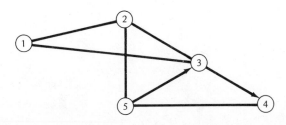

Figure 9.1

Nodes generally represent locations of some type (cities, relay stations, and so forth) and are displayed graphically by circles with numbers or letters enclosed. *Arcs* or *branches* connect nodes and establish their relationship to each other. Arcs represent such quantities as distance, time, flow capacity, and so forth, and are represented as lines between nodes. An arc with specified direction, such as arc (5, 3) is known as a *directed arc;* if no direction is specified, it is an *undirected arc.* A *chain,* or directed chain, is a sequence of nodes and directed arcs connecting two nodes. Nodes 5 and 4, in Figure 9.1, are connected by chain (5, 3, 4). A *path* is a sequence of nodes and directed or undirected arcs connecting two nodes, such as path (1, 2, 5, 3). If a path starts from a node and returns to that node, it becomes a *loop*, or *cycle*. A *connected network* is one in which every pair of nodes is connected by a path. A *tree* is a connected network with no loops. The number of arcs in a tree is always one fewer than the number of nodes, as you can easily convince yourself. Figure 9.1 is a connected network, but not a tree, since it contains a number of loops.

9.1   THE SHORTEST ROUTE PROBLEM

The shortest route problem is concerned with finding the shortest route from an origin to a destination through a connected network, given the nonnegative distance associated with each branch of the network. This "distance" could also represent travel time, activity completion time, cost, and so forth, so that finding the shortest route could actually involve time or cost minimization. Although this problem could be solved by linear programming, more efficient specialized algorithms have been developed. The one by Dantzig is perhaps the easiest to understand.

Dantzig's method basically involves working outward from the origin and always selecting the next closest node (or nodes, in case of ties) to the origin and tabulating its distance from the origin. This process continues until the destination node is reached. In a network containing n nodes, it can be demonstrated that the maximum number of comparisons needed to determine the shortest route from a given origin to all other nodes is $n(n - 1)/2$. In practice, the number of comparisons tends to be much less, since all arcs leading to nodes previously evaluated are eliminated from further consideration.

The computational process for this algorithm can best be understood by taking a numerical example.

EXAMPLE 9.1

The Keepon Trucking Company has to deliver a shipment of goods from city A to city G, and the feasible routes pass through cities B through F, as shown in the diagram of Figure 9.2. The numbers on the arcs represent the estimated driving times, in hours, between adjacent cities. Owing to major construction work, the driving times between cities C and D and between cities C and E differ, depending on the direction of travel. The remainder of the travel times are independent of the direction. Keepon Trucking would like to determine the route requiring the shortest travel time.

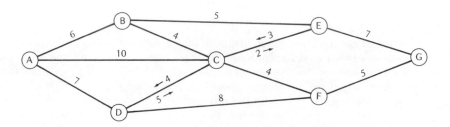

Figure 9.2

Before starting the calculations, we construct what can be called an adjacent node table. For each given node, Table 9.1 contains all adjacent nodes, followed by their arc values, listed in order of increasing arc value. We exclude arcs into the origin or out of the destination, since they would never be used. Above each node, as the computations proceed we will place the shortest distance (travel time) to that node.

Table 9.1   Adjacent Node Table

		Node					
	A	B	C	D	E	F	G
Adjacent Nodes and Arc Values	AB–6	BC–4	CE–2	DC–5	EC–3	FC–4	
	AD–7	BE–5	CB–4	DF–8	EB–5	FG–5	
	AC–10		CD–4		EG–7	FD–8	
			CF–4				

In the iterations that follow, only arcs leading from "established" nodes, those whose shortest distance to the origin is already determined, can be considered. Candidate arcs will be underlined, and the distance to each established node will be shown in parentheses above that node.

In iteration 1, the only established node is A, which is obviously 0 units from the origin, and the only candidate arc is (AB). The next closest node to the origin is then node B, which has a shortest distance of 6 + 0 = 6 units. This value is placed above node B, and the chosen arc is circled. Then, all arcs leading into the newly chosen node are crossed out, as indicated, because they would never be used.

For iteration 2, with nodes A and B established, there are two candidate arcs underlined, arcs (AD) and (BC). Node D becomes the next established node, since its distance from the origin is 0 + 7 = 7, whereas the distance to node C is 6 + 4 = 10. A 7 is placed over node D, arc (AD) is circled, and arcs leading into arc D are crossed out. (Arcs crossed out earlier have been deleted.)

Iteration 1

| Shortest Distance | (0) | 6 | | | | | |
Node	A	B	C	D	E	F	G
	(AB)–6	BC–4	CE–2	DC–5	EC–3	FC–4	
Adjacent	AD–7	BE–5	C̶B̶–̶4̶	DF–8	E̶B̶–̶5̶	FG–5	
Nodes	AC–10		CD–4		EG–7	FD–8	
			CF–4				

Iteration 2

| Shortest Distance | (0) | (6) | | 7 | | | |
Node	A	B	C	D	E	F	G
	(AB)–6	<u>BC–4</u>	CE–2	DC–5	EC–3	FC–4	
Adjacent	(AD)–7	BE–5		DF–8		FG–5	
Nodes	AC–10		C̶D̶–̶4̶		EG–7	F̶D̶–̶8̶	
			CF–4				

At iteration 3, with established nodes A, B, and D, underlined arcs (AC), (BC), and (DC) must be considered. Since the distance to node C using arc (AC) is $0 + 10 = 10$ and the distance to node C using arc (BC) is $6 + 4 = 10$, the shortest distance to node C is 10, and there are alternative shortest paths to node C. All arcs leading into node C are crossed out, including arc (DC), which was just a candidate.

Iteration 3

| Shortest Distance | (0) | (6) | 10 | (7) | | | |
Node	A	B	C	D	E	F	G
	(AB)–6	(BC)–4	CE–2	D̶C̶–̶5̶	E̶C̶–̶3̶	F̶C̶–̶4̶	
Adjacent	(AD)–7	<u>BE–5</u>		DF–8		FG–5	
Nodes	(AC)–10				EG–7		
			CF–4				

Iteration 4 has four established nodes but only three arcs to be considered, since there are no longer any eligible arcs leading from node A. Arc (BE), giving a distance of $6 + 5 = 11$, establishes node E, and arc (CE) is crossed out.

Iteration 4

Shortest Distance Node	(0) A	(6) B	(10) C	(7) D	11 E	F	G
Adjacent Nodes	(A B)-6 (A D)-7 (A C)-10	(B C)-4 (B E)-5	~~CE-2~~	DF–8	EG–7	FG–5	
			CF–4				

The candidate arcs at iteration 5 are arcs (CF), (DF), and (EG), and arc (CF) gives a shortest distance to node F of 14. Arc (DF) is crossed out.

Iteration 5

Shortest Distance Node	(0) A	(6) B	(10) C	(7) D	(11) E	14 F	G
Adjacent Nodes	(AB)-6 (AD)-7 (AC)-10	(BC)-4 (BE)-5	(CF)-4	~~DF–8~~	EG–7	FG–5	

Iteration 6 is the final iteration. With candidate arcs (EG) and (FG), node G is established at a shortest distance of 18, using arc (EG).

Iteration 6

Shortest Distance Node	(0) A	(6) B	(10) C	(7) D	(11) E	(14) F	18 G
Adjacent Nodes	(AB)-6 (AD)-7 (AC)-10	(BC)-4 (BE)-5	(CF)-4		(EG)-7		~~FG–5~~

Now, tracing the route from the *destination* back to the *origin*, the shortest route uses arcs (EG), (BE), and (AB). Figure 9.3 shows the shortest routes from the origin to all nodes, and the results of the analysis are summarized in Table 9.2. The shortest time required to travel from city A to city G is 18 hours, and the optimal route is A–B–E–G.

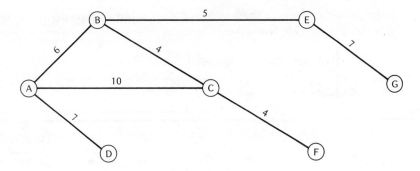

Figure 9.3   Shortest route from city A

Table 9.2   Shortest Route Analysis

Node	Shortest Distance from Node A	Shortest Route(s)
B	6	A–B
D	7	A–D
C	10	A–B–C, A–C
E	11	A–B–E
F	14	A–B–C–F, A–C–F
G	18	A–B–E–G

To summarize this shortest route algorithm (which starts with the origin having an established distance of zero), the following steps are required for each iteration.

1. For each established node, add its distance to the distance of its shortest remaining adjacent node arc (if any) to get a test distance.
2. Considering all established nodes, find the shortest test distance. This distance now becomes the established distance for the second node of the arc associated with the shortest test distance. (If there is a tie for the shortest test distance, there will be more than one new established node and/or alternative paths to a newly established node.)
3. Excluding the arc(s) just chosen, cross off all arcs leading into the node(s) just established.

Continue these iterations until the destination node is reached. Find the shortest route(s) by tracing the chosen arcs from the destination back to the origin. As a by-product of this analysis, the shortest distance from the origin to all nodes will be obtained.

It is not actually necessary to handle each iteration separately. The algorithm has been shown in this manner to make it easier to follow. The entire network can be readily evaluated with a single adjacent node table, as shown in Table 9.3, where the superscripts indicate the order of solution.

Table 9.3   Determination of Shortest Routes

Shortest Distance	0	6	10	7	11	14	18
Node	A⁰	B¹	C³	D²	E⁴	F⁵	G⁶

	¹(AB)-6	³(BC)-4	⁴CE-2	³DE-5	³EC-3	³FE-4
Adjacent	²(AD)-7	⁴(BE)-5	¹CB-4	⁵DF-8	¹EB-5	⁶FG-5
Nodes	³(AC)-10		²CD-4		⁶(EG)-7	²FD-8
			⁵(CF)-4			

9.2 THE MINIMAL SPANNING TREE PROBLEM

Suppose we have a set of nodes and we know the arc distances between the nodes that can be connected. We wish to find that set of arcs which will connect all nodes and have minimum total length when all the arc lengths are added together. These arcs will form a tree, which, as we discussed at the beginning of this chapter, is a connected network which contains no loops.

This problem has practical applications in the planning of communications and transportation networks. If, for example, we wished to establish a communications network of minimum total length between several different sites, we would like to find that network "tree" of minimum length which spanned all the sites. Or, suppose we were interested in constructing a road to connect several remote locations. The minimal spanning tree would be the network which minimized the total road mileage to be constructed. It should be clear that, in the context of this problem, all network arcs must be undirected.

The computational procedure conceptually involves selecting any node as the starting node and then choosing the shortest arc to any adjacent node. From that point on, we choose the unconnected node closest to any connected node. As noted earlier, for a network with n nodes, any tree in that network must contain exactly $n - 1$ arcs.

A computational algorithm which essentially operates in this fashion and minimizes the number of comparisons required, is given in the following steps.

1. Find the minimum length arc. Place its nodes in what can be called a "selected node" list. If there is more than one such arc of minimum length, choose any one of them at random.
2. Find the next shortest arc. (If there are ties, select any one of those arcs tied.)
   a) If one, but not both, of its nodes is in the selected node list, add the other node to the selected node list. Go to step 3.

b) If both of its nodes are already in the selected node list, delete this arc. Go to step 3.
c) If neither of its nodes is in the selected node list, go back to step 2, but reconsider this arc (and all other such arcs that have been temporarily passed over) after the selection of every new arc.
3. If all nodes are now in the selected node list, stop. If not, return to step 2.

This mathematical model will now be illustrated with an example.

EXAMPLE 9.2

The Peoples Power Company is in the process of designing a low-voltage communications network to tie together eight large and widely scattered substations in a large metropolitan area. The company wishes to determine the minimum network length required to provide a control path between all these substations, utilizing existing power poles to carry the necessary cables. Figure 9.4 shows the substations, designated as A through H, and the available power pole routes connecting them, with the numbers indicating the distances in miles.

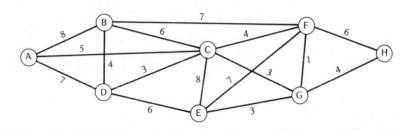

Figure 9.4

The solution to this problem involves the determination of the minimal spanning tree. In performing the analysis, it is most helpful to set up the arc distances in tabular or array form, and this has been done in Table 9.4. Since the arc distances are symmetric, only the upper or lower triangular array is required.

By use of superscripts attached to the arcs, to indicate the order in which they were chosen, the entire process will be completed in a single table, Table 9.5. Working from Table 9.4 and following the steps of the algorithm.

1. The minimum length arc is (FG), with length 1, so the initially selected nodes are F and G.
2. There is a three-way tie for the next shortest arc, which has a length of 3. The three arcs are (CD), (CG), and (EG). Since neither C nor D is in the selected node list, arc (CD) must be passed over for now, because it cannot be connected to an existing arc. The next arc considered is arc (CG). Since node G is in the selected node list, we now add node C to that list. Going back to those

arcs passed over previously, only arc (CD) in this case, we observe that node C is now in the selected node list. Arc (CD) must now be chosen, thereby adding node D to the selected node list. Arc (EG) next contributes node E.

The process continues in the same fashion. The next shortest arcs are (BD), (CF), and (GH), all with a length of 4. Arc (BD) contributes node B to the selected node list.

Table 9.4 Arc Distances between Nodes (Nodes represent substations; arc lengths are in miles)

Node	A	B	C	D	E	F	G	H
A	–	8	5	7				
B		–	6	4		7		
C			–	3	8	4	3	
D				–	6			
E					–	7	3	
F						–	1	6
G							–	4
H								–

Table 9.5 Determination of Minimal Spanning Tree

Arc	*Length (miles)*	*Selected Nodes* A	B	C	D	E	F	G	H
FG[1]	1						×	×	
CD[3]	3				×				
CG[2]	3			×					
EG[4]	3					×			
BD[5]	4		×						
~~CF~~	4								
GH[6]	4								×
AC[7]	5	×							

The next arc considered is (CF), but since nodes C and F are already in the selected node list, arc (CF) must be deleted, because it would form a loop, rather than add a new node. The next two arcs, (GH) and (AC), each add a node to the selected node list, thereby completing it.

The resulting minimal spanning tree is shown in Figure 9.5. The total arc length of this tree is 23 units (miles). Observe the efficiency of this method, as it considers only those arcs which are likely candidates. In the simple example chosen, only 8 of the 16 arcs were considered, and 7 of those 8 were selected.

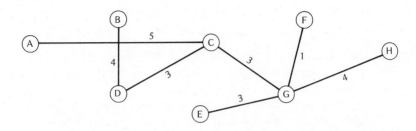

Figure 9.5

In some situations, we might be interested in finding the maximal spanning tree. For this case, the same basic algorithm can be used either by setting all arc values negative or by starting with the maximum length arc, and then selecting the next longest arc, and so on.

9.3   MAXIMAL FLOW IN A CAPACITATED NETWORK

Given a network consisting of directed or undirected arcs, each with a stated flow capacity, we wish to determine the maximum achievable flow from a specified source node to a specified destination node. This problem is of interest in various types of transportation and communication networks. For instance, given the number of messages which can be transmitted simultaneously in each link of a communications network, we can determine the maximum number of messages which can be transmitted simultaneously from any node in that network to any other node, using all feasible routes. Or, in a network of pipelines connecting refineries, the maximal flow possible between any two refineries can be determined.

Let c_{ij} = maximum allowable flow (arc capacity), in units, between nodes i and j
$\quad\quad x_{ij}$ = actual units of flow between nodes i and j.

If nodes i and j are unconnected, $c_{ij} = c_{ji} = 0$. Observe that flow must be conserved at each node, since the total flow into a node must exactly balance the total flow out of that node. If we designate node 1 as the source node and node N as the destination node in a network with N nodes, the conservation of flow at any node j can be expressed as

$$\sum_{i=1}^{N} x_{ij} = \sum_{k=1}^{N} x_{jk} \qquad i \neq j, \quad k \neq j.$$

To maximize the total flow in the network, we can maximize the flow out of the origin, node 1, or, equivalently, into the destination, node N. Given the capacity constraints c_{ij}, our problem can then be stated as:

$$\text{maximize} \sum_{j=2}^{N} x_{1j} = \sum_{i=1}^{N-1} x_{iN}$$

$$\text{subject to} \quad \sum_{i=1}^{N} x_{ij} - \sum_{k=1}^{N} x_{jk} = 0 \qquad j = 2, 3, \ldots, N-1 \quad i, k \neq j$$

$$0 \leq x_{ij} \leq c_{ij} \qquad \text{for all } i, j \quad i \neq j.$$

This problem can be solved by linear programming techniques, but again, there are more specialized and efficient techniques.

The technique to be shown involves a computational algorithm which is quite satisfactory for the manual solution of small networks, up to perhaps 20 nodes. Actually, the more sophisticated methods, used for the computer solution of large network flow problems, are generally refinements of the simple algorithm to be presented. For any given source and destination node pair, this algorithm not only finds the maximal flow in the network but also determines an optimal (not necessarily unique) flow in all arcs of the network.

The algorithm consists of four steps.

1. Find a chain between source and destination which has positive flow capacity on all arcs. If no such chain can be found, an optimal solution has been achieved, and the algorithm is terminated. The maximal flow is that out of the source node or into the destination node.
2. If such a chain is found, locate the lowest arc capacity in that chain. Call this value c.
3. For every arc in this chain, subtract c from its current flow capacity.
4. For every arc in the chain from destination to source passing through the same nodes in reverse order, add c to its current flow capacity. Go to step 1.

EXAMPLE 9.3

The Direct Distribution Company has a data network linking its six distribution centers. The arrowed numbers in Figure 9.6 represent send-only communication units which connect the various distribution centers. Data communication devices automatically route data through intermediate points, given any specified routing from a particular originating unit. DDC wants to determine the maximum number of communication paths which can be set up at any one time to transmit data from distribution center 1 to distribution center 6.

We will apply the maximal flow algorithm to this network, again using the notation c_{ij} to represent the flow capacity from node i to node j. The computations

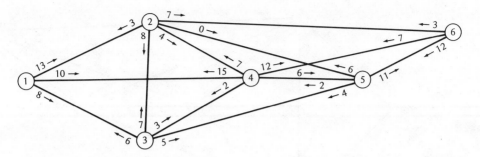

Figure 9.6

are performed directly on the network, and superscripts are used to indicate the number of the iteration on which a given value resulted. It should be made clear that the order of selection of the chains enumerated is completely arbitrary.

Examining Figure 9.6, suppose we choose chain 1–2–6 for the first iteration. Since the minimum arc capacity is 7, we subtract 7 from c_{12} and c_{26} and add 7 to c_{21} and c_{62}. At the end of iteration 1, the changed values are $c_{12} = 6$, $c_{21} = 10$, $c_{26} = 0$, and $c_{62} = 10$. These values are shown in Figure 9.7, and all are labeled with a superscript 1, denoting the first iteration.

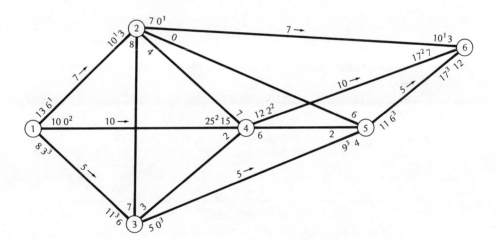

Figure 9.7   Iterations 1 to 3

Choosing chain 1–4–6 for the second iteration, the minimum arc capacity is 10, so $c_{14} = 10 - 10 = 0$, $c_{41} = 15 + 10 = 25$, $c_{46} = 12 - 10 = 2$,   and $c_{64} = 7 + 10 = 17$. These values, labeled with a superscript 2, are shown in Figure 9.7. The third iteration results, using chain 1–3–5–6, are also shown in Figure 9.7. For clarity, the results of the next three iterations, using in turn chains 1–2–4–5–6, 1–2–3–4–5–6, and 1–3–4–6, are shown separately in Figure 9.8.

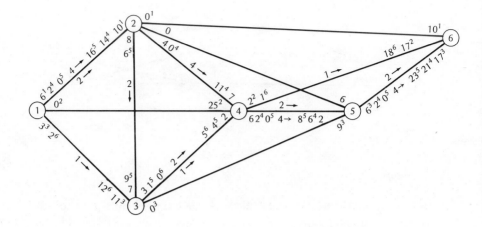

Figure 9.8 Iterations 4 to 6

After the sixth iteration, the only flow capacity remaining at node 1 is $c_{13} = 2$. At node 3, the only available flow capacity is $c_{32} = 9$. At node 2, however, the only possible flows are back to node 3 or node 1. Thus, no more flow can pass from node 1 to node 6, so the maximal flow of 29 units has been achieved, as summarized in Table 9.6.

Table 9.6 Determination of Maximal Flow

Iteration	Chain	Arc Values	Minimum
1	1–2–6	13, 7	7
2	1–4–6	10, 12	10
3	1–3–5–6	8, 5, 11	5
4	1–2–4–5–6	6, 4, 6, 6	4
5	1–2–3–4–5–6	2, 8, 3, 2, 2	2
6	1–3–4–6	3, 1, 2	1
		Maximal flow	29

The entire process can actually be performed on a single diagram, as shown in Figure 9.9.

Utilizing the results shown in Figure 9.9, we can now specify the flows in all arcs of the network. For all arc capacities which have decreased, we calculate the flow on a given directed arc by subtracting the final remaining capacity from the original flow capacity. For example, the actual flow from node 1 to node 3 is $8 - 2 = 6$. The summarization of all flows in the network is shown in Table 9.7 and diagrammed in Figure 9.10. Observe that for all nodes except the source and destination nodes (nodes 1 and 6), the row and column totals in Table 9.7 are equal. This shows the

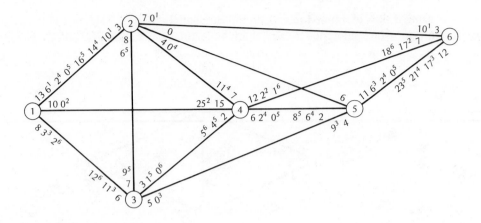

Figure 9.9   All iterations

Table 9.7   Value of Directed Flows

			To Node			
From Node	2	3	4	5	6	Total
1	13	6	10			29
2		2	4		7	13
3			3	5		8
4				6	11	17
5					11	11
Total	13	8	17	11	29	

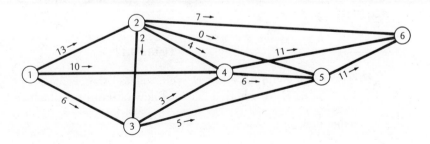

Figure 9.10

conservation of flow at each node, which is also evident from Figure 9.10, as you can readily verify. For nodes 1 and 6, the flow out of node 1 equals the flow into node 6, 29 units.

Although step 4 of the algorithm turned out to have no effect on the solution of this particular problem, since we would have arrived at the same answer without using it, it is of interest to explain the rationale behind it. This step is, in essence, an artifice which allows us to correct any unfortunate selection of chains by permitting a reverse flow along an arc to partially or completely cancel out a flow in the opposite direction. As an example, consider the simple network of Figure 9.11.

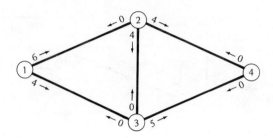

Figure 9.11

In attempting to determine the maximal flow between nodes 1 and 4, suppose we chose the chains specified in Table 9.8, resulting in the network of Figure 9.12, but did *not* employ step 4 to adjust the reverse flows. The maximal flow between nodes 1 and 4 appears to be 7 units.

Table 9.8

Chain	Arc Values	Minimum
1–2–3–4	6, 4, 5	4
1–3–4	4, 1	1
1–2–4	2, 4	2
		$\overline{7}$

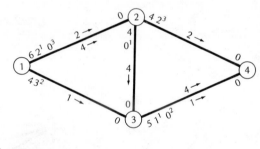

Figure 9.12

However, we could have just as well selected the chains shown in Table 9.9, resulting in Figure 9.13, where a maximal flow of 9 units is obtained.

Table 9. 9

Chain	Arc Values	Minimum
1–2–4	6, 4	4
1–2–3–4	2, 4, 5	2
1–3–4	4, 3	3
		$\overline{9}$

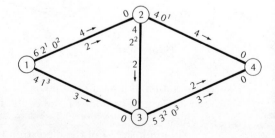

Figure 9.13

If we had chosen the chains in the same order as in Table 9.8 and had properly utilized step 4 to adjust the reverse flows, the results would have been as shown in Table 9.10 and Figure 9.14. The ability to send flow through arc (3, 2) has the effect of decreasing the final net flow through arc (2, 3) by the selection of chain 1–3–2–4. Figure 9.14 then shows the same net flows as those of Figure 9.13.

Table 9.10

Chain	Arc Values	Minimum
1–2–3–4	6, 4, 5	4
1–3–4	4, 1	1
1–2–4	2, 4	2
1–3–2–4	3, 4, 2	2
		9

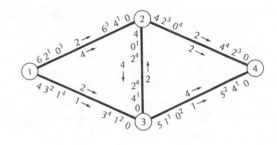

Figure 9.14

9.4 MULTITERMINAL MAXIMAL FLOWS

Instead of being interested only in the maximal flow between a single source-destination node pair, suppose we wanted to know the maximal flow between any two nodes of a network. We could, of course, apply the procedure just shown to the analysis of each node pair. With N nodes, there are $N(N - 1)/2$ such node pairs. For *undirected* networks, however, a highly efficient algorithm, which evaluates all maximal flows in only $N - 1$ iterations, has been developed by Gomory and Hu. The end result of the algorithm is the development of what is termed a flow-equivalent tree. At each iteration, we generate an arc of this tree.

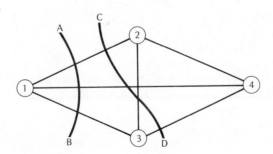

Figure 9.15

Before going into the specific solution process, we will need to establish some important network concepts. These concepts are valid for either directed or undirected networks. It should be noted that any undirected arc with capacity c can always be replaced by two oppositely directed arcs, each with capacity c. Referring to Figure 9.15, suppose we partition the set of nodes into two sets S and $\bar{S}$, where $\bar{S}$ is the complement of S. Such a partition is called a *cut*, which we denote by $[S|\bar{S}]$. Each arc which is cut will have one node in S and one node in $\bar{S}$. A cut completely disconnects the source node from the destination node. The *cut capacity* equals the sum of the capacities of the arcs of the cut. To illustrate, in Figure 9.15, the constructed arc (AB) produces cut $[1|2, \ 3, \ 4]$ with cut capacity $c_{12} + c_{14} + c_{13}$. Arc (CD) generates cut $[1, \ 3|2, \ 4]$ with cut capacity $c_{12} + c_{14} + c_{32} + c_{34}$.

For any source node and any destination node, the cut giving the minimum cut capacity is called the *minimum cut*. Ford and Fukerson proved that the maximal flow is always equal to the minimum cut. This result is stated as the well-known *max-flow min-cut theorem*: for any network, the maximal flow from source to destination is equal to the flow capacity of the minimum cut separating the source and the destination.

EXAMPLE 9.4

The Goodie Company has five manufacturing plants which communicate with one another by means of leased telephone lines, as shown in Figure 9.16, which indicates that there are 12 leased lines between plants 1 and 2, and so forth. Calls from one plant to another can be routed through intermediate plants if necessary. If all required lines are made available, what is the maximum number of connections that can be made simultaneously between any two of the five manufacturing plants?

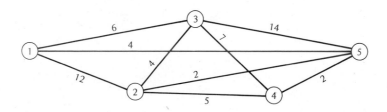

Figure 9.16

We start by choosing arbitrarily any two source-destination (s–d) nodes and finding the minimum cut capacity. Suppose we choose nodes 1 and 3 and evaluate the minimum cut capacity. The constructed arcs are shown in Figure 9.17 and evaluated in Table 9.11.

In the evaluation of the cuts, it may appear difficult to determine the proper direction of flow in each of the cut arcs. The rule is actually quite straightforward, however: the flows in all cut arcs on the source side must be toward the nodes on the opposite side of the cut, since the flows must be from source to destination. For example, consider cut $[1, 2, 4|3, 5]$, shown as the dashed line in Figure 9.17. All flows from nodes 1, 2, and 4 must be directed toward nodes 3 and 5, so, from the top of the network, the directed arcs must then be (1, 3), (2, 3), (1, 5) (4, 3), (2, 5), and (4, 5).

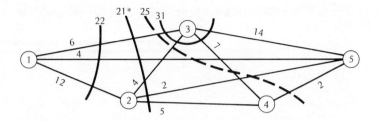

Figure 9.17

Table 9.11

s–d Nodes	Cut	Capacity
1, 3	$[1\|2, 3, 4, 5]$	$6 + 4 + 12 = 22$
	$[1, 2\|3, 4, 5]$	$6 + 4 + 4 + 2 + 5 = 21^*$
	$[1, 2, 4\|3, 5]$	$6 + 4 + 4 + 7 + 2 + 2 = 25$
	$[1, 2, 4, 5\|3]$	$6 + 4 + 7 + 14 = 31$

Since a cut must divide the network into two sets, both of which are connected networks, it is not possible to have a cut which would divide the network into three or more parts. Another way of looking at this is to note that each constructed arc representing a cut, such as those in Figure 9.17, starts outside the network, slices through it, and emerges again on the outside. Such a constructed arc cannot again enter the network and then leave it, as would be required if that network were partitioned into $[1, 4|2, 3, 5]$, for example.

We now form what is termed a condensed network. Nodes 1 and 2 are condensed into a single node, as are nodes 3, 4, and 5, and the arc connecting them has a capacity equal to the minimum cut capacity, or 21. This network forms a tree, as shown in Figure 9.18.

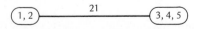

Figure 9.18

The next step is to pick any pair of nodes from one of the condensed nodes and determine the minimum cut capacity for that node pair. In doing this, we can use the condensed nodes to simplify the network, although we can always use the original network if we wish. Suppose we pick nodes 1 and 2 as the next source-destination node pair. Referring back to the values in Figure 9.16, the flow capacity from node 1 to condensed node 3, 4, 5 is $c_{13} + c_{14} + c_{15} = 10$. From node 2 to condensed node 3, 4, 5, the flow capacity is $c_{23} + c_{24} + c_{25} = 11$. Redrawing the network, we have Figure 9.19.

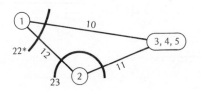

s–d Nodes	Cut	Capacity
1, 2	$[1\,|\,2, 3, 4, 5]$	22*
	$[1, 3, 4, 5\,|\,2]$	23

Figure 9.19

Treating nodes 3, 4, and 5 together, as a single condensed node, simplifies the solution considerably. This minimum cut puts node 1 in one set and all the other nodes in the complementary set, and the results of this iteration are as shown in Figure 9.20.

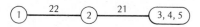

Figure 9.20

Now, considering nodes 1 and 2 as a condensed node, we pick a source-destination node pair from among nodes 3, 4, and 5. Choosing nodes 3 and 4, we have Figure 9.21.

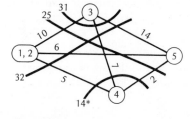

s–d Nodes	Cut	Capacity
3, 4	$[3\,|\,1, 2, 4, 5]$	31
	$[3, 5\,|\,1, 2, 4]$	25
	$[1, 2, 3\,|\,4, 5]$	32
	$[1, 2, 3, 5\,|\,4]$	14*

Figure 9.21

Since the minimum cut splits off node 4 from the remainder of the network, we now have the condensed network of Figure 9.22.

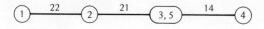

Figure 9.22

The final step is to assign nodes 3 and 5 as the source-destination pair. We can handle nodes 1, 2, and 4 as a condensed node, as shown in Figure 9.23.

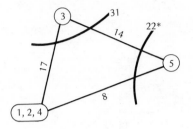

s–d Nodes	Cut	Capacity
3, 5	$[3\mid 1, 2, 4, 5]$	31
	$[1, 2, 3, 4\mid 5]$	22*

Figure 9.23

The evaluation is now complete, and, observing that the minimum cut separates node 5 from all the other nodes, the flow-equivalent tree (termed a cut tree by Gomory and Hu) is seen in Figure 9.24.

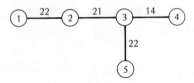

Figure 9.24

The final network, which is clearly a tree, has the property that the maximal flow between any pair of nodes is equal to the maximal flow between those two nodes in the original network; thus the term *flow-equivalent tree*. With this remarkably simple network, we can now immediately specify the maximal flow from any node to any other node by determining the minimum capacity on the unique path joining the two nodes. The results are most easily presented in tabular form, as in Table 9.12. This table is, of course, symmetrical, since the network is undirected. The minimum cuts in the final solution are shown in Figure 9.25.

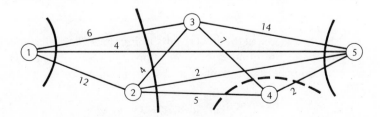

Figure 9.25

Table 9.12   Maximum Number of Connections between
Manufacturing Plants

				Plant		
		1	2	3	4	5
	1	—	22	21	14	21
	2	22	—	21	14	21
Plant	3	21	21	—	14	22
	4	14	14	14	—	14
	5	21	21	22	14	—

For any particular pair of source-destination nodes, the flows on all arcs can be determined by working from Figure 9.25. For example, suppose we wish to know a specific pattern of connections such that the number of connections between plants 1 and 4 is maximized. We can employ the iterative technique presented earlier, but we start with the knowledge that the maximal flow between nodes 1 and 4 is 14 (from Table 9.12), and, more importantly, that the applicable minimum cut, shown as a dashed line in Figure 9.25, indicates that the capacities of arcs (4, 2), (4, 3), and (4, 5) are completely utilized. Since this is the case, we know that we must have flows of 5, 7, and 2 units, respectively, on those arcs. On this basis, the iterations were performed as shown in Figure 9.26 and Table 9.13. (A direction of flow from node 4 to node 1 was assumed for computational convenience.)

Table 9.13   Determination of Maximal Flow

Iteration	Chain	Arc Values	Minimum
1	4–2–1	5, 12	5
2	4–3–1	7, 6	6
3	4–3–2–1	1, 4, 7	1
4	4–5–1	2, 4	2
		Maximal flow	14

From an analysis of the final results in Figure 9.26 (similar to the earlier analysis of Figure 9.19), the number of connections between all plants is as follows, when the connections between plants 1 and 4 are maximized.

Between	Plant	1	1	1	2	2	2	3	3	4
	Plant	2	3	5	3	4	5	4	5	5
Number of connections		6	6	2	1	5	0	7	0	2

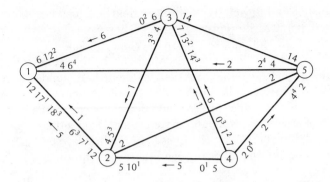

Figure 9.26

Figure 9.27, shows these results graphically. A similar analysis would have to be performed to obtain the same detailed breakdown of the connection pattern required to maximize the number of connections between any other two plants.

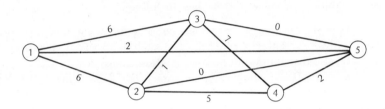

Figure 9.27

9.5 PROJECT SCHEDULING

A typical project-scheduling problem involves a large-scale, one-time project comprised of many highly interrelated activities. The coordination and scheduling of such large, complex projects has always been difficult. The two network-oriented techniques that will be presented were developed to answer such questions as these: What happens to the anticipated project completion date if activity j is delayed one week? When must a component be delivered in order not to delay the project? How much leeway is there in the completion of certain activities which may experience delays, perhaps due to weather or other uncontrollable factors? If extra manpower becomes available, on which task or tasks can it be most effectively used to shorten project completion time? The capability to answer such questions knowledgeably is vitally important when a project can well involve thousands of tasks, years of time, and costs in the millions of dollars.

We will first discuss an approach to these problems using the PERT (Project

Evaluation and Review Technique) method developed in 1958 in connection with the United States Navy's Polaris program. Then we will describe another method, CPM (Critical Path Method), which was developed independently from and almost concurrently with PERT. From a conceptual viewpoint, these methods are very similar in approach, and successive versions of them have tended to converge even more. Highly successful applications of PERT and CPM have been made in the construction industry, new product research and development, military weapons systems, installation of large-scale computer systems, and many other areas.

For these network techniques to be applicable, a certain problem structure must exist. Basically, the following conditions are required.

1. The project must be broken down into a set of activities such that it is completely clear as to what constitutes the start and the completion of each activity.
2. Each activity, once started, continues directly to its completion independently of the state of completion or rate of progress of any other activity.
3. The entire sequence in which activities are to be performed must be known.

PERT (Project Evaluation and Review Technique)

We will start by assuming that there is a single value for the completion time of each given task. Later, we discuss the analysis of PERT networks when there is a probabilistic distribution of task completion times.

In Figure 9.28 is shown an elementary PERT diagram, which always consists of a network of directed arcs. Each arc, labeled with a letter, represents an *activity*, or task. The numbers represent activity times (durations). The nodes represent *events*, points in time when certain activities have been completed and other activities may be started. An event occurs when all the inwardly directed activities at a given event node have been completed. Only at that time can the outwardly directed activities at that node begin.

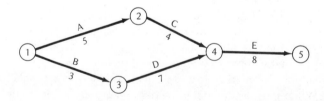

Figure 9.28

A *path* is defined as an unbroken sequence of activities directed from the origin node to the terminal node. In Figure 9.28, there are just two paths, A–C–E and B–D–E. The project duration is determined by the longest path, or what we call the *critical path*. Finding the critical path amounts to finding the longest path in a network containing no cycles, or loops.

The activities comprising the critical path are termed *critical activities*. Any delay in the completion of a critical activity will delay the entire project. In this example, we can see by inspection that the critical path is B–D–E, with a total time of 18 units. The critical activities are then B, D, and E. A delay in any one of them would delay project completion. Activities A and C, which are not on the critical path, are called noncritical activities. Noncritical activities can be delayed by some amount without delaying project completion. For a given activity, when considered by itself, the maximum permissible delay is termed its *slack*. Activities A and C each have 1 unit of slack. Either one, but not both, could be delayed 1 time unit without delaying the project.

When developing a Pert diagram, we need to know, for each activity, its duration and its immediate predecessors, those activities which immediately precede it. If we use the "$<$" symbol to mean "precedes," we can conveniently and succinctly express the so-called precedence relationships for any PERT network. As an example, the network of Figure 9.28 has the following precedence relationships:

$$A < C \qquad B < D \qquad C, D < E.$$

In the construction of PERT networks, it is sometimes necessary to add additional fictitious activities called "dummy" activities. These dummy activities take zero time and are generally indicated by dashed arcs. There are two situations, in particular, where dummy activities are required.

1. Since each activity's position in a PERT network is uniquely identified by its starting and ending nodes, no two activities may both start at the same node and end at the same node. Thus, if we have a network with activities A, B, C, and D, such that

    $$A < B \qquad A < C \qquad B, C < D,$$

    Figure 9.29a is not a feasible representation. A dummy activity must be placed between nodes 2 and 3 so that it precedes or follows either activity B or C, as shown in Figure 9.29b. As indicated by the double-ended arrows in Figure 9.29b, the positions of the dummy and labeled activities could be interchanged.

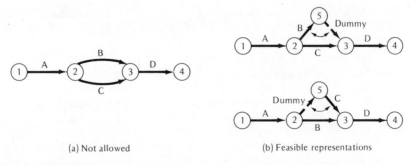

(a) Not allowed   (b) Feasible representations

Figure 9.29

2. It may be necessary to add dummy activities to properly show relationships between activities. Suppose we have the following precedence relationships:

$$A < C \qquad B < D \qquad C < E \qquad C, D < F.$$

The diagram of Figure 9.30a is then incorrect, since it shows that activities C and D both precede activity E. The correct diagram requires a dummy activity, as shown in Figure 9.30b.

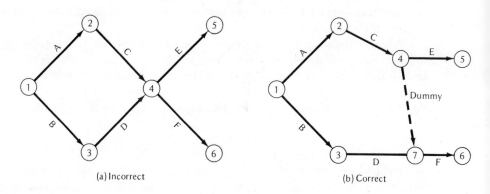

(a) Incorrect   (b) Correct

Figure 9.30

Let us now develop and analyze a simple scheduling problem using PERT.

EXAMPLE 9.5

A new product, which is quite similar to one already being produced, is going into production at the Multiproduct Company. On the basis of the information in Table 9.14, the company would like to determine the critical path, its duration, and the time relationships between the different activities.

Table 9.14   Activity Data

Activity	Description	Time (days)	Immediate Predecessors
A	Prepare bill of materials	1	—
B	Prepare assembly charts	3	A
C	Order and await delivery of materials	4	A
D	Organize production line	2	B
E	Specify inspection procedures	1	B
F	Set up inspection stations	2	D, E
G	Train workers	3	C, D
H	Assemble product	7	F, G

The first step is to construct the PERT diagram. This diagram is shown as Figure 9.31, with the activity times in parentheses. With a little practice, facility is readily gained in constructing such diagrams for small problems. When the diagram has been drawn, a careful check should be made to ensure that all precedence relationships are satisfied. Observe the use of the dummy activity here.

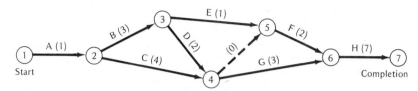

Figure 9.31

The next step is to determine the time relationship between the different activities. For a given activity, its earliest finish (EF) time is equal to its earliest start (ES) time plus its duration. Its ES time is equal to the latest EF time of its immediate predecessors, or zero, if it has no predecessors. In Figure 9.32, the ES value is labeled above the tail, and the EF value above the head, of each activity arrow.

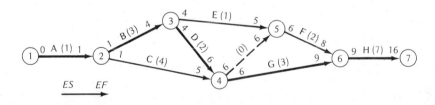

Figure 9.32

In analyzing Figure 9.32, it is easy to see that activity A starts at time 0, B and C start at 1, and D and E start at 4. Activity G cannot start until both C and D are finished, which is at time 6. Similarly, activity F cannot start until time 6 and activity H cannot start until time 9. The project completion time is 16 days, and the critical path is A–B–D–G–H, indicated by the heavy line for each of the critical activities. Any one of these five activities, if delayed, would delay the entire project.

Now, we wish to determine the latest time each activity can start without delaying project completion. We do this by working backward through the network, starting with the node representing project completion. For a given activity, its latest start (LS) time is equal to its latest finish (LF) time minus its duration. Its LF time is equal to the earliest LS time of its immediate followers, or the project completion time, if it is the final activity on the critical path. In Figure 9.33, the LF value is labeled below the head, and the LS value below the tail, of each activity arrow.

Starting at node 7, activity H must finish no later than time 16 and must,

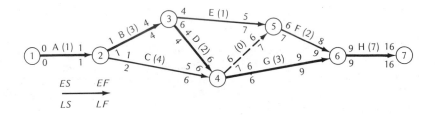

Figure 9.33

therefore, start no later than time 9. At node 6, for both F and G, LF must not exceed 9, or H will be delayed. At node 5, LS for F will be 7, so that LF for E and the dummy activity is also 7. At node 4, LS for G is 6 and for the dummy activity it is 7. In order not to delay either of these activities, then, both C and D must have LF values of 6. Then, with LS values of 6 and 4 for E and D, respectively, the LF value for B, at node 3, must be no greater than 4, or D would be delayed. The analysis proceeds in the same manner, working backward until node 1, the starting point, is reached.

All this information is summarized in Table 9.15. In addition, we will add the slack values for each activity. For any activity, its slack will be equal to its $LF - EF$ or $LS - ES$ value. Any activity with zero slack is a critical activity and is so noted.

Table 9.15 PERT Computations

Activity	Time	ES	EF	LS	LF	Slack	Critical Activity?
A	1	0	1	0	1	0	✕
B	3	1	4	1	4	0	✕
C	4	1	5	2	6	1	
D	2	4	6	4	6	0	✕
E	1	4	5	6	7	2	
F	2	6	8	7	9	1	
G	3	6	9	6	9	0	✕
H	7	9	16	9	16	0	✕

The results in Table 9.15 give all the basic information for this PERT network. Multiproduct can now see which activities are critical and which are noncritical. For each noncritical activity, its slack value tells how much its start could be delayed without extending the 16 days required for project completion. Thus, for example, the start of activity E could be delayed up to 2 days without affecting the completion time of the project.

Probabilistic Activity Times   The discussion of PERT has, up to now, assumed a single value for each activity time. This is useful in explaining the basic concepts and the development of PERT networks. In its original development, however, PERT did make provision for the uncertainty in the estimates of activity times. It was assumed that each activity time follows a beta probability distribution. There is no reason to believe that the beta distribution represents the "true" probability distribution of activity times, but it has certain convenient features. The beta distribution is a fairly "rich" distribution, which means that it can assume a wide range of shapes, as shown in Figure 9.34, and it possesses finite endpoints. (The normal distribution, as an example, possesses neither of these properties.) It is also relatively easy to define the required numerical estimates, as will be shown.

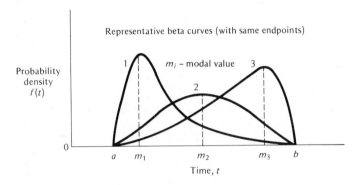

Figure 9.34

PERT uses three time estimates to define the beta distribution of a given activity time. The optimistic time a is the shortest feasible time in which the activity could be completed. The pessimistic time b is the longest time the activity would take, barring unforeseen difficulties. The most likely time m is the modal value. In PERT, the expected time t_e of an activity is approximated by weighting the most likely time twice as heavily as the sum of the optimistic and pessimistic times, which are equally weighted. The standard deviation is assumed to be one-sixth the range, so that all the values of the random variable would lie within plus or minus three standard deviations from the mean if the distribution is symmetrical. With a normal probability distribution, for example, about 99.7 percent of the values fall within this range, so, from this standpoint, the PERT assumption seems reasonable. For the expected time t_e and the variance V, we then have

$$t_e = \frac{a + 4m + b}{6} \quad \text{and} \quad V = \left(\frac{b - a}{6}\right)^2.$$

PERT uses the probability information in the following manner: after constructing the network diagram, t_e values are calculated for every activity and then used to determine the critical path in the same manner as was done previously for the deterministic case. Then, for each event (node) on the critical path, the mean time at which that event occurs is equal to the earliest finish (EF) time of the critical activity leading to that event. The variance of the event time is equal to the sum of the variances of all critical activities from the project start up to that event, based on the assumption that all activities on the critical path are independent. It should be noted that the assumption of independent activity times is not always a valid one. We will discuss additional weaknesses in the PERT probability assumptions later.

To avoid structuring an entirely new problem, suppose we take the previous problem, replacing the single time estimate with the three time estimates, a, b, and m, shown in Table 9.16. We then calculate the expected time t_e and the variance V. The values of a, b, and m have been deliberately manipulated to give t_e values the same as the original activity times in Table 9.14. Thus, the critical activities will be the same as those noted in Table 9.15.

Table 9.16 Probabilistic PERT Values

| Activity | Time Estimates, Days | | | | Variance |
	a	b	m	t_e	V
A	0.6	1.8	0.9	1.0	0.04
B	2.0	4.0	3.0	3.0	0.11
C	2.0	8.0	3.5	4.0	1.00
D	1.2	3.6	1.8	2.0	0.16
E	0.7	1.3	1.0	1.0	0.01
F	1.0	5.0	1.5	2.0	0.44
G	2.0	3.6	3.1	3.0	0.07
H	6.0	8.0	7.0	7.0	0.11

We now define E_i as the earliest expected time that event i can occur. E_i will equal the latest EF value for all activities ending at node i. Let V_i be the variance of the earliest time that event i occurs. V_i will be equal to the sum of the activity variances V for all activities on the longest path to event i. If event i is on the critical path, these activities will all be critical activities. Should there be a tie in longest path lengths, we choose the path with the highest variance when we calculate V_i.

Letting T_i represent the random variable for the actual time event i occurs, we will assume that T_i has a normal probability distribution with mean E_i and variance V_i. We base this on the *central limit theorem*, which states that the sum of independent random variables drawn from distributions with finite mean and variance tends to be normally distributed with mean equal to the sum of the means of the given distributions and variance equal to the sum of their variances.

Given some scheduled time S_i for the occurrence of event i, we can now compute the probability of meeting the schedule. Having assumed a normal probability distribution, we calculate how many normalized standard deviations k_i by which S_i exceeds, or is exceeded by, E_i, given a standard deviation of $\sqrt{V_i}$. Let $Z_i = (T_i - E_i)/\sqrt{V_i}$ be the normalized value of the random variable T_i. With $k_i = (S_i - E_i)/\sqrt{V_i}$, the probability of on-time occurrence of event i is

$P(T_i \leq S_i) \equiv P(Z_i \leq k_i)$, the probability area to the left of S_i, as shown in Figure 9.35. This probability is easily found in the standardized normal probability table, Appendix A.

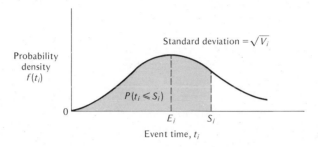

Figure 9.35

Given the scheduled event times S_i shown in Table 9.17, we determine the event time values E_i and V_i. We can then calculate the normalized standard deviations k_i and determine the probability of meeting the scheduled time.

Table 9.17

Event i	Longest Path	Event Time Values E_i	V_i	$\sqrt{V_i}$	Scheduled Time S_i	Normalized Standard Deviation, k_i $(S_i - E_i)/\sqrt{V_i}$	Probability of Meeting Schedule $P(Z_i \leq k_i)$
1	—	0	0	0	0	—	—
2	A	1	0.04	0.20	1	0.00	0.50
3	A–B	4	0.15	0.39	5	2.56	0.99
4	A–B–D	6	0.31	0.56	7	1.79	0.96
5	A–B–D–Dummy	6	0.31	0.56	6	0.00	0.50
6	A–B–D–G	9	0.38	0.62	10	1.61	0.95
7	A–B–D–G–H	16	0.49	0.70	17	1.43	0.92

According to the results of Table 9.17, the probability of completing the entire project in the scheduled 17 days is 0.92, which is quite high. The scheduled times for events 2 and 5 would appear to be not too realistic, as there is only 0.50 probability of meeting them. These computations, then, furnish information on the reasonableness of project schedules. It should also be noted that this type of analysis can be used to determine the project start date which will provide a predetermined probability of project completion by a specified date.

Actually, the PERT probability assumptions leave quite a bit to be desired. Since the variances are only calculated along a single path (the critical path, when considering critical activities), no account is taken of the effect of variance along alternate paths which may have expected time values only slightly smaller than the longest path. As an example, Van Slyke takes the case of a single-activity network with a t_e of 10 and V of 1.[1] If 5 such identical activities are in parallel, t_e becomes 11.24 and V becomes 0.57. With 10 such activities, t_e = 11.65 and V = 0.41. As the number of these activities in parallel increases without limit, $t_e \rightarrow 14.06$ and $V \rightarrow 0$. By calculating a critical path (or, paths) and assuming that noncritical activities never will delay the project (become critical), it should be clear that PERT will tend to be overly optimistic about meeting scheduled times. In addition, as mentioned earlier, the assumption of independent activity times does not stand up in many cases. Thus, in a construction project, poor weather will tend to delay a number of different activities. The same holds true for a strike or a work slowdown. About all we can really say about the PERT probability calculations is that they give us some feeling about how realistic our scheduling is. These calculations are anything but definitive.

When computationally feasible (perhaps up to several hundred activities), simulation is a much more meaningful approach for evaluating the probabilities of meeting schedule times. Each simulation trial consists of drawing a random time for each activity and determining the simulated time that each event actually occurs. After many trials, perhaps a thousand or more, we have a meaningful probability distribution for each event time and the fraction of time that each activity is critical. In addition, the probability distribution for the individual activity times can be of any form, rather than being limited to a beta distribution or any other particular probability distribution. (Such a simulation approach is described by Van Slyke in the article referred to in the footnote.)

CPM (Critical Path Method)

Unlike PERT, CPM makes no provision for probabilistic activity times, but uses a single estimate comparable to the expected time (t_e) of PERT. CPM also uses a different diagrammatic representation of activities, representing them as *nodes*, rather than as arrows connecting event nodes, as in PERT. In CPM, the arrows between nodes indicate precedence relationships only. One advantage of the nodal representation of activities is that no dummy activities are ever required. A disadvantage is that events are no longer clearly delineated in the CPM diagram, as they are in a PERT diagram.

The major difference between CPM and the *basic* version of PERT is that CPM introduces variable cost factors in the analysis. However, other versions of PERT, such as PERT-COST, also consider cost factors. From an overall point of view, there is really little difference between the most general versions of PERT and CPM, but cost analysis was first introduced in CPM, so it will be discussed here in that context.

In the simplest version of CPM, two costs and two times are specified for each activity. The "normal cost" C_n is the cost of performing the activity in the "normal

---

[1]R. M. Van Slyke, "Monte Carlo Methods and the PERT Problem," *Operations Research*, Vol. 11, No. 5, 1963, pp. 839–860.

time" T_n; the "crash cost" C_c is the cost of "crashing," or accelerating, the activity (generally by using overtime and/or additional personnel) so as to complete the activity in "crash time" T_c. A graph of activity cost versus activity time would look like

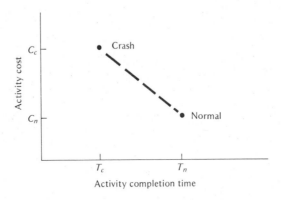

Figure 9.36

Figure 9.36. The significance of the dashed line connecting the two points in Figure 9.36 is that we assume that the cost of reducing activity time is a linear function of the reduction in time. However, as shown in Figure 9.37, it would be possible to represent a function by linear segments, a so-called piecewise-linear representation. This graph illustrates a most likely situation, that of decreasing returns to scale from allocating additional funds.

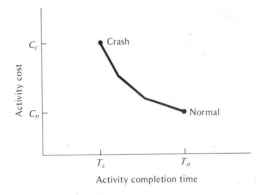

Figure 9.37

To show how CPM uses cost information of the nature discussed, we will work a sample problem. To permit direct comparison with the PERT calculations, we will again obtain the solution to the production problem of the Multiproduct Company in

Example 9.5, but we will augment that problem by later adding cost information. For convenience, the problem statement and data values are repeated here.

EXAMPLE 9.6

A new product, which is quite similar to one already being produced, is going into production at the Multiproduct Company. The required production activities are specified in Table 9.18.

Table 9.18   Activity Data

Activity	Description	Time (Days)	Immediate Predecessors
A	Prepare bill of materials	1	—
B	Prepare assembly charts	3	A
C	Order and await delivery of materials	4	A
D	Organize production line	2	B
E	Specify inspection procedures	1	B
F	Set up inspection stations	2	D, E
G	Train workers	3	C, D
H	Assemble product	7	F, G

a) Use CPM to determine the critical path, the project completion time, and the slack for noncritical activities.

The CPM diagram is drawn as Figure 9.38 (after some preliminary work on scratch paper). Each node is labeled with the activity letter designation, and the activity time, in days, appears below that designation. Observe that activities B and C are preceded by A, activities D and E by B, and so on, according to the precedence relationships specified in Table 9.18.

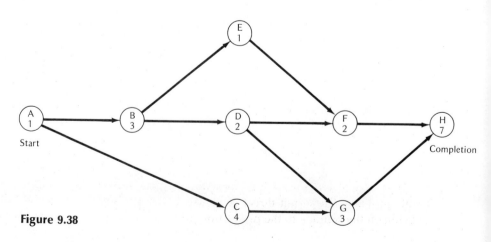

Figure 9.38

Just as with the PERT solution, we will use the designations ES (earliest start), EF (earliest finish), LS (latest start), and LF (latest finish). The ES and EF values are shown above each activity node in Figure 9.39.

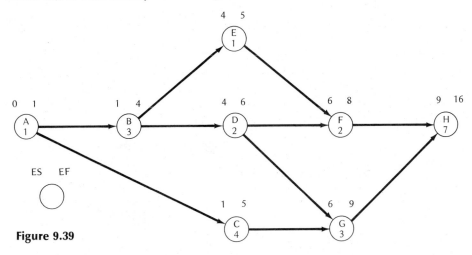

Figure 9.39

Starting with activity A, the value of EF for A (ES plus activity time) is obviously the same as the value of ES for activities B and C. In a similar fashion, ES for D and E is the same as EF for B. For activity F, ES is 6, since it cannot start until both activities D and E have been completed, and D is not completed until time 6. Activity G has an ES value of 6 too, since activity D has a later completion time than activity C. ES for activity H must then be 9, the greater of the EF values for activities F and G. Project completion time will be 16 days.

Just as was done in PERT, the process is now reversed to get the LS and LF values and then determine the critical path. The results are shown in Figure 9.40.

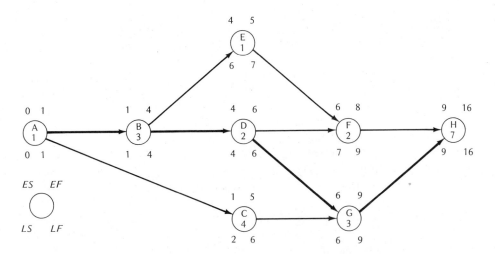

Starting with activity H, its *LF* value must be 16, if the project is not to be delayed. Its *LS* value of 9 then becomes the *LF* value for activities F and G. This generates *LS* values of 7 and 6, respectively, for activities F and G. The process continues until all the *LS* and *LF* values have been determined.

The critical activities are those with the same *ES* and *LS* (or *EF* and *LF*) values. The critical path is shown by a heavy line. (Figure 9.40 can be directly compared with Figure 9.33, the PERT solution.) For any activity not on the critical path, its slack is just its *LS* − *ES* or *LF* − *EF* value. If we combined all this information in a table, we would simply duplicate Table 9.15. To summarize, the critical path is A–B–D–G–H, and the project completion time is 16 days. Noncritical activity slacks are 1 day for activities C and F, and 2 days for activity E.

(b) Given the cost versus time information in Table 9.19, determine the most efficient allocation of additional funds to reduce the project completion time. Graph the results in the form of a total cost versus project completion time curve.

Table 9.19   Relationship between Activity Completion Times and Costs

Activity	Days Normal Time, T_n	Crash Time, T_c	Maximum Reduction	Normal Cost, C_n ($)	Crash Cost, C_c ($)	Cost per Day Saved ($)
A	1	1	0	100	100	—
B	3	2	1	400	650	250
C	4	2	2	600	850	125
D	2	1	1	150	300	150
E	1	1	0	120	120	—
F	2	2	0	300	300	—
G	3	2	1	300	500	200
H	7	4	3	800	1250	150
				2770		

The column labeled Maximum Reduction is just the value of $T_n − T_c$. A linear cost versus time relationship has been assumed, so the cost per day saved for a given activity is $(C_c − C_n)/(T_n − T_c)$. With a 16-day completion time, the total cost is $2770. Note that activities A, E, and F cannot be shortened, so only activities B, C, D, G, and H will be examined in the following analysis.

The cost analysis is an iterative approach, with each iteration based on an updated CPM diagram. The initial diagram is that of Figure 9.40. For each iteration of the network, the only activities which are candidates for reduction will be those on the critical path. If there is a single critical path, we choose the most cost-effective activity, the one with the lowest cost per day saved, and we reduce that activity time until another path becomes critical or the maximum allowable reduction of that activity time is achieved, whichever comes first. (If there is more than one critical path, we must make a comparison between any activity on *all* critical paths or any combination of activities which will reduce all critical paths. This particular procedure will become clearer when the example problem is worked.) The network is then updated as required and the next iteration performed. This continues until the project time cannot be further reduced.

Iteration 1

Activity	B	*C	D	G	H
Cost per day saved ($)	250	125	150	200	150
Allowable reduction (days)	1	2	1	1	3
Actual reduction (days)			1		3
Additional cost ($)			150		450

Total project cost: 2770 + 600 = $3370.
Project completion time: 16 − 4 = 12 days.

*Not on the critical path.

Activities D and H are the critical activities with the lowest cost per day saved. Since activity H is the final activity, its time can be reduced the maximum amount without affecting the critical path. Activity D can also be reduced by 1 day, at which point the 1-day slack in activity C will disappear, making C a critical activity on the new critical path A–C–G–H. Figure 9.41 is the updated network.

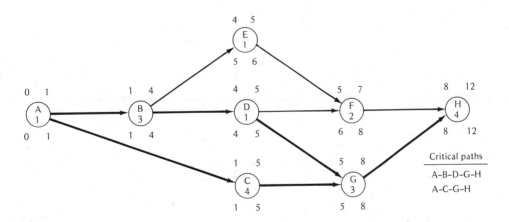

Figure 9.41

Iteration 2

Activity	B	C	D	G	H
Cost per day saved ($)	250	125		200	
Allowable reduction (days)	1	2	0	1	0
Actual reduction (days)				1	
Additional cost ($)				200	

Total project cost: 3370 + 200 = $3570.
Project completion time: 12 − 1 = 11 days.

Minimum cost per day saved is not a sufficient criterion for selection when there is more than one critical path. Activities B, C, and G are all critical activities with reduction possibilities, but only G is on *all* critical paths. It would take a simultaneous 1-day reduction in both B and C activity times to shorten project time by a day, and this would add a cost of $375, therefore, shortening activity G is clearly preferable. After this change, all activities become critical, and there are four critical paths, as can be seen from Figure 9.42.

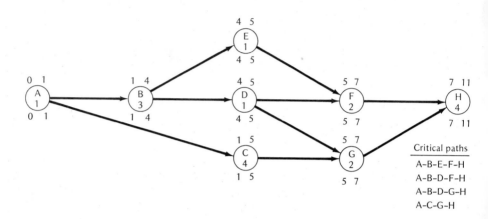

Figure 9.42

<u>Iteration 3</u>

Activity	B	C	D	G	H
Cost per day saved ($)	250	125			
Allowable reduction (days)	1	2	0	0	0
Actual reduction (days)	1	1			
Additional cost ($)	250	125			

Total project cost: 3570 + 375 = $3945.
Project completion time: 11 − 1 = 10 days.

Both activity B and activity C must be simultaneously reduced by 1 day to shorten project completion time by another day. Activity B is on three critical paths, and activity C is on the fourth. It would be of no value to reduce the activity time of only one of these activities. The final network is shown in Figure 9.43.

The one remaining possible reduction in the time of activity C would not shorten project completion time, so the iterations are completed. The results of the analysis are summarized in Table 9.20 and graphed in Figure 9.44. Multiproduct Company now has the necessary information on which to base a decision. For any feasible number of days reduction in project completion time, the firm knows how much it will cost and which activities to speed up. It can also observe, from Figure 9.44, the increased cost per day as project completion time is compressed.

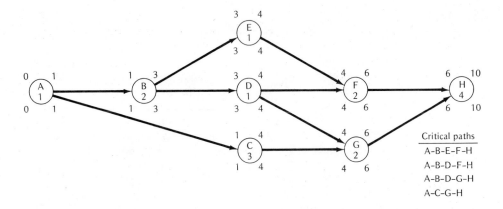

Critical paths

A–B–E–F–H

A–B–D–F–H

A–B–D–G–H

A–C–G–H

Figure 9.43

Table 9.20   Project Cost versus Completion Time Analysis

Cost ($)	Activities Shortened	Project Completion Time (Days)
2770		16
3370	D (1 day), H (3 days)	12
3570	G (1 day)	11
3945	B (1 day), C (1 day)	10

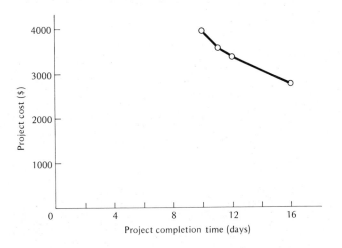

Figure 9.44

SUMMARY

Although the network models studied here represent only a handful of the many types of network models developed, they are representative of certain fairly common classes of such models, and they are intended to serve as an introduction to some of the basic terminology and concepts associated with network models. As in the previous two chapters, an iterative approach was employed in the computational algorithms for several different types of problems. In addition, step-by-step tables and diagrams were used to clarify both the procedural and the conceptual nature of the various algorithms specifically developed for the efficient solution of the models studied.

After demonstrating a technique for determining the shortest route through a network, a network tree problem, that of finding the minimal spanning tree, was solved. The next model was that involving the maximal flow between any two nodes in a capacitated network consisting of directed and/or undirected arcs. Then, utilizing the concepts of cut sets and the max-flow min-cut theorem, a very efficient algorithm was developed for the determination of the maximal flows between all nodes of an undirected capacitated network. The computational procedure involved the reduction of the original network to a so-called flow-equivalent tree.

The final topic concerned project scheduling. The PERT method was discussed first, starting with deterministic activity times, to illustrate the basic concepts and methodology, and then considering probabilistic activity times and their effect on the probability of meeting the project schedule deadline. The use of simulation models for project scheduling was mentioned, and the general nature of such models will become clearer after the chapter on Simulation Models has been studied. CPM was shown to be a project-scheduling method very similar to PERT, but it was primarily used as a vehicle to analyze the tradeoff between cost and project completion time using network techniques.

EXERCISES

9.1   At the end of the section on the shortest-route problem, the complete solution for the example problem is shown in a single table. From a table of that nature, explain how the shortest route(s) can be traced from the origin node to any given node by working backward from the given node. Illustrate by tracing the routes from node A to node G.

9.2   The Hyflying Company has a small aircraft which is used to fly its executives to plant locations in other cities. The airline distances, in miles, are shown in the accompanying figure. The limited range of the aircraft precludes any lengthier nonstop flights.

    The executive office is located in city B. Determine the shortest distance from city B to each of the other cities. Specify the routing for each such shortest distance.

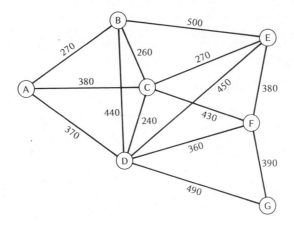

9.3 Keepon Trucking Company (Example 9.1) has just found out that the new
bypass route between city A and city C, reducing the driving time from 10 to 8
hours, will be opened before they have to deliver a return shipment from city
G to city A. Find the shortest route, and its travel time, from city G to city A.
Also specify the shortest routes to each of the other cities, along with the
associated travel times.

9.4 In the accompanying diagram, the nodes represent the plant locations of a large
corporation, and the directed arcs represent the data connections between
plants. The values on the arcs are the relative costs of transmitting data. Using
the shortest-route algorithm, determine the minimum relative cost data
transmission path from plant A to each of the other plant locations.

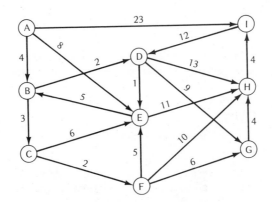

9.5   Distances between six islands in the Pacific Ocean are given in the accompanying table. The government of the islands would like to establish telephone connections between all the islands, using the smallest possible amount of submarine telephone cable. To help them, find the minimal spanning tree for the six islands. Specify which islands should be connected and the total length of telephone cable needed.

| | | | Distance (miles) | | | |
From / To A	A	B	C	D	E	F
A	—	100	70	80	90	140
B	100	—	170	180	190	250
C	70	170	—	10	20	70
D	80	180	10	—	10	60
E	90	190	20	10	—	50
F	140	250	70	60	50	—

9.6   There are five villages in a tropical jungle region, and the government is planning to construct an all-weather road to connect these villages. Since road construction in the jungle is particularly time-consuming and costly, it is desired to construct the minimal length road such that any one of the villages can be reached from any other village. The lengths of the feasible direct routes, as determined by a helicopter survey, are as follows, with all distances in kilometers.

| | | | To Village | | |
From Village	A	B	C	D	E
A	—	5.7	5.8	10.5	7.2
B		—	6.7	8.8	10.8
C			—	5.1	7.6
D				—	9.2
E					—

(a)   Completely specify the minimal length road network and its total length.
(b)   Suppose that normal road construction costs are $100,000 per km. If road construction between villages C and D would be particularly difficult, how much additional cost could the government afford before abandoning this route?

9.7   Explain why a minimal spanning tree can never contain a loop, and illustrate with a sketch.

9.8   An irrigation district has four reservoirs connected by waterways, as shown in the diagram below. The number on each arc is the capacity of that waterway, in thousands of gallons per hour. Determine the maximal flow between reservoirs A and C using the algorithm for capacitated networks. Specify the direction and volume of flow on each waterway.

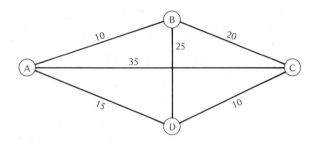

9.9 The Shorthaul Steamship Company has an opportunity to deliver oil from port X to port Y, and it is attempting to determine the maximum amount of oil it could deliver over the time period during which the oil will be required. The oil would be shipped from port X to port Y through intermediate reshipping points at ports A, B, C, D, and E. The available cargo capacities for shipment from one port to another are given in the accompanying table. Missing table entries indicate that no cargo capacity is available. Capacities are in thousands of bbl (barrels).

	To					
From	A	B	C	D	E	Y
X	20	25	32			
A	—	18		12		
B	7	—	16	30	8	
C		22	—		15	
D	14	5		—	24	40
E		10	18	16	—	35

(a) Determine the maximum amount of oil that could be shipped from port Y. Specify the routes over which it would be shipped and the cargo capacity utilized on each such route.

(b) Determine the maximum additional amount of cargo capacity which could be effectively utilized *between* the reshipping ports of A, B, C, D, and E *only*. If this capacity could be allocated to just one route, to which route (or routes) should it be allocated in order to permit the maximum possible delivery of oil? Specify the complete route(s) for this additional quantity of oil.

9.10 The Direct Distribution Company, Example 9.3, now wishes to know the maximum number of communication paths which can be set up at any one time to transmit data from distribution center 5 to distribution center 2.

(a)   Sketch the network and show the number and direction of communication paths on each arc.

(b)   On a separate sketch, show an alternative solution that is equally good.

9.11   Coal slurry (a liquefied mixture of coal particles) is piped between locations A and H, which are interconnected by pumping stations B through G, as shown in the accompanying network diagram. The values on the directed arcs are pumping capacities, in hundreds of gallons per hour.

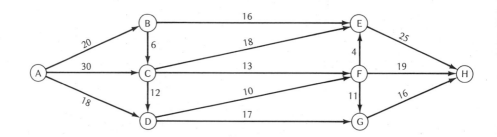

(a)   Determine the maximal allowable flow from location A to location H.

(b)   Draw a sketch of the network. On each arc, specify the actual flow, and, in parentheses, the remaining capacity.

9.12   In Exercise 9.8, the irrigation district problem, determine the maximal flow between reservoirs A and C by determining all feasible cuts and then using the max-flow min-cut theorem.

9.13   Solve Example 9.3, involving the data network of the Direct Distribution Company, by evaluating all the feasible cuts between nodes 1 and 6 and then employing the max-flow min-cut theorem.

9.14   For the coal slurry network in Exercise 9.11, use the max-flow min-cut approach to determine the maximum allowable flow from location A to location H.

9.15   Use the Gomory-Hu algorithm to determine the maximal flow between all reservoirs in the irrigation district problem of Exercise 9.8.

9.16   The Desert Oil Company has four refineries, and the pipelines between these refineries have the following capacities, in bbls (barrels) per day:

(a)   Using the Gomory-Hu algorithm, determine the maximum possible daily amount of oil which can be piped between any two refineries, utilizing all possible flow paths. State your answers in the form of a table.

(b)   From your results in part (a), if the flow capacity for the pipeline between refinery 2 and refinery 3 were increased by 150 bbl/day, by how much would the maximum possible flow from refinery 1 to refinery 2 increase?

Verify this by directly evaluating this maximum flow from the revised network.

| | To Refinery | | | |
From Refinery	1	2	3	4
1	—	150	370	240
2		—	190	310
3			—	280
4				—

9.17 The Desert Oil Company, Exercise 9.16, has just sustained an outage of the pipeline between refineries 2 and 4.
  (a) During the time this pipeline is undergoing repairs, what is the maximum possible daily amount of oil which can be piped between any two refineries, utilizing all possible flow paths?
  (b) Draw a diagram showing the minimum cuts associated with the optimal flows determined in part (a).
  (c) Determine the flow on all arcs when the flow from refinery 1 to refinery 4 is maximized.

9.18 In your own words, define the following PERT terms:
  (a) Activity
  (b) Event
  (c) Critical activity
  (d) Critical path
  (e) Slack
  (f) Dummy activity.

9.19 A certain professional organization prepares an annual program each fall giving the monthly meeting dates, background on the speakers, an abstract of their talks, and an alphabetic listing, both by name and company affiliation, of all dues-paying members. The program is mailed to these members as well as to selected individuals and organizations. The tasks to be performed have been detailed as shown in the accompanying table.

  (a) Develop a PERT diagram to show the relationship between all tasks.
  (b) For each task, determine the earliest and latest start times and the earliest and latest finish times. Specify the tasks on the critical path and the project completion time.
  (c) The program chairman now claims that it will take him 6 weeks to get commitments and abstracts from the speakers. Will this delay the project completion time? How will it affect the critical path?

Task	Description	Immediately Preceding Tasks	Estimated Time, Weeks
A	Decide on general orientation for this year's program	—	1
B	Get commitments from speakers and abstracts of their talks	A	4
C	Solicit advertising to appear in the program	A	3
D	Mail out dues notices and wait for response	—	6
E	Prepare list of dues-paying members	D	1
F	Get copy to printer and proofread	B, C, E	2
G	Get program printed and assembled	F	2
H	Prepare final mailing list	E	1
I	Stuff envelopes and mail programs	G, H	0.5

9.20 A manufacturing company has determined that additional equipment is needed to meet increasing customer demand. The company has decided to expand its present facility and phase in the new equipment over a period of time. The relevant information for this expansion project is given in the following table.

Activity	Description	Predecessor Activities	Expected Activity Time (months)
A	Prepare plans for expanded building	—	3
B	Construct additions to building	A	6
C	Evaluate equipment suppliers and order new equipment	—	3
D	Install and test new equipment	C	2
E	Formulate hiring plans	A	1
F	Integrate new equipment into operations	D	5
G	Train new employees on new equipment	D, E	7
H	Relocate equipment to new part of building and integrate operations	B, F, G	4

(a) Construct a PERT diagram.
(b) For activity, determine the earliest and latest start and finish times; specify the critical path activities and the project completion time.

(c)   Comment on the managerial implications of the critical path activities.

9.21   For the plant expansion problem of Exercise 9.20, use CPM
       (a)   to draw a project diagram.
       (b)   to determine the earliest and latest start and finish times, the critical path
             activities, and the project completion time.

9.22   How does PERT provide for uncertainty in activity time estimates? What is the
       rationale for using beta probability distributions?

9.23   Describe briefly how the Central Limit Theorem comes into play in the analysis
       of probabilistic PERT networks.

9.24   The UUA is gearing up for its next big invitational track meet. It has listed the
       required activities and their time estimates as follows.

| | | Immediately | Time Estimates, Days | | |
Activity	Description	Preceding Activities	Most Optimistic	Most Pessimistic	Most Likely
A	Select teams and individuals	—	1	5	3
B	Select site	A	3	8	4
C	Mail out invitations and receive acceptances	B	10	20	15
D	Arrange accommodations for participants	C	5	11	8
E	Print tickets	B	4	8	6
F	Sell tickets	E	20	20	20
G	Complete detailed meet arrangements	C	5	12	7
H	Work out practice schedules	D	2	5	3
I	Practice sessions for participants	G, H	2	2	2
J	Conduct meet	F, I	1	1	1

(a)   Draw a PERT diagram and determine the critical path. What is the
      expected time from initiation to completion?
(b)   If the meet is to be held on May 15, on what date would the first activity
      have to begin in order for the probability to be at least 0.90 that the meet
      would be held as scheduled?

9.25   A publisher is preparing to produce the second edition of a mathematics textbook. The activities required and their estimated times follow.

Activity	Description	Immediately Preceding Activities	Most Optimistic	Most Pessimistic	Most Likely
				Time Estimates (months)	
A	Assess market	—	1	3	2
B	Get reviews from users of first edition	A	1	2	1.5
C	Revamp old material and add new material	B	3	9	5
D	Obtain reviews and prepare final draft	C	4	12	6
E	Revise and expand problems	B	2	7	4
F	Copyedit final draft	D	1	2.5	1.5
G	Copyedit problems	E	0.5	1.5	1
H	Set type, proof, and print book	F, G	5	9	6
I	Prepare instructor's manual	E	2	4	3
J	Produce instructor's manual	I	1	2	1.5
K	Completion of book and instructor's manual	H, J	0	0	0

(a)   Draw a PERT or CPM diagram and determine the critical path. For each activity not on the critical path, state the value of its slack. What is the expected length of this project?

(b)   What is the probability that the project will be completed within 21 months? 24 months? 27 months?

9.26   A family living in a hot desert community decides on June 1 to have a backyard pool constructed. The builder cannot begin work until June 12. The required sequential activities are listed below, along with data on their associated normal and crash times and costs.

   If there are 16 working days between June 12 and June 30, what is the least cost for which all pool construction could be completed by June 30?

		Time (days)		Cost ($)	
Task	Description	Normal	Crash	Normal	Crash
A	Excavation	2	1	550	750
B	Steel installation	1	0.5	500	700
C	Plumbing installation	1	0.5	1000	1300
D	Inspection	2	2	200*	200
E	Gunnite	4	2	1500	2000
F	Gas and electrical connections	2	1	950	1200
G	Inspection	2	2	—	—
H	Decking	4	2	1700	2000
I	Tiling	1	1	450	450
J	Fence and gate inspection	2	2	—	—
K	Plastering	1	0.5	700	850

This fee covers the cost of all inspections.

9.27 Normal and crash times and costs are given below for the plant expansion project of Exercise 9.20.

Activity	Normal Time (months)	Crash Time (months)	Normal Cost ($1000s)	Crash Cost ($1000s)
A	3	2	40	50
B	6	4	200	300
C	3	2	20	35
D	2	1	20	32
E	1	1	20	20
F	5	3	150	190
G	7	6	120	150
H	4	3	160	195

(a) If the company has $776,000 available for this project, how should the funds be allocated to minimize overall completion time, to the nearest 0.1 month? What is that minimum completion time?

(b) Repeat part (a) if $800,000 is available.

9.28 In the problem of Exercise 9.19, the professional organization is considering the use of additional manpower (unpaid) to speed up the preparation of the annual program. For each activity, the table below shows the normal and crash times as a function of the manpower available. The organization has received a commitment of 9 additional man-days. How should this additional manpower be used to minimize the completion time of the project? What is the new project completion time?

Task	Time (weeks)		Man-days Required	
	Normal	Crash	Normal	Crash
A	1	0.5	1	2
B	4	3	2	4
C	3	2	3	5
D	6	3	2	7
E	1	0.5	1	3
F	2	1.5	3	5
G	2	1.5	2	4
H	1	0.5	2	5
I	0.5	0.5	3	3

CHAPTER 10

DYNAMIC PROGRAMMING

In linear programming, we studied a class of problems which fitted into a more or less standard form of a particular mathematical model. Once a given problem was formulated as a linear programming problem, its solution was essentially straightforward. That is, we merely had to put it into the linear programming format and solve by a standard technique. In dynamic programming, by contrast, each problem represents a separate challenge. *Dynamic programming is a way of looking at problems as multistage decision processes.* The actual stages may represent real time intervals, as when we attempt to optimize monthly production quantities over a given production period, or they may be a computational artifice, as when we are attempting to determine the optimal allocation of salesmen to several different sales territories. In this latter case, although the overall allocation would, of course, be made at one time, the dynamic programming approach will be to consider the allocation to each territory as a stage and to solve the problem stage by stage, with the optimal allocation determined when the computations for the final stage are completed. The first part of this chapter will cover deterministic models; the second part will discuss probabilistic models.

A substantial number of problems, covering many diverse areas, have been solved utilizing the techniques of dynamic programming. The following examples may give some feeling for the breadth of applicability.

Production Planning   A manufacturing plant has certain production requirements during the next six months. How many production runs should there be during this period, and what should the number of units be on each run, in order to minimize the sum of the cost of production setups and the cost of holding inventory in stock?

Resource Allocation   A company has a limited amount of funds to be invested in several different projects. Given the estimated return from each project as a function of the amount invested in that project, what is the optimal allocation of funds to each project?

Equipment Reliability   An unmanned spacecraft contains a number of critical components, and the failure of any one of them would cause failure of the mission. Spare units can be provided to cut into the circuit automatically when a given component fails. Given the component failure probabilities and assuming independent failures, how many spares of each type should be provided, on the basis of such constraints as allowable weight, available funds, and required mission reliability?

Equipment Replacement   Given the estimated maintenance cost per time period, where this cost changes for each time period, and the estimated salvage or trade-in value of this equipment as a function of time, what is the optimal time for replacing this equipment?

10.1 DETERMINISTIC DYNAMIC PROGRAMMING

We will start by working a network problem to illustrate the general conceptual approach used in dynamic programming. The example chosen is the Keepon Trucking Company problem of determining the minimal-time route between two cities. We solved this problem earlier in Example 9.1 by using a shortest route algorithm.

In this initial problem, we will avoid notation and will concentrate on explaining some of the basic principles of dynamic programming.

EXAMPLE 10.1 (*Shortest Route Problem*)

The Keepon Trucking Company has to deliver a shipment of goods from city A to city G, and the feasible routes pass through cities B through F, as shown in Figure 10.1. The numbers on the arcs represent the estimated driving times in hours between adjacent cities. Because of major construction work, the driving times between cities C and D and between cities C and E differ, depending on the direction of travel. The remainder of the travel times are independent of the direction. Keepon Trucking would like to determine the route requiring the shortest travel time.

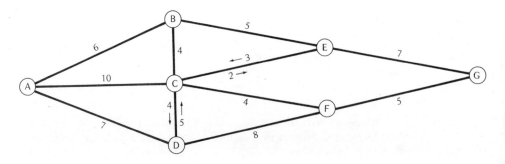

Figure 10.1

To solve this problem using dynamic programming, we must put it in the form of a multistage decision process. To do this, we first define the stages at which decisions are to be made and the nature of the possible decisions. In this problem, we will define stage k as the set of cities from which city G can be reached by a *minimum* of k arcs, or city-to-city routes.

For reasons which will become clearer later, this problem will, in essence, be solved backward. We will work stage by stage from the destination to the origin. For each city at a given stage, our decision involves the selection of the optimal route from that city to the destination, city G.

Stage 1 consists of cities E and F, both a minimum of one arc from city G. We start by determining the optimal routes from those cities to city G. The necessary information appears in Table 10.1. It is obvious that at cities E and F the direct routes to city G are optimal in both cases.

Table 10.1 Stage 1

City	Shortest Time to City G (hr)	Optimal Route from Given City
E	7	E–G
F	5	F–G

Cities B, C, and D make up stage 2, since all are a minimum of two arcs from city G. From Figure 10.1, we first determine the shortest time to travel from each of these three cities to stage 1 cities E and F. From city B to city E, for example, the candidate shortest routes are B–E, with a time of 5 hours, and B–C–E, with a time of 6 hours. Thus, route B–E is preferred. From city B to city F, the shortest route is B–C–F, with a time of 8 hours. The other candidate route, B–C–D–F, takes 16 hours. Now, as shown in Table 10.2, we can utilize the optimal route information already available for the stage 1 cities.

Table 10.2 Stage 2

From City	To City	Shortest Time Route	Shortest Time Hours	Shortest Additional Time to City G (hr)	Total Time (hr)	Optimal Route(s) from Given City
B	E	B–E	5	7	12 (optimal)	B–E–G
	F	B–C–F	8	5	13	
C	E	C–E	2	7	9 (optimal)	C–E–G
	F	C–F	4	5	9 (optimal)	C–F–G
D	E	D–C–E	7	7	14	
	F	D–F	8	5	13 (optimal)	D–F–G

From city B, the shortest route to city E takes 5 hours, and the optimal route from that point adds another 7 hours, for a total of 12 hours. The shortest route from city B to city F requires 8 hours, giving a total of 13 hours when the optimal route time of 5 hours from city F to city G is added. Therefore, if leaving from city B, the optimal route is B–E–G, taking 12 hours. From city C, there are two optimal 9-hour routes to city G, while the single optimal route from city D takes 13 hours and goes through city F.

Now, moving to stage 3 and city A, we need determine only the shortest distance from city A to stage 2 cities B, C, and D. Then, from the stage 2 results, we can utilize the optimal route from each of those cities to determine the overall optimal route or routes, as shown in Table 10.3.

Table 10.3   Stage 3

From City	To City	Shortest Time Route	Shortest Time Hours	Shortest Additional Distance to City G (hr)	Total Time (hr)	Optimal Route
A	B	A–B	6	12	18 (optimal)	A–B–E–G
	C	A–C	10	9	19	
		or A–B–C				
	D	A–D	7	13	20	

From city A to city B, the shortest route takes 6 hours and the optimal route from city B an additional 12 hours, for a total of 18 hours. In a similar fashion, the shortest route from city A through city C takes 19 hours, 10 hours to city C and then, using an optimal route from city C, another 9 hours. The shortest route from city A to city D takes 7 hours, with a total time of 20 hours when the optimal route is followed from city D to city G. The optimal solution is to use route A–B–E–G, with a total time of 18 hours.

The stage 3 calculations show the real power of the dynamic programming approach. For each of the three cities directly linked to city A, we first determined their shortest distance from city A. Then, we utilized the optimal routing from each of those cities to destination city G. In other words, we had to consider only the final stage possibilities and the associated optimal results from the previous stage.

We will now analyze a second example, this time an allocation problem. In this problem, we will develop a more structured approach, including notation and terminology appropriate to a dynamic programming model. Later on, we will show a unifying approach that is useful in the formulation and solution of a large class of dynamic programming problems.

An Allocation Problem Solved by Dynamic Programming

EXAMPLE 10.2 (*Allocation of Salesmen*)

A company has five salesmen to cover three territories. It wishes to determine the most profitable allocation, based on estimates of monthly profit as a function of the number of salesmen assigned to each territory. This information is shown in Table 10.4.

Table 10.4 Estimated Return
(Monthly Profit, $1000s)

Territory	Number of Salesmen Assigned					
	0	1	2	3	4	5
1	0	0.5	2.0	2.9	3.3	3.4
2	0	0.7	1.5	2.3	3.2	4.0
3	0	1.1	2.1	3.0	3.9	4.7

To formulate this problem as a multistage decision process, we consider each territory as a stage. We will work backward, starting with territory 1 as stage 1.

Let M = number of territories (stages),

N = total number of salesmen available for assignment,

N_i = total number of unassigned salesmen at stage i $(0 \leqslant N_i \leqslant N)$,

n_i = number of salesmen to be assigned to territory i at stage i $(0 \leqslant n_i \leqslant N_i)$,

$R_i(n_i)$ = immediate return function (in $1000s),

= return from assigning n_i salesmen to territory i,

$f_i(N_i)$ = optimal return function (in $1000s),

= maximum return when N_i salesmen are allocated in an optimal, fashion at stage i and *all* preceding stages.

The immediate return function is just the amount obtained from assigning n_i salesmen to territory i at stage i. For instance, if 3 salesmen are assigned to territory 2, the immediate return would be 2.3, from Table 10.4. The optimal return function involves maximizing the total return given N_i salesman available at stage i. Thus, as we will show, if 4 salesmen are available at stage 2, the optimal return is 3.6, obtained by assigning 1 salesman to territory 2 and 3 salesmen to territory 1.

The objective in this problem is to maximize the total profit subject to the limitation on the number of salesmen available, and we can state this as

$$\text{maximize} \sum_{i=1}^{M} R_i(n_i)$$

subject to

$$\sum_{i=1}^{M} n_i \leqslant N$$

and $\qquad n_i = 0, 1, 2, \ldots, 5 \qquad$ for all i,

since the number of salesmen allocated to any territory must obviously be an integer.

Let us work this example stage by stage, utilizing both a tabular and a graphical presentation of results.

Stage 1, where we begin our computations, is actually the last stage in the allocation process. At that stage, there could be anywhere from 0 to 5 unassigned salesmen. Obviously, there is only one choice for any unassigned salesmen. We would assign them to territory 1, and the optimal return would equal the immediate return, as shown in Table 10.5.

Table 10.5   Stage 1 (Territory 1)

Unassigned Salesmen N_1	Salesmen Assigned n_1	Immediate Return $R_1(n_1)$	Optimal Return $f_1(N_1)$
5	5	3.4	3.4
4	4	3.3	3.3
3	3	2.9	2.9
2	2	2.0	2.0
1	1	0.5	0.5
0	0	0	0

At stage 2, we can again have from 0 to 5 unassigned salesmen, N_2. Now, however, we have a number of possibilities, as shown in Table 10.6. For example, if there are 4 unassigned salesmen ($N_2 = 4$), we could assign 3 to territory 2, ($n_2 = 3$), with an immediate return of 2.3, and the remaining 1 ($N_2 - n_2 = 1$) to territory 1 with a return of 0.5, for a total return of 2.8. With $N_2 = 4$, there are five possible combinations of n_2 and $N_2 - n_2$ to evaluate. We are looking for that combination which gives us the optimal return, $f_2(4)$. This turns out to be 1 salesman to territory 2 and 3 salesmen to territory 1, with a total return of 3.6.

For each possible number of unassigned salesmen at stage 2, N_2, we must evaluate the return from all combinations of n_2, the number of salesmen assigned to territory 2, and the assignment of the remaining $N_2 - n_2$ salesmen to territory 1. The desired result is the determination of the assignment yielding the optimal return $f_2(N_2)$ for each of the six possible values of N_2, 0 through 5. The resulting values of $f_2(0), f_2(1), \ldots , f_2(5)$ are indicated in the last column of Table 10.6.

Stage 3 is the final stage in our evaluation, but the first stage in the actual allocation process. Thus, all salesmen are available for assignment at stage 3, so $N_3 = N = 5$. For each of the six possible allocations to stage 3, namely, $n_3 = 0$ to 5 salesmen, we can now add the immediate return from n_3 salesmen and the optimal return at stage 2 from $N_3 - n_3$ salesmen. The calculations are shown in Table 10.7.

Again, as in the previous example, we can observe the efficiency of the dynamic programming approach. For each possible immediate return from a given allocation of salesmen to stage 3, we had only to add the optimal return at the previous stage, stage 2, for the remainder of the available salesmen. As can be seen, there are two optimal policies, both yielding a total return of 5.0 ($5000 per month).

Table 10.6   Stage 2 (Territory 2)

Unassigned Salesmen N_2	Salesmen Assigned n_2	Immediate Return $R_2(n_2)$	Remaining Salesmen $N_2 - n_2$	Optimal Return at Previous Stage $f_1(N_2 - n_2)$	Total Return $R_2(n_2) + f_1(N_2 - n_2)$
5	0	0	5	3.4	3.4
	1	0.7	4	3.3	4.0
	2	1.5	3	2.9	$4.4 = f_2(5)$
	3	2.3	2	2.0	4.3
	4	3.2	1	0.5	3.7
	5	4.0	0	0	4.0
4	0	0	4	3.3	3.3
	1	0.7	3	2.9	$3.6 = f_2(4)$
	2	1.5	2	2.0	3.5
	3	2.3	1	0.5	2.8
	4	3.2	0	0	3.2
3	0	0	3	2.9	$2.9 = f_2(3)$
	1	0.7	2	2.0	2.7
	2	1.5	1	0.5	2.0
	3	2.3	0	0	2.3
2	0	0	2	2.0	$2.0 = f_2(2)$
	1	0.7	1	0.5	1.2
	2	1.5	0	0	1.5
1	0	0	1	0.5	0.5
	1	0.7	0	0	$0.7 = f_2(1)$
0	0	0	0	0	$0 \ \ = f_2(0)$

Table 10.7   Stage 3 (Territory 3)

Unassigned Salesmen N_3	Salesmen Assigned n_3	Immediate Return $R_3(n_3)$	Remaining Salesmen $N_3 - n_3$	Optimal Return at Previous Stage $f_2(N_3 - n_3)$	Total Return $R_3(n_3) + f_2(N_3 - n_3)$
5	0	0	5	4.4	4.4
	1	1.1	4	3.6	4.7
	2	2.1	3	2.9	$5.0 = f_3(5)$
	3	3.0	2	2.0	$5.0 = f_3(5)$
	4	3.9	1	0.7	4.6
	5	4.7	0	0	4.7

To determine the optimal allocation of salesmen, we start at the beginning stage, stage 3 in this example, and work forward, just the reverse of the order in which the problem was solved. With the initial number of unassigned salesmen $N_3 = 5$, Table 10.7 shows that there are two optimal assignments at stage 3, $n_3 = 2$ or $n_3 = 3$. Suppose we choose $n_3 = 2$ initially. That leaves 3 of the 5 salesmen to be assigned at stage 2, so $N_2 = 3$. From Table 10.6, the optimal allocation for $N_2 = 3$ is $n_2 = 0$, so 3 salesmen still remain to be assigned at stage 1. Then, for $N_1 = 3$, referring to Table 10.5, the optimal assignment is, of course, $n_1 = 3$. We can show this procedure more clearly by a tabular approach, as in Table 10.8, which develops the optimal solution and the alternate optimal solution starting with $n_3 = 3$. By a similar procedure, the optimal allocations can also be readily traced in the diagram of Figure 10.2. Table 10.9 summarizes the optimal solutions for this example.

Table 10.8   Procedure for Determining Optimal Solution(s)

Territory	Stage i	Unassigned Salesmen N_i	Optimal Assignment Based on N_i n_i	Remaining Unassigned Salesmen N_{i-1}
3	3	5	2	3
2	2	3	0	3
1	1	3	3	0
3	3	5	3	2
2	2	2	0	2
1	1	2	2	0

Table 10.9   Summarization of Optimal Solutions

Territory	Allocation 1		Allocation 2	
	Salesmen	Return	Salesmen	Return
3	2	2.1	3	3.0
2	0	0.0	0	0.0
1	3	2.9	2	2.0
		5.0		5.0

For this problem, as for all dynamic programming problems, we have established a basic *recursion* relationship, whereby the return at each stage is expressed as

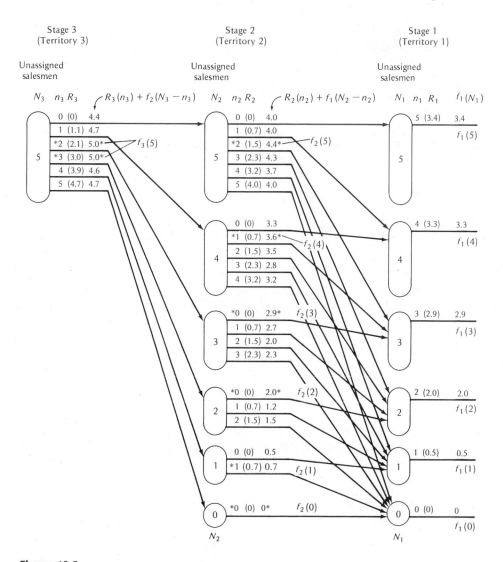

Figure 10.2

a function of data relevant to that stage and the optimal return function of the previous stage. In this problem, the optimal return function is

$$f_i(N_i) = \max_{0 \leqslant n_i \leqslant N_i} \left[R_i(n_i) + f_{i-1}(N_i - n_i) \right] \qquad 1 < i \leqslant M.$$

Expressed in words, the optimal return at stage i, given that N_i salesmen are available, is obtained by finding the value of n_i, the salesmen allocated to territory i, which maximizes the sum of the immediate return $R_i(n_i)$ and the optimal return from allocating the remainder of the salesmen, $N_i - n_i$, at the previous stage. At stage 1, we optimize by allocating all available salesmen, so

$$f_1(N_1) = R_1(n_1), \text{ where } n_1 = N_1.$$

From the work already done, it is quite easy to evaluate the optimal assignment for a smaller number of salesmen. For example, if only 4 salesmen were available, we could immediately go to stage 3, with $N_3 = 4$, and then utilize the optimal assignments previously determined at stage 2. This is shown in Table 10.10. Verify that the optimal allocation is 2 salesmen to territory 3 and 2 salesmen to territory 1.

Table 10.10   Stage 3 (Territory 3)

Unassigned Salesmen N_3	Salesmen Assigned n_3	Immediate Return $R_3(n_3)$	Remaining Salesmen $N_3 - n_3$	Optimal Return at Previous Stage $f_2(N_3 - n_3)$	Total Return $R_3(n_3) + f_2(N_3 - n_3)$
4	0	0	4	3.6	3.6
	1	1.1	3	2.9	4.0
	2	2.1	2	2.0	$4.1 = f_3(4)$
	3	3.0	1	0.7	3.7
	4	3.9	0	0	3.9

If we determine the optimal allocation of salesmen when the number available ranges from 1 to 5, we get the results shown in Table 10.11. Because the return function, as given in Table 10.4, is quite nonlinear for some of the territories, notably territory 1, the optimal allocation of salesmen exhibits some interesting changes. Thus, with 2 salesmen, both are assigned to territory 3, but when a third salesman becomes available, 2 salesmen are now assigned to territory 1 and only 1 to territory 3. With a fourth salesman, however, 2 salesmen are again assigned to territory 3. The final column in Table 10.11 shows the incremental return from adding one more salesman. As you can appreciate, this type of information could be quite useful to management, which might well be in the position of determining how many salesmen to allocate to the three territories combined. Thus, the problem of optimal allocation of the salesmen to these three territories could be a subproblem of a much larger optimization problem.

Incidentally, if there had been a requirement for at least 1 salesman to be allocated to each territory, the allocation problem would have become relatively trivial, since only the allocation of the fourth and fifth salesmen would remain to be determined. Table 10.4 could then be modified to show the additional return from allocating more than one salesman in each territory. If the problem is then reworked to allocate only the final 2 salesmen, the optimal allocation can be readily determined, perhaps from an abbreviated diagram similar to Figure 10.2, as 2 salesmen to

Table 10.11

Salesmen Available	Optimal Allocation Territory 1	2	3	Total Return	Incremental Return from Last Salesman
1	0	0	1	1.1	1.1
2	0	0	2	2.1	1.0
3	2	0	1	3.1	1.0
4	2	0	2	4.1	1.0
5	2	0	3	5.0	0.9
	3	0	2		

territory 1, 1 salesman to territory 2, and 2 salesmen to territory 3. The optimal return, under the given restriction of allocating at least 1 salesman to each territory, is now 4.8, instead of 5.0, as it was in the unrestricted case.

General Concepts of Dynamic Programming

The foundation of dynamic programming is built upon *Bellman's principle of optimality*, which states: "An optimal policy has the property that, whatever the initial state and initial decision are, the remaining decisions must constitute an optimal policy with regard to the state resulting from the first decision." Let us now carefully define the important terms in the study of multistage decision processes.

Stage   Each point in the problem where a decision must be made. For the shortest route problem, a stage was a group of cities with a common property (minimum number of arcs from the destination). In the salesmen allocation problem, each territory represented a stage.

State   Information describing the problem at each stage, generally in the form of specific values of state variables. In the shortest route problem, the state at any stage was a specific city. Each stage in the salesmen allocation problem had one state variable, the number of salesmen still available. The state was the specific value of that number. Conceptually, the state variable links together the stages in a multistage decision problem.

Policy   A decision-making rule which, at any stage, permits a feasible sequence of decisions. In effect, a policy transforms the state at a given stage into a state associated with the next stage. The policy at any stage of the shortest route problem was the selection of the routes to the next group of cities. At any stage in the salesmen allocation problem, a policy would be the allocation of some specific number of the available salesmen to the territory represented by that stage.

Optimal Policy   A policy which optimizes the value of a criterion, objective, or return function. Starting in any given state of any stage, the optimal policy depends only upon that state and not upon how it was reached. In other words, in accordance with the principle of optimality, the optimal decision at any stage is in no way dependent on the previous history of the system. (This is the so-called Markovian property, which will be discussed in depth in Chapter 13, Markov Analysis.)

In both the earlier problems, we determined the optimal policy for each possible state of every stage. Here is a specific example of an optimal policy: If, at stage 2 of the salesmen allocation problem, 4 salesmen were yet to be assigned, the optimal policy at that point would be (as determined from Figure 10.2) to allocate 1 salesman to territory 2 and 3 salesmen to territory 1. This is the best that we can do if we have 4 unassigned salesmen at that point.

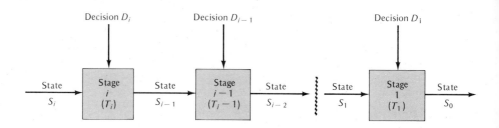

Figure 10.3

The general relationship between state, stage, and policy (or decision) can be illustrated by a diagram such as that of Figure 10.3. At any stage i, the next state (moving backward through the system) S_{i-1} is a function only of the state S_i at stage i and the decision D_i made at that stage. What we call the state transformation function T_i transforms state S_i to state S_{i-1}, given decision D_i. We can write this as $S_{i-1} = T_i(S_i, D_i)$. The form of the state transformation function T_i depends on the particular problem to be solved.

In the salesmen allocation problem, the state transformation function is a very simple one. The state variable S_i represents the number of salesmen remaining to be allocated at stage i and the decision variable D_i represents the number of salesmen allocated to territory i at stage i. Thus, the state transformation function is $S_{i-1} = S_i - D_i$. In the notation of that problem, $N_{i-1} = N_i - n_i$.

In problems which can be formulated as dynamic programming problems, the solution process is initiated by determining the optimal policy for the last stage, which we label as stage 1, since we analyze it first. With the state transformation function and the recursive criterion function developed for the particular problem, we then work backward stage by stage to find the optimal policy for each state of every stage i, given the optimal policy for each state of stage $i - 1$. The optimal policy for the entire problem is determined when this process terminates at the initial stage. This procedure is called *backward recursion*.

It is also possible to solve some dynamic programming problems by forward recursion. Whereas in backward recursion we express the output state as a function of the input state and the decision at that stage, in forward recursion the input state is expressed as a function of the output state and the decision. Using backward recursion, $S_{i-1} = T_i(S_i, D_i)$, as we saw earlier. With forward recursion, we perform what is called *state inversion*, of the form $S_i = \bar{T}_i(S_{i-1}, D_i)$, where $\bar{T}_i$ represents the inverse state transformation at stage i.

As an example of a forward recursion relationship, consider the salesmen allocation problem. In that problem, the state transformation function T_i was $N_{i-1} = N_i - n_i$. The inverse state transformation function would then be $N_i = N_{i-1} + n_i$. That problem could have been solved by forward recursion just as easily as it was by backward recursion. In general, backward recursion is usually preferred, because the state transformations tend to be less complicated and more natural than when using forward recursion. In the next chapter, we will utilize forward recursion to solve a simple inventory problem.

In general, dynamic programming attempts to reduce a single problem involving a relatively large number of decision variables, frequently integer-valued, into a series of smaller problems, each with a small number of decision variables. By so doing, it avoids the frequently formidable computational problem of evaluating all possible combinations of variables, since, as is usually the case, most of these combinations need not be evaluated if some reasonably perceptive weeding-out process is performed. It should be pointed out, however, that dynamic programming is by no means a computational panacea for large problems. If there are more than a very few state variables (perhaps two) at each stage, unless they have a very small number of possible states, the number of required values to be retained in computer memory rapidly becomes excessive, even for the largest computers. Thus, if we had three state variables, each with 100 possible states, we would have to retain $(100)^3$ or $1,000,000$ values in computer memory at one time. Bellman calls this factor the "curse of dimensionality," where dimensionality refers to the number of state variables. There are, in practice, several different methods by which the number of state variables can be reduced. Probably the best known method of state variable reduction is through the use of Lagrange multipliers. The interested reader is referred to the text by Nemhauser (1966).

In this chapter, the emphasis is on the approach to dynamic programming and its methodology, so we will confine ourselves primarily to problems with only a single state variable.

Formulation and Solution of Dynamic Programming Problems

The procedure generally followed is given below.

1. Define the problem variables, determine the objective function to be minimized or maximized, and specify the problem constraints.
2. Define the stages of the particular multistage decision problem. Determine the state variables, whose values constitute the state at each stage, and what constitutes the decisions required (policy) at each stage. Specify the state transformation function, the relationship by which the state at one stage is determined as a function of the state and decision at the next stage.

3. Develop the recursion relationship, the optimal return function, which permits computation of the optimal policy given the state at any stage. Specify the optimal return function at stage 1, since this function is usually slightly different in form from the general optimal return function for the other stages.
4. When appropriate, carefully devise tabular presentations which will clearly show the required values and calculations for each stage. Solve manually or by developing the necessary computer program.
5. For the specific numerical values and relationships in the problem, perform the required stage-by-stage computations and determine the overall optimal policy and its value. There may be more than one such optimal policy.

As we go through the various example problems in the remainder of this chapter, observe how this approach focuses attention on the vital problem elements which are common to all dynamic programming problems.

Two examples of deterministic problems will now be worked out in detail.

EXAMPLE 10.3 *(Manpower Scheduling)*

Consider the situation of a company which has manpower commitments to a certain project. Each month a certain required minimum manpower level has been determined. Changing this level each month results in employment or layoff costs, depending on the direction of the change. If the manpower level is higher than required in any month, the company is paying for idle manpower. Over the time span of the project, the company wishes to determine the least-cost manpower schedule.

As a simple version of this problem, suppose that the cost of changing manpower levels is proportional to the square of the monthly change in manpower level (either up or down) and that the cost of excess personnel is a linear function of the number of such personnel. Each period's minimum manpower requirement must be met.

Let M_i = minimum manpower requirement in period i,
n_i = manpower assigned in period i,
C_1 = cost factor for a change in monthly manpower between periods,
C_2 = cost for each excess person per period.

For month i, the cost of changing the manpower level is $C_1(n_i - n_{i-1})^2$, and the cost of excess personnel is $C_2(n_i - M_i)$, where $n_i \geq M_i$. If there are N periods and the manpower level n_0 is known prior to the start of the project, then our objective is

$$\text{minimize} \sum_{i=1}^{N} \left[C_1(n_i - n_{i-1})^2 + C_2(n_i - M_i) \right]$$

subject to $\qquad\qquad\qquad n_i \geq M_i, \qquad i = 1, 2, \ldots, N.$

To formulate this as a dynamic programming problem, let each stage represent a time period. The state at stage i, S_i, is the manpower level at the beginning of period i, and the decision at stage i, D_i, is the manpower level during period i. We will work backward, as usual, so stage 1 represents the last period.

The manpower at the beginning of any period must be the manpower assigned in the previous period, so the state S_i at period i is n_{i+1}, the manpower assigned in period $i + 1$, the immediately preceding period (using the backward numbering scheme).

At period N, with state $S_1 = n_2$, we must minimize the sum of the two cost components for each feasible manpower level n_1, so the optimal return function is

$$f_1(n_2) = \min_{n_1 \geqslant M_1} \left[C_1(n_2 - n_1)^2 + C_2(n_1 - M_1) \right].$$

For any period earlier than period N, the lowest achievable cost associated with a given manpower level n_i at that stage is calculated by summing the cost of changing from manpower level n_{i+1} to n_i, the excess manpower cost for n_i, and the minimum cost for all lower numbered stages (later periods) when starting with manpower level n_i at this stage.

Let $f_i(n_{i+1}) =$ minimum cost when manpower level n_{i+1} exists at the beginning of period i and an optimal manpower allocation is made to stage i and all lower numbered stages.

By definition, the minimum cost for all lower numbered stages is then $f_{i-1}(n_i)$ when manpower level n_i is chosen. The general optimal return function can now be expressed as

$$f_i(n_{i+1}) = \min_{n_i \geqslant M_i} \left[C_1(n_{i+1} - n_i)^2 + C_2(n_i - M_i) + f_{i-1}(n_i) \right], \qquad 1 < i \leqslant N.$$

The following numerical example will serve to illustrate the approach.

Period	Minimum Required Manpower Level	Stage
1	14	4
2	11	3
3	12	2
4	10	1

C_1, cost factor for a manpower change between periods = \$50,
C_2, unit cost of excess manpower per period = \$100.

The manpower level of 14 in period 1 is actually the starting point, and we are required to determine the minimum-cost combination of manpower levels in periods 2, 3, and 4. Since the maximum manpower requirement in any period is 14, no higher manpower level need ever be considered. On the other hand, the manpower level at the beginning of any period cannot be less than the minimum manpower level required in the preceding period.

For stage 1, which represents period 4, the manpower level n_1 must be at least 10, and the manpower level at the beginning of the period must be at least 12 and will not exceed 14. The required calculations are shown in Table 10.12.

Table 10.12 Stage 1 (Period 4)   (Minimum Level $M_1 = 10$)

Beginning Level n_2	Period Level n_1	Change Cost $50(n_2 - n_1)^2$ ($)	Excess Level Cost $100(n_1 - M_1)$ ($)	Total Cost ($)	Optimal Cost $f_1(n_2)$
14	14	0	400	400	
	13	50	300	350	$= f_1(14)$
	12	200	200	400	
	11	450	100	550	
	10	800	0	800	
13	13	0	300	300	
	12	50	200	250	$= f_1(13)$
	11	200	100	300	
	10	450	0	450	
12	12	0	200	200	
	11	50	100	150	$= f_1(12)$
	10	200	0	200	

At stage 2, as we noted in the discussion of the stage 1 calculations, the manpower level n_2 must range between 12 and 14. The beginning manpower level n_3 could fall between 11 and 14, since the minimum manpower level at stage 3 (period 2) is 11. The stage 2 calculations are in Table 10.13. Observe that, for any manpower level n_2 chosen, we must include the cost of using this level as the input state for the prior stage, with an optimal manpower level allocation for all prior stages.

Table 10.13 Stage 2 (Period 3)   (Minimum Level $M_2 = 12$)

Beginning Level n_3	Period Level n_2	Change Cost $50(n_3 - n_2)^2$ ($)	Excess Level Cost $100(n_2 - M_2)$ ($)	Optimal Cost for Prior Stages $f_1(n_2)$ ($)	Total Cost ($)	Optimal Cost $f_2(n_3)$
14	14	0	200	350	550	
	13	50	100	250	400	
	12	200	0	150	350	$= f_2(14)$
13	13	0	100	250	350	
	12	50	0	150	200	$= f_2(13)$
12	12	0	0	150	150	$= f_2(12)$
11	12	50	0	150	200	$= f_2(11)$

For stage 3, as we observed, the manpower level n_3 could range from 11 to 14. The beginning manpower level n_4, however, will be 14. Assuming that the project starts in period 1 and requires a minimum manpower level of 14, there is no point to starting with any more than 14, since this is the maximum manpower level ever required. (Note that, if the minimum manpower levels in periods 1 and 2 were interchanged, we would have to investigate beginning manpower levels from 12 to 14 at stage 3, but only a single beginning manpower level of 14 at stage 2.)

Table 10.14   Stage 3 (Period 2)   (Minimum Level $M_3 = 11$)

Beginning Level n_4	Period Level n_3	Change Cost $50(n_4 - n_3)^2$ ($)	Excess Level Cost $100(n_3 - M_3)$ ($)	Optimal Cost for Prior Stages $f_2(n_3)$ ($)	Total Cost ($)	Optimal Cost $f_3(n_4)$
14	14	0	300	350	650	
	13	50	200	200	450	$= f_3(14)$
	12	200	100	150	450	$= f_3(14)$
	11	450	0	200	650	

At stage 4, as we have already discussed, we will use a manpower level of 14, incurring no penalty costs whatsoever. Then, as can be seen in Table 10.14, there are two optimal solutions with the same minimal cost of $450.

Table 10.15   Optimal Solutions

Period	Stage i	Beginning Manpower Level n_{i+1}	Manpower Level This Period n_i
1	4	—	14
2	3	14	13
3	2	13	12
4	1	12	11
1	4	—	14
2	3	14	12
3	2	12	12
4	1	12	11

By tracing back through the calculations for each stage, we can easily determine the period manpower levels associated with each optimal solution. Since the optimal stage 4 (period 1) manpower level n_4 is 14, this is the beginning manpower level at stage 3 (period 2). From Table 10.14, the optimal period manpower level n_3 is either 13 or 12. Examining Table 10.13, if the beginning manpower level n_3 at stage 2 (period 3) is 13, the optimal period manpower level n_2 is 12. Coincidentally, n_2 is also 12 if the value of n_3 is 12. Finally, from Table 10.12, with a beginning manpower level n_2 of 12 at stage 1 (period 4), the optimal period manpower level n_1 is 11. The development of the optimal solutions is shown in Table 10.15.

EXAMPLE 10.4 *(Cargo-Loading Problem)*

Suppose we have several different items to be shipped as cargo. The total allowable weight is limited to a given amount, and we wish to determine the number of units of each item to ship so as to maximize the total profit. This type of problem is also known as the *knapsack* or *fly-away kit* problem, in which it is desired to maximize the value (in some consistent units) of items carried subject to a weight or capacity limitation, or both, and generally a limitation on the number of items of a given type.

Let v_i = profit of item i,
  w_i = weight of item i,
  x_i = number of items of type i taken,
  A = total allowable weight.

With N different items to be considered, the problem is

$$\text{maximize} \sum_{i=1}^{N} v_i x_i$$

subject to

$$\sum_{i=1}^{N} w_i x_i \leq A$$

and

$$x_i = 0, 1, 2, \ldots \text{ for all } i.$$

This last restriction states that only integer quantities of each item can be carried. Were it not for this restriction, the optimal solution would obviously be to load the maximum allowable weight of the item with the highest profit-to-weight ratio. The discrete nature of the decision variables (x_i's) precludes such a simple solution. If the decision variables could assume continuous values, as would be the case if we had tons of wheat, gallons of oil, and so forth, this problem would be trivial.

To solve this problem by dynamic programming, we will consider each item as a stage. The state S_i at stage i will be the weight remaining to be allocated, which we will denote as a_1. The decision at stage i, D_i, is the number of units chosen of item i, x_i. The state transformation function is then $S_{i-1} = S_i - w_1 D_i$, or, in terms of the problem variables, $a_{i-1} = a_i - w_i x_1$. Stated in words, the weight remaining at state $i - 1$ is the weight remaining at state i less the weight accounted for by x_i units each with weight w_i.

Let $f_i(a_i)$ = profit when available weight a_i is distributed optimally over stages (items) 1, 2, . . . , i.

The recursive dynamic programming relationship is then

$$f_i(a_i) = \max_{0 \le x_i \le [a_i/w_i]} \left[v_i x_i + f_{i-1}(a_i - w_i x_i) \right] \qquad \text{for } 1 < i \le N,$$

where x_i assumes only integer values and $[a_i/w_i]$ denotes the largest integer value of the bracketed expression.

We can interpret this optimal return function in the following manner: given any weight a_i ($\le A$), the optimal number of units x_i (in the permissible range $0 \le x_i \le [a_i/w_i]$) is that which maximizes the sum of the profit contribution from x_i and that from units 1 through $i - 1$ when allocating the remaining weight of $a_i - w_i x_i$ in an optimal fashion.

Finally, allocating all available weight at stage 1,

$$f_1(a_1) = v_1 x_1, \text{ where } x_1 = [a_1/w_1].$$

Consider a numerical example where the maximum allowable weight A is 10 pounds and the item data is given in Table 10.16.

Table 10.16

Item, i	Weight, w_i (lb)	Profit, v_i ($)
1	3	5
2	4	7
3	2	3

Table 10.17 Stage 1 (Item 1)
(Weight $w_1 = 3$ lb, Profit $v_1 = \$5$/unit)

Available Weight (lb) a_1	Optimal Units of Item 1 x_1	Weight of Item 1 (lb) $w_1 x_1$	Total Profit $v_1 x_1$	$=$	Optimal Return $f_1(a_1)$
10	3	9	$15		
9	3	9	15		
8	2	6	10		
7	2	6	10		
6	2	6	10		
5	1	3	5		
4	1	3	5		
3	1	3	5		
2	0	0	0		
1	0	0	0		
0	0	0	0		

As noted, we will solve this problem by considering each item as a stage, with item i as stage i. At stage 3, we will have 10 pounds available, but at stages 2 and 1, the remaining available weight could be any amount between 0 and 10 pounds. At stage 1, all remaining available weight would be allocated to item 1, the last item to be considered, since we are working backward. The calculations are in Table 10.17.

At stage 2, for each possible value of the available weight a_2, the total profit must be evaluated for each feasible combination of units of item 2 and an optimal allocation

Table 10.18   Stage 2 (Item 2)
(Weight $w_2 = 4$ lb, Profit $v_2 = \$7$/unit)

Available Weight (lb) a_2	Units of Item 2 x_2	Weight of Item 2 (lb) w_2x_2	Remaining Weight (lb) $a_2 - w_2x_2$	Profit of Item 2 ($) v_2x_2	Optimal Profit from Remaining Weight ($) $f_1(a_2 - w_2x_2)$	Total Profit ($)
10	2	8	2	14	0	14
	1	4	6	7	10	$17 = f_2(10)$
	0	0	10	0	15	15
9	2	8	1	14	0	14
	1	4	5	7	5	12
	0	0	9	0	15	$15 = f_2(9)$
8	2	8	0	14	0	$14 = f_2(8)$
	1	4	4	7	5	12
	0	0	8	0	10	10
7	1	4	3	7	5	$12 = f_2(7)$
	0	0	7	0	10	10
6	1	4	2	7	0	7
	0	0	6	0	10	$10 = f_2(6)$
5	1	4	1	7	0	$7 = f_2(5)$
	0	0	5	0	5	5
4	1	4	0	7	0	$7 = f_2(4)$
	0	0	4	0	5	5
3	0	0	3	0	5	$5 = f_2(3)$
2	0	0	2	0	0	$0 = f_2(2)$
1	0	0	1	0	0	$0 = f_2(1)$
0	0	0	0	0	0	$0 = f_2(0)$

of the remaining weight among items previously evaluated. This process is shown in Table 10.18.

At stage 3, the available weight a_3 is 10 pounds, so the calculations, which are similar to those in Table 10.18, are minimal, as seen in Table 10.19.

To determine the optimal allocations, Table 10.20 can be readily constructed by working backward through the tables just developed, as was done for earlier examples. Both optimal allocations utilize all the available resource (the weight of 10 pounds) in this example. Table 10.21 summarizes these optimal allocations.

Table 10.19 Stage 3 (Item 3)
(Weight $w_3 = 2$ lb, Profit $v_3 = \$3$/unit)

Available Weight (lb) a_3	Units of Item 3 x_3	Weight of Item 3 (lb) $w_3 x_3$	Remaining Weight (lb) $a_3 - w_3 x_3$	Profit of Item 3 ($) $v_3 x_3$	Optimal Profit from Remaining Weight ($) $f_2(a_3 - w_3 x_3)$	Total Profit ($)
10	5	10	0	15	0	15
	4	8	2	12	0	12
	3	6	4	9	7	16
	2	4	6	6	10	16
	1	2	8	3	14	$17 = f_3(10)$
	0	0	10	0	17	$17 = f_3(10)$

Table 10.20 Procedure for Determining Optimal Solution(s)

		Optimal Solutions			
Item	Stage i	Available Weight (lb)	Units of Item i	Weight of Item i (lb)	Remaining Weight (lb
3	3	10	1	2	8
2	2	8	2	8	0
1	1	0	0	0	0
3	3	10	0	0	10
2	2	10	1	4	6
1	1	6	2	6	0

Table 10.21 Optimal Solutions

Item	Units	Profit $	Units	Profit $
1	0	0	2	10
2	2	14	1	7
3	1	3	0	0
		17		17

Formulation of a Problem with Two State Variables

Suppose in the cargo-loading problem, we had not only a weight limitation, but also a volume limitation. Now we would have two constraints instead of just one. Expanding the notation of Example 10.3,

Let v_i = profit of item i,
  w = weight of item i,
  t_i = volume of item i,
  x_i = number of items of type i taken,
  A = total allowable weight,
  C = total allowable capacity.

Given N different items, the problem becomes

$$\text{maximize } \sum_{i=1}^{N} v_i x_i$$

subject to

$$\sum_{i=1}^{N} w_i x_i \leq A$$

$$\sum_{i=1}^{N} t_i x_i \leq C$$

and

$$x_i = 0, 1, 2, \ldots \text{ for all } i.$$

The state variables are a_i, the remaining weight at stage i, and c_i, the remaining capacity at state i. The state transformation functions are

$$a_{i-1} = a_i - w_i x_i$$
$$c_{i-1} = c_i - t_i x_i.$$

Then, the optimal return function involves the two state variables a_i and c_i.

$$
\begin{aligned}
f_i(a_i, c_i) &= \text{profit when available weight } a_i \text{ and available volume } c_i \text{ are distributed} \\
&\quad \text{optimally over stages (items) } 1, 2 \ldots, i \\
&= \max_{\text{all } x_i} \left[v_i x_i + f_{i-1}(a_i - w_i x_i, c_i - t_i x_i) \right] \quad \text{for } 1 < i \leq N,
\end{aligned}
$$

where x_i assumes only integer values in the range

$$0 \leq x_i \leq \min \left([a_i/w_i], [c_i/t_i] \right).$$

Also,

$$f_1(a_1, c_1) = v_1 x_1, \text{ where } x_1 = \min \left([a_1/w_1], [c_1/t_1] \right).$$

Note that the maximum value of x_i is constrained to be the lesser of the maximum number of units possible, given the available weight a_i, and the maximum number of units possible, given the available volume c_i.

As you can see, the addition of just one more constraint, which adds one state variable, not only complicates the mathematical model but also multiplies the number of computations of the optimal return, since the return function must, at each stage, be calculated for all possible combinations of the two state variables. Contrast this situation with that in a linear programming problem, where the addition of a single constraint does not affect the mathematical model at all and generally has the effect of increasing the computational time only slightly.

10.2 PROBABILISTIC DYNAMIC PROGRAMMING

Thus far, we have considered only deterministic dynamic programming problems. In such problems, having worked through the computations leading up to those of any given stage, we could, for each possible state of that stage, completely specify the optimal decisions (selection of states) at each lower numbered stage. Now, however, we will consider the situation where there is a probabilistic distribution of possible outcomes, so that a decision at any particular stage results in a probability distribution of states at lower numbered stages.

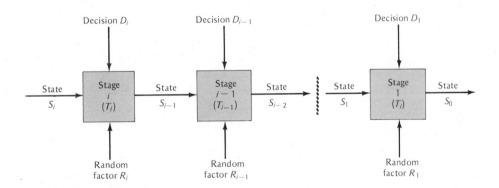

Figure 10.4

The structure of a probabilistic dynamic programming problem is illustrated in Figure 10.4, which is similar to Figure 10.3. At any stage i, we not only have a decision D_i, but some type of random factor R_i, so that the next state S_{i-1} may assume a set of values, according to some probability distribution, rather than a single value, as in the deterministic case. The state transformation equation can then be written as $S_{i-1} = T_i(S_i, D_i, R_i)$ where S_{i-1} now becomes a random variable. The form of the state transformation function T_i again is dependent on the particular problem.

As an example of a probabilistic dynamic programming problem, suppose, in the manpower scheduling problem of Example 10.3, that it was not always possible to obtain the exact manpower level decided upon at the beginning of a period. For instance, if a manpower level of 12 were specified, we might have 0.1 probability of ending up with 13, 0.7 probability of 12, and 0.2 probability of 11. (Differences from the specified manpower level could occur through unanticipated transfers to or from the particular project, or by employees leaving the company.) Then, for each feasible manpower level at the beginning of a period, the change in manpower level and the costs of excess, as well as too little, manpower would have to be evaluated for each of the possible manpower levels resulting from a given decision. These costs would be weighted according to the given probability values and then summed. The problem is still solvable by the same approach as that used previously, but the computations are considerably more involved than in the deterministic case.

It should be pointed out that there are situations where probabilistic distributions add little, if any, additional complexity, as we will show. Typically, this occurs when the random elements in the problem do not affect the actual state transformations. For example, in the problem of allocating salesmen to territories, suppose that the returns from assigning a certain number of salesmen to each territory were represented by probability distributions, rather than by single values. If we wished to optimize in terms of expected monetary value, the optimal solution would be determined by replacing each probability distribution by its mean value and solving exactly as in the deterministic case.

Having already indicated how two of the previously discussed dynamic programming problems could contain stochastic elements, we will examine in some detail two additional examples of probabilistic dynamic programming problems. The first problem will serve to illustrate a particular approach, utilizing a decision tree, which is applicable to multistage decision processes of a rather general nature. The second problem involves a multistage version of the so-called optimal lot size problem (which will be discussed in considerable detail in the following chapter).

Decision Tree Approach

Suppose we are faced with a decision process where, at certain points in time, we must make a decision involving two or more alternatives, or acts. After we choose a particular act, one or more possible events may occur, each with a given probability. An event may be an act of nature, such as a storm; a competitor's action, such as a price decrease or the introduction of a new product; the awarding of a contract; and so forth. Given a particular situation involving some sequence of possible acts and events, we wish to determine that sequence of acts which will optimize an appropriate objective.

The procedure involves the construction, as in Chapter 4, of a decision tree where either the nodes represent decision forks or chance forks and the branches represent acts or events. We start with the part of the network associated with the latest chronological time. Then, working backward (as in the dynamic programming problems previously solved) through the tree, we choose the optimal act at each decision fork (stage) where such a decision is made. When this process reaches the initial decision fork, we will be able to determine the optimal solution to the entire problem.

EXAMPLE 10.6

A small parts manufacturer has an opportunity to bid on a preproduction study contract worth $20,000 net profit, exclusive of bidding expenses, which are estimated at $10,000. The chances of winning the contract are estimated as 50–50. If the contract is won, the company must decide on the level of effort it wishes to expend to increase its chances of getting the follow-on production contract worth $50,000 net profit. No further bid effort will be required. A high level of effort will cost $16,000 and will result in a 0.80 probability of winning the production contract. A moderate level of effort will cost $10,000, with a 0.70 probability of winning the production contract. With a low level of effort, the figures are $6000 and 0.60 probability. If the study contract is bid on and lost, there will be another chance to bid on the production contract, and an additional bid expense of $5000 will be incurred if a decision to bid is made. The probability of winning the production contract is estimated as 0.40. If the study contract was never bid on, a bid on the production contract may be prepared, at a cost of $15,000. In this case, the probability of winning the production contract is estimated as only 0.20.

This problem becomes much clearer when we draw a decision tree and show the relationship of the various components of the problem. Figure 10.5 shows the decision tree, with the initial decision point at the left and subsequent decisions at the right. Using the same terminology and notation as in Chapter 4, the squares represent decision forks, and the circles represent chance forks. The values on the branches represent profits (in thousands of dollars), and negative values represent expenditures. The numbers in parentheses are event probability values. All these values are conditional probabilities. The net profit values at the right are obtained by adding the dollar values along the branches connecting the given point to the initial decision fork at the extreme left. These net profit values are primarily conditional values, dependent on the occurrence of one or more chance events.

Let us work backward from the right and from top to bottom, calculating the expected value for each alternative at the decision fork nearest the right-hand side. Starting with decision fork 2, if we choose the high level of effort, we have an 80 percent chance of winning the production contract, and the expected net profit is then $(0.8)(44) + (0.2)(-6) = 34$ ($34,000). Evaluating the other two alternatives in the same manner, we find, as shown in Figure 10.6, that the moderate level of effort is most favorable, with an expected value of 35. If we should arrive at decision fork 2, the optimal decision would then be to employ a moderate level of effort. At decision

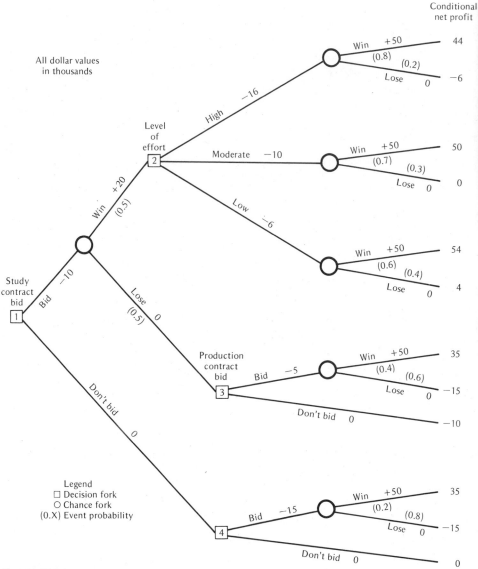

Figure 10.5

fork 3, the optimal decision would be to bid, with an expected value of 5. The optimal decision at decision fork 4 would be "don't bid," with a value of 0.

We are now in a position to evaluate the expected value at decision fork 1, since we know the optimal decision to make at all the other controllable decision points. Taking the expected values of the optimal decisions at decision forks 2 and 3 and weighting them by their probabilities, we find that the expected value of bidding on

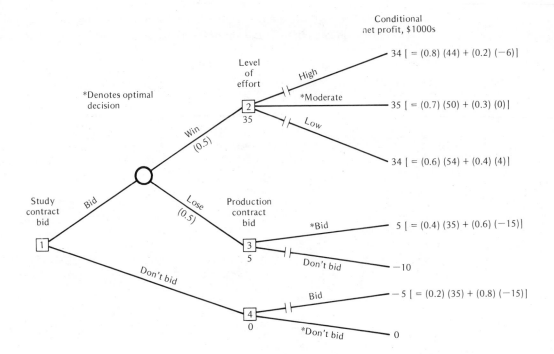

Figure 10.6

the study contract and then, depending on the outcome, making the succeeding decisions in an optimal manner, is $(0.5)(35) + (0.5)(5) = 20$, as shown in Figure 10.7. This is clearly preferable to the alternative of never bidding at all, with a value of 0. The overall optimal policy must be specified completely, as follows.

> Bid on the study contract. If you win, use a moderate level of effort. If you lose, bid on the production contract.

The expected value of this policy is $20,000.

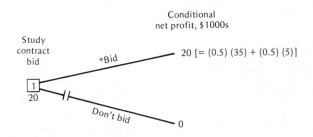

Figure 10.7

Another way of performing the required calculations is to omit the initial calculation of the net profit on each branch and simply work backward with the dollar values as given. Thus, at decision fork 2, for example, the expected value for the high level of effort would be $(0.8)(50) + (0.2)(0) - 16 = 24$. For the moderate level, it would be $(0.7)(50) + (0.3)(0) - 10 = 25$, and for the low level, it would be $(0.6)(50) + (0.4)(0) - 6 = 24$. The optimal decision would, of course, be to use the moderate level of effort. The detailed results are shown in Figure 10.8, where the expected value is shown beneath each fork, for both decision forks and chance forks. At decision forks, the underlined value represents the value of the optimal decision at that point, given an optimal policy for the remainder of the decisions and no knowledge as to any earlier decisions or associated monetary values.

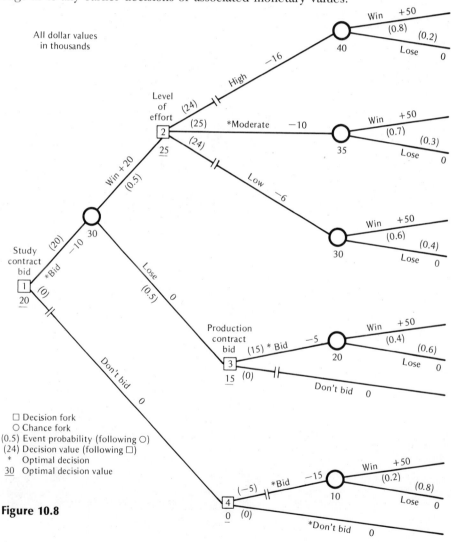

All dollar values
in thousands

□ Decision fork
○ Chance fork
(0.5) Event probability (following ○)
(24) Decision value (following □)
  *   Optimal decision
30 Optimal decision value

Figure 10.8

This problem can also be solved using a tabular presentation generally similar to that employed in the earlier examples, but with differences due to the probabilistic events in the problem. However, because the structure of this problem is not readily apparent, the determination as to what constitutes the stages and states and the development of a suitable notation and presentation all require careful thought. We will define the stage by the number of sequential decisions to be made starting at that stage. Thus, at stage 1, only a single decision remains to be made, so that, if we relate the tabular presentation to the decision tree of Figure 10.8, for convenience in comparing the two approaches, stage 1 includes decision forks 2, 3, and 4. At stage 2 two sequential decisions are to be made, one at decision fork 1 and the other at one of the three other decision forks. The states will be the conditions by which a particular decision fork is reached. The analysis of stage 1 is shown in Table 10.22. The expected immediate return (profit) values are developed from the data in the original statement of the problem.

Table 10.22 Stage 1

State S_1	Decision D_i	Expected Immediate Return ($1000s)	Optimal Return $f_1(S_1)$
A, win bid on study contract	D_1, high effort on study contract	$-16 + (0.8)(50)$ $+ (0.2)(0) = 24$	
	D_2, moderate effort on study contract	$-10 + (0.7)(50)$ $+ (0.3)(0) = 25$	$= f_1(A)$
	D_3, low effort on study contract	$-6 + (0.6)(50)$ $+ (0.4)(0) = 24$	
B, lose bid on study contract	D_4, bid on production contract	$-5 + (0.4)(50)$ $+ (0.6)(0) = 15$	$= f_1(B)$
	D_5, don't bid on production contract	0	
C, don't bid on study contract	D_4, bid on production contract	$-15 + (0.2)(50)$ $+ (0.8)(0) = -5$	
	D_5, don't bid on production contract	0	$= f_1(C)$

Observe that the probabilities involved at stage 1 affect only the expected immediate return resulting from a given decision D_i. At stage 2, there is only a single state, but there is a probability distribution of outcomes resulting from one of the possible decisions, as can be seen from Table 10.23.

The probabilities involved in the stage 2 analysis have a considerably different effect than those in stage 1. Here, they actually affect the state transformation resulting from a particular decision, D_6. This was not true at stage 1, as we have noted.

Table 10.23 Stage 2

State S_2	Decision D_i	Next State, S_1	Probability of S_1	Immediate Return ($1000s)	Optimal Return from Previous Stage, $f_1(S_1)$ ($1000s)	Weighted Total Return ($1000s)
Chance to bid on study contract	D_6, bid on study contract	A	0.5	20 − 10 = 10	25	17.5
		B	0.5	−10	15	2.5
						20.0 = $f_2(S_2)$
	D_7, don't bid on study contract	C	1.0	0	0	0

From Tables 10.22 and 10.23, the optimal policy is

D_6, bid on the study contract. If you win, use D_2, moderate effort on the study contract. If you lose, use D_4, bid on the production contract.

The expected return from this policy is $20,000, and this solution is, of course, identical to that obtained using a decision tree.

We will now consider a more structured type of probabilistic dynamic programming problem. In this problem, the random state transformations are a function of a theoretical probability distribution, rather than a set of empirical probabilities.

EXAMPLE 10.7 (Reject Allowance Problem)

In most production operations, the problem of spoilage is an ever-present factor. When a company must manufacture a specified quantity of a complicated part, there is a distinct possibility that one or more items in the production lot will be defective. Therefore, the size of the lot is generally made greater than the required quantity; the additional number of units added is called the reject allowance.

Consider a manufacturer's situation where a production run for a certain part requires a setup cost in addition to the production cost of each unit. Any defective units will not be found until some time after the production run has been completed. If the number of good units after the production run is less than the desired quantity, a second production run can be made, incurring another setup cost. If there still are insufficient good units after a second production run, a shortage cost will be charged for each unit short. Surplus units have no value. On the basis of the economic factors involved, the sequence of production run quantities which minimizes the expected total cost is to be determined. We will examine only policies such that the first production run is for a lot size at least equal to the required quantity of good units, and a second production run, if needed, will be made for at least the number of units short.

Let C = unit production cost,
C_1 = setup cost (independent of number of units produced),
C_2 = unit shortage cost,
N_i = number of good units still required prior to production run i
n_i = number of units produced in production run i,
$P(k_i|n_i)$ = probability that k_i defective units are produced in a lot of n_i units.

The objective in this problem is to minimize the expected sum of all relevant costs. These include the cost of all units produced, the cost of a possible second setup, and a shortage cost if the final number of good units is less than the required number. Excluded is the cost of the first setup, which will be incurred regardless of any other decisions. At this point, let us introduce a numerical example for this mathematical model.

Each unit of a production item is produced according to a Bernoulli process, and the probability of a defective unit is 0.20, so that the probability distribution of defectives is binomial. Two units of this item are required, and two production runs are possible, if needed. Setup cost is $30, production cost is $10 per unit, and shortage cost is $50 per unit. Determine the minimum expected cost sequence of production quantities.

From the given data,

$$C = \$10,$$
$$C_1 = \$30,$$
$$C_2 = \$50,$$
$$N_1 = 2,$$
$$P(k_i|n_i) = P(k_i|B:n_i, 0.20) \text{ (binomial probability notation).}$$

In this problem, unlike most of the previous examples, we will first develop a tabular presentation and then the formal recursion formulas. This is done because these formulas are complicated by the probabilistic nature of this type of problem. Their development will be easier to follow after the problem has been solved by the tabular approach.

Each production run will be treated as a stage, and the state at each stage is the number of good units still required. The decision is the lot size, the number of units to manufacture. As usual, we will work backward, so that stage 1 is the second production run and stage 2 is the first production run. The calculations for stage 1 are shown in Table 10.24 and will be discussed in detail.

Table 10.24 Stage 1 (Production Run 2)

(1)	(2)	(3)	(4)	(5)	(6)	(7)	(8)	(9)
		Setup and Production	Defective Units				Weighted	Total
Units Needed N_1	Lot Size n_1	Cost ($) $C_1 + n_1 C$	Number k_1	Probability $P(k_1\|n_1)$	Units Short $N_1 - n_1 + k_1$	Shortage Cost ($)	Shortage Cost ($) (5) × (7)	Expected Cost ($) (3) + Σ(8)
2	2	50	0	0.64	0	0	0	
			1	0.32	1	50	16	
			2	0.04	2	100	4	70.0
	3	60	0	0.512	0	0	0	
			1	0.384	0	0	0	
			2	0.096	1	50	4.8	
			3	0.008	2	100	0.8	$65.6 = f_1(2)$
	4	70	—	—	—	—	—	70+
1	1	40	0	0.8	0	0	0	
			1	0.2	1	50	10	$50.0 = f_1(1)$
	2	50	—	—	—	—	—	50+

On a column-by-column basis, Table 10.24 can be explained as follows.

(1) Units needed at stage 1 will be 2, at most, for the case where no good units were produced on the first production run.

(2) Lot size must be at least as large as the number of units needed.

(3) $30 setup cost plus $10 per unit produced.

(4) For a given lot size n_1, the number of defectives is a random variable, with possible values 0, 1, . . . , n_1.

(5) Binomial probabilities for n_1 trials, k_1 successes (defectives), and 0.2 success probability per trial.

(6) Units needed minus good units produced.

(7) $50 per unit short.

(8) Shortage cost multiplied by the probability of that shortage. For a given n_1 value, the summation of the column (8) values is the expected shortage cost.

(9) Setup and production cost plus expected shortage cost.

For $N_1 = 2$, 2 good units needed after the first production run, lot size $n_1 = 3$ has a lower total expected cost, $65.6, than for $n_1 = 2$. Since the setup and production cost alone for a lot size of 4 or more is at least $70, there is no need to proceed further; $n_1 = 3$ must be optimal. Similarly, for $N_1 = 1$, 1 good unit needed after production run 1, the optimal number to produce is 1, at an expected cost of $50.0. Any lot size greater than 1 will have an expected cost exceeding $50. The optimal return function $f_1(N_1)$ is the expected cost of the optimal policy when N_1 good units are needed. Thus, $f_1(2) = \$65.6$ and $f_1(1) = \$50.0$.

We are now ready to perform the stage 2 calculations, as shown in Table 10.25.

Table 10.25 Stage 2 (Production Run 1)

(1)	(2)	(3)	(4)	(5)	(6)	(7)	(8)	(9)
			Defective Units		Units Still	Optimal Cost from Previous	Weighted	Total Expected
Units Needed	Lot Size	Production Cost ($)	Number	Probability	Needed	Stage ($)	Cost ($)	Cost ($)
N_2	n_2	n_2C	k_2	$P(k_2\|n_2)$	$N_2 - n_2 + k_2$	$f_1(N_2 - n_2 + k_2)$	$(5) \times (7)$	$(3) + \Sigma(8)$
2	2	20	0	0.64	0	0	0	
			1	0.32	1	50.0	16.0	
			2	0.04	2	65.6	2.6	38.6
	3	30	0	0.512	0	0	0	
			1	0.384	0	0	0	
			2	0.096	1	50.0	4.8	
			3	0.008	2	65.6	0.5	$35.3 = f_2(2)$
	4	40	—	—	—	—	—	40+

The stage 2 calculations are similar to those of stage 1, with these differences: The setup cost has been omitted in column (3) because the first production run will always be required. In column (6), we have the units still needed after the first production run, and for this number the column (7) value is the optimal return from stage 1, when the optimal policy is followed at that stage. The summation of the column (8) values for a given n_2 value is now the expected value of the cost of the second production run. The optimal solution at stage 2 is to produce 3 units, and the total expected cost of the entire process, excluding the setup cost on production run 1, is $35.3.

The complete statement of the optimal solution follows.

Produce 3 units in production run 1.
If 0 or 1 defective, no additional units are required. Stop.
If 2 defectives, 1 additional unit is required. Produce 1 unit in production run 2.
If 3 defectives, 2 additional units are required. Produce 3 units in production run 2.

The optimal solution can also be presented in the form of a decision tree, as in Figure 10.9.

Observe how the stochastic nature of the problem multiplies the calculations, as compared to deterministic problems. Each decision (lot size chosen) results in several probabilistic outcomes (good units actually produced). In addition, the calculations themselves tend to be more involved than for deterministic problems, since certain values must be weighted by probabilities and summed.

At this point, let us return to the task of developing the appropriate recursion formulas for this problem. First of all, the general form of the state transformation function is $N_{i-1} = N_i - n_i + k_i$, since the number of units needed at one stage is the number needed at the previous stage less the number of good units produced at the

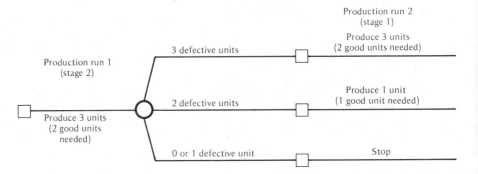

Figure 10.9

previous stage. If N_1 good units are still needed after the first production run, the optimal return function at stage 1 (the second production run) is

$$f_1(N_1) = \min_{n_1 = N_1, \, N_1 + 1, \ldots} \left\{ C_1 + n_1 C + C_2 \sum_{k_1 = n_1 - N_1}^{n_1} \left[(N_1 - n_1 + k_1) P(k_1 | n_1) \right] \right\}$$

$$\text{for } N_1 > 0,$$

$$= 0 \quad \text{for } N_1 = 0.$$

The first two terms are just the setup and production costs. The complicated third term is the expected shortage cost. For each possible number of units short, the shortage cost is multiplied by the number of units short and weighted by its probability of occurrence.

The optimal return function at stage 2 (the first production run) is somewhat less complicated.

$$f_2(N_2) = f_2(N) = \min_{n_2 = N_2, \, N_2 + 1, \ldots} \left\{ n_2 C + \sum_{k_2 = 0}^{n_2} \left[P(k_2 | n_2) f_1(N_2 - n_2 + k_2) \right] \right\}$$

For each feasible production quantity n_2, we add its production cost and the summation of the optimal return values for the number of good units produced $(N_2 - n_2 + k_2)$, each weighted by its probability of occurrence.

As we have demonstrated, this problem is more difficult to formulate mathematically than it is to solve numerically, although the numerical computations, if done manually, can be quite tedious. It would be a straightforward process, however, to develop a computer program to perform computations for practical situations where a reject allowance must be determined.

10.3 PRACTICAL APPLICATIONS

Three applications are presented. The first two applications show how dynamic programming models can be used in the decision analysis of large-scale energy systems, although one model is concerned with a capital budgeting problem and the other with engineering design. The third application is a small-scale example of an interesting resource allocation problem.

1. Electric power system expansion[1] At the National Energy Board, Ottawa, Canada, a dynamic programming model has been developed to determine an optimal expansion plan for the generating capacity of an electric power system. The model solves for the least-cost combination of hydro, nuclear, thermal, and peaking turbine plants, the size of the plants to be added, and the timing of these additions. In its original form, the problem involved four state variables (the additional capacity of each plant type added up to period t) and four decision variables (the change in capacity of each plant type during period t). In this form, the problem is an extremely large one, as you should appreciate at this point. However, by taking careful advantage of the mathematical structure of the problem, the number of computations per period was reduced from approximately n^8, where n is the average number of values each decision and state variable can assume, to about $n^5 + 3n^4$. For $n = 20$, this is a reduction by a factor of nearly 2000, and the number of computations required becomes feasible on a large computer. The model, a 3000-statement FORTRAN program, was applied to a study of the expansion of the Maritime Power Pool System in Canada. Compared to an existing 17-year expansion plan, the model showed that present worth costs could be decreased by approximately 5 percent, indicating potential savings of millions of dollars.

2. Gas pipeline design[2] In late 1967, the National Energy Board (NEB) of Canada denied the application of Westcoast Transmission Company Limited (Westcoast) to export 200 million cubic feet of natural gas per day to the United States Pacific Northwest, although there was extreme pressure on many sides to approve the application. The denial was based on extensive studies and innovative approaches by NEB's O-R Branch, which showed that the contract price offer from the United States Federal Power Commission (FPC) was unrealistically low. Playing a critical role in NEB's management science analyses was a dynamic programming model for

[1]E. R. Petersen, "A Dynamic Programming Model for the Expansion of Electric Power Systems," *Management Science*, Vol. 20, No. 4, Pt. II, December 1973, pp. 656–664.

[2]J. G. Debanne, "Management Science in Energy Policy—A Case History and Success Story," *Interfaces*, Vol. 5, No. 2, Pt. 2, February 1975, pp. 1–21.

the optimal design and expansion of natural gas pipeline systems. This model, developed by P. T. Taylor,[3] was utilized to optimally expand Westcoast's facilities over time in order to meet the immediate and anticipated gas export requirements. For a given set of market forecasts, engineering and financial assumptions, Taylor's model gives that design and expansion program over time, throughout the system, which results in the lowest discounted cost of transportation when accumulated over the period of the study. The final outcome of the controversy, one of national scope in both countries, was a compromise solution between NEB and FPC which set a higher and more realistic price for Canadian gas.

3. Periodical selection[4] As an aid to research, the Bureau of Business Research and Services reading room at the School of Business Administration of the University of Connecticut maintains a current periodical collection. This collection is entirely separate from the more complete collection in the main university library. The bureau's list of journals is revised from time to time according to the uses and preferences of the business faculty. Because budgetary limitations and rapidly increasing subscription prices have mandated elimination of a number of journals, the problem is to determine which journals should be eliminated and which ones added, given an annual allocation for reading room periodicals. The procedure is to maximize the sum of the utilities of the individual periodicals in the collection, where the utility of a periodical is defined as the number of faculty contacts with the issues of the most recent volume. To implement this procedure, the probability distribution of contacts by users with a given periodical is obtained empirically. The problem of choosing an optimal periodical collection is then formulated as a capital budgeting problem and solved by dynamic programming. A specific solution, showing the 50 periodicals selected out of 76 candidates, is given for an annual budget of $700. It is suggested that the model has possible alternative uses, such as media selection in advertising and allocation among research and development projects.

SUMMARY

As noted at the beginning of this chapter, dynamic programming models are based upon the consideration of problems as multistage decision processes. Although each different dynamic programming problem generally results in a different mathematical

---

[3]P. T. Taylor, "A Dynamic Programming Approach to the Design of Natural Gas Pipelines," paper presented at the 14th Annual TIMS Conference, August 1967, Mexico City; also issued as a *National Energy Board Report* (Canada).

[4]Marvin Rothstein, "A Dynamic Programming Model for Periodical Selection," *Decision Sciences*, Vol. 4, No. 2, April 1973, pp. 237–246.

model, we have attempted to delineate the concepts and elements common to most problems which can be formulated as dynamic programming models. We have done this by carefully defining the terminology and general mathematical relationships in such problems.

To formulate dynamic programming problems, it is almost imperative that one have a clear understanding of fundamental concepts such as those of stages, states, optimal policies, state variables, decision variables, and state transformation functions. To solve dynamic programming problems, the concepts underlying recursive solution procedures must be mastered, since these procedures form the heart and soul of dynamic programming models. In addition, the reasons for the extensive use of backward recursion should be understood.

Throughout the detailed formulation and solution of a number of different dynamic programming problems in this chapter, the general approach is similar and the reader should begin to get a fairly good idea of how to handle relatively simple dynamic programming problems with a single-state variable. Once the criterion function has been optimized, the specific values of the variables in the optimal solution can be readily obtained by tracing back through the solutions for each stage, as shown in the example problems. Both deterministic and probabilistic dynamic programming problems have been considered, and it should be apparent that, in general, the stochastic problems become more involved from a computational standpoint, but their actual model complexity is little changed from that of deterministic problems. Decision trees, first covered in Chapter 4, are shown to represent a probabilistic multistage decision process, and the approach to obtaining an associated tabular presentation is also discussed.

Constructing models of dynamic programming problems tends to be much more of an art than that of constructing other types of mathematical models discussed in this text (with the possible exception of simulation models, covered in Chapter 14), since there is no standard form, as such, for dynamic programming problems.

EXERCISES

Note: For those exercises requiring the formulation of a dynamic programming model, the following are included: establishing a suitable notation for all required variables not specified in the exercise, specifying the objective function and constraints, and determining the optimal return functions (recursion relationships) for the general case and for the specific case where there is one stage to go.

10.1   Discuss briefly:
   (a)   The general similarities between dynamic programming and linear programming.
   (b)   How dynamic programming differs conceptually from linear programming.

10.2   Define in your own words the following dynamic programming terms.
- (a) Stage
- (b) State
- (c) State variable
- (d) Decision variable
- (e) Immediate return
- (f) Optimal return
- (g) State transformation function

10.3   What is a recursion relationship? Describe the general process of backward recursion.

10.4   Why is it frequently desirable to solve a problem with a number of decision variables by dividing it into a series of subproblems?

10.5   Freddie's Pickled Pizzas has four pizza parlors operating in the metropolitan area. Staffing for the four outlets is handled centrally. Sales and profit at each outlet is a function of the number of staff working, as shown by the accompanying table. Each parlor needs at least two persons.

Use dynamic programming to determine the optimal staff assignment if 12 persons are available.

Staff size	Net Profit per Day ($)			
	Parlor 1	Parlor 2	Parlor 3	Parlor 4
2	100	80	70	60
3	150	120	115	125
4	175	135	145	155
5	180	150	160	165
6	170	150	170	170
7	160	145	175	165

10.6   The Optimull Marketing Company is attempting to determine the best way to allocate the amount A they have available for the test marketing of M products. They are unwilling to allocate more than K dollars to any one product.
- (a) Develop a general dynamic programming model to optimize the test marketing effort, assuming the company wishes to maximize total profit.
- (b) For the accompanying profit table, optimize the allocation for the three products, given that $A = \$15,000$ and $K = \$8000$.

Profit Table, $1000s

Product	Allocation, $1000s							
	1	2	3	4	5	6	7	8
1	0.08	0.20	0.38	0.48	0.52	0.54	0.56	0.58
2	0	0	0.30	0.42	0.50	0.56	0.60	0.64
3	0.14	0.28	0.38	0.44	0.47	0.50	0.52	0.54

10.7   The Trific Tractor Company is ending production of its Model 29 tractor. In the next three months, it is scheduled to deliver 3, 2, and 4 units, respectively. For a certain part, which is needed at the beginning of each month, each unit costs $3, and there is a $10 cost for each order placed. This part requires special handling while in inventory, so that its holding cost of $2 for each part carried over from one month to the next is very high compared to the cost of the part. None of these parts are currently on hand, and none are desired to be on hand at the end of the three-month period.

Determine the optimal sequence of order quantities using dynamic programming. [*Hint:* Using backward recursion, the state variable is the number of units on hand at the beginning of each period.]

10.8   In the cargo-loading problem of Example 10.4, suppose that it is desired to minimize the total weight of the cargo items subject to the requirement of a given profit minimum.
(a)   Formulate the revised dynamic programming model, given that the minimum profit is R and the required minimum profit at stage i is V_i.
(b)   Solve this model for the given problem data in Example 10.4, with $R = \$15$.

10.9   In a certain piece of electronic equipment, there are N different components. Each individual component i has a weight w_i and a reliability r_i, which is the probability of its survival over some stipulated time period. It is possible to increase the reliability R_i associated with the ith component by providing additional identical units in parallel. If there are n_i units of component i in parallel, then the reliability associated with component i is

$$R_i = 1 - (1 - r_i)^{n_i}$$

(Note that, for $n_i = 1$, R_i is, of course, equal to r_i.) The overall equipment reliability is equal to the product of the component reliabilities, since it is assumed that the components are independent in their operation and that at least one unit of each component must function in order for the equipment to remain operational.
(a)   Formulate a dynamic programming model to maximize the overall equipment reliability subject to a maximum allowable weight of W.
(b)   Solve this model, given a total allowable weight of 12 pounds and the following data:

Component i	1	2	3
Unit reliability r_i	0.8	0.9	0.7
Unit weight w_i, lb.	2	3	1

10.10   In the previous exercise, suppose that each individual component i has an associated cost c_i. Formulate a dynamic programming model to maximize the overall equipment reliability subject to a maximum allowable weight of W and a maximum allowable cost of C.

10.11   In a state with a single legislative body, it is desired to allocate the total number of legislators M to each of the N districts in such a way as to minimize, considering all districts, the maximum difference between the actual number m_i allocated to any district and the theoretical number t_i which should be allocated to that district, where this theoretical number is equal to M times the fraction of the state's population residing in that district. Thus, if district i contained 1.5 percent of the state's population and M were 100, then t_i would be 1.5, whereas the value of m_i would, of course, have to be an integer.

(a) Formulate an appropriate dynamic programming model.

(b) Solve this model for the state of Bliss, which can afford only 10 legislators for its population of 1,000,000. The district populations are as follows:

District 1—160,000   District 3—430,000
District 2—270,000   District 4—140,000.

10.12   A company has just purchased a new special-purpose machine at a cost of C dollars. Over the next N years, the company wishes to know the optimal schedule of replacement for this machine. Replacement is evaluated on an annual basis. When the machine is j years old, the cost of the maintenance contract for the coming year is m_j dollars, and this machine has no salvage value. There is a limiting age of L years for the machine; at that time, the machine must be replaced.

(a) Develop a dynamic programming model which will minimize the total cost over a period of N yr. [*Hint:* Use a decision variable d_i which, at the start of year i, is set to 1 if the decision is to retain the machine, and set to 0 if the decision is to replace the machine.]

(b) Solve this model for the case where N is 7 years, L is 5 years, C = $1000, and the annual maintenance contract costs are as follows.

Age of machine, yr.	0	1	2	3	4	5
Annual maintenance contract, $	50	100	170	300	500	—

10.13   Do nonlinear return functions complicate dynamic programming calculations, as compared to linear return functions? Explain.

10.14   Why does an additional constraint in a dynamic programming problem complicate the computational process?

10.15   In terms of the relationship between states at successive stages, what is the effect of a probabilistic state transformation function? How does this affect the calculations as compared to a deterministic state transformation function?

10.16   What are the general relationships portrayed by a decision tree? Explain briefly how this is accomplished graphically.

10.17   The Gnu Products Company is attempting to decide on the best allocation of its new product development budget for this year. The company has a total amount A available, and it is considering M different development projects which would be completed within the year. If amount a_i is invested in development project i, the probability of a successful product is $p_i(a_i)$. The

expected present value of a successful product is R_i. Gnu Products wishes to maximize the expected return from its new product development budget.
(a) Formulate a dynamic programming model.
(b) Suppose that a total expected return of at least R dollars is required. Formulate a dynamic programming model to minimize the new product development budget under this constraint. Let S_i be the value of the expected return still required at stage i.

10.18 In the manpower scheduling problem of Example 10.3, suppose that there is no guarantee that the manpower assigned will actually be available when assigned. If n_i is the manpower assigned in period i, let there be a probability p that n_i will actually be available and a probability $1 - p$ that only $n_i - 1$ persons will be available. Since the minimum manpower requirement of M_i in period i must be met, this means that at least $M_i + 1$ persons must be assigned to that period.
(a) Develop a dynamic programming model for determining the manpower schedule which minimizes expected cost.
(b) Using the data of Example 10.3 and starting with period 2 rather than period 1, solve this model, given that $p = 0.8$. Assume that the beginning manpower level n_3 (for stage 3, which is period 2) can be set to any desired level.
Express the answer in decision tree form.

10.19 A traveler wishes to fly from Los Angeles to Miami. Because of a shortage of funds, however, he can afford to fly only on Stochastic Airlines, which guarantees the fare but not the destination.
   He has a choice of two flights from Los Angeles, arriving in either Salt Lake City, Denver, or Chicago, according to the probability distribution in the accompanying table. From Salt Lake City or Denver, he has a choice of two flights from either point, arriving in Chicago, St. Louis, or ?. From Chicago or St. Louis, only one flight operates, flying directly to Miami and arriving there most of the time.
   Based on the flight information in the table, determine, by dynamic programming, the traveler's optimal selection of flights to maximize the probability of reaching Miami. What is this probability? [*Hint:* You may find it helpful to work out the calculations on a crude map.]

Probability of Arrival at Possible Destinations

Flight	Leaves	Salt Lake City	Denver	Chicago	St. Louis	Miami	?
1A	Los Angeles	0.8	0.1	0.1			
1B	Los Angeles	0.6	0.4				
2A	Salt Lake City			0.8	0.2		
2B	Salt Lake City			0.3	0.7		

Probability of Arrival at Possible Destinations (continued)

Flight	Leaves	Salt Lake City	Denver	Chicago	St. Louis	Miami	?
3A	Denver			0.7	0.3		
3B	Denver			0.4	0.5		0.1
4	Chicago					0.8	0.2
5	St. Louis					0.9	0.1

10.20 The Jensun Company has been offered a study contract to refine a device for reducing automobile exhaust emissions. Following the study contract, there will be awards for prototype production contracts for a few preliminary models and then awards for production contracts. All contracts are for fixed dollar amounts; the study contract is for $10,000, the prototype contract for $10,000, and the production contract for $50,000.

Jensun has decided to consider two levels of effort, high and low, on the study contract. A high level of effort will cost more, but it will increase chances of getting the prototype contract. The probability of getting the production contract depends on the level of effort on the study contract and also on the level of effort (again high or low) on the prototype contract, if one is received. If Jensun receives a production contract, it will incur additional production expenses unless a high level of effort was employed on the prototype contract. All this information, with probability and cost figures, is summarized in the accompanying table.

Study Contract Level of Effort	Probability of Winning Prototype Contract	Prototype Contract Level of Effort	Probability of Winning Production Contract	Cost, $1000s		
				Study Contract	Prototype Contract	Additional Production Expense
High	0.7	High	0.8	15	10	0
		Low	0.6	15	6	5
		None*	0.2	15	0	10
Low	0.4	High	0.7	5	10	0
		Low	0.5	5	6	5
		None*	0.1	5	0	15

*Prototype contract not received

Develop a decision tree. Utilize it to produce tables such as Tables 10.27 and 10.28. From your tables, determine the optimal strategy and specify it completely. What is the expected value of the optimal strategy?

10.21 On certain TV "giveaway" shows, a contestant gets an initial prize and then gets at least one chance to trade in that prize for a chance at another, hopefully better, prize. The contestant may decide to quit and retain the prize at any point. Suppose that 10 prizes are always available, with the following monetary values

Prize value	$100	$200	$500	$1000	$2000	$5000
Number of prizes	4	2	1	1	1	1

(Any prize drawn is always replaced by one of comparable value, so that the expected value of the prize drawn remains the same for any draw.)

Using a dynamic programming approach, determine a contestant's optimal strategy and expected monetary value, for any possible outcome, if the number of opportunities to trade in a prize is limited to (a) 1, (b) 2, (c) 3, (d) 4.

Specify the required decisions in the form of instructions (or a table) that a contestant could understand.

CHAPTER 11

INVENTORY MODELS

Inventory plays a vital role in the operation of any business or enterprise. The primary reason for the existence of inventory is that it is completely impractical, for many reasons, to produce an item upon demand. Some of the most important reasons for carrying inventory are listed below.

1. Economic—a manufacturer carries stocks of raw material so that they will be available when needed. He cannot have material mined and processed upon demand, because the expense and time delays would be prohibitive.
2. Customer satisfaction—every retail and wholesale firm carries inventories of goods for sale. Without such inventories, it would lose sales to competitors able to immediately supply customer demand, which, of course, cannot be perfectly predicted.
3. Maintenance of operational capability—in order to keep equipment operational, without excessive "down time," an inventory of spare parts must be available for on-the-spot repairs.
4. Seasonal factors—some food products are harvested only at certain times of the year. If they are to be distributed at other times of the year, they must be processed and stored.
5. Convenience—every household carries an inventory of food. It would be extremely inconvenient (and essentially impossible in remote areas) to shop at the store for every meal.

Our study of inventory models will be conducted from the point of view of making good (economical) managerial decisions on inventory policies. For a given item, these policies primarily involve the decisions *when* to reorder and *how much* to reorder. The models to be analyzed will be categorized as either deterministic, when the demand is known, although it may vary from period to period, and stochastic, or probabilistic, when the demand is a random variable.

11.1   FACTORS INVOLVED IN INVENTORY ANALYSIS

A number of factors must be considered in the analysis of inventory problems. Among the most important are the following.

Economic

Ordering or setup cost   If an item is purchased, an ordering cost is incurred each time an order is placed. This cost consists primarily of administrative costs incident to the preparation of an order and the administrative and handling costs on receipt of that order. When an item is produced internally, the setup cost includes both paperwork costs and the physical preparation costs attendant to the initiation and termination of a production run.

Holding or carrying cost   This cost includes the opportunity cost of the money invested in inventory, the cost of physical storage, depreciation, insurance, and possibly obsolescence. Holding cost is expressed as a cost per unit time which, in order to simplify decision making, is generally taken to be proportional to the average number of units in inventory.

Shortage penalty cost   When an item cannot be supplied on demand, we say that a shortage has occurred. The actual penalty cost associated with a shortage may be rather difficult to determine. If the customer is willing to wait, there are administrative costs, frequently called "back order" costs. They are associated with such things as the extra paperwork, possible expediting of the order, and customer notification when the item arrives in stock. If the customer is unwilling to wait, the profit on the item is lost, and an additional cost, that of "goodwill," may be incurred. That is, the customer may be so displeased that he takes all or part of his future business elsewhere. To minimize shortage penalty costs, additional inventory, called buffer or safety stock, is generally carried.

Purchase price or production cost   As the lot size is increased, it may be possible to take advantage of lowered prices or production costs (price breaks) for larger quantities. In such a situation, it is necessary to evaluate the economic tradeoff between the savings in purchase cost and ordering cost and the increased cost of holding inventory.

Salvage value   When an item remains unsold at the end of some time period and it is undesirable, for any reason, to carry it over to the next time period, it often has a value to someone. This value is frequently less than its actual cost. For example, retail merchandise is frequently sold at half price, say at the end of the selling season, in order to make room for new merchandise.

Demand   Knowledge of customer demand for a given item is extremely important in the determination of an optimal inventory policy for that item. Although the

demand distribution almost always has some degree of inherent randomness, so that it is probabilistic in nature, we will find that some worthwhile information can be obtained regarding different ordering policies and their costs by assuming that demand is known and constant. We will show, primarily through the techniques of sensitivity analysis, that such a simplifying assumption is well justified in many cases. We will also develop models involving both discrete and continuous probability distributions of demand.

Lead Time or Delivery Lag   Lead time measures the time delay between initiation of a replenishment order and the actual delivery of the items ordered. We will consider both constant lead times and those defined by a probability distribution. For models involving probabilistic demand distributions, we will be particularly concerned with demand during the lead time as a primary factor in the determination of optimal inventory policies when shortages are permitted.

Ordering Policy

Order point systems   A so-called "perpetual" inventory record (frequently computerized) is generally maintained, so that the number of units on hand is always known. This is also called a continuous review policy. When the inventory level drops to a certain point, called the order point or reorder level, a replenishment order for a fixed quantity is placed. With slight modifications, an order point system can also be used in some situations where only periodic stock counts are available, rather than a continuous record of disbursements.

Order point systems are often used where the number of units demanded per transaction is relatively large and where inventory costs are significant. Order point systems also tend to minimize, compared to other ordering policies, the safety stock required to protect against possible shortages, and they are, therefore, generally used when the unit costs of items are high. An example of a crude, but effective, order point system is the *two-bin system*. Items are taken from the first bin, and the quantity in the second bin is set equal to the order point. When the first bin becomes empty, an order is placed and the stock in the second bin is used until receipt of the order. This procedure is frequently followed for relatively small, inexpensive items, such as screws, nails, and so forth. In many cases, the items are not even counted, but only weighed.

Periodic review systems   Orders are placed at predetermined points in time, generally representing fixed time intervals. The quantity ordered varies, depending on the inventory on hand and on order at the time of the review. This policy is sometimes referred to as a replenishment or replenishment level system.

Although, as we will discuss later, periodic replenishment does require a higher safety stock than an order point system for the same level of protection against shortages, there are a number of compensating advantages. Different requests for the same item, coming from a company's retail stores to its warehouse, can be readily consolidated, and quantity discounts may be obtained. A vendor may have carload lot restrictions, requiring a single order to be placed for a number of items, or he may ship only at fixed dates. In the use of a computer system, periodic replenishment allows batch processing of transactions, which is usually more economical than the transaction-by-transaction processing required to maintain perpetual inventory records.

Optional replenishment systems   Such systems basically combine a periodic review policy with a minimum order quantity restriction. If the calculated order quantity is less than the minimum value stipulated, no order is placed. This avoids the placement of small orders. This type of ordering policy tends to be more complicated to administer than the previously described ordering policies, but it can be quite effective for many applications.

11.2   DETERMINISTIC MODELS

We will consider two different types of deterministic inventory models, wherein the demand for an item is assumed to be known. In the first type, demand is assumed to occur at a constant rate for an indefinite time into the future. We wish to determine the order or lot size and the ordering frequency that will minimize the total relevant cost, which is the sum of the ordering cost, the holding cost, and the shortage penalty cost. In the second type of model, although the demand is known, it can vary from period to period, and we wish to determine the order size or production quantity in each period that will minimize the total relevant cost. For this type of model, we will consider only a finite number of periods, utilizing the techniques of dynamic programming.

Simplest Optimal Lot Size Model

Demand is assumed to be known and steady. No shortages are allowed, and the lead time is zero. This model is also known as the basic EOQ (economic order quantity) or Wilson model. Figure 11.1 shows how the inventory level changes over time. We assume that a replenishment of Q units arrives just as the last unit is demanded.

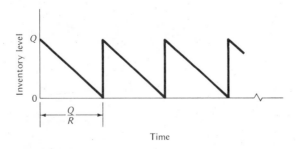

Figure 11.1

The notation used follows.

Let Q = lot size per order,

       Q^* = optimal lot size per order,

       R = units required (demand) per unit time,

      C_o = constant cost of ordering or setup per order placed,

      C_h = constant cost of holding (or carrying) a unit of inventory per unit time,

   $C(Q)$ = total relevant cost (ordering + holding) per unit time for lot size Q.

As indicated in Figure 11.1, the time between orders is that fraction of the time period equal to the lot size divided by the rate of demand per unit time. For example, if demand is 1000 units per year and the lot size is 200, the time between orders will be 200/1000 = 0.2 year.

The number of orders per unit time is the total number of units required divided by the lot size on each order, or R/Q. The average number of units in inventory is half the lot size, or $Q/2$, since the average height of a triangle is just half the total height. The cost factors are then

Ordering cost = (cost per order) × (orders per unit time)

$$= C_o \frac{R}{Q}.$$

Holding cost = (per unit holding cost per unit time) × (average units in inventory)

$$= C_h \frac{Q}{2}.$$

The total relevant cost is the sum of these two costs.

$$C(Q) = \frac{C_o R}{Q} + \frac{C_h Q}{2}. \tag{11.1}$$

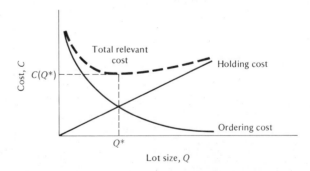

Figure 11.2

A generalized graph of the ordering cost, holding cost, and total relevant cost is shown in Figure 11.2. From this graph, we can see that the total relevant cost is minimized at a value of Q which appears to be at the point where the holding and ordering costs are equal. In Appendix 11A, it is shown analytically that this is so, and the expressions are derived for the optimal lot size Q^* and the associated minimum total relevant cost $C(Q^*)$. From those results,

$$Q^* = \sqrt{2RC_o/C_h} \tag{11.2}$$
$$C(Q^*) = \sqrt{2RC_oC_h} = C_hQ^*. \tag{11.3}$$

Observe that the optimal lot size is determined by the ratio of the ordering cost to the holding cost, rather than their absolute values. Although the absolute values of C_o and C_h directly affect the value of the total relevant cost, the *decision* to be made is that of determining the lot size and here, it is only the ratio of C_o to C_h which is a factor. This is an important point, since the ratio of C_o to C_h may be easier to estimate than the actual values of C_o and C_h. Also, if C_o and C_h both double, say, the total relevant cost also doubles, according to Equation (11.3), but the optimal lot size is unchanged. The point here is that we have done the best we can if we select the lot size which minimizes the total relevant cost. The actual value of that cost, as such, is not a factor in our decision.

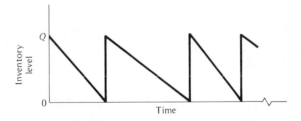

Figure 11.3

Although this model may seem too simple to have any practical use, several factors lead to its applicability in a number of situations. If the annual (say) demand for an item can be reasonably estimated, and this is certainly true in many cases, then the requirement for essentially steady demand need hold only during each time period between the receipt of orders. As shown in Figure 11.3, this would then dictate a variable time period between orders, but the given value of Q^* would still be optimal, since the average inventory and the number of orders would be unchanged, and thus the total relevant cost would still be at a minimum. Furthermore, if the lead time is constant, but not zero, this adds no complication, so long as the demand during the lead time is known and constant, as we have assumed. For example, suppose the annual demand for a seasonal item is 1200 units, the lead time is 5 days, and the optimal lot size Q^* is 100 units. If the demand during winter is 2 units per day, an order would last for 50 days, and the reorder would have to be placed when the inventory level reached 10 units. If the summer demand were 5 units per day, an order would last 20 days, and it would be necessary to reorder at an inventory level of 25 units. This situation is depicted in Figure 11.4. The lead time could even change from period to period, but its value would have to be known.

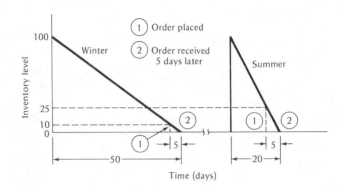

Figure 11.4

Actually, the requirement of known and steady demand, even between order periods, is rarely met in practice, but the solution is rather insensitive to any changes or errors in the problem variables, as we will show in the following section on sensitivity analysis. Thus this model, in spite of its simplicity, does have a reasonable range of applicability.

Let us now take an example to show the usage of the lot size formulas.

EXAMPLE 11.1

The Little Shaver Company purchases the motors for its Model 777 electric shavers from an outside vendor. During the coming year, the company wishes to manufacture, at essentially a constant rate, 100,000 units of the Model 777. The cost of placing each order for the motors is $16. For any item in inventory, Little Shaver uses an annual holding cost equal to 20 percent of the item's cost. The motors cost $4 each.

a)   What is the optimal order size?

From the problem data and Equation (11.2),

$$C_o = \$16, \; C_h = (0.20)(4) = \$0.8/\text{yr}$$
$$R = 100,000 \text{ units/yr}$$
$$Q^* = \sqrt{2RC_o/C_h} = \sqrt{(2)(100,000)(16)/(0.8)}$$
$$= \sqrt{4,000,000} = 2000.$$

Each order should be for 2000 units (motors).

b)   What is the total relevant inventory cost?

From Equation (11.3),

$$C(Q^*) = C_h Q^* = (0.8)(2000) = \$1600.$$

c) Verify that the ordering and holding costs are equal.

$$\text{Ordering cost} = C_o \frac{R}{Q^*} = (16)\frac{100,000}{2000} = \$800.$$

$$\text{Holding cost} = C_h \frac{Q^*}{2} = (0.8)\frac{2000}{2} = \$800.$$

d) How many orders will be placed in the next year?

$$\text{Number of orders} = \frac{R}{Q^*} = \frac{100,000}{2000} = 50.$$

e) If Little Shaver decided to order the motors only twice a month, how much of a cost penalty would it suffer, in percent?

$$Q = \frac{100,000 \text{ units/yr}}{24 \text{ orders/yr}} = 4167 \text{ units/order.}$$

Using Equation (11.1), the total relevant cost would be

$$C(Q) = C_o \frac{R}{Q} + C_h \frac{Q}{2}$$

$$= (16)\frac{100,000}{4167} + (0.8)\frac{4167}{2}$$

$$= 384 + 1666 = \$2050.$$

Cost penalty $= (2050 - 1600)/1600 = 450/1600 = 0.28 = 28$ percent.

f) Suppose that an ordering cost of only \$8 had been used, instead of the correct value of \$16.

1. What would the order size have been?

Let the new value of Q be Q', a supposedly optimal lot size value, but calculated with incorrect data.

$$Q' = \sqrt{2RC_o/C_h} = \sqrt{(2)(100,000)(8)/(0.8)}$$

$$= \sqrt{2,000,000} = 1414 \text{ units.}$$

A factor of 2 error in C_o changed the calculated lot size value by $\sqrt{2}$, as would be expected from the formula.

2. How would the total relevant cost have changed in this situation? Since the order size Q' is nonoptimal, Equation (11.1) must be employed, using the correct ordering cost of $16.

$$C(Q') = C_o\frac{R}{Q'} + C_h\frac{Q'}{2}$$

$$= (16)\frac{100,000}{1414} + (0.8)\frac{1414}{2}$$

$$= 1131 + 566 = \$1697.$$

The change in the total relevant cost was $1697 - 1600 = \$97$, or only a 6.1 percent increase, despite an ordering cost 50 percent too low.

g) After determining the optimal order quantity of 2000 units, the company finds that the required annual production has been increased to 110,000 units.

1. What change is required in the order size?

$$Q^* = \sqrt{2RC_o/C_h} = \sqrt{(2)(110,000)(16)/(0.8)}$$

$$= \sqrt{4,400,000} = 2098 \text{ units}.$$

The order size should be increased by 98 units.

2. What is the new optimal total relevant cost?

$$C(Q^*) = C_hQ^* = (0.8)(2096) = \$1678.$$

3. What would the total relevant cost have been if Little Shaver had continued to use an order quantity of 2000 units?

2000 units would now be nonoptimal, again requiring the use of Equation (11.1), rather than the optimal lot size equation.

$$C(2000) = (16)\frac{110,000}{2000} + (0.8)\frac{2000}{2}$$

$$= 880 + 800 = \$1680.$$

Retaining an order size of 2000 units would cost only an additional 0.1 percent, even though the annual demand changed by 10 percent. Note that the annual number of orders would now be $110,000/2000 = 55$, instead of the 50 orders formerly required to provide 100,000 units annually.

Sensitivity Analysis   In previous chapters, sensitivity analysis has been discussed on several occasions. In the coverage of Bayesian decision models, including decision trees, we were interested in determining the range over which certain variables, such as subjective probabilities, could vary without changing the optimal decision. In linear programming models, which are deterministic, we investigated the sensitivity of the optimal solution to changes in certain of the problem values and also examined the range over which these values could change without changing the set of basic (nonzero) variables in the optimal solution. In both these models, their general complexity limited consideration to just one change at a time, and the changes examined generally resulted in linear effects over the range of analysis.

For the basic inventory models in this section, we will be interested primarily in exploring the effect of changes in certain variables and problem constraints on the total relevant cost, as in Example 11.1. We will find two significant differences from the earlier sensitivity analyses. First, changes in the problem variables will usually induce nonlinear, rather than linear, changes in the total relevant cost. Second, because of the relatively simple relationships between the variables in the optimal lot size formula, the effect of changing more than one variable at a time can be readily determined.

We will be particularly interested in answering questions such as the following.

1. How is the total relevant cost affected by departures from the optimal lot size?

   The optimal lot size calculated may not be achievable, because a certain minimum order quantity is stipulated by the supplier, or because the item must be ordered in units of 10. Also, the optimal time between orders may not be convenient to use because of administrative complications, thereby forcing a change from the optimal lot size. Thus, if the optimal time between orders turns out to be 23.5 days, then ordering once a month would probably be preferred, requiring a compensating increase in the lot size.

2. What is the effect on the decision variable, the lot size chosen, if an error is made in any of the model factors or if their values should change?

   In this type of inventory model, the determination of the optimal lot size is, as we have seen, dependent on the value of the demand per unit time, the ordering or setup cost, and the cost of holding inventory. We have implicitly assumed that these factors are all known with certainty, but in reality each one of them is usually an estimate.

The effect of changing the lot size on the total relevant cost will now be examined in some detail.

Sensitivity of Total Relevant Cost to Lot Size   In Equation (11.1), the total relevant cost $C(Q)$ is expressed as

$$C(Q) = \frac{C_o R}{Q} + \frac{C_h Q}{2},$$

the sum of the ordering and holding costs, respectively. At the optimal lot size $Q = Q^*$, let the value of $C(Q^*)$ be \$100. Since the ordering and holding costs are equal at $Q = Q^*$, $C_o R/Q^* = C_h Q^*/2 = \$50$. Now, suppose that a lot size Q' was chosen which was exactly double the optimal lot size, so $Q' = 2Q^*$. With half the optimal number of orders placed and twice the optimal lot size, the ordering cost would be halved and the holding cost doubled. The value of $C(Q')$ would be

$$C(Q') = C\left(\frac{Q^*}{2}\right) = \frac{50}{2} + (2)(50) = \$125.$$

Since $C(Q^*/2)/C(Q^*) = 125/100 = 1.25$, the total relevant cost would increase by only 25 percent if the lot size were double the optimal lot size. If the lot size Q' were half the optimal lot size, the cost increase would be the same, since the ordering cost would double, but the holding cost would be halved. For this case,

$$C(Q') = C(2Q^*) = (2)(50) + \frac{50}{2} = \$125.$$

In this example, for any lot size $Q' = kQ^*$, where k is any positive value,

$$C(Q') = C(kQ^*) = \frac{50}{k} + 50k = \$50\left(k + \frac{1}{k}\right),$$

and $C(Q')/C(Q^*) = 50(k + 1/k)/100 = (k + 1/k)/2$.

To generalize this relationship, given that $Q' = kQ^*$,

let $r(k)$ = ratio of total relevant cost with a lot size of Q' to the optimal total relevant cost.

$$r(k) = \frac{C(Q')}{C(Q^*)} = \frac{C(kQ^*)}{C(Q^*)} = \frac{k + 1/k}{2}. \tag{11.4}$$

When $Q' = Q^*$, $k = 1$, and $r(k)$ is of course 1.0, its minimum value. For any other value of k, $r(k)$ is greater than 1.0. Observe the *ratio symmetry* in $r(k)$, whereby the value of $r(k)$ is the same for a given value k and its reciprocal. Thus, if $k = 2$, $1/k = 0.5$, and $r(k)$ is 1.25; if $k = 0.5$, $1/k = 2$, and $r(k)$ is again 1.25.

Table 11.1   Sensitivity Analysis of the Optimal Lot Size Formula

	$k = \dfrac{Q'}{Q^*}$	$r(k) = \dfrac{C(Q')}{C(Q^*)} = \dfrac{k + 1/k}{2}$			
If k Is:	Percentage Change in Lot Size Is:	$k + 1/k$	$r(k)$		Percentage Increase in Total Relevant Cost
1.100 or 0.909	+ 10 or −9.1	2.009	1.0045		0.45
1.250 or 0.800	+ 25 or −20	2.050	1.025		2.5
1.500 or 0.667	+ 50 or −33.3	2.167	1.083		8.3
2.000 or 0.500	+ 100 or −50	2.500	1.250		25.0
2.500 or 0.400	+ 150 or −60	2.900	1.450		45.0
3.000 or 0.333	+ 200 or −66.7	3.333	1.667		66.7

In Table 11.1, $r(k)$ is tabulated for a few values of k, and it can be seen that the total relevant cost is quite insensitive to variations from the optimal lot size. Thus, for example, if Q' is 25 percent too high or 20 percent too low, the total relevant cost will increase only by 2.5 percent. If Q' is 100 percent too high or 50 percent too low, the total relevant cost still increases only by 25 percent. Since $r(k)$ is the same for any value k and for its reciprocal $1/k$, $r(k)$ will be symmetrical, with respect to $k = 1$, when plotted against k on a logarithmic scale, as shown in Figure 11.5. (A logarithmic scale is linear in terms of ratios. Thus, if you measured along the abscissa in Figure 11.5, you would find, for example, that k values of 0.25, 0.5, 1, 2, 4, and 8 are equally spaced.)

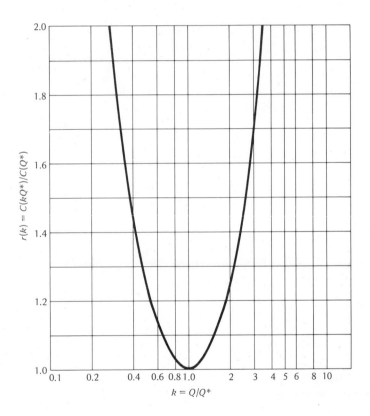

Figure 11.5

If the value of Q is limited to certain discrete values, as it often is, the ratio symmetry of $r(k)$ enables us to readily select the optimal value of Q. We calculate Q^* as though Q were continuous. Then, for the closest allowable values of Q on either side of Q^* (call them Q^- and Q^+), we choose the lower value if Q^*/Q^- is less than

Q^+/Q^*, and the upper value otherwise. (If these two ratios are equal, we will be indifferent.)

To illustrate, suppose $Q^* = 247$ units, but we can order units in quantities of only 100. Thus, our choice would be to order either 200 or 300 units. Then, $Q^- = 200$ and $Q^+ = 300$, so $Q^*/Q^- = 1.235$ and $Q^+/Q^* = 1.215$. We should order 300 units, rather than the 200 units we would have ordered had we rounded to the nearest allowable order quantity. The cost penalty, because of being unable to order Q^*, will be only 1.9 percent. You should check this number to make sure you know where it comes from.

Knowing the direct effect on total relevant cost of a change from the optimal lot size, we can now determine the effect of a change in the time between orders. Since t^*, the optimal time between orders, is equal to Q^*/R (the reciprocal of the number of orders per unit time), a change in the time between orders to a value t' will require a commensurate change in the lot size to a value Q' such that

$$\frac{t'}{t^*} = \frac{Q'}{Q^*} = k.$$

Thus, if $t^* = 23.5$ days, and an order is instead placed once a month, so that $t' = 365/12 = 30.4$ days,

$$k = \frac{30.4}{23.5} = 1.29$$

$$r(k) = \frac{1.29 + 1/1.29}{2} = 1.033.$$

Only a 3.3 percent increase in the total relevant cost results from a 29 percent increase in the time between orders.

Sensitivity of Lot Size to Model Factors. In order to determine the sensitivity of the total relevant cost to possible errors or changes, as discussed earlier, it is instructive to evaluate the effect of such errors or changes on the decision variable, the actual lot size chosen. Then, for any change from the optimal lot size, the increase in the total relevant cost can be expressed as a function of the ratio of the actual lot size to the optimal lot size.

Consider now the sensitivity analysis of the factors directly involved in the determination of the optimal lot size, namely, R, demand per unit time, C_o, order or setup cost, and C_h, holding cost per unit time.

Let $R' =$ estimated value of R,
$C_o' =$ estimated value of C_o,
$C_h' =$ estimated value of C_h,
$Q' =$ lot size calculated from the optimal lot size formula.

Using the optimal lot size formula, the lot size calculated from these values will be

$$Q' = \sqrt{\frac{2R'C_o'}{C_h'}}.$$

Now, let $k = Q'/Q^*$, as before.

Since

$$Q^* = \sqrt{\frac{2RC_o}{C_h}}$$

then

$$k = \sqrt{\left(\frac{R'}{R}\right)\left(\frac{C_o'}{C_o}\right)\Big/\left(\frac{C_h'}{C_h}\right)} \qquad \textbf{(11.5)}$$

The factor k (which permits us to express Q' as kQ^*, in which form it is most convenient for determining the change in total relevant cost) can then be evaluated, given the ratios R'/R, C_o'/C_o, and C_h'/C_h.

Because of the square root factor in Equation (11.5), the calculated lot size value $Q' = kQ^*$ is relatively insensitive to changes in the values of R, C_o, and C_h. Thus, if the actual ordering cost C_o turns out to be 56.2 percent greater than the estimated ordering cost C_o', so that $C_o'/C_o = 1/1.562 = 0.64$, the value of k will be 0.80, and the actual lot size Q' represents only a 20 percent decrease from the optimal lot size Q^*. Furthermore, as we have seen, the total relevant cost will increase only 2.5 percent for a 20 percent decrease from the optimal lot size!

To show the power of the sensitivity analysis approach, we will, for comparative purposes, work with Example 11.1, without recalculating the optimal solution.

EXAMPLE 11.2

The Little Shaver Company purchases the motors for its Model 777 electric shavers from an outside vendor. During the coming year, the company wishes to manufacture, at essentially a constant rate, 100,000 units of the Model 777. The cost of placing each order for the motors is $16. For any item in inventory, Little Shaver uses an annual holding cost equal to 20 percent of the item's cost. The motors cost $4 each.

From the problem statement,

$$C_o = \$16, \; C_h = \$0.8/\text{yr}, \; R = 100,000 \text{ units/yr}.$$

As worked out in Example 11.1,

$$Q^* = 2000 \text{ units}, \; C(Q^*) = \$1600,$$

and the optimal number of orders per year is 50.

a) If Little Shaver decided to order the motors only twice a month, how much of a cost penalty would it suffer, in percent?

Since $Q' = 100,000/24 = 4167$ units, and $Q^* = 2000$ units, $k = Q'/Q^* = 2.08$. From Equation (11.4),

$$r(k) = \frac{C(Q')}{C(Q^*)} = \frac{k + 1/k}{2} = \frac{2.08 + 0.48}{2} = 1.28.$$

As in Example 11.1e, the cost increase will be 28 percent. The sensitivity analysis approach is easier than the calculations using the basic formula for total relevant cost.

b) Suppose an ordering cost of only $8 had been used instead of the correct value of $16.

1. What would the order size have been?

The factor k, from Equation (11.5), is expressed as

$$k = \sqrt{\left(\frac{R'}{R}\right)\left(\frac{C_o'}{C_o}\right)\Big/\left(\frac{C_h'}{C_h}\right)}$$

Since neither the demand nor the holding cost is affected, the ratio C_o'/C_o is in the proportion of 8 to 16, or 0.5. Therefore, $k = \sqrt{(1)(0.5)} = 0.707$. Then,

$$Q' = kQ^* = (0.707)(2000) = 1414 \text{ units.}$$

2. How would the total relevant cost have changed?

Since $k = 0.707$,

$$r(k) = \frac{k + 1/k}{2} = \frac{2.121}{2} = 1.061$$

$$C(Q') = (1.061)(1600) = \$1697,$$

an increase of $97, or 6.1 percent.

These answers check with those of Example 11.1f.

c) After determining the optimal order quantity of 2000 units, the company finds that the required annual production has been increased to 110,000 units.

1. What change is required in the order size?

The value of 2000 units is no longer Q^*, but now becomes Q'. The former R value of 100,000 units is now R', and R is 110,000 units. Therefore,

$$k = \sqrt{\left(\frac{R'}{R}\right)\left(\frac{C_o'}{C_o}\right)\Big/\left(\frac{C_h'}{C_h}\right)} = \sqrt{\frac{100,000}{110,000}(1.0)}$$

$$= \sqrt{0.909} = 0.9535$$

$$Q^* = \frac{Q'}{k} = \frac{2000}{0.9535} = 2098 \text{ units/order,}$$

an increase of 8 units per order.

2. What would the total relevant cost have been if Little Shaver had continued to use an order quantity of 2000 units?

For a Q' value of 2000, $k = 0.9535$, as we just determined. We then calculate $r(k)$.

$$r(k) = \frac{0.9535 + 1/0.9535}{2} = \frac{2.0022}{2} = 1.0011,$$

$$C(Q') = r(k)C(Q^*) = r(k)C_h Q^* = (1.0011)(0.8)(2098) = \$1680.$$

The answers in Example 11.1g are the same as these answers.

Uniform Replenishment

Up to this point, we have been considering the case where the entire order was received just as we ran out of stock. In a production situation, however, the production run may take a significant time to complete, so that we have an inventory history such as that shown in Figure 11.6. We will assume that production is at a uniform rate for t_1 time units during each period between the start of production runs.

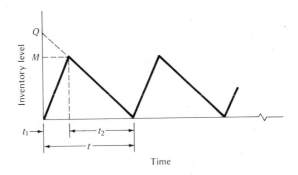

Figure 11.6

Recalling that R is the number of units required per unit time,

let R' = maximum production possible per unit time, $(R' > R)$
  M = maximum inventory level,
  Q = production quantity per period.

The fraction of time production is actually required will be R/R'. From Figure 11.6, the ratio t_2/t represents the fraction of time there is no production, namely, $1 - R/R'$. From elementary trigonometric relationships (similar triangles), $M/t_2 = Q/t$, so $M/Q = t_2/t = 1 - R/R'$. Now, for convenience,

let $v = 1 - R/R'$.

Then, $$M = Qv,$$

and,
$$\text{Average inventory} = M/2 = Qv/2$$
$$\text{Holding cost} = C_h Qv/2$$
$$\text{Ordering cost} = C_o R/Q$$
$$\text{Total relevant cost, } C(Q) = C_o R/Q + C_h Qv/2.$$

Clearly, the equation for $C(Q)$ is of precisely the same form as for the case of instantaneous replenishment, given in Equation (11.1). The only difference is the factor v which is a constant, independent of Q. The solution is then

$$Q^* = \sqrt{2RC_o/C_h v} \tag{11.6}$$
$$C(Q^*) = \sqrt{2RC_o C_h v} = C_h v Q^* \tag{11.7}$$
$$t^* = \sqrt{2C_o/(RC_h v)}. \tag{11.8}$$

When $R' \to \infty$, so that $v \to 1$, these equations, of course, are identical to those for the instantaneous replenishment case.

Optimal Lot Size Model When Shortages Are Allowed

Demand is again assumed to be known and steady, lead time is zero, and replenishment is instantaneous. Now, however, shortages are allowed, and the cost of a shortage is assumed to be directly proportional to the mean number of units short. In addition to the notation used previously,

let C_s = cost per unit short per unit time,
   M = maximum inventory on hand.

The change in inventory level over time will then be as shown in Figure 11.7.

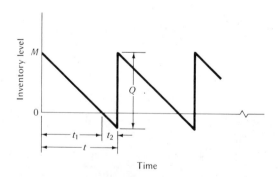

Figure 11.7

From an analysis of Figure 11.7:

Fraction of time no shortages exists = $t_1/t = M/Q$ (by similar triangles)
Average inventory when no shortage exists = $M/2$

Average inventory over time $= (M/Q)(M/2) = M^2/2Q$
Maximum shortage $= Q - M$
Fraction of time shortage exists $= t_2/t = (Q - M)/Q$
Average shortage when short $= (Q - M)/2$
Average shortage over time $= [(Q - M)/Q][(Q - M)/2] = (Q - M)^2/2Q$
Ordering cost $= C_o(R/Q)$
Holding cost $= C_h(M^2/2Q)$
Shortage cost $= C_s[(Q - M)^2/2Q]$.

The total relevant cost $C(Q, M)$ is the sum of these three costs:

$$C(Q, M) = \frac{C_oR}{Q} + \frac{C_hM^2}{2Q} + \frac{C_s(Q - M)^2}{2Q}. \tag{11.9}$$

In order to solve for $C(Q^*, M^*)$, the minimum value of $C(Q, M)$, we must solve for both Q^* and M^*. The procedure is generally similar to that shown in Appendix 11A but is more involved (although not difficult), since Q and M must be optimized simultaneously. Using the calculus, the process involves partial differentiation and the solution of two simultaneous equations.

To simplify the form of the results:

Let $w = C_s/(C_h + C_s)$.

The formulas are

$$Q^* = \sqrt{2RC_o/(C_hw)} \tag{11.10}$$
$$M^* = wQ^* = \sqrt{2RC_ow/C_h} \quad \left.\right\}\text{Instantaneous replenishment} \tag{11.11}$$
$$C(Q^*, M^*) = \sqrt{2RC_oC_hw} = C_hwQ^* \tag{11.12}$$

When the optimal lot size is used, the cost components become:

$$\text{Ordering cost} = C_o\frac{R}{Q^*} = \frac{C_oR}{\sqrt{2RC_o/(C_hw)}} = \frac{\sqrt{2RC_oC_hw}}{2}$$

$$= \frac{C(Q^*, M^*)}{2} \tag{11.13}$$

$$\text{Holding cost} = C_h\frac{(M^*)^2}{2Q^*} = \frac{C_h(2RC_ow/C_h)}{2\sqrt{2RC_o/(C_hw)}}$$

$$= \frac{w\sqrt{2RC_oC_hw}}{2} = \frac{wC(Q^*, M^*)}{2} \tag{11.14}$$

$$\text{Shortage cost} = C_s\frac{(Q^* - M^*)^2}{2Q^*}$$

$$= C(Q^*, M^*) - \text{ordering cost} - \text{holding cost}$$
$$= \frac{(1 - w)C(Q^*, M^*)}{2} \tag{11.15}$$

Thus, the ordering cost equals the sum of the holding and shortage costs.

If replenishment occurs at a uniform rate, rather than instantaneously, the only change is the introduction of the factor $v(= 1 - R/R')$, as in the previous section. For this case, the basic formulas become

$$Q^* = \sqrt{2RC_o/(C_h wv)}$$

$$M^* = wvQ^* = \sqrt{2RC_o wv/C_h}$$

$$C(Q^*, M^*) = \sqrt{2RC_o C_h wv} = C_h wvQ^*$$

$\left.\vphantom{\begin{array}{c}a\\b\\c\end{array}}\right\}$ Uniform replenishment

(11.16)
(11.17)
(11.18)

It can be shown that, at the optimal solution point, the factor v has no effect on the relationship between the cost components, so that Equations (11.13) to (11.15) are again applicable. Furthermore, if the shortage cost C_s is infinite, so that $w = 1$, all formulas involving w reduce to the comparable expressions developed earlier for the no-shortage case.

When a shortage is allowed, you should verify that the optimal lot size increases and the maximum inventory on hand and the total relevant cost both decrease, as compared to the no-shortage case.

EXAMPLE 11.3

Each unit of the Model 777 electric shaver of the Little Shaver Company requires an on-off switch, which is manufactured at the company's plant. In the coming year 100,000 units of the Model 777 are to be produced, at a constant rate. For each production run of the switch, there is a $40 setup cost. The switch production capacity would be 200,000 per year, if switches were being produced on a continuous basis. The annual holding cost per unit is considered to be 20 percent of the item cost, which, for this switch, is $0.25. If a shortage of switches should occur at any time, the annual cost per unit short is estimated as $0.20.

a)   What is the optimal lot size and the associated total relevant inventory cost?

Given the problem data,

$$R = 100,000, \ R' = 200,000,$$
$$C_o = \$40, \ C_h = (0.20)(0.25) = \$0.05, \ C_s = \$0.20.$$

Then,

$$\text{Uniform replenishment factor } v = 1 - \frac{R}{R'} = 1 - \frac{100,000}{200,000} = 0.5$$

$$\text{Shortage factor } w = \frac{C_s}{C_h + C_s} = \frac{0.20}{0.05 + 0.20} = 0.8.$$

Therefore, from Equations (11.16) and (11.18):

$$Q^* = \sqrt{\frac{2RC_o}{C_h wv}} = \sqrt{\frac{(2)(100,000)(40)}{(0.05)(0.8)(0.5)}} = \sqrt{400,000,000} = 20,000$$

$$C(Q^*, M^*) = C_h wvQ^* = (0.05)(0.8)(0.5)(20,000) = \$400/\text{yr}.$$

b) What is the maximum inventory level if the optimal lot size is used?

From Equation (11.17),

$$M^* = wvQ^* = (0.8)(0.5)(20,000) = 8000.$$

c) What are the setup, holding, and shortage costs associated with the optimal inventory policy?

From Equations (11.13) to (11.15):

$$\text{Setup cost} = \frac{C(Q^*, M^*)}{2} = \frac{400}{2} = \$200/\text{yr}$$

$$\text{Holding cost} = \frac{wC(Q^*, M^*)}{2} = \frac{(0.8)(400)}{2} = \$160/\text{yr}$$

$$\text{Shortage cost} = \frac{(1-w)C(Q^*, M^*)}{2} = \frac{(0.2)(400)}{2} = \$40/\text{yr}.$$

d) If the switches could be purchased on the outside, so that replenishment could be assumed to be instantaneous, what would the ordering cost have to be in order to have the same total relevant inventory cost as that previously calculated?

With a shortage allowed, we have, according to Equation (11.12),

$$C(Q^*, M^*) = \sqrt{2RC_oC_hw}$$

$$= \sqrt{(2)(100,000)C_o(0.05)(0.8)} = 400$$

$$C_o = \frac{(400)^2}{8000} = \$20 \text{ per order.}$$

Since the production factor v, with a value of 0.5, is not in this $C(Q^*, M^*)$ equation, for the value of C_o, originally \$40, would have to be halved to give the same value for $C(Q^*, M^*)$.

If the shortage cost is not known, but it is decided to order a quantity greater than the optimal lot size when no shortage is allowed, then the implied shortage cost can be readily calculated.

Let Q_0^* = optimal lot size when shortage is allowed,
Q^* = lot size assumed to be optimal with unknown shortage cost.

For either uniform or instantaneous replenishment,

$$\frac{Q^*}{Q_0^*} = \sqrt{\frac{1}{w}} = \sqrt{\frac{C_h + C_s}{C_s}}.$$

We can now square both sides and solve for the unknown C_s value:

$$C_s = C_h \frac{(Q_0^*)^2}{(Q^*)^2 - (Q_0^*)^2} = \frac{C_h}{(Q^*/Q_0^*)^2 - 1}.$$

In Example 11.1, for the case of instantaneous replenishment, suppose that the shortage cost was not known, but a decision had been made to order 3000 units each time. Then, since the "no-shortage" optimal lot size was 2000 units and the annual holding cost was $0.8, the implied shortage cost is

$$C_s = \frac{0.8}{(3000/2000)^2 - 1} = \frac{0.8}{1.25} = \$0.64 \text{ per unit per yr.}$$

A considered judgment can then be made whether this is a reasonable value for the shortage cost. If not, the lot size should be modified accordingly.

Price Breaks

In many commercial and industrial situations, the seller or producer of an item offers a lower unit price if the item is ordered in larger quantities. A price break occurs at the point where the unit price drops, and a given item may have several price breaks. The optimal lot size will be that which minimizes the *total* cost of *purchasing*, ordering, and holding the item.

In regard to the holding cost, we have noted in the earlier example problems that it is generally expressed as a fraction of the unit cost of the item. This fraction represents the cost of money and is frequently chosen to be the estimated internal rate of return for the company or the interest rate at which the company could make investments of comparable risk. Then, $C_h = C_i I$, where

$$C_i = \text{unit cost of the item,}$$
$$I = \text{estimated cost of money per unit time.}$$

Typical values of I are in the range of 15 to 30 percent per year.

In the determination of the optimal lot size when there are multiple price breaks, it is useful to visualize the total cost curve for each different unit price. Figure 11.8 shows representative total cost curves for three different unit prices. The solid lines show the regions where the individual curves apply. The notation will be discussed in ensuing paragraphs.

In particular, Figure 11.8 is intended to bring out two important factors:

1. The curve for a given unit price is, at every lot size value, always below that for a higher unit price. This is so because the purchasing and holding costs are lower, while the ordering cost is the same.
2. As the unit price decreases, the minimum of each curve shifts to the right. This occurs because, in the formula for Q^*, the only factor that is changing is the holding cost, and Q^* is inversely proportional to the square root of the holding cost.

There are three possible relationships for the lot size range over which a given unit price applies. Figure 11.8 has been "doctored" specifically to illustrate all three relationships. In the upper curve, the price break occurs before the minimum cost point is reached. In the middle curve, the applicable range includes the minimum cost point. In the bottom curve, the minimum cost point occurs at a lot size below the lower limit for that unit price and is therefore not feasible.

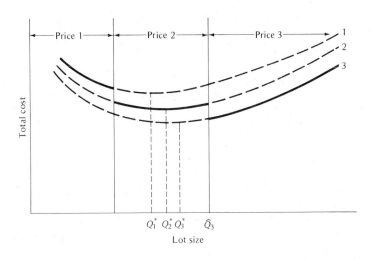

Figure 11.8

Let us now show a logical procedure for calculating the optimal lot size when there are multiple price breaks.

Let R = units required (demand) per unit time

C_j = jth unit price,

$\hat{Q}_j$ = minimum lot size for which unit price C_j applies,

Q_j^* = "unrestricted" optimal lot size for unit price C_j, *disregarding* the range of lot sizes over which C_j applies (in other words, Q_j^* may not be *feasible*),

$C(Q_j)$ = cost of ordering, holding, and shortage for any lot size Q_j,

$T(Q_j)$ = total inventory cost (purchasing, ordering, holding, and shortage) for any lot size Q_j,

$= RC_j + C(Q_j)$,

Q^* = optimal lot size associated with the lowest total inventory cost.

The procedure can be most succinctly stated in the form of an algorithm.

1. Starting with the *lowest* unit price, find the first unit price C_j for which the "unrestricted" optimal lot size Q_j^* is feasible. Calculate the total inventory cost for that lot size. Note that no *higher* unit price could possibly yield a lower total inventory cost. If the optimal lot size for the lowest unit price is feasible, stop. This is the optimal solution.

2. Now, working down from unit price C_j, for each lower unit price, in turn, calculate the total inventory cost at the minimum lot size for which that unit

price applies. To calculate the $C(\hat{Q}_j)$ value for unit price C_j, use the sensitivity analysis formula for $r(k)$ in Equation (11.4), with Q' replaced by $\hat{Q}_j$ and Q^* by Q_j^*. Then, $C(\hat{Q}_j) = r(k)C(Q_j^*)$, where Q_j^* will already have been calculated in step 1. $T(\hat{Q}_j) = RC_j + C(\hat{Q}_j)$.

The optimal lot size Q^* will be that associated with the lowest total inventory cost calculated in steps 1 and 2.

Relating the algorithm to Figure 11.8, C_2 is the lowest unit price for which the unrestricted lot size is feasible. We then compare $T(Q_2)$ with $T(\hat{Q}_3)$, since $\hat{Q}_3$ is the minimum lot size for which the next lower unit price C_3 is feasible. Since $T(\hat{Q}_3) < T(Q_2)$, $\hat{Q}_3$ is the optimal lot size.

EXAMPLE 11.4

The Minny Computer Company purchases a component for which it has a steady usage of 1000 units per year. The ordering cost is \$10 per order, and the estimated cost of money invested in inventory is 25 percent per year. The unit cost for this component is \$8 for orders up to 149 units, \$7.80 for orders from 150 to 499 units, and \$7.60 for orders of 500 units or more. What is the optimal lot size to order if no shortage is allowed?

From the information supplied, $R = 1000$ units/yr, $C_o = \$10$, and $I = 0.25$, since the time unit is years. $C_1 = \$8$, with $\hat{Q}_1 = 1$; $C_2 = \$7.80$, with $\hat{Q}_2 = 150$; and $C_3 = \$760$, with $\hat{Q}_3 = 500$. We can now apply the algorithm.

1. The lowest unit price is $C_3 = \$7.60$.
    $$C_h = C_3 I = (7.60)(0.25) = \$1.90.$$
    $$Q_3^* = \sqrt{2RC_o/C_h} = \sqrt{(2)(1000)(10)/1.90} = 102.6.$$
    Since $\hat{Q}_3 = 500$, Q_3^* is not feasible.

    The next higher unit price is $C_2 = \$7.80$.
    $$C_h = C_2 I = (7.80)(0.25) = \$1.95.$$
    $$Q_2^* = \sqrt{(2)(1000)(10)/1.95} = 101.3.$$
    Since $\hat{Q}_2 = 150$, Q_2^* is not feasible.

    The next higher unit price is $C_1 = \$8$.
    $$C_h = C_1 I = (8)(0.25) = \$2.$$
    $$Q_1^* = \sqrt{(2)(1000)(10)/2} = 100, \text{ which is feasible.}$$
    $$C(Q_1^*) = C_h Q_1^* = (2)(100) = \$200.$$
    $$T(Q_1^*) = RC_1 + C(Q_1^*) = (1000)(8) + 200 = \$8200.$$

2. Now, working down in unit price from C_1, $C_2 = \$7.80$.
    $$\text{For } \hat{Q}_2 = 150, k = \hat{Q}_2/Q_2^* = 150/101.3 = 1.481.$$
    $$r(k) = (1.481 + 1/1.481)/2 = 1.078.$$
    $$C(\hat{Q}_2) = r(k)C_h Q_2^* = (1.078)(1.95)(101.3) = \$213.$$
    $$T(\hat{Q}_2) = RC_2 + C(\hat{Q}_2) = (1000)(7.80) + 213 = \$8013.$$

The next lower unit price is $C_3 = \$7.60$.

$$\text{For } \hat{Q}_3 = 500, k = \hat{Q}_3/Q_3{}^* = 500/102.6 = 4.873.$$
$$r(k) = (4.873 + 1/4.873)/2 = 2.539.$$
$$C(\hat{Q}_3) = r(k)C_hQ_3{}^* = (2.539)(1.90)(102.6) = \$495.$$
$$T(\hat{Q}_3) = RC_3 + C(\hat{Q}_3) = (1000)(7.60) + 495 = \$8095.$$

The lowest total inventory cost is $T(\hat{Q}_2) = \$8013$. $Q^* = \hat{Q}_2 = 150$ units.

Observe that the \$200 saving in purchase cost at a unit price of \$7.80 more than offsets the slight increase of \$13 in ordering and holding costs, but the substantial increase in these costs at the next price break of \$7.60 more than nullifies the additional \$200 saving in purchase cost.

Multiperiod Model with Changing Demand

In the optimal lot size models just studied, we assumed that demand was steady during some indefinite time interval. Furthermore, we implicitly assumed a continuous review inventory policy, so that we would always schedule a replenishment order (or, perhaps, start a new production run) at the exact time when the inventory level reached some predetermined value. Such models, in which the demand is assumed to be constant, are called static inventory models. Now, however, we will consider the situation where the demand is still deterministic but changes from period to period. We will assume that there is a periodic review inventory policy, such that the inventory level is measured only at the beginning of each time period (the end of the preceding time period). Only a finite number of such time periods will be considered. A model of this nature is called a dynamic inventory model. The manpower scheduling problem, Example 10.3, was of this general type, with the inventory not goods but manpower.

Suppose we have a situation where an item is ordered once each time period to supply a known demand which changes from period to period. Units of this item are carried in inventory. There is an ordering cost for the item and a holding cost associated with each unit which is carried over from one period to the next.

Let n_i = number of units ordered for delivery at the beginning of period i,
   $C(n_i)$ = total cost, including ordering cost, for a supply of n_i units,
   N_i = number of units on hand at the end of period i,
   C_h = cost of holding a unit from one period to the next,
   d_i = number of units demanded during period i,
   M = total number of time periods.

We assume that no shortage is allowed in any period and that after M periods we wish to end up with zero inventory. Then, to minimize total cost,

$$\text{minimize } \sum_{i=1}^{M} \left[C(n_i) + C_h N_i \right]$$

subject to
$$N_i \geqslant 0 \text{ for all } i < M$$
$$N_M = 0$$
and
$$n_i = 0, 1, 2, \ldots \text{ for all } i.$$

We must determine the optimal sequence of order quantities n_i such that total cost is minimized. This is a multistage decision process amenable to a dynamic programming approach.

To solve this problem by dynamic programming, each stage will represent a time period. For convenience in comparing the results with a subsequent analysis, we will use a forward recursion, although a backward recursion could have been performed just as readily.

We start by numbering the stages the same as the periods, so that stage i represents period i. At stage i, the state will be the units of inventory carried over from the previous period, or N_{i-1}. The decision is the units to be ordered in period i, or n_i. The state transformation function is $N_i = N_{i-1} + n_i - d_i$, so that the required inverse transformation function for forward recursion is

$$N_{i-1} = N_i - n_i + d_i.$$

With N_i units in inventory at the end of period i, the minimal cost is determined by the value of n_i which minimizes the sum of the ordering cost for n_i units, the holding cost for N_i units, and the cost from the optimal solution for $N_i - n_i + d_i$ units in inventory at the end of the previous period. The optimal return function is then

$$f_i(N_i) = \min_{0 \leqslant n_i \leqslant N_i + d_i} \left[C(n_i) + C_h N_i + f_{i-1}(N_i - n_i + d_i) \right] \qquad 1 < i \leqslant M.$$

At stage 1 (period 1),

$$f_1(N_1) = C(n_1) + C_h N_1 \qquad \text{where} \qquad n_1 = N_1 + d_1 - N_0$$

and N_0 is the initial inventory on hand.

EXAMPLE 11.5

The Trific Tractor Company is ending production of its Model 29 tractor. In the next three months, it is scheduled to deliver 3, 2, and 4 units, respectively. For a certain part, which is needed at the beginning of each month, each unit costs $3 and there is a $10 cost for each order placed. This part requires special handling while in inventory, so that its holding cost of $2 for each part carried over from one month to the next is very high compared to the cost of the part. None of these parts are currently on hand, and none are desired to be on hand at the end of the three-month period. Trific wants to determine the optimal sequence of order quantities for this period.

From the problem statement,

$$C_h = 2, M = 3 \quad \text{and} \quad \begin{array}{ll} C(n_i) = 10 + 3n_i & n_i > 0 \\ = 0 & n_i = 0 \end{array}$$

$$d_1 = 3, d_2 = 2, d_3 = 4.$$

The state at stage 1 (period 1), which is the inventory N_1 at the end of period 1, cannot exceed 6, the total number of units required in the remaining periods, since the ending inventory must be zero. The stage 1 calculations are shown in Table 11.2. These calculations are minimized because there is a single value, in this case zero, for the inventory at the end of the previous period. It seems somewhat unnatural to obtain a value of the input state, $N_1 + d_1 - n_1$, as a function of the output state N_1, but this is typical of dynamic programming models solved by forward recursion.

Table 11.2   Stage 1 (Period 1)

	Demand $d_1 = 3$ Units, Initial Inventory $N_0 = 0$	
Inventory at End of Period N_1	Units Ordered $(N_1 + d_1 - N_0)$ n_1	Total Cost (\$) (= Immediate Cost) $C(n_1) + C_h N_1$
0	3	$19 + 0 = 19 = f_1(0)$
1	4	$22 + 2 = 24 = f_1(1)$
2	5	$25 + 4 = 29 = f_1(2)$
3	6	$28 + 6 = 34 = f_1(3)$
4	7	$31 + 8 = 39 = f_1(4)$
5	8	$34 + 10 = 44 = f_1(5)$
6	9	$37 + 12 = 49 = f_1(6)$

At stage 2 (period 2), the ending inventory N_2 can be between 0 and 4 units, the demand in the one remaining period. For each value of N_2, the units ordered n_2 can range from $N_2 + d_2$ down to zero. The calculations for stage 2 are shown in Table 11.3.

Since the inventory at the end of period 3 must be zero, there is a single state at stage 3. With a maximum beginning inventory of 4 units, the order size n_3 can range from 0 to 4 units, as shown in Table 11.4.

The optimal solution can now be found by working backward through the computations for each stage. The optimal solution at period 3 is to order 4 units, so that the inventory at the end of the previous period must be equal to zero. Then, going back to the period 2 calculations, with an ending inventory of zero, the optimal total

Table 11.3 Stage 2 (Period 2)

		Demand d_2 = 2 Units			
Inventory at End of Period N_2	Units Ordered n_2	Inventory at End of Previous Period $N_2 + d_2 - n_2$	Immediate Cost (\$) $C(n_2) + C_h N_2$	Optimal Cost from Previous Period (\$) $f_1(N_2 + d_2 - n_2)$	Total Cost (\$)
0	2	0	$16 + 0 = 16$	19	35
	1	1	$13 + 0 = 13$	24	37
	0	2	$0 + 0 = 0$	29	$29 = f_2(0)$
1	3	0	$19 + 2 = 21$	19	40
	2	1	$16 + 2 = 18$	24	42
	1	2	$13 + 2 = 15$	29	44
	0	3	$0 + 2 = 2$	34	$36 = f_2(1)$
2	4	0	$22 + 4 = 26$	19	45
	3	1	$19 + 4 = 23$	24	47
	2	2	$16 + 4 = 20$	29	49
	1	3	$13 + 4 = 17$	34	51
	0	4	$0 + 4 = 4$	39	$43 = f_2(2)$
3	5	0	$25 + 6 = 31$	19	$50 = f_2(3)$
	4	1	$22 + 6 = 28$	24	52
	3	2	$19 + 6 = 25$	29	54
	2	3	$16 + 6 = 22$	34	56
	1	4	$13 + 6 = 19$	39	58
	0	5	$0 + 6 = 6$	44	$50 = f_2(3)$
4	6	0	$28 + 8 = 36$	19	$55 = f_2(4)$
	5	1	$25 + 8 = 33$	24	57
	4	2	$22 + 8 = 30$	29	59
	3	3	$19 + 8 = 27$	34	61
	2	4	$16 + 8 = 24$	39	63
	1	5	$13 + 8 = 21$	44	65
	0	6	$0 + 8 = 8$	49	57

Table 11.4 Stage 3 (Period 3)

		Demand d_3 = 4 Units			
Inventory at End of Period N_3	Units Ordered n_3	Inventory at End of Previous Period $N_3 + d_3 - n_3$	Immediate Cost (\$) $C(n_3) + C_h N_3$	Optimal Cost from Previous Period (\$) $f_2(N_3 + d_3 - n_3)$	Total Cost (\$)
0	4	0	$22 + 0 = 22$	29	$51 = f_3(0)$
	3	1	$19 + 0 = 19$	36	55
	2	2	$16 + 0 = 16$	43	59
	1	3	$13 + 0 = 13$	50	63
	0	4	$0 + 0 = 0$	55	55

cost $f_2(0)$ is achieved by ordering zero units, requiring an inventory of 2 units at the end of the previous period. Finally, at period 1, since the ending inventory is 2 units, the solution for $f_1(2)$ dictates an order of 5 units in period 1. The optimal solution is then

Period	Units Ordered
1	5
2	0
3	4

The minimum achievable cost is $51, from Table 11.4.

If the cost function $C(n_i)$ can be of any form, problems of this general nature can be solved by the ordinary methods of dynamic programming, as illustrated in Example 11.5. However, when the per unit holding cost is constant and the ordering cost is a linear function, this problem becomes what has been called a Wagner-Whitin inventory model. We can take advantage of the particular structure of this model to greatly simplify the calculations, since it can be shown that:

1. Provided that the starting inventory N_0 is zero, it can never be optimal both to order in period i and to carry over inventory into period i.
2. If an order is placed in period i, the quantity ordered can be optimal only if it is exactly equal to the demand in period i or to the demand in period i plus the demand in one or more successive periods.

If an order were required in period i, but inventory units were being carried over from the previous period, then it would have been less costly if those units had been added to the order in period i, since their ordering cost would be the same and their holding cost would be avoided. Thus, the first condition must be met. The second condition follows directly from the first condition. The requirement for a starting inventory of zero is readily met by using up any starting inventory as soon as possible and readjusting the demand for the first period when the starting inventory is used up. For example, if 10 and 12 units are demanded in the first two periods, and the starting inventory is 15 units, we would then start the calculations in period 2 with a starting inventory of zero and a demand of $10 + 12 - 15 = 7$ units.

Since the Wagner-Whitin model applies to the Trific Tractor example, we could have considered far fewer alternatives in that example. Thus, in the stage 1 computations shown in Table 11.2, the only values of N_1 which could possibly be optimal would be 0, 2 (the demand in period 2), or 6 (the sum of the demands in periods 2 and 3). Similarly, in Table 11.3, only N_2 values of 0 and 4 need have been considered. Also, for each N_2 value, the number of units ordered, n_2, could assume only the value zero or a value such that the value of the previous period's ending inventory was zero, according to the first condition stated earlier. Thus, for $N_2 = 0$, n_2 could have values only of 2 and 0, while for $N_2 = 4$, the possible values of n_2 would be 6 and 0. In Table 11.4, only n_3 values of 4 and 0 would have been of interest.

Although it is now apparent that the computations in the previous example could have been reduced considerably, knowledge that it was a Wagner-Whitin model allows us to formulate the solution from a somewhat different viewpoint, one which yields additional insights.

If we start with zero inventory, the demand d_1 in period 1 can be met by ordering only d_1 units in period 1. Considering period 2, d_2 units can be ordered in period 2 or added to the order in period 1. In general, the demand d_i in any period i can be supplied either in that period or in an earlier period, but it is unnecessary to go back beyond the most recent period in which an order turned out to be optimal. Any order placed at an earlier period would require inventory to be carried over into a period when an order would be placed, and such a solution could not be optimal.

The procedure involves the calculation of several candidate total costs. We calculate the total cost of ordering d_i units in period i and the cost of the optimal solution for periods 1 through $i - 1$. Then, we calculate the total cost of adding d_i units to the order, if any, in period $i - 1$ plus the cost of the optimal solution for periods 1 through $i - 2$, and so on, stopping after evaluating a period in which an order was placed. The optimal solution for the first i periods is that which gives the minimum total cost.

This procedure is best illustrated with an example, so, for comparative purposes, let us take again the data from the Trific Tractor Company example. In addition, to show how straightforward additional computations are, suppose we add demands of 8, 4, and 7 in monthly periods 4, 5, and 6, respectively. The results are shown in Table 11.5.

In period 1, the demand of 3 units can be satisfied only by ordering 3 units in that period, so that the total cost of $19 is optimal for period 1 considered by itself. When the demand of 2 units in period 2 is added, this additional demand could be supplied by increasing the order in period 1 to 5 units, at a total cost of $29, including the holding cost. Alternatively, an order could be placed in period 2 for 2 units, at a cost of $16. Adding the optimal cost of $19 from period 1, the total cost would be $35. Considering only periods 1 and 2, the optimal policy is then to order all 5 units in period 1, at a total cost of $29.

Three cases must now be evaluated for the demand of 4 units in period 3. We could order 9 units in period 1 to cover the demand for all three periods, incurring an ordering cost of $37 and a holding cost of $20, with 6 units held over from period 1 to 2 and 4 units held from period 2 to 3, for a total cost of $57. Or, in period 2, an order could be placed for 6 units, covering the demand for periods 2 and 3, and then the optimal solution for period 1 only would be added, at a total cost of $55. The third possibility would be to order the 4 units in period 3, at a cost of $22, and then employ the optimal solution for the first two periods, costing $29, resulting in a total cost of

Table 11.5 Analysis Using Wagner-Whitin Model

Period i	Demand d_i	Place Order in Period	Units Ordered n_i	Ordering Cost, $ $C(n_i)$	Holding Costs for This Order ($)	Optimal Cost ($) for Periods Prior to Order	Total Cost ($)
1	3	1	3	19	0	—	$19 = f_1$
2	2	1	5	25	$(2)(2) = 4$	—	$29 = f_2$
		2	2	16	0	19	35
3	4	1	9	37	$(6)(2) + (4)(2) = 20$	—	57
		2	6	28	$(4)(2) = 8$	19	55
		3	4	22	0	29	$51 = f_3$
4	8	3	12	46	$(8)(2) = 16$	29	91
		4	8	34	0	51	$85 = f_4$
5	4	4	12	46	$(4)(2) = 8$	51	$105 = f_5$
		5	4	22	0	85	107
6	7	4	19	67	$(11)(2) + (7)(2) = 36$	51	154
		5	11	43	$(7)(2) = 14$	85	142
		6	7	31	0	105	$136 = f_6$

$51, which is optimal for the demands in the first three periods. This solution is, of course, identical with that found earlier using conventional dynamic programming.

From the results of the analysis of the first three periods, in period 4 we need consider only two possible ordering policies, rather than the four that might appear to be possible. Since it is optimal to satisfy period 3 demand by placing an order in period 3, rather than in an earlier period, it cannot possibly be optimal to satisfy period 4 demand by ordering it before period 3, because that would require units carried over into period 3 even though an order would be placed in period 3. Thus, we need only examine the policies of ordering in period 3 or in period 4 to satisfy the demand in period 4. This situation illustrates what Wagner and Whitin term the *Planning Horizon Theorem*, which states, in effect, that the problem can be broken up into a series of subproblems, with a so-called planning horizon starting at any period i where the optimal policy is to supply the demand for period i by ordering in period i. At that point, the demands from period 1 through $i - 1$ have no effect on the optimal ordering policy from period i onward. In this example, planning horizons begin at periods 1, 3, 4, and 6. This feature of the model clearly reduces the computational effort significantly.

From the computations shown in Table 11.5, the optimal ordering policy for the six periods is determined by working backward through the table, taking each optimal period solution in turn which results in an order being placed in a new period. Thus, from the period 6 optimal solution, 7 units should be ordered in period 6. In

the period 5 optimal solution, 12 units should be ordered in period 4. The period
optimal solution, which again requires an order in period 4, is ignored, since th
optimal order for period 4 was determined in the optimal solution for period
Continuing this process, the period 3 optimal solution dictates an order of 4 units i
period 3, the period 2 optimal solution requires an order of 5 units in period 1, an
the period 1 optimal solution is not of interest by itself. The optimal ordering policy
with a cost of $136, is then

Period	Units Ordered
1	5
2	0
3	4
4	12
5	0
6	7

The solution technique just illustrated does not require that the ordering co
and holding cost be the same for each period. We could have different ordering cos
and holding costs, just as long as the ordering cost is a linear function and the per-un
holding cost is constant for a given period. In addition, these procedures are al:
applicable for the more general case where the marginal cost for each additional un
ordered or held is a constant or a decreasing function of the number of units, althoug
the Planning Horizon Theorem may no longer be applicable.

11.3 PROBABILISTIC MODELS

Consider now the situation where demand is a random variable, as described b
either a discrete or a continuous probability distribution. We will examine first th
case where a decision is to be made as to the optimal order quantity of an item whic
will be demanded over a single period of time. Then, we will study multiple-peri
models where lead time is also a random variable. Both order point and period
review models will be considered.

Single-Period Models

Suppose an inventory of an item must be on hand at the beginning of a give
time period. Demand is a random variable, described by a probability distributio
Initially, we will assume that no reordering is possible during the period if more uni
should be demanded than have been stocked. Later, we will relax this assumptio
Based on the relevant monetary factors, such as unit cost, holding cost, selling pric
shortage penalty cost, and salvage value, we wish to determine the initial invento

level which will optimize the expected monetary value. It will be assumed that all monetary factors remain constant over the analysis period and are not a function of the number of units demanded or supplied. We will also assume that the inventory level prior to ordering is zero and that there is no ordering cost. Both these restrictions will be removed later.

This type of problem has frequently been called the "newsboy" problem, as characterized by a newsboy who wishes to determine the number of papers to stock at the beginning of a day so as to maximize his expected profit. He pays for his papers and makes a profit on each paper sold, but demand is random, and unsold papers are worthless. On the other hand, for each paper demanded which he is unable to supply, he loses the potential profit and may also incur a penalty cost. Similar situations occur, for example, in the stocking of seasonal goods, when no resupply is possible or is very expensive, and in the determination of the optimal number of spare parts when the spares can be manufactured economically only at the time the original equipment is manufactured.

In the study of this class of models, we will use an incremental analysis (also called marginal analysis) approach and view the decision procedure as consisting of a sequence of steps. In a profit maximization situation, for example, the expected profit of each additional unit (or, when applicable, group of units) is evaluated in turn. Units are added to inventory until the point is reached where an additional unit would contribute negative expected profit. As will be shown, it is possible to determine quickly and directly the optimal number of units to stock without actually calculating each unit's expected profit contribution. This is one of the major advantages of the incremental analysis approach.

We will show that this approach really involves the comparison of expected opportunity losses and is therefore applicable to a wide range of problems. We will consider both discrete and continuous probability distributions of demand. Discrete probability distributions serve to illustrate more clearly the principles involved, so they will be discussed first.

Let D = number of units of the item demanded (a random variable),

$\quad d$ = number of units of the item stocked,

$\quad d^*$ = optimal number of units to stock,

$\quad c_o$ = unit cost of overordering (an opportunity loss associated with each unit left over at the end of the time period),

$\quad c_u$ = unit cost of underordering (an opportunity loss associated with each unit demanded but not available).

Both c_o and c_u represent opportunity losses incurred when the number of units stocked is not exactly equal to the number of units actually demanded.

We will assume that c_o and c_u are constants over the analysis period. We will discuss later the factors involved in the makeup of c_o and c_u.

Incremental Analysis for Discrete Probability Distributions of Demand   Suppose we have determined that it is advisable to stock at least $d - 1$ units. Now we wish to determine if it is advisable to stock an additional unit. To do this, we need to calculate two values. They are $\Delta L'$, the expected incremental opportunity loss if the next unit *is not* stocked, and ΔL, the expected incremental opportunity loss if the next unit *is* stocked. We should stock the additional unit if $\Delta L'$ exceeds ΔL. Let us now explain how $\Delta L'$ and ΔL are calculated.

If an additional unit is stocked, it will be needed if the actual demand turns out to be d units or greater. The conditional opportunity loss of not having this needed unit is the cost of underordering. The expected incremental opportunity loss of not stocking the dth unit is then

$$\Delta L' = c_u P(D \geq d).$$

The additional unit will not be needed if the actual demand is less than d units. The conditional opportunity loss of having this unneeded unit is the cost of overordering. The expected incremental opportunity loss of stocking the dth unit is

$$\Delta L = c_o P(D < d).$$

If $\Delta L'$ is greater than ΔL, we should stock the additional unit, since the expected opportunity loss from not stocking is greater than that from stocking. The decision-maker will be indifferent to the addition of the dth unit if $\Delta L' = \Delta L$, or when

$$c_u P(D \geq d) = c_o P(D < d) = c_o \left[1 - P(D \geq d) \right] = c_o - c_o P(D \geq d).$$

Let us now define the so-called "critical" probability, p_c.

$$p_c = \text{value of } P(D \geq d) \text{ for which } \Delta L' = \Delta L.$$

Solving for p_c,

$$c_u p_c = c_o - c_o p_c,$$

$$p_c = \frac{c_o}{c_o + c_u} = \frac{1}{1 + c_u/c_o}. \tag{11.19}$$

We should keep increasing the value of d, the number of units stocked, as long as $P(D \geq d) > p_c$. The value for the optimal number of units to stock is then

$$d^* = \text{largest } d \text{ such that } P(D \geq d) > p_c. \tag{11.20}$$

If $P(D \geq d) = p_c$, we would be indifferent to stocking d^* or $d^* - 1$ units. In the calculations of p_c, note that we do not need the actual values of c_u and c_o but only their *ratio*. (It should be noted that some texts define the critical probability as $c_u/(c_o + c_u)$, which is just $1 - p_c$.)

At this point, let us consider the factors involved in the determination of c_o and c_u. For a given item,

let S = unit selling price,
      C = unit purchase cost,
      C_h = unit holding cost for the entire period,
      V = salvage value,
      C_p = shortage penalty cost.

If the item is for sale, any shortage penalty cost generally represents a so-called "goodwill" (sometimes called "ill will") cost, since it usually is an estimate of the average dollar amount of future profits foregone because of a customer's current displeasure at not being served. If the item is not for sale but is consumed within the organization, as would be the case for an assembly part or a spare part, the shortage penalty cost typically reflects the cost of not having the item immediately available (that is, cost of assembly delay or machine down time) plus the cost of making or ordering the item, since we assume we must have the item.

To show where the conditional opportunity loss values come from, let us first consider the conditional profit associated with stocking or not stocking the dth unit, as a function of the demand D. If the demand is at least as great as the number of units stocked d, the profit from the dth unit will be the unit selling price less the sum of the unit purchase cost and, we will assume, half the unit holding cost. (Unit d could be sold anywhere within the period, depending on the distribution of demand D and by how much D exceeds d; we are assuming unit d is sold at the midpoint of the period. Holding cost, in this model, is generally small compared to other cost factors, so the assumption made is not a significant factor.) If the dth unit is not stocked but is demanded, there will be a loss equal to the shortage penalty cost. On the other hand, if demand is less than d units, the profit of the dth unit will be equal to the salvage value less the sum of the unit purchase cost and unit holding cost if the dth unit is stocked, and zero if it is not. This information is presented in Table 11.6.

Table 11.6

Demand	Conditional Profit	
	Stock Unit d	Don't Stock Unit d
$D \geqslant d$	$S - C - C_h/2$	$-C_p$
$D < d$	$V - C - C_h$	0

In any practical situation, the quantity $V - C - C_h$ will be negative, since the salvage value will not exceed the unit purchase cost, much less the sum of the unit purchase cost and holding cost.

Since it is clearly desirable to stock the dth unit when it will be demanded and not otherwise, the conditional opportunity losses are as shown in Table 11.7.

Table 11.7

Demand	Conditional Opportunity Loss	
	Stock Unit d	Don't Stock Unit d
$D \geqslant d$	0	$S - C - (C_h/2) + C_p$
$D < d$	$C + C_h - V$	0

The unit costs of underordering and overordering are then

$$c_u = S - C - (C_h/2) + C_p. \tag{11.21}$$
$$c_o = C + C_h - V. \tag{11.22}$$

To illustrate this model, we will now take two numerical examples. The first involves an item which is sold and the second an item which is consumed within the organization.

EXAMPLE 11.6

A merchant stocks a particular item at the beginning of summer and cannot reorder. This item costs him $30 and he sells it for $60. For any items which are demanded but cannot be supplied, the merchant feels that he incurs a goodwill cost of $20. Any items unsold by fall have a salvage value of $12. He estimates his holding cost during the inventory period as 5 percent of his item cost. The probability distribution of demand is shown in Table 11.8 and represents his best (subjective) estimate of the actual demand. How many units should he stock?

Table 11.8

(1) Units Stocked d	(2) Demand Probability $P(D = d)$	(3) Cumulative Probability $P(D \geq d)$
2	0.4	1.0
3	0.3	0.6
4	0.1	0.3
5	0.2	0.2

From the given data,

$$S = 60, \ C = 30, \ C_h = (0.05)(30) = 1.5, \ V = 12, \ C_p = 20.$$

We then have, from Equations (11.21) and (11.22):

$$c_u = S - C - \frac{C_h}{2} + C_p = 60 - 30 - 0.75 + 20 = \$49.25,$$
$$c_o = C + C_h - V = 30 + 1.5 - 12 = \$19.5,$$

and

$$p_c = \frac{c_o}{c_o + c_u} = \frac{19.5}{68.75} = 0.284.$$

Looking down column (3) in Table 11.8, the lowest cumulative probability value which exceeds p_c is 0.3, so the optimal number to stock, d^*, is 4 units.

Some insight into the incremental analysis of this problem can be gained if we evaluate the expected net gain from stocking as the number of units stocked is increased from 2 to 5. The required computations are shown in Table 11.9.

Table 11.9

Units Stocked d	Cumulative Demand P(D ⩾ d)	Expected Incremental Opportunity Loss		Expected Incremental Net Gain from Stocking ΔL' − ΔL
		of Underordering ΔL' = $c_u P(D ⩾ d)$	of Overordering ΔL = $c_o P(D < d)$	
2	1.0	(49.25)(1.0) = $49.25	(19.50)(0.0) = $ 0	$49.25
3	0.6	(49.25)(0.6) = 29.55	(19.50)(0.4) = 7.80	21.75
4	0.3	(49.25)(0.3) = 14.78	(19.50)(0.7) = 13.65	1.13
5	0.2	(49.25)(0.2) = 9.85	(19.50)(0.8) = 15.60	−5.75

Through the fourth unit, each additional unit stocked results in an expected incremental net gain. For the fifth unit, however, the expected incremental net gain is negative, so it is uneconomical to stock 5 units. Once the expected incremental net gain from stocking goes negative, it can become only more negative for any additional units stocked. This is true because the expected incremental opportunity loss of underordering is a monotonically decreasing function of the number of units stocked, since c_u remains constant and $P(D ⩾ d)$ continually decreases. At the same time, the expected incremental opportunity loss of overordering is a monotonically increasing function of the number of units stocked, since c_o remains constant and $P(D < d)$ continually increases. The expected incremental net gain, therefore, must be a monotonically decreasing function of the number of units stocked.

EXAMPLE 11.7

A certain piece of equipment is to be purchased for a construction project at a remote location. This equipment contains an expensive part which is subject to random failure. Spares of this part can be purchased at the same time the equipment is purchased. Their unit cost is $1000, and they have no scrap value. If the part fails on the job and no spare is available, the part will have to be manufactured on a special-order basis and flown in. If this is required, the total cost, including down time of the equipment, is estimated as $8000 for each such occurrence. Based on previous experience with similar parts, the following probability estimates of the number of failures expected over the duration of the project are provided: $P(0$ failures$) = 0.80$, $P(1$ failure$) = 0.15$, $P(2$ failures$) = 0.05$. The probability of more than two failures is considered to be negligible.

a) What is the optimal number of spares to stock?

The probability data, in a form suitable for incremental analysis, is shown in Table 11.10.

To calculate the unit costs of underordering and overordering, note first that the item is consumed internally, so the selling price S is zero. The salvage value V is zero, and, in the absence of any information, we will assume that the holding cost C_h is also

Table 11.10

Units Stocked d	Demand Probability $P(D = d)$	Cumulative Probability $P(D \geq d)$
0	0.80	1.00
1	0.15	0.20
2	0.05	0.05

zero. (The sensitivity of the optimal solution to any holding cost or other cost factor could be explored through sensitivity analysis of this mathematical model, to be discussed shortly.) The shortage penalty cost C_p is \$8000, and the unit purchase cost is \$1000. Therefore, from Equations (11.21) and (11.22):

$$c_u = S - C - \frac{C_h}{2} + C_p = 0 - 1000 - 0 + 8000 = \$7000$$

$$c_o = C + C_h - V = 1000 + 0 - 0 = \$1000$$

and

$$P_c = \frac{c_o}{c_o + c_u} = \frac{1000}{8000} = 0.125.$$

Since the lowest cumulative probability value exceeding p_c is 0.20, the optimal number of units to stock, d^*, is 1. Thus, one spare should be purchased at the same time the equipment is purchased.

    b) The cost of an emergency (a part failure and no spare available) was esti-mated as \$8000. At what emergency cost e would the contractor be indifferent to stocking one or two spares?

For this situation, c_u becomes $-1000 + e$, while c_o is unchanged at 1000. The p_c value for indifference between one and two units stocked is 0.05, from Table 11.10. Therefore,

$$p_c = \frac{c_o}{c_o + c_u} = \frac{1000}{1000 - 1000 + e} = \frac{1000}{e} = 0.05.$$

The emergency cost e would be $1000/0.05 = \$20,000$.

Summarization of the Procedure   We can now summarize the basic steps in the incremental analysis approach.

    1. From the given monetary values, determine c_u and c_o, the costs of under-ordering and overordering.

    2. Calculate the critical probability value p_c.

3. Select the optimal number of units to stock, d^*, based on the given probability distribution of demand.

Sensitivity Analysis In a given situation, having determined the optimal number to stock d^*, we would generally be quite interested in knowing how sensitive our solution is to possible errors or changes in the input data. As a good example, the shortage penalty cost, in particular, usually represents only an educated guess. It would be of value to determine the sensitivity of our decision (number of units to stock) to the shortage penalty cost. Let us illustrate the procedure by utilizing the data of Example 11.6, where $S = 60$, $C = 30$, $C_h = 1.5$, and $V = 12$.

Examining Table 11.8, the given probability distribution of demand is such that the optimal number of units to stock can change only at the points where p_c takes on the values of 0.6, 0.3, and 0.2. We will call these "break-point" p_c values.

As before, let C_p = shortage penalty cost in dollars for each unit demanded but not supplied. With C_p as a variable, $c_u = 29.25 + C_p$, c_o is unchanged, and $p_c = 19.50/(48.75 + C_p)$. Since the shortage cost will never be negative, the minimum value of C_p is zero, so that p_c can never exceed $19.50/48.74 = 0.400$, and the optimal number of stock must be at least 3. We have

$$p_c = \frac{19.50}{48.75 + C_p}, \qquad 0 \leqslant C_p \leqslant \infty$$

Solving for C_p in terms of p_c,

$$p_c(48.75 + C_p) = 19.50$$

$$C_p = \frac{19.50 - 48.75 p_c}{p_c}.$$

We can now solve this equation for the values of C_p which yield the feasible break-point p_c values of 0.3 and 0.2:

$$\begin{aligned} \text{for } p_c = 0.3, \qquad & C_p = \$16.25 \\ \text{for } p_c = 0.2, \qquad & C_p = \$48.75. \end{aligned}$$

The decision ranges on C_p are then

$$\begin{aligned} \$0 \leqslant C_p \leqslant \$16.25, \qquad & d^* = 3 \\ \$16.25 \leqslant C_p \leqslant \$48.75, \qquad & d^* = 4 \\ C_p \geqslant \$48.75, \qquad & d^* = 5. \end{aligned}$$

The decision maker does not *know* what the shortage penalty cost (goodwill cost) is, but armed with this additional information, he is better able to make a rational decision. If he feels that the shortage cost is somewhere between \$20 and \$40, then stocking 4 units would be his best decision. If he is quite sure that his shortage cost does not exceed \$15, then he should stock 3 units. He will not stock 5 units unless his shortage cost appears to exceed \$50.

The shortage cost is not the only factor of interest. We might be interested in exploring the sensitivity of the decision to changes in the purchase cost or salvage value. For example, suppose the unit purchase cost C were subject to change. Since the holding cost $C_h = 0.05C$, and $C_p = 20$,

$$c_u = 60 - C - \frac{0.05C}{2} + 20 = 80 - 1.025C$$

$$c_o = C + 0.05C - 12 = 1.05C - 12$$

$$p_c = \frac{1.05C - 12}{68 + 0.025C}.$$

Solving for C in terms of p_c,

$$(68 + 0.025C)p_c = 1.05C - 12$$

$$C = \frac{12 + 68p_c}{1.05 - 0.025p_c}$$

Since p_c is a probability, its value must lie between 0 and 1. The corresponding values of C are 78.05 and 11.43. Values of C outside these limits make no sense. A value lower than $11.43 would make it profitable to carry an infinite stock, since all items not sold could be salvaged at a profit. A value greater than $78.05 would be so high that stocking and selling would result in an opportunity loss, even if all items could be sold.

Given the break-point p_c values and solving the above equation for the corresponding values of C:

$$
\begin{array}{ll}
\text{for } p_c = 0.2, & C = \$24.50 \\
\text{for } p_c = 0.3, & C = \$31.08 \\
\text{for } p_c = 0.6, & C = \$51.01.
\end{array}
$$

Therefore, the decision ranges on C are

$$
\begin{array}{ll}
\$11.43 \leqslant C \leqslant \$24.50, & d^* = 5, \\
\$24.50 \leqslant C \leqslant \$31.08, & d^* = 4, \\
\$31.08 \leqslant C \leqslant \$51.01, & d^* = 3, \\
\$51.01 \leqslant C \leqslant \$78.05, & d^* = 2.
\end{array}
$$

We see that the given purchase cost of $30 could increase by $1.08 or decrease by $5.50 without changing the optimal number to stock, all other factors remaining the same. This is certainly useful information.

We could, of course, examine other factors, such as the holding cost or salvage value, in a similar fashion. The incremental analysis approach makes such sensitivity analyses straightforward.

Reordering   Up to this point, considering an item which is sold, we have been concerned only with situations where the sale is lost if the item demanded cannot be supplied immediately. In many instances, however, the customer will still buy if the item can be supplied within a short period. We will consider only the case where a constant cost is associated with each unit reordered. This will occur, for example, if there is a cost of expedited delivery for each unit reordered or if the unit cost is higher for reorders. We will assume that a fraction f of customers, when faced with an out-of-stock situation, will wait for the item to be reordered.

Consider again the decision to be made by the merchant who buys an item at $30, sells it for $60, and can salvage unsold units for $12. His holding cost is 5 percent of the unit purchase cost. Suppose he is now able to place a reorder, at an additional cost of $15 per unit, over and above the purchase cost, when a customer will wait for a reorder if the item is out of stock. If the sale is lost, there is a shortage penalty cost of $20. If an estimated half of the out-of-stock units can be reordered, what is the optimal number of units to stock?

When an out-of-stock item will be reordered, the cost of underordering no longer includes the gross profit foregone, $S - C$, and the shortage penalty cost C_p, since the gross profit will now be received and there will not be any shortage. Thus the cost of underordering includes only the reorder cost, which we will denote as C_r, less the holding cost. With a fraction f of customers who will wait for a reorder, the weighted cost of underordering becomes

$$c_u = fC_r + (1 - f)(S - C + C_p) - \frac{C_h}{2}.$$

Substituting the given numerical values,

$$c_u = (0.5)(15) + (0.5)(60 - 30 + 20) - 0.75 = \$31.75.$$

Since reordering has no effect on the cost of overordering, $c_o = \$19.5$. Then,

$$p_c = \frac{c_o}{c_o + c_u} = \frac{19.5}{51.25} = 0.381.$$

With the demand distribution given in Table 11.8, the optimal number to stock is now 3, compared to the original value of 4. When loss of an immediate sale can result in a profit reduced by the amount of the reorder cost, rather than complete loss of profit plus a possible shortage penalty (goodwill cost), it should be clear that the tendency will be to stock fewer items.

Continuous Probability Distributions of Demand Suppose the probability distribution of demand is continuous or can be assumed to be continuous, for all practical purposes. The incremental analysis approach is equally applicable to this type of probability distribution.

Consider a representative cumulative distribution function (cdf) of demand, as shown in Figure 11.9. $F(d)$ is the probability that the random demand D is less than or equal to any specified value d.

For any given amount d which is stocked, the probability of selling that amount is just the probability that demand is at least that high, or $P(D \geq d)$. For any value of d, this probability can be determined from Figure 11.9, since $P(D \geq d) = 1 - F(d)$. The optimal quantity to stock, d^*, is at the point where the value of $F(d)$ is equal to $1 - p_c$. This is the same p_c derived earlier, dependent only on the ratio of the costs of underordering to overordering.

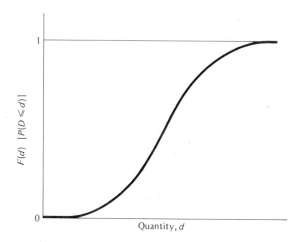

Figure 11.9

Let us now take a numerical example. For convenience only, we will assume that demand is normally distributed, although the approach is applicable to any continuous probability distribution.

EXAMPLE 11.8

An item sells for $5.50 per pound, costs $2.50 per pound, and unsold quantities are worth $1.50 per pound. This item is stocked at the beginning of the week and cannot be reordered. We will assume there is no shortage penalty cost, and we will ignore the holding cost, since the holding period is so short. Weekly demand is normally distributed, with a mean value of 200 pounds and a standard deviation of 10 pounds. What is the optimal quantity of this item to stock?

From the problem data,

$$S = 5.5, \; C = 2.5, \; V = 1.5, \; C_h = 0, \; C_p = 0.$$

Then,

$$c_u = S - C - \frac{C_h}{2} + C_p = 5.5 - 2.5 - 0 + 0 = \$3/\text{lb}$$

$$c_o = C + C_h - V = 2.5 + 0 - 1.5 = \$1/\text{lb}$$

$$p_c = \frac{c_o}{c_o + c_u} = \frac{1}{4} = 0.25.$$

Since $1 - p_c = 0.75$, we now consult the standardized normal distribution table, looking for the value of the standardized normal variate for which the cdf is 0.75. This value is very close to +0.67. Thus, the optimal quantity to stock, d^*, lies 0.67 standard deviations to the right of the mean. Therefore,

$$d^* = 200 + (0.67)(10) = 206.7 \text{ lb.}$$

Ordering Policy Suppose there are units already on hand at the beginning of the period during which the inventory will be required. The number of additional units to order will then depend on the magnitude of the ordering or setup cost, if any.

Let d_o = number of units of inventory already on hand,

$\quad$ C_o = fixed ordering (or setup) cost, independent of the number of units ordered.

Case I: $C_o = 0$

If there is no ordering cost, the policy should clearly be to have the optimal number on hand unless already overstocked.

If $d_0 \geq d^*$, order nothing.

If $d_0 < d^*$, order $d^* - d_0$ units.

Case II: $C_0 > 0$

If there is an ordering cost and $d_0 < d^*$, it will be preferable not to order at all if the improvement in expected monetary value by having d^* units on hand, compared to d_0 units, is less than C_o. If it is preferable to order, $d^* - d_0$ units should be ordered. The policy is then:

If $d_0 \geq d^*$, order nothing.

If $d_0 < d^*$, order nothing if $EMV(d^*) - EMV(d_0) < C_o$; otherwise, order $d^* - d_0$ units.

To illustrate the situation where there is an ordering cost and $d_0 < d^*$, consider the merchant's problem in Example 11.6. In that problem, we found that d^* was 4. Suppose there had been an ordering cost of $10 for any order placed, regardless of its size, in addition to the purchase cost of $30 per unit. If three units of the item were on hand already ($d_0 = 3$), would it pay to place an order?

Having performed the calculations of incremental net gains in Table 11.9, we need not calculate $EMV(d^*)$ and $EMV(d_0)$, since we are only interested in their difference. From Table 11.9, the fourth unit stocked contributes an expected net incremental gain of $1.13, so $EMV(4) - EMV(3) = \$1.13$. Since this is less than the ordering cost C_o of $10, we should not order. An order of size 1 would reduce the expected profit by $10.00 - 1.13$ or $8.87. If only 2 units had been on hand, $EMV(2)$ would be less than $EMV(4)$ by the expected net incremental gains of both the third and fourth unit stocked, or $1.13 + 21.75 = \$22.88$. Then, $EMV(4) - EMV(2) > C_o$, and stocking the 2 additional units required to increase the inventory to d^* units would increase the expected profit by $22.88 - 10.00 = \$12.88$.

Multiple-Period Models

In the deterministic multiple-period models discussed at the beginning of this chapter, we assumed that demand occurred at a constant rate and that lead time was zero, although we noted that we could readily handle the situation with a known lead time. Now, however, we will consider the customary business situation where both demand and lead time are random variables, and we will reasonably assume that they are independent of each other.

A stockout occurs when inventory is completely depleted. To decrease the chances of a stockout, it is customary to incorporate into the inventory system a safety stock, or buffer stock, an additional amount of inventory whose function is solely to protect against higher-than-expected demand during the period when the item is vulnerable to the occurrence of a stockout. As we will show, this period is different for order-point and periodic-review inventory systems.

In the determination of the appropriate quantity of buffer stock, we would like to balance the cost of holding this additional stock and the estimated cost of shortages. Since the shortage cost is generally quite difficult to determine, management often chooses to define a measure of system performance and then arbitrarily establishes a performance level considered to be satisfactory. Among a number of different measures of system performance which have been employed in the absence of information on shortage costs, we will examine two which are frequently used.

1. Fraction of replenishment periods in which no stockout occurs
2. Fraction of units which are supplied upon demand

We will also develop a model for optimizing the buffer stock level when a shortage cost is given.

Order Point System   In this type of system, also called a continuous review system, the count of the number of units in inventory is continuously maintained. When the inventory level drops to a certain point, called the order point or reorder level, an order is placed for a fixed order quantity, which should be as close as feasible to the optimal lot size.

In Figure 11.10, a representative inventory history is charted. During the first lead time, demand rate and lead time are at their average values, so that the replenishment order arrives just as the buffer stock level is reached. During the next lead time, the demand rate is higher than its average value, so that the lead-time demand cuts into the buffer stock. In the third lead-time period, both demand rate and lead-time values are high, and a stockout occurs just before the replenishment order arrives.

Based on the given problem data and on the measure of system performance selected, the optimal order point and order quantity can be determined. Their values are actually interdependent, but, fortunately, a change in one has only a small effect on the other. Because the expected total relevant cost curve is quite flat near the minimum cost point, we can get a very good approximation to the desired values by calculating the order quantity and the order point separately.

We will work an example problem using three different performance measures. The first, which we will call the service level criterion, requires that the fraction of replenishment periods in which no shortage occurs be at least equal to the service level, a high probability value, typically around 0.95. The second, which we term the

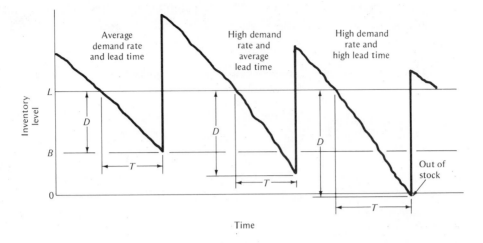

Figure 11.10

service fraction criterion, specifies that the fraction of customer orders supplied on demand shall be at least the service fraction, again a relatively high value, such as 0.95 or even higher. Both these criteria are easiest to explain by going through the example. The third performance measure is the minimization of the expected total relevant cost when the shortage penalty cost is expressed as a cost for each unit short, a cost which is not a function of the length of time a shortage exists. We will now develop a mathematical model for this third performance measure.

Let D = actual demand during lead time,
       $\overline{D}$ = average lead-time demand,
       B = buffer stock or safety stock,
       L = reorder level or order point,
       R = units required (demand) per time period,
       C_o = cost of ordering per order placed,
       C_h = cost of holding a unit of inventory per time period,
       C_p = penalty cost per unit short in any replenishment period,
    $C(Q, L)$ = expected total relevant cost (ordering, holding, and shortage) per time period,
       $\overline{S}$ = expected units short in any replenishment period.

As before,

$$\text{Ordering cost} = C_o R/Q.$$

The holding cost covers the average working inventory $Q/2$ and the average buffer stock, which is very close to $L - \overline{D}$, as can be visualized from Figure 11.10. This value for the average buffer stock is actually slightly lower than the true value, since it includes the effect of all values of the random variable for demand D, even though the stock level never actually goes negative when the value of D exceeds L, as in the last replenishment cycle shown in Figure 11.10.

$$\text{Holding cost} = C_h\left(\frac{Q}{2} + L - \bar{D}\right).$$

The shortage penalty cost equals the expected penalty cost per replenishment period multiplied by the number of replenishment periods, or

$$\text{Shortage penalty cost} = C_p\bar{S}\frac{R}{Q}$$

Then, the expected total relevant cost is

$$C(Q, L) = \frac{C_oR}{Q} + C_h\left(\frac{Q}{2} + L - \bar{D}\right) + \frac{C_p\bar{S}R}{Q}.$$

Grouping like terms,

$$C(Q, L) = \frac{R}{Q}(C_o + C_p\bar{S}) + C_h\left(\frac{Q}{2} + L - \bar{D}\right). \tag{11.23}$$

The optimal value of Q will be approximated by using the optimal lot size formula of Equation (11.2). This is generally a very acceptable approximation.

To find the optimal value of L, we can employ the same approach as that used earlier for the single-period probabilistic inventory model where the optimal number to stock was to be determined. We will need to calculate the opportunity losses, c_u and c_o, which are the unit cost of underordering and overordering, respectively. The opportunity loss of underordering will be the penalty cost of a one-unit shortage during each replenishment period less the amount saved by holding one less unit. The opportunity loss of overordering will be just the cost of holding one additional item. Therefore,

$$c_u = C_p\frac{R}{Q^*} - C_h$$

$$c_o = C_h.$$

As before, the critical probability $p_c = c_o/(c_o + c_u)$, so, for this model,

$$p_c = \frac{C_hQ^*}{C_pR} \tag{11.24}$$

We solve for the value of L such that

$$P(D > L) = p_c. \tag{11.25}$$

If L is fractional, we truncate (round down) to the integer value. (If we rounded up, $P(D > L)$ would be less than p_c.)

EXAMPLE 11.9

A certain item has an annual demand of 1000 units. The cost of placing an order is \$10, and the annual holding cost is \$2 per unit. Daily demand tends to be randomly distributed throughout a working day, so that a Poisson distributed may be assumed. There are 250 working days per year, and lead time is 5 working days.

a) Determine the optimal order quantity.

From the given data, $R = 1000$, $C_o = \$10$, and $C_h = \$2$.

$$Q^* = \sqrt{2RC_o/C_h} = \sqrt{(2)(1000)(10)/2} = 100 \text{ units.}$$

b) Determine the order point if a service level of 0.95 is required.

With this criterion, a shortage is permitted in no more than 5 percent of the replenishment periods. The order point L must be high enough so that the probability that the demand D is greater than L does not exceed 0.05. With a mean daily demand of $1000/250 = 4$ units and a lead time of 5 days, $\overline{D} = (4)(5) = 20$ units. The demand will then have a Poisson distribution with a mean of 20. Now, a table can be prepared of cumulative Poisson probability values from Appendix D. This information is tabulated in the first two columns of Table 11.11. (For the moment, disregard the remainder of the table.)

Table 11.11 Order Point Inventory System Calculations

(1)	(2)	(3)	(4)	(5)	(6)	(7)
			Order Point = 20		Order Point = 24	
Lead Time Demand d	Cumulative Demand Probability $P(D \geqslant d)$	Demand Probability $P(D = d)$	Units Short $(d - 20)$	Weighted Units Short $(3) \times (4)$	Units Short $(d - 24)$	Weighted Units Short $(3) \times (6)$
21	0.441	0.085	1	0.085		
22	0.356	0.077	2	0.154		
23	0.279	0.066	3	0.198		
24	0.213	0.056	4	0.224		
25	0.157	0.045	5	0.225	1	0.045
26	0.112	0.034	6	0.204	2	0.068
27	0.078	0.025	7	0.175	3	0.075
28	0.053	0.019	8	0.152	4	0.076
29	0.034	0.012	9	0.108	5	0.060
30	0.022	0.008	10	0.080	6	0.048
31	0.014	0.006	11	0.066	7	0.042
32	0.008	0.003	12	0.036	8	0.024
33	0.005	0.002	13	0.026	9	0.018
34	0.003	0.001	14	0.014	10	0.010
35	0.002	0.001	15	0.010	11	0.011
				1.757		0.477
				$\cong 1.8$		$\cong 0.5$

Since the probability of demand exceeding the order point value is not to be greater than 0.05, it will be necessary to set the order point L at 28. Although a stockout would occur for a demand D of 28 units, no *shortage* would occur until D exceeded 28 units. Therefore, we have actually considered the protection level to be $1 - P(\text{shortage})$ rather than $1 - P(\text{stockout})$, so that the protection level would be $1 - P(D > 28) = 1 - P(D \geqslant 29) = 1 - 0.034 = 0.966$, or 96.6 percent.

c) Determine the order point if the service fraction must be at least 0.98.

To get the service fraction, we need to calculate $\bar{S}$, the expected number of units short in any replenishment period. For a given order point L, the probability of a shortage of n units is $P(D = L + n)$. If this probability is multiplied by n and these products are summed for all reasonable values of n (those, say, for which the probability is at least 0.001), the total will be $\bar{S}$. Since this is a trial-and-error process, suppose we perform the necessary calculations for a buffer stock B of 0, so that the trial value of L is 20.

The calculations are shown in columns (3), (4), and (5) of Table 11.11. The individual probability values in column (3) are obtained by taking successive differences of the column (2) cumulative probabilities. For example, $P(D = 21) = P(D \geqslant 21) - P(D \geqslant 22) = 0.441 - 0.356 = 0.085$. The column (4) and (5) values are self-explanatory. The result is an expected shortage of 1.8 units. With $R/Q^* = 1000/100 = 10$ orders per year, the expected annual shortage would be $(10)(1.8) = 18$ units. The fraction of units supplied upon demand is then $(1000 - 18)/1000 = 0.982$. Since this exceeds the required fraction of 0.98, no buffer would be required, so an order point of 20 would be acceptable. From the first entry in column (2) of Table 11.11, a shortage could be expected in about 44 percent of the replenishment periods.

d) For each unit which cannot be supplied upon demand, there is an estimated shortage penalty cost of $1. Find the order point if the total relevant cost is to be minimized.

Given that $C_p = \$1$,

$$p_c = \frac{C_h Q^*}{C_p R} = \frac{(2)(100)}{(1)(1000)} = 0.200.$$

In Table 11.11, column (2), we look for the cumulative probability value which just exceeds the p_c value of 0.200. That value is 0.213, so the optimal order point L is 24. (This is the same procedure as was used in the earlier section on incremental analysis.)

e) Calculate the expected total relevant cost for all three selection criteria, assuming a shortage penalty cost C_p of $1 per unit. The formula to be used is Equation (11.23),

$$C(Q, L) = \frac{R}{Q}\left(C_o + C_p\bar{S}\right) + C_h\left(\frac{Q}{2} + L - D\right).$$

1. Service level $\geqslant 0.95$

   With $L = 29$, $\bar{S}$ can be calculated as 0.1. (These calculations are not shown, but are of exactly the same form as the earlier $\bar{S}$ calculations.)

   $$C(100, 29) = \frac{1000}{100}\left[10 + (1)(0.1)\right] + 2\left(\frac{100}{2} + 29 - 20\right)$$
   $$= (10)(10.1) + (2)(59) = 101 + 118 = \$219.$$

2. Service fraction $\geqslant 0.98$

   For $L = 20$ (zero buffer stock), $\bar{S}$ was 1.8.

   $$C(100, 20) = \frac{1000}{100}\left[10 + (1)(1.8)\right] + 2\left(\frac{100}{2} + 20 - 20\right)$$
   $$= (10)(11.8) + (2)(50) = 118 + 100 = \$218.$$

3. Minimum expected total relevant cost

   No shortage occurs until D exceeds 24 units, so the calculations are as shown in columns (6) and (7) of Table 11.11. The value of $\bar{S}$ is 0.5.

   $$C(100, 24) = \frac{1000}{100}\left[10 + (1)(0.5)\right] + 2\left(\frac{100}{2} + 24 - 20\right)$$
   $$= (10)(10.5) + (2)(54) = 105 + 108 = \$213.$$

As would be expected, of the three alternative approaches to setting the order point, the third was the minimum cost alternative. The cost curve is so flat, however, that the cost differences between these alternatives are very small.

Sensitivity Analysis   Since the shortage penalty cost C_p is rarely known with any degree of confidence, we can perform a sensitivity analysis to determine the optimal order point as a function of C_p, based on the relationship between C_p and the critical probability p_c, as expressed in Equation (11.24). From that equation,

$$p_c = \frac{C_h Q^*}{C_p R}.$$

Solving for C_p as a function of p_c,

$$C_p = \frac{C_h Q^*}{p_c R} = \frac{(2)(100)}{p_c(1000)} = \frac{0.2}{p_c}.$$

The necessary calculations are shown in Table 11.12, taking the cumulative probability values from Table 11.11.

From the results of Table 11.12, an order point L of 24, which minimized total relevant cost, would be optimal for a shortage penalty cost in the range of $0.94 to $1.27. For the service fraction measure of performance, the chosen value of $L = 29$ implies a shortage penalty cost between about $6 and $9, while the service level criterion, with $L = 20$, implies a shortage penalty cost under $0.45.

If management chooses to avoid making an estimate of the shortage penalty cost

Table 11.12 Sensitivity Analysis of the Shortage Penalty Cost C_p

Lead Time Demand d	Breakpoint Values $P_c = P(D \geqslant d)$	C_p ($)	Implied Range of C_p Values for Which $L = d$ is Optimal ($)
21	0.441	0.45	0.45 to 0.56
22	0.356	0.56	0.56 to 0.72
23	0.279	0.72	0.72 to 0.94
24	0.213	0.94	0.94 to 1.27
25	0.157	1.27	1.27 to 1.79
26	0.112	1.79	1.79 to 2.56
27	0.078	2.56	2.56 to 3.77
28	0.053	3.77	3.77 to 5.88
29	0.034	5.88	5.88 to 9.09
30	0.022	9.09	9.09 to 14.3
31	0.014	14.3	14.3 to 25
32	0.008	25	25 to 40
33	0.005	40	40 to 67
34	0.003	67	67 to 100
35	0.002	100	Over 100

and determines the order point by some performance measure other than minimum total relevant cost, the value of the implied shortage cost can be determined. Then, management can look at the cost implications of the order point decision and can adjust the order point in appropriate fashion if the implied shortage cost seems unreasonably high or low.

Periodic Review System   In this type of model, as discussed at the beginning of this chapter, the inventory situation is reviewed only at periodic intervals, rather than continuously, as with most order point models. We will consider here a replenishment level inventory system. This system basically functions as follows: At the time of the periodic review, an order is placed for a quantity equal to the difference between the replenishment level (sometimes called the maximum liability) and the number of units on hand plus those on order. The only decision variable in this model is the replenishment level.

Let M = replenishment level, in units,
B = buffer stock, in units,
$\bar{d}$ = average demand rate, units per day,
$\bar{T}$ = average lead time, days,
V = specified review period, days,
I = inventory on hand at the time of the review.

Assuming that the lead time is less than the review period, so that an order placed at a review period will be received prior to the next review period, the variable order quantity q at any review period can be stated as

$$q = M - I.$$

If the lead time exceeded the review period, the order quantity would be reduced by the quantity of any order or orders outstanding (placed, but not yet received).

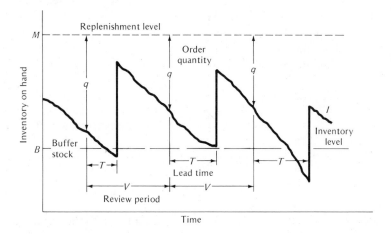

Figure 11.11

Figure 11.11 illustrates the general way in which a replenishment level inventory system functions. Once an order of size $q = M - I$ has been placed, at the time of a periodic review, the inventory level will continue to drop until that order is received T time units later. At that point, the on-hand inventory increases by the amount just ordered. The average inventory $\bar{I}$ will be equal to the buffer stock plus half the average number of units demanded in each period between replenishments. Thus,

$$\bar{I} = B + \frac{\overline{dV}}{2}.$$

Since an order quantity must be adequate to cover demand over the review period and the ensuing lead time, the buffer stock level must be adequate to cover variations in demand during that entire period. Thus, the value of the buffer stock depends on the distribution of demand over the actual period $V + T$. (This contrasts with the situation for a continuous review system, where the buffer stock is only required to protect against above-average demand during the lead time. Replenishment level systems, therefore, tend to require larger buffer stocks than order point systems.) As an approximation, we can base the required buffer stock on the distribution of demand over the mean period $V + \overline{T}$. Once the buffer stock B is determined, the replenishment level M is then easily calculated by the following formula:

$$M = B + \overline{d}(V + \overline{T}). \tag{11.26}$$

To solve for the required buffer stock of a periodic review system, we could set up an equation similar in nature to that of Equation (11.23), which expresses the total relevant cost of an order point system. This would require jointly optimizing the review period V and the buffer stock B. This process becomes somewhat involved, so we will assume that the time between reviews is a value fixed, say, by administrative considerations. Then, we will use an earlier measure of performance, the service level (sometimes called the protection level), which was defined as the fraction of replenishment periods in which no stockout occurs.

Let p = probability that no stockout occurs during a replenishment period.

Consider the case where a Poisson distribution of daily demand can be assumed. If we also make the assumption that the variability in the lead time is small compared to the sum of the review time V and the mean lead time $\overline{T}$, we can then assume that the demand D over that time period has a mean $\overline{D} = \overline{d}(V + \overline{T})$ units, with a Poisson distribution. The standard deviation σ of that demand distribution will be

$$\sigma = \sqrt{\overline{d}(V + \overline{T})}.$$

For $\overline{D} \geq 3\sigma$, we can use the normal approximation to the Poisson distribution. Then, we have

$$B = z\sigma,$$

where z is the number of standard deviations such that the probability the actual demand does not exceed the mean demand plus the buffer stock is at least equal to the specified protection level, or

$$P(D \leq \overline{D} + B) \geq p.$$

To illustrate the computations required to determine the proper replenishment level, consider the following example.

EXAMPLE 11.10

The Friendlee Discount Store, open seven days a week, reorders a certain portable typewriter every two weeks, according to a replenishment level system. Sales of this typewriter appear to be random, averaging 3.5 per day. Resupply is from the warehouse and always takes either one or two days. The mean lead time is very close to 1.5 days. What replenishment level should be specified if it is desired to have a stockout protection level of at least 95 percent?

The expected demand over the review period and the mean lead time is

$$\begin{aligned}
\overline{D} &= \overline{d}(V + \overline{T}) \\
&= (3.5)(14 + 1.5) \\
&= 54.25 \text{ units.}
\end{aligned}$$

Assuming a Poisson distribution of demand,

$$\sigma = \sqrt{\overline{D}} = \sqrt{54.25}$$
$$= 7.37 \text{ units.}$$

Since $\overline{D} > 3\sigma$, we can use the normal approximation to the Poisson distribution, with mean 54.25 units and standard deviation 7.37 units. Then, as shown in Figure 11.12, the value of the buffer stock B must be such that

$$P(D \leqslant \overline{D} + B) \geqslant 0.95.$$

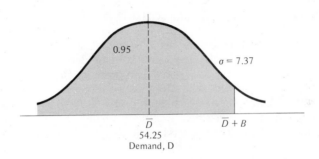

Figure 11.12

With $B = z\sigma$, since a normal probability distribution has been used as an approximation, z is determined from the normal probability table, Appendix A. The value of z is that for which 0.95 of the probability area lies to the left.

Thus,
$$z = 1.645,$$
$$B = z\sigma = (1.645)(7.37)$$
$$= 12.1 \text{ units.}$$

Then, from Equation (11.26), the replenishment level is

$$M = B + \overline{d}(V + \overline{T})$$
$$= 12.1 + 54.2$$
$$= 66.3 \text{ units.}$$

Since the replenishment level must be an integer and the protection level must be at least 0.95, the value of M must be rounded up to the next higher integer. Therefore,

$$M = 67 \text{ units.}$$

With an M value of 67 rather than 66.3, the buffer stock B will be increased by $67 - 66.3 = 0.7$, so $B = 12.1 + 0.7 = 12.8$. Since $B = z\sigma$, z can now be recalculated:

$$z = \frac{B}{\sigma} = \frac{12.8}{7.37} = 1.74.$$

From the normal probability tables, for a z value of 1.74, the protection level will be 0.959.

SUMMARY

In the study of inventory models, we are primarily concerned with the determination of optimal inventory policies, which generally involve the minimization of the total relevant cost, consisting primarily of the components of ordering cost, holding cost, and shortage penalty cost. The optimal lot size models studied initially were deterministic models with a number of simplifying assumptions, including known and constant demand, but we showed, through sensitivity analyses, that the optimal solutions tend to be quite insensitive even to fairly significant changes in the cost and demand factors. Thus, these models tend to have more general applicability than one might suppose. A deterministic model with known but changing demand was also presented, and it was shown that the techniques of dynamic programming could be utilized to develop a particularly efficient algorithm for this type of problem.

In the second part of the chapter, probabilistic models were discussed. For models covering inventory decisions applicable to only a single time period, the factor of random demand was introduced, including both discrete and continuous probability distributions of demand, and the technique of incremental analysis was shown to be a powerful tool in the study of such models. Sensitivity analysis was again employed to explore the effects of errors or changes in the data inputs. For multiple-period probabilistic models, the additional factor of random lead time was considered, and the effect on ordering policy of the combination of random demand and random lead time was shown in pictorial form. The need for buffer stock was clearly demonstrated. Both an order point and a periodic review model were presented. In the order point model, three different measures of system performance were used in the calculation of the order point. One of these involved the minimization of the expected total relevant cost, given an estimated shortage penalty cost. In the periodic review model, an iterative approach was described which led to the determination of both the optimal lot size and the optimal reorder level. In the periodic review model, a noneconomic approach was followed, in that the optimal replenishment level was based on an arbitrarily established protection level related to the fraction of periods in which a shortage could be tolerated.

The inventory models covered in this chapter should give an appreciation of some of the different classes of inventory models, but only a basic introduction of such models has been presented. The chapter references give some indication of the extensive work that has been done on inventory models.

Optimal Lot Size Model—No Shortages Allowed

Assuming that demand is known and steady and that lead time is zero:

Let Q = lot size per order,

Q^* = optimal lot size per order,

R = units required (demand) per unit time,

C_o = cost of ordering or setup per order placed,

C_h = cost of holding (or carrying) a unit of inventory per unit time,

$C(Q)$ = total relevant cost (ordering + holding) per unit time for lot size Q.

As shown earlier (Equation 11.1):

$$C(Q) = \frac{C_o R}{Q} + \frac{C_h Q}{2}.$$

Since Q^* is the optimal lot size, $C(Q^*)$ must represent the minimum cost point, so that the slope of the $C(Q)$ curve, as shown in Figure 11.2, is zero at the point $Q = Q^*$. Using the calculus, we first take the derivative of this expression with respect to Q.

$$\frac{dC(Q)}{dQ} = -\frac{C_o R}{Q^2} + \frac{C_h}{2}$$

At the optimal lot size Q^*, the derivative is equal to zero, so

$$-\frac{C_o R}{(Q^*)^2} + \frac{C_h}{2} = 0, \qquad (Q^*)^2 = 2RC_o/C_h, \qquad Q^* = \sqrt{2RC_o/C_h}.$$

As for the minimum total relevant cost, substituting the value of Q^* in Equation (11.1),

$$C(Q^*) = \frac{C_o R}{\sqrt{2RC_o/C_h}} + \frac{C_h\sqrt{2RC_o/C_h}}{2}$$

$$= \frac{\sqrt{2RC_oC_h}}{2} + \frac{\sqrt{2RC_oC_h}}{2} = \sqrt{2RC_oC_h} = C_h Q^*.$$

We see that the holding and ordering costs are indeed equal for $Q = Q^*$. As a matter of fact, it can be easily shown that, if the product of two values is a constant, then their sum is minimized by setting them equal. In this case, $(C_o R/Q)(C_h Q/2) = RC_oC_h/2$, which is a constant, independent of Q.

EXERCISES

11.1   Explain in your own words the general nature of the following cost factors:
(a)   Holding or carrying costs
(b)   Ordering or setup cost
(c)   Shortage penalty cost

11.2   In the deterministic optimal lot size models discussed, a known and constant rate of demand is assumed. If this assumption is only approximately true, are these models invalid? Explain.

11.3   The state of Sur-tan-tee would like to improve its inventory management policies for its supply of paint used for highway markings. Annual demand for such paint is 4000 gallons, and the paint, which costs $2 per gallon, is used at a constant rate. Annual paint holding costs are estimated to be 10 percent of the value of paint held. Each order costs $25.
(a)   How much paint should be ordered each time?
(b)   How often should paint be ordered?
(c)   What is the total annual cost (including the cost of the paint) associated with this policy?
(d)   Verify that the ordering and holding costs are equal.

11.4   Demand for a certain part ordered by the Shorte Company tends to be constant, at a monthly rate of 1000 units. The per-unit holding cost of this item is $5 per year, and the cost of placing an order is $20.
(a)   What is the optimal order size? How often should an order be placed, to the nearest day?
(b)   Show that the annual holding cost and ordering cost are equal when the optimal order size is used. What is the total relevant cost?
(c)   The company wishes to order only once every other week. By what percentage would this increase the total relevant cost?
(d)   Suppose that this part can be ordered only in multiples of 100 units. What is the annual total relevant cost?

11.5   Describe at least two factors which can make the theoretical optimal lot size impracticable or impossible to use in an actual business situation. What is the value of sensitivity analysis in such situations?

11.6   In optimal lot size models, explain why the average inventory level is lower when replenishment is at a uniform rate than when it is instantaneous.

11.7   A furniture manufacturer makes 25 chairs of a certain model daily, so 100 legs are needed each day to continue production. The machine which makes chair legs can produce 200 legs per day. Setup cost for this machine is $100. The annual holding cost is $0.40 per chair leg.
  (a) Assuming 250 business days per year, how many chair legs should be made in each production lot if it is desired to minimize setup and holding costs?
  (b) How many working days will there be between production runs? How many days does a production run last?
  (c) Determine the total relevant cost of setting up production runs and holding chair legs in inventory.

11.8   If no shortages are allowed, what is the implied shortage cost? Is this generally realistic? Discuss.

11.9   In Exercise 11.3, if the state of Sur-tan-tee allows shortages, at a cost of 60 cents per gallon per year, how much paint should be ordered each time? What is the total annual cost (including the cost of the paint) associated with this policy?

11.10 The Shorte Company (Exercise 11.4) has decided to manufacture the part they have been ordering. They can produce this part at a monthly rate of 2500 units, and the setup cost per run is $20.
  (a) If no shortages are allowed, what is the optimal time, to the nearest day, between production runs, assuming 300 working days per year?
  (b) How many units must be produced in each run?
  (c) What is the total relevant cost?
  (d) What is the average inventory investment, in dollars, if each unit costs $25?
  (e) Suppose that shortages are allowed, and it is felt that the optimal production run size is 500 units. What is the implied annual shortage cost per unit short?

11.11 The Belle Cam Company can manufacture a certain type of cam at the rate of 1480 per month. Demand for this cam is quite steady, at an annual rate of 9000 units. The unit cost of the cam is $3, and the setup cost per production run is $100. The annual cost per unit short is $4. The company has determined the optimal production lot size to be 3000 units.
  (a) If the annual inventory holding cost is expressed as a percentage of the unit cost, what must this percentage be?
  (b) What are the total relevant cost and the maximum inventory level?

11.12 A large furniture distributor purchases bedroom sets for which he has an annual, essentially constant, demand of 250 units. For each order, he estimates his costs of ordering and handling as $36. Each set costs the distributor $400. His annual cost for money tied up in inventory is 15 percent, and there is also an annual storage charge of $12 per unit, as well as a per unit yearly insurance cost of 2 percent of the unit cost.

(a) If shortages are not allowed, what are the optimal order quantity and associated total relevant cost?

(b) What would be the optimal order quantity if the sets could be ordered only in quantities of 10 units? How much would the total relevant cost increase?

(c) Suppose that annual demand increased by 44 percent. What would be the percentage change in the optimal order quantity and total relevant cost, as compared to the answers in part (a)? (Work from basic relationships—do not recalculate the values.)

(d) If the order quantity determined in part (a) were used, even though the demand increased 44 percent, what would be the percentage change in total relevant cost, as compared to the answer in part (a)?

11.13 In deterministic lot size models, what additional cost factor must be considered when price breaks are involved, as compared to those models with no price breaks? Explain.

11.14 In Exercise 11.3, regarding the inventory policy for highway marking paint, shortages are not permitted, and the supplier offers a discount of five cents per gallon on orders of 1500 gallons or more and a discount of ten cents per gallon for orders of at least 4000 gallons. How much paint should be ordered each time? What is the total annual cost?

11.15 For the inventory problem of the Minny Computer Company, Example 11.4, suppose that shortages are now allowed, and the annual shortage cost is $2 per unit.

(a) Determine the optimal lot size and the total annual cost.

(b) Briefly explain the numerical differences between the answers in part (a) and the comparable answers in Example 11.4, in which shortages are not allowed.

11.16 For three different unit prices, draw a sketch, similar to Figure 11.8, showing total inventory cost versus lot size. For now, omit the price break between price 2 and price 3.

(a) Show a price break between unit prices C_2 and C_3 such that $\hat{Q}_2$ is the optimal lot size.

(b) Add a fourth curve at a still lower unit price C_4, and show its price break at a point such that $\hat{Q}_4$ is the optimal lot size.

11.17 Given an inventory situation where demand is known but changes from period to period, explain how a Wagner-Whitin model, where applicable, simplifies the dynamic programming calculations.

11.18 The Ketchup Queen is a wholesale food distributor who usually buys her entire year's supply of the red sauce in late September when the bulk tomato crop is processed. Her bright young son-in-law, the Ketchup Prince, has suggested that the Queen might save money by purchasing ketchup several times a year, instead of just once. Quarterly demand and cost figures are given below.

	4th Quarter	1st Quarter	2nd Quarter	3rd Quarter
Demand (1000s of gallons)	50	50	60	70
Cost (cents per gallon)	40	54	66	72

It costs 11 cents to hold a gallon of ketchup in inventory for one quarter.
(a)   Find the optimal purchasing strategy by solving this problem as a Wagner-Whitin model. Assume that the supply of ketchup is not a limiting factor.
(b)   What is the total cost? How much money has the Prince saved the Queen?

11.19 In the next eight weeks, the E. Lectric Company has contracted to build specialty transformers in the following quantities

Week	1	2	3	4	5	6	7	8
Units required	25	33	18	32	49	40	27	41

Each unit costs $50 to manufacture, and there is an inventory holding cost of $1 per week. Setup cost is $80 per production run, except in the last two weeks, when it will be $90. There are presently 30 units on hand.
       Determine the optimal production schedule and its cost.

11.20 Suppose that the E. Lectric Company (Exercise 11.19) can realize manufacturing economies in the production of large lots. After the first 100 units in any production run, the unit cost drops to $45.
       Determine the optimal production schedule and its cost.

11.21 In the production scheduling problem of the Trific Tractor Company, Example 11.4, suppose that the inventory holding cost C_h were unknown. By solving this problem as a Wagner-Whitin model:
(a)   Determine the maximum allowable value of C_h such that the optimal production schedule would be to produce all 9 items in period 1.
(b)   What is the minimum value of C_h, such that it would never be economical to hold inventory from one period to another?

11.22 Explain the general concept of incremental analysis as applied to single-period probabilistic inventory models.

11.23 In an incremental analysis problem involving a discrete probability distribution, when the critical probability p_c is calculated, how is the optimal number of units to stock chosen? What is the rationale behind this selection?

11.24 Flatt Tire Company has just been informed of the availability of a new line of radial tires. These tires would cost Flatt $35 each and would sell for $70. If the tires stocked are not sold within a three-month period, Flatt would wholesale them at an estimated price of $25 per tire. Annual holding costs are calculated as 20 percent of unit costs. Based on previous experience with radial tire sales, Flatt estimates the following probability distribution of demand.

Sets of 4 Tires	10	15	20	25
Demand probability	0.4	0.3	0.2	0.1

(a) What is the optimal number of tires for Flatt Tire Company to stock?

(b) How many tires can Flatt expect to sell if it stocks the number of tires determined in part (a)?

(c) If there is a goodwill cost associated with each set of tires Flatt is unable to supply upon demand, how much would this cost have to be before Flatt would be indifferent to stocking 20 or 25 sets of tires?

(d) If there is no goodwill cost, how high would the salvage value have to be before stocking at least 20 sets of tires could be justified?

11.25   The Makeshift Company has just placed an order for 20 units of a special machine part which is difficult to manufacture and has a very high setup cost. From past experience, parts similar to these have averaged 3 percent defective from this supplier. The cost of each unit is $30. If this special part is not available when needed, there is an estimated cost of $200 in machine downtime and labor cost incurred while a defective part is reworked. This problem can be alleviated by ordering spare units, guaranteed to be good, at a cost of $50 each. Excess units, however, have no salvage value. The holding cost during the period of interest is 10 percent of the unit cost.

(a) How many spare units should be ordered, assuming a binomial distribution of defectives?

(b) What is the expected value of the shortage penalty cost incurred if the optimal number of spares is stocked?

(c) For what value of the shortage penalty cost would it be optimal to stock *no* spares?

11.26   Demand for a certain daily newspaper appears to be random, with a mean of 1.5. This newspaper costs $0.06 and sells for $0.15. Unsold papers receive a rebate of 50 percent of their cost. An estimated goodwill cost of $0.10 is associated with each unfilled demand. Holding cost can be considered negligible.

(a) What is the optimal number of papers to stock?

(b) What would be the optimal number of papers to stock if unsold papers were worthless?

(c) Perform a sensitivity analysis to determine the decision ranges on the value of unsold papers.

11.27   In the spares problem of Example 11.7, the expected cost of the spares furnished can be estimated as follows.

E(spares cost) = (expected units used) $\times$ $(C + C_h/2)$
        + (expected units not used) $\times$ $(C + C_h - V)$
        + (expected units short) $\times$ C_p.

(a) If 1 spare, the optimal number, is stocked, show that the expected number of units used is 0.20, the expected number of units not used is 0.80, and the expected number of units short is 0.05. Find the expected cost of stocking 1 spare.

(b) Suppose that a failure detector has been developed which will give advance warning of an incipient failure in time to special-order a spare, thereby avoiding the downtime cost entirely. The cost of manufacturing and shipping a spare on a special-order basis is $2000. Determine the optimal number of spares. How much would such a failure detector be worth?

11.28 Referring to the spares problem of Example 11.7, perform a sensitivity analysis of the emergency cost e to determine the range of e over which 0, 1, or 2 spares are optimal.

11.29 A newsstand receives its weekly order of Glimpse magazine on Monday and cannot reorder. Each copy costs $0.15 and sells for $0.25. Unsold copies may be returned the following week and are worth $0.10 each. When the newstand runs out of copies and cannot supply a customer wanting a Glimpse, it estimates its goodwill loss as $0.20 in future profits, figuring that the customer will take his business elsewhere for a couple of weeks, on the average. Demand has been remarkably constant, ranging between 7 and 10 copies, as shown below.

Demand, copies	7	8	9	10
Fraction of time	0.3	0.4	0.2	0.1

(a) Determine the optimal number of copies to stock.
(b) If none of the customers were regular customers, so that a lost sale resulted only in a profit foregone, with no additional goodwill cost, what would be the optimal number of copies to stock?
(c) In the original problem, suppose that it were now possible to reorder, at a unit cost of $0.20, and a would-be purchaser would return the following day to purchase the magazine. Find the optimal number of copies to stock.
(d) Given the data in part (c), if only a fraction f of purchasers would wait for a reorder, perform a sensitivity analysis to determine the optimal number of copies to stock as a function of f.

11.30 A florist buys long-stemmed roses every morning for $5.50 per dozen and sells them fresh for $15 per dozen. On Valentine's Day and Mother's Day, he pays $7.50 per dozen, but raises his selling price to $20 per dozen. At the end of the day, including holidays, unsold roses are sold to Wilt's Flowers for $3 per dozen. On days other than special holidays, demand for roses is uniformly distributed between 21 and 30 dozen. On special holidays, rose demand is uniformly distributed between 31 and 40 dozen.
(a) How many roses should the florist stock on special holidays such as Valentine's Day?
(b) How many roses should the florist stock on ordinary days?
(c) Compare your answers to (a) and (b) and discuss their difference.

11.31 In the spring, a retail store receives its shipment of men's summer suits. The best estimate of the seasonal demand for these suits appears to be in the range of 80 to 120, with any quantity in that range being equally likely. The average cost of these suits is $40, and the average selling price is $60. Any suits unsold at the end of summer can be sold at half price. The annual cost of holding inventory is estimated as 15 percent, and the holding period is about four months. Assuming a uniform probability distribution of demand

(as a good approximation to the actual discrete distribution):
(a)   What is the optimal number of suits to stock?
(b)   Suppose the average cost of the suits were a variable. Express the critical probability p_c as a function of this variable. Find the limiting values of this variable for which the optimal number of suits to stock would be (1) 80, (2) 120. Briefly explain the rationale for these limiting values.

11.32   The Looksee Company sells calendar year appointment books to doctors and dentists. Each appointment book costs $6 and sells for $10. Unsold books are worthless. A single order is placed in the fall and it is not possible to reorder. If a potential customer orders an appointment book and none is available, Looksee estimates a goodwill cost of $8 due to the potential loss of future orders. Annual demand for these appointment books appears to be normally distributed, with a mean of 1200 and a standard deviation of 100. Disregarding the holding costs for the short holding period:
(a)   What is the optimal number of appointment books to stock?
(b)   Sketch the (mixed) cumulative probability distribution of sales.
(c)   Suppose it becomes possible to reorder, at a cost of $8 per book, and 80 percent of customers will wait for a reorder. Under these conditions, determine the optimal number of appointment books to stock.

11.33   What is buffer stock, and what function does it serve?

11.34   Explain the basic method of operation for the followimg inventory systems:
(a)   Order point systems
(b)   Periodic review systems

11.35   For a given inventory item, why is the buffer stock requirement greater if a periodic review ordering policy is used than if a continuous review ordering policy is used?

11.36   A tropical fish store buys its goldfish from a supplier that delivers an order two weeks after it is placed. Goldfish demand for two weeks is approximately normally distributed with a mean of 800 and a standard deviation of 50. If it is desired to keep the probability of running out of goldfish to not more than 0.05, what should the reorder point be?

11.37   A department store sells electric fans over about a four-month period. During that time, the store expects to sell 400 units. Each order placed with its warehouse costs $30 and the annual cost of carrying a unit in inventory is estimated as 40 percent of the unit cost, which is $15. During the three-day order lead time, daily demand appears to have a Poisson distribution, with a mean of 5 units.
    Determine the optimal order quantity and the reorder level for a service level of 0.96.

11.38   For the problem of Exercise 11.37, determine the value of the service fraction if the reorder level is set equal to the expected lead-time demand, so that there is no buffer stock, and an order is placed each month in the four-month period.

11.39   For the data of Exercise 11.37, perform a sensitivity analysis to determine the implied value of the shortage penalty cost C_p as a function of the optimal order point. Use order point values from 15 to 28.

11.40 The Daisy Bicycle Shop reorders its most popular line of ten-speed bicycles every week, using a replenishment level system. Demand appears to be Poisson, averaging 5 units per day. Daisy is open 6 days a week. Lead time for orders from the local warehouse is from 3 to 5 working days, averaging 4 days.

   (a)   What replenishment level is required to achieve a stockout protection level of at least 99 percent?

   (b)   What is the stockout protection level associated with a replenishment level of 60?

CHAPTER 12

QUEUEING MODELS

A queue is nothing more or less than a waiting line. Queues are with us in all aspects of our existence. We wait in lines at stop signs and traffic lights, at supermarkets and the post office, at the doctor's office and at the tennis court. We also encounter less obvious queueing delays when we call an airlines reservation office and get a busy signal, when we have car trouble and the tow truck is delayed because of a backlog of service calls, when our income tax refund request waits in line behind thousands of other such requests, and so on, ad infinitum.

Queueing problems arise primarily because of economic considerations. It is indeed a rare situation in which the cost of service is so low that enough service facilities can be provided so that no arrival ever has to wait. The only situation of this nature that comes to mind is that of self-service! (In some cases, however, a queue can improve efficiency, as when pedestrians wait at a traffic light to cross the street, thereby avoiding interference with the flow of vehicular traffic and reducing pedestrian fatalities.) In general, an attempt is made to balance the cost of providing service and that associated with obtaining it, including the cost of waiting time. In the application of queueing theory to practical problems, we strive to minimize the total cost of service and waiting time by manipulating the controllable variables, such as number of servers, speed of service, and order of service. A good illustration of the practical application of queueing theory is given in the following example.

In most banks, supermarkets, post offices, and other public places, a customer requiring service but finding all servers busy joins what he hopes will be the shortest, that is, fastest-moving, queue. He may be lucky and wait only a few minutes, but he may also be delayed by someone with a time-consuming transaction, while he observes later arrivals entering a different line and receiving service while he is still waiting. As a result, he may switch from line to line and become even more frustrated.

A number of banks and post offices, as well as other service organizations, have initiated a special type of service with a single queue for all customers. Entering customers follow a marked path and join a single line (well clear of the clerks' positions), if all clerks are busy. They are then served, in turn, by the first clerk who becomes available. This type of service has two main advantages over the usual service: it is fair, offering first-come, first-served service, and it affords the individual customer privacy, since there is only one customer at a time at each clerk's position. In some such installations, tests have indicated an average customer time saving of 10 percent and more over the conventional multiple-queue system. Generally, both customers and clerks strongly favor this type of service.

Given the numerical data in a particular situation, such as arrival rates, service rates, their probability distributions, and the number of servers, queueing models can be particularly useful in determining the effect of changes on the operation of a system in which queues form.

12.1 ANALYSIS OF QUEUEING SITUATIONS

Queues form when units receiving some type of service cannot be serviced immediately. The type of units being serviced, the actual service performed, and the queue itself all can take many different forms, as shown in Table 12.1.

Table 12.1 Representative Queueing Situations

Arriving Units	Servers	The Queue
Cars	Left-turn lane	Cars waiting to turn
Airplanes	Runways	Planes waiting to land or to take off
Ships	Repair docks	Ships awaiting repair
Parcels	Postal clerks	Parcels awaiting distribution
Computer jobs	Computer	Jobs awaiting processing
Students	Scholarships	List of applicants
Diners	Restaurant tables	Waiting diners
Customers	Clerks	Waiting customers
Tennis players	Tennis courts	Waiting players
Library patrons	Books	Waiting list
Commuters	Buses	Waiting passengers
Disabled machines	Repairmen	Machines awaiting repair
Telephone calls	Airline reservations clerk	Calls on "hold"
Trouble calls	Police cars	Unanswered calls
Budgetary requests	Budget	Unfunded requests
Orders for merchandise	Inventory	Back orders
Criminal cases	Criminal courts	Cases awaiting trial

These examples are designed to be "mind expanders," clearly illustrating the great conceptual diversity of queueing situations. For instance, there are arrivals (cars, people) that are mobile, arrivals (parcels) that are moved by outside forces, arrivals (disabled machines) that are immobile and which "arrive" only in the sense that they require service at some point in time, arrivals (telephone calls) not in a physical form, and arrivals (orders for merchandise) that can possibly be considered requests for some particular resource. As for the servers, we have servers (runways) that represent a capacity of some sort, servers (airline reservation clerks) that are stationary or essentially so, servers (police cars) that are mobile, and servers (clerks) that can be stationary or mobile. There are queues in which the queue (ships awaiting repair) requires some type of waiting space, in which the queue (disabled machines) requires no waiting space as such, in which the queue (unanswered trouble calls) is nonphysical, and in which the queue (back orders) essentially represents a list of some nature. These categorizations are far from exhaustive and by no means mutually exclusive.

In some queueing situations, the arriving units and the servers interchange positions, under certain conditions. Consider, for example, the situation with taxis and waiting passengers. At a given hotel, there are times when the doorman flags down a passing taxi for a waiting passenger. At other times, there is a line of cabs at the hotel waiting for passengers. In the first case, the taxi is serving the passenger, but in the second case, from a queueing standpoint, the passenger is "serving" the taxi. A similar situation occurs in a store in which the customers usually outnumber the salesmen, except for slack periods, when the salesmen are waiting for customers.

As diagrammed in Figure 12.1, a queueing system consists of arriving units, a queue of some nature, the queue discipline (method of selecting the next unit to be served), and the so-called service mechanism.

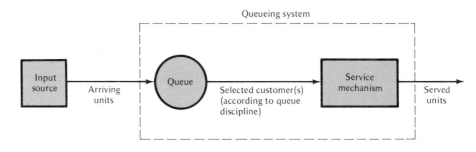

Figure 12.1

Any queueing system can be described by a particular set of characteristics, so let us now list and briefly describe some of the more important characteristics of queueing systems, with regard to the input source, the queue, and the service mechanism. By doing this we sometimes find that a system that is quite different, to outward appearances, from any system we are familiar with, is really not different from a queueing standpoint and is thus amenable to the same general mathematical approaches.

12.2 CHARACTERISTICS OF QUEUEING SYSTEMS

Input Source

Calling Population   When the number of potential arrivals is dependent on the number of units currently in the system (those being serviced plus those in queue), the calling population is limited, or *finite*. If there are five lathes which occasionally require servicing, and three of them are inoperative, then, at that point in time, there are only two units which could possibly require service.

The calling population is considered to be unlimited (no inherent limitation), or *infinite*, when the number of potential arrivals is independent of the number of units currently in the system. The number of cars arriving at a toll booth is not a function of the number of cars being served or awaiting service at that toll booth.

Arrival Distribution   The probability distribution of the time between successive arrivals defines the arrival distribution. There is an unlimited number of possible arrival distributions, ranging from equally spaced arrivals to distributions where the time between arrivals is extremely variable.

If, in any small interval of time (small compared with the average time between arrivals), the probability of an arrival is the same as for all such intervals and independent of other arrivals, then we have *Poisson* arrivals. Telephone calls to a business firm during any relatively short time period, such as a half hour, tend to arrive in such a random fashion.

Arrivals   A customer waiting to check out at a supermarket represents a *single* arrival. A family entering a restaurant represents a *bulk* arrival.

Degree of Control of Customers   For customers of retail stores, the control is *insignificant,* since customers can enter at any time these stores are open. There is a *significant* degree of control over aircraft scheduled to land at a large airport; we call this air traffic control. However, aircraft arrival times can change appreciably as a result of weather and other factors outside the airport's control. There is *almost total* control over patients arriving at a dentist's office.

Customer Behavior   Arriving customers are considered to be *patient* when they will wait for service regardless of the number in queue. Jobs arriving to be processed through a computer can be considered as patient "customers." A customer, dissatisfied by the delay in service, who leaves the queue (reneges) is termed *impatient.* Customers who move from one queue to another hoping to receive service more quickly are said to be *jockeying.* A customer who *balks* will not wait for service if the queue is too long. He may or may not return later. A driver *balks* when he is unwilling to stop at a busy service station. If service is not immediately available, an arrival can be *lost*, at least temporarily. When a telephone caller receives a busy signal, he must hang up and try again before he can possibly complete the call. When arrivals collaborate to reduce overall waiting time, their behavior is termed *collusive*. There is collusion when one person gets in line at a ticket window to buy tickets for three other persons also waiting to buy tickets.

Queue

Size   Calls for airline information are often put on "hold" while reservations clerks are busy. The queue of waiting calls is limited, or *finite*, because the number of available lines is limited. When traffic backs up at a railroad crossing, the queue is essentially unlimited, or *infinite*.

Queue Discipline   When the first customer in line is the next customer served, we have a *first-come, first-served* (also called FIFO, for first-in, first-out) queue discipline. When the last customer in line is the next customer served, we have a *last-come, first served* (also called LIFO, for last-in, first-out) queue discipline. At the end of the working day in an office building, the last person to enter an elevator is frequently the first to leave at the ground floor. Customers in a busy store frequently tend to be served in *random* order. When units requiring service receive partial service in sequential order, such as programs being run on time-shared terminals, we have a *round-robin* queue discipline. Under a *preemptive priority* queue discipline, service is interrupted to start service for a special customer. Police officers conducting spot vehicle inspections will leave immediately if called to the aid of fellow officers. Under a *nonpreemptive priority* queue discipline, special service is started immediately on completion of the current service. Thus a "hot" computer job is readied to start as soon as the current job is completed. There are many other possible queue disciplines in addition to those described here.

Queues for Multiple Servers   When there is a *single queue*, all arrivals enter a single line and are served by the first available server. Some stores give customers a number when they arrive. They are then served by the first available salesperson when their number comes up. In supermarkets, as in many establishments, there is *one queue per server*. Sometimes, there is a *combination* of single and multiple queues, as in the morning rush for elevators on the ground floor in a busy office building. Some persons wait in front of a specific elevator, while others stand around waiting to make a dash for the next elevator to arrive.

Service Mechanism

Number of Service Channels   The box office of a small movie theater represents a *single* service channel, whereas the check-out stands at a supermarket represent *multiple* service channels (as do the seats in a movie theater).

Arrangement of Service Channels   With *parallel noncooperative* service channels, the servers perform independently, as would be the case with checkout clerks in a supermarket. With *parallel cooperative* service channels, the servers help one another if they can, as in the case of service station attendants working together to service a single car. When the service channels are in *series* (or tandem), units proceed from one server to the next, possibly waiting in queue between services. Products manufactured in a machine shop typically go through a series of operations, frequently waiting in a queue prior to each operation. An example of *series-parallel* service channels is found at sports stadiums where there are multiple ticket windows at which to buy tickets and then multiple gates at which to present tickets.

Service Capacity per Channel   Most types of service with which we are familiar handle only *one* customer at a time. However, in many types of service, such as buses, restaurants, and so forth, *more than one* customer can be handled at the same time.

Service Time Distribution   If, in any small interval of time (small compared with the average service time), the probability that service is completed is the same as for all such intervals and is independent of the length of time that service has been in process, we have *random* (negative exponential) service completions. The completion time of some types of telephone calls tends to be random. Parts baked in an annealing oven for a fixed time period would have a *constant* service time. Sometimes, the service is *dependent on queue length.* Thus, when a service station is very busy, attendants tend to skip nonessential services in order to speed up the service rate. Literally, there is an infinite number of possible service time distributions.

Priority

Sometimes, a *deliberate* priority is established, as when supermarkets have a quick checkout counter for customers buying only a few items. In certain situations, a *nondeliberate* priority can be established. For example, during the peak departure period, buses in a downtown area may fill up at the first few stops, so that would-be passengers a little farther out on the route watch full buses go by until the downtown rush eases.

12.3   OVERVIEW

Having indicated the broad scope of queueing problems, discussed the general characteristics of such systems, and introduced some of the terms in common usage, we now develop the basic concepts of queueing and apply them to simple single-server and multiple-server models. As you will see, queueing formulas become rather involved even for elementary queueing models, and for queueing situations of any real complexity we are almost forced to turn to the technique of simulation, discussed in Chapter 14. However, a knowledge of analytical queueing models frequently enables us to utilize these models, by making simplifying but often quite adequate assumptions, to determine, at least roughly, the operating characteristics of a given queueing system. We are concerned with such operating characteristics as mean waiting times, mean queue lengths, and fraction of server idle time. Economic analysis is developed in the latter part of the chapter, and the important concept of sensitivity analysis and its application to queueing problems is also discussed.

Almost all the models to be developed are based on the assumption of Poisson arrivals and exponential service times. In Appendix 12A, the Poisson distribution of arrivals is derived, based on the assumption of completely random arrivals, and the exponential service distribution is derived from the assumption of completely random service departures. Both these distributions were also discussed in Chapter 3.

12.4   STEADY-STATE ANALYSIS

When a queueing system has recently begun operation, as, for example, when a bank opens its doors, the state of the system (number of units in the system) is greatly affected by the initial state and the elapsed time. During this period, the system is said to be in a *transient* condition. However, after sufficient time has elapsed, the state of the system becomes essentially independent of the initial state and of the elapsed time, except under unusual circumstances. The system has now reached a *steady-state* condition. Queueing theory has tended to focus largely on the steady-state case, primarily for two reasons: (1) Systems usually operate in the steady state most of the time and (2) the transient case is much more difficult to model analytically. We will concentrate entirely on the analysis of steady-state conditions. (The transient case can be analyzed through the use of simulation techniques, presented in Chapter 14.)

The basic notation used is as follows.

Let λ = mean arrival rate per unit time,
  μ = mean service rate per unit time (if the server were continually busy),
  $(1/\mu$ = mean service time),
  ρ = traffic intensity,
   $= \lambda/\mu$,
  S = number of service channels,
  n = number of calling units in system (waiting and in service),
   = state of system,
  P_n = probability of n calling units in system,
   = probability that the system is in state n,
  L = mean number of calling units in system (waiting and in service),
  L_q = mean number of calling units in queue,
  W = mean time in system (queue time plus service time),
  W_q = mean time in queue.

For our analytical results to be valid, the traffic intensity per server, ρ/S, must be less than unity (the arrival rate must be less than the overall service rate), or queues will tend to build up without limit. The queueing system would then no longer be in the steady state.

In some models, to be discussed later, there is no such limitation on the value of the traffic intensity. These models represent a situation in which the queue length is limited, generally because of some type of space or capacity limitation, or in which customers balk when the queue becomes too long for their liking. In another class of models, the traffic intensity is inherently limited by the nature of the process itself. Thus, for example, if a group of machines suffer individual breakdowns, at any given time the potential arrivals for service are limited to those machines which are operable.

In our analyses, we assume Poisson (completely random) arrivals. There is a considerable degree of justification for doing so, as many arrival processes tend toward complete randomness. Consider, for instance, the breakdown of machines, the arrival of customers at a store in a given half-hour time period, and so forth. Although in real-world systems the arrival rate is rarely constant over any appreciable time period, we can often validly assume that it is constant in a long enough interval to be meaningful. The assumption of Poisson arrivals is reasonable, unless we have good reasons or evidence to doubt it, and it permits us to develop a number of worthwhile analytical models.

In most cases, we make the assumption of exponential service time. This assumption is much harder to justify than that of Poisson arrivals, since it implies that the probability of service completion in any short time period is constant and independent of the length of time that service has been in progress. The duration of a local telephone call seems to be a reasonably good example of an exponential service distribution. Our primary reason for assuming exponential service is that it enables us to formulate simple mathematical models that can aid us in gaining insight into a number of aspects of queueing problems. It should be noted that exponential service represents an extreme case, that of completely random service departures. (The opposite extreme is the case of constant service, which we briefly touch on.)

There are a number of ways in which empirical data can be tested statistically to determine whether they reasonably fit a Poisson or exponential distribution. As a rough check, one particularly straightforward method can be used for both these distributions, by virtue of their equivalence, discussed earlier. In testing data on arrivals, given the actual arrival times, we determine the mean and variance of the resulting interarrival times. If the variance is approximately equal to the square of the mean, as would be the case for exponentially distributed interarrival times, then the assumption of Poisson arrivals is probably reasonable. A better feeling as to the validity of the exponential distribution assumption can be obtained if the cumulative distribution function of the interarrival times is plotted and compared with that of the theoretical exponential distribution with the same mean. These same approaches can be used to test whether service times appear to follow an exponential distribution.

12.5 SINGLE-SERVER MODELS

Exponential Service—Unlimited Queue

In the following section, the basic relationships are developed for a single-server queueing system with exponential service. In the succeeding section, the resulting formulas are summarized and used to solve an example problem.

In the major sections on single-server and multiple-server models which follow we will find that some of the most important formulas cannot be derived without knowing the state probability equation(s) for P_n, the probability that there are n calling units (customers) in the system. To avoid an overemphasis on mathematical detail, the theoretical development of the state probability equations for the various models has been placed in appendices at the end of the chapter. The material on each new model then starts with the determination of the required basic relationships between and among state probabilities and system operating characteristics, followed by a summarization of the important formulas, and a numerical example.

Basic Relationships   The fundamental state probability formula, which is derived in Appendix 12B, is

$$P_n = \rho^n(1 - \rho) \qquad n \geqslant 0 \qquad \rho < 1 \tag{12.1}$$

where P_n = probability of n calling units (customers) in the system
  ρ = traffic intensity
    = λ/μ, ratio of arrival rate to service rate.

Starting with Equation (12.1), several important relationships can be determined.

1. L, mean number of units in the system
   L is simply the weighted average of all system states, so

$$L = \sum_{n=0}^{\infty} nP_n = \sum_{n=0}^{\infty} n\rho^n(1 - \rho) = (1 - \rho)\sum_{n=0}^{\infty} n\rho^n.$$

The quantity inside the summation is the infinite series

$$\rho + 2\rho^2 + 3\rho^3 + \cdots = \rho(1 + 2\rho + 3\rho^2 + \cdots),$$

which, for $\rho < 1$, converges to the sum $\rho/(1 - \rho)^2$. (See any calculus text.) Therefore

$$L = (1 - \rho)\frac{\rho}{(1 - \rho)^2} = \frac{\rho}{1 - \rho} = \frac{\lambda}{\mu - \lambda}.$$

2. L_q, mean number of units in the queue
   L_q must equal the mean number in the system L minus the mean number in service. With a single server, the mean number of units in service is simply equal to the fraction of time that the server is busy, or $1 - P_0$. Thus

$$L_q = L - (1 - P_0) = L - (1 - 1 + \rho) = L - \rho$$

$$= \frac{\rho}{1 - \rho} - \rho = \frac{\rho^2}{1 - \rho} = \frac{\lambda^2}{\mu(\mu - \lambda)}.$$

We can also calculate L_q by a different approach. The mean number of units waiting is the weighted average of all queue lengths. With a single server, the number in queue at any time is one less than the number in the system, provided there is at least one unit in the system. Thus, we have

$$L_q = \sum_{n=1}^{\infty} (n - 1)P_n = \sum_{n=1}^{\infty} nP_n - \sum_{n=1}^{\infty} P_n$$

$$= (L - 0P_0) - (1 - P_0) = L - (1 - P_0)$$

$$= L - \rho,$$

as before.

3. W_q, mean time a unit spends in queue

To determine W_q, we use the following intuitive argument: in a long time period T, the mean number of arrivals is λT. If the mean number in queue is L_q, then the total time that all units spend waiting is $L_q T$. The mean waiting time equals the total waiting time divided by the number of calling units during the entire time period, so

$$W_q = \frac{L_q T}{\lambda T} = \frac{L_q}{\lambda} = \frac{\rho^2}{\lambda(1 - \rho)} = \frac{\lambda}{\mu(\mu - \lambda)} = \frac{\rho}{\mu - \lambda}.$$

For example, suppose that $\lambda = 10$ arrivals per hour and $L_q = 1.8$. In a period of 100 hours, the total time in queue is $(1.8)(100) = 180$ hours. With an expected 1000 arrivals during the period, the mean time in queue $W_q = 180/1000 = 0.18$ hours $= L_q/\lambda$.

4. W, mean time a unit spends in the system

Following the same line of reasoning, the mean system time W equals L/λ. From another viewpoint, the mean system time is the sum of the mean time in queue and the mean time in service. The mean service time is just $1/\mu$, the reciprocal of the mean service rate. Therefore,

$$W = W_q + \frac{1}{\mu} = \frac{L_q}{\lambda} + \frac{1}{\mu} = \frac{1}{\lambda}\left(L_q + \frac{\lambda}{\mu}\right)$$

$$= \frac{1}{\lambda}(L_q + \rho) = \frac{L}{\lambda}, \qquad \text{since } L_q = L - \rho, \text{ as shown earlier.}$$

The two relationships, namely, $W_q = L_q/\lambda$ and $W = L/\lambda$, have been proved, by Little (1961) and Jewell (1967), to hold over quite general conditions for any steady-state queueing process in which the arrival rate is independent of the service rate.[1] (With suitable modifications, as we will see, these relationships also hold when this condition is not met.) Knowing any one of the quantities L, L_q, W, or W_q, we can readily determine the other three values.

---

[1] J. D. C. Little, "A Proof for the Queuing Formula: $L = \lambda W$." *Operations Research*, Vol. 9, 1961, pp. 383–387. W. S. Jewell, "A Simple Proof of: $L = \lambda W$," *Operations Research*, Vol. 15, 1967, pp. 1109–1116.

5. $\hat{P}_n$, probability of n or more units in the system

It is not difficult to determine the probability $\hat{P}_n$ of n or more units in the system:

$$\hat{P}_n = \sum_{i=n}^{\infty} P_i = (1 - \rho) \sum_{i=n}^{\infty} \rho^i = (1 - \rho)(\rho^n + \rho^{n+1} + \rho^{n+2} + \cdots).$$

The infinite geometric series in the second term sums to $\rho^n/(1 - \rho)$, as given by the $A/(1 - R)$ formula presented in Appendix 12B. Then

$$\hat{P}_n = (1 - \rho)\frac{\rho^n}{1 - \rho} = \rho^n.$$

Summarization of Formulas   For Poisson arrivals, exponential service, and no limit on the queue length, the useful formulas are as follows. (*Note:* $\rho < 1$.)

Fraction of time n units in system:

$$P_n = (1 - \rho)\rho^n. \tag{12.1}$$

Fraction server idle time:

$$P_0 = 1 - \rho. \tag{12.2}$$

Fraction of time n or more units in system:

$$\hat{P}_n = \rho^n. \tag{12.3}$$

Mean number of units in system:

$$L = \frac{\rho}{1 - \rho} = \frac{\lambda}{\mu - \lambda} = L_q + \rho = \lambda W. \tag{12.4}$$

Mean number of units in queue:

$$L_q = \frac{\rho^2}{1 - \rho} = \frac{\lambda^2}{\mu(\mu - \lambda)} = L - \rho = \lambda W_q. \tag{12.5}$$

Mean number of units in service $= \rho$.

Mean time in system:

$$W = \frac{\rho}{\lambda(1 - \rho)} = \frac{1}{\mu - \lambda} = W_q + \frac{1}{\mu} = \frac{L}{\lambda}. \tag{12.6}$$

Mean time in queue:

$$W_q = \frac{\rho^2}{\lambda(1 - \rho)} = \frac{\rho}{\mu - \lambda} = W - \frac{1}{\mu} = \frac{L_q}{\lambda} \tag{12.7}$$

Let us now utilize these results to solve an example problem.

EXAMPLE 12.1

The owner of a small service station operates it by himself. On Friday afternoon, customers arrive randomly at the rate of 12 per hour. On the average service takes 3 minutes and tends to be exponentially distributed.

a) What is the mean number of customers waiting at any time?

$$\lambda = 12/\text{hr}.$$

Mean service time $= 1/\mu = 3 \text{ min} = 0.05 \text{ hr}, \ \mu = 1/0.05 = 20/\text{hr}.$

$$\rho = \lambda \mu = 12/20 = 0.6$$

$$L_q = \frac{\rho^2}{1 - \rho} = \frac{(0.6)^2}{0.4} = 0.9.$$

b) What is the mean customer waiting time, in minutes?

$$W_q = L_q/\lambda = 0.9/12 = 0.075 \text{ hr} = 4.5 \text{ min}.$$

c) What is the mean time that a customer spends in the station?

$$W = W_q + 1/\mu = 4.5 + 3 = 7.5 \text{ min}.$$

d) What is the mean number of customers in the station?

$$L = \lambda W = 12(7.5/60) = 1.5.$$

e) What fraction of time is the owner idle?

$$P_0 = 1 - \rho = 0.4.$$

f) What fraction of time will there be customers waiting?
Let $n =$ number of customers in the station. Customers wait if $n > 1$.

$$P(n > 1) = P(n \geqslant 2) = \hat{P}_2 = \rho^2 = 0.36.$$

Arbitrary Service Time Distribution—Unlimited Queue

It has been shown by Saaty (1961) that the following formula, which is known as the Pollaczek-Khintchine formula, gives the mean queue length for any service distribution with finite variance σ^2.

$$L_q = \frac{\rho^2 + \lambda^2\sigma^2}{2(1 - \rho)}. \tag{12.8}$$

(For any random variable with a negative exponential distribution, the variance equals the square of the mean. Thus, for exponential service, the variance of the service time equals $1/\mu^2$, and the Pollaczek-Khintchine formula reduces to the expression $\rho^2(1 - \rho)$, derived earlier.)

Once we have calculated L_q, the other operating characteristics can be easily determined, since

$$L = L_q + \rho, \qquad W_q = L_q/\lambda, \qquad W = W_q + 1/\mu.$$

Observe that, for a given λ and μ, all these operating characteristics decrease linearly with decreasing variance. (P_0, fraction server idle time, is independent of the variance.) Even if it is not possible or practicable to reduce the average service time, improvement in system performance can be achieved by reduction of the variability of service times. Consider, for instance, the previous example involving the service station owner. Suppose that his mean service time remained at 3 minutes, but that he was able to reduce his standard deviation from its original 3 minutes (based on the exponential distribution) to just 1 minute. Converting the variance to units consistent with λ, $\sigma^2 = (1/60)^2$. Then, recalling that λ was 12 arrivals per hour, so that ρ was 0.6,

$$L_q = \frac{(0.6)^2 + (12)^2(1/60)^2}{2(0.4)} = \frac{0.36 + 0.04}{0.8} = 0.5,$$

$$L = L_q + \rho = 0.5 + 0.6 = 1.1.$$

Thus, compared with the case of exponential service, the mean queue length decreased from 0.9 to 0.5, and the mean number in the system decreased from 1.5 to 1.1. The mean time in queue W_q would drop from 4.5 to 2.5 minutes, and the mean system time W would be reduced from 7.5 to 5.5 minutes.

Let us now examine two particular service time distributions.

Constant Service Time   If the service time is the same for every unit served, the service time variance is zero. Substituting $\sigma^2 = 0$ in the Pollaczek-Khintchine formula,

$$L_q = \frac{\rho^2}{2(1 - \rho)}. \tag{12.9}$$

Note that this value is exactly one-half that for the case of exponential service. The assumption of constant service time places an absolute lower bound on the value of the mean queue length, and a reasonable upper bound can be obtained by assuming exponential service, since the negative exponential distribution can be considered a high-variance distribution. (It is possible, but quite unlikely, that a service distribution with a higher variance than the exponential distribution would be encountered.) Observe that, since L_q is halved, W_q is also halved.

Erlang Service Time   The Erlang distribution represents the summation of k random variates drawn from a negative exponential distribution. An Erlang service distribution, with parameters μ and k, consists of k identical exponential services (phases) in series, each with mean service time $1/(k\mu)$. A new service does not start until all k phases have been completed.

Let the random variable T denote the total service time and t_i the service time in phase i:

$$T = t_1 + t_2 + \cdots + t_k = \sum_{i=1}^{k} t_i.$$

The expected value of T is

$$E(T) = k \left(\frac{1}{k\mu} \right) = \frac{1}{\mu}.$$

Recalling that the variance of the exponential distribution is equal to the square of the mean, the variance of the Erlang distribution, $V(T)$, is

$$V(T) = k \frac{1}{(k\mu)^2} = \frac{1}{k\mu^2}.$$

Observe that we get the exponential distribution when $k = 1$ and constant service time when $k = \infty$.

The Erlang distribution is considered to be a fairly "rich" distribution, since it can assume a rather wide range of shapes, as shown in Figure 12.2. Many empirical service time distributions can be represented by an Erlang distribution with the appropriate value of k. It should be clearly noted that the number of phases k does not have to have any physical significance.

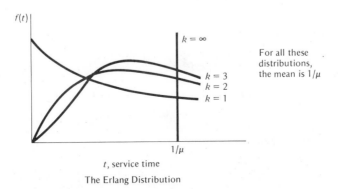

For all these distributions, the mean is $1/\mu$

The Erlang Distribution

Figure 12.2

Substituting the Erlang variance in the Pollaczek-Khintchine formula,

$$L_q = \frac{\rho^2 + \lambda^2 \left[1/(k\mu^2) \right]}{2(1 - \rho)} = \frac{\rho^2(1 + k)}{2k(1 - \rho)}. \qquad \textbf{(12.10)}$$

Exponential Service—Finite Queue

Up to this point, we have placed no limit on the number of units that can be present in the system. Suppose now that no more than M units can be accommodated at any time in the system. A unit arriving when the system already contains M units does not enter the system and is "lost." A situation such as this generally arises because of space or capacity limitations. Visualize, for instance, a small one-man barber shop, in which the barber has, in addition to his barber chair, three chairs for waiting customers. Any potential customer who looks in and sees the barber busy and three seated customers waiting takes his business elsewhere. In this example, $M = 4$.

Basic Relationships   As derived in Appendix 12B, the state probability formulas are

$$P_n = \begin{cases} \left(\dfrac{1 - \rho}{1 - \rho^{M+1}}\right)\rho^n & \rho \neq 1 \\[2ex] \dfrac{1}{M + 1} & \rho = 1 \end{cases}$$

where $n = 0, 1, 2, \ldots, M$.

1. L, mean number of units in the system

For $\rho \neq 1$, the mean number of units in the system L is determined as follows:

$$L = \sum_{n=0}^{M} nP_n = \sum_{n=0}^{M} n\left(\frac{1 - \rho}{1 - \rho^{M+1}}\right)\rho^n = \frac{1 - \rho}{1 - \rho^{M+1}} \sum_{n=0}^{M} n\rho^n$$

$$= \frac{1 - \rho}{1 - \rho^{M+1}} (\rho + 2\rho^2 + 3\rho^3 + \cdots + M\rho^M).$$

The sum of this finite series is, from Morse (1958),

$$\frac{\rho}{(1 - \rho)^2}\left[1 - (M + 1)\rho^M + M\rho^{M+1}\right].$$

Therefore,

$$L = \frac{\rho}{1 - \rho}\left(\frac{1 - (M + 1)\rho^M + M\rho^{M+1}}{1 - \rho^{M+1}}\right) = \frac{\rho}{1 - \rho} - \frac{(M + 1)\rho^{M+1}}{1 - \rho^{M+1}} \qquad \rho \neq 1.$$

For $\rho < 1$ and M large, L converges to $\rho/(1 - \rho)$, as would be expected. For $\rho \gg 1$, the system becomes saturated, and L approaches M.

For the case in which $\rho = 1$,

$$L = \sum_{n=0}^{M} nP_n = \sum_{n=0}^{M} n\left(\frac{1}{M + 1}\right) = \frac{1}{M + 1}\sum_{n=0}^{M} n = \left(\frac{1}{M + 1}\right)\frac{M(M + 1)}{2}$$

and so,

$$L = \frac{M}{2} \qquad \rho = 1.$$

2. L_q, mean number of units in the queue

As for the mean queue length, we know that

$$L_q = L - (1 - P_0),$$

so we need only substitute the proper value of P_0, depending on ρ.

Discussion and Summarization of Formulas   For Poisson arrivals, exponential service, and a finite queue limit, the waiting and system times must be carefully defined. Since system capacity is limited, all units arriving when the system is full depart without entering the system. The effective arrival rate—considering only units which actually enter the system—is then equal to the fraction of time the system is *not* full multiplied by the arrival rate. Therefore:

$$\text{Fraction of customers lost} = P_M$$
$$\text{Effective arrival rate } \lambda_e = \lambda(1 - P_M).$$

It seems reasonable to consider that mean waiting and system times should be specified for only those arrivals which actually enter the system, rather than all arrivals which attempt to enter the system. On this basis, then,

$$W = \frac{L}{\lambda_e} = \frac{L}{\lambda(1 - P_M)}$$

and

$$W_q = \frac{L_q}{\lambda_e} = \frac{L_q}{\lambda(1 - P_M)}.$$

For this model, the traffic intensity ρ is not required to be less than 1, since no more than M units can be in the system at any time, regardless of the value of ρ. Also, since the denominator in the basic equation for P_0 vanishes when $\rho = 1$, there are different formulas for $\rho = 1$ and $\rho \neq 1$. The formulas are summarized below.

Fraction of time n units in system:

$$P_n = \begin{cases} P_0\rho^n & \rho \neq 1 \\ \dfrac{1}{M+1} & \rho = 1. \end{cases} \quad n = 0, 1, 2, \ldots, M \qquad (12.11)$$

Fraction server idle time:

$$P_0 = \begin{cases} \dfrac{1-\rho}{1-\rho^{M+1}} & \rho \neq 1 \\ \dfrac{1}{M+1} & \rho = 1. \end{cases} \qquad (12.12)$$

Fraction of potential customers "lost" (= fraction of time system full):

$$P_M = P_0\rho^M. \qquad (12.13)$$

Effective arrival rate:

$$\lambda_e = \lambda(1 - P_M). \tag{12.14}$$

Mean number of units in system:

$$L = \begin{cases} \dfrac{\rho}{1-\rho} - \dfrac{(M+1)\rho^{M+1}}{1-\rho^{M+1}} & \rho \neq 1 \\[2mm] \dfrac{M}{2} & \rho = 1. \end{cases} \tag{12.15}$$

Mean number of units in queue:

$$L_q = L - (1 - P_0). \tag{12.16}$$

Mean time in system:

$$W = \frac{L}{\lambda(1 - P_M)}. \tag{12.17}$$

Mean time in queue:

$$W_q = \frac{L_q}{\lambda(1 - P_M)}. \tag{12.18}$$

EXAMPLE 12.2

In the service station problem of Example 12.1, suppose that the owner is considering enlarging the station. During the construction period, there will be space to accommodate a maximum of only three cars at any one time. Again, consider the situation where customers arrive randomly at the rate of 12 per hour and service is exponentially distributed, averaging 3 minutes per customer.

a) What is the mean number of customers in the station?

$$\lambda = 12/hr \qquad \mu = 20/hr \qquad \rho = \frac{\lambda}{\mu} = 0.6.$$

Maximum units in the system $M = 3$.

$$\text{Since } \rho \neq 1, L = \frac{\rho}{1-\rho} - \frac{(M+1)\rho^{M+1}}{1-\rho^{M+1}} = \frac{0.6}{0.4} - \frac{(4)(0.6)^4}{1-(0.6)^4}$$
$$= 1.500 - 0.595 = 0.905.$$

b) What fraction of the time will the owner be idle?

$$\text{Fraction idle time} = P_0 = \frac{1-\rho}{1-\rho^{M+1}} = \frac{1-0.6}{1-(0.6)^4} = \frac{0.4}{0.8704} = 0.460.$$

c) What fraction of potential customers will be lost?

$$P_M = P_3 = P_0\rho^3 = (0.460)(0.6)^3 = 0.0995.$$

d) What is the mean number of customers entering the service station per hour?

$$\lambda_e = \lambda(1 - P_M) = (12)(1 - 0.0995) = 10.8/\text{hr}.$$

e) What is the mean number of customers waiting at any time?

$$L_q = L - (1 - P_0) = 0.905 - (1 - 0.460) = 0.365.$$

f) What is the mean customer waiting time, in minutes?

$$W_q = \frac{L_q}{\lambda_e} = \frac{0.365}{10.8} = 0.0338 \text{ hr} = 2.0 \text{ min.}$$

g) What is the mean time that a customer spends in the station?

$$W = \frac{L}{\lambda_e} = \frac{0.905}{10.8} = 0.0838 \text{ hr} = 5.0 \text{ min.}$$

or

$$W = W_q + \frac{1}{\mu} = 2.0 + 3.0 = 5.0 \text{ min.}$$

h) What fraction of time will there be customers waiting?

$$P(n > 1) = 1 - (P_0 + P_1) = 1 - (P_0 + P_0\rho) = 1 - P_0(1 + \rho).$$
$$= 1 - (0.0460)(1.6) = 1 - 0.736 = 0.264.$$

Comparing these results with those of Example 12.1, where $M = \infty$, since there is no limitation on queue length:

	M, Maximum Units in System	
	∞	3
L	1.5	0.905
L_q	0.9	0.365
W	7.5 min	5.0 min
W_q	4.5 min	2.0 min
P_o	0.4	0.46
λ_e	12.0/hr	10.8/hr

Thus, at the cost of losing 10 percent of the would-be customers, the values of the operating characteristics L, L_q, W, and W_q are all reduced, while the idle time increases from 40 to 46 percent.

12.6   MULTIPLE-SERVER MODELS

Exponential Service—Unlimited Queue

As an approximation, a multiple-servier system with S servers can be analyzed as S single-server systems operating independently, each with an arrival rate of λ/S. Since calling units can be waiting for a particular server while other servers are idle, this represents an inefficient use of the available service facilities. It does, however, tend to give an upper bound for mean waiting times and mean queue lengths, using the formulas for the single-server case. On the other hand, the assumption of a single queue for all servers represents the most efficient use of service facilities. Although customers do not generally form a single queue, unless they are constrained to do so or are given a number on arrival and are served in numerical order, their behavior tends toward this if they can observe all servers and can move more or less freely from one line to another.

One general comment about servers is in order. For all the models discussed in this text, a server can handle only one calling unit at a time. This does not, however, restrict the general nature of the server. By this, we mean that the server can represent some type of multiple function. For example, a crew is assigned to service an aircraft to ready it for departure. The crew, which services only one aircraft at a time, functions as a single server.

In the material that follows, we will assume that there are S identical servers, all having exponential service times with mean $1/\mu$. Customers enter a single queue and are served, in turn, by the first available server.

Basic Relationships   In Appendix 12C, the state probability equations are derived as

$$P_n = \begin{cases} \dfrac{\rho^n}{n!} P_0 & 0 \le n \le S \\[2ex] \dfrac{\rho^n}{S! S^{n-S}} P_0 & n > S. \end{cases} \tag{12.19}$$

Solving for the mean queue length,

$$L_q = \sum_{n=S}^{\infty} (n - S)P_n = \sum_{n=S}^{\infty} \frac{(n - S)\rho^n}{S! S^{n-S}} P_0 = \frac{P_0}{S!} \left(\frac{\rho^{S+1}}{S} + \frac{2\rho^{S+2}}{S^2} + \frac{3\rho^{S+3}}{S^3} + \cdots \right)$$
$$= \frac{P_0}{S!} \left(\frac{\rho^{S+1}}{S} \right) \left[1 + 2\frac{\rho}{S} + 3\frac{\rho^2}{S} + \cdots \right].$$

The infinite series term converges to $1/(1 - \rho/S)^2$, for $\rho/S < 1$, so

$$L_q = \frac{\rho^{S+1}}{S! S (1 - \rho/S)^2} P_0 = \frac{\rho^{S+1}}{(S - 1)!(S - \rho)^2} P_0 \qquad \rho/S < 1. \tag{12.20}$$

Since the general expression for P_0 is quite complicated, as shown in Appendix 12C, we will leave Equation (12.20) in this form.

Proceeding as for the single-server case,

$$W_q = L_q/\lambda$$
$$W = W_q + 1/\mu$$
$$L = \lambda W = \lambda W_q + \rho = L_q + \rho.$$

Discussion and Summarization of Formulas   For the multiple-server model with Poisson arrivals, exponential service, and no queue limit, the basic equations become very complicated.

For the case of two or three servers, substitution in the formulas for P_0 and L_q yields the following simplified results:

For $S = 2$ and $\rho < 2$: $P_0 = \dfrac{2 - \rho}{2 + \rho}$ **(12.21)**

$$L_q = \frac{\rho^3}{(2 - \rho)^2} P_0 = \frac{\rho^3}{4 - \rho^2}$$ **(12.22)**

For $S = 3$ and $\rho < 3$: $P_0 = \dfrac{2(3 - \rho)}{6 + 4\rho + \rho^2}$ **(12.23)**

$$L_q = \frac{\rho^4}{2(3 - \rho)^2} P_0 = \frac{\rho^4}{(3 - \rho)(6 + 4\rho + \rho^2)}$$ **(12.24)**

For more than three servers, the formulas become rather messy, and we can turn to graphs and/or tables. A tabular presentation that seems quite useful for the type of problems we will be concerned with is that of Table 12.2, showing the dimensionless quantity μW_q $\left[W_q/(1/\mu)\right.$, or mean time in queue as a multiple of mean service time$\left.\right]$ as a function of ρ/S, traffic intensity per server. (In Appendix 12D, a more comprehensive graphical presentation will be found. The accuracy of this graph is good even for ρ/S values of 0.9 and higher.) Note that ρ/S must be less than 1, so that the combined service rate of all servers exceeds the arrival rate.

For given values of ρ and S, W_q can be directly obtained by multiplying the dimensionless μW_q value read from the table by the mean service time $1/\mu$, since $(\mu W_q)(1/\mu) = W_q$. The other three operating characteristics can then be determined by utilizing the standard relationships, as in the single-server case.

$$W = W_q + 1/\mu$$ **(12.25)**
$$L_q = \lambda W_q$$ **(12.26)**
$$L = \lambda W = \lambda W_q + \rho = L_q + \rho.$$ **(12.27)**

If it is required to calculate the probability P_0 that *all* servers are idle, this can be done by first finding L_q and using the following relationship between P_0 and L_q, developed by inverting Equation (12.20).

$$P_0 = \frac{(S - 1)(S - \rho)^2}{\rho^{S+1}} L_q \qquad S > 1 \qquad \rho/S < 1.$$ **(12.28)**

Table 12.2 μW_q, Mean Waiting Time as a Multiple of Mean Service Time

					Servers, S				
ρ/S	2	3	4	5	6	7	8	9	10
0.20	0.042	0.010	0.003	0.001	0.000	0.000	0.000	0.000	0.000
0.22	0.051	0.014	0.004	0.001	0.001	0.000	0.000	0.000	0.000
0.24	0.061	0.017	0.006	0.002	0.001	0.000	0.000	0.000	0.000
0.26	0.073	0.022	0.008	0.003	0.001	0.001	0.000	0.000	0.000
0.28	0.085	0.027	0.010	0.004	0.002	0.001	0.000	0.000	0.000
0.30	0.099	0.033	0.013	0.006	0.003	0.001	0.001	0.000	0.000
0.32	0.114	0.040	0.017	0.008	0.004	0.002	0.001	0.001	0.000
0.34	0.131	0.048	0.021	0.010	0.005	0.003	0.001	0.001	0.000
0.36	0.149	0.057	0.026	0.013	0.007	0.004	0.002	0.001	0.001
0.38	0.169	0.067	0.031	0.016	0.009	0.005	0.003	0.002	0.001
0.40	0.190	0.078	0.038	0.020	0.011	0.006	0.004	0.002	0.001
0.42	0.214	0.091	0.045	0.025	0.014	0.008	0.005	0.003	0.002
0.44	0.240	0.105	0.054	0.030	0.018	0.011	0.007	0.004	0.003
0.46	0.268	0.121	0.063	0.036	0.022	0.014	0.009	0.006	0.004
0.48	0.299	0.138	0.074	0.044	0.027	0.017	0.012	0.008	0.005
0.50	0.333	0.158	0.087	0.052	0.033	0.022	0.015	0.010	0.007
0.52	0.371	0.180	0.101	0.062	0.040	0.027	0.019	0.013	0.009
0.54	0.412	0.204	0.117	0.073	0.048	0.033	0.023	0.017	0.012
0.56	0.457	0.231	0.135	0.086	0.058	0.040	0.029	0.021	0.016
0.58	0.507	0.262	0.156	0.101	0.069	0.049	0.036	0.027	0.020
0.60	0.563	0.296	0.179	0.118	0.082	0.059	0.044	0.033	0.025
0.62	0.624	0.334	0.206	0.138	0.097	0.071	0.053	0.041	0.032
0.64	0.694	0.377	0.236	0.160	0.114	0.085	0.064	0.050	0.039
0.66	0.772	0.427	0.271	0.186	0.135	0.101	0.078	0.061	0.049
0.68	0.860	0.483	0.311	0.217	0.159	0.120	0.094	0.075	0.060
0.70	0.961	0.547	0.357	0.252	0.187	0.143	0.113	0.091	0.074
0.71	1.017	0.583	0.383	0.272	0.202	0.156	0.124	0.100	0.082
0.72	1.076	0.621	0.411	0.293	0.220	0.170	0.135	0.110	0.091
0.73	1.141	0.663	0.441	0.316	0.238	0.186	0.148	0.121	0.100
0.74	1.210	0.708	0.474	0.342	0.259	0.203	0.163	0.133	0.111
0.75	1.286	0.757	0.509	0.369	0.281	0.221	0.178	0.147	0.123
0.76	1.367	0.810	0.548	0.400	0.306	0.242	0.196	0.162	0.136
0.77	1.456	0.868	0.591	0.433	0.333	0.264	0.215	0.178	0.150
0.78	1.554	0.932	0.637	0.469	0.362	0.289	0.236	0.197	0.166
0.79	1.660	1.002	0.689	0.510	0.395	0.316	0.260	0.217	0.184
0.80	1.778	1.079	0.746	0.554	0.431	0.347	0.286	0.240	0.205
0.81	1.908	1.164	0.809	0.604	0.472	0.381	0.315	0.266	0.227
0.82	2.053	1.259	0.879	0.659	0.518	0.420	0.349	0.295	0.253
0.83	2.214	1.366	0.958	0.722	0.569	0.463	0.386	0.328	0.282
0.84	2.397	1.486	1.047	0.792	0.627	0.512	0.428	0.365	0.315
0.85	2.604	1.623	1.149	0.873	0.693	0.569	0.477	0.408	0.353
0.86	2.840	1.780	1.265	0.965	0.770	0.633	0.533	0.457	0.397
0.87	3.114	1.961	1.400	1.072	0.858	0.709	0.599	0.515	0.449
0.88	3.433	2.172	1.558	1.197	0.962	0.797	0.675	0.582	0.509
0.89	3.810	2.423	1.745	1.346	1.085	0.902	0.767	0.663	0.581
0.90	4.263	2.724	1.969	1.525	1.234	1.029	0.877	0.761	0.669
0.91	4.817	3.092	2.245	1.744	1.416	1.184	1.012	0.881	0.776
0.92	5.510	3.553	2.589	2.019	1.644	1.379	1.183	1.031	0.912
0.93	6.402	4.146	3.033	2.374	1.939	1.631	1.403	1.226	1.087
0.94	7.591	4.938	3.626	2.847	2.333	1.968	1.697	1.488	1.321
0.95	9.256	6.047	4.457	3.511	2.885	2.441	2.110	1.855	1.651
0.96	11.755	7.711	5.705	4.508	3.716	3.152	2.732	2.407	2.148
0.97	15.920	10.487	7.786	6.172	5.102	4.340	3.771	3.329	2.978
0.98	24.253	16.041	11.950	9.503	7.877	6.718	5.851	5.178	4.641
0.99	49.251	32.706	24.448	19.501	16.207	13.858	12.098	10.730	9.637

In any queueing system, the mean number of busy servers must equal $L - L_q$, so the fraction of servers busy is $(L - L_q)/S$. Thus, in general,

$$\text{Fraction server idle time} = 1 - \frac{L - L_q}{S}.$$

For this specific model, since $L - L_q = \rho$,

$$\text{Fraction server idle time} = 1 - \rho/S. \qquad \text{(12.29)}$$

EXAMPLE 12.3

A bank has three equally competent tellers, and each one handles all types of transactions. Suppose that customers arrive randomly at the rate of 72 per hour. On the average it requires 2 minutes to serve a customer, and we will assume an exponential distribution. There is a single queue for waiting customers.

a) What is the mean customer waiting time, in minutes?

$$\lambda = 72/\text{hr}, \ 1/\mu = 2 \text{ min}, \ \mu = 30/\text{hr}.$$
$$\rho = \lambda/\mu = 72/30 = 2.4, \ \rho/S = 2.4/3 = 0.80.$$

From Table 12.2, for $S = 3$ and $\rho/S = 0.80$, $\mu W_q = 1.079$,

$$W_q = 1.079/30 = 0.036 \text{ hr} = 2.2 \text{ min}.$$

b) What is the mean customer system time, in minutes?

$$W = W_q + 1/\mu = 2.2 + 2 = 4.2 \text{ min}.$$

c) What is the mean queue length?

$$L_q = \lambda W_q = (72)(0.036) = 2.59$$

d) What is the mean number of customers in the bank?

$$L = L_q + \rho = 2.59 + 2.4 = 4.99.$$

e) What proportion of time are the tellers idle, on the average?

$$\text{Fraction idle time} = 1 - \rho/S = 1 - 0.80 = 0.20.$$

f) What is the probability that all tellers are idle?

Using Equation (12.23), the special formula for P_0 for the case of three servers,

$$P_0 = \frac{2(3 - \rho)}{6 + 4\rho + \rho^2} = \frac{2(3 - 2.4)}{6 + (4)(2.4) + (2.4)^2}$$

$$= \frac{1.2}{21.36} = 0.056.$$

For comparative purposes, using the value of L_q previously determined, the general formula of Equation (12.28) gives

$$P_0 = \frac{(S-1)(S-\rho)^2}{\rho^{S+1}} L_q = \frac{(3-1)(3-2.4)^2}{(2.4)^4} \quad (2.59)$$

$$= \frac{(2)(0.36)(2.59)}{33.18} = 0.056.$$

The system can be expected to be empty about 6 percent of the time.

g) What is the probability that all tellers are busy, with no one waiting in line?

With three servers, this is the probability of exactly three customers in the system, so we need the value of P_n, for $n = 3$. Since $n = S$, the first formula of Equation (12.25) applies.

$$P_n = \frac{\rho^n}{n!} P_0$$

$$P_3 = \frac{(2.4)^3}{3!} (0.056) = 0.129.$$

h) What is the probability that there are two customers waiting in line?

With all three servers busy, the value needed is P_n, with $n = 5$. Since $n > S$, the second formula of Equation (12.25) must be used.

$$P_n = \frac{\rho^n}{S! S^{n-S}} P_0$$

$$= \frac{(2.4)^5}{3! 3^2} (0.056) = 0.083.$$

i) What happens to the mean waiting time and system time if customers randomly select one of the three tellers, so that, in effect, each teller handles an average of one-third of the customers?

Each teller can now be considered independently as a single server, with $\lambda = 24/\text{hr}$, and $\mu = 30/\text{hr}$, so $\rho = 0.80$, as before.

$$W_q = \frac{\rho}{\mu - \lambda} = \frac{0.80}{30 - 24} = 0.133 \text{ hr} = 8.0 \text{ min.}$$

$$W = W_q + 1/\mu = 8.0 + 2 = 10.0 \text{ min.}$$

Service has obviously degraded. Why?

j) What happens to the mean number in queue in the bank now?

For each server, $L_q = \lambda W_q = (24)(8.0/60) = 3.2$. Considering all servers, mean number in queue $= (3)(3.2) = 9.6$.

Queueing Systems in Series—Exponential Service, Unlimited Queue

In the preceding section, we considered a multiple-server system having Poisson input with arrival rate λ and S servers, all with the same exponential service time distribution. For such a system, Saaty (1961) shows that, in the steady state, the output is also Poisson, with rate λ. If we have several such systems in series and if each operates independently, so that the operations in any one system do not affect those of any other system, then all will have Poisson arrivals with rate λ. We can then analyze each system independently and combine the results.

EXAMPLE 12.4

A motor vehicle inspection station is set up to perform two sequential inspections. At Station 1, a mechanic checks and, if necessary, adjusts headlight aim. On the average, this takes 1 minute. At Station 2, where two cars can be serviced simultaneously, two mechanics work independently, each able to check the condition and adjustment of brakes in an average time of 3 minutes. There is adequate space for cars to wait between Station 1 and Station 2. If the service times are exponentially distributed and cars arrive randomly at an average rate of 30 per hour, what is the mean time that a customer spends getting his car inspected?

At Station 1, $\lambda = 30$/hr and $1/\mu = 1$ min $= 1/60$ hr, so that $\mu = 60$/hr. With a single server,

$$W = \frac{1}{\mu - \lambda} = \frac{1}{60 - 30} = \frac{1}{30} \text{ hr} = 2.0 \text{ min.}$$

Since the output from Station 1 will be Poisson, the input to Station 2 will also be Poisson, with an arrival rate of 30/hour.

At Station 2, $1/\mu = 3$ min $= 1/20$ hr, so that $\mu = 20$/hr. With $\lambda = 30$/hr, $\rho = 30/20 = 1.5$. With $S = 2$, $\rho/S = 0.75$, and $\mu W_q = 1.286$, from Table 12.2.

$$W_q = 1.286/\mu = 1.286/20 \text{ hr} = 3.9 \text{ min,} \quad W = W_q + 1/\mu = 3.9 + 3 = 6.9 \text{ min.}$$

Therefore, the mean time that a customer spends in the entire inspection process is $2.0 + 6.9 = 8.9$ minutes.

Self-Service—Exponential Service

A special multiple-server case is one in which all units are to be served immediately. Theoretically, we would have to have an infinite number of servers. Although, on the surface this situation seems farfetched, it is approached, for example, in the situation in which each customer serves himself.

For this case, $S = \infty$, so that n is always less than S, and thus

$$P_n = \frac{\rho^n}{n!} P_0.$$

Summing the state probabilities and solving for P_0.

$$P_0 = \frac{1}{\displaystyle\sum_{n=0}^{\infty} \frac{\rho^n}{n!}} = \frac{1}{1 + \rho + \dfrac{\rho^2}{2!} + \dfrac{\rho^3}{3!} + \cdots} = \frac{1}{e^{\rho}} = e^{-\rho}, \tag{12.30}$$

Therefore

$$P_n = \frac{\rho^n e^{-\rho}}{n!}. \tag{12.31}$$

which is just the Poisson distribution with mean ρ. Since no one waits for service, W_q and L_q are both zero. W is $1/\mu$, just the mean service time, and $L = \lambda W = \lambda(1/\mu) = \rho$, the mean of this distribution, as would be expected.

EXAMPLE 12.5

Customers arrive randomly at the U-Pick-M orange grove at a rate of 9 per hour. Each customer picks his own tree-ripened oranges, requiring an average of 10 minutes to do so. This time varies widely, however, and can be assumed to be exponentially distributed.

a) What is the mean number of customers picking oranges?

From the data, $\lambda = 9/\text{hr}$, $\mu = 6/\text{hr}$, and $\rho = 1.5$. Since each customer serves himself, with no waiting, the self-service model applies, so

$$L = \rho = 1.5.$$

b) What is the probability that there are no customers serving themselves?

From the Poisson tables in Appendix D, locate the column for a mean of 1.5. Then, denoting the number of customers by the random variable X,

$$P_0 = P(X = 0 \mid \text{Pn}:1.5) = 1 - P(X \geq 1 \mid \text{Pn}:1.5)$$
$$= 1 - 0.7769 = 0.2231.$$

c) What is the probability that three customers are busy picking oranges?

$$P_3 = P(X = 3 \mid \text{Pn}:1.5) = P(X \geq 3 \mid \text{Pn}:1.5) - P(X \geq 4 \mid \text{Pn}:1.5)$$
$$= 0.1912 - 0.0656 = 0.1256.$$

Exponential Service—No Queue Allowed

If no queue is allowed, the number of calling units cannot exceed the number of servers, so $n \leq S$. This feature is sometimes called absolute truncation. An example of this situation is a downtown parking lot, because customers must go elsewhere when the lot is full. Since no queue is allowed to build up, there is no requirement that $\rho/S < 1$.

The equations for the state probabilities P_n are the same as for the unlimited queue case where n does not exceed S.

$$P_n = \frac{\rho^n}{n!} P_0$$

and

$$\sum_{n=0}^{S} P_n = 1.$$

Therefore,

$$\sum_{n=0}^{S} \frac{\rho^n}{n!} P_0 = 1$$

and

$$P_0 = \frac{1}{\sum_{n=0}^{S} \frac{\rho^n}{n!}}$$

Since no queue forms,

$$L_q = W_q = 0.$$

As we did earlier in the case of a system with a finite queue limit, we calculate mean system time only for those arrivals which actually enter the system. With no queue permitted, mean system time is equal to mean service time, and so

$$W = \frac{1}{\mu}.$$

Since arrivals do not enter when the system is full, or in state S,

fraction of customers lost $= P_S$.
effective arrival rate $\lambda_e = \lambda(1 - P_S)$.

Solving for the mean number of units in the system,

$$L = \lambda_e W = \frac{\lambda(1 - P_S)}{\mu} = \rho(1 - P_S).$$

Since $L_q = 0$,

$$\text{fraction server idle time} = 1 - \frac{L - L_q}{S} = 1 - \frac{L}{S}.$$

Summarization of Formulas   For a multiple-server system with Poisson arrivals, exponential service, and no queue allowed.

Fraction of time system is empty:

$$P_0 = \frac{1}{\sum_{n=0}^{S} \frac{\rho^n}{n!}} \tag{12.32}$$

Fraction of time n units in system:

$$P_n = \frac{\rho^n}{n!} P_0 \tag{12.33}$$

Fraction of potential customers lost:

$$P_S = \frac{\rho^S}{S!} P_0 \tag{12.34}$$

Effective arrival rate:

$$\lambda_e = \lambda(1 - P_S) \tag{12.35}$$

Mean time in system:

$$W = \frac{1}{\mu} \tag{12.36}$$

Mean number of units in system:

$$L = \lambda_e W = \rho(1 - P_S) \tag{12.37}$$

Fraction server idle time $= 1 - L/S$. $\tag{12.38}$

Also, since no queue is permitted, $L_q = W_q = 0$.

Computational Procedure For a problem of this nature, with a finite number of states, the computations can be handled by a tabular approach. We take advantage of the fact that there is a simple relationship between successive state probabilities, whereby each term can be expressed as a function of the previous term. This is called a recursion relationship, as we learned in the study of dynamic programming in Chapter 10. To show this relationship, substitute $n - 1$ for n in Equation (12.33) to get the probability of state $n - 1$:

$$P_{n-1} = \frac{\rho^{n-1}}{(n-1)!} P_0.$$

Dividing P_n by P_{n-1}, we get

$$\frac{P_n}{P_{n-1}} = \frac{\rho^n P_0}{n!} \frac{(n-1)!}{\rho^{n-1} P_0} = \frac{\rho}{n} \qquad n > 0.$$

Therefore, each state probability is equal to the previous state probability multiplied by ρ/n. Suppose we now calculate successive P_n/P_0 values for $n = 0$ to S. Their sum will equal the reciprocal of P_0, as shown below, since the state probabilities must add to 1.

$$\sum_{n=0}^{S} \frac{P_n}{P_0} = \frac{1}{P_0} \sum_{n=0}^{S} P_n = \frac{1}{P_0}(1) = \frac{1}{P_0}.$$

Once the value $1/P_0$ is determined, we divide all P_n/P_0 ratios by $1/P_0$ to get the desired probability values, since $P_n/P_0 \div 1/p_0 = P_n$.

To clarify and formalize this procedure, consider the following example.

EXAMPLE 12.6

A small store has a parking lot with six spaces. Potential customers arrive randomly at the rate of 10 per hour and leave immediately if no parking space is available. Occupancy of a parking space is 30 minutes on the average, and tends to be exponentially distributed.

a) What fraction of the arriving customers will leave immediately?

This fraction will be $P_S = P_6$. The required calculation of the state probabilities is shown in Table 12.3.

Table 12.3 Multiple-Server Problem with No Queue Allowed

| | $\lambda = 10/\text{hr}$, | $1/\mu = 0.5$ hr, | $S = 6$ |
| | $\mu = 2/\text{hr}$, | $\rho = \lambda/\mu = 5$ | |

| (1) | (2) | (3) | (4) |
| | | | (3)/Σ (3) |
n	ρ/n	P_n/P_o	P_n
0	——	1.0	0.009
1	5.00	5.0	0.044
2	2.50	12.5	0.111
3	1.67	20.8	0.184
4	1.25	26.0	0.230
5	1.00	26.0	0.230
6	0.83	21.6	0.192
		$\dfrac{1}{P_o} = 112.9$	1.000

With the exception of the initial P_n/P_0 value, which must be 1.0 for $n = 0$, each column (3) value is obtained by multiplying the associated column (2) value by the previous column (3) value, since $P_n/P_0 = (\rho/n)(P_{n-1}/P_o)$. The summation of the P_n/P_0 values is equal to $1/P_0$. Then, the P_n values can be obtained by a normalizing process, namely, dividing the P_n/P_0 values by their sum, $1/P_0$. From the results, 19.2 percent of potential customers will be lost, since $P_S = P_6 = 0.192$.

b) What is the effective arrival rate?

$$\lambda_e = \lambda(1 - P_6) = (10)(1 - 0.192) = 8.08 \text{ arrivals/hr.}$$

c) What is the average fraction of empty spaces?

The average number of spaces occupied is L, and

$$L = \rho(1 - P_6) = (5)(0.808) = 4.04.$$

Average fraction of empty spaces $\equiv$ fraction server idle time

$$= 1 - \frac{L}{S} = 1 - \frac{4.04}{6} = 0.327.$$

d) What fraction of customers would be lost if only five spaces were available? How much does the sixth parking space contribute to the reduction in the fraction of customers lost?

From the data in Table 12.3, $\Sigma_{n=0}^{5} P_n/P_0 = 1/P_0 = 91.3$. With only five spaces,

$$\text{fraction of customers lost} = P_5/P_0 = 26.0/91.3 = 0.285.$$

The sixth parking space therefore reduces the fraction of lost customers from 28.5 to 19.2 percent, a reduction of 9.3 percent.

Exponential Service—Finite Queue Limit

Suppose that no more than M calling units are allowed in the system, where $M > S$. The maximum possible queue length is then $M - S$. This model is a more general case of the previous model, in which no queue was allowed. The state probabilities are the same, in terms of P_0, as for the unlimited queue model, except that n can never exceed M. We then have

$$P_n = \begin{cases} \dfrac{\rho^n}{n!} P_0 & n \leq S \\[2mm] \dfrac{\rho^n}{S!S^{n-S}} P_0 & S \leq n \leq M \end{cases}$$

and

$$P_0 = \frac{1}{\displaystyle\sum_{n=0}^{S-1} \frac{\rho^n}{n!} + \frac{\rho^S}{S!} \sum_{n=S}^{M} \left(\frac{\rho}{S}\right)^{n-S}}$$

We choose not to solve for P_0 from the preceding rather formidable closed-form expression. Instead, we will draw upon our experience in the previous problem and solve for the state probabilities recursively. When the state probabilities are determined, L_q can be readily calculated, since it is, by definition, just the sum of the products of each possible queue length and associated probability, or,

$$L_q = \sum_{n=S}^{M} (n - S) P_n.$$

Summarization of Formulas   For a multiple-server system with Poisson arrivals, exponential service, and a finite system limit M exceeding the number of servers S, the maximum possible queue length will be $M - S$. Once having solved for the state probabilities P_n and the mean number in queue L_q, the following formulas are useful.

Effective arrival rate:

$$\lambda_e = \lambda(1 - P_M) \tag{12.39}$$

Mean time in queue:

$$W_q = \frac{L_q}{\lambda_e} \tag{12.40}$$

Mean time in system:

$$W = W_q + \frac{1}{\mu} \tag{12.41}$$

Mean number of units in the system:

$$L = \lambda_e W \tag{12.42}$$

Fraction server idle time $= 1 - \dfrac{L - L_q}{S} = 1 - \dfrac{\rho}{S}(1 - P_M). \tag{12.43}$

Computational Procedure To determine the recursion relationships, observe that:

$$\text{For } 0 < n \leqslant S: P_n = \frac{\rho^n}{n!} P_0 \text{ and } P_{n-1} = \frac{\rho^{n-1}}{(n-1)!} P_0, \qquad \text{so } P_n = \frac{\rho}{n} P_{n-1}.$$

$$\text{For } n \geqslant S: P_n = \frac{\rho^n}{S!S^{n-S}} P_0 \text{ and } P_{n-1} = \frac{\rho^{n-1}}{S!S^{n-S-1}} P_0, \qquad \text{so } P_n = \frac{\rho}{S} P_{n-1}.$$

EXAMPLE 12.7

Consider a barber shop with three barbers and two additional chairs for waiting customers. Customers arrive randomly at an average rate of 8 per hour, and haircuts take an average of 15 minutes, with an exponential distribution. Arriving customers who find the barbers busy and two customers waiting leave immediately.

a) What is the mean number of customers waiting at any time?

From the problem data, $S = 3$, $M = 5$, $\mu = 4$/hr., and $\rho = 8/4 = 2$, so that $\rho/S = 2/3$. As shown in Table 12.4, we first calculate values of P_n/P_0 recursively, multiplying the previous value by ρ/n or ρ/S, depending on the value of n. Then we sum these P_n/P_0 values to get $1/P_0$ and divide each P_n/P_0 value by $1/P_0$ to get the P_n values. L_q is calculated by summing the products of $(n - S)P_n$ for $n > S$.

The mean number of customers in queue is 0.269.

b) What is the effective arrival rate?

Since 7.7 percent of the potential arrivals are lost,

$$\lambda_e = \lambda(1 - P_M) = 8(1 - 0.077) = 7.38 \text{ arrivals/hr.}$$

Table 12.4 Multiple Server Problem with Queue Limit of 5

		$\lambda = 8/hr,$	$\mu = 4/hr,$	$\rho = 2.0,$	$S = 3$	
n	ρ/n	ρ/S	P_n/P_0	P_n	$n - S$	$(n - S)P_n$
0			1	0.128		
1	2		2	0.255		
2	1		2	0.255		
3		2/3	1.333	0.170		
4		2/3	0.889	0.115	1	0.115
5		2/3	0.602	0.077	2	0.154
			$\dfrac{1}{P_0} = 7.824$	1.000		$L_q = 0.269$

c) Find the mean customer waiting time.

$$W_q = L_q/\lambda_e = 0.269/7.38 = 0.0365 \text{ hr} = 2.2 \text{ min.}$$

d) What is the mean time a customer spends in the barber shop?

$$W = W_q + 1/\mu = 0.036 + 0.25 = 0.286 \text{ hr} = 17.2 \text{ min.}$$

e) What fraction of the time are the barbers idle, on the average?

$$\text{Fraction server idle time} = 1 - (\rho/S)(1 - P_M) = 1 - \frac{2}{3}(1 - 0.077) = 0.383.$$

f) Determine the mean number of customers in the barber shop.

$$L = \lambda_e W = (7.38)(0.286) = 2.11.$$

Exponential Service—Finite Population of Arrivals

Up to this point, we have analyzed only situations in which the calling units came from an essentially unlimited population of arrivals. Now, however, consider the case in which there are only a finite number of calling units. Such a situation occurs, for example, when machines break down in a factory and require service by a repairman. The rate at which machines arrive for service is clearly a function of the number of machines that are operable at any time, and this, in turn, is a function of the repair time (in relation to the running time) and the number of repairmen. This particular model is sometimes called the machine interference model.

Think of this queueing system as including only those calling units needing service or being serviced. At any point in time, those calling units not requiring service (machines still running) are considered outside the system.

In this particular model, as noted, the number of calling units is a function of the system state. Since the calling population is not constant, it makes sense to define λ as the arrival (failure) rate per unit time of an *individual* calling unit (machine). This is the only model in this chapter for which the arrival rate has been so defined.

If there are M machines and n of them are in the queueing system, either being serviced or awaiting service, the size of the calling population at that instant (the machines subject to failure) is equal to $M - n$. The effective arrival rate λ_e is equal to the average number of arrivals per unit time. Since the instantaneous arrival rate at any point in time is $(M - n)\lambda$, λ_e will be equal to the expected value of $M - n$ multiplied by λ. The expected value of $M - n$ is $M - E(n)$, and $E(n)$ is just L, the expected number of units in the system. Thus,

$$\lambda_e = \lambda(M - L).$$

The effective arrival rate, therefore, equals the arrival rate for one calling unit multiplied by the average number of operable calling units.

Once again we will find that the state probabilities can be determined by utilizing recursion relationships, as indicated in Appendix 12C. Along with those computations, the value of L can be readily calculated, since, by definition,

$$L = \sum_{n=0}^{M} nP_n,$$

the summation of the weighted system states.

Summarization of Formulas   With a multiple-server system having Poisson arrivals, exponential service time, and a finite calling population, we will determine the state probabilities recursively and, at the same time, calculate the value of L. Then, we have:

Effective arrival rate:

$$\lambda_e = \lambda(M - L). \tag{12.44}$$

Mean time in system:

$$W = \frac{L}{\lambda_e}. \tag{12.45}$$

Mean time in queue:

$$W_q = W - \frac{1}{\mu}. \tag{12.46}$$

Mean number of units in the queue:

$$L_q = \lambda_e W_q. \tag{12.47}$$

Computational Procedure   The recursion relationships can be developed from the state probability formulas in Appendix 12C.

$$P_n = (M - n + 1)\left(\frac{\rho}{n}\right)P_{n-1} \qquad 0 < n \leq S.$$

$$P_n = (M - n + 1)\left(\frac{\rho}{S}\right)P_{n-1} \qquad S \leq n \leq M.$$

We can then solve for the state probabilities and L recursively.

EXAMPLE 12.8

In a certain factory, five machines are serviced by two repairmen. On the average these machines break down randomly every 5 hours. The mean repair time is 2.5 hours, exponentially distributed. We wish to calculate all values which might yield useful information in a problem of this nature.

The calculations for the state probabilities and L are shown in Table 12.5. These calculations form the starting point for the determination of all the values of interest.

Table 12.5   Finite Arrival Population Problem

				$M = 5$ Machines, $S = 2$ Repairmen			
				$\lambda = 0.2$/hr, $\mu = 0.4$/hr, $\rho = \lambda/\mu = 0.5$			
(1)	(2)	(3)		(4)	(5)	(6)	(7)
n	$M - n + 1$	ρ/n	ρ/S	$(2) \times (3)$	P_n/P_0	P_n	nP_n
0					1	0.111	0
1	5	0.5		2.5	2.5	0.276	0.28
2	4		0.25	1.0	2.5	0.276	0.55
3	3		0.25	0.75	1.88	0.208	0.62
4	2		0.25	0.50	0.94	0.104	0.42
5	1		0.25	0.25	0.23	0.025	0.13
					$\frac{1}{P_0} = 9.05$	1.000	$L = 2.00$

In the calculation of P_1/P_0, the second multiplicative factor, that in column (3), is $\rho/n = \rho/1 = \rho$, since the state $n = 1$ is the only state for which $n < S$. Thereafter this factor is $\rho/S = \rho/2$. Once the state probabilities have been evaluated by the normalizing process of dividing each P_n/P_0 value by $1/P_0$, then nP_n terms can be calculated and summed to get L.

The following information can now be determined:

Mean number of machines inoperable $= L = 2.00$.
Effective arrival rate $= \lambda_e = \lambda(M - L) = (0.2)(5 - 2.00) = 0.60$/hr.

Mean time a machine is inoperable $= W = \dfrac{L}{\lambda_e} = \dfrac{2.00}{0.60} = 3.33$ hr.

Mean time a machine waits for service $= W_q = W - \dfrac{1}{\mu} = 3.33 - 2.5 = 0.83$ hr.

Mean number of machines awaiting service $= L_q = \lambda_e W_q = (0.60)(0.83) = 0.50$.

Mean number of machines being serviced $= L - L_q = 2.00 - 0.50 = 1.50$.

Mean number of machines operable $= M - L = 5 - 2.00 = 3.00$.

Fraction of machines operable $= \dfrac{M - L}{L} = \dfrac{3.00}{5} = 0.60$.

Mean time between breakdowns $= \dfrac{1}{\lambda_e} = \dfrac{1}{0.60} = 1.67$ hr.

Mean number of repairmen idle $= S - (L - L_q) = 2 - 1.50 = 0.50$.

Fraction repairmen idle time $= 1 - \dfrac{L - L_q}{S} = 1 - \dfrac{1.50}{2} = 0.25$.

An extensive set of tables, the Finite Queueing Tables, by Peck and Hazelwood (1958), has been developed to aid in the solution of such problems. These tables cover finite population sizes from 4 to 250.[2] Among other quantities, the calculations use a system efficiency factor F which is equal to $(M - L_q)/M$. This factor is a measure of the reduction of the average number of machines operable because of the formation of a queue, and it permits ready calculations of quantities of interest for this model.

12.7   ECONOMIC ANALYSIS

As noted at the beginning of this chapter, queueing situations occur primarily because it is uneconomical to provide enough service capacity to completely avoid such situations. In the determination of the most economical queueing system, for a given situation, we attempt to balance the cost of providing service, the cost of obtaining service, and the cost of lost business, if any. Most of the cost models discussed involve only the costs of providing and obtaining service, and the general relationship of these cost factors is illustrated in Figure 12.3.

The cost of obtaining service is generally not very easy to determine, but some reasonable estimate generally must be made if we are to have any hope of designing an economical queueing system. The determination of this cost is discussed in some detail by Hillier and Lieberman (1974). If the calling units are external to the organization providing service, the cost of obtaining service is, in many situations, the cost associated with customer waiting time. This tends to be of the nature of a goodwill (or ill-will) cost, usually attributed to future lost business due to annoyance at being delayed. As can well be imagined, such a cost is quite difficult to estimate. We will show, however, that with the technique of sensitivity analysis, we are able to deter-

[2]L. G. Peck and R. N. Hazelwood, *Finite Queueing Tables*, John Wiley and Sons, Inc., New York, 1958.

mine the range over which this cost, as well as other factors, can vary without changing the solution. This can give us considerably more confidence in our solution. (Rather than attempting to place any direct value on the cost of obtaining service, we may choose, as an alternative, to impose a limit on the mean waiting time. Then, using sensitivity analysis, we can evaluate the implied cost of obtaining service and judge its reasonableness.) If service is provided to calling units within the organization, the costs of obtaining service may be easier to quantify. For example, the waiting time cost chargeable to a machine awaiting repair may well be the profit associated with this amount of production time on the machine. In the simplified cost models that we consider, we will assume that the cost of waiting is a linear function of the waiting (or system) time.

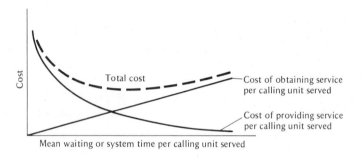

Figure 12.3

The cost of providing service is generally much easier to determine. It is usually just the cost per unit time of the server(s). For short waiting times, the cost of providing service tends to be quite high. If waiting times are permitted to increase, service costs can sometimes be lowered appreciably, either by decreasing the number of servers or by decreasing the service rate, perhaps by using less experienced servers. If the service level becomes rather low, waiting times tend to rise quite sharply. The optimal point of operation is that at which the total cost of providing and obtaining service is a minimum. If the cost of obtaining service is linear with waiting or system time, the minimum cost is theoretically achieved at the point at which the slopes of the two cost curves are equal in magnitude. Actually, however, these curves are not usually continuous, since we are frequently attempting to determine the optimal number of servers, and this is clearly a discrete variable. The use of continuous curves, then, is meant to be indicative of the general shape of these cost functions.

In developing and analyzing cost models, we attempt to keep them as general as possible. In order to minimize the required number of input parameters, we use ratios as much as feasible. The advantage of doing this will become apparent. (Earlier, we did this in the sensitivity analysis of optimal lot size models in Chapter 11 on Inventory Models.)

In these models, we use the following notation for costs.

Let C_s = cost per server per unit time,
$\quad C_w$ = cost of waiting (or being served) per unit time,
$\quad\quad$ = cost per unit time of being in the system,
$\quad R = C_w/C_s$.

We are interested only in the incremental or marginal costs of providing or obtaining service. That is, we are concerned only with those costs which affect our decision. Any other costs are simply not relevant to our analysis. We will assume Poisson arrivals and exponential service for all cost models discussed.

Cost Model 1—Optimal Number of Servers

Given the traffic intensity ρ and the cost ratio $R = C_w/C_s$, we wish to determine the optimal number of servers $S*$. We assume that there is no limit either on the calling population or on queue length.

The cost per unit time of providing service is $C_s S$. Over a given time interval the cost of obtaining service is proportional to the total system time for all calling units. Since the mean system time for each calling unit is W, and there are λ arrivals per unit time, the total system time per unit time is $\lambda W = L$. The cost per unit time of obtaining service is then $C_w L$. Therefore, our objective appears to be:

$$\text{minimize } C_s S + C_w L(S, \rho),$$

where the notation $L(S, \rho)$ serves to remind us that L is a function of both S and ρ. We will, however, divide through by C_s, so we need consider only the cost ratio R, and not the actual values of C_w and C_s. Our objective becomes:

$$\text{minimize } S + RL(S, \rho).$$

Now we will perform a breakeven analysis and come up with a general solution of relatively wide applicability.

Let $\hat{R}(S, \rho)$ = value of R which makes us indifferent to the choice of either S or $S + 1$ servers when the traffic intensity is ρ.

Then,

$$S + \hat{R}(S, \rho)L(S, \rho) = S + 1 + \hat{R}(S, \rho)L(S + 1, \rho).$$

Solving for $\hat{R}(S, \rho)$, we obtain the expression:

$$\hat{R}(S, \rho) = \frac{1}{L(S, \rho) - L(S + 1, \rho)}.$$

Using this formula, it is straightforward to compute L values over a reasonable range of S and ρ values and plot a family of indifference curves. These curves can then be used to directly determine the optimal number of servers. The curves also facilitate sensitivity analyses, an important advantage, as we will show shortly. A family of such curves is drawn in Figure 12.4. On the graph, note that the value of $S*$, from 1 to 10, applies to the region *between* the indicated curves. $S^* = 1$ for the region beneath the lowest curve.

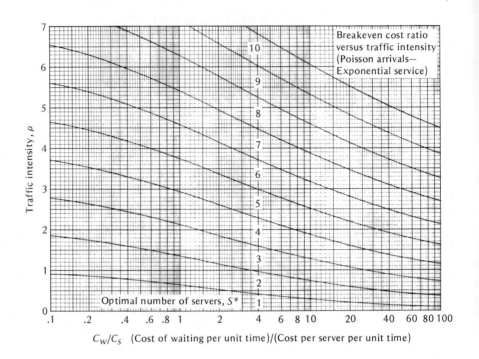

Figure 12.4

EXAMPLE 12.9

Suppose that, during a certain period of operation, a bank anticipates random arrivals at the rate of 87 per hour. Service takes an average of 2 minutes, exponentially distributed. The cost of customer waiting time is assumed to be $6 per hour, and tellers receive $3 per hour. What is the optimal number of tellers during this period? We will assume a single queue.

With $\lambda = 87$/hr and $\mu = 30$/hr, $\rho = 2.9$. Since $C_w = \$6$/hr and $C_s = \$3$/hr, $R = C_w/C_s = 2.0$. If we visualize two lines on Figure 12.4, one at $\rho = 2.9$ and the other at $R = 2.0$, their intersection is clearly in the region for which $S^* = 5$. Therefore, five tellers are optimal.

If we did not have a graph such as Figure 12.4, we could perform a cost analysis with the aid of values obtained from Table 12.2. We look for the value of S for which $C_w L + C_s S$ is a minimum. Since C_w and C_s are given and S is to be varied, we need to find L as a function of S, for the given value of ρ.

We start with a minimum of $S = 3$ servers, since ρ/S must be less than 1. Then, for any S and associated ρ/S, the value of μW_q can be read from Table 12.2. To find L, we can utilize a rather simple relationship between L and μW_q. Working from basic relationships and using a little algebra,

$$L = \lambda W = \lambda \left(W_q + \frac{1}{\mu}\right) = \lambda \left(\frac{\mu W_q + 1}{\mu}\right) = \rho(\mu W_q + 1).$$

The necessary calculations are shown in Table 12.6. The μW_q values were obtained from Table 12.2.

Table 12.6 Determination of Optimal Number of Servers

| | | $\rho = 2.9,$ | $C_w = \$6/hr,$ | $C_s = \$3/hr$ | | |
| | | | | $C_w L$ | $C_s S$ | Total Cost |
S	ρ/S	μW_q	$\rho(\mu W_q + 1) = L$	($/hr)	($/hr)	($/hr)
3	0.97	10.5	33.4	200	9.00	209
4	0.72	0.41	4.09	24.54	12.00	36.54
5	0.58	0.10	3.19	19.14	15.00	34.14
6	0.48	0.03	2.99	17.94	18.00	35.94

With a minimum total cost of $34.14/hour, the optimal number of servers (tellers) S^* is 5.

As additional servers are added, the cost of waiting time decreases sharply at first and then more and more slowly. As $\mu W_q \to 0$, $L = \rho(\mu W_q + 1) \to \rho$, and $C_w L \to C_w \rho \to (6)(2.9) = \$17.4$. This is an irreducible minimum; it is the cost of the mean time spent in service. (Actually, since this cost is the same regardless of the number of servers, it could be omitted from the analysis.) Meanwhile, the cost of providing service increases by a constant amount $C_s = \$3/$hour for each additional server. Note that a seventh server would bring the total cost to at least $17.4 + (7)(3) = \$38.4/$hour.

This cost model is not limited to the case where the arrival population is essentially unlimited. Exactly the same reasoning applies for the case of a finite population M of arrivals. L is now, however, a function of S, ρ, and M. Thus, if we are going to plot curves, we need a set of curves for every value of M which is of interest. As before, our objective will be

$$\text{minimize } S + RL(S, \rho, M).$$

If either or both of the cost factors are nonlinear, it is necessary to calculate the optimal number of servers by a trial-and-error solution, minimizing $C_s S + C_w L$.

For the model with unlimited arrivals but a finite queue limit such that the maximum number of calling units in the system is M, to determine the optimal number of servers,

$$\text{minimize } C_s S + C_w L(S, \rho, M) + C_d \lambda P_M(S, \rho, M),$$

where C_d is the cost associated with each calling unit denied or refusing entry to the queueing system, and λP_M is the number of such calling units per unit time. It should be pointed out that the value of C_d may be difficult to estimate.

Cost Model 2—Least Cost Service Alternative

In this model, a number of alternative methods exist for providing the necessary service. Alternative i is characterized by (S_i, μ_i, C_{s_i}), denoting S_i servers, each with service rate μ_i and cost C_{s_i} per unit time. Given the arrival rate λ, the objective is to choose the alternative whose total relevant cost is lowest.

EXAMPLE 12.10

A tool crib in a certain factory services mechanics, who arrive randomly at the average rate of 30 per hour. Service times tend to be exponentially distributed and there are currently two tool clerks, both with an average service time of 1.5 minutes and both paid $2.50 per hour. The manager of the tool crib has an opportunity to transfer the two clerks and replace them with a more experienced clerk, earning $4 per hour, who should be able to cut the average service time to 1 minute.

a) Is it economical for the manager to make this replacement if the time required by the mechanics to get tools is estimated to cost $6 per hour in lost production time?

For both alternatives, $\lambda = 30$/hr and $C_w = \$6$/hr. Let alternative 1 be the use of two clerks. We have

$$S_1 = 2 \qquad \mu_1 = \frac{60}{1.5} = 40\text{/hr} \qquad C_{s_1} = \$2.5\text{/hr}.$$

L_1, the value of L for alternative 1, can be obtained by first calculating L_q using Equation (12.22), since there are two servers.

$$L_q = \frac{\rho^3}{4 - \rho^2} = \frac{(0.75)^3}{4 - (0.75)^2} = 0.123$$

$$L_1 = L_q + \rho = 0.123 + 0.75 = 0.873.$$

$$\text{Total relevant cost} = C_{s_1}S_1 + C_w L_1$$
$$= (2.5)(2) + (6)(0.873) = \$10.24\text{/hr}.$$

Alternative 2 is the use of the more experienced clerk.

$$S_2 = 1 \qquad \mu_2 = \frac{60}{1} = 60\text{/hr} \qquad C_{s_2} = \$4\text{/hr}$$

$$L = \frac{\lambda}{\mu - \lambda} = \frac{30}{60 - 30} = 1.0 = L_2$$

$$\text{Total relevant cost} = C_{s_2}S_2 + C_w L_2$$
$$= (4)(1) + (6)(1) = \$10\text{/hr}.$$

There would be a small economic advantage in obtaining the more experienced tool clerk.

b) At what value of the cost of mechanics' waiting time would the manager be indifferent to the two alternatives?

Let $\hat{C}_w$ be the breakeven value of C_w. Equating the total relevant cost of the two alternatives,

$$C_{s_1} S_1 + \hat{C}_w L_1 = C_{s_2} S_2 + \hat{C}_w L_2$$
$$(2.5)(2) + \hat{C}_w (0.873) = (4)(1) + \hat{C}_w (1)$$
$$0.127 C_w = 1.0, \qquad \hat{C}_w = \$7.87/\text{hr}.$$

Above this value of C_w, the first alternative would be preferred.

There is a special case of this cost model which can be evaluated in a manner similar to that for cost model 1.

Cost Model 2a—Least Cost Crew Size

Service is to be performed by a single crew of size N. Both the service rate μ and the service cost C_s are directly proportional to the crew size. Thus, if μ_1 is the service rate for one man and C_{s_1} is the service cost per unit time per man, $\mu = N\mu_1$ and $C_s = NC_{s_1}$. Given the arrival rate λ and C_w, the cost of waiting time per unit time, we wish to determine the optimal crew size N^*.

We must minimize $NC_{s_1} + C_w L(N, \rho_1)$, where $\rho_1 = \lambda/\mu_1$. If we divide through by C_{s_1} and let $R = C_w/C_{s_1}$, we then

$$\text{minimize } N + RL(N, \rho_1).$$

We can now perform a breakeven analysis to solve for $\hat{R}(N, \rho_1)$, the value of R for which we are indifferent between a crew size of N or $N + 1$.

$$N + \hat{R}(N, \rho_1) L(N, \rho_1) = N + 1 + \hat{R}(N, \rho_1) L(N + 1, \rho_1),$$

and

$$\hat{R}(N, \rho_1) = \frac{1}{L(N, \rho_1) - L(N + 1, \rho_1)}.$$

For the case of an essentially unlimited arrival population,

$$L(N, \rho_1) = \frac{\lambda}{N\mu_1 - \lambda} = \frac{\rho_1}{N - \rho_1},$$

and, with a little algebra,

$$\hat{R}(N, \rho_1) = \frac{(N - \rho_1)(N + 1 - \rho_1)}{\rho_1}.$$

The optimal crew size is the value N^* for which

$$R(N^* - 1, \rho_1) < R < \hat{R}(N^*, \rho_1).$$

If there is a value N such that $R = \hat{R}(N, \rho_1)$ then $N^* = N$ or $N + 1$.

EXAMPLE 12.11

Consider the situation where a crew is assigned to load trucks. The minimum crew size is 4. Trucks arrive randomly, on the average of 1 per hour. The 4-man crew can service an average of 1 truck per hour, and service is approximately exponential. A larger crew can service trucks at a rate proportionate to the crew size. Each man is paid $4 per hour. Idle cost of a truck and driver is $20 per hour. What is the optimal crew size?

From the problem data, $\lambda = 1/\text{hr}$ and $\mu_1 = 0.25/\text{hr}$, so $\rho_1 = 4.0$, and at least a 5-man crew will be required to make $\rho < 1$. Since it gives us additional information, we will solve for the breakeven $\hat{R}(N, \rho_1)$ values which bracket the given R value of $C_w/C_{s_1} = 20/4 = 5.0$. The calculations are shown in Table 12.7. From these results, we should be indifferent to the choice of an 8-man or a 9-man crew, since the given R value just happens to equal the breakeven value between 8 and 9 men. As a check, suppose we calculate their costs directly.

$$\text{Cost of 8-man crew} = NC_{s_1} + C_w L(N) = (8)(4) + 20\,\frac{1}{(8)(0.25) - 1} = \$52/\text{hr}.$$

$$\text{Cost of 9-man crew} = (9)(4) + 20\,\frac{1}{(9)(0.25) - 1} = \$52/\text{hr}.$$

Table 12.7 Breakeven Analysis for Crew Size

N	$N - \rho_1$	$N + 1 - \rho_1$	$\hat{R}(N, \rho_1)$
5	1.0	2.0	0.50
6	2.0	3.0	1.50
7	3.0	4.0	3.00
8	4.0	5.0	5.00
9	5.0	6.0	7.50

It should be apparent that many different queueing cost models can be developed, and we will now discuss briefly two additional cost models. These models are not accompanied by numerical examples, since the required calculations are quite tedious. The purpose of including these models is simply to indicate how such models can be structured.

Cost Model 3—Most Economical System Capacity (Queue Limit)

Given the arrival rate λ, the service rate μ, the number of servers S, the service cost C_s, the waiting time cost C_w, and costs C_c and C_d,

where $C_c =$ cost per unit time (possibly over some payoff period) of adding one unit of system capacity, and

$C_d =$ cost associated with each calling unit denied or refusing entry to the queueing system,

we want to determine the optimal queue limit M^*.

Recalling that λP_M is the loss rate per unit time for calling units which do not enter the system, the objective would be

$$\text{minimize } C_s S + C_w L + C_d \lambda P_M + M C_c.$$

If we assume that the servers cannot be used for other work during their idle time, the cost of service can be dropped as a factor in this model, since the number of servers is not a variable. The objective then becomes

$$\text{minimize } C_w L + C_d \lambda P_M + M C_c.$$

Cost Model 4—Optimal Number of Servers When No Queue Allowed

This situation is what we termed absolute truncation. Given the arrival rate λ, the service rate μ, the service cost C_s, and the cost C_d for each calling unit not entering the system, we want to find the optimal number of servers S^*.

The objective is then to

$$\text{minimize } C_s S + C_d \lambda P_S.$$

Note that the cost of service C_s may well relate to the cost of some type of capacity and thus could conceptually be very similar to the cost factor C_c used in the previous case. Thus, in the parking lot example, the number of servers actually represented the capacity of the parking lot.

Sensitivity Analysis

In the study of queueing models, sensitivity analysis can play an important role. Sometimes, the solution is relatively insensitive to certain changes. As an example, consider the total cost curve in Figure 12.3. If we were operating at the optimal value of mean waiting time to give minimum total cost, a required decrease of 25 percent in the mean waiting time could well result in a cost increase of only 5 percent or less. On the other hand, for the simplest single-server queueing model, if the system is operating at a traffic intensity ρ of 0.8, increasing the arrival rate by 12.5 percent, so that ρ becomes 0.9, will increase the mean number in queue from 3.2 to 8.1, a change of $+153$ percent. Obviously, in this operating region, queue length is extremely sensitive to changes in traffic intensity.

Let us now consider in some detail the case where the solution value is discrete, as in the determination of the optimal number of servers. We would like to know how much the input variables could change without changing our solution.

In Example 12.9, the input data values were

$$\lambda = 87/\text{hr}, \ \mu = 30/\text{hr}, \ C_w = \$6/\text{hr}, \text{ and } C_s = \$3/\text{hr}.$$

The derived values were

$$\rho = 2.9, \ C_w/C_s = 2.0.$$

From Figure 12.4, the optimal solution was found to be $S^* = 5$ servers. We can, however, derive a great deal more information from the data presented in that graph.

Let us analyze changes in both basic parameters, C_w/C_s, and ρ.

1. Knowing the value of C_w, the cost of waiting time, is at best an estimate and at worst a wild guess, how much could C_w vary from the given value before the solution would change? In other words, how sensitive is our solution to the value of C_w?

In Figure 12.4, we locate the ρ value of 2.9 and construct an imaginary line from that point parallel to the C_w/C_s axis. At the points where that line intersects the two curves bounding the region $S^* = 5$, we have the extreme values. These values of C_w/C_s are approximately 1.1 and 4.8. The solution $S^* = 5$ applies anywhere within this range. Therefore,

$$5 \text{ servers are optimal for } 1.1 \leqslant C_w/C_s \leqslant 4.8.$$

To get this into the desired form, in terms of C_w, we multiply the inequality by the value of $C_s = \$3$, so

$$5 \text{ servers are optimal for } \$3.3/\text{hr} \leqslant C_w \leqslant \$14.4/\text{hr}.$$

This knowledge should give us more confidence in our answer, as we see that our original estimate of \$6/hr could be decreased by \$2.7/hr or increased by \$8.4/hr without changing the optimal value of S.

2. What would the range of values for C_s be (assuming C_w remained at \$6/hr) in order that the optimal value S^* remains at 5?

Given the range of C_w/C_s values for which $S^* = 5$, we can invert the inequality to get C_s into the numerator. In this process, the inequality signs must be reversed, so we get

$$S^* = 5 \text{ for } \frac{1}{1.1} \geqslant \frac{C_s}{C_w} \geqslant \frac{1}{4.8}.$$

Reversing the order and simplifying,

$$S^* = 5 \text{ for } 0.21 \leqslant \frac{C_s}{C_w} \leqslant 0.91.$$

The desired result is now obtained by multiplying through by the value of $C_w = \$6/\text{hr}$.

$$S^* = 5 \text{ for } \$1.3/\text{hr} \leqslant C_s \leqslant \$5.5/\text{hr}.$$

3. Looking at the other basic parameter ρ, how much would the service rate have to increase before we could cut the optimal number of servers from 5 to 4?

Again referring to Figure 12.4, we find the given C_w/C_s value of 2.0 and draw another imaginary line parallel to the ρ axis. The range over which ρ may vary and still have $S^* = 5$, is determined by the intersection with the curves bounding the region for which 5 servers is optimal. The values are approximately 2.6 and 3.4. We can then state that $S^* = 5$ for $2.6 \leqslant \rho \leqslant 3.4$. Given that λ was 87 per hour,

$$5 \text{ servers are optimal for } \frac{87}{3.4} \leqslant \mu \leqslant \frac{87}{2.6}, \text{ or } 26 \text{ per hr} \leqslant \mu \leqslant 33 \text{ per hr.}$$

Therefore, we would have to increase the service rate to 33 per hour (a 10 percent increase) before we could economically justify one less server. Conversely, the service rate would have to drop to less than 26 per hour before a sixth server could be justified. We could, of course, perform the same type of analysis for λ, holding μ constant.

Implied Costs   There is another case of considerable interest where sensitivity analysis can give us valuable information. Suppose that we are more concerned with the mean waiting time W_q than with the cost of waiting time C_w, or we are in a situation where it is extremely difficult or quite impractical to measure C_w. For instance, a drive-in restaurant may attempt to hold the average waiting time for each car's occupants to no more than one minute before their orders are taken. Although a mean waiting time has been specified, rather than a waiting cost, the limiting value of mean waiting time chosen actually implies a waiting cost, as we will show.

Let us specify the required value of W_q in terms of the mean service time, or as μW_q, which is dimensionless, allowing our analysis to be more general. We wish to find the smallest value of S for which μW_q will not exceed whatever value is specified.

Suppose we continue with the same example problem.

4. Assuming that the value of C_w is really unknown, what is the implied waiting cost if the mean time in queue is not to exceed 1.5 minutes?

With $\mu = 30/\text{hr} = 0.5/\text{min}$, the limiting value of μW_q is $(0.5/\text{min})(1.5 \text{ min}) = 0.75$.

From the data of Table 12.6, we observe that 4 servers are the minimum required in order that μW_q not exceed 0.75. If we utilize 4 servers, the given value of ρ enables us to determine the *implied* range of C_w/C_s for which 4 servers is optimal. Referring to Figure 12.4, for $\rho = 2.9$ and $S^* = 4$, we see that $0.1 \leqslant C_w/C_s \leqslant 1.1$. For the given value C_s value of \$3/hr, our choice of 4 servers then implies a waiting cost somewhere between \$3.3/hr and a value less than \$0.3/hr.

SUMMARY

In this chapter, we have tried to give some insight into queueing problems and the development and analysis of basic queueing models. We set the stage by analyzing the characteristics common to all queueing situations, namely, the arriving units, the servers, and the queue. Then we studied single-server and multiple-server models with the objective of determining such system operating characteristics as mean queue length, mean time in queue, and fraction server idle time. We considered models with unlimited queues, with limited queues, and with a limited source of arrivals. In the section on economic analysis, we stressed the concept of breakeven analysis as a general solution approach and the ease of developing and using graphs based on cost and service ratios. Finally, we used these same graphs to perform sensitivity analyses of optimal solutions to determine the range of values over which our solution would remain optimal.

Conceptually, the models studied have been quite fundamental, although many of the resulting formulas tend to look rather complicated. (We have demonstrated, however, that most of the complicated-looking formulas can be readily evaluated using recursion relationships.) We have really only scratched the surface, as far as model complexity goes. Books have been written on the subject of queueing, and many hundreds of different queueing models have been developed. Some of the topics we have not covered relate to the assignment of priorities in queues, the situation where the service rate is a function of queue length (called state-dependent service), and queue disciplines other than first-come, first-served. Nevertheless, you should have gained a general understanding of the basic nature and wide scope of queueing systems. In Chapter 14, we will study the subject of simulation, and we will show, among other things, how we can model queueing situations that we could not begin to handle analytically.

12.8   PRACTICAL APPLICATIONS

In the following paragraphs, three queueing situations are described. The first considers an application with a direct payoff to the company; the second describes an important approach to economically improving emergency customer service; the third analyzes the causes and possible cures for the extreme congestion during the 1974 gas shortage.

1. Optimal size of customer service teams[3]   When the Xerox Corporation brought out a powerful new offset duplicating system, it soon became apparent that its traditional approach, that of assigning a service technical representative (commonly called a "Tech Rep") to be completely responsible for servicing a group of machines, would not provide an adequate level of service for such duplicating systems. Instead, a relatively straightforward multiple-server queueing model, assuming random arrivals and exponential service, based on the analysis of available data on service calls, showed that so-called mini-teams of three Tech Reps could meet the requirement for short response times to customer service calls and appreciably increase the productivity of the service work force. This is almost a classic case of improving the efficiency of a multiple-server system by utilizing a single queue rather than a separate queue for each server. For one of the copy volume markets, the savings over the program life in labor-dollars per thousand copies was estimated to be 90 percent, and the savings over the program life in total service cost was estimated as 46 percent.

2. Emergency ambulance service[4]   In many areas, emergency ambulance service is frequently provided by a single agency. Vehicle utilization tends to be low, margi-

[3]W. H. Bleuel, "Management Science's Impact on Service Strategy," *Interfaces*, Vol. 6, No. 1, Pt. 2, November 1975, pp. 4–12.

[4]Keith A. Stevenson, "Emergency Ambulance Transportation," in *Analysis of Public Systems*, A. W. Drake, R. L. Keeney, and P. M. Morse (editors), M. I. T. Press, Cambridge, Mass., 1972, Chap. 8.

nal improvements in service are expensive, and other community resources are often underutilized. An approach is described which is designed to aid the administrator of emergency ambulance services in determining the most cost-effective number of vehicles, taking into account legally mandated requirements to meet certain minimum operations standards. Considering one measure of system effectiveness, if the service level is defined as the fraction of emergency calls for which an ambulance can be dispatched immediately, the number of vehicles required goes up rapidly as the service level is increased from, say, 0.95 to 0.99. There is another way of achieving high service levels which should be less costly than increasing the permanent fleet of ambulances. It is to fall back on a secondary source of ambulances, such as private ambulance services or police or fire department emergency units. When the primary system of N ambulances is busy, a secondary source would be called upon. The appropriate queueing model is a multiple-server model where queues are not allowed. Then, instead of "lost" customers, the "overflow" customers would be served by the secondary source ambulances. To make it financially attractive to the secondary source(s), the hourly rate paid would be much higher than that for the primary source, perhaps several hundred percent higher. Since the secondary source would be paid only when used, the overall cost could be minimized by determining, for each ambulance duty shift, the preferred number of primary ambulances as a function of the traffic intensity and the cost ratio of secondary source to primary source hourly charges.

3. A queueing analysis of the 1974 gas shortage[5]

Utilizing a simple single-server queueing model with Poisson arrivals and exponential service, the author shows that the long lines at service stations during the 1974 gas shortage could be explained by analyzing the queueing effect of consumer behavior under the threat of a real or an implied gas shortage. Instead of customers filling their tanks when near empty, suppose they would fill up when only half empty. This would tend both to roughly double the arrival rate and to increase short-term demand, since cars, on the average, would be carrying three-quarters of a tank of gas rather than half a tank. As waits grew longer because of the increased arrival rate, drivers would tend to fill up when only down by a few gallons, thereby increasing the arrival rate even more, leading to inordinate line lengths and excessive waits. All these phenomena actually occurred, demonstrating the fact that the queue length tends to grow without limit as the arrival rate approaches the service rate. The author also discusses, from a queueing theory viewpoint, the probable effects of various measures designed to alleviate the congestion, such as price increases, gallon or dollar limits, the requirement that the tank be at least half empty, and odd/even license numbers used to determine the days on which gas could be purchased.

[5]Warren J. Erikson, "Management Science and the Gas Shortage," *Interfaces*, Vol. 4, No. 4, August 1974, pp. 47–51.

Poisson Arrival Distribution and Exponential Service Distribution

POISSON ARRIVALS

Suppose that customers arrive completely randomly, so that the probability of an arrival during the time interval between time t and time $t + \Delta t$ is the same regardless of the value of t and the history of any earlier arrivals. Let Δt be an infinitesimally small time increment, so that there is a very small probability of an arrival in any given interval and an absolutely negligible probability of more than one arrival in such an interval. In a unit time interval, let there be n intervals of width Δt. Since Δt is infinitesimally small, n is very large.

Let p = probability of an arrival in Δt,
   λ = expected number of arrivals in a unit time interval
     = np,
   k = actual number of arrivals in a unit time interval.

If at most one arrival can occur in an interval Δt and the probability of an arrival is the same for any interval, the actual number of arrivals k in n such intervals is given by the binomial distribution probability function $P(k \mid B{:}n, p)$. As shown earlier,

$$P(k \mid B{:}n, p) = \frac{n!}{k!(n-k)!}\, p^k (1-p)^{n-k}.$$

Now, for the case of no arrivals, $k = 0$, and

$$P(0 \mid B{:}n, p) = (1-p)^n = \left[1 - (\lambda/n)\right]^n.$$

Expanding $\left[1 - (\lambda/n)\right]^n$ in an infinite series (refer to any standard mathematics or statistics handbook), as n becomes very large,

$$P(0|B{:}n, p) \cong 1 - \lambda + \frac{\lambda^2}{2!} - \frac{\lambda^3}{3!} + \cdots.$$

This is called an exponential series, and it converges to the value $e^{-\lambda}$. Thus,

$$P(0|B{:}n, p) \cong e^{-\lambda}.$$

Going back to the general expression for $P(k|B{:}n, p)$ and taking the ratio of successive terms,

$$\frac{P(k + 1|B{:}n, p)}{P(k|B{:}n, p)} = \frac{n!}{(k + 1)!(n - k - 1)!} \cdot \frac{k!(n - k)!}{n!} \cdot \frac{p^{k+1}(1 - p)^{n-k-1}}{p^k(1 - p)^{n-k}}$$

$$= \frac{n - k}{k + 1}\left(\frac{p}{1 - p}\right),$$

so that

$$P(k + 1|B{:}n, p) = \frac{n - k}{k + 1}\left(\frac{p}{1 - p}\right) P(k|B{:}n, p).$$

Therefore, for large n,

$$P(1|B{:}n, p) = \frac{np}{1 - p} P(0|B{:}n, p) = \frac{\lambda}{1 - (\lambda/n)} e^{-\lambda}.$$

Since the interval Δt was chosen to make $\lambda/n = p$ very small, we have

$$P(1|B{:}n, p) \cong \lambda e^{-\lambda}.$$

Similarly,

$$P(2|B{:}n, p) = \frac{(n - 1)p}{2(1 - p)} P(1|B{:}n, p) = \frac{\lambda - \lambda/n}{2[1 - (\lambda/n)]} \lambda e^{-\lambda}$$

$$\cong \frac{\lambda^2 e^{-\lambda}}{2}.$$

Proceeding in the same fashion,

$$P(k|B{:}n, p) \cong \frac{\lambda^k e^{-\lambda}}{k!}.$$

This is the well-known Poisson approximation to the binomial distribution. In the limit, as Δt goes to zero, p goes to zero, and n becomes infinitely large. The probability of k arrivals in a unit time interval, when the expected number of arrivals is λ, is then, modifying the probability notation,

$$P(k|Pn{:}\lambda) = \frac{\lambda^k e^{-\lambda}}{k!}.$$

This is the Poisson distribution with parameter λ. (The Poisson distribution can be derived directly, rather than as a limiting case of the binomial distribution, but this derivation requires the use of calculus.)

During a period of t time units, the expected number of arrivals is λt, and

$$P(k \mid Pn:\lambda t) = \frac{(\lambda t)^k e^{-\lambda t}}{k!}.$$

Relationship between Poisson and Exponential Distributions

Suppose that we now designate the time of an arrival as time zero. We are interested in determining the distribution of the random variable T, the time to the next arrival. We call this distribution the interarrival time distribution.

In the time interval from 0 to t, the probability of no arrival is

$$P(0 \mid Pn:\lambda t) = e^{-\lambda t}. \tag{12.48}$$

The probability that there is an arrival in this interval is the complementary probability, so that

$$P\{T < t\} = 1 - e^{-\lambda t} \qquad t \geq 0,$$

and this is simply the cumulative distribution function of T, $F(t)$. This distribution is the negative exponential distribution, commonly referred to as the exponential distribution. The mean of this distribution is the expected time between arrivals, $E(T)$. With λ arrivals per unit time,

$$E(T) = \frac{1}{\lambda}.$$

Thus, if, on the average, 10 customers arrive per hour, the expected time between arrivals is 0.1 hour.

At this point, we have shown that the Poisson distribution of arrivals with arrival rate λ is exactly equivalent to the negative exponential distribution of interarrival times with mean interarrival time $1/\lambda$.

EXPONENTIAL SERVICE

Suppose that the probability of a service ending during the time interval between time t and time $t + \Delta t$ is the same regardless of the time t and the history of earlier service completions. Let Δt be infinitesimally small, so that there is a very small probability of completing service in any given interval. In a unit time interval, let there be n intervals of width Δt.

Let p = probability that service ends in Δt,
   μ = expected number of services completed in a unit time interval, given that the server is busy continuously,
   = np.

This case is entirely analogous to the previous case in which we derived the expressions of interest for arrivals. Thus, if we consider time zero as the start of service, the probability that service is *not* completed by time t is, substituting μ for λ in Equation (12.48),

$$P(0 \mid Pn:\mu t) = e^{-\mu t}.$$

If we let the random variable T now represent the service time, the probability of service completion within t time units is

$$P\{T < t\} = 1 - e^{-\mu t} \quad t \geq 0.$$

Thus we have shown that the assumption of entirely random service completions leads to a negative exponential distribution of service times. The mean of this distribution is $1/\mu$.

Single-Server Models— State Probability Equations

EXPONENTIAL SERVICE—UNLIMITED QUEUE

We assume that arrivals are completely random, are served in arrival order, and there is no limitation on any queue that may build up.

Let Δt be a time interval so short that there is a very low probability of either an arrival or a service completion. The probability of both an arrival and a service completion, or of multiple arrivals or service completions, is absolutely negligible. The number of arrivals during Δt is then Poisson-distributed with a mean of $\lambda \Delta t$, but since Δt is so small, we assume that there is either one arrival, with probability $\lambda \Delta t$, or no arrivals, with probability $1 - \lambda \Delta t$. As an example of the closeness of this approximation, suppose that $\lambda = 10$ arrivals per minute and $\Delta t = 0.0001$ minutes. Then the exact probability distribution of arrivals in 0.0001 minute is Poisson-distributed with a mean of $\lambda \Delta t = 0.001$. The approximation represents a binomial distribution with a sample size of 1 and a success (arrival) probability of 0.001. Comparison of the exact and approximate distributions is shown in Table 12.7. Clearly the approximation is an excellent one for very small Δt.

Now consider some derived quantities of interest:

$\lambda \Delta t$ = probability of an arrival during Δt
$\mu \Delta t$ = probability of a service completion during Δt.

Since we assume that arrivals and service completions are independent:

Probability of an arrival and no service completion during Δt

$$= (\lambda \Delta t)(1 - \mu \Delta t) = \lambda \Delta t - \lambda \mu (\Delta t)^2 \cong \lambda \Delta t,$$

since we can drop all terms involving $(\Delta t)^2$, which is very small compared to Δt. (The notation "$\cong$" denotes "approximately equal to.")

Probability of no arrival and a service completion during Δt

$$= (1 - \lambda\Delta t)(\mu\Delta t) = \mu\Delta t - \lambda\mu(\Delta t)^2 \cong \mu\Delta t.$$

Probability of no arrival and no service completion during Δt

$$= (1 - \lambda\Delta t)(1 - \mu\Delta t) = 1 - \lambda\Delta t - \mu\Delta t + \lambda\mu(\Delta t)^2$$
$$\cong 1 - \lambda\Delta t - \mu\Delta t.$$

Probability of an arrival and a service completion during Δt

$$= (\lambda\Delta t)(\mu\Delta t) = \lambda\mu(\Delta t)^2 \cong 0.$$

Table 12.7 Comparison of Exact and Approximate
Probability Distributions

	$\lambda = 10$ Arrivals per min	$\Delta t = 0.0001$ min	
	Probability		Error Using
Arrivals	Exact (Poisson)	Approximate (Binomial)	Approximation
0	0.9990005	0.9990000	−0.0000005
1	0.0009990	0.0010000	0.0000010
2	0.0000005	0.0000000	−0.0000005

Suppose that we now enumerate all possible ways of arriving in state n, for $n > 0$, at time $t + \Delta t$, considering the state at time t.

Events during Next Δt Leading to a Transition to State n

State at Time t	Arrival	Service Completion	Probability
$n - 1$	Yes	No	$\lambda\Delta t$
n	No	No	$1 - \lambda\Delta t - \mu\Delta t$
$n + 1$	No	Yes	$\mu\Delta t$

The relationship of the system states and the transition probabilities is shown pictorially in Figure 12.5.

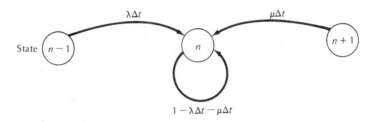

Figure 12.5

We can now write the general equation

$$P_n(t + \Delta t) = P_{n-1}(t)(\lambda\Delta t) + P_n(t)(1 - \lambda\Delta t - \mu\Delta t) + P_{n+1}(t)(\mu\Delta t).$$

In the steady state, $P_n(t)$ is independent of t, so $P_n(t + \Delta t) = P_n(t)$. Writing P_n for $P_n(t)$, the general equation becomes

$$P_n = \lambda\Delta t P_{n-1} + P_n(1 - \lambda\Delta t - \mu\Delta t) + \mu\Delta t P_{n+1}.$$

Canceling out P_n, which appears on both sides, and factoring out Δt,

$$0 = \left[\lambda P_{n-1} - (\lambda + \mu)P_n + \mu P_{n+1}\right]\Delta t$$

Now, since Δt is positive, we can divide it out, arriving at the final result.

$$\lambda P_{n-1} - (\lambda + \mu)P_n + \mu P_{n+1} = 0.$$

For the limiting case, in which the system is in state 0 (empty) at time $t + \Delta t$, it is clearly impossible to have a service completion during Δt if the system was in state 0 at time t. For this special case, we have only two possiblities, instead of three, as illustrated in Figure 12.6.

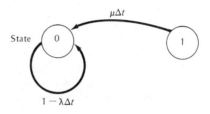

Figure 12.6

Events during Next Δt Leading to a Transition to State 0

State at Time t	Arrival	Service Completion	Probability
0	No	Impossible	$1 - \lambda\Delta t$
1	No	Yes	$\mu\Delta t$

The resulting equation is

$$P_0(t + \Delta t) = P_0(t)(1 - \lambda\Delta t) + P_1(t)(\mu\Delta t).$$

In the steady state, $P_0(t + \Delta t) = P_0(t)$. Writing P_0 for $P_0(t)$,

$$P_0 = P_0(1 - \lambda\Delta t) + \mu\Delta t P_1.$$

Canceling out P_0 and factoring out Δt,

$$0 = (-\lambda P_0 + \mu P_1)\Delta t.$$

Finally, dividing by Δt,

$$-\lambda P_0 + \mu P_1 = 0.$$

In the steady state, then, we get a series of what are termed difference equations.

$$\lambda P_0 - \qquad \mu P_1 \qquad\qquad\qquad\qquad = 0.$$
$$\lambda P_0 - (\lambda + \mu)P_1 + \qquad \mu P_2 \qquad\qquad = 0.$$
$$\lambda P_1 - (\lambda + \mu)P_2 + \qquad \mu P_3 \qquad = 0.$$
$$\lambda P_2 - (\lambda + \mu)P_3 + \mu P_4 \quad = 0.$$
$$\cdot$$
$$\cdot$$
$$\cdot$$

Suppose that, in the first difference equation, we now solve for P_1 in terms of P_0:

$$\lambda P_0 = \mu P_1, \qquad P_1 = \frac{\lambda}{\mu} P_0.$$

By substituting μP_1 for λP_0 in the second equation, we can solve for P_2 as a function of P_1:

$$\mu P_1 - (\lambda + \mu)P_1 + \mu P_2 = 0$$
$$\mu P_2 = \lambda P_1, \qquad P_2 = \frac{\lambda}{\mu} P_1 = \left(\frac{\lambda}{\mu}\right)^2 P_0.$$

Similarly, in the third equation, substituting μP_2 for λP_1, we get

$$\mu P_2 - (\lambda + \mu)P_2 + \mu P_3 = 0.$$
$$\mu P_3 = \lambda P_2, \qquad P_3 = \frac{\lambda}{\mu} P_2 = \left(\frac{\lambda}{\mu}\right)^3 P_0.$$

By induction, it becomes apparent that

$$P_n = \frac{\lambda}{\mu} P_{n-1} = \left(\frac{\lambda}{\mu}\right)^n P_0.$$

This process, by which the solution is obtained by solving the set of equations one at a time in successive order, is termed a recursive solution procedure. We encountered such procedures earlier, in the study of dynamic programming models.

Since the possible system states are mutually exclusive and exhaustive, it must be true that

$$P_0 + P_1 + P_2 + P_3 + \cdots = 1 \qquad \text{or} \qquad \sum_{n=0}^{\infty} P_n = 1,$$

and this fundamental relationship now enables us to solve for P_0 and thus P_n. Since the traffic intensity ρ is λ/μ, $P_n = \rho^n P_0$, and

$$P_0 + \rho P_0 + \rho^2 P_0 + \rho^3 P_0 + \cdots = 1$$

The series $(1 + \rho + \rho^2 + \rho^3 + \cdots)$, with $\rho < 1$, which must hold in the steady-state case, is an infinite converging geometric series, summing to the value $A/(1 - R)$, where A is the first term and R is the common ratio of terms. (See any calculus text.)

For this case, $A = 1$ and $R = \rho$. Therefore

$$P_o\left(\frac{1}{1-\rho}\right) = 1 \qquad P_0 = 1 - \rho.$$

Thus P_o, the fraction of time the system is empty, or idle, is just 1 minus the traffic intensity. Then, for $\rho < 1$

$$P_n = \rho^n(1 - \rho) \qquad n \geq 0.$$

EXPONENTIAL SERVICE—FINITE QUEUE

A little thought should convince you that the basic difference equations developed for the unlimited queue case are unchanged, except that we now have a finite number $M + 1$ of such equations, and the final equation is

$$-\lambda P_{M-1} + \mu P_M = 0.$$

Solving these equations recursively, as before, the expression for P_n is the same:

$$P_n = \rho^n P_0.$$

Since the $M + 1$ terms must sum to unity,

$$P_0 + P_1 + \cdots + P_M = 1$$

and so

$$P_0(1 + \rho + \rho^2 + \cdots + \rho^M) = 1.$$

The term inside the parentheses represents a geometric progression with first term $A = 1$, last term $L = \rho^M$, and common ratio $R = \rho$. As such, its sum is $(A - LR)/(1 - R) = (1 - \rho^{M+1})/(1 - \rho)$, for $\rho \neq 1$, since the denominator goes to zero at $\rho = 1$. Therefore,

$$P_0 = \frac{1 - \rho}{1 - \rho^{M+1}} \qquad \rho \neq 1$$

and

$$P_n = \left(\frac{1 - \rho}{1 - \rho^{M+1}}\right)\rho^n \qquad n = 0, 1, 2, \cdots, M \qquad \rho \neq 1.$$

Note that ρ is *not* constrained to be less than unity, since no more than M units can be in the system at one time, regardless of the traffic intensity ρ.

If ρ is exactly unity, the expression $(1 + \rho + \rho^2 + \cdots + \rho^M)$ becomes just $M + 1$, so that

$$P_0(1 + \rho + \rho^2 + \cdots + \rho^M) = P_0(M + 1) = 1.$$

Thus

$$P_0 = \frac{1}{M + 1} \qquad \rho = 1.$$

Finally,

$$P_n = \rho^n P_0 = 1^n P_0 = \frac{1}{M + 1} \qquad \rho = 1.$$

Thus all states are equally likely if $\rho = 1$.

Multiple-Server Models—State Probability Equations

EXPONENTIAL SERVICE—UNLIMITED QUEUE

We assume that all arrivals enter a single queue and are served in turn by the first available server. Each of the S servers has the same exponential service time distribution, with mean $1/\mu$. To determine the operating characteristics of such a system, we must solve the applicable set of difference equations. The approach is just the same as that for the single-server case, but the system service rate is no longer equal to μ.

If there are n units in the system (system is in state n),

$$
\begin{aligned}
\text{system service rate} &= n\mu \qquad 0 < n < S \\
&= S\mu \qquad n \geq S.
\end{aligned}
$$

This simply states that the service rate is proportional to the number of service channels that are busy.

Just as we did for the single-server case, we can now enumerate all possible ways of arriving in state n ($n > 0$) at time $t + \Delta t$, considering the state at time t. We again assume that Δt is so small that we can have, in any Δt, only a single arrival, or a single service completion, or neither. In this analysis, we must differentiate between the situation in which some servers are idle ($0 < n < S$) and that in which all servers are busy ($n \geq S$).

Events During Next Δt Leading to a Transition to State n

			$0 < n < S$	$n \geqslant S$
State at Time t	Arrival	Service Completion	Probability	Probability
$n - 1$	Yes	No	$\lambda \Delta t$	$\lambda \Delta t$
n	No	No	$1 - \lambda \Delta t - n\mu \Delta t$	$1 - \lambda \Delta t - S\mu \Delta t$
$n + 1$	No	Yes	$(n + 1)\mu \Delta t$	$S\mu \Delta t$

If the system is in state 0 (empty) at time $t + \Delta t$, a little thought should convince you that we have a situation identical with that in the single-server case.

In the steady state, the set of difference equations becomes

$$
\begin{cases}
\lambda P_o - \mu P_1 = 0 \\
\lambda P_{n-1} - (\lambda + n\mu)P_n + (n + 1)\mu P_{n+1} = 0 & 0 < n < S \\
\lambda P_{n-1} - (\lambda + S\mu)P_n + S\mu P_{n+1} = 0 & n \geqslant S.
\end{cases}
$$

We can solve these equations recursively, just as we did for the single-server case. When we do, we find that

$$
P_n = \begin{cases}
\dfrac{\rho^n}{n!} P_0 & 0 \leqslant n \leqslant S \\[2mm]
\dfrac{\rho^n}{S! S^{n-S}} P_0 & n > S,
\end{cases}
$$

where $\rho = \lambda/\mu$, the traffic intensity and also the expected number of servers busy. Since the state probabilities P_n must sum to unity, we can now solve for P_0:

$$
P_0 = \frac{1}{\displaystyle\sum_{n=0}^{S-1} \frac{\rho^n}{n!} + \frac{1}{S!} \sum_{n=S}^{\infty} \frac{\rho^n}{S^{n-S}}} = \frac{1}{\displaystyle\sum_{n=0}^{S-1} \frac{\rho^n}{n!} + \frac{\rho^S}{(S-1)!(S-\rho)}} \qquad \rho/S < 1.
$$

In the steady state, it is required that ρ/S be less than unity, so that the mean arrival rate does not exceed the mean system service rate.

EXPONENTIAL SERVICE—FINITE POPULATION OF ARRIVALS

Let M = number of calling units (machines),
S = number of servers (repairmen),
λ = mean arrival (failure)rate per unit time for an *individual* calling unit,
μ = mean service (repair) rate per unit time when server is busy continuously,
n = number of calling units in the system (being served and waiting for service),
= system state.

When there are n units in the system,

$$\text{system arrival rate} = (M - n)\lambda \quad 0 \leqslant n \leqslant M.$$

$$\text{system arrival rate} = \begin{cases} n\mu & 1 \leqslant n \leqslant S \\ S\mu & S \leqslant n \leqslant M. \end{cases}$$

The applicable set of difference equations can be derived in the same fashion as shown earlier for the unlimited arrival population case. The results are

$$-M\lambda P_0 + \mu P_1 = 0$$

$$(M - n + 1)\lambda P_{n-1} - \left[(M - n)\lambda + n\mu\right]P_n + (n + 1)\mu P_{n+1} = 0 \quad 1 \leqslant n < S$$

$$(M - n + 1)\lambda P_{n-1} - \left[(M - n)\lambda + S\mu\right]P_n + S\mu P_{n+1} = 0 \quad S \leqslant n < M,$$

$$\lambda P_{M-1} - S\mu P_M = 0.$$

Solving these equations recursively,

$$P_n = \begin{cases} \dfrac{M!}{(M - n)!n!}\rho^n P_0 & 0 < n \leqslant S \\[3mm] \dfrac{M!}{(M - n)!S!S^{n-S}}\rho^n P_0 & S \leqslant n \leqslant M \end{cases}$$

and

$$P_0 = \frac{1}{\displaystyle\sum_{n=0}^{S-1}\frac{M!}{(M - n)!n!}\rho^n + \sum_{n=S}^{M}\frac{M!}{(M - n)!S!S^{n-S}}\rho^n}.$$

Comprehensive Graph of μW_q Values for 1 to 10, 20, 40, 60, 80, and 100 Servers

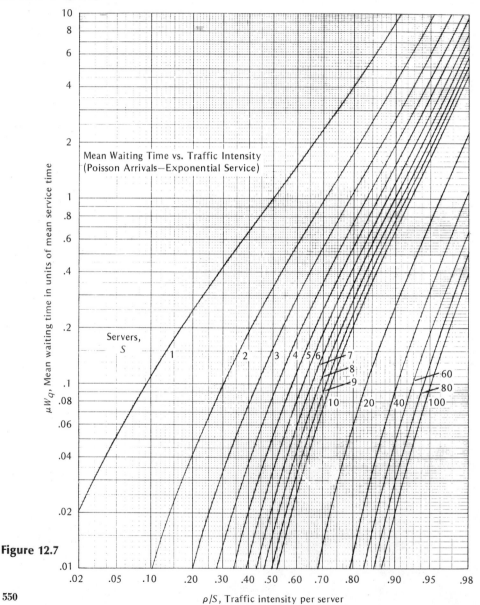

Figure 12.7

EXERCISES

12.1   In your own words, state briefly the meaning of the following queueing terms: infinite calling population, finite population of arrivals, queue discipline, mean system time, steady-state analysis, the state of a queueing system, effective arrival rate, recursion relationship.

12.2   Given a single-server model with Poisson arrivals, exponential service, and no queue limit:
(a)   For a service rate of 6 units per hour solve for L, L_q, W, and W_q for arrival rates of 2, 4, and 5.7 per hour.
(b)   For a service rate of 12 units per hour solve for L, L_q, W, and W_q for arrival rates of 4, 8, and 11.4 per hour.
(c)   What general conclusions regarding the dependence of line lengths and waiting times upon traffic intensity can you draw from this exercise?

12.3   Arrivals to the office of the student counselor at Small College appear to be random, with a mean time of 25 minutes between arrivals. The time spent with each student averages 15 minutes and there is enough variation in these times so that they can be assumed to be exponentially distributed.
(a)   What fraction of time will the counselor be idle?
(b)   What fraction of the time will there be at least 2 students waiting for interviews?
(c)   What is the average number of students in the office at any time?
(d)   What is the mean time a student waits in line?

12.4   The tuition payment window at the registrar's office is staffed by one clerk. Service times are exponentially distributed, averaging 6 minutes. Student arrivals at this window are approximately Poisson with an average of 8 per hour.
(a)   What is the mean time a student waits before service starts?
(b)   What is the mean interval between the time a student arrives and departs?
(c)   What is the mean number of students awaiting service?
(d)   What is the mean number of students either in line or at the window?
(e)   What proportion of the time will there be no student at the window?

12.5   In the situation of Exercise 12.4, suppose the supervisor wishes to speed up the service process to the point where the clerk will be busy only 60 percent of the time. Assuming that the service times will remain exponentially distributed:
(a)   Determine the mean service time required.
(b)   What is the mean time spent waiting for service?
(c)   What is the mean number of students awaiting service?

12.6   A busy general aviation airport has just one runway for landings. The arrival rate of incoming aircraft averages 8 per hour, and arrivals may be assumed to be Poisson. Runway usage times for arriving aircraft cleared for landing have a mean of 4 minutes, with a standard deviation of 1.5 minutes.

(a) What is the mean time an arriving plane spends waiting to be cleared for landing?

(b) What is the overall mean fraction of time that runway is tied up by an aircraft in the process of landing, considering only time periods when landings are permitted? [*Hint:* The distribution of service times is not a factor.]

(c) If runway usage times were exponentially distributed, with a mean of 4 minutes, what would be the mean landing clearance time for an arriving aircraft?

12.7 An apartment complex has a single tennis court. Player groups (either two or four persons) appear to arrive randomly at the rate of 0.9 groups per hour. Play, which is limited to one set, appears to take a mean time of 50 minutes, with a standard deviation of 15 minutes.

(a) What is the expected number of groups waiting at any time?

(b) What is the expected waiting time per group?

(c) What percentage of time will the court be idle?

(d) Suppose play is limited to a maximum of 50 minutes. What is the upper limit for the mean waiting time?

12.8 A soft-drink vending machine has a constant service time of 30 seconds. Customers arrive randomly to purchase drinks.

(a) If customers arrive at the rate of 1 per minute, what will be the mean system time per customer?

(b) Given an allowable mean waiting time per customer W_q and a service rate μ, derive a general expression for the allowable arrival rate λ.

(c) At what arrival rate will the mean waiting time be 1.0 minute?

(d) If the service time could be reduced to 20 seconds, at what arrival rate would the mean waiting time again be 1.0 minute?

12.9 Smith and Jones, who are good friends, both operate their own one-man TV repair shops. TV sets to be repaired appear to arrive randomly, with an arrival rate of 1 per hour for each of them. Again, for each of them, service consists of diagnosis, with a mean time of 20 minutes, exponentially distributed, followed by repair, which again has a mean time of 20 minutes, exponentially distributed.

Since Smith prefers diagnosis and Jones prefers repair, Smith has proposed that they merge their operation, with Smith handling all the diagnosis work and Jones the repair work. They believe the arrival rates and service times would be unchanged. (Thus, the total arrival rate would be 2 per hour.)

If they wish to minimize the time the average TV set spends in the shop, should they merge or not?

12.10 The counselor's secretary (Exercise 12.3) has decided to limit the number of waiting students to 2, to relieve the congestion. Recalculate the answers to parts (a) through (d) of Exercise 12.3.

12.11   A drive-in bank has only five spaces for cars to wait for service at its one teller's window. Not included is the space taken by the car of the customer being served. Customer service times are exponentially distributed with a mean of 3 minutes. Customers arrive in a Poisson fashion at the mean rate of 18 per hour. If a customer arrives and sees all five waiting spaces occupied, the customer leaves.

(a)   What proportion of customers are turned away by the lack of available waiting space?

(b)   What is the average time a customer spends waiting for and receiving service?

(c)   What proportion of customers would be turned away if the bank had six spaces for waiting customers?

12.12   Give a system with S essentially identical servers, why is it preferable for the customers to form a single queue rather than a queue in front of each server?

12.13   Consider a system with two servers having the same service rate of 1 per minute, exponentially distributed, and random arrivals. For system traffic intensity values of 0.4, 0.8, 1.2, 1.6, and 1.8, calculate the values of L_q and W_q for two different arrangements: (1) the two servers operate completely independently, with the arrival rate to each one half the system arrival rate, and (2) the two servers service a single queue. Discuss your results briefly.

12.14   The AAAce Company offers "while-you-wait" carry-in TV service at three of its stores in a metropolitan area. At each of these stores, service (by a single repairman) takes approximately 30 minutes, exponentially distributed. TV sets arrive randomly at the stores, with rates of 1.0 per hour, 0.8 per hour, and 1.2 per hour, respectively.

(a)   What is the overall mean time that a customer spends getting his TV set repaired by the AAAce Company?

(b)   It has been proposed that all three repairmen be assigned to just one store. An estimate has been made that this would add, on the average, an additional 20 minutes of driving time for customers. If the arrival and service rates remained unchanged, what would the new value be for the overall mean time spent by a customer, including the additional driving time? Would the proposed change be beneficial to AAAce's customers?

12.15   In the bank teller problem of Example 12.3, part (i) considered the situation where customers randomly selected one of the three tellers, so that each functioned as a single server. What would each teller's service rate have to become before the mean customer system time would be reduced to the same value (4.2 minutes) as when all three tellers serviced a single queue?

12.16   Renaissance Rental Realty has observed a recent decline in customer activity and is considering a reduction in staff from the present five agents. The most recent data indicate that customers arrive in a Poisson fashion at the mean rate of 4.8 per hour. The mean service time is 30 minutes, and service appears to be exponentially distributed. Managerial policy is that the mean customer waiting time shall not exceed 10 minutes.

(a) How many agents are needed?

(b) What will the mean waiting time be?

(c) What is the current mean waiting time with five agents?

12.17 All-American Airlines is attempting to determine the minimum number of reservation clerks required at one of its reservations offices. Incoming calls are put on hold for the first available clerk, and management has decided that a customer should not have to wait more than 60 seconds, on the average, before being connected with a clerk. Customer calls arrive randomly at the mean rate of 4 per minute, and service tends to be exponentially distributed with a mean time of 40 seconds per call.

(a) What is the minimum number of clerks needed?

(b) With the number of clerks determined in part (a), what is the expected mean waiting time per customer?

(c) How many customers, on the average, will be waiting at any one time?

(d) What fraction of the time would all operators be idle?

(e) What fraction of the time would all operators be busy, with no customers waiting?

12.18 A very small fast-food lunch counter has four seats for customers but no standing room for additional customers to wait. Arriving customers turn away when all four seats are full. Customers arrive randomly at a mean rate of 15 per hour at lunchtime. Customer seat occupancy times are distributed exponentially with a mean of 10 minutes.

(a) What fraction of the time will the lunch counter be empty?

(b) What proportion of arriving customers will turn away? What is the effective arrival rate?

(c) What is the mean number of seats occupied?

12.19 Yallhaul Camper Rental Service has four campers available for rent. The average rental time is 9 days, and customers arrive randomly every 3 days, on the average. Rental times tend to be exponentially distributed. If a camper is not available, the customer will go elsewhere to obtain a rental.

(a) What fraction of arriving customers will be lost?

(b) What is the mean number of campers in use?

(c) What is the average fraction of campers in use?

(d) What fraction of arriving customers will be lost if one of the campers is in the shop for repairs?

12.20 Moonlight Travel Reservation Service has two agents and three telephone lines. When both agents are busy, the next caller is placed on hold on the remaining line. When all three lines are busy, callers receive a busy signal and call elsewhere for reservations. Service appears to be exponentially

distributed, with a mean of 3 minutes. Calls arrive randomly, at the rate of 30 per hour.
- (a)   Find the effective arrival rate.
- (b)   Determine the mean customer waiting time.
- (c)   What is the fraction of time all three lines are in use?

12.21   A small auto parts store, manned by 2 clerks, can accommodate only 6 customers at one time. Customers arriving when the store is full take their business elsewhere. Service time takes, on the average, 3 minutes and appears to be exponentially distributed. Customers arrive randomly at the rate of 20 per hour.
- (a)   What fraction of potential customers will be lost?
- (b)   What is the mean number of customers in the store?
- (c)   What is the mean waiting time per customer, in minutes?
- (d)   What fraction of the time will the clerks be idle, on the average?

12.22   What type of queueing systems will remain in the steady state even though the traffic intensity per server is equal to or greater than unity? Explain why.

12.23   In the machine repair problem in Example 12.8, each machine can produce 150 units per hour while it is operating. The factory operates 8 hours per day.
- (a)   What is the expected number of units produced per day?
- (b)   How many units per day can be produced with one additional machine?

12.24   Suppose that, in Exercise 12.23, an additional repairman is added, rather than an additional machine. How many units can now be produced daily?

12.25   In Example 12.5, involving the store with the small parking lot, suppose that the incremental profit associated with each customer and potential customer is $1.50. The store is open 8 hours a day, 5 days a week.
- (a)   What is the weekly value of having the sixth parking space?
- (b)   What would be the weekly value of having a seventh parking space?

12.26   In the machine repair problem of Example 12.8, suppose that machine downtime costs $10 per hour per machine, and each repairman is paid $5 per hour.
- (a)   What is the total hourly cost of service and machine downtime?
- (b)   What would the total hourly cost be if there were only 1 repairman?

12.27   Renaissance Rental Realty, Exercise 12.16, pays its agents $5 per hour and places a value of $6 per hour on customer waiting time.
- (a)   Determine the optimal number of agents if there is no constraint on the maximum value of mean customer waiting time.
- (b)   What is the mean customer waiting time for this number of agents?
- (c)   What is the hourly cost of providing and obtaining service?
- (d)   What would be the hourly cost if an additional agent were employed?

12.28   All-American Airlines pays its reservation clerks $4 per hour. Customer calls arrive randomly at the mean rate of 4 per minute, and service tends to be exponentially distributed with a mean time of 40 seconds per call. Incoming calls are put on hold for the first available clerk. If customer time is valued at $6 per hour:
  (a)   What is the optimal number of reservations clerks?
  (b)   What is the expected number of callers on hold?
  (c)   Verify your answer in part (a) by determining the combined cost of providing and obtaining service for the optimal number of clerks, as well as the combined costs for one less clerk and for one more clerk.

12.29   A large company advertises for a machinist who will be able to recondition and reassemble a highly specialized part. Two candidates apply. The first wants $100 per day and claims to be able to recondition and reassemble 3 parts per day. The second wants $150 per day but claims to be able to recondition and reassemble 4 parts per day. Service times tend to be exponentially distributed for both machinists. Arrival of failed parts (from the company's own equipment) is random, averaging 2 per day.
        If the company estimates that the time during which the failed part is being worked on (or is awaiting repair) costs $50 per day in lost profits, which machinist should be hired?

12.30   The ZYX Company is contemplating building its own garage facilities for the service and maintenance of company cars. The company is currently using the facilities of a private garage. The cars arrive for service randomly, at the average rate of 2 per day. Only one car can be serviced at a time, and service takes a mean time of 2 hours, exponentially distributed. A flat fee of $500 per month is paid for these services. If ZYX builds its own facilities, it estimates that it can reduce the mean service time to 1.5 hours, still servicing one car at a time. The company attaches a cost of $2 per hour for each hour a car is tied up at a garage. The ZYX Company and the garage work an 8-hour day and a 22-day month.
  (a)   If the cost of building and operating the new garage facilities, averaged out over the life of those facilities, is C dollars per month, at what value of C would the ZYX Company be indifferent to building its own garage facilities?
  (b)   The private garage is considering expanding its service facilities so that it could handle two cars at a time. What is the maximum amount by which the garage could increase its monthly fee if the current expected total cost to ZYX cannot be exceeded?

12.31   Eight machines in a factory require servicing. These machines break down randomly, on the average of once every 2.5 hours. Service tends to be exponentially distributed, with a mean of 40 minutes. Repairmen are paid $6 per hour, and inoperative machines are estimated to cost $40 per hour. A computer program gives the following results.

Number of repairmen	1	2	3	4	5
Mean number of inoperative machines	4.337	2.294	1.796	1.701	1.686

Determine the optimal number of repairmen.

12.32 In Exercise 12.31, suppose that absenteeism among the repairmen averages 5 percent, with absences among the repair crew being random and independent. What is the optimal number of repairmen? (Note that a repairman must be paid even though he is absent.) [Hint: If S repairmen are hired, there will be a probability distribution of repairmen actually on the job.] For each possible number of repairmen on the job, determine the total cost and then weight it by its probability of occurrence. Start with $S = 3$, and ignore the very low probability of all repairmen being absent.

12.33 The Exxoff Service Station has three attendants and three pumps. Cars in the station are limited to 5 and those awaiting service can be considered to be in a single queue. Customers arrive randomly at the rate of 60 per hour, and service takes 3 minutes on the average, exponentially distributed. Each attendant is paid $3 per hour. The incremental profit per customer is estimated as $1.

The owner is contemplating going to a self-service operation, in which only one attendant would be needed to collect for the gasoline purchases and help out as required. Since the price of gasoline will be dropped slightly, the estimated incremental profit per customer would be $0.95. It is believed that the arrival rate would decrease to 50 per hour, because some people will not stop at a self-service station. On the other hand, the mean service time would be expected to decrease to 2 minutes, again exponentially distributed.

Determine if the owner should go to the self-service system or continue using three attendants.

12.34 The Testem Company has many units of a certain type of equipment which tends to break down randomly. These failures occur at an average rate of 1 per hour, and the major problem is diagnosing the particular type of failure. Testem is considering leasing an equipment tester. Three types of equipment testers are available. Type A is fully automatic and takes a constant 30 minutes to diagnose the failure. Type B is partially automated and takes a mean time of 36 minutes, with a standard deviation of 6 mimutes. Type C is manually operated and takes a mean time of 40 minutes, exponentially distributed. If the downtime of the equipment which fails costs $10 per hour, which type of equipment should be leased? The hourly leasing charges are: Type A—$20, Type B—$15, and Type C—$10.

12.35 When an economic analysis is performed to determine the optimal number of servers for a queueing system, why are concurrent sensitivity analyses important?

12.36 In Exercise 12.16, what is the range of the implied cost of customer waiting time if Renaissance Rental Realty maintains a staff of 5 agents, each paid $5 per hour? Does this cost range seem reasonable to you? Discuss.

12.37   Suppose that Renaissance Rental Realty, Exercise 12.16, pays each agent $5 per hour and values customer time at $15 per hour. If customers arrive randomly at the mean rate of 4.8 per hour and service times are exponentially distributed, over what range of service times, in minutes, will 4 servers be optimal?

12.38   In the problem involving the staffing of the All-American Airlines reservations office (Exercise 12.28), the clerks are paid $4 per hour. Determine the range of the implied customer goodwill cost per minute of waiting time if the number of clerks is: (a) 3   (b) 4   (c) 5.

12.39   If the All-American Airlines reservations clerks (Exercise 12.28) are paid $4 per hour and customer goodwill cost is assumed to be $6 per hour, determine the range of arrival rates for which the following number of servers is optimal: (a) 3   (b) 4   (c) 5.

12.40   In Example 12.11, in which a crew can service trucks at a rate proportionate to crew size, suppose that the cost of an idle truck and driver is not known with certainty. Determine the range for this idle cost such that the optimal crew size would be: (a) 5   (b) 6   (c) 7   (d) 8   (e) 9.

CHAPTER 13

MARKOV ANALYSIS

In the earlier discussions of dynamic programming and queueing models, we defined the state of a given system as a particular measure of some property of that system. For example, in the dynamic programming salesmen allocation model, the state was the number of salesmen still unallocated. In queueing models, the state was the total number of customers in the queueing system.

If the state of a given system can change in some probabilistic fashion at fixed or random intervals in time, we have what is called a *stochastic process*. The queueing systems we studied were models of stochastic processes. A *Markov process* is a stochastic process which has the property that the probability of a transition from a given state to any future state is dependent only on the present state and not on the manner in which it was reached. This is also called the *Markovian property*.

In the analysis of problems which can be viewed as Markov processes, it is necessary to be able to define each possible state and to develop or obtain a set of transition probabilities between states. To illustrate the nature of Markov processes, consider the following two examples.

A truck rental company operates agencies in several large cities. Trucks rented at one location may be returned to any location that the company operates. Considered as a Markov process, the states would be the different rental locations. A particular transition probability P_{ij} would be the probability that a truck rented at location i would be returned to location j, where j could equal i. Estimates of the transition probabilities could be obtained from an examination of customer invoices. Markov analysis could be used to determine such values as the expected long-term fraction of trucks at each location and the mean number of trips a truck would make, starting from location i, before returning to that location.

A certain CPA examination is offered once a year. A qualified applicant is permitted to take the examination up to four times within a six-year period, upon payment of the examination fee each time. A Markov model of this process would include four states, one for each possible number of failures (zero to three), plus a state representing passing the examination, and a state denoting that the applicant has terminated (failed four times or given up). For each possible number of failures, estimates would be needed of the probability of passing the examination and the probability of failing it and giving up. Some of the required transition probabilities (such as the probability of passing after two failures) could be based on data from files which would have to be kept for each applicant still eligible and which would be presumably be kept, probably in summary form, for applicants who had passed. Other transition probabilities would have to be carefully estimated on the basis of all available information. From an analysis of this model, the average number of times an applicant takes the examination could be calculated, leading directly to the determination of the average fee paid per applicant. The probability of an applicant's eventually passing the examination could also be computed. This model could be quite helpful in analyzing the effects of contemplated changes in the degree of difficulty of the examination.

The mathematical models to be developed in this chapter necessitate a basic understanding of matrix representation of data, and some models require the use of elementary matrix multiplication concepts. The use of matrix operations has been minimized, but those needing review or unfamiliar with matrices should refer to Appendix 13A.

13.1 BASIC CONCEPTS

A Markov process which meets the following conditions is termed a finite-state first-order Markov chain.

1. There is a finite set of states numbered 1, 2, . . . , n. The process can be in one, and only one, of these states at a given time.
2. The so-called transition probability p_{ij}, the probability of a transition from state i to state j, is given for every possible combination of i and j, including $i = j$. These transition probabilities are assumed to be stationary (unchanging) over the time period of interest and independent of how state i was reached.
3. Either the initial state in which the process begins is known, or a probability distribution of initial states is specified.

The transition probabilities p_{ij} can be arranged in the form of what is termed a one-step stationary transition probability matrix **P**:

$$
\mathbf{P} = \begin{array}{c} \\ \text{From} \\ \\ 1 \\ 2 \\ \\ \\ \\ n \end{array}
\begin{array}{c} \text{To} \quad 1 \quad\;\; 2 \quad\;\; 3 \quad \cdots \quad n \\
\left[\begin{array}{ccccc}
p_{11} & p_{12} & p_{13} & \cdots & p_{1n} \\
p_{21} & p_{22} & p_{23} & \cdots & p_{2n} \\
\cdot & \cdot & \cdot & & \cdot \\
\cdot & \cdot & \cdot & & \cdot \\
\cdot & \cdot & \cdot & & \cdot \\
p_{n1} & p_{n2} & p_{n3} & \cdots & p_{nn}
\end{array} \right]
\end{array}
$$

P is a square matrix with nonnegative elements and row elements that sum to unity. Such a matrix is called a *stochastic matrix*. Any stochastic matrix can serve as a matrix of transition probabilities; together with an initial probability distribution of states it completely defines a Markov chain.

If the probability of reaching a particular state depends on the two previous states, we have a second-order Markov chain. We will consider only first-order Markov chains, since the topic of higher-order Markov chains is much more advanced.

We will now illustrate some of the basic concepts with an example of a Markov chain for a brand-switching problem with just two states.

EXAMPLE 13.1

The B. A. Wheel family purchases a new car every two years. The Wheels prefer a brand A car but sometimes buy another brand. For simplicity, suppose we designate as brand B any other car which they may purchase. To add a little spice to their car buying, the Wheels have devised a method of randomly selecting each new car. They place ten slips, numbered 1 through 10, in a bowl and draw one slip. If their present car is brand A and the number on the slip is 8 or less, they will again purchase brand A. Thus, there is a probability of 0.8 that their next car will also be brand A. If they presently own a brand B car and the number on the slip is 6 or less, they will next purchase a brand A car. The probability they switch back to a brand A car is then 0.6.

Let state 1 be the condition of owning a brand A car and state 2 that of owning a brand B car. The transition probabilities are then

$$p_{11} = 0.8, \qquad p_{12} = 0.2, \qquad p_{21} = 0.6, \qquad p_{22} = 0.4.$$

The transition probability matrix can be structured as in Table 13.1.

Table 13.1 Brand-Switching Transition Probabilities

Current State i	Next State j	
	1	2
	P_{i1}	P_{i2}
1 (Brand A)	0.8	0.2
2 (Brand B)	0.6	0.4

The transition probabilities can also be represented by what is called a transition diagram, which was presented earlier in the derivations of queueing models in the appendices to Chapter 12. For this example, the transition diagram is shown as Figure 13.1. The nodes indicate states, and the directed line segments, branches, or arcs represent the allowable transitions between states. The transition probability is specified for each possible transition.

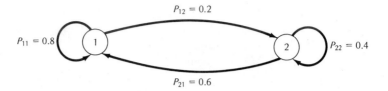

Figure 13.1   Brand-Switching Transition Diagram

We wish to investigate the probabilistic behavior of this Markov chain over a number of transitions.

Let $s_{kj}(n)$ = probability the system occupies state j after n transitions, given that it started in state k at time 0,

$S(n)$ = the state row vector of probabilities after n transitions, with components $s_{kj}(n)$.

With N possible states,

$$\sum_{j=1}^{N} s_{kj}(n) = 1, \qquad \text{for all } k. \tag{13.1}$$

At transition $n + 1$, the probability of being in state j is equal to the probability of being in state i on the previous transition weighted by the probability of a transition from state i to state j, for all possible values of i. Thus,

$$s_{kj}(n + 1) = s_{k1}(n)p_{1j} + s_{k2}(n)p_{2j} + \cdots + s_{kN}(n)p_{Nj}.$$

Expressing this in a more convenient notational form,

$$s_{kj}(n + 1) = \sum_{i=1}^{N} s_{ki}(n)p_{ij} \qquad n = 0, 1, 2, \ldots . \tag{13.2}$$

If the Wheels start by buying a brand A car, $s_{11}(0) = 1$ and $s_{12}(0) = 0$, so

$$S(0) = \begin{bmatrix} 1 & 0 \end{bmatrix}.$$

After the first transition,

$$S(1) = S(0)P = \begin{bmatrix} 1 & 0 \end{bmatrix} \begin{bmatrix} 0.8 & 0.2 \\ 0.6 & 0.4 \end{bmatrix} = \begin{bmatrix} 0.8 & 0.2 \end{bmatrix}.$$

Continuing this procedure through three more transitions,

$$S(2) = S(1)P = \begin{bmatrix} 0.8 & 0.2 \end{bmatrix} \begin{bmatrix} 0.8 & 0.2 \\ 0.6 & 0.4 \end{bmatrix} = \begin{bmatrix} 0.76 & 0.24 \end{bmatrix}$$

$$S(3) = S(2)P = \begin{bmatrix} 0.76 & 0.24 \end{bmatrix} \begin{bmatrix} 0.8 & 0.2 \\ 0.6 & 0.4 \end{bmatrix} = \begin{bmatrix} 0.752 & 0.248 \end{bmatrix}$$

$$S(4) = S(3)P = \begin{bmatrix} 0.752 & 0.248 \end{bmatrix} \begin{bmatrix} 0.8 & 0.2 \\ 0.6 & 0.4 \end{bmatrix} = \begin{bmatrix} 0.7504 & 0.2496 \end{bmatrix}.$$

If we let $s_{1j}(\infty)$ be the probability of being in state j after a large number of transitions, starting in state 1 at time 0, it appears that the state probabilities are converging rapidly to limiting values $s_{11}(\infty) = 0.75$ and $s_{12}(\infty) = 0.25$. A little later, we will show that this is indeed true.

Now, suppose that the initial state had been one in which the Wheels owned a brand B car, so that $s_{21}(0) = 0$ and $s_{22}(0) = 1$, giving

$$\mathbf{S}(0) = \begin{bmatrix} 0 & 1 \end{bmatrix}.$$

The first four state row vectors are then

$$\mathbf{S}(1) = \begin{bmatrix} 0 & 1 \end{bmatrix} \begin{bmatrix} 0.8 & 0.2 \\ 0.6 & 0.4 \end{bmatrix} = \begin{bmatrix} 0.6 & 0.4 \end{bmatrix}$$

$$\mathbf{S}(2) = \begin{bmatrix} 0.6 & 0.4 \end{bmatrix} \begin{bmatrix} 0.8 & 0.2 \\ 0.6 & 0.4 \end{bmatrix} = \begin{bmatrix} 0.72 & 0.28 \end{bmatrix}$$

$$\mathbf{S}(3) = \begin{bmatrix} 0.72 & 0.28 \end{bmatrix} \begin{bmatrix} 0.8 & 0.2 \\ 0.6 & 0.4 \end{bmatrix} = \begin{bmatrix} 0.744 & 0.256 \end{bmatrix}$$

$$\mathbf{S}(4) = \begin{bmatrix} 0.744 & 0.256 \end{bmatrix} \begin{bmatrix} 0.8 & 0.2 \\ 0.6 & 0.4 \end{bmatrix} = \begin{bmatrix} 0.7488 & 0.2512 \end{bmatrix}.$$

Again, we see that the limiting values of the state probabilities appear to be $s_{21}(\infty) = 0.75$ and $s_{22}(\infty) = 0.25$.

As a third case, suppose we knew that the Wheels were about to purchase a new car, but we had no information as to the brand of their present car. We could then assume a probability distribution for the initial state such that $\mathbf{S}(0) = \begin{bmatrix} r & 1-r \end{bmatrix}$, denoting that the probability of being in state 1 is r and the probability of being in state 2 is the complementary probability $1 - r$. Since $s_{11}(\infty) = s_{21}(\infty) = 0.75$, and $s_{12}(\infty) = s_{22}(\infty) = 0.25$, as we have seen previously, the limiting state probabilities are the same regardless of the initial state, so the value of the probability r has no effect on the limiting state probabilities. When the limiting state probabilities become independent of the initial state as n becomes relatively large, such a Markov process is called an *ergodic process*.

We can also calculate the state row vectors in a different way. Since $\mathbf{S}(2) = \mathbf{S}(1)\mathbf{P}$, and $\mathbf{S}(1) = \mathbf{S}(0)\mathbf{P}$,

$$\mathbf{S}(2) = \mathbf{S}(1)\mathbf{P} = \mathbf{S}(0)\mathbf{P}\cdot\mathbf{P} = \mathbf{S}(0)\mathbf{P}^2$$

and, in general,

$$\mathbf{S}(n) = \mathbf{S}(0)\mathbf{P}^n. \tag{13.3}$$

$\mathbf{P}^n$ is called the multistep transition probability matrix.

In this example,

$$\mathbf{P} = \begin{bmatrix} 0.8 & 0.2 \\ 0.6 & 0.4 \end{bmatrix}$$

$$\mathbf{P}^2 = \mathbf{P}\cdot\mathbf{P} = \begin{bmatrix} 0.8 & 0.2 \\ 0.6 & 0.4 \end{bmatrix} \begin{bmatrix} 0.8 & 0.2 \\ 0.6 & 0.4 \end{bmatrix} = \begin{bmatrix} 0.76 & 0.24 \\ 0.72 & 0.28 \end{bmatrix}$$

$$P^3 = P \cdot P^2 = \begin{bmatrix} 0.8 & 0.2 \\ 0.6 & 0.4 \end{bmatrix} \begin{bmatrix} 0.76 & 0.24 \\ 0.72 & 0.28 \end{bmatrix} = \begin{bmatrix} 0.752 & 0.248 \\ 0.744 & 0.256 \end{bmatrix}$$

$$P^4 = P^2 \cdot P^2 = \begin{bmatrix} 0.76 & 0.24 \\ 0.72 & 0.28 \end{bmatrix} \begin{bmatrix} 0.76 & 0.24 \\ 0.72 & 0.28 \end{bmatrix} = \begin{bmatrix} 0.7504 & 0.2496 \\ 0.7488 & 0.2512 \end{bmatrix}.$$

It is apparent that in the limit, as $n \to \infty$,

$$P^\infty = \begin{bmatrix} 0.75 & 0.25 \\ 0.75 & 0.25 \end{bmatrix}.$$

To find the state row vector $S(3)$ for the first case, where $S(0) = \begin{bmatrix} 1 & 0 \end{bmatrix}$, we could have calculated

$$S(3) = S(0)P^3 = \begin{bmatrix} 1 & 0 \end{bmatrix} \begin{bmatrix} 0.752 & 0.248 \\ 0.744 & 0.256 \end{bmatrix} = \begin{bmatrix} 0.752 & 0.248 \end{bmatrix},$$

which is, of course, the same as the earlier result.

To summarize the results of the analysis, regardless of whether the Wheels start with a brand A or a brand B car, you could give odds of approximately 3 to 1 that, after about three transitions (purchases over a six-year period) their next car would be a brand A car. Furthermore, over succeeding periods, 75 percent of the cars they own can be expected to be of brand A.

Before going on, we will now differentiate between the various types of states in a Markov chain.

Recurrent State   State j is recurrent, or persistent, if the probability is 1 that the process will eventually return to state j, having started in state j.

In Example 13.1, assuming that the Wheels (or their heirs) continue purchasing new cars in the same fashion into the indefinite future, both states are recurrent. A purchase (at any point in time) of a brand A car will eventually be followed by another purchase of a brand A car, and, likewise, a purchase of a brand B car must at some time be followed by another brand B car purchase.

Transient State   State j is transient, or nonrecurrent, if the probability is 1 that the process will eventually *not* return to state j, having started in state j.

Absorbing State   State j is absorbing, or trapping, if $p_{jj} = 1$. Once the process reaches state j, it can never leave.

To illustrate these last two state types, consider a modification of Example 13.1. Suppose that the Wheels start by purchasing a brand A car, but when they purchase a brand B car for the first time, they never again go back to brand A. The transition diagram would then be as shown in Figure 13.2. Although the process may remain in state 1 for a number of transitions, state 1 now becomes a transient state, because once the process leaves state 1, it can never return. State 2 is an absorbing state. When the process reaches state 2, as it eventually must, it remains in state 2.

We will have much more to say later about Markov processes with transient and absorbing states, but at this point let us return to the analysis of a process with only recurrent states.

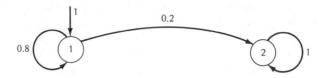

Figure 13.2   Brand-Switching Transition Diagram
with Absorption

Example 13.1 concentrated on the transient behavior of a Markov process and indicated the limiting probability values as the number of transitions became large. Now, let us directly analyze the limiting, or steady-state, behavior of such a two-state process.

13.2   STEADY-STATE ANALYSIS

In many situations, we may be primarily interested in what occurs in the long run when the process achieves a steady-state condition. To show what occurs, suppose we work with a two-state Markov process which, if in state 1, has a probability $p_{12} = a$ of moving to state 2. If in state 2, it has a probability $p_{21} = b$ of moving to state 1. Therefore, the transition probability matrix $\mathbf{P}$ can be expressed as

$$\mathbf{P} = \begin{bmatrix} 1-a & a \\ b & 1-b \end{bmatrix}.$$

As we have shown in Example 13.1, as the number of transitions n becomes large, the state probability row vector $\mathbf{S}(n)$ reaches a limiting value $\mathbf{S}(\infty)$, which we hereafter denote as just $\mathbf{S}$. Then, the following relationship must apply.

$$\mathbf{S} = \mathbf{SP} \qquad \text{for } n \text{ large.} \tag{13.4}$$

If we now denote s_1 and s_2 as the limiting state probabilities for a two-state process and use the preceding transition probability matrix, we can write

$$\begin{bmatrix} s_1 & s_2 \end{bmatrix} = \begin{bmatrix} s_1 & s_2 \end{bmatrix} \begin{bmatrix} 1-a & a \\ b & 1-b \end{bmatrix}.$$

Separating this into individual equations,

$$\begin{aligned} s_1 &= (1-a)s_1 + & bs_2, \\ s_2 &= & as_1 + (1-b)s_2. \end{aligned}$$

Combining terms,

$$\begin{aligned} as_1 - bs_2 &= 0 \\ -as_1 + bs_2 &= 0. \end{aligned}$$

Because of the complementary probabilities in the transition matrix, these equations are dependent, so we have only one independent equation in two unknowns. If we solved that equation, we would obviously be able to determine only the ratio of s_1 to s_2. To solve for s_1 and s_2 as probabilities, we drop one of the preceding equations and add the constraint that $s_1 + s_2 = 1$, since the limiting state probabilities must sum to 1. The resultant equations are

$$as_1 - bs_2 = 0$$
$$s_1 + \ \ s_2 = 1.$$

Solving, we find that

$$s_1 = \frac{b}{a + b}, \qquad s_2 = \frac{a}{a + b},$$

so that, for the general two-state Markov chain,

$$S = \left[\frac{b}{a + b} \ \frac{a}{a + b} \right] = \left[\frac{p_{21}}{p_{12} + p_{21}} \ \frac{p_{12}}{p_{12} + p_{21}} \right]. \qquad \textbf{(13.5)}$$

We can also arrive at Equation (13.5) by working from the transition diagram of Figure 13.3 and applying the principle of what Howard (1971) terms the equilibrium of probabilistic flows. This procedure should lead to additional insights. It is somewhat similar in concept to the conservation of flow approach utilized in the study of multiterminal network flows in Chapter 9.

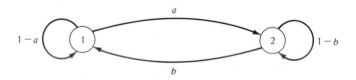

Figure 13.3   General Two-State Transition Diagram

In the steady state, the probability of a transition into state i must be the same as the probability of a transition out of state i. For example, the probability of leaving state 1 is equal to the probability s_1 of being in state 1 multiplied by the probability a of leaving state 1. The probability of entering state 1 is the probability s_2 of being in state 2 multiplied by the probability b of entering state 1. We can express this as

$$as_1 = bs_2.$$

This equation, in combination with the requirement for s_1 and s_2 to sum to 1, gives the same two equations used earlier to derive Equation (13.5).

The limiting multistep transition probability matrix will be of the following form for the general case.

$$\mathbf{P}^{\infty} = \begin{bmatrix} \dfrac{b}{a+b} & \dfrac{a}{a+b} \\ \dfrac{b}{a+b} & \dfrac{a}{a+b} \end{bmatrix} = \begin{bmatrix} \dfrac{p_{21}}{p_{12}+p_{21}} & \dfrac{p_{12}}{p_{12}+p_{21}} \\ \dfrac{p_{21}}{p_{12}+p_{21}} & \dfrac{p_{12}}{p_{12}+p_{21}} \end{bmatrix}. \tag{13.6}$$

This is so because, in the steady state, the following relationship must hold for *any* initial state probability vector $S(0)$.

$$S = S(0)\mathbf{P}^{\infty}.$$

Let $S(0)$ be of the form $\begin{bmatrix} r & 1-r \end{bmatrix}$, where $0 \leqslant r \leqslant 1$. Then,

$$S(0)\mathbf{P}^{\infty} = \begin{bmatrix} r & 1-r \end{bmatrix} \begin{bmatrix} \dfrac{b}{a+b} & \dfrac{a}{a+b} \\ \dfrac{b}{a+b} & \dfrac{a}{a+b} \end{bmatrix}$$

$$= \begin{bmatrix} \dfrac{b}{a+b}(r+1-r) & \dfrac{a}{a+b}(r+1-r) \end{bmatrix}$$

$$= \begin{bmatrix} \dfrac{b}{a+b} & \dfrac{a}{a+b} \end{bmatrix} = S,$$

independent of the value of r.

Going back to Example 13.1 to check the results, the one-step transition probability matrix was

$$\mathbf{P} = \begin{bmatrix} 0.8 & 0.2 \\ 0.6 & 0.4 \end{bmatrix}.$$

The limiting state probability vector would then be, from Equation (13.5),

$$S = \begin{bmatrix} \dfrac{0.6}{0.2+0.6} & \dfrac{0.2}{0.2+0.6} \end{bmatrix} = \begin{bmatrix} 0.75 & 0.25 \end{bmatrix}.$$

The limiting multistep transition probability matrix, from Equation (13.6), would be

$$\mathbf{P}^{\infty} = \begin{bmatrix} 0.75 & 0.25 \\ 0.75 & 0.25 \end{bmatrix}.$$

These answers, of course, are the same as the limiting values found in Example 13.1.

For a Markov chain with n recurrent states, the matrix relationship in Equation (13.4), with any one individual equation replaced by an equation where all the state probabilities are required to sum to 1, can be utilized to determine the steady-state probability vector. It is necessary only to solve a system of n simultaneous linear equations in n unknowns. Almost every computer software system has a "canned" program to do this with a minimum of effort on the user's part.

A queueing system with a finite number of states and a constant service time can be analyzed as another example of a Markov process with recurrent states. We consider the state of the system (the number of customers) to change only at multiples of the service time. Thus, any service begun in one period must be completed in the succeeding period. As an illustration of the analysis, we will take an earlier queueing example, Example 12.2, which involved a single-server queueing system with a finite queue limit. This time, however, we will assume a constant service time.

EXAMPLE 13.2

The owner of a small service station operates it by himself. On Friday afternoon, customers arrive randomly at the rate of 12 per hour. The owner is currently enlarging the station, and there is space enough to accommodate only a maximum of three cars at any one time. Any customers arriving when the station is full depart immediately and take their business elsewhere. Service time tends to be essentially constant at 3 minutes per customer. We would like to determine the effective arrival rate λ_e of customers actually receiving service and the operating characteristics L (mean number in the system), L_q (mean number in queue), W (mean time in the system), and W_q (mean time in queue).

The distribution of arrivals in any 3-minute period will be Poisson with a mean of $(12)(3/60) = 0.6$. By differencing successive terms in the Poisson cumulative probability tables in Appendix D, we can arrive at the following values, rounded to three decimal places.

Number of arrivals, k	0	1	2	3 or more
Probability, $P(k)$	0.549	0.329	0.099	0.023

We can now enumerate the feasible state changes, as shown in Table 13.2, to facilitate setting up the transition probability matrix. For convenience, we will number the states to correspond with the number of customers in the system.

The state transition probability matrix is then

$$
\mathbf{P} = \begin{array}{c c} & \begin{array}{cccc} 0 & 1 & 2 & 3 \end{array} \\ \begin{array}{c} 0 \\ 1 \\ 2 \\ 3 \end{array} & \left[\begin{array}{cccc} 0.549 & 0.329 & 0.099 & 0.023 \\ 0.549 & 0.329 & 0.099 & 0.023 \\ 0 & 0.549 & 0.329 & 0.122 \\ 0 & 0 & 0.549 & 0.451 \end{array} \right] \end{array}
$$

The transition diagram is shown in Figure 13.4.

We can now determine the steady-state probabilities by utilizing the principle of the equilibrium of probabilistic flows.

$$
\begin{aligned}
\text{At state 0:} \quad & 0.451 s_0 - 0.549 s_1 && = 0. \\
\text{At state 1:} \quad & -0.329 s_0 + 0.671 s_1 - 0.549 s_2 && = 0. \\
\text{At state 2:} \quad & -0.099 s_0 - 0.099 s_1 + 0.671 s_2 - 0.549 s_3 = 0. \\
& s_0 + \quad s_1 + \quad s_2 + \quad s_3 = 1.
\end{aligned}
$$

From the first equation, $s_0 = 1.217s_1$. Using this relationship in the second equation, $s_2 = 0.493s_1$. Substituting these values in the last two equations, we get

$$0.111s_1 - 0.549s_3 = 0,$$
$$2.71 \; s_1 + \qquad s_3 = 1.$$

Solving these two equations,

$$s_1 = 0.343, \qquad s_3 = 0.070.$$

Then,

$$s_0 = (1.217)(0.343) = 0.418, \qquad s_2 = (0.493)(0.343) = 0.169.$$

Table 13.2 Feasible State Changes for Queueing Example

Current State (Number of Customers)	Next Time Interval		Next State (Number of Customers)	State Transition Probability
	Completions	Arrivals		
0	0	0	0	0.549
	0	1	1	0.329
	0	2	2	0.099
	0	≥3	3	0.023
1	1	0	0	0.549
	1	1	1	0.329
	1	2	2	0.099
	1	≥3	3	0.023
2	1	0	1	0.549
	1	1	2	0.329
	1	≥2	3	0.122
3	1	0	2	0.549
	1	≥1	3	0.451

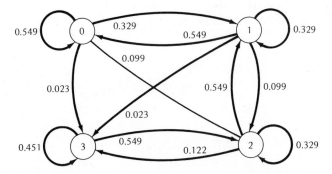

Figure 13.4 Transition Diagram for Queueing Example

Working from the state probability values thus determined, the quantities of interest can now be calculated, based on the fundamental queueing relationships developed in Chapter 12. First of all, using standard queueing notation, the state probabilities P_n, where n is the number of customers in the system, are

$$P_0 = 0.418, \qquad P_1 = 0.343, \qquad P_2 = 0.169, \qquad P_3 = 0.070.$$

Since the expected fraction of customers lost is P_3, the fraction of time the system is full, we have:

$$\text{effective arrival rate } \lambda_e = \lambda(1 - P_3) = (12)(1 - 0.070)$$
$$= 11.16 \text{ customers/hr.}$$

The operating characteristics are

$$L = \sum_{n=1}^{3} nP_n = (1)(0.343) + (2)(0.169) + (3)(0.070) = 0.891.$$

$$L_q = L - (1 - P_0) = 0.891 - (1 - 0.418) = 0.309.$$

$$W_q = \frac{L_q}{\lambda_e} = \frac{0.309}{11.16} = 0.0277 \text{ hr} = 1.66 \text{ min.}$$

$$W = W_q + \frac{1}{\mu} = 1.66 + 3 = 4.66 \text{ min.}$$

These values can be compared with those obtained in Example 13.2 for the same problem with exponentially distributed service times. It will be found that, with constant service time, there is a reduction in the fraction of customers lost from 10 to 7 percent, a corresponding decrease of the server idle time from 46 to 42 percent, and a decrease in mean queue length from 0.365 to 0.309. These reductions can be attributed to the elimination of all variability in the service time.

13.3   FIRST-PASSAGE TIMES

The number of transitions required to leave state i and to reach state j for the first time has come to be known as the *first-passage time*, a random variable. We will show how expected first-passage times can be determined and then will demonstrate their applicability to problems involving recurrent states and also problems where there are absorbing states.

Systems with Recurrent States

In the brand-switching problem, for example, the expected time between the purchase of a brand A car and the next purchase of a brand B car is just the expected first-passage time from state 1 to state 2. We will now show how such expected first-passage times can be calculated.

Let $\mu_{ij} =$ expected first-passage time (number of transitions) from state i to state j.

For systems containing only recurrent states, the value of μ_{ij} can be expressed in the form of the following relationship.

$$\mu_{ij} = p_{ij} + \sum_{k \neq j} p_{ik}(1 + \mu_{kj}). \tag{13.7}$$

The first term, which is really p_{ij} multiplied by 1, expresses the fact that the transition from state i to state j will be made in one step with probability p_{ij}. Each term in the summation may be explained as follows: It takes one step to go from state i to state $k(k \neq j)$ and then an additional expected value of μ_{kj} steps to get to state j for the first time. For each possible value of k (excluding $k = j$), the expected number of steps of the path from state i to state k and then on to state j for the first time must then be weighted by the one-step transition probability p_{ik} of going from state i to state k. By breaking the summation in Equation (13.7) into two parts and then observing that all transition probabilities out of state i must sum to 1, a simpler result can be obtained.

$$\mu_{ij} = p_{ij} + \sum_{k \neq j} p_{ik} + \sum_{k \neq j} p_{ik} \mu_{kj}$$

$$= 1 + \sum_{k \neq j} p_{ik} \mu_{kj}. \tag{13.8}$$

To solve for the first-passage times to a given state j from all other states, this equation enables us to set up one equation for each of the other states. For a system with n states, the result is a set of $n - 1$ linear equations in $n - 1$ unknowns.

In Example 13.1, the expected first-passage time from state 1 to state 2 is the expected number of periods between the purchase of a brand A car and a brand B car. From Equation (13.8),

$$\mu_{12} = 1 + p_{11}\mu_{12}, \qquad \mu_{12} = \frac{1}{1 - p_{11}}.$$

Since $p_{11} = 0.8$,

$$\mu_{12} = \frac{1}{1 - 0.8} = 5$$

The expected time between the purchase of a brand A car and the next purchase of a brand B car is 5 periods, which is 10 years. Similarly,

$$\mu_{21} = 1 + p_{22}\mu_{21}, \qquad \mu_{21} = \frac{1}{1 - p_{22}} = \frac{1}{1 - 0.4} = 1.67.$$

The expected number of periods between purchase of a brand B car and the next purchase of a brand A car is 1.67 periods, or 3.33 years.

In Equation (13.7), when $j = i$, we call the quantity μ_{ii} the expected *recurrence* time, the expected number of steps between a start in state i and the next return to that same state. It is not difficult to show that the expected recurrence time μ_{ii} is inversely proportional to the limiting state occupancy probability s_i, so that

$$\mu_{ii} = \frac{1}{s_i}. \tag{13.9}$$

In the brand-switching example, with limiting state probabilities of $s_1 = 0.75$ and $s_2 = 0.25$, the recurrence times would be

$$\mu_{11} = \frac{1}{s_1} = \frac{1}{0.75} = 1.333$$

$$\mu_{22} = \frac{1}{s_2} = \frac{1}{0.25} = 4.0.$$

Since a transition is made every 2 years, the mean time between purchases of a brand A car would be 2.67 years, and the mean time between purchases of a brand B car would be 8.0 years.

For the service station example, we could determine the mean time between successive idle periods by calculating μ_{00}, since state 0 represented no customers in the station. With $s_0 = 0.418$,

$$\mu_{00} = \frac{1}{s_0} = \frac{1}{0.418} = 2.39.$$

With state transitions occurring every 3 minutes, the constant service time, the expected time between idle periods is $(2.39)(3) = 7.2$ minutes. This is sometimes called the mean busy period.

Systems with Transient and Absorbing States

We will usually be interested in the expected number of steps from a given transient state i until absorption (by *any* absorbing state) and the probability of reaching a *specific* absorbing state starting from state i. In the next example (Example 13.3), which involves door-to-door sales, in order to determine the estimated cost per sale, we will need to calculate the expected number of calls until a sale is either completed or lost. We will also have to know the probability of making a successful sale.

Suppose we now combine all absorbing states into a composite absorbing state q. The first-passage time μ_{iq} is then the expected number of steps to absorption.

$$\mu_{iq} = 1 + \sum_{k \neq q} p_{ik} \mu_{kq}, \tag{13.10}$$

where q represents a composite state consisting of all absorbing states. This equation permits us to form an $m \times m$ set of linear simultaneous equations, where m is the number of transient states.

Since we generally need to differentiate between absorbing states, let us calculate the probability of reaching a given absorbing state.

Let p'_{ij} = probability that absorbing state j is eventually reached when starting in transient state i.

Using the same conceptual approach as in the derivation of the first-passage times, and employing the one-step transition probabilities,

$$p'_{ij} = p_{ij} + \sum_{k \neq j} p_{ik} p'_{kj} \qquad \text{for all transient states } k. \tag{13.11}$$

The first term is the probability of a direct transition to absorbing state j. Each product in the summation is the probability of a direct transition to transient state k multiplied by the probability of eventually getting from state k to state j. Again, the result is a set of linear equations, with as many equations and unknowns as there are transient states.

Let us now solve an example problem involving a Markov process with transient and absorbing states.

EXAMPLE 13.3

Screem Security Systems markets a standard home security system by using door-to-door salesmen as demonstrators. A sales call will be either to a new prospect or to a prospect previously called on and showing enough interest to warrant another sales call. After the sales call has been made, the result will be either a completed sale, enough interest shown to justify an additional call, or a lost sale. Screem concentrates its sales efforts on likely prospects only.

A salesman receives \$40 for each Screem system sold, and the salesman's estimated cost per call is \$10. We wish to find the expected profit from calling on a new prospect and from calling on an interested prospect.

It will be assumed that the selling process can be represented as a Markov process with the following states.

State 1: New prospect
State 2: Interested prospect, based on previous sales call(s)
State 3: Sale lost on this call
State 4: Sale completed on this call

The following probability data are believed to be representative: For a new customer, there is 0.30 probability of losing the sale, 0.20 probability of making the sale, and 0.50 probability that the prospect will be interested enough to make another sales call worthwhile. For a previously interested customer, the probability of losing the sale is 0.25, the probability of completing the sale is 0.50, and the probability of the prospect's retaining interest is 0.25. From these data and assuming that the probabilities applying to an interested customer do not change if he receives more than one sales call before coming to a final decision, the following matrix of one-step transition probabilities can be constructed.

$$
\mathbf{P} = \begin{array}{c} \\ 1 \\ 2 \\ 3 \\ 4 \end{array}
\begin{array}{cccc}
1 & 2 & 3 & 4 \\
\left[\begin{array}{cccc}
0 & 0.50 & 0.30 & 0.20 \\
0 & 0.25 & 0.25 & 0.50 \\
0 & 0 & 1 & 0 \\
0 & 0 & 0 & 1
\end{array}\right]
\end{array}
$$

Since the process always starts in state 1, with a new prospect, the starting row vector is

$$
S(0) = \begin{bmatrix} 1 & 0 & 0 & 0 \end{bmatrix}.
$$

To calculate the expected profit, we must determine the expected number of calls until the customer is either sold or lost. We also need to determine the probability that a sale is successfully completed.

Let us start by constructing a transition diagram, Figure 13.5, so as to get a picture of the process. The process always starts in state 1. States 1 and 2 are transient states, since the process eventually ends in either state 3 or state 4, the absorbing states.

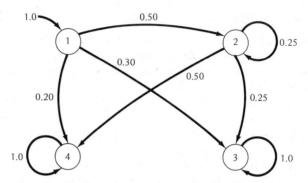

Figure 13.5 Transition Diagram, Screem Security
Systems

To find the expected number of calls until the prospect makes a decision, we must combine the two absorbing states into a single composite state. This is done in the transition diagram of Figure 13.6, where the composite absorbing state is denoted as state 5.

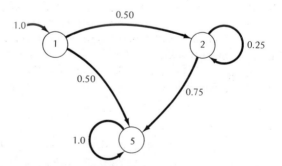

Figure 13.6 Transition Diagram with
Composite Absorbing State,
Screem Security Systems

Observe that

$$p_{15} = p_{13} + p_{14} = 0.30 + 0.20 = 0.50$$
$$p_{25} = p_{23} + p_{24} = 0.25 + 0.50 = 0.75.$$

Now, we are ready to apply Equation (13.10):

$$\mu_{15} = 1 + p_{11}\mu_{15} + p_{12}\mu_{25}$$
$$\mu_{25} = 1 + p_{21}\mu_{15} + p_{22}\mu_{25}.$$

Noting that p_{11} and p_{21} are zero, and substituting the values of p_{12} and p_{22},

$$\mu_{15} = 1 + 0.50\mu_{25}$$
$$\mu_{25} = 1 + 0.25\mu_{25}.$$

We solve the second equation, which has only one unknown, and then the first equation.

$$\mu_{25}(1 - 0.25) = 1, \ \mu_{25} = 1/0.75 = 1.333$$
$$\mu_{15} = 1 + (0.50)(1.333) = 1.667.$$

For a new customer, the expected number of calls is 1.67 before a decision is reached. When calling on an interested prospect, the comparable figure is 1.33 calls.

The probability of a successful sale (reaching state 4) can be determined by using Equation (13.11) and the transition diagram of Figure 13.5.

$$p'_{14} = p_{14} + p_{11}p'_{14} + p_{12}p'_{24}$$
$$p'_{24} = p_{24} + p_{21}p'_{14} + p_{22}p'_{24}.$$

State 3 is an absorbing state, so transitions to it are not involved. At this point, we can substitute the values of the one-step transition probabilities, including $p_{11} = p_{21} = 0$.

$$p'_{14} = 0.20 + 0.50p'_{24}$$
$$p'_{24} = 0.50 + 0.25p'_{24}.$$

Again solving the easy second equation first,

$$p'_{24}(1 - 0.25) = 0.50, \ p'_{24} = 0.50/0.75 = 0.67$$
$$p'_{14} = 0.20 + (0.50)(0.67) = 0.53.$$

The probability of a successful sale is 0.53 for a new prospect, increasing to 0.67 if the prospect has previously shown interest.

Now we are ready to calculate the expected profit values, using the following relationship.

Expected profit = (profit per sale)(probability of a successful sale)
$$- \text{(cost per call)(expected number of calls)}.$$
Expected profit for a new prospect = $(40)(0.53) - (10)(1.67) = \$4.5$.
Expected profit for an interested prospect = $(40)(0.67) - (10)(1.33) = \$13.5$.

Given the data of this problem, if a salesman is limited to fewer calls than there are prospects, he should concentrate on previously interested prospects, which, on the average, will yield three times the expected profit for a new prospect.

13.4 MARKOVIAN DECISION ANALYSIS

In many situations, a decision maker may have the opportunity to consider alternative courses of action, each with associated cost and/or payoff relationships. For Markov processes, alternative actions will generally result in changes to the original transition probability matrix. For example, an advertising campaign could be expected to increase the probability of a customer remaining with brand A, in preference to switching to brand B. If meaningful data on the statistical population of potential customers were available, along with the expected profit per customer, the desirability of the advertising campaign, given its cost, could be determined.

We will now work through two examples, the first a production reject allowance problem and the second an accounts receivable problem.

EXAMPLE 13.4

A certain manufactured part has to go through a critical finishing operation. On completion of this operation, the part is inspected. If it passes inspection, it goes into inventory. If it does not pass inspection, it is either scrapped or sent back to go through the operation again. A diagram of this process is shown as Figure 13.7.

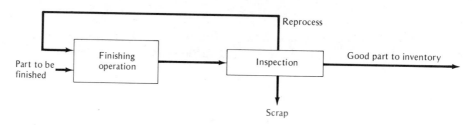

Figure 13.7 Processing Flow

When a part goes through the finishing operation (regardless of whether it is the first time or not), there is an 85 percent chance it is a good part, a 5 percent chance it must be scrapped, and a 10 percent chance it can be reprocessed. By the time the part gets to the finishing operation, it is valued at $50, including materials and labor. The direct costs of the operation and inspection are estimated as $10 per part processed. Any parts scrapped have a value of only $5; 1000 good parts are required annually.

A modification of the equipment has been proposed which, at an annual cost of $2000, would be expected to decrease the fraction of scrapped parts from 5 to 2 percent, but would increase the fraction of parts to be reprocessed from 10 to 15 percent. It is desired to determine if the equipment modification is economically justifiable.

For each individual part, the finishing operation and inspection can be considered as a three-state Markov process.

Ĩ State 1: Being processed or inspected
Ĩ State 2: Scrapped
Ĩ State 3: Passed inspection

States 2 and 3 are clearly absorbing states, with state 1 a transient state, resulting in the simple transition diagram of Figure 13.8.

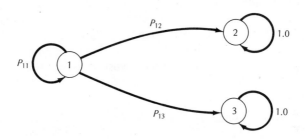

Figure 13.8 Transition Diagram, Production Problem

The total relevant annual cost will be a function of the number of parts required to go through the finishing operation in order to end up with an expected number of 1000 parts, the mean number of times each part is processed, and the expected fraction of parts scrapped. We will therefore need to determine, for this Markov process, the expected number of steps to absorption from state 1, which is always the initial state. In addition, we must find the absorption probabilities for both absorbing states.

Since there are two sets of transition probabilities, and we have a very simple Markov chain, we will derive the desired values in general terms and then substitute the given numerical data.

First, from Figure 13.7 and Equation (13.10), the probabilities of eventually reaching the two absorbing states are

$$p'_{12} = p_{12} + p_{11}p'_{12}, \qquad p'_{12} = \frac{p_{12}}{1 - p_{11}}.$$

$$p'_{13} = p_{13} + p_{11}p'_{13}, \qquad p'_{13} = \frac{p_{13}}{1 - p_{11}}.$$

Now, we combine the two absorbing states into a single composite absorbing state, state 4, as in Figure 13.9.

The expected number of steps until absorption, μ_{14}, can be determined from Equation (13.10).

$$\mu_{14} = 1 + p_{11}\mu_{14}, \qquad \mu_{14} = \frac{1}{1 - p_{11}}.$$

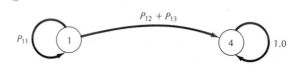

Figure 13.9   Transition Diagram with Composite
Absorbing State, Production Problem

In order to meet the annual requirement for the expected number of good parts to be 1000, the number of parts entering the finishing operation must be 1000 divided by the fraction which pass inspection, or $1000/p'_{13}$. The number of parts scrapped (worth \$5 each) will then be $(1000/p'_{13})p'_{12}$, the number of parts beginning the finishing operation multiplied by the fraction scrapped. The relevant cost per part processed is \$50 plus the expected cost of going through the finishing operation, $\$10\mu_{14}$. We then have:

$$\text{expected annual total relevant cost } C = \frac{1000}{p'_{13}}(50 + 10\mu_{14}) - 5\left(\frac{1000}{p'_{13}}\right)p'_{12}.$$

Based on the general equations derived for this problem, the values of interest for the two alternatives are developed in Table 13.3.

Table 13.3   Comparative Values for Production Alternatives

Quantity	Present Equipment	Modified Equipment
p_{11}	0.10	0.15
p_{12}	0.05	0.02
p_{13}	0.85	0.83
$p'_{12} = p_{12}/(1 - p_{11})$	0.056	0.024
$p'_{13} = p_{13}/(1 - p_{11})$	0.944	0.976
$\mu_{14} = 1/(1 - p_{11})$	1.111	1.176
Initial parts required $= 1000/p'_{13}$	1059	1025
Expected parts scrapped $= 1000p'_{12}/p'_{13}$	59	25
Expected operation cost per part $= 10\mu_{14}$	\$11.11	\$11.76

$$C(\text{present equipment}) = (1059)(50 + 11.11) - (5)(59)$$
$$= 64,715 - 295 = \$64,420.$$

$$C(\text{modified equipment}) = (1025)(50 + 11.76) - (5)(25) + 2000$$
$$= 63,304 - 125 + 2000 = \$65,179.$$

At an annual cost of \$2000, the equipment modification is too expensive, by the amount of \$65,179 - \$64,420 = \$759. At the present annual production rate, the modification is not economically worthwhile.

By equating the total relevant cost for the two alternatives, we can readily solve for the required production quantity for which we would be indifferent between the two alternatives.

Let m = number of good parts required annually for indifference.

$$C(\text{present equipment}) = 61.11m/0.944 - (5)(0.056m)/0.944$$
$$= 64.74m - 0.30m = 64.44m.$$

$$C(\text{modified equipment}) = 61.76m/0.976 - (5)(0.024m)/0.976 + 2000$$
$$= 63.28m - 0.12m + 2000 = 63.16m + 2000.$$

Equating the two costs,

$$64.44m = 63.16m + 2000,$$
$$m = \frac{2000}{1.28} = 1560 \text{ parts.}$$

Above a mean annual requirement of 1560 good parts, the modified equipment could be economically justified.

As a second example of Markovian decision analysis, we now consider an accounts receivable situation which can be formulated as a Markov process with recurrent states.

EXAMPLE 13.5

The Reed M. Enweep Book Club classifies its customers accounts as current, 30 days past due, 60 days past due, and delinquent (90 days or more past due). All delinquent accounts are turned over to the Thuggee Collection Agency and denied any further credit.

Enweep currently has 100,000 accounts, and it wishes to remain at this level, so it has a policy of adding just enough new accounts to replace those which become delinquent. From an analysis of its records, the club has obtained the following information on the probability of an account in one classification moving to another classification: 20 percent of current accounts will become 30 days past due; 30 percent of accounts 30 days past due will become 60 days past due; 40 percent of accounts 60 days past due will become delinquent, while 60 percent will pay up and become current.

We can visualize the behavior of customer accounts as a Markov process with four account states.

        State 1: Current
        State 2: 30 days past due
        State 3: 60 days past due
        State 4: Delinquent

Given the numerical data in the problem and the stipulation that each delinquent account will be replaced by a new account, the following transition probability matrix is obtained.

$$
\mathbf{P} = \begin{array}{c} \\ 1 \\ 2 \\ 3 \\ 4 \end{array}
\begin{array}{c} \begin{array}{cccc} 1 & 2 & 3 & 4 \end{array} \\
\left[\begin{array}{cccc}
0.8 & 0.2 & 0 & 0 \\
0.7 & 0 & 0.3 & 0 \\
0.6 & 0 & 0 & 0.4 \\
1 & 0 & 0 & 0
\end{array} \right]
\end{array}
$$

It should be carefully noted that the transition probability data given in this problem is aggregate data, not data on individual accounts. If the transition probability matrix were incorrectly interpreted as applying to an individual account, then each such account would eventually end up as delinquent, and this is clearly not the case.

For each account which is not delinquent, the net revenue, excluding any collection expense, averages $2 per month. The average collection expense is $0.50 for accounts 30 days past due and $1 for accounts 60 days past due. For delinquent accounts, Enweep has managed to recover its expenses through Thuggee's efforts, so a delinquent account contributes neither to profit nor to loss.

A proposal has been made to give an incentive, in the form of lowered prices, to customers remaining current. This would have the effect of lowering the expected net revenue on current accounts from $2 to $1.80 per month. It is estimated that more customers would remain current, and accounts past due would be more likely to become current, according to the following revised transition probability matrix.

$$
\mathbf{P} = \begin{array}{c} \\ 1 \\ 2 \\ 3 \\ 4 \end{array}
\begin{array}{c} \begin{array}{cccc} 1 & 2 & 3 & 4 \end{array} \\
\left[\begin{array}{cccc}
0.85 & 0.15 & 0 & 0 \\
0.8 & 0 & 0.2 & 0 \\
0.7 & 0 & 0 & 0.3 \\
1 & 0 & 0 & 0
\end{array} \right]
\end{array}
$$

We wish to evaluate the economic desirability of the proposed change. To do so, we will have to determine the steady-state proportion for each account classification. To do this, we can develop a set of equations based on the equilibrium of probabilistic flows. For this problem, we will develop and solve a general set of equations based on the transition diagram of Figure 13.10. Then, we can readily substitute the given transition probabilities for both cases.

Writing equilibrium flow equations for the three least complicated nodes, 2, 3, and 4, and adding the constraint that all limiting state probabilities s_i must sum to 1:

State 2 flows: $p_{12} s_1 = (p_{21} + p_{23})s_2.$

State 3 flows: $p_{23} s_2 = (p_{31} + p_{34})s_3.$

State 4 flows: $p_{34} s_3 = p_{41} s_4 = s_4$

$$s_1 + s_2 + s_3 + s_4 = 1.$$

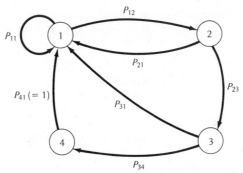

Figure 13.10   Transition Diagram for Accounts Receivable

Since $p_{21} + p_{23} = 1$, and $p_{31} + p_{34} = 1$, we can simplify the first three equations to

$$s_2 = p_{12}s_1.$$
$$s_3 = p_{23}s_2 = p_{23}p_{12}s_1.$$
$$s_4 = p_{34}s_3 = p_{34}p_{23}p_{12}s_1.$$

Substituting in the probability summation equation,

$$s_1 + p_{12}s_1 + p_{23}p_{12}s_1 + p_{34}p_{23}p_{12}s_1 = 1$$

$$s_1 = \frac{1}{1 + p_{12} + p_{23}p_{12} + p_{34}p_{23}p_{12}}.$$

The other three steady-state probabilities are then easily determined from the previous relationships.

The comparative numerical data for the two alternatives are developed in Table 13.4.

Table 13.4   Comparative Values for Accounts Receivable Alternatives

Quantity	Present Situation	Proposed Change
p_{12}	0.2	0.15
p_{23}	0.3	0.2
p_{34}	0.4	0.3
$s_1 = 1/(1 + p_{12} + p_{23}p_{12} + p_{34}p_{23}p_{12})$	0.778	0.841
$s_2 = p_{12}s_1$	0.156	0.126
$s_3 = p_{23}s_2$	0.047	0.025
$s_4 = p_{34}s_3$	0.019	0.008
Expected customers current $= 100{,}000s_1$	77,800	84,100
Expected customers 30 days past due $= 100{,}000s_2$	15,600	12,600
Expected customers 60 days past due $= 100{,}000s_3$	4,700	2,500
Expected customers delinquent = expected new customers $= 100{,}000s_4$	1,900	800
Expected monthly collection expense $= (0.5)(100{,}000s_2) + (1.0)(100{,}000s_3)$	$12,500	$8,800

Present situation: Expected monthly net revenue
$$= (2.0)(77,800 + 15,600 + 4,700) - 12,500$$
$$= 196,200 - 12,500 = \$183,700.$$

Proposed change: Expected monthly net revenue
$$= (1.8)(84,100) + (2.0)(12,600 + 2,500) - 8,800$$
$$= 151,380 + 30,200 - 8,800 = \$172,780.$$

The proposed change gives up too much in revenue for the expected decrease in collection costs. The existing situation is preferable.

SUMMARY

Many different types of problems involving probabilistic elements can be viewed as Markov processes. Viewing them from this perspective frequently yields valuable insights into the mathematical structure of such problems, particularly from the standpoints of defining appropriate states and determining the allowable state transitions.

In this chapter, we have examined only finite-state, first-order Markov chains. After presenting the transition probability matrix and the transition diagram, we initially analyzed the transient and steady-state behavior of Markov chains containing only recurrent states. Then, after developing the concept of first-passage times, we considered problems involving only transient and absorbing states. In these problems, we showed how to determine the eventual probability of reaching a particular absorbing state, along with finding the expected number of transitions required to reach any absorbing state. To obtain this latter value, a transition diagram with a composite absorbing state was used.

In the discussion of Markovian decision analysis, basic approaches to the economic comparison of alternative actions were presented. In both the examples in this section, the structure of the particular mathematical model was the same for both alternatives, with only the transition probabilities and economic factors differing. This, of course, will not always be true, but we have considered only rather elementary models. More complex decision models, such as those involving the value iteration and policy iteration approaches of Howard (1971), are beyond the scope of this text.

The presentation of finite-state Markov processes in this chapter has barely scratched the surface of a topic as comprehensive as Markov analysis. Powerful transform methods have been utilized to tackle problems involving finite-state, infinite-state, and continuous-time Markov and semi-Markov processes. The interested reader is particularly referred to Howard's two volumes on dynamic probabilistic systems, surely the definitive work in this area.

Matrices, Vectors, and Matrix Multiplication

The material in this appendix is intended to cover only those aspects of matrix algebra actually used in the preceding chapter on Markov analysis. For more complete coverage, the reader can refer to any one of the many available business mathematics or finite mathematics texts.

A *matrix* is a rectangular array of numbers, or elements, arranged in rows and columns. The numbers or elements are enclosed in brackets, and the matrix is generally designated by a capital letter, frequently set in bold type. As examples, we have matrices **A** and **B:**

$$\mathbf{A} = \begin{bmatrix} 5 & 0 & 1 & 2 \\ 2 & 8 & -3 & 9 \\ 0 & 1 & 10 & 3 \end{bmatrix} \qquad \mathbf{B} = \begin{bmatrix} b_{11} & b_{12} & b_{13} \\ b_{21} & b_{22} & b_{23} \end{bmatrix}.$$

Matrix **A** is a 3×4 matrix. The number of rows is always given first, followed by the number of columns. Matrix **B** is a 2×3 matrix, with the element subscripts denoting row and column, in that order. A square matrix is obviously a matrix with the same number of rows and columns.

A *vector* is a matrix consisting of either one row or one column. Matrix **C** is a row vector; matrix **D** is a column vector.

$$\mathbf{C} = \begin{bmatrix} 2 & -5 & 8 & 1 \end{bmatrix}, \qquad \mathbf{D} = \begin{bmatrix} 5.3 \\ 1.2 \\ 9.7 \end{bmatrix}.$$

In elementary Markov analysis, our primary interest is in matrix multiplication. The use of matrix notation permits us to express in a very compact form what would otherwise be a time- and space-consuming enumeration of required multiplications and additions.

Matrix multiplication is an operation which is only defined if the number of columns in the first matrix is equal to the number of rows in the second matrix. A 4×3 matrix may be multiplied by a 3×2 matrix, but a 3×2 matrix cannot be multiplied by a 4×3 matrix; this latter operation is simply undefined. For two matrices that can be multiplied, the resultant matrix will have the same number of rows as the first matrix and the same number of columns as the second matrix. Thus, multiplication of an $m \times n$ matrix by an $n \times k$ matrix results in a matrix of size $m \times k$. A square matrix can always be multiplied by itself or by another square matrix of the same size. The product is again square and of the same size.

The actual process of matrix multiplication involves the summation of the product of row elements of the first matrix and column elements of the second matrix. To illustrate, consider the multiplication of 3×2 matrix **A** by 2×3 matrix **B** to get 3×3 matrix **C**.

$$\mathbf{A} = \begin{bmatrix} a_{11} & a_{12} \\ a_{21} & a_{22} \\ a_{31} & a_{32} \end{bmatrix}, \qquad \mathbf{B} = \begin{bmatrix} b_{11} & b_{12} & b_{13} \\ b_{21} & b_{22} & b_{23} \end{bmatrix}.$$

The matrix product $\mathbf{C} = \mathbf{AB}$ is:

$$\mathbf{C} = \begin{bmatrix} a_{11}b_{11} + a_{12}b_{21} & a_{11}b_{12} + a_{12}b_{22} & a_{11}b_{13} + a_{12}b_{23} \\ a_{21}b_{11} + a_{22}b_{21} & a_{21}b_{12} + a_{22}b_{22} & a_{21}b_{13} + a_{22}b_{23} \\ a_{31}b_{11} + a_{32}b_{21} & a_{31}b_{12} + a_{32}b_{22} & a_{31}b_{13} + a_{32}b_{23} \end{bmatrix}$$

The element in row i and column j of matrix **C** is the summation of the products of the corresponding elements in row i of matrix **A** and column j of matrix **B**. For example, the element in row 2 and column 3 of matrix **C** is the summation of the products of the corresponding elements in row 2 of matrix **A** and column 3 of matrix **B**.

Let us now take numerical examples illustrating the two types of matrix multiplication used in this chapter.

1. Multiplication of a row vector by a square matrix

$$\mathbf{A} = \begin{bmatrix} 2 & -1 & 1 \end{bmatrix} \qquad \mathbf{B} = \begin{bmatrix} 1 & 5 & 2 \\ 3 & 7 & 4 \\ 0 & -1 & -2 \end{bmatrix}$$

The matrix product $\mathbf{C} = \mathbf{AB}$ is a row vector of the same size as vector **A**.

$$\mathbf{C} = \begin{bmatrix} (2)(1) + (-1)(3) + (1)(0) & (2)(5) + (-1)(7) + (1)(-1) & (2)(2) + (-1)(4) + (1)(-2) \end{bmatrix}$$
$$= \begin{bmatrix} -1 & 2 & -2 \end{bmatrix}.$$

2. Multiplication of a square matrix by another square matrix of the same size

$$\mathbf{A} = \begin{bmatrix} 0.6 & 0.4 \\ 0.8 & 0.2 \end{bmatrix} \qquad \mathbf{B} = \begin{bmatrix} 0.9 & 0.1 \\ 0.3 & 0.7 \end{bmatrix}$$

The matrix product $C = AB$ will again be a square matrix of order (size) 2.

$$C = \begin{bmatrix} (0.6)(0.9) + (0.4)(0.3) & (0.6)(0.1) + (0.4)(0.7) \\ (0.8)(0.9) + (0.2)(0.3) & (0.8)(0.1) + (0.2)(0.7) \end{bmatrix}$$

$$= \begin{bmatrix} 0.66 & 0.34 \\ 0.78 & 0.22 \end{bmatrix}.$$

Note that, if A and B are both stochastic matrices (elements in each row sum to 1.0), $C = AB$ will also be a stochastic matrix. Also, observe that the matrix product $BA \neq AB$.

EXERCISES

13.1   In your own words, state briefly the meaning of the following terms: Markov process, first-order Markov chain, transition probability matrix, transition diagram, ergodic process.

13.2   What are the three fundamental properties of a finite-state, first-order Markov chain?

13.3   From a problem-solving standpoint, what is the importance of the so-called Markovian property?

13.4   Clearly specify the conditions which must be met for a state in a Markov chain to be: (a) recurrent   (b) transient   (c) absorbing.

13.5   The accompanying transition diagram contains five states.

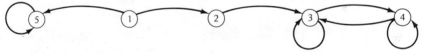

        Identify each state as either recurrent, transient, or absorbing, and briefly discuss your reasons.

13.6   All faculty teaching a required junior level business course use one of two textbooks. The number of students in the course is essentially constant from quarter to quarter. Considering the number of copies of the older text in use at the beginning of a quarter, 50 percent as many copies will be used the following quarter, and the remaining 50 percent will be copies of the newer text. Given the number of copies of the newer text at the quarter's beginning, 70 percent as many copies of that text will be used during the succeeding quarter, with the remaining 30 percent being copies of the older text.
        (a)   Specify the transition probability matrix.
        (b)   At the beginning of the school year of three quarters, 80 percent of the total copies are of the older text. What is its expected share for the second quarter? for the third quarter? for the first quarter of the next school year? Calculate each required state row vector as a function of the previous state row vector.

(c)   Determine the two-step and three-step transition probabilities. Use them, in conjunction with the initial state row vector from part (b), to calculate the state probabilities for the third quarter and for the first quarter of the next school year.

13.7   Two famous magazines compete for the same audience. Of the subscribers who order only one of the magazines each year, 70 percent renew magazine A annually, while 30 percent change to magazine B. At annual renewal time, 80 percent of subscribers retain magazine B, while 20 percent switch to magazine A.

(a)   Specify the annual transition probability matrix for magazine subscriptions.

In parts (b) and (c) below, calculate the expected proportion of subscribers to each magazine after one year, after two years, and after three years, given the following extreme initial states:

(b)   All subscribers are ordering magazine A.
(c)   All subscribers are ordering magazine B.
(d)   Compare the results in (b) and (c), and discuss the implications.
(e)   Estimate the limiting state probabilities. What would you say is the maximum error in your estimates?

13.8   A large state university system has been studying the aggregate flow of faculty through the three ranks of assistant professor, associate professor, and full professor. The number of faculty in the system has stabilized. Currently, 40 percent of the faculty are assistant professors, 30 percent are associate professors, and 30 percent are full professors. Only when full professors die, retire, or resign are new assistant professors hired. The accompanying transition probability matrix reflects the proportion of annual movement among the three academic ranks. (The transition from full professor to assistant professor represents the replacement of a full professor by an assistant professor.)

From	To Asst. Prof.	Assoc. Prof.	Full Prof.
Asst. Prof.	0.9	0.1	0
Assoc. Prof.	0	0.8	0.2
Full Prof.	0.05	0	0.95

(a)   Calculate the expected proportion in each of the three ranks one year from now and two years from now.
(b)   The current average salaries for the three ranks are $14,000, $18,000, and $24,000, respectively. What is the average salary per faculty member this year?
(c)   If the average salary for each rank is anticipated to increase at the rate of 5 percent each year (compounded), what will be the expected salary per faculty member two years from now?
(d)   What fraction of the increase in average salary two years from now can be attributed to the change in the proportion in each faculty rank?

13.9 A company has salespersons at four different locations. Every two years, a fraction of the salespersons are reassigned to other locations, according to the accompanying transition probability matrix.

		Location			
	From \ To	A	B	C	D
Location	A	0.6	0.4	0	0
	B	0.3	0	0.7	0
	C	0.2	0	0	0.8
	D	0.1	0	0	0.9

(a) Are the states in this Markov chain recurrent, transient, or absorbing?
(b) Compute the two-step transition probability matrix.
(c) Compute the four-step transition probability matrix.
(d) How does your result in part (c) corroborate your answer in part (a)?

13.10 State the principle of the equilibrium of probabilistic flows in a steady-state Markov process.

13.11 In the textbook selection problem of Exercise 13.6, if the process continued over a period of time, what would be the steady-state fraction of books used for each text?

(a) Draw a transition diagram and use the principle of the equilibrium of probabilistic flows.
(b) Use the formula for a general two-state Markov chain.

13.12 In Exercise 13.8, involving the distribution of faculty ranks for a university, construct a transition diagram and use it to help determine the steady-state proportion in each faculty rank.

13.13 The Model T Truck Rental Company has agencies in cities A, B, and C. From an analysis of its records, the fraction of trucks rented in a given city and returned in each of the three cities is as shown in the following table.

		City to Which Returned		
		A	B	C
City at Which Rented	A	0.6	0.1	0.3
	B	0.3	0.4	0.3
	C	0.1	0.1	0.8

What is the expected long-term fraction of trucks at each city?

13.14 Briefly explain the concept of the first-passage time. Why is a first-passage time a random variable?

13.15 What is the difference between expected first-passage time and expected recurrence time?

13.16 For what purpose do we generally combine absorbing states in a Markov chain?

13.17 For the truck rental company of Exercise 13.13, it can be determined that the mean fraction of trucks in city A is 0.257. If a truck is rented at city A, what is the expected number of trips
(a)   until the first arrival at city C?
(b)   until the truck first returns to city A?

13.18 From the data of Exercise 13.8, what is the expected number of years
(a)   until an assistant professor is promoted to associate professor?
(b)   until an assistant professor is promoted to full professor?
(c)   until an associate professor is promoted to full professor?

13.19 A study of armed robbers yielded the approximate transition probability matrix shown below. This matrix gives the probability that a robber currently free, on probation, or in jail would, over a period of a year, make a transition to one of the three states.

From \ To	Free	Probation	Jail
Free	0.7	0.2	0.1
Probation	0.3	0.5	0.2
Jail	0	0.1	0.9

Assuming that transitions are recorded at the end of each one-year period:
(a)   For a robber who is now free, what is the expected number of years before going to jail?
(b)   For a robber now on probation, what is the expected number of years before going to jail?
(c)   What proportion of time can a robber expect to spend in jail?

13.20 A famous university has been studying the annual progress of its upper division undergraduate students. Data analyzed over the past several years reveals the following annual transition probabilities.

From \ To	Junior	Senior	Bachelor's Degree	Dropout
Junior	0.1	0.8	0	0.1
Senior	0	0.2	0.7	0.1
Bachelor's Degree	0	0	1	0
Dropout	0.4	0.4	0	0.2

The university is concerned about the time some of these students are taking to graduate.
(a) Calculate the average number of years for a junior to obain a bachelor's degree.
(b) Find the average number of years for a senior to graduate.

13.21 A certain 3-minute person-to-person telephone call costs $3.55, and there is no charge unless the called party is reached. That same 3-minute call, on a station-to-station basis, costs $1.95 if anyone answers the phone. Let state 1 be the process of placing the call on a station-to-station basis, and let state 2 be the successful completion of the connection to the called party. Assume that p_{12}, the probability of reaching the called party, is the same for each call.
(a) Determine the expected number of station-to-station calls for which you should be indifferent between paying for just one person-to-person call and paying for that number of station-to-station calls.
(b) Draw a generalized transition diagram for the process of attempting to reach the called party by a station call. From the results of part (a), for what value of p_{12} should you be indifferent between calling on a station-to-station basis and making a person-to-person call?

13.22 A furniture factory which makes cabinets considers each cabinet to be in one of four states: in work, in rework, scrapped, or finished. The weekly transition probability matrix reflecting movement between these states is shown below.

From \ To	Work	Rework	Scrap	Finish
Work	0	0.2	0.1	0.7
Rework	0	0.1	0.3	0.6
Scrap	0	0	1	0
Finish	0	0	0	1

(a) Draw a transition diagram and show all numerical probability values.
(b) Draw a modified transition diagram and use it to help determine the average manufacturing time per cabinet (until it is either finished or scrapped).
(c) What proportion of cabinets will be scrapped?
(d) If each finished cabinet yields a profit of $100 and each cabinet scrapped results in a loss of $50, what is the expected profit per cabinet constructed?

13.23 A congressional team has been formed to look into the progress of bills in the House of Representatives. For the past 30 months the team has been noting the location of bills on the first day of each month. Each bill can be in one of four states: in committee, on the floor of the House, rejected by the House, or passed by the House. The team found that 80 percent of bills in committee one month were still there the next month, the other 20 percent having moved on to the floor. Of those bills on the floor of the House on the first of the month, by the end of the month 30 percent were sent back to committee, 40 percent were still on the floor, 10 percent were rejected, and 20 percent were passed.

(a) Form the transition probability matrix for the monthly movement of bills in the House. Draw a transition diagram showing numerical probability values.

(b) Determine the expected length of time from the start of committee action until a decision (acceptance or rejection) is made. Start by drawing a modified transition diagram.

(c) What fraction of bills can be expected to pass?

13.24 Briefly discuss the general idea of Markovian decision analysis.

13.25 A firm is reviewing its procedures for maintaining, repairing, and buying new equipment. A certain piece of equipment costs $500 new and requires $50 per month in regular maintenance costs when it is running well. When the piece is running poorly, regular maintenance costs $75 per month. When it is broken down, it must be replaced. Let the three states be: (1) running well, (2) running poorly, and (3) broken down. The one-month transition probability matrix P is

$$\mathbf{P} = \begin{matrix} & \begin{matrix} 1 & \quad 2 & \quad 3 \end{matrix} \\ \begin{matrix} 1 \\ 2 \\ 3 \end{matrix} & \begin{bmatrix} 0.8 & 0.2 & 0 \\ 0 & 0.7 & 0.3 \\ 0 & 0 & 1 \end{bmatrix} \end{matrix}$$

(a) Construct a transition diagram.

(b) What is the expected number of months that a machine runs well?

(c) What is the expected number of months until a poorly running machine breaks down?

In parts (d) and (e), assume that when the machine breaks down, it is immediately replaced (at a cost of $500), so that it spends no time in a failed state.

(d) Including equipment replacement cost, what is the expected monthly operating cost?

(e) Preventive maintenance could be performed, at an additional cost of $20 per month, on a machine that is running well. Such preventive maintenance would change the transition probabilities p_{11} to 0.9 and p_{12} to 0.1. Would this preventive maintenance be worth its cost? If so, how much would it save?

13.26 The state university system, Exercise 13.8, is considering a proposal to raise the annual salaries of full professors by $2000 if they will retire earlier. It is believed that implementation of this proposal will lead to 10 percent of full professors vacating their positions each year, instead of the current 5 percent.

(a) Determine the steady-state proportion of faculty in each rank if the new proposal is adopted.

From the solution to Exercise 13.12, the steady-state proportion in each faculty rank is currently 2/7, 1/7, and 4/7, respectively, for assistant, associate, and full professors.

(b) If the current average salaries for the three ranks are $14,000, $18,000, and $24,000, would the proposal have been worthwhile if it had been in effect at this salary scale? Make this determination by comparing the expected annual costs of the two alternatives.

(c) At what increase in the annual salary of full professors should the university be indifferent between the status quo and the proposal?

13.27 Suppose that Screem Security Systems, Example 13.5, is considering incorporating additional selling aids which would raise the estimated cost per customer call from $10 to $12. Management believes that, for a new customer, the probability of losing the sale would drop from 0.30 to 0.25, and the probability of making the sale would increase from 0.20 to 0.25. For a previously interested customer, it is estimated that the probability of losing the sale would decrease from 0.25 to 0.20, and the probability of the prospect retaining interest would increase from 0.25 to 0.30.

Calculate the expected profit for a new prospect and for an interested prospect. Can the cost of the additional selling aids be justified?

CHAPTER 14

SIMULATION MODELS

In the second part of this book, we have studied many different types of mathematical models. In many of these models, especially those involving probabilistic occurrences, we have had to make simplifying assumptions in order to come up with analytic solutions. Consider just two examples.

1. In Chapter 12, Queueing Models, we developed the solution for the so-called machine interference model, where there is a finite population of arrivals. In that model, we made several assumptions which may not be appropriate in many situations. For instance, we assumed that failures of operating machines were completely random, having a constant failure rate, whereas a certain fraction of the failures will likely be of a wearout nature, so that the failure probability increases as operating time is accumulated. Also, the repair time was assumed to be exponentially distributed, which is generally not the case, since some minimum amount of time is usually required to diagnose the problem and go through standard repair and maintenance procedures. There may well be different types of repair, some requiring a short time and some requiring much longer.

2. The probabilistic order point model, in Chapter 11 on Inventory Models, assumed that demand during the lead time could be represented by a Poisson probability distribution, and there are certain situations where this may not be a reasonable approximation, such as those where an appreciable number of orders are for multiple unit quantities or where demand tends to be concentrated at certain points in time. In addition, the shortage penalty cost was assumed to be directly proportional to the expected number of units short in any replenishment period, whereas it could well be that the shortage penalty cost would be a nonlinear function of the actual number of units short or would be dependent on the duration of the shortage.

We will now describe a very general problem-solving approach, referred to as simulation, which enables us to drop some of these simplifying assumptions and create mathematical models which can be made to more nearly represent real-world situations.

There have been a number of definitions of simulation, and there are many different types of simulation. For our purposes, simulation can best be described, in a pragmatic way, as a technique for developing a mathematical model of a system and utilizing that mathematical model to perform simulated experiments on that system. We will be concerned with what is generally called Monte Carlo simulation, and our approach is highly oriented toward the use of digital computers.

Monte Carlo simulation (which we will hereafter mean when we refer to simulation) involves experimentation with mathematical models involving one or more probabilistic elements, such as random customer arrivals, random sales quantities, random service times, and so forth. The emphasis will be on time-oriented simulations, primarily queueing, where the temporal relationships between the elements of a particular system are of vital importance in analyzing the performance of that system. Since simulation is a sampling method, simulation models yield statistical estimates, not optimal solutions.

The actual process of simulation involves constructing a mathematical model and then "playing it through" either for a relatively long simulated time (long in relation to the customary time spacing between events) or for many separate trials. We do not "solve" a simulation model; we "exercise" it. We will demonstrate this with numerical examples.

14.1 SIMULATION MODELING

EXAMPLE 14.1

Prestige Rent-a-Car has gathered the following statistics on its operation.

Number of cars demanded daily	0	1	2	3	4
Probability	0.10	0.15	0.20	0.30	0.25

Length of rental, days	1	2	3	4
Probability	0.50	0.30	0.15	0.05

Prestige realizes an average net profit of $40 per day for each car rented. When there is a demand for a car, and no car is available, the goodwill cost is estimated as $80. Each day a car is unused represents a cost of $5.

Develop a simulation model for a fleet of 4 cars, starting with all 4 cars initially available. If a car is rented for 1 day, assume that it is available the next day, and so on. Simulate 10 days of operation, and estimate the mean daily profit from the results of the simulation run.

To model Prestige's operations, we must generate random customer arrivals for each simulated day and, for each customer renting a car, a random rental period. It will obviously be necessary to set up a "bookkeeping" procedure to keep daily track of the number of cars available, the number of cars not rented, and the number of unfilled demands for a car. First, let us discuss the process of simulating random customer arrivals.

From the data given in the problem, we expect no customers to show up on 10 percent of the days, 1 customer arrival on 15 percent of the days, and so on. Suppose we took 100 slips of paper and numbered them as follows: 10 0s, 15 1s, 20 2s, 30 3s, and 25 4s. The slips would then be placed in a bowl. For each simulated day, we could draw a numbered slip whose value would represent the number of arrivals for that day. The slip would then be replaced in the bowl before the next draw. Assuming that the slips were thoroughly mixed in the bowl, the procedure described would be expected to give the proper distribution of daily customer arrivals. That is, if the simulated period were relatively long, say at least 100 days, we could expect a demand of 0 to occur about 10 percent of the time, a demand of 1 around 15 percent of the time, and so on. Although this procedure would certainly work, it is time-consuming and inefficient. We will now describe a more practical computer-oriented approach, since practical simulation models almost mandate the use of computers.

We will assume that we have available a sequence of random numbers r which are uniformly distributed between 0 and 1, sometimes called the unit interval and denoted as $(0, 1)$. (Such a random number program is available in almost all computer software packages, typically generating a number of at least eight digits. There is a table of three-digit uniformly distributed random numbers in Appendix E. These three-digit numbers are convenient and quite adequate for our manual simulation needs.) The uniform distribution, discussed earlier in Chapter 3, has the property that, for any subinterval of a given width, the probability that a random number falls within that subinterval is independent of the subinterval's location. To illustrate, when sampling from a uniform distribution between 0 and 1, we are just as likely to draw a random number between 0.07 and 0.08 as between 0.83 and 0.84 or between 0.4113 and 0.4213, since all have the same interval width of 0.01.

Given the discrete probability distribution of daily demand, it is convenient to construct a cumulative probability table, as shown in Table 14.1. Then, for any random number r, uniform on $(0, 1)$, the value of r determines the value of the daily demand, according to the final column of Table 14.1. If, for example, $r = 0.631$, a demand of 3 cars is indicated. We should expect r to fall within the interval 0.45 to 0.75 30 percent of the time, and this, of course, is just what is wanted. For any value of r between 0 and 1, the ranges in the final column specify a selection rule which simulates the draw of what we call *random variates* (specific values) from the probability distribution of the given random variable, daily demand for cars.

From a conceptual standpoint, the scheme selected for defining the ranges on r in this example is only one of many possibilities. For example, if the probabilities had been accumulated in the opposite direction, the ranges shown in Table 14.2 would have resulted. Random variates selected on the basis of the ranges in the last column of Table 14.2 would have exactly the same properties as those based on the ranges in Table 14.1.

Table 14.1   Data for Simulation of Daily Demand

Daily Demand Cars	Probability	Cumulative Probability	Value of Random Number r
0	0.10	0.10	$0 \ < r \leqslant 0.10$
1	0.15	0.25	$0.10 < r \leqslant 0.25$
2	0.20	0.45	$0.25 < r \leqslant 0.45$
3	0.30	0.75	$0.45 < r \leqslant 0.75$
4	0.25	1.00	$0.75 < r \leqslant 1.00$

Table 14.2   Alternative Simulation Scheme for Daily Demand

Daily Demand Cars	Probability	Cumulative Probability	Value of Random Number r
0	0.10	1.00	$0.90 < r \leqslant 1.00$
1	0.15	0.90	$0.75 < r \leqslant 0.90$
2	0.20	0.75	$0.55 < r \leqslant 0.75$
3	0.30	0.55	$0.25 < r \leqslant 0.55$
4	0.25	0.25	$0 \ < r \leqslant 0.25$

This particular procedure of generating random variates from a discrete probability distribution can be summarized as follows.

1. Construct a cumulative probability table.
2. Specify a proper range of uniform random numbers for selecting each possible random variate.
3. Get random numbers uniform on (0, 1) and select the associated random variates.

Using this procedure, Table 14.3 can be easily developed for simulation of the random variable representing the rental period. The ranges specified for the random number r should result in selecting the rental period according to the desired probability distribution.

At this point, we are ready to structure the simulation model itself. Each simulated day, we will first find the number of cars available and then determine the random demand for cars. Then, for *each* car demanded *and* available, we will randomly select a rental period and then record when that car will again be available for rental. At the end of each day, we tally the number of cars not rented, or demanded but unavailable.

Table 14.3 Data for Simulation of the Rental Period

Rental Period Days	Probability	Cumulative Probability	Value of Random Number r
1	0.50	0.50	$0 < r \leq 0.50$
2	0.30	0.80	$0.50 < r \leq 0.80$
3	0.15	0.95	$0.80 < r \leq 0.95$
4	0.05	1.00	$0.95 < r \leq 1.00$

As stipulated in the problem, we start with a fleet of 4 cars, all available at the beginning of the simulation. To make the work a little easier to follow, we will retain separate identities for each car, although this is not a requirement. Random number r will be used to select the value of daily demand, and random number r_i to select the rental period length for car i. The random numbers actually used in the simulation are taken from the third and fourth columns (an arbitrary selection) of the table in Appendix E. It is unnecessary to randomize the selection within the table. Since the numbers themselves are randomly ordered, a systematic selection process is easiest to implement.

A simulation of 10 days' operation is presented in Table 14.4 and will be explained in detail.

Table 14.4 Simulation of Prestige Rent-a-Car Operations with Four Cars

				Random Number r_i and Rental Period								
Day	*Cars Available*	*Random Number r*	*Demand for Cars*	Car 1 r_1	Days	Car 2 r_2	Days	Car 3 r_3	Days	Car 4 r_4	Days	*Number of Cars Over (+) Short (−)*
1	4	0.911	4	0.851	3	0.534	2	0.822	3	0.985	4	0
2	0	0.082	0	—		—		—		—		0
3	1	0.448	2	—		0.779	2	—		—		−1
4	2	0.697	3	0.872	3	—		0.002	1	—		−1
5	3	0.153	1	—		0.595	2					+2
6	2	0.328	2	—		—		0.391	1	0.313	1	0
7	4	0.629	3	0.128	1	0.002	1	0.801	3			+1
8	3	0.981	4	0.610	2	0.596	2	—		0.226	1	−1
9	1	0.691	3	—		—		—		0.715	2	−2
10	3	0.564	3	0.062	1	0.767	2	0.753	2	—		0
	23		25									Over 3 Short 5

An explanation of the first few days of the simulation is now presented.

Day 1: 4 cars are available, and all are needed, since the initial random number $r = 0.911$, drawn from column 3 of the table in Appendix E, selects a demand for 4 cars, as determined from Table 14.1. The four random numbers r_i, taken from column 4 of the random number table, generate, according to the decision rule in Table 14.3, successive rental periods of 3, 2, 3, and 4 days, as indicated. (You should verify this.) Car 1 will not be available again until day 4, so dashes are drawn to indicate its unavailability on days 2 and 3. A similar procedure is followed for the other three cars. At the end of the day, we record the fact that there are no cars unused (over) or short (demanded but unavailable).

Day 2: No cars are available, but no shortage occurs, since the random number $r = 0.082$ generates a demand of 0 cars.

Day 3: Only 1 car is available, whereas 2 cars are needed, so the first shortage is recorded.

Day 4: A shortage again occurs, with 3 cars demanded and only 2 available.

Day 5: The pendulum swings the other way. Three cars are available, but only 1 is required, so a surplus of 2 cars is recorded. The blank spaces in the table indicate cars available but not demanded.

The simulation continues in this manner for an additional five days.

Analysis of Results   It should be obvious that the manual simulation of only ten days' operations is far too short to provide meaningful results. A simulation of at least 100 days would have been desirable, from the standpoint of obtaining statistically meaningful results. Nevertheless, we can derive some useful information from even these abbreviated results. (Our major objective at this point, of course, is not to obtain statistically significant results, but to illustrate the development and use of a simulation model.)

With 37 out of a possible 40 car-days (to coin a unit) rented, 3 car-days unused, and a shortage of 5 car-days, the total profit is $(37)(40) - (3)(5) - (5)(80) = \$1065$. On a daily basis, the estimated profit is $1065/10 = \$106$.

It is not a bad idea to check the random variates generated to see if they conform reasonably closely to what would be expected. For example, the total of 25 cars demanded during the 10-day period, an average of 2.5 per day, can be compared with the expected value of daily demand.

$$E(\text{daily demand}) = (0.10)(0) + (0.15)(1) + (0.20)(2) + (0.30)(3) + (0.25)(4)$$
$$= 2.45 \text{ cars.}$$

Also, if we add the total rental period for the 20 cars rented, we get 39 days, an average of 1.95 days per car. The expected rental period is:

$$E(\text{rental period}) = (0.50)(1) + (0.30)(2) + (0.15)(3) + (0.05)(4)$$
$$= 1.75 \text{ days.}$$

Thus, over the simulation period, the random variates appear to have been quite representative of the random variables being simulated.

We will now consider a second simulation model which differs from the previous model in two important respects.

1. A simulation run consists of a number of repetitive trials, instead of a single simulation running for a simulated time period.
2. The random variable of interest has a continuous probability distribution rather than a discrete probability distribution.

Since simulation tends to be as much an art as a science, we will also try to point out some of the approaches to improving the ease and efficiency of the simulation process.

The following problem was presented earlier, as Example 4.8, where it was solved by using the linear loss integral to approximate the exact solution.

EXAMPLE 14.2

A manufacturing company has received a production contract from the government. It has 100 days to complete the contract. For each day or fraction of a day past the deadline, there is a penalty cost of $1000. The production manager feels that the company does not have much leeway, but the best estimate is 90 days for completion of the contract. Because of possible delays in getting material, production problems, and so forth, his uncertainty regarding this estimate is reflected by his belief that the time to contract completion can be represented by a normal probability distribution with a mean of 90 days and a standard deviation of 10 days.

Estimate the expected penalty cost by developing and running a manual simulation model.

In this problem, there is a single random variable, the completion time, which is normally distributed with a mean of 90 days and a standard deviation of 10 days. To simulate the completion of the contract, visualize a simulation trial as the draw of a random variate from a normal probability distribution with the given mean and standard deviation, and the subsequent determination of the associated penalty cost, if any. The simulation then consists of many such trials, and the estimate of the expected penalty cost would be the average cost per trial.

To obtain a random variate from a normal probability distribution, we can utilize available tables of normal random variates drawn from a standardized normal distribution with mean 0 and standard deviation 1, such as the table in Appendix F. (We can also generate such standardized normal random variates from uniformly distributed random numbers, as will be shown in section 14.3.) Such a standardized normal random variate can then be transformed into a variate from the desired distribution by multiplying it by the given standard deviation and adding the value of the mean. For example, if the normal random variate were $+1.151$, it would be transformed into a value of $(1.151)(10) + 90 = 101.51$ days, with an associated penalty cost of $2000, since the contract would be completed on the second day late.

From the preceding analysis of the problem, we see that a simulation could be performed by conducting a series of trials, for each one drawing a standardized normal random variate and then transforming it into a completion time value. If this value were greater than 100 days, the penalty cost would be specified. A table showing such simulation trials could be readily constructed. Before doing this, however, let us consider what can be done to simplify the simulation procedure and to increase its computational efficiency.

Several improvements can be made to the basic simulation model just described.

1. Instead of converting *each* standardized normal random variate into a completion time value, we can make *one* conversion from the target completion time of 100 days to a standardized normal variate of +1.0 standard deviations. Then, the value of each random variate can be compared directly with the target value of +1.0.

2. We are interested only in random variates exceeding the value of +1.0, so there is no point in even recording the value of random variates less than that value. We need only count the total number of trials. For a normal probability distribution, note that over 84 percent of the random variates can be expected to be less than +1 standard deviations from the mean, so we will need to record information on only about one-sixth of the total number of trials, a considerable time-saver.

3. For each random variate exceeding +1.0, a direct linear transformation can be made into penalty cost by almost "eyeballing" the value of the random variate. The following procedure is much easier to do than to express: subtract 1, multiply by 10, and round up if fractional. The resultant number is the penalty cost in $1000s. Example: $1.213 \rightarrow 0.213 \rightarrow 2.13 \rightarrow 3$ ($3000). Or, you can go to the trouble of constructing a conversion table such as that of Table 14.5. In either case, the simulation table then needs only two entries, the random variate and the associated penalty cost, for each trial of interest (random variate exceeding 1.0).

Table 14.5 Conversion from Normal Random Variate to Penalty Cost

Random Variate Value	Completion Time (days)	Days Late	Penalty Cost ($)
1.001–1.100	101	1	1,000
1.101–1.200	102	2	2,000
1.201–1.300	103	3	3,000
1.301–1.400	104	4	4,000
1.401–1.500	105	5	5,000
1.501–1.600	106	6	6,000
1.601–1.700	107	7	7,000
1.701–1.800	108	8	8,000
1.801–1.900	109	9	9,000
1.901–2.000	110	10	10,000
2.001–2.100	111	11	11,000
2.101–2.200	112	12	12,000
2.201–2.300	113	13	13,000
2.301–2.400	114	14	14,000

4. We can take advantage of the symmetry of the normal probability distribution by utilizing all normal random variate values *less than* -1.0 and taking their absolute

value to get the associated penalty cost. On the average, this will mean a "success" (a random variate resulting in a penalty cost) about every three trials instead of every six trials. From a given table of normal random variates, we can then generate twice as many useful numbers. Using this scheme, the estimate of the expected penalty cost will then be the total cost for all trials divided by *twice* the number of trials, since the penalty cost values have been inflated by a factor of 2.

With all this preliminary work, the actual simulation becomes extremely easy, as shown in Table 14.6. The normal random variates are taken from the first five columns of the table in Appendix F, a total of 100 values. The associated penalty costs are then obtained by "eyeballing" the random variates or from Table 14.5. For compactness, the table is of triple width.

Table 14.6   Simulation of Contract Penalty Cost

Total Random Variates Examined = 100

Normal Random Variate	Penalty Cost, ($1000s)	Normal Random Variate	Penalty Cost, ($1000s)	Normal Random Variate	Penalty Cost, ($1000s)
1.049	1	1.454	5	1.196	2
1.691	7	1.786	8	1.416	5
2.151	12	−1.664	7	2.201	13
−1.248	3	−1.943	10	1.607	7
−1.344	4	−1.186	2	−1.194	2
−1.317	4	−1.467	5	1.384	4
1.123	2	−1.479	5	−1.049	1
1.307	4	1.422	5	−1.127	2
2.352	14	−1.784	8	1.757	8
				Grand Total =	150

From the results of the simulation, total cost = $150,000.

$$\text{Average penalty cost} = \frac{150,000}{(2)(100)} = \$750.$$

Now that we have an estimate of the expected penalty cost, we could ask ourselves how meaningful the figure of $750 is, from a statistical viewpoint. With a total of 200 penalty cost values, all but 27 of which are zero, the variance of the 200 penalty cost values can be readily calculated by the formula of Equation (3.8), where X would be the penalty cost in $1000s. From that equation, $V(X) = E(X^2) - [E(X)]^2$. $E(X)$ has been calculated, and $E(X^2)$, the expected value of the square of the penalty cost, is easily computed from the data in Table 14.6 by squaring each penalty cost value and weighting it by 1/200, since the effective number of trials is 200. When this is done,

$V(X) = 5.84 - 0.75^2 = 5.278$, so the standard deviation σ_x is $\sqrt{5.278} = 2.30$ ($2300). The well-known formula for $\sigma_{\bar{x}}$, the standard deviation of the mean value, is $\sigma_x/\sqrt{n}$, where n is the sample size. (See any statistics text.) In this simulation, $\sigma_{\bar{x}} = 2.30/\sqrt{200} = 0.163$($163). From the earlier analysis of Example 4.8, the actual value of the expected cost was determined to be $912, so our estimate is certainly in line with that value, since the estimated mean from the simulation results turned out to be just one standard deviation from the true mean. ($912 - $750 = $162.)

14.2 GENERATION OF RANDOM NUMBERS

Although tables of random numbers are available for manual simulations, it is generally impractical, unnecessary, and undesirable to store random number tables in computer memory for use in computer simulation models.

For simulation computer programs, we generate what are known as *pseudo-random* numbers. These numbers are not random at all, but they "look" random, as judged by various types of statistical tests used to evaluate the distribution of the numbers (and their individual digits), statistical independence between numbers, and so forth. Given any number in a sequence of pseudorandom numbers and the computational algorithm used, any other number (following or preceding) in the sequence can be determined. For any given starting number, the sequence is completely reproducible.

From the standpoint of simulation, pseudorandom numbers are better than "pure" random numbers, since they allow experiments to be performed under completely controlled conditions. We will see this in Example 14.4, where we will simulate the exact same sequence of customer arrivals for two different system configurations.

A frequently used method of generating pseudorandom numbers is the multiplicative congruential method, whereby each pseudorandom number r_{n+1} is determined by multiplying the previous random number r_n by a constant and retaining only part of the resulting digits. The formula is stated as

$$r_{n+1} = kr_n(\text{modulo } m),$$

where k is a constant and "modulo m" means to divide the product kr_n by m and retain only the remainder. Examples of modular arithmetic are 18 (modulo 10) = 558 (modulo 10) = 8; 111 (modulo 1000) = 10111 (modulo 1000) = 4503111 (modulo 1000) = 111. The value of r/m always lies between 0 and 1. The choice of k and m is important in determining the randomness properties of the pseudorandom number sequence and establishing its period, which is the number of values generated before the sequence repeats itself, which it must do eventually. The value of r_0, called the seed, is also important to a lesser degree. Selection of the same seed for different simulation runs guarantees the same pseudorandom number sequences. We will not discuss the determination of particular values for k, m, and r_0, since we are primarily interested in simulation concepts, rather than specific computer implementation details.

Using the multiplicative congruential method or other generally similar methods, it is possible to readily generate statistically satisfactory pseudorandom number sequences with periods of a billion or more. We will assume, hereafter, that a random number generator is available which will generate a random number r, uniform over the interval (0, 1), which means that the random variable R is uniformly distributed between 0 and 1. Neither of the endpoints, 0 or 1, is included. Almost every computer system library has such a random number generator available.

14.3 GENERATION OF RANDOM VARIATES

For use in computer simulations, it will be necessary to generate random variates from different probability distributions, both continuous and discrete. We will discuss, in some detail, the generation of variates from some of the most frequently encountered probability distributions, starting first with continuous probability distributions.

As we learned in Chapter 3, $F(x)$, the cumulative distribution function (cdf) for any random variable X, is a nondecreasing function with increasing x, and the value of $F(x)$ always lies between 0 and 1. The uniformly distributed random number r also falls between 0 and 1. Suppose we now associate a random number r_a with a random variate x_a by setting $F(x_a) = r_a$. We call x_a the inverse transformation of r_a. Now, since the probability that the value of the random variable X will fall between x_a and x_b, where $x_a < x_b$, is $F(x_b) - F(x_a) = r_b - r_a$, as illustrated in Figure 14.1, the randomly generated values of X will have exactly the desired probability of falling in the given interval (x_a, x_b). If $F(x)$ is a mathematically tractable function, then the inverse

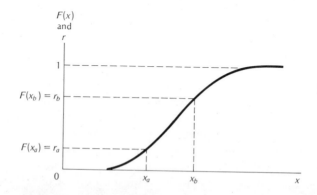

Figure 14.1

transformation method consists of setting r equal to that function and solving for x in terms of r. This method should become clearer after a few examples. We will start first with continuous probability distributions. Other approaches to random variate generation will also be discussed.

Continuous Probability Distributions

Uniform Distribution   Suppose we wish to generate random variates from a distribution uniform over the interval (a, b), $b > a$. It is then necessary to convert from the random number r uniform over $(0, 1)$ to the random variate x, uniform over (a, b). Figure 14.2 (a) and (b) shows $f(x)$, the probability density function (pdf), and $F(x)$, the cdf. These functions were discussed and derived in Chapter 3.

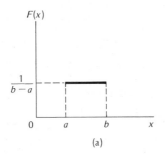
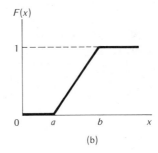

(a)   (b)

Figure 14.2

In the region of interest, between a and b,

$$F(x) = \frac{x - a}{b - a} \qquad a \leq x \leq b.$$

If we now set $F(x) = r$ and solve for x, we get

$$x = a + (b - a)r.$$

As we should expect, having a linear cdf, we simply get a linear transformation. Thus, if $a = 40$ and $b = 50$, a value of $r = 0.3$ gives $x = 43.0$, 30 percent of the distance between 40 and 50.

Negative Exponential Distribution   As we saw in Chapter 12 on Queueing Models, this distribution arises naturally where the probability of a given event, such as a customer arrival or service completion, is the same in each time interval. In that chapter, we found that

$$F(x) = 1 - e^{-\alpha x} \qquad x > 0,$$

where α is the single distribution parameter, so that the mean of the exponential distribution is $1/\alpha$. Using the inverse transformation method,

$$F(x) = r = 1 - e^{-\alpha x}$$
$$e^{-\alpha x} = 1 - r$$
$$-\alpha x = \ln(1 - r)$$
$$x = -\frac{\ln(1 - r)}{\alpha},$$

where ln is the natural logarithm, or $\log_e$. Since the uniform distribution is symmetrical, the probability distribution of $1 - R$ is the same as that of R, so for computational speed we replace $1 - r$ by r, so that

$$x = -\frac{\ln r}{\alpha}.$$

If we had random customer arrivals at the rate of 6 per hour, $1/\alpha = 1/6$ hr $= 10$ min, and an r value of 0.5 would give -0.693 for the natural logarithm of r, so that $x = 6.93$ min.

Erlang Distribution   As we saw in Chapter 12, the Erlang distribution, with parameters k and α, results from the summation of k random variates drawn from a negative exponential distribution with mean $1/(k\alpha)$. It seems natural, then, to use what is called the *composition method*, which involves the independent generation of random variates and their summation. We could thus generate k random exponential variates, getting

$$x = -\frac{1}{k\alpha} \sum_{i=1}^{k} \ln r_i.$$

If we take advantage of the properties of logarithms, there is no need to compute k logarithms, a relatively slow process on the computer. Recall that $\ln r_1 + \ln r_2 + \cdots + \ln r_k = \ln(r_1 r_2 \ldots r_k)$. A more efficient calculation could then be

$$x = -\frac{1}{k\alpha} \ln \left(\prod_{i=1}^{k} r_i \right),$$

where the capital Greek pi represents the operation of multiplication, just as capital Greek sigma represents the operation of summation.

Normal Distribution   The density function for the standardized normal distribution, with mean 0 and variance 1, is of the following form.

$$f(z) = \frac{1}{\sqrt{2\pi}} e^{-z^2/2} \qquad -\infty < z < \infty.$$

Unfortunately, the cdf for this density function cannot be obtained in closed form, so the cdf cannot be expressed analytically. However, several methods can be used to generate random normal variates, and we will show two, the first approximate and the second exact, but slower.

Approximate method—the central limit theorem states that the probability distribution of the sum of N independent and identically distributed random variates X_i, from *any* finite distribution with mean μ_i and variance σ_i^2, approaches asymptotically a normal distribution with mean μ and variance σ^2, where

$$\mu = \sum_{i=1}^{N} \mu_i \quad \text{and} \quad \sigma^2 = \sum_{i=1}^{N} \sigma_i^2.$$

Suppose we utilize the composition method and generate N random uniform variates over the interval $(0, 1)$. Then

$$E\left(\sum_{i=1}^{N} r_i\right) = \frac{N}{2}, \quad V\left(\sum_{i=1}^{N} r_i\right) = \frac{N}{12},$$

since the variance of a uniform distribution over $(0, 1)$ is $1/12$. Recalling that the conversion from a random variate X normally distributed with mean μ and standard deviation σ to a standardized random variate Z normally distributed with mean 0 and standard deviation 1 was

$$Z = \frac{X - \mu}{\sigma},$$

we then get

$$z = \frac{\sum_{i=1}^{N} r_i - \frac{N}{2}}{\sqrt{\frac{N}{12}}}.$$

For computational speed, N should be small, but for accuracy, N should be relatively large. N should be at least 6, but 12 is generally used, since the radical is eliminated, thereby speeding up the computation.

$$\text{For } N = 12, z = \sum_{i=1}^{12} r_i - 6.$$

If we are generating random variates x from a normal distribution with mean μ and standard deviation σ, then, for each random value z,

$$x = \mu + z\sigma.$$

Using this approximate method, the normal distribution generated will be truncated at six standard deviations from the mean, and values in the tails, beyond about three standard deviations from the mean, will be rather inaccurate. Nevertheless, this method can be quite adequate for many applications.

Exact method—using two random variates, R_1 and R_2, uniform on the interval $(0, 1)$, pairs of independent standardized random normal variates, with mean 0 and standard deviation 1, can be generated by calculating:

$$z_1 = \sqrt{-2 \ln r_1} \, (\cos 2\pi r_2), \quad z_2 = \sqrt{-2 \ln r_1} \, (\sin 2\pi r_2).$$

Discussion regarding the generation of random variates from other continuous probability distributions, such as the beta, gamma. Weibull, lognormal, and so forth, can be found in simulation textbooks and other references given at the end of this text.

Discrete Probability Distributions

For generating such random variates, the inverse transformation method is frequently used. Given a probability mass function $P(x)$, we construct the cumulative density function $F(x)$, as shown in Figure 14.3. Then, we set $F(x) = r$ and select the indicated discrete value. Let us now consider empirical discrete distributions and the binomial probability distribution.

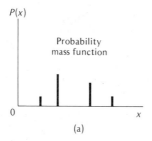 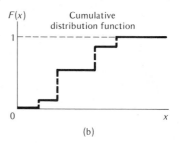

Figure 14.3

Empirical Discrete Distributions   Given the probability mass function $P(x)$, we construct the cumulative probability function $F(x)$. Then, we go through what is called a "table lookup" procedure. To illustrate this, consider the numerical example in Table 14.7.

Given a specific value r of a random variable R, uniform over $(0,1)$, we compare that value, in turn, with each $F(x_i)$ value, starting with $i = 1$. When we find the first $F(x_i)$ value that exceeds r, the associated x_i value is the random variate chosen. For instance, if $r = 0.83$, we find that r exceeds $F(x_1)$ and $F(x_2)$, but it does not exceed $F(x_3)$. Thus, our random variate is $x_3 = 6.5$. It should be clear that this procedure will select each of the four values with the required probability. It is the same procedure as that used in Example 14.1.

Binomial Distribution   We will show two methods of generating random variates from a binomial distribution. The first is more straightforward, using the composition method; the second is faster, using the inverse transformation method. Recall that the binomial distribution represents the probability of k successes in n independent trials if the probability of success on an individual trial is p. We have

$$P(k) = \left(\frac{n}{k} \right) p^k (1 - p)^{n-k} \quad k = 0, 1, 2, \ldots, n.$$

Table 14.7

Index i	Value x_i	Probability $P(x_i)$	Cumulative Probability $F(x_i)$
1	2.0	0.15	0.15
2	3.8	0.48	0.63
3	6.5	0.24	0.87
4	8.3	0.13	1.00

Composition method.   We simply sample n times and count the number of successes k. On each trial, we generate a new random number r, uniform over $(0,1)$, and compare its value with the success probability p. If $r < p$, we tally a success. After n such Bernoulli trials, the total number of successes on those trials gives us a single random binomial variate.

Inverse transformation.   We program the calculation for $P(k)$, form the cumulative probability function $F(k)$, and then use the table lookup procedure previously described. The relationship between successive terms of the binomial distribution is such as to make it easy to calculate the terms by recursion. Thus, letting $q = 1 - p$, $P(0) = q^n$. As can be readily shown,

$$\frac{P(k + 1)}{P(k)} = \frac{n - k}{k + 1}\left(\frac{p}{q}\right).$$

Then,

$$P(1) = n\left(\frac{p}{q}\right)P(0), \qquad P(2) = \frac{n - 1}{2}\left(\frac{p}{q}\right)P(1), \qquad \text{and so forth.}$$

The distribution can be truncated when $P(k)$ becomes sufficiently small, say less than 0.00001. At the truncation point, the final term must then be set equal to one minus the sum of all previous terms.

The discussion of generating random variates from other discrete probability distributions, such as the hypergeometric, geometric, negative binomial, and so forth is left to the references at the end of the text.

14.4   MOVING A SIMULATION THROUGH TIME

Let us consider now how we can keep track of all the events (such as arrivals, departures, failures, customer orders, and so forth) occurring with the passage of time in a simulation. Two basic approaches have been used in the great majority of simulation models. Both employ the concept of a system "clock," which is just a memory location containing the numerical value representing the simulated time.

Variable-time-increment methods (also called event sequencing).   The system clock is advanced to the time of the most imminent event, regardless of whether it be microseconds or months away in simulated time. An internal "calendar" must be kept for each event which is to take place, and action occurs only when an event is scheduled.

With event sequencing, good computational efficiency is achieved, since actions are taken only as they are required. The disadvantage is that an event calendar must be maintained in proper chronological order at all times. It must be updated every time an event is added, deleted, shifted in time, or temporarily suspended.

The majority of simulation languages and simulation programs use event-sequencing methods. Not only are they more efficient than time slicing from a computational standpoint, but they are more meaningful from a conceptual viewpoint.

Fixed-time-increment methods (also called time slicing).   The system clock is advanced a fixed time increment, and at each successive point in simulated time, the entire system is scanned to determine if any events have occurred during that time increment. Generally, there will be a number of timing counters in the model for such events as time until service completion, time until order arrives, and so forth. At each time increment, all timing counters are decremented (decreased) by one time unit. When a timing counter gets down to zero or when it first goes negative, then the event it represents occurs in that time interval.

The major advantage of time slicing is that the actual sequence of events need not be recorded in any way, since the possible occurrence of each event is checked at each time increment. The disadvantages are twofold. The time increment must be short in comparison to the average time between events, or inaccuracies and loss of information will result. The smaller the time increment, however, the longer and more costly the simulation run. In addition, if events are quite unevenly spaced over time, there will be relatively long intervals where nothing is happening, yet scanning must continue at each small time interval.

When time slicing is used, the time increment Δt must be chosen with reasonable care. As noted, the smaller Δt, the longer the simulation run time. A rough rule of thumb is to make Δt just small enough so that the probability of any one type of event occurring in a given interval does not exceed 0.1.

Event-Sequencing Simulation

We will now examine two event-sequencing models, both of which happen to be single-server queueing models. (It can be noted that the majority of event-sequencing models tend to involve queueing problems in some form.) The first example is designed to give a "cutaway" view of what goes on deep within a typical event-sequencing simulation model; the second is a more conventional example of the analysis of a particular queueing problem.

EXAMPLE 14.3

A gross (minimum detail) flow chart of a simple queueing simulation model using event sequencing is shown as Figure 14.4. A model of this nature could be used to provide estimates of the probability distribution of waiting times and queue lengths, for any arrival and service time distributions. From such information, we could readily determine, for example, the probability of having to wait more than t minutes for service, or the fraction of time more than n customers would be waiting for service.

Referring to Figure 14.4, we now describe how such a simulation is performed. We start with an initialization phase, which is always required in any simulation program. The total idle time, total waiting time, number of customers in queue, and the system clock are all set to zero. Service facility status is set to idle, by setting a so-called indicator variable to zero. A random variate is generated to get the first customer's arrival time. (Sometimes the first customer is assumed to arrive at time zero.) The first arrival time is placed on the event calendar. Now, we are ready to begin the simulation itself.

For generality, suppose that the simulation has been running for some time and the next event is an arrival. The first thing done is to set the clock time to this "next event" time. This customer's arrival time is recorded for possible later use in determining the waiting time, if any. If the service facility is busy, the customer is placed in queue. If the service facility is not busy, it now becomes busy and its status is so changed, by setting its indicator variable to 1, say. The customer service time is now randomly generated from the given probability distribution of service time. The customer's departure time is set equal to the service time plus the clock time, and this event is entered in the event calendar. The idle time since the facility was last busy is then added to the cumulative idle time. At this point, we generate the next interarrival time, add it to the current clock time to get the next arrival time, and file this arrival time in the event calendar. Observe that each arrival has the effect of triggering the next arrival. Thus, we never have to generate more than one arrival at a time. The calendar is now examined to determine the next event.

When the next event is a departure, the clock time is set to this "next event" time. If there are no customers in queue, the facility is set to idle status and the time recorded so that the idle time can be accumulated the next time the facility becomes busy. We then move to the next event on the calendar. If there are customers in queue, the waiting time of the first customer is added to the cumulative customer waiting time. Since service will start immediately, the service time is added to the current clock time to get the departure time, which is immediately placed on the event calendar. This customer is removed from the queue, and all remaining customers, if any, are moved up one position. We then return to the event calendar.

In this simplified flow chart, one important event has not been shown. There is no way to end the simulation. This can be done in several ways. We can terminate the simulation at a given time, by stopping when the next-event time first exceeds the end-of-simulation time, or we can actually schedule an end-of-simulation event.

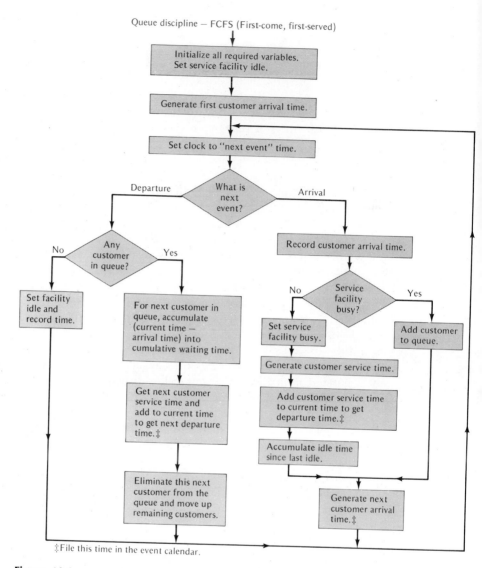

Queue discipline — FCFS (First-come, first-served)

Initialize all required variables. Set service facility idle.

Generate first customer arrival time.

Set clock to "next event" time.

What is next event?

Departure — Arrival

Any customer in queue?
No / Yes

Record customer arrival time.

Service facility busy?
No / Yes

Set facility idle and record time.

For next customer in queue, accumulate (current time — arrival time) into cumulative waiting time.

Set service facility busy.

Add customer to queue.

Generate customer service time.

Get next customer service time and add to current time to get next departure time.‡

Add customer service time to current time to get departure time.‡

Accumulate idle time since last idle.

Eliminate this next customer from the queue and move up remaining customers.

Generate next customer arrival time.‡

‡File this time in the event calendar.

Figure 14.4

Alternatively, we may keep a count of the number of arrivals and terminate the simulation after a specified number have arrived and all arriving customers have been served.

In Table 14.8, a numerical example has been "manufactured" to illustrate the workings of this simulation model. No attempt has been made to randomly generate arrival or service times, but the numbers have been chosen to show the buildup of a queue and the occurrence of facility idle time and customer waiting time.

Table 14.8 Single-Server Queueing Simulation

| Event Calendar* | Event | Customer Number | Clock Time | Change Facility Status to | Number in Queue After Event | Arrival | | | | | | | Departure | | | | |
| | | | | | | Idle Time Increment | Scheduled Departure Time | Next Customer | | | Idle Time Starts | Waiting Time Increment | Next Customer | | | Idle Time Increment | Waiting Time Increment |
								Number	Δt	Service Time			Number	Service Time	Departure Time		
0(A1)	Arr.	1	0	Busy	0	0	2	2	25	6							
2(D1), 25(A2)	Dep.	1	2	Idle	0						2						
25(A2)	Arr.	2	25	Busy	0	23	31	3	10	7							
31(D2), 35(A3)	Dep.	2	31	Idle	0						31						
35(A3)	Arr.	3	35	Busy	0	4	42	4	3	6							
38(A4), 42(D3)	Arr.	4	38		1			5	1	14							
39(A5), 42(D3)	Arr.	5	39		2			6	3	9							
42(D3), 42(A6)	Dep.	3	42		1								4	6	48		4
42(A6), 48(D4)	Arr.	6	42		2			7	38	10							
48(D4), 80(A7)	Dep.	4	48		1								5	14	62		9
62(D5), 80(A7)	Dep.	5	62		0								6	9	71		20
71(D6), 80(A7)	Dep.	6	71	Idle	0						71						
80(A7)	Arr.	7	80	Busy	0	9	90	"Doors closed"									
90(D7)	Dep.	7	90	Idle	0						90						

Total idle time = 36   Total waiting time = 33

*Notation: First number is time; letter A is for arrival, D for departure; second number is customer number.
Example: 48(D4)—customer 4 due to depart at time 48.

The first customer is scheduled to arrive at time 0 and has a service time of 2 time units. Thus, the initial event on the event calendar is the arrival of customer 1 at time 0. The service facility is then placed in busy status and the departure of customer 1 is scheduled to be at time 2. For customer 2, an interarrival time of 25 results in scheduling customer 2's arrival at time 25. The service time is 6 time units. The next event is the departure of customer 1 at time 2. This event is the earliest of all the events on the event calendar. In this model, there can never be more than two events on the event calendar, namely, the scheduled arrival of the next customer and the scheduled departure of the customer being served by the single service facility, if it is busy. When customer 1 departs, the service facility becomes idle at time 2. The arrival of customer 2 at time 25 then results in an idle time increment of 23 time units.

Customer 4, arriving at time 38, is the first to encounter a wait, since the facility is still serving customer 3. When customer 3 departs at time 42, customer 4 starts service immediately, having waited 4 time units. At time 42, we have a coincident arrival and departure. In this example, it makes no difference which we handle first, although general practice is to consider first the event which tends to release system capacity. In this case, that would be a departure. (To see the reason for this practice, consider the case where the queue is limited to a maximum of three and there are three customers currently in queue. Then, if there is a simultaneous arrival and departure, the queue really stays at three. If, however, we take the arrival first, we will be forced to reject that arrival and then reduce the queue to two.)

After the arrival of customer 7, we "close the doors," permitting no additional customers to enter. The simulation then terminates upon the departure of customer 7.

Figure 14.5 shows a graphic presentation of the simulation time history, including cumulative plots of facility idle time and customer waiting time. During idle-time and waiting-time periods, these values are, of course, accumulated linearly. They are, however, only recorded at the time of a status change (for either facility or customer), as shown in Figure 14.5.

EXAMPLE 14.4

Sam, the proprietor of Sam's Lunch Counter, has room for four seats at his lunch counter. He is contemplating expansion to five seats, because he has observed that customers who cannot be seated immediately will leave without waiting to be served. During the 11:00 A.M. to 2:00 P.M. weekday lunch period, Sam has observed that customers appear to arrive randomly, with a mean time of about 10 minutes between arrivals. Sam's rough estimate of the length of time a person occupies his seat (the service time) is given in Table 14.9.

We wish to develop a simulation model to help Sam estimate the fraction of customers lost with the present four seats and the expected improvement if a fifth seat is added. To do this, we must generate random arrivals and, for each customer served, random service times. At the time of each arrival, we want to know how many seats are available. This requires a knowledge as to whether any departures have

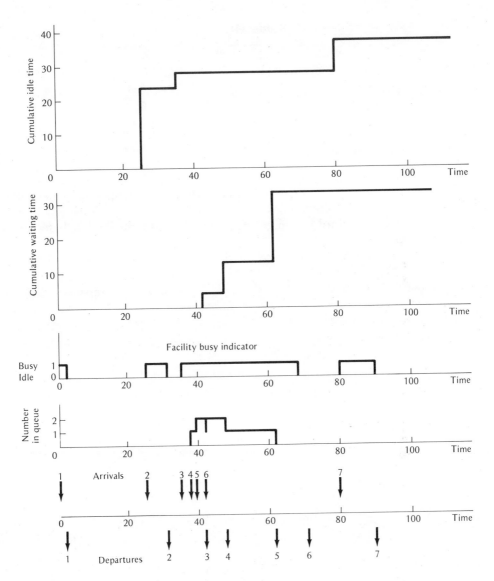

Figure 14.5

occurred since the previous arrival, so we must note the departure time of each customer served.

To generate random arrivals, we will take advantage of the fact that, as we learned in Chapter 12 on Queueing Models, for completely random (Poisson) arrivals, the interarrival time (time between successive arrivals) has a negative exponential distribution. We will assume that we have a table of random exponentially distributed numbers with mean 1.0, as shown in Appendix G. Given one of these random

Table 14.9

Service Time (min)	Probability
5–15⁻	0.10
15–25⁻	0.40
25–35⁻	0.25
35–45⁻	0.15
45–55	0.10

numbers, the time Δt to the next arrival will be that number multiplied by the mean interarrival time, 10 minutes in this example. (Earlier, in Section 14.3, we showed how straightforward it is to generate random exponentially distributed numbers on the computer.)

With the given empirical distribution of service times, let us make the simplification, only for clarity in presentation, of using just the mean time value in each specified time interval. Then, we construct a cumulative probability distribution, as shown in Table 14.10, to enable us to select the range of random numbers for which we will choose a given time value. The expected service time is 27.5 minutes, as can be readily calculated.

Table 14.10

Service Time (min)	Probability	Cumulative Probability
10	0.10	0.10
20	0.40	0.50
30	0.25	0.75
40	0.15	0.90
50	0.10	1.00

We will assume the availability of a random number uniform on the unit interval. Given any particular random number r, determination of the service time is straightforward. The service time will be that value in Table 14.10 associated with the first cumulative probability value which exceeds r.

Now, we must specify how the simulation will be performed. Suppose we start the simulation with the first customer's arrival precisely at 11:00 A.M., when Sam opens for business. The simulation will be terminated when a customer arrives after 2:00 P.M., to find the door locked. For convenience, we will use a three-digit random decimal number to generate service times, and we will also round the interarrival times to the nearest 0.1 min.

Look now at Table 14.11, which has the simulation results for both four seats and five seats. With the exception of those numbers appearing in parentheses, which apply to the five-seat case only, all single-valued column entries apply to both cases. We will discuss the four-seat case first.

The first arrival is at 11:00 A.M., at which time there are four seats available. The random number 0.289 drawn for the service time is first exceeded by the cumulative probability value 0.50. The service time chosen is then 20 minutes, so that service completion will occur at 11:20.0. This seat will become available to the first customer arriving after 11:20.0. We do not yet know which customer this will be, so the next column is blank at this point in the simulation. The first exponential random number 0.396 is multiplied by the mean interarrival time of 10 minutes and, for convenience, rounded to give a Δt of 4.0 minutes, so that the second customer arrives at 11:04.0, 4.0 minutes after the previous customer. During this time interval, no seats have become available through a service completion, so we have one less seat available than when the previous customer arrived. With a random number of 0.171, the service time is again 20 minutes, with service completion set to occur at 11:24.0.

Continuing in this fashion, we find the fourth arrival occurring at 11:23.0, and we now note that the first customer will have left just prior to this time, at 11:20.0. At this time, and not until then, we can record the number of the customer first following customer 1's departure. The number of seats available for customer 4 is the same as that for customer 3, since customer 3 took one seat, but one was made available in the time interval before customer 4's arrival. At the time of customer 8's arrival, at 11:52.5, no seats are available, so customer 8 is lost. By the time customer 9 arrives, some 41 minutes later, the lunch counter is empty, and all four seats are available. Proceeding, we observe that five of the last nine customers are lost. The simulation terminates with the first arrival after 2:00 P.M. Of the 22 customers arriving between 11:00 A.M. and 2:00 P.M., 6, or 27 percent, were lost.

For the five-seat case, the identical sequence of customers was used, and the service times of all customers served in the four-seat case also were unchanged. With the fifth seat, we can now serve the eighth customer, who was the first to be lost in the four-seat case. When the ninth customer arrives, all five seats have become available. The final result for this case is that the number of customers lost is halved, going from six to three.

As a rough check of the random numbers generated, note that 21 cutomers arrived after the initial arrival at 11:00.0. The mean interarrival time was $180/21 = 8.6$ min, whereas the expected interarrival time was 10.0 minutes. Thus, in this simulation run, the number of customers lost would tend to be higher than if the interarrival time had been closer to its expected value. Checking the service times, for the maximum of 19 customers served in the five-seat case, the average value was $470/19 = 24.7$ min, compared to the expected value of 27.5 minutes. Shorter-than-expected service times tend to have the opposite effect to shorter-than-expected interarrival times, from the standpoint of customers lost, so that in this simulation run we have random factors which tend to be counterbalancing.

The use of the same randomly generated sequence of customer arrivals and service times (whenever possible), is termed "correlated sampling," which is an

Table 14.11 Simulation of Sam's Lunch Counter Operation with Four Seats
(Values in parentheses represent the changes when a fifth seat is added.)

(1) Customer Number	(2) Exponential Random Number	(3) Time Since Last Arrival, Δt (min)	(4) Arrival Time	(5) Seats Available	(6) Uniform Random Number	(7) Service Time (min)	(8) Service Completion Time	(9) First Customer Following This Service Completion	(10) Cumulative Customers Lost
1	—	—	11:00.0	4 (5)	0.289	20	11:20.0	4	
2	0.396	4.0	11:04.0	3 (4)	0.171	20	11:24.0	5	
3	0.809	8.1	11:12.1	2 (3)	0.101	20	11:32.1	6	
4	1.090	10.9	11:23.0	2 (3)	0.722	30	11:53.0	9	
5	0.583	5.8	11:28.8	2 (3)	0.806	40	12:08.8	9	
6	1.126	11.3	11:40.1	2 (3)	0.244	20	12:01.1	9	
7	0.165	1.6	11:41.7	1 (2)	0.391	20	12:01.7	9	
8	1.077	10.8	11:52.5	0 (1)	(0.436)	(20)	(12:12.5)	(9)	1 (0)
9	4.111	41.1	12:33.6	4 (5)	0.058	10	12:43.6	10	
10	2.433	24.3	12:57.9	4 (5)	0.512	30	1:27.9	17	
11	0.264	2.6	1:00.5	3 (4)	0.817	40	1:40.5	19	
12	1.312	13.1	1:13.6	2 (3)	0.823	40	1:53.6	21	
13	0.217	2.2	1:15.8	1 (2)	0.176	20	1:35.8	18	
14	0.531	5.3	1:21.1	0 (1)	(0.398)	(20)	(1:41.1)	(19)	2 (0)
15	0.185	1.8	1:22.9	0	—	—	—	—	3 (1)
16	0.292	2.9	1:25.8	0	—	—	—	—	4 (2)
17	0.600	6.0	1:31.8	1	0.645	30	2:01.8	—	
18	0.800	8.0	1:39.8	1	0.123	10	1:49.8	20	
19	0.413	4.1	1:43.9	1 (2)	0.631	30	2:13.9	—	
20	0.920	9.2	1:53.1	1 (2)	0.312	20	2:13.1	—	
21	0.136	1.4	1:54.5	0 (1)	(0.715)	(30)	(2:24.5)	—	5 (2)
22	0.535	5.4	1:59.9	0	—	—	—	—	6 (3)
	0.077	0.8	2:00.7		Simulation ends				

important technique used to eliminate, to a great degree, variability between simulation runs due only to differences in random number sequences. We will have more to say about this later.

Time-Slicing Simulation

There are some models where it is logical to use a fixed-time-increment approach. One of these is a periodic review inventory model, which we now utilize as a second example of a time-slicing simulation. Although it was not emphasized earlier, you should now be able to recognize that Example 14.1, the Prestige Rent-a-Car simulation, was a time-slicing simulation, with an effective time increment of one day.

EXAMPLE 14.5

The Spiffy Department Store stocks a certain item whose sales appear to vary randomly from day to day and have averaged 2.5 units per day. Rather than keep track of each unit sold, Spiffy takes an inventory count every Monday evening at closing time and then determines how many units to reorder. The vendor who supplies this item has sent the order after two days 45 percent of the time, after three days 25 percent of the time, and after four days 30 percent of the time. The order is phoned in to the vendor on Monday evening, and if the lead time is two days, for example, the order arrives before the store opens Thursday morning, with the units available for sale when the store opens. Spiffy is open seven days a week.

The cost of holding a unit overnight is estimated as $0.10, and the estimated shortage penalty cost is $1.00 for each day a customer waits if the item is out of stock. It is assumed that all customers will wait if the item is not in stock. (This assumption is chosen only to simplify the calculations in this example, and it could be easily modified.)

Spiffy wishes to evaluate a proposal to order 25 units minus the number of units on hand at the inventory count. This is a replenishment level inventory policy, which we discussed in Chapter 11. Since an order is placed every week, the cost of placing an order is not relevant to the decision as to the best replenishment level.

It is desired to develop a simple simulation model which can be used to estimate the average daily total relevant cost under this inventory policy. As we will demonstrate, the model can be used to readily evaluate the effect of using other replenishment levels and cost factors.

In the simulation model, the time increment is, in effect, a half day, since the computations are performed at the beginning and at the end of each day. At the beginning of each day, a check is made to see if a replenishment order is due. If so, the quantity due in is added to the inventory on hand. At the end of each day, the inventory is equal to the inventory that morning less the current day's demand. If it is Monday, an order is placed for the quantity determined by the given decision rule. The delivery of that order is then scheduled according to the lead time value chosen.

Each day, a random demand must be generated, and every Monday, a random lead time value is needed. For these purposes, the cumulative probability values are tabulated in Table 14.12. The demand probability values are based on the assumption of a Poisson distribution of daily demand, which was stated to be of a random nature with a mean of 2.5 units. The demand probability values were derived from Appendix D. The lead time probability values come from the given data on the vendor's delivery performance. Each required random variate will be generated by the inverse transformation method, using the appropriate cumulative probability table.

Table 14.12   Probability Distributions

	Item Demand			Lead Time	
Demand d	Probability $P(d)$	Cumulative Probability $F(d)$	Days t	Probability $P(t)$	Cumulative Probability $F(t)$
0	0.08	0.08	2	0.45	0.45
1	0.21	0.29	3	0.25	0.70
2	0.26	0.55	4	0.30	1.00
3	0.21	0.76			
4	0.13	0.89			
5	0.07	0.96			
6	0.03	0.99			
7	0.01	1.00			

The simulation of a four-week period is detailed in Table 14.13. An initial inventory of 10 units is arbitrarily assumed. At the start of the simulation, the first random number 0.211 generates a demand of 1 unit, as determined from the cumulative probability values for item demand in Table 14.12. This leaves 9 units on hand at the end of the first day. Since it is a Monday, an order is placed for $25 - 9 = 16$ units. With a random number 0.330, the lead time is 2 days, referring to the lead time cumulative probability values in Table 14.12. With 9 units to be held overnight, the holding cost is $0.90, and there is no shortage cost. On the next day, the random number 0.932 results in a demand of 5 units, from Table 14.12, and the 9 units in inventory Tuesday morning are reduced to 4 units by Tuesday evening. On Thursday, the 16 units ordered on Monday arrive. The timing is perfect in this instance, since the inventory had dropped to zero Wednesday evening. Continuing in this fashion, the first shortage occurs on Wednesday of the third week, but a supply of 18 units arrives the next morning, leaving 17 units available after the 1 unit is set aside for the customer who found the item out of stock on the previous day. In the fourth week, no units were available from sometime Tuesday until the replenishment order arrived on Friday.

Based on this simulation, the estimated average daily total relevant cost is $1.30. As we noted earlier, the order cost is not relevant to the decision as to the optimal replenishment level, since an order is placed every week and we assume that the ordering cost is constant, independent of the number of units ordered.

If we continued to run this simulation for a reasonably long period, perhaps 100 weeks, we would get a fairly good estimate of the costs when using a replenishment

Table 14.13 Spiffy Department Store Inventory Simulation

			Demand				Lead Time		Costs ($)	
Week	Day	Beginning on Hand	Random Number	Units	Ending on Hand	Units Ordered	Random Number	Days	Holding	Shortage
1	M	10	0.211	1	9	16	0.330	2	0.90	0.00
	T	9	0.932	5	4				0.40	0.00
	W	4	0.878	4	0				0.00	0.00
	T	16*	0.531	2	14				1.40	0.00
	F	14	0.227	1	13				1.30	0.00
	S	13	0.514	2	11				1.10	0.00
	S	11	0.908	5	6				0.60	0.00
2	M	6	0.279	1	5	20	0.195	2	0.50	0.00
	T	5	0.525	2	3				0.30	0.00
	W	3	0.199	1	2				0.20	0.00
	T	22*	0.893	5	17				1.70	0.00
	F	17	0.295	2	15				1.50	0.00
	S	15	0.693	3	12				1.20	0.00
	S	12	0.866	4	8				0.80	0.00
3	M	8	0.173	1	7	18	0.041	2	0.70	0.00
	T	7	0.917	5	2				0.20	0.00
	W	2	0.657	3	−1				0.00	1.00
	T	17*	0.400	2	15				1.50	0.00
	F	15	0.642	3	12				1.20	0.00
	S	12	0.456	2	10				1.00	0.00
	S	10	0.919	5	5				0.50	0.00
4	M	5	0.566	3	2	23	0.469	3	0.20	0.00
	T	2	0.869	4	−2				0.00	2.00
	W	−2	0.699	3	−5				0.00	5.00
	T	−5	0.399	2	−7				0.00	7.00
	F	16*	0.239	1	15				1.50	0.00
	S	15	0.269	1	14				1.40	0.00
	S	14	0.334	2	12				1.20	0.00
									21.30	15.00
							Daily average		0.76	0.54

*Includes order quantity just received.

level of 25. Without testing other replenishment levels, however, we would have no real idea as to the optimal replenishment level value. We could, of course, run similar simulations using different replenishment level values, but suppose we take a close look at this simulation and see if there is some way of utilizing some of the calculations already performed.

First, observe that the random variables in this simulation, namely, demand and lead time, are independent of the replenishment level value. We can, therefore, use the same sequence of random variates to make comparative tests involving other replenishment level values. We could, for example, try a replenishment level of 24. The first order would then be for $24 - 9 = 15$ units, and the first change in inventory levels would come on Thursday, which would now start with 15 units instead of 16. Then, with 4 units, instead of 5, on hand at the end of the following Monday, we would order 20 units, and so on, for the remainder of the four-week period. The net result, compared with a replenishment level of 25, is a reduction of $2.10 in total holding costs but an increase of $4.00 in total shortage costs, giving an average daily total relevant cost of $1.37, an increase of $0.07. Since we are using the same sequence of random variates for both cases, this is again correlated sampling, just as in the simulation of Sam's Lunch Counter. The results for the two different replenishment levels are thus directly related. All other things remaining the same (and we made sure they did), a lower replenishment level should lower the average number of units held but should increase the average shortage cost, and this is what our results showed. This very possibly would not have been the case had we run two entirely separate simulations, with differing sequences of random variates, since the sample size is quite small.

By extending the simulation results of Table 14.13, we could test other replenishment levels and find the optimal value for this inventory situation. We will explore this shortly, but for now, let us consider the aspect of cost values. Suppose we had different holding and shortage cost factors; how could we investigate their effect? It is most helpful if we recognize that the optimal replenishment level is really determined by the *ratio* of the shortage cost to the holding cost, rather than the absolute values of these costs. (Recall that this was also the case for the optimal lot size models discussed in Chapter 11.) It should be clear, for example, that if we doubled both costs, the optimal replenishment level would not change. Once we do realize that the ratio of these costs is the important factor, we can develop a straightforward simulation model which can readily be utilized to determine the optimal replenishment level for any feasible ratio of shortage to holding cost.

One way of using the basic logic of this simulation model to determine the optimal replenishment level, as a function of a range of cost ratios, is as follows. We assume a convenient cost ratio, such as 1:1. Then, for each replenishment level to be tested, we keep a separate daily record of inventory amounts and cumulative holding and shortage costs, as well as a weekly record of order quantities. We use a single random demand variate each day and a single random lead time variate each Monday. At the end of the simulation, having generated only eight random variates for each simulated week, the simulation results will enable us to determine the re plenishment level yielding the lowest average total relevant cost for a 1:1 cost ratio. Having kept the holding cost and shortage cost totals separately, we are now in a position to vary their ratio and thereby determine the optimal replenishment level for any given cost ratio.

To illustrate these ideas, a simulation model was programmed to consider simultaneously a number of different replenishment levels through a period of 100 simulated weeks' operation. The results, based on an assumed shortage cost of $1.00 and a shortage cost to holding cost ratio of 1.0, are given in Table 14.14. The optimal replenishment level is 18 units, with an average daily total relevant cost of $5.47.

Table 14.14 Replenishment Level Inventory Simulation

Shortage Cost = $1		Shortage Cost to Holding Cost Ratio = 1.0					
		Average Daily Costs ($)					
Replenishment Level	16	17	18	19	20	21	22
Holding	1.86	2.30	2.79	3.33	3.91	4.55	5.25
Shortage	3.74	3.19	2.68	2.23	1.82	1.46	1.16
Total	5.60	5.49	5.47	5.56	5.73	6.01	6.41

			Average Daily Costs ($)				
Replenishment Level	23	24	25	26	27	28	29	30
Holding	5.99	6.78	7.61	8.47	9.36	10.28	11.21	12.16
Shortage	0.91	0.70	0.53	0.40	0.30	0.22	0.15	0.11
Total	6.90	7.48	8.14	8.87	9.66	10.50	11.36	12.27

By holding the shortage cost at $1.00 and varying the ratio of shortage cost to holding cost from 2 to 20 (by dividing the holding costs in Table 14.14 by each ratio used), Table 14.15 was developed. As an example, taking the cost ratio of $1.00/0.10 = 10.0$ used in the four-week simulation, the average holding cost for a replenishment level of 25 is $7.61/10.0 = \$0.76$. The average daily total relevant cost is then $0.76 + 0.53 = \$1.29$. For each specified cost ratio, the average daily total relevant cost associated with the optimal replenishment level(s) is underlined.

From the data of Table 14.15, the most meaningful observation is that the optimal replenishment level changes very slowly as the cost ratio changes. This is quite important, because the cost ratio is, in practice, seldom known very accurately, primarily because the shortage cost is hard to pinpoint. The Spiffy Department Store now knows that the choice of the optimal replenishment level is not sensitive to its estimate of the cost ratio, and this should give the store management a good deal of confidence in its choice of replenishment level, which should be 27 units based on the estimated shortage cost to holding cost ratio of 10. See Table 14.15.

Table 14.15   Replenishment Level Inventory Simulation

Average Daily Total Relevant Cost (in $) for Shortage Cost of $1

Replenishment Level	20	21	22	23	24	25	26	27	28	29	30
Shortage Cost / *Holding Cost*											
2	3.77	3.74	3.78	3.91	4.09	4.33	4.63	4.98	5.36	5.76	6.19
3	3.12	2.98	2.91	2.91	2.96	3.06	3.22	3.42	3.65	3.89	4.16
4	2.79	2.60	2.47	2.41	2.40	2.43	2.51	2.64	2.79	2.95	3.15
5	2.60	2.37	2.21	2.11	2.06	2.05	2.09	2.17	2.28	2.39	2.54
6	2.47	2.22	2.03	1.91	1.83	1.80	1.81	1.86	1.93	2.02	2.13
7	2.37	2.11	1.91	1.76	1.67	1.62	1.61	1.63	1.69	1.75	1.84
8	2.30	2.03	1.81	1.66	1.55	1.48	1.45	1.47	1.50	1.55	1.63
9	2.25	1.97	1.74	1.57	1.45	1.37	1.34	1.34	1.36	1.40	1.46
10	2.21	1.92	1.68	1.51	1.38	1.29	1.24	1.23	1.25	1.27	1.32
12	2.14	1.84	1.60	1.41	1.27	1.16	1.10	1.08	1.08	1.08	1.12
14	2.10	1.79	1.53	1.34	1.18	1.07	1.00	0.96	0.95	0.95	0.98
16	2.06	1.74	1.49	1.28	1.12	1.00	0.92	0.88	0.86	0.85	0.87
18	2.03	1.71	1.45	1.24	1.08	0.95	0.87	0.82	0.79	0.77	0.78
20	2.01	1.69	1.42	1.21	1.04	0.91	0.82	0.76	0.73	0.71	0.72

The approach shown here demonstrates how a thoughtful analysis of a problem can sometimes greatly extend the usefulness, from a decision-making standpoint, of a simple mathematical model. From the viewpoint of making the decision as to the optimal replenishment level, note that the dollar values in Tables 14.14 and 14.15 are not really meaningful in an absolute sense. Thus, for each cost ratio, we are interested only in locating the replenishment level which gives the lowest average daily total relevant cost and not in the cost value itself. However, given the best estimate of the actual holding and shortage costs, the data in Table 14.15 permit the ready calculation of the average daily total relevant cost associated with the optimal replenishment level.

14.5   SIMULATION LANGUAGES

Simulation can certainly be done without special programming languages, but to do so requires extensive modeling and programming experience. As can be seen from the simple queueing model simulation previously discussed, many tedious details are involved in a simulation model, not the least of which is the correct and efficient maintenance of an event calendar when using event sequencing.

Special simulation languages cut program preparation time and cost with features specifically designed for simulation. Such features generally include a master sequencing routine to automatically maintain an event calendar and to keep track of simulated time, routines to handle queue arrivals and departures, the capability to readily generate different types of random variates, straightforward or even automatic generation of certain types of statistical reports, flexible report generators for the effective presentation of output data, and numerous other features.

Simulation "packages" range from the special-purpose program which requires no programming ability and is easy to use, but only for one specific application (such as the simulation of PERT networks), to a full-fledged simulation language which can be used over a wide range of simulation models by those who have at least a reasonable amount of simulation programming experience. For a given user, the choice of a simulation package will depend to a great extent on the specific application, the availability of simulation languages on the particular computer or computers, the user's training and experience in simulation modeling and programming, and the availability of experienced programmers.

We will not attempt to describe particular simulation languages, an exercise in futility, since these languages frequently tend to change fairly substantially, both in capability and availability, over a relatively short period of time. Over the past few years, however, the most-used simulation languages have been SIMSCRIPT and GPSS (General Purpose Systems Simulator), both of which have appeared in a number of different versions. (Technically, GPSS is a program, rather than a language, since a simulation model is actually constructed through the detailed specification of data selected from a set of data inputs designed to facilitate the performance of highly sophisticated computer simulation operations.) A great deal of simulation programming has been done in FORTRAN, which is a general scientific programming language. FORTRAN has an almost unlimited range of applicability, because it is general purpose, but it has no features to aid simulation, so it requires considerable skill in both programming and simulation modeling.

With the exception of the programming of small simulation models, simulation programming is not for the uninitiated. It seems to require almost as much art as the skill which comes only with experience.

4.6   USES OF SIMULATION

Having previously covered the general concepts and implementation of simple simulation models, we are now in a better position to discuss the important role of simulation models in the study of various types of systems.

Simulation models can be manipulated in ways which would otherwise be impossible, impractical, too expensive, too hazardous, and so forth. For example, we can simulate the operation of systems not yet built; we can "try out" different warehouse locations without actually building any; we can simulate the effect of substantial changes in a complex logistics system without physically making such changes; and we can evaluate the potential of an air-traffic control system without the enormous expense and possible hazards involved in actually installing and testing such a system.

From a conceptual viewpoint, it may be of value to look at some of the more important ways in which simulation models are employed. Let us now briefly discuss the use of simulation models to perform the functions of systems analysis, systems design, systems synthesis, and training or teaching.

Systems analysis involves the manipulation of a simulation model and observation of the effects. Thus, if we were modeling the operation of a machine shop, we might investigate the effect on job delays of adding another lathe and a drill press, or we might test different decision rules regarding the order in which jobs are processed. We could perform sensitivity analyses, changing certain problem parameters and noting the effect on important output variables and the interaction between variables. As a rule, systems analysis is used in an attempt to answer the question: "What happens if —?"

Systems design involves the determination of the optimal system configuration based on a given measure of system performance, often called the measure of effectiveness, or M.E. Optimizing the measure of effectiveness can involve cost minimization or profit maximization under time and resource constraints, minimization of task completion time under resource (including financial) constraints, and so forth. The inputs are generally known, at least in a probabilistic sense, and we attempt to design an optimal system to generate the required outputs. For example, consider the determination of the optimal number of tellers in a bank. The measure of effectiveness could be the cost associated with a given level of service, as defined by average customer waiting time until served. Given data on the probability distribution of customer service and interarrival times, we could develop a simulation model and "exercise" it with different values for the number of tellers. The optimal number of tellers would then be determined as the minimum number required to achieve the specified service level.

Systems synthesis is generally a very difficult process. Given particular data inputs *and* outputs, we attempt to develop a simulation model which will reproduce, to a statistically significant degree, the given output data from the given input data. Simulation models of a national economy represent attempts to construct a mathematical model which will take given inputs and transform them into observed outputs. The validity of such a model is measured by the degree to which it faithfully reproduces known outputs over a range of known inputs. A valid model can then hopefully, be used to generate the outputs given some hypothesized set of inputs thereby extrapolating from the original model.

Training involves the use of simulation models to perform functions under what is often a completely controlled environment. As an example, a complicated communications network can be simulated with random failures at various points. Operators can then be informed, say, by printed messages or visual displays, of the problems and can be required to reroute messages according to specified procedures. These messages then become inputs to the simulation program, thereby forming a feedback loop. As a teaching device, simulation models are used for many different kinds of business games. Teams of players are required to make a set of decisions on certain variables (frequently expenditures of different types) and this information is fed into the simulation program and combined with random variables representing demand, production, and so forth. The resulting outputs are displayed, and the team, by a process similar to systems synthesis, attempts to develop an approach to the selection of those system inputs which will optimize their particular measure of effectiveness, such as total profit, over a specified number of time periods.

14.7   OVERVIEW OF SIMULATION MODELING

In the development of simulation models, one of the first steps required is the construction of a gross flow chart. Such a flow chart should show the elements making up the system (the system components), the points at which decisions must be made, and the logical flow of operations within the system. This is shown in Figure 14.6, a highly simplified representation of a supermarket. Flow charts are as fundamental to simulation models as are equations to analytic models.

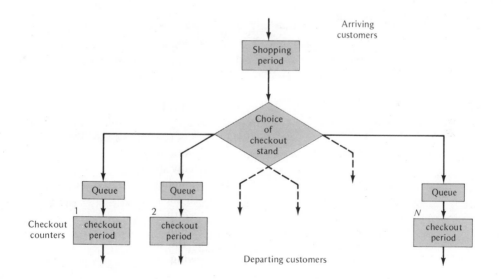

Figure 14.6

After constructing the flow chart and prior to the development of the actual computer program, several steps should be taken. Considering the quantitative level of information desired from the simulation model, whether this be gross effects, "a good feel for," or relatively precise numerical values, the variables and parameters of interest should be specified. By *variables*, both independent and dependent, we mean those quantities which fluctuate during a simulation run; by *parameters*, we mean those quantities which are fixed during a given simulation run but which may change over a set of simulation runs. For example, in a queueing simulation, instantaneous and mean queue lengths, individual and mean waiting times, and individual customer interarrival times are all variables. The number of servers, the *mean* service rate, and the *mean* arrival rate are parameters which can be deliberately varied from run to run. Note that some parameters, such as mean arrival rate, may not actually be controllable in the real situation.

The functional relationships between the system components should now be detailed. Preliminary solutions should be obtained, if at all possible, by manual simulation and/or simplified analytical models. These preliminary solutions are useful in determining the range of values of the expected results and in aiding in the validation of the computer program through the obtaining of numerical results for particular cases.

We will not discuss development, checkout, and analysis of computer simulation programs. These topics are too detailed for this book but are well covered in several different textbooks on simulation.

14.8 SIMULATION APPLICATIONS

The range of application of computer simulation models is enormous, since simulation represents an approach, rather than an application of a specific technique such as linear programming. We will first discuss a representative range of applications relating to models presented earlier in this book and then some other applications.

Perhaps the major use of computer Monte Carlo simulation models has been in the solution of complex queueing problems. As a matter of fact, the General Purpose Systems Simulator (GPSS) program is essentially structured as a queueing simulation vehicle. As was seen in Chapter 12 on Queueing Models, many of the analytical formulas are complicated enough even with the simplified assumption of Poisson arrivals and exponential service times. Since either or both of these assumptions are untenable in many cases, and since, in addition, there can be complex interactions between system components, simulation is the only recourse in the modeling of many queueing problems, such as the following.

1. Determination of the optimal number of repairmen required to maintain a number of different types of machines subject to both "purely random" (Poisson) and wearout failures.
2. Determination of the optimal division of labor for an automobile production line so as to maximize the flow of completed cars by avoiding bottlenecks at various points in the assembly process. This is known as the assembly line balancing problem.
3. Analysis of the transient behavior of elevator queues which form during peak

arrival and departure periods in a large office building and the effect on waiting times of assigning elevators to serve only a subset of floors rather than all floors.

4. Advance scheduling of the manning of toll booths in such a manner as to minimize expected vehicle delays and the expected idle time of toll booth collectors.

5. Evaluating and optimizing the performance of a production facility, commonly known as a job shop, which handles a wide mix of order types.

A number of job shop simulation programs have been written, generally involving *deterministic* times for the individual operations of a given order. In spite of the lack of probabilistic elements in such a model, the high degree of interaction between orders, due to their different processing times for similar operations and to different order operation sequences, makes it impossible to predict the waiting time for a particular order at any given work center. Since orders must be scheduled with an allowance for waiting at the various work centers they will pass through, simulation is the only way to make reasonably accurate estimates of such allowances, which are required for efficient scheduling. Simulation models, employed on a day-by-day basis, have actually been used to dynamically forecast manpower and machine workloads, thereby facilitating efficient manpower and machine utilization.

A good deal of work has been done in the development of inventory simulation models of fairly wide applicability, as well as those for specialized use. As we noted earlier, parts of many inventory models have a strong queueing flavor. Thus, a problem concerned with the optimal inventory of rental cars can be viewed as a queueing problem where the servers are the cars. Some inventory applications are indicated below:

1. Determination of optimal reorder level and order quantity under conditions of probabilistic demand and lead time, where analytical models are not suitable because of nonlinearities and/or the form of the given probability distributions.

2. Study of transient effects in inventory systems, such as occur when demand patterns change markedly over a short period, a new product is introduced, or a new warehouse is opened.

3. Determination of the optimal review period and ordering policy for continuous review inventory models under conditions of random demand and lead time.

A number of network simulation models have also been developed. Again, some of them have definite queueing aspects. The following are some network applications.

1. Study of the message-handling capabilities of large communication networks under conditions of random message inputs and random breakdowns of

communications facilities and links. (Note that messages waiting to be transmitted at some point in the network form a queue, with the available transmission circuits acting as the servers.)

2. Simulation of probabilistic task times in PERT networks, as mentioned in Chapter 9 on Network Models. (With a randomly selected task time for each task, the critical path can be evaluated and its length determined. Repeating this process many, many times, the probability distribution of project completion time can be obtained, as well as the probability that each given task is on the critical path.)

3. Study of traffic flow patterns in a road network as a function of traffic signal timing.

A variety of other applications of simulation models includes the following.

1. Simulation of the operation of computer hardware and software systems with various job mixes, evaluating different computer configurations and testing job scheduling rules.

2. Military studies of logistics, support planning, deployment strategies, and weapons systems effectiveness.

3. Studies of individual and group behavior.

4. Financial studies involving risky investments.

5. Testing of decision rules for hospital admissions and operating policies;

6. Man-machine simulations where the computer program is responsible for generating random events, doing all the required computations, and presenting the outputs in printed or displayed form so that required manual decisions can be made and entered as inputs to the program. Such simulations have been used to evaluate the performance of personnel in large, complex logistics systems, in air defense systems, and in space flight operations.

As an illustration of the power of simulation models to aid in the development of effective solutions to complex and costly business problems, consider the following two examples of successfully implemented simulation models in the 1970s.

1. Solid-waste management operations in Cleveland, Ohio[1]   Faced with an economic crisis brought about by higher equipment, facility, and labor costs, coupled with a decreasing tax base resulting from the urban exodus, the Cleveland Division of Solid-Waste Collection and Disposal developed a solid-waste management simulation model which utilizes information from a comprehensive data acquisition and analysis system. This simulation models the complex interrelationships between solid-waste generation, collection, transportation, and disposal. The insights gained from the simulation studies permitted a reduction of the solid-waste work force from

[1]Robert M. Clark and James I. Gillean, "Analysis of Solid Waste Management Operations in Cleveland, Ohio: A Case Study," *Interfaces*, Vol. 6, No. 1, Pt. 2, November 1975, pp. 32–42.

1640 to 850, led to a total redesign of the collection routing system, and prompted a complete reorganization of the solid-waste management structure. Over a four-year period, the total savings, based on the 1970 budget, were $14.6 million.

2. A new Federal Reserve District check-clearing system[2]   In 1972, Federal Reserve Banks were ordered to provide overnight clearing services for all intra-district checks. This required each district to specify the number, location, and capacity of processing centers, as well as the transportation network, including timetables. A comprehensive *deterministic* simulation model of the Philadelphia Federal Reserve district was developed by the Management and Behavioral Science Center at the Wharton School of the University of Pennsylvania to evaluate such performance measures as total costs, services provided, and number of late checks. The simulation model linked detailed submodels of transportation, check volume, commercial bank clearing practices, and facility sizing. A deterministic model was used because there was no point in simulating the individual flow of the thousands of daily checks processed; the primary problem was to determine how the volume and distribution (both in space and time) of checks influenced processing times and costs for different system configurations. The recommendation from the studies was for a single RCPC (Regional Check Processing Center), instead of the three RCPCs that were believed necessary. The recommended system was implemented very early in 1973, actually earlier than planned. The two unneeded RCPCs would have added $70,000 per month in fixed costs. In addition, the Philadelphia Federal Reserve Bank was able to see the advantages of the systems approach to its decision making. As a direct result, the Philadelphia Fed formed its own operations research group. Also, four other in-house operations research groups were formed within the Federal Reserve System.

By now, it should be quite obvious that there is no inherent limitation in the employment of computer simulation models. This is by no means meant to imply that computer simulation is the universal problem-solving tool. Many computer simulation models have been poorly conceived and poorly implemented, and the term GIGO (garbage in, garbage out) is directly applicable to such models. If the necessary modeling and programming skills are available, computer simulation models can be quite valuable *when* analytical models are inapplicable. In addition, "quick and dirty" simulation models sometimes yield valuable insights which can aid the modeler to formulate an adequate analytical model.

14.9 OPERATIONAL CONSIDERATIONS

As we have stated earlier, computer simulation is an experimental method. It behooves us, then, to conduct a simulation "experiment" in a reasonably efficient

[2]Sidney W. Hess, "Design and Implementation of a New Check Clearing System for the Philadelphia Federal Reserve District," *Interfaces*, Vol. 5, No. 2, Pt. 2, February 1975, pp. 22–36.

manner. Although we cannot go into any depth of detail regarding the design of computer simulation experiments, we can discuss some common simulation problems and some relatively straightforward approaches designed to generally improve the efficiency of a computer simulation model.

Initial Conditions

Many simulations are started with the system "empty and idle" and this may be quite realistic for some situations. Thus, when a bank opens, all tellers are idle and immediately available for service. If we are not interested in the start-up of the system, but only in its steady-state operation, we must run the simulation through the transient phase and discard the statistics collected during that time. Some simulation languages provide this capability almost automatically. The transient phase statistics, if not eliminated, can significantly bias the overall results. Identifying the end of the transient phase is no easy task, but it can sometimes be approximated by measuring, at "reasonable" intervals of simulated time, a well-behaved variable, such as average waiting time in a queueing model. When the period-to-period change in this variable becomes less than some stipulated value, or, perhaps, when the sign of the change reverses several times, the transient phase can be considered as over.

In some cases, it may be possible to start with a "representative" initial load, and this avoids what can be a very long transient period. For example, assume we are simulating a job shop that we know has an average of approximately 200 orders in process at one time. If the average number of orders introduced daily is 10, it will generally require far longer than 20 simulated days to approach a steady-state condition. This is so because the first few days' orders will go through with practically no delays. It might take 40 to 100 or more days, depending on the numerical data of the particular problem. Suppose, instead of starting "empty and idle," we immediately introduce 200 orders into the shop. For each of these orders, we generate a random number uniform on the interval (0, 1). This number represents the fraction of the order completed when simulation starts. To show how this value is used, consider a certain order which has operations to be performed at machine groups A, B, and C, in that order. These operations take 3 hours, 2 hours, and 5 hours, respectively. If a random number of 0.40 is generated, this order is tentatively assumed to be 40 percent completed, which means that it is placed at machine group B, since it would have completed 4 hours out of its total processing time of 10 hours. Once located at machine group B, there are two possibilities. If a machine is available, this order is then placed on that machine with 1 hour of processing time remaining, and the number of available machines is reduced by one. If all machines are already busy, this order is placed in queue with its full processing time of 2 hours at machine group B. If the 200 orders introduced are representative orders, this initialization process should give reasonable results, for all practical purposes eliminating any transient phase.

In queueing simulations, another way of establishing an initial load is to initiate arrivals and delay service until a "representative" queue builds up. In the case of a bank, we might delay service until the doors had been open for five minutes. This approach obviously requires good judgment and may be suitable for the case where each customer receives a single type of service. It is completely unsuitable for the previous example of a job shop simulation. Why?

Again, in queueing simulations, if a series of runs is being performed, it is sometimes possible to use the final state of one run as the initial state for the next run, thereby shortening (but not eliminating) the transient period. This is frequently acceptable if we are changing rates (average arrival rate or service rate) but not if we are changing quantities such as the number of servers or the maximum queue limit.

Variance Reduction

Many of the values resulting from a simulation run are sample means. We would like the variance of these sample means to be as small as possible, thereby increasing the precision of these statistical estimates.

Where the primary objective is to choose the best of several alternative decision rules, designs, and so forth, the emphasis is on relative comparisons rather than the determination of absolute values. If $\bar{X}_1$ and $\bar{X}_2$ are the sample means to be compared from the results of two simulation runs, it can be shown that

$$V(\bar{X}_1 - \bar{X}_2) = V(\bar{X}_1) + V(\bar{X}_2) - 2\gamma\sqrt{V(\bar{X}_1)\,V(\bar{X}_2)},$$

where γ is the correlation coefficient. Thus, the variance of the difference between sample means is an inverse function of the degree of correlation between the samples. We can reduce this variance by inducing a highly positive correlation through the use of identical sequences of pseudorandom numbers for these simulation runs. This technique, mentioned earlier, is called *correlated sampling*. It eliminates what can be a significant source of variability, permitting the effect of changing controllable variables to be measured under the same set of conditions. For example, suppose we are trying to determine the optimal reorder point and reorder quantity in an inventory system. Through the use of correlated sampling, the identical sequence of random demands and lead times is generated for each reorder point and reorder quantity combination. The cost for each combination can then be compared without concern for any difference which might be masked or amplified by differences in the sequence of random demands and lead times.

While correlated sampling reduces the variance between the difference of sample means, it does not reduce the variance of the estimate of individual means. To accomplish this, the method of *antithetic variates* can be used to generate negatively correlated replications of the same experiment. The estimate of the mean is then taken as the average of the means resulting from the two replications. If the ith random variate in the first replication is some function $f(r_i)$, where r_i is a pseudorandom number uniform on the interval $(0, 1)$, then the ith random variate in the second replication becomes $f(1 - r_i)$, thereby inducing the desired negative correlation. As an illustration, suppose the time between customer arrivals was uniformly distributed in the interval 10 to 30 minutes. An r value of 0.20 would then generate an interarrival time of $10 + 0.20(30 - 10) = 14$ minutes, which is less than the mean interarrival time of 20 minutes. In the second replication, for the same customer arrival, we would use $r = 1 - 0.20 = 0.80$. This time, the interarrival time would be $10 + 0.80(30 - 10) = 26$ minutes, which is higher than the mean interarrival time. Thus, customer arrivals tending to bunch together in the first replication would tend to be spread apart in the second replication, and vice versa.

Selective sampling is a technique, developed by Brenner (1963), which is based on the concept that the relative frequency of simulated events should conform as closely as possible to their actual probability of occurrence.[3] Suppose that, in a particular simulation, a total of n events is to be simulated (perhaps customer arrivals). These n events consist of m different types of event (such as the customer's priority classification).

Let p_j = desired probability that a type j event occurs
v_j = actual occurrences of a type j event.

As the value of n increases, the relative frequency of the jth event, v_j/n, will converge to the value p_j. For small or moderate values of n, however, v_j/n can vary considerably from p_j. Through the technique of selective sampling, the values of v_j can be made to conform closely to the value of p_j. In fact, if np_j assumes integer values for all j, then the desired probability distribution can be reproduced exactly. The selective sampling process is actually one of random sampling without replacement. A count is stored for the desired number of occurrences of each type of event. Each time a particular event type is selected, its count is decreased by one. Each type of event is randomly selected in proportion to the ratio of its remaining count to the total number of remaining events. Again, selective sampling, when applicable, can eliminate an important source of variability between comparative simulation runs.

Additional variance-reduction techniques, such as stratified sampling, importance sampling, and the method of control variates, are somewhat more involved than those presented here and may be found in other references.

Computer Runs

There are no hard and fast rules for determining the proper length of a computer run or of the number of replications which may be required. These factors generally depend both on the statistical behavior of the model and on the desired precision of the statistical outputs from the simulation. One very long simulation run can be divided into segments and the variable of interest (such as mean queue length) calculated for each segment. The variance of the overall mean value can then be estimated using the central limit theorem.

In many cases, simulation variables of interest are well-behaved functions of problem parameters. Through the use of smoothing techniques, often purely graphical, it should be possible in such cases to reduce accuracy requirements, thereby permitting shorter simulation runs and/or fewer replications. As an example of a

---

[3]M. E. Brenner, "Selective Sampling—A Technique for Reducing Sample Size in Simulation for Decision Making Problems," *Journal of Industrial Engineering*, Vol. 14, No. 6, 1963, pp. 291–296.

well-behaved function, consider, in almost any queueing study, the variation of mean time in queue as a function of customer arrival rate, for any given combination of system configuration, decision rules, and parameter values. Mean time in queue must be a monotonically increasing function of customer arrival rate, and the information to be determined is the particular shape of this function. Very rarely are highly precise data required in the estimation of the function. (Indeed, this is true of most data generated in simulation studies.) A curve plotted from the data shown in Figure 14.7a may be just as meaningful as that plotted from the data of Figure 14.7b, and the less precise data may reduce total run time by a factor of two or more.

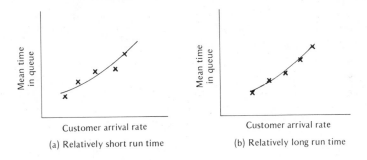

Figure 14.7

Validation

How can we tell if the simulation model is a valid representation of the system to be simulated? Unfortunately, there is no clear-cut answer to this question. If historical data are available, the ability of the model to reproduce previous results with reasonable faithfulness lends credibility to the model. This is, however, no guarantee that the model will produce valid predictions in the future. In the situation where no historical or other related data are available to help check out the model, the problem is more difficult. In any case, those most familiar with the system being simulated should concur with the model structure and should help establish appropriate ranges for the model parameters. In practice, a number of things can be done to investigate the credibility of a simulation model.

During the development of the computer program for the simulation model, the computer output should be compared with the results of manual simulations using the same random variates or with the results of analytical calculations (when possible) under identical conditions. This is part of the so-called "debugging" process. When debugging is successfully completed, it validates the computer program, not the model. This is a necessary first step prior to model validation.

The validity of the model itself can be tested in several ways. For example, are the results reasonable under limiting conditions? In a queueing model, for instance, with a low traffic intensity (when the system arrival rate is low compared to the system service rate), the system should function very smoothly, with a minimum of delays. Conversely, when the traffic intensity is high, there should be significant service delays. If these conditions do not obtain, then something is wrong with the model. Are trends reasonable? Large parameter changes should be tested initially to determine the sensitivity of the model to such changes. Frequently, there will be at least a good feeling as to which parameter changes should affect the results significantly. As the parameters are varied, there should be no unexpected abrupt changes in the results. On the other hand, any expected significant changes should be present.

In the final analysis, the real validation of a simulation model occurs only when the predicted results agree satisfactorily with the "real world" results, and that may be a long time after the required completion of the simulation model. Some simulations, such as those analyzing situations involving natural disasters or evaluating the effectiveness of military weapons systems, never do get validated, fortunately.

SUMMARY

Computer Monte Carlo simulation is an important and powerful problem-solving tool in its own right, and not just a last resort "when all else fails," as some believe. This can be attributed primarily to the advent of the high-speed digital computer and the availability of powerful simulation languages. (It should be noted that simulation can sometimes provide insights leading to the formulation of analytical models which are satisfactory for a given problem and which generally provide solutions of wider applicability than simulation solutions.)

The intent in this chapter has been to provide a basic understanding of the formulation and structuring of computer simulation models, as well as an appreciation of their limitations, since simulation is an experimental technique. The general concept of pseudorandom numbers and their usage in preference to "pure" random numbers should be understood, especially in regard to correlated sampling. The generation of random variates from continuous probability distributions and from discrete probability distributions, including empirical distributions, is fundamental to most simulation models. The approach used to keep track of the time sequence of events in a simulation model is also most important. Although both time-slicing and event-sequencing methods are used, the latter appears to be preferable for the majority of simulation models, and a fairly detailed exposition of a simple queueing model using event sequencing was illustrated.

Fortunately, simulation languages embody many features which greatly simplify simulation modeling and allow concentration on simulation, rather than programming, aspects. Operational considerations, however, such as initial conditions of simulation runs, variance reduction for comparative computer runs, and validation of simulation models, are still the responsibility of the simulation modeler-programmer.

The reader should be able to formulate and exercise small manual simulation models, and should have a general comprehension of what is involved in computer simulation. Actual skill in simulation modeling, however, is acquired only with practice and experience.

EXERCISES

Note: In the following exercises, all random variates are to be generated manually, based on random number tables, and all simulations are to be performed manually.

14.1 What is the conceptual difference between solutions derived from simulation models and solutions derived from analytical models?

14.2 Using the multiplicative congruential method of generating pseudorandom numbers, each random number r is obtained by multiplying the previous random number by a constant k and retaining the remainder after dividing by a second constant m. The length and apparent randomness of the sequence generated is sensitive to the choice of k, m, and the initial random number r_0.

Let the value of m be 100, so that r is limited to two-digit numbers. Starting with $r_0 = 7$, generate random numbers using the formula $r_{n+1} = kr_n$ (modulo n). Continue until the number 7 shows up again, at which point the sequence repeats itself. As an example of the procedure, suppose k were 23. Then, $r_1 = (23)(7)(\text{modulo } 100) = 161 \text{ modulo } 100 = 61$, $r_2 = (61)(7)(\text{modulo } 100) = 427 \text{ modulo } 100 = 27$, and so on. Use the following values of k: (a) $k = 9$ (b) $k = 17$. Compare the sequences generated in (a) and (b) from the standpoint of length and apparent randomness. In particular, comment upon the exclusion of certain digit values.

14.3 Two methods frequently used to generate random variates are
(a) the inverse transformation method,
(b) the composition method.
For each of these methods, describe briefly how it works and give an example of its usage.

14.4 Starting with random numbers uniform on the interval (0, 1), generate two random variates from each of the following continuous probability distributions.
(a) Uniform, over the interval -20 to $+30$.
(b) Normal, with mean 10 and standard deviation 2:
    1. Use the approximate method, with $N = 12$.
    2. Use the exact method.
(c) Erlang, with a mean of 6 and 3 phases, using the composition method.
    1. Use the additive process.
    2. Use the multiplicative process.

14.5 Starting with random numbers uniform on the interval (0, 1), generate two random variates from each of the following discrete probability distributions.
(a) Empirical:

Value	Probability
-2	0.25
0	0.37
5	0.08
8	0.30

(b)   Binomial, with 5 trials and individual success probability 0.2.
1.   Use the composition method.
2.   Use the inverse transformation method, utilizing the cumulative probability tables in Appendix C.
(c)   Geometric, with individual success probability 0.1. (The geometric distribution represents the distribution of the number of trials until the first success occurs.) Use the composition method.

14.6   A random variate x is to be drawn from a distribution which is uniform on the interval (a, b) with probability p and uniform on the interval (b, c) with probability $1 - p$.
(a)   Sketch and algebraically state the probability density function $f(x)$ and the cumulative distribution function $F(x)$.
(b)   Draw a simple flow chart to show the process of generating random variates from this distribution by the inverse transformation method.
(c)   Using 20 random numbers uniform on the interval $(0, 1)$, generate 20 random variates from a distribution of the nature described and with parameters $a = 2, b = 4, c = 14$, and $p = 0.8$. Calculate the expected value of X and compare it with the mean value obtained from the simulation.

14.7   It is desired to generate random variates from a Poisson distribution of equipment failures having a mean of 1.2 per day.
(a)   From the table of the cumulative Poisson distribution, Appendix D, tabulate the probability of 0 through 6 failures.
(b)   Since a Poisson distribution of failures means that a failure is equally likely in any small time interval throughout the day, approximate the desired distribution by dividing the day into small enough time intervals that the probability of a failure in any such interval is less than 0.10. Suppose we use 20 intervals, so that the failure probability in any interval is $1.2/20 = 0.06$. A single Poisson variate can then be generated, using the composition method, by examining 20 random numbers uniform on $(0, 1)$ and counting a failure for each random number less than 0.06. Generate ten Poisson variates by using the uniform random number table of Appendix E. Each column of 20 numbers will yield one random variate. Calculate the mean and tabulate the probability distribution, as in (a).
(c)   Generate ten Poisson variates by using the inverse transformation method in conjunction with the cumulative Poisson distribution values for a mean of 1.2. Use the first ten uniform random numbers in the first column of Appendix E. If a number falls between 1.0000 and 0.6988, select 0 as the random variate, and so on. Calculate the mean and tabulate the probability distribution.
(d)   Compare the two methods used in parts (b) and (c) as to speed and accuracy.

14.8   Suppose that between the initial and final phases of a particular project there are four activities which can be performed in parallel. If the PERT method is used to analyze and schedule this project, only the longest of the four activities will be considered to be on the critical path, even if the activity completion times are probabilistic in nature. With simulation, however, we can determine the probability that any given activity will be on the critical path.

The activities listed below can be performed in parallel. (For computational convenience, assume that their probabilistic completion times are from a uniform distribution, although a number of other distributions could be readily simulated.)

Activity A: 6 to 8 days
Activity B: 5 to 7 days
Activity C: 6 to 7 days
Activity D: 5.5 to 6 days

Using random numbers uniform on (0, 1), generate a random time for each activity and choose the longest time, noting the activity thus selected. Repeat this process 20 times and, from the results, estimate the probability of each activity being on the critical path. Calculate the mean time of the critical path activity. Compare this mean time with the mean time of activity A, which would have been the critical path activity in conventional PERT.

14.9   State in your own words the meaning of the following simulation terms.
  (a)   Pseudo-random numbers
  (b)   Time-slicing
  (c)   Event-sequencing

14.10   For most time-oriented simulations, why is an event-sequencing approach preferred to a time-slicing approach?

14.11   In an event-sequencing simulation, what is the purpose of the event calendar? Describe briefly how it functions.

14.12   A traveler wishes to fly from Los Angeles to Miami. Because of a shortage of funds, however, he can only afford to fly on Stochastic Airlines, which guarantees the fare but not the destination.

The flight from Los Angeles arrives in either Salt Lake City, Denver, or Chicago, according to the probability distribution in the accompanying table. From Salt Lake City or Denver, he may arrive in Chicago, St. Louis, or ?. From Chicago or St. Louis, he can fly directly to Miami, and the flight arrives there most of the time.

Probability of Arrival at Possible Destinations

Flight	Leaves	Salt Lake City	Denver	Chicago	St. Louis	Miami	?
1	Los Angeles	0.8	0.1	0.1			
2	Salt Lake City			0.8	0.2		
3	Denver			0.4	0.5		0.1
4	Chicago					0.8	0.2
5	St. Louis					0.9	0.1

(a) Based on the flight information in the table, simulate 20 departures from Los Angeles, and from your results estimate the probability of arrival in Miami. Each flight will have two or three legs, and a random number is required for each leg. It is suggested that cumulative probability tables be associated with each flight number.

(b) Sketch a crude map of the cities and routes involved. Using elementary probability theory, calculate the theoretical probability of reaching Miami, assuming independence between flights.

14.13 The Model T Truck Company, Exercise 13.13, has agencies in cities A, B, and C. From an analysis of their records, the fraction of trucks rented in a given city and returned in each of the three cities is as shown in the following table.

<table>
<tr><td></td><td></td><td colspan="3">City to Which Returned</td></tr>
<tr><td></td><td></td><td>A</td><td>B</td><td>C</td></tr>
<tr><td></td><td>A</td><td>0.6</td><td>0.1</td><td>0.3</td></tr>
<tr><td>City</td><td></td><td></td><td></td><td></td></tr>
<tr><td>at Which</td><td>B</td><td>0.3</td><td>0.4</td><td>0.3</td></tr>
<tr><td>Rented</td><td></td><td></td><td></td><td></td></tr>
<tr><td></td><td>C</td><td>0.1</td><td>0.1</td><td>0.8</td></tr>
</table>

Starting at city A, simulate successive truck rentals until city C is reached for the first time. Repeat this process a total of ten times. From your results, estimate the mean number of trips until a truck first reaches city C, given that it started at city A.

A suggested approach is to form the cumulative probabilities for each row and then use values from the table of uniform random numbers in Appendix E to select successive destinations. For example, the cumulative probabilities for the first row would be 0.6, 0.7, and 1.0, for cities A, B, and C, respectively. Then, if the first random number were greater than 0.7, city C would be reached on the first trip, ending this simulation trial. If the number were between 0.6 and 0.7, the truck would go to city B, and a second random number would be used to determine the next destination, based on the cumulative probability values in the second row. This simulation trial would be concluded when city C was reached.

14.14 A congressional team has been formed to look into the progress of bills in the House of Representatives. For the past 30 months the team has been noting the location of bills on the first day of each month. Each bill can be in one of four states: in committee, on the floor of the House, rejected by the House, or passed by the House. The team found that 80 percent of bills in committee one month were still there the next month, the other 20 percent having moved on to the floor. Of those bills on the floor of the House on the first of the month, by the end of the month 30 percent were sent back to committee, 40 percent were still on the floor, 10 percent were rejected, and 20 percent were passed.

Simulate the monthly progress of two separate bills from their start in committee until they are either rejected or passed. For each bill, state whether or not it passed and how many months it was in process.

14.15   A student has several different routes to take to Ye Olde College. Each time
she is at a point where she has a choice, she makes her choice randomly,
according to the probability values shown in parentheses for each labeled
route segment in the accompanying diagram.

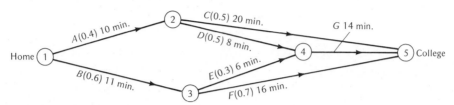

(a)   Given a table of random numbers, uniform on (0, 1), specify the
complete procedure for random selection of a route.
(b)   Simulate ten trips. From your results, estimate the average trip time.
(c)   Repeat part (b) with the following change: For each random number r_i,
substitute the complementary random number $1 - r_i$. (This is the method
of antithetic variates.)
(d)   Calculate the expected trip time from the given problem data. Compare
it with the value obtained by averaging the results of parts (b) and (c).

14.16   Suppose a company has bid on a total of N different contracts. The expected
return from contract i is R_i, and the estimated probability of getting contract i
is P_i.
(a)   What is the expected value of all contracts?
(b)   It may be quite important to know something about the distribution of
the total amount from all contracts, rather than just their expected value.
For example, we may wish to know a value D such that there is 90
percent confidence of a total amount of at least D dollars. Or, we may
wish to know the probability that the total amount lies between E and F
dollars.
      Flow chart a simple simulation model which would facilitate
obtaining such a distribution, and explain briefly how it operates.

14.17   As a numerical example of the type of situation described in Exercise 14.16,
the company has bid on the following five contracts.

Contract	1	2	3	4	5
Value ($1000s)	10	50	20	35	62
Probability of winning	0.8	0.5	0.6	0.7	0.4

(a)   Calculate the expected value of all contracts received.
(b)   For each contract, a random number is to be drawn to determine if that
contract was won. A simulation trial is completed when this is done for
each contract. Perform ten such trials and plot a cumulative probability
distribution of the value of all contracts received (after sorting the
individual totals from the ten simulation trials).
(c)   From your results, what dollar value would be exceeded at least 20
percent of the time? at least 50 percent of the time? at least 80 percent of
the time?

14.18   A hard-working cab driver has studied his varying monthly income and monthly expenditures and has arrived at the following empirical distributions.

Monthly Income ($)	Probability	Monthly Expenses ($)	Probability
1000	0.6	900	0.2
1100	0.2	1000	0.4
1200	0.15	1100	0.25
1300	0.05	1200	0.15

(a)   The cab driver now has $100 in the bank. Simulate his income and expenses over a twelve-month period. Assume that the cabbie uses credit to cover any negative balances.

(b)   How much money does the cab driver have at the end of the year?

(c)   What was the low point in his finances during the year?

14.19   An article in a statistics journal was entitled "On the Incidence of Swept Double-Headers."[4] (The term "double-header" generally refers to two back-to-back baseball games, but the term is not restricted to the sport of baseball.) A swept double-header occurs when one team wins both games. Suppose that team A is playing team B, and has, according to past performance, a record of winning a fraction f of the games it plays with team B. Assume that the games in a double-header can be considered as independent events.

(a)   Simulate, on a game-by-game basis, the results of 25 double-headers (50 games) between the two teams. Use random numbers uniform on the interval (0, 1). Clearly indicate the process by which you perform the simulation and list all random numbers and resultant outcomes for f values of 0.6, 0.7, and 0.8. Use only one set of random numbers, rather than three sets. From your results, estimate the probability of a swept double-header for each value of f.

(b)   Repeat part (a), using the method of antithetic variates. Thus, if the ith random number in part (a) was r_i, the ith random number now becomes $1 - r_i$. Again estimate the probability of a swept double-header for each value of f.

(c)   Derive a formula for the theoretical probability of a swept double-header as a function of f.

(d)   Plot a continuous curve showing the theoretical probability of a swept double-header as a function of f. On this graph, plot the results from parts (a) and (b). Finally, for each of the three values of f, calculate and plot the mean of the two values in parts (a) and (b). Comment briefly on your results.

(e)   The article pointed out that the number of double-headers swept was greater than the number split and that this difference was statistically significant. Briefly explain the reason.

[4]M. L. Goodman, "On the Incidence of Swept Double-Headers," *The American Statistician*, Vol. 23, No. 5, December 1969, pp. 15–17.

14.20 A certain piece of electronic component is subject to two types of failure, catastrophic and wearout. Catastrophic failures occur in a completely random fashion, with an expected time between failures of 100 hours. Wearout failures are normally distributed with a mean of 100 hours and a standard deviation of 10 hours. When a failure of either type occurs, the component is replaced with a new component.

(a) Develop a flow chart to show how the distribution of the time between replacements can be simulated.

(b) Starting with a new component, simulate a total of 25 failures. From the results of the simulation, estimate the expected time between replacements.

(c) From your simulation results, plot the cumulative distribution function for the time between replacements.

(d) In order to avoid (for all practical purposes) the problem of wearout failures, which result in deteriorating equipment performance when nearing the point of failure, it has been proposed that a component surviving 70 hours be replaced at that point. Using your calculations in part (b), estimate the expected time between replacements using this proposed policy.

14.21 The manager of an auto repair shop is concerned about lines of cars awaiting wheel alignment. He is interested in simulating the operation of the wheel alignment facility and has gathered data for the arrival and service time distributions for this facility. There is a single waiting line and two alignment stations (servers).

Interarrival Time (minutes)	Frequency	Service Time (minutes)	Frequency
10	8	15	5
11	18	16	10
12	30	17	15
13	20	18	45
14	19	19	25
15	5		___
	___		100
	100		

(a) Convert the distributions to cumulative probability distributions.

(b) Using a simulated sample of 15 customer arrivals, estimate the average time a car spends waiting for wheel alignment. State clearly any assumptions you may make.

(c) Estimate the mean fraction of time each server is idle.

14.22 At a small one-man service station containing a single service island with two pumps, one for regular gasoline and the other for ethyl gasoline, customers arrive randomly and service is exponentially distributed. If one customer requires ethyl gasoline and the next customer regular gasoline, or vice versa, both can be served immediately. Otherwise, the second customer cannot be served until the first car leaves. An estimated fraction f of the customers use regular gasoline.

(a) Develop, in the form of a flow chart similar to Figure 14.4, a simple simulation model for this problem. Assume the availability of both uniform and exponentially distributed random variates.

(b) Suppose that the mean customer arrival rate is 12 per hour, the mean service time is 3 minutes, and an estimated 60 percent of the customers use regular gasoline. Simulate the arrival of 20 customers, starting at time zero, using random variates from the appropriate tables. Estimate the fraction of idle time for the attendant and the mean waiting time per customer.

14.23 A balanced assembly line has an average of 5.5 minutes of work at each station. Management has been concerned because the output is far below the expected 10.9 (60/5.5) completed units per hour. Two adjacent stations suspected of being the bottleneck are selected for study. Arrival of parts at the first station follows the empirical distribution below.

Time between arrivals (minutes)	4	5	6	7
Probability	0.2	0.3	0.3	0.2

Operation time at the first station is equally likely to be 4, 5, 6, or 7 minutes. Parts leaving that station immediately move to the second station. No inventory of parts is permitted between the two stations. Operation time at the second station appears to have the distribution shown below.

Second-station operation time (minutes)	4	5	6	7
Probability	0.1	0.4	0.4	0.1

(a) Simulate the movement of eleven units through these two stations. Estimate the average hourly output from the time required to process ten parts, the elapsed time from the completion of the first part to the completion of the eleventh part. Processing of the first part serves to initialize the system.

(b) Discuss the possible reasons for the average hourly output to be appreciably less than 10.9.

(c) What might be suggested to management regarding alleviation of this bottleneck condition?

14.24 State the general concept of correlated sampling. Give at least two examples of the types of problems where the concept would be helpful, and specify how it would improve the results, as compared to the situation where correlated sampling was not used.

14.25 Describe how the method of antithetic variates is used to replicate a simulation run. What is the purpose of this technique?

14.26 Using antithetic variates, repeat the Prestige Rent-a-Car simulation of Example 14.1. For each random number r used to generate a daily demand value, substitute the complementary value $1 - r$. Since the daily demand values will now be changed, the distribution of the required daily number of rental period random numbers r_i will be quite different than for the original simulation. Nevertheless, as each rental period random number is required, use the complement of an r_i value from the original simulation. Doing this will tend to make the actual distribution of rental periods over the two simulations conform quite closely to the theoretical distribution. The first new r_i value, then, should be $1 - 0.851 = 0.149$, and so on.

(a)   Calculate the new statistics, comparable to those in Example 14.1.

(b)   Combine the statistics of both simulation runs.

(c)   Compare the statistics of the combined simulation runs and the individual runs.

14.27   In the simulation of an automatic elevator system, it is desired, for comparative purposes, to have the number of passengers boarding on the ground floor be exactly the same for each of the floors above the ground floor.

     For a four-story building, it is desired to have the destination floors of the next nine passengers equally split between floors 2, 3, and 4, but in random order. To accomplish this, use the method of selective sampling to simulate the random ordering of these three different destination floors and to make sure that each floor is called out exactly three times. [Hint: If there are n passenger destinations remaining to be selected, a random integer between 1 and n can be generated by multiplying n by a random number uniform on $(0, 1)$ and rounding up the result to the next integer value.]

14.28   A machine turns out a certain part with thickness t, normally distributed with mean M, the desired value, and standard deviation S. Parts with the value of t in the range of $M \pm 2S$ are judged acceptable; those outside this range are rejected. Acceptability is judged by measuring each part with a gage which is not perfectly accurate. The gage has a measurement error which is normally distributed with standard deviation G and mean 0. Thus, when a part is tested, there will be four possible results: The part is good and test good, and so forth.

     A little thought should convince you that the test results are independent of the value of M and dependent only on the ratio of G and S, rather than their absolute values.

(a)   Develop a simple and concise simulation model which can be used to evaluate the probability of each possible test result as a function of the ratio of G/S. Draw a flow chart for this process.

(b)   Simulate the test of 20 parts, using a G/S ratio of 1.0, and tally the result of each test. (Let both G and S equal 1.0.) Without drawing any additional random numbers, determine what the results would have been had the G/S ratio been 0.1.

(c)   Illustrate how you would present, as a function of the G/S ratio, the results of N simulation trials using this model. Show tabular headings only.

CHAPTER 15

DECISION ANALYSIS IN THE BUSINESS WORLD

It should come as no great surprise to the reader that there is quite a gap to be bridged between learning about the tools and techniques of decision analysis and actually applying them to the successful solution of real business problems. This situation is hardly peculiar to the study of decision analysis; it is a fact of life for anyone receiving an academic education, rather than learning a trade. A good education in any area represents only a foundation, and the individual attempting to apply that education in a practical manner is building a structure on that foundation. This takes both time and experience. There are really no short cuts.

In this final chapter, we will take a closer look at quantitative problem solving as it is practiced in the business world, emphasizing application rather than theory. The aim is to give a sense of direction, a feeling for some of the difficulties and pitfalls, an appreciation of the nonquantitative and human aspects, and an overview of the field at this point in time.

In the following section, which provides a brief description of some of the important aspects of the decision analysis process, an example of an implemented decision analysis study is used to illustrate the discussion of the various facets of such studies. The example is that of a financial analysis system developed for a major oil company.[1] There is no thought of presenting this as a "representative" decision analysis, since each decision analysis is different; the intent is to give some feeling for the relationship between the generalities presented and the specifics of a particular application.

---

[1]D. O. Cooper, L. B. Davidson, and W. K. Denison, "A Tool for More Effective Financial Analysis," *Interfaces*, Vol. 5, No. 2, Pt. 2, February 1975, pp. 91–103.

15.1   THE DECISION ANALYSIS PROCESS

The initiation of a decision analysis study of any system obviously cannot occur until it is recognized either that a problem exists or that there may be a "better" way to operate that system. In the first case, it may become apparent that costs are getting out of hand, or inventories are piling up at warehouses, or bottlenecks are occurring, or that there are other visible manifestations of difficulties. In the second case, those who run the system may well be quite satisfied with its operation or at least content to live with a system which has "done the job" for an appreciable period of time. But the competition may be doing a significantly more effective job, or there is a possible operational approach which has the potential for significant improvement. Regardless of the way in which the need for a decision analysis study may be indicated, it is vitally important that the key decision makers involved recognize that there is a problem. Without this recognition, a study is almost certainly doomed to failure. Experience has also shown that the likelihood of successful implementation depends strongly on management's understanding of the capabilities and limitations of decision analysis, as well as on management's willingness to participate actively in the study.

The aforementioned oil company spends hundreds of millions of dollars annually in capital investments, primarily in the areas of petroleum exploration and production. Long-range corporate planning for capital programs is obviously of vital importance. However, so much time was required with computational procedures, including numerous uncoordinated computer programs and substantial hand computations, that it was only possible to generate one "most likely" five-year plan each year. Yet it was felt that several such plans were needed in order to properly analyze future corporate strategies. In addition, about 100 major investment opportunities are recommended each year, most of them in the multi-million dollar category, and management was dissatisfied with slow, costly, and often inconsistent and confusing analyses of investment proposals. Rather than put together one computer program for overall long-range planning and another for investment analysis, the decision was made to develop a generalized financial analysis system that would facilitate rapid consolidation of long-term program projections, permit effective investment analysis, and be readily adaptable to changes.

Once a problem area has been recognized and a knowledgeable management has committed itself to support a decision analysis study, the decision analysts, whether they be within or outside the organization, must develop a good understanding of the system under study, as it currently exists. With such knowledge, they will be able to see how and why the system has evolved into its present state. They will be able to appreciate its strengths, as well as its weaknesses, and the extent of personal involvement of the individuals operating and managing the system. At this point, initiation of a team effort can commence. The project has little hope of success unless there is major participation by the using organizations. The study requires their inputs, their criticisms, and their mental and physical involvement throughout its course. They are the consumers, and if they are not involved in the design of the product (the solution to be implemented), they are almost certain not to buy (accept) it. Even an excellent solution to a problem cannot be successfully implemented if the users are opposed to acceptance of the solution or it is forced upon them by higher management. Not only does the team approach get the using organizations involved in what they must feel is "their" project, but it helps to keep the decision analysis team on the path to successful implementation, avoiding the temptation to develop overly sophisticated models or to pursue intriguing, but nonproductive, approaches.

The oil company's Management Science Department conducted a thorough study of all the different analyses that were being performed. Then, development of what it called the Plan Analysis and Modeling System (PAMS) was begun, with the analysts working closely with those who would be the users of this system. Throughout all aspects of the PAMS development, the project was directed toward providing an operational system that would be completely user-oriented.

When the study team has been formed and has reached agreement on the scope of the problem to be attacked, the objectives of the project should then be defined as clearly as possible. These objectives will almost always involve economic and noneconomic considerations. For example, in the design of a large-scale computerized inventory control system, one objective would undoubtedly be to minimize the total operational system cost, including such factors as administrative, handling, and performance monitoring costs, plus the cost of money tied up in inventory. Nonmonetary objectives might be to have the control system design as flexible as possible, in order to facilitate possible system changes and future expansion, and to have the system developed in-house, if at all possible, rather than by an outside agency.

Once a consensus has been reached on objectives, appropriate performance measures must be selected so that it will be possible to evaluate the extent to which the objectives have been met. Generally, the most-used economic performance measure is cost or profit, or a benefit/cost ratio. But even here, care must be exercised. If expenditures and/or receipts occur over a period of months or years, the time value of money should be taken into account, as by converting all amounts to present value at an appropriate interest rate, or perhaps a range of rates, depending on the uncertainties involved. Noneconomic performance measures may be much more difficult to quantify. The flexibility desired for the aforementioned computerized inventory control system may have to be judged by the degree of modularity of the computer programs developed and the ease with which modules can be modified, added, or removed.

In the development of PAMS, the primary objective was to produce a financial analysis system which would lead to better decisions and higher expected profits. From this very general objective, the following specifics were formulated: the system must be straightforward and natural to apply, by virtue of being highly user-oriented; the new things to be learned were to be minimized; and the computer must do as much of the work as possible, freeing the user from requirements to manipulate the input data before submitting the problem for analysis. PAMS also had to be very flexible, able to handle a number of different types of analyses, and capable of being readily modified and expanded. Measures of effectiveness were related to such factors as the length of time required for a new user to use the system effectively (get meaningful results), the expected number of computer runs before a new model was "debugged," and the completeness, understandability, and helpfulness of the diagnostic error messages provided.

Actual development of the mathematical model is again a user-oriented approach. While the analysts will be primarily responsible for determining the mathematical relationships between the various problem factors, with the users' concurrence, many of the system constraints will tend to be supplied by the users. (However, the analysis should consider solutions with modified constraints, since it may be worthwhile to pay to remove or decrease certain constraints where possible if the incremental cost of doing this is less than the improvement in the payoff.) During the model development process, there must be a continual critical examination and challenge of all facets of the model. The model assumptions, both explicit and implicit, must be clearly spelled out for all to see, and user agreement as to their applicability obtained. Input data requirements need to be established, in conjunction with a clear perception of the form and availability of such data currently. If the desired data are either unavailable or are in the wrong form, either too aggregated or not aggregated enough, it will be necessary to consider revising the current data collection system. If this does not appear to be possible or is not economically feasible, then the model will have to be revised. There is an interdependence between model development and data gathering which must be taken into consideration in any practical problem; the two cannot be handled independently. The model should have the capability of considering all reasonable alternatives, and provisions for comprehensive sensitivity analyses are most important if the model is to provide a meaningful comparison of the feasible alternatives.

As PAMS evolved, specifications for the system were worked out with the users in considerable detail. A number of potential applications were set up and pretested, before any programming was done, in order to insure that PAMS would meet the company's needs. Specific design weaknesses were uncovered and corrected at this early stage. Program routines were developed to facilitate data filing and retrieval, to provide hand-tailored tabular and graphical presentations, to incorporate frequently used computational routines, such as different depreciation methods, and to minimize debugging problems, by providing diagnostics pinpointing program or data errors. Extensive capabilities to perform sensitivity analyses were built into the system.

The model should undergo extensive testing to make sure that it operates as intended. Numerous test cases should be run and the reasonableness of the solutions verified. Depending on the particular problem, as well as on the attitudes and needs of the users, it may be desirable to run the new system in parallel with the existing system for some time (several weeks or months) in order to evaluate how well it would have performed had it been implemented. This may not be necessary if enough data exists so that the new system can be applied, after the fact, to determine how it would have performed if it had been available in the past.

After the testing phase has been completed satisfactorily, then implementation can begin. The implementation phase is the most important part of the project; if it is not successful, the entire project has become an exercise in futility. One of the biggest mistakes that can be made by the decision analysts is to assume that their work is completed when the solution and/or procedure is turned over to the users. The decision analysis team must be committed from the beginning to work toward effective implementation, generally geared to the lowest level of sophistication of the users. Thus, a system requiring complicated measurements, manual calculations, and/or complex charts in a factory environment is not likely to survive in that form, if it survives at all.

By its very nature, successful implementation tends to be an evolutionary process. There always seems to be at least one particular set of conditions that were either overlooked or which never occurred before, requiring some type of adjustment to the system. On the other hand, operation of the system frequently leads to more effective procedures which can often be incorporated at little or no additional cost. Thus, the process of implementation is a continuing one. The implemented system must be monitored, to some degree, over its entire life, to make sure that it is working as it was designed to work, doing the job it was intended to do, and still serving the need for which it was developed. After all, needs do change over time, and a successful implementation may require substantial modifications over a period of time.

In the implementation of PAMS, careful attention was given to both communications and education. Management personnel were well informed about the capabilities of PAMS, and a comprehensive and readable User's Manual was developed. Workshops were given throughout the company, with each attendee bringing his own application problem. He then learned PAMS by planning, preparing, and running his own model on the computer. In addition, the Management Science Department is on call for special problems or emergency help. As a result of PAMS' extensive capabilities and ease of use, it has had a pervasive influence upon the company's financial analyses. By 1974, at least 15 separate groups were using PAMS throughout the oil company. Many domestic and all international oil exploration and production ventures are analyzed using the system. Successful implementation of PAMS has brought verified savings of millions of dollars through more informed decision making based on timely and comprehensive decision analyses. Additional benefits have accrued as the system has led to more effective use of management science techniques, such as risk analysis, decision tree analysis, and sensitivity analysis, throughout the company.

15.2   DECISION ANALYSIS IN THE DIFFERENT ECONOMIC SECTORS

Defense Sector

As brought out in Chapter 1, decision analysis got its start in what we now term the defense sector. Today, there are decision analysis groups within all branches of the Armed Forces, and there are also a number of civilian agencies which work closely with the military in such studies. Decision analysis, frequently called weapons systems analysis when appropriate, is a government requirement in many areas, and it is usually highly structured and heavily computer-oriented. Objectives and measures of effectiveness tend to be quite straightforward, at least in general terms. For example, the objective might be to develop a logistics system to fully integrate the Aardvark air-to-ground missile into the Whippet tactical bomber system, with the measure of effectiveness related to the availability of fully operable missiles under given usage patterns and the associated logistics costs. The development of many of the required mathematical models also tends to be well structured (although by no means routine), since similar analyses have generally been performed in the past for other systems. Data gathering can be a real problem, for many reasons. It may involve operations in unfamiliar areas, educated guesses as to enemy capabilities (especially for future time periods), and assumptions (such as the degree of target damage or the probability of putting a target out of action) based on considerable extrapolation from existing data. In some projects, such as logistics systems, the primary orientation is toward efficient utilization. In other studies, such as those involving wartime operations, implementation cannot occur unless a wartime situation develops. Because of the classified nature of most of the work, relatively little in the way of defense sector decision analysis has been published in the open literature. To summarize, we can say that decision analysis in the defense sector is widely accepted, highly structured, and very specialized. From an overall standpoint, "defense preparedness" is the major consideration; cost minimization, while very important, is not the primary goal.

Private Sector

In the world of business and industry, there has been and continues to be a tremendous diversity in the applications, or attempted applications, of decision analysis. These range all the way from the use of basic optimal lot size models to the simulation of complex, large-scale, production and operating systems. There is also a great difference in the results achieved, all the way from vitally important successes (as illustrated by some of the examples cited in earlier chapter sections on practical applications) to dismal failures, usually studies where the users were not thoroughly involved. The most successful studies have generally been in those companies where management was knowledgeable about decision analysis, a team approach was employed throughout the study, and the decision analysts were fully committed to successful implementation. For a number of reasons, however, some of which will be discussed in the following section, decision analysis has not achieved the high degree of acceptability and usage in the private sector which were predicted for it ten years or so ago by professionals in the field. Nevertheless, decision analysis is making a definite impact on the operations of a number of companies, notably large companies with their own internal decision analysis group(s). In the private sector, then, we can characterize decision analysis as an approach which is far from pervasive, differs markedly in its level of sophistication, and is judged almost entirely upon its financial impact.

Public Sector

Decision analysis in the public sector, as compared to either the defense or the private sector, is "a whole new ballgame." Organizational authority structure is generally much less well defined, and there are conflicting social, political, and organizational pressures. Considerations of cost effectiveness, or benefit-to-cost ratios, are often outweighed by noneconomic considerations, although the era of tighter budgets is changing this to a marked extent in some locales. In the problem recognition phase, it is frequently difficult even to get agreement as to the nature of the problem, much less as to how it should be tackled. The team approach is still very important, but it may suffer from the lack of clearcut leadership, half-hearted user participation and commitment, and too many conflicting points of view. Development of quantitative models may well be a continuing battle between the decision analysts and those who feel that social and political factors are not amenable to quantification. Obtaining substantial agreement upon basic objectives may be extremely difficult. Prior to obtaining the results of the decision analysis, groups affected by it may have already taken strong positions favoring a particular solution. In addition, any proposed solution may have to be greatly modified to satisfy the various organizations involved, and there are frequently strong pressures to come up with solutions in a relatively short time period. Since laymen often actively participate in the decisions and are frequently suspicious of "high-powered" analyses, the difficulties are further compounded. Thus, in the public sector, decision analysis must be applied to organizations which are frequently not well structured, where meaningful measures of effectiveness are often very difficult to quantify, and where social, political, and organizational considerations frequently dominate economic factors. In spite of all these difficulties, there have been some notably successful studies. Some of these are mentioned in Chapters 10 and 14, in particular, and the Drake, Keeney, and Morse book, *Analysis of Public Systems*, referenced at the end of this chapter, also has some good examples.

15.3   SOME REFLECTIONS ON DECISION ANALYSIS AND ITS FUTURE PROSPECTS

A few short years ago, it was strongly suggested that decision analysis models, easily accessible through time-sharing computer terminals, would soon be of major importance at the highest executive levels. By the late 1970s, however, this type of achievement was still very much in the minority. Although many effective and important decision analysis studies have been performed over the years, there is a strong feeling, among both professionals in the field and business executives, that decision analysis has not made the contribution to business that it could have. One of the major reasons for this appears to be the communications gap between decision analysts and management. Too often, decision analysts have been guilty of such things as overuse of technical jargon in both oral and written communication, use of oversimplified or unwarranted assumptions because they really did not understand the problem, and failure to understand or even to really care about the implementation phase. Analysts with a particular expertise, such as linear programming or simulation, have also been known to make strenuous efforts to make the problem fit the model, instead of vice versa, and modelers have often developed overly sophisticated models, extending them far beyond the point of diminishing returns. For their part, managers have sometimes had unrealistic expectations as to what decision analysis could do, and, once disappointed, have refused to have anything further to do with it. Some managers, particularly those in a factory environment, seem to feel that no one without extensive experience in that particular environment can possibly understand their problems, and they may also be quite suspicious of anyone with a high degree of technical training.

As an example of the usage of decision analysis, a relatively recent and carefully conducted survey in the manufacturing area, published by Gaither in 1975,[2] indicated that 133 out of 275 manufacturing firms used one or more operations research techniques. More than half used PERT, CPM, linear programming, exponential smoothing and regression analysis, and computer simulation, in that order. Almost 30 percent used queueing theory.

The future holds many challenges for decision analysis, especially with regard to ill-structured problems. In this respect, the greatest challenge is undoubtedly in the public sector, where very large amounts of money are being spent (and misspent) at almost every level of government. Decision analysts in this area need not only the technical skills but also a good measure of "savvy" when it comes to people, politics, and meaningful compromise solutions. The author holds no crystal ball, but does believe that decision analysis must and will become more oriented toward implementation—less technical and more practical. This will require a more conscious and dedicated effort toward truly meaningful user involvement and the team approach. Management can be expected to become more knowledgeable about the field of decision analysis, and decision analysts must come down to earth and become much more user-oriented, with successful implementation and cost effectiveness as their primary goals. If these things do happen, decision analysis, which is certainly needed in many areas, has a bright future indeed.

For discussions in more depth, some of them in lighter vein, the interested reader is directed to the following references.

[2]Norman Gaither, "The Adoption of Operations Research Techniques by Manufacturing Organizations," *Decision Sciences*, Vol. 6, No. 4, October 1975, pp. 797–813.

SELECTED REFERENCES

Arnoff, E. Leonard, "Successful Models I Have Known," *Decision Sciences*, Vol. 2, No. 2, April 1971, pp. 141–148.

Drake, A. W., R. L. Keeney, and P. M. Morse (editors), *Analysis of Public Systems*, M. I. T. Press, Cambridge, Mass., 1972.

Grayson, C. Jackson, Jr., "Management Science and Business Practice," *Harvard Business Review*, July–August 1973, pp. 41–48.

Magee, John F., "Progress in the Management Sciences," *Interfaces*, Vol. 3, No. 2, February 1973, pp. 35–41.

Raitt, Robert A., "Must We Revolutionize Our Methodology?," *Interfaces*, Vol. 4, No. 2, February 1974, pp. 1–9.

Shycon, Harvey L., "Perspectives on MS Applications," *Interfaces*, Vol. 6, No. 1, November 1975, pp. 64–66.

Turban, Efraim, and N. Paul Loomba (editors), *Readings in Management Science*, Business Publications, Inc., Dallas, Texas, 1976, Chapter 12 (Implementation) and Chapter 13 (The Future of OR/MS).

Woolsey, Robert E. D., "O Tempora, O Mores, O C. Jackson Grayson, Jr.," *Interfaces*, Vol. 4, No. 3, May 1974, pp. 76–78.

———, "The Measure of M.S./O.R. Applications or Let's Hear It for the Bean Counters," *Interfaces*, Vol. 5, No. 2, February 1975, pp. 74–78.

Appendices

Appendix A

Cumulative Standardized Normal Distribution Function

z	.00	.01	.02	.03	.04	.05	.06	.07	.08	.09
−.0	.5000	.4960	.4920	.4880	.4840	.4801	.4761	.4721	.4681	.4641
−.1	.4602	.4562	.4522	.4483	.4443	.4404	.4364	.4325	.4286	.4247
−.2	.4207	.4168	.4129	.4090	.4052	.4013	.3974	.3936	.3897	.3859
−.3	.3821	.3783	.3745	.3707	.3669	.3632	.3594	.3557	.3520	.3483
−.4	.3446	.3409	.3372	.3336	.3300	.3264	.3228	.3192	.3156	.3121
−.5	.3085	.3050	.3015	.2981	.2946	.2912	.2877	.2843	.2810	.2776
−.6	.2743	.2709	.2676	.2643	.2611	.2578	.2546	.2514	.2483	.2451
−.7	.2420	.2389	.2358	.2327	.2297	.2266	.2236	.2206	.2177	.2148
−.8	.2119	.2090	.2061	.2033	.2005	.1977	.1949	.1922	.1894	.1867
−.9	.1841	.1814	.1788	.1762	.1736	.1711	.1685	.1660	.1635	.1611
−1.0	.1587	.1562	.1539	.1515	.1492	.1469	.1446	.1423	.1401	.1379
−1.1	.1357	.1335	.1314	.1292	.1271	.1251	.1230	.1210	.1190	.1170
−1.2	.1151	.1131	.1112	.1093	.1075	.1056	.1038	.1020	.1003	.09853
−1.3	.09680	.09510	.09342	.09176	.09012	.08851	.08691	.08534	.08379	.08226
−1.4	.08076	.07927	.07780	.07636	.07493	.07353	.07215	.07078	.06944	.06811
−1.5	.06681	.06552	.06426	.06301	.06178	.06057	.05938	.05821	.05705	.05592
−1.6	.05480	.05370	.05262	.05155	.05050	.04947	.04846	.04746	.04648	.04551
−1.7	.04457	.04363	.04272	.04182	.04093	.04006	.03920	.03836	.03754	.03673
−1.8	.03593	.03515	.03438	.03362	.03288	.03216	.03144	.03074	.03005	.02938
−1.9	.02872	.02807	.02743	.02680	.02619	.02559	.02500	.02442	.02385	.02330
−2.0	.02275	.02222	.02169	.02118	.02068	.02018	.01970	.01923	.01876	.01831
−2.1	.01786	.01743	.01700	.01659	.01618	.01578	.01539	.01500	.01463	.01426
−2.2	.01390	.01355	.01321	.01287	.01255	.01222	.01191	.01160	.01130	.01101
−2.3	.01072	.01044	.01017	$.0^2 9903$	$.0^2 9642$	$.0^2 9387$	$.0^2 9137$	$.0^2 8894$	$.0^2 8656$	$.0^2 8424$
−2.4	$.0^2 8198$	$.0^2 7976$	$.0^2 7760$	$.0^2 7549$	$.0^2 7344$	$.0^2 7143$	$.0^2 6947$	$.0^2 6756$	$.0^2 6569$	$.0^2 6387$
−2.5	$.0^2 6210$	$.0^2 6037$	$.0^2 5868$	$.0^2 5703$	$.0^2 5543$	$.0^2 5386$	$.0^2 5234$	$.0^2 5085$	$.0^2 4940$	$.0^2 4799$
−2.6	$.0^2 4661$	$.0^2 4527$	$.0^2 4396$	$.0^2 4269$	$.0^2 4145$	$.0^2 4025$	$.0^2 3907$	$.0^2 3793$	$.0^2 3681$	$.0^2 3573$
−2.7	$.0^2 3467$	$.0^2 3364$	$.0^2 3264$	$.0^2 3167$	$.0^2 3072$	$.0^2 2980$	$.0^2 2890$	$.0^2 2803$	$.0^2 2718$	$.0^2 2635$
−2.8	$.0^2 2555$	$.0^2 2477$	$.0^2 2401$	$.0^2 2327$	$.0^2 2256$	$.0^2 2186$	$.0^2 2118$	$.0^2 2052$	$.0^2 1988$	$.0^2 1926$
−2.9	$.0^2 1866$	$.0^2 1807$	$.0^2 1750$	$.0^2 1695$	$.0^2 1641$	$.0^2 1589$	$.0^2 1538$	$.0^2 1489$	$.0^2 1441$	$.0^2 1395$
−3.0	$.0^2 1350$	$.0^2 1306$	$.0^2 1264$	$.0^2 1223$	$.0^2 1183$	$.0^2 1144$	$.0^2 1107$	$.0^2 1070$	$.0^2 1035$	$.0^2 1001$

The notation $.0^2$ signifies .00. Example: $.0^2 1350$ is .001350.

Appendix A

Cumulative Standardized Normal Distribution Function

z	.00	.01	.02	.03	.04	.05	.06	.07	.08	.09
.0	.5000	.5040	.5080	.5120	.5160	.5199	.5239	.5279	.5319	.5359
.1	.5398	.5438	.5478	.5517	.5557	.5596	.5636	.5675	.5714	.5753
.2	.5793	.5832	.5871	.5910	.5948	.5987	.6026	.6064	.6103	.6141
.3	.6179	.6217	.6255	.6293	.6331	.6368	.6406	.6443	.6480	.6517
.4	.6554	.6591	.6628	.6664	.6700	.6736	.6772	.6808	.6844	.6879
.5	.6915	.6950	.6985	.7019	.7054	.7088	.7123	.7157	.7190	.7224
.6	.7257	.7291	.7324	.7357	.7389	.7422	.7454	.7486	.7517	.7549
.7	.7580	.7611	.7642	.7673	.7703	.7734	.7764	.7794	.7823	.7852
.8	.7881	.7910	.7939	.7967	.7995	.8023	.8051	.8078	.8106	.8133
.9	.8159	.8186	.8212	.8238	.8264	.8289	.8315	.8340	.8365	.8389
1.0	.8413	.8438	.8461	.8485	.8508	.8531	.8554	.8577	.8599	.8621
1.1	.8643	.8665	.8686	.8708	.8729	.8749	.8770	.8790	.8810	.8830
1.2	.8849	.8869	.8888	.8907	.8925	.8944	.8962	.8980	.8997	.90147
1.3	.90320	.90490	.90658	.90824	.90988	.91149	.91309	.91466	.91621	.91774
1.4	.91924	.92073	.92220	.92364	.92507	.92647	.92785	.92922	.93056	.93189
1.5	.93319	.93448	.93574	.93699	.93822	.93943	.94062	.94179	.94295	.94408
1.6	.94520	.94630	.94738	.94845	.94950	.95053	.95154	.95254	.95352	.95449
1.7	.95543	.95637	.95728	.95818	.95907	.95994	.96080	.96164	.96246	.96327
1.8	.96407	.96485	.96562	.96638	.96712	.96784	.96856	.96926	.96995	.97062
1.9	.97128	.97193	.97257	.97320	.97381	.97441	.97500	.97558	.97615	.97670
2.0	.97725	.97778	.97831	.97882	.97932	.97982	.98030	.98077	.98124	.98169
2.1	.98214	.98257	.98300	.98341	.98382	.98422	.98461	.98500	.98537	.98574
2.2	.98610	.98645	.98679	.98713	.98745	.98778	.98809	.98840	.98870	.98899
2.3	.98928	.98956	.98983	$.9^2$0097	$.9^2$0358	$.9^2$0613	$.9^2$0863	$.9^2$1106	$.9^2$1344	$.9^2$1576
2.4	$.9^2$1802	$.9^2$2024	$.9^2$2240	$.9^2$2451	$.9^2$2656	$.9^2$2857	$.9^2$3053	$.9^2$3244	$.9^2$3431	$.9^2$3613
2.5	$.9^2$3790	$.9^2$3963	$.9^2$4132	$.9^2$4297	$.9^2$4457	$.9^2$4614	$.9^2$4766	$.9^2$4915	$.9^2$5060	$.9^2$5201
2.6	$.9^2$5339	$.9^2$5473	$.9^2$5604	$.9^2$5731	$.9^2$5855	$.9^2$5975	$.9^2$6093	$.9^2$6207	$.9^2$6319	$.9^2$6427
2.7	$.9^2$6533	$.9^2$6636	$.9^2$6736	$.9^2$6833	$.9^2$6928	$.9^2$7020	$.9^2$7110	$.9^2$7197	$.9^2$7282	$.9^2$7365
2.8	$.9^2$7445	$.9^2$7523	$.9^2$7599	$.9^2$7673	$.9^2$7744	$.9^2$7814	$.9^2$7882	$.9^2$7948	$.9^2$8012	$.9^2$8074
2.9	$.9^2$8134	$.9^2$8193	$.9^2$8250	$.9^2$8305	$.9^2$8359	$.9^2$8411	$.9^2$8462	$.9^2$8511	$.9^2$8559	$.9^2$8605
3.0	$.9^2$8650	$.9^2$8694	$.9^2$8736	$.9^2$8777	$.9^2$8817	$.9^2$8856	$.9^2$8893	$.9^2$8930	$.9^2$8965	$.9^2$8999

The notation $.9^2$ signifies .99. Example: $.9^2$8650 is .998650.

Appendix B
Unit Normal Linear Loss Integral N(D)

D	.00	.01	.02	.03	.04	.05	.06	.07	.08	.09
.0	.3989	.3940	.3890	.3841	.3793	.3744	.3697	.3649	.3602	.3556
.1	.3509	.3464	.3418	.3373	.3328	.3284	.3240	.3197	.3154	.3111
.2	.3069	.3027	.2986	.2944	.2904	.2863	.2824	.2784	.2745	.2706
.3	.2668	.2630	.2592	.2555	.2518	.2481	.2445	.2409	.2374	.2339
.4	.2304	.2270	.2236	.2203	.2169	.2137	.2104	.2072	.2040	.2009
.5	.1978	.1947	.1917	.1887	.1857	.1828	.1799	.1771	.1742	.1714
.6	.1687	.1659	.1633	.1606	.1580	.1554	.1528	.1503	.1478	.1453
.7	.1429	.1405	.1381	.1358	.1334	.1312	.1289	.1267	.1245	.1223
.8	.1202	.1181	.1160	.1140	.1120	.1100	.1080	.1061	.1042	.1023
.9	.1004	.09860	.09680	.09503	.09328	.09156	.08986	.08819	.08654	.08491
1.0	.08332	.08174	.08019	.07866	.07716	.07568	.07422	.07279	.07138	.06999
1.1	.06862	.06727	.06595	.06465	.06336	.06210	.06086	.05964	.05844	.05726
1.2	.05610	.05496	.05384	.05274	.05165	.05059	.04954	.04851	.04750	.04650
1.3	.04553	.04457	.04363	.04270	.04179	.04090	.04002	.03916	.03831	.03748
1.4	.03667	.03587	.03508	.03431	.03356	.03281	.03208	.03137	.03067	.02998
1.5	.02931	.02865	.02800	.02736	.02674	.02612	.02552	.02494	.02436	.02380
1.6	.02324	.02270	.02217	.02165	.02114	.02064	.02015	.01967	.01920	.01874
1.7	.01829	.01785	.01742	.01699	.01658	.01617	.01578	.01539	.01501	.01464
1.8	.01428	.01392	.01357	.01323	.01290	.01257	.01226	.01195	.01164	.01134
1.9	.01105	.01077	.01049	.01022	$.0^2 9957$	$.0^2 9698$	$.0^2 9445$	$.0^2 9198$	$.0^2 8957$	$.0^2 8721$
2.0	$.0^2 8491$	$.0^2 8266$	$.0^2 8046$	$.0^2 7832$	$.0^2 7623$	$.0^2 7418$	$.0^2 7219$	$.0^2 7024$	$.0^2 6835$	$.0^2 6649$
2.1	$.0^2 6468$	$.0^2 6292$	$.0^2 6120$	$.0^2 5952$	$.0^2 5788$	$.0^2 5628$	$.0^2 5472$	$.0^2 5320$	$.0^2 5172$	$.0^2 5028$
2.2	$.0^2 4887$	$.0^2 4750$	$.0^2 4616$	$.0^2 4486$	$.0^2 4358$	$.0^2 4235$	$.0^2 4114$	$.0^2 3996$	$.0^2 3882$	$.0^2 3770$
2.3	$.0^2 3662$	$.0^2 3556$	$.0^2 3453$	$.0^2 3352$	$.0^2 3255$	$.0^2 3159$	$.0^2 3067$	$.0^2 2977$	$.0^2 2889$	$.0^2 2804$
2.4	$.0^2 2720$	$.0^2 2640$	$.0^2 2561$	$.0^2 2484$	$.0^2 2410$	$.0^2 2337$	$.0^2 2267$	$.0^2 2199$	$.0^2 2132$	$.0^2 2067$

The notation $.0^2$ signifies .00. Example: $.0^2 1350$ is .001350.

These Tables of "Unit Normal Loss Function" appear in *Introduction to Statistics for Business Decisions* by Robert Schlaifer, published by McGraw-Hill Book Company, Inc., 1961. They are reproduced here by specific permission of the copyright holder, The President and Fellows of Harvard College.

Appendix B
Unit Normal Linear Loss Integral N(D)

D	.00	.01	.02	.03	.04	.05	.06	.07	.08	.09
2.5	$.0^{2}2004$	$.0^{2}1943$	$.0^{2}1883$	$.0^{2}1826$	$.0^{2}1769$	$.0^{2}1715$	$.0^{2}1662$	$.0^{2}1610$	$.0^{2}1560$	$.0^{2}1511$
2.6	$.0^{2}1464$	$.0^{2}1418$	$.0^{2}1373$	$.0^{2}1330$	$.0^{2}1288$	$.0^{2}1247$	$.0^{2}1207$	$.0^{2}1169$	$.0^{2}1132$	$.0^{2}1095$
2.7	$.0^{2}1060$	$.0^{2}1026$	$.0^{3}9928$	$.0^{3}9607$	$.0^{3}9295$	$.0^{3}8992$	$.0^{3}8699$	$.0^{3}8414$	$.0^{3}8138$	$.0^{3}7870$
2.8	$.0^{3}7611$	$.0^{3}7359$	$.0^{3}7115$	$.0^{3}6879$	$.0^{3}6650$	$.0^{3}6428$	$.0^{3}6213$	$.0^{3}6004$	$.0^{3}5802$	$.0^{3}5606$
2.9	$.0^{3}5417$	$.0^{3}5233$	$.0^{3}5055$	$.0^{3}4883$	$.0^{3}4716$	$.0^{3}4555$	$.0^{3}4398$	$.0^{3}4247$	$.0^{3}4101$	$.0^{3}3959$
3.0	$.0^{3}3822$	$.0^{3}3689$	$.0^{3}3560$	$.0^{3}3436$	$.0^{3}3316$	$.0^{3}3199$	$.0^{3}3087$	$.0^{3}2978$	$.0^{3}2873$	$.0^{3}2771$
3.1	$.0^{3}2673$	$.0^{3}2577$	$.0^{3}2485$	$.0^{3}2396$	$.0^{3}2311$	$.0^{3}2227$	$.0^{3}2147$	$.0^{3}2070$	$.0^{3}1995$	$.0^{3}1922$
3.2	$.0^{3}1852$	$.0^{3}1785$	$.0^{3}1720$	$.0^{3}1657$	$.0^{3}1596$	$.0^{3}1537$	$.0^{3}1480$	$.0^{3}1426$	$.0^{3}1373$	$.0^{3}1322$
3.3	$.0^{3}1273$	$.0^{3}1225$	$.0^{3}1179$	$.0^{3}1135$	$.0^{3}1093$	$.0^{3}1051$	$.0^{3}1012$	$.0^{4}9734$	$.0^{4}9365$	$.0^{4}9009$
3.4	$.0^{4}8666$	$.0^{4}8335$	$.0^{4}8016$	$.0^{4}7709$	$.0^{4}7413$	$.0^{4}7127$	$.0^{4}6852$	$.0^{4}6587$	$.0^{4}6331$	$.0^{4}6085$
3.5	$.0^{4}5848$	$.0^{4}5620$	$.0^{4}5400$	$.0^{4}5188$	$.0^{4}4984$	$.0^{4}4788$	$.0^{4}4599$	$.0^{4}4417$	$.0^{4}4242$	$.0^{4}4073$
3.6	$.0^{4}3911$	$.0^{4}3755$	$.0^{4}3605$	$.0^{4}3460$	$.0^{4}3321$	$.0^{4}3188$	$.0^{4}3059$	$.0^{4}2935$	$.0^{4}2816$	$.0^{4}2702$
3.7	$.0^{4}2592$	$.0^{4}2486$	$.0^{4}2385$	$.0^{4}2287$	$.0^{4}2193$	$.0^{4}2103$	$.0^{4}2016$	$.0^{4}1933$	$.0^{4}1853$	$.0^{4}1776$
3.8	$.0^{4}1702$	$.0^{4}1632$	$.0^{4}1563$	$.0^{4}1498$	$.0^{4}1435$	$.0^{4}1375$	$.0^{4}1317$	$.0^{4}1262$	$.0^{4}1208$	$.0^{4}1157$
3.9	$.0^{4}1108$	$.0^{4}1061$	$.0^{4}1016$	$.0^{5}9723$	$.0^{5}9307$	$.0^{5}8908$	$.0^{5}8525$	$.0^{5}8158$	$.0^{5}7806$	$.0^{5}7469$
4.0	$.0^{5}7145$	$.0^{5}6835$	$.0^{5}6538$	$.0^{5}6253$	$.0^{5}5980$	$.0^{5}5718$	$.0^{5}5468$	$.0^{5}5227$	$.0^{5}4997$	$.0^{5}4777$
4.1	$.0^{5}4566$	$.0^{5}4364$	$.0^{5}4170$	$.0^{5}3985$	$.0^{5}3807$	$.0^{5}3637$	$.0^{5}3475$	$.0^{5}3319$	$.0^{5}3170$	$.0^{5}3027$
4.2	$.0^{5}2891$	$.0^{5}2760$	$.0^{5}2635$	$.0^{5}2516$	$.0^{5}2402$	$.0^{5}2292$	$.0^{5}2188$	$.0^{5}2088$	$.0^{5}1992$	$.0^{5}1901$
4.3	$.0^{5}1814$	$.0^{5}1730$	$.0^{5}1650$	$.0^{5}1574$	$.0^{5}1501$	$.0^{5}1431$	$.0^{5}1365$	$.0^{5}1301$	$.0^{5}1241$	$.0^{5}1183$
4.4	$.0^{5}1127$	$.0^{5}1074$	$.0^{5}1024$	$.0^{6}9756$	$.0^{6}9296$	$.0^{6}8857$	$.0^{6}8437$	$.0^{6}8037$	$.0^{6}7655$	$.0^{6}7290$
4.5	$.0^{6}6942$	$.0^{6}6610$	$.0^{6}6294$	$.0^{6}5992$	$.0^{6}5704$	$.0^{6}5429$	$.0^{6}5167$	$.0^{6}4917$	$.0^{6}4679$	$.0^{6}4452$
4.6	$.0^{6}4236$	$.0^{6}4029$	$.0^{6}3833$	$.0^{6}3645$	$.0^{6}3467$	$.0^{6}3297$	$.0^{6}3135$	$.0^{6}2981$	$.0^{6}2834$	$.0^{6}2694$
4.7	$.0^{6}2560$	$.0^{6}2433$	$.0^{6}2313$	$.0^{6}2197$	$.0^{6}2088$	$.0^{6}1984$	$.0^{6}1884$	$.0^{6}1790$	$.0^{6}1700$	$.0^{6}1615$
4.8	$.0^{6}1533$	$.0^{6}1456$	$.0^{6}1382$	$.0^{6}1312$	$.0^{6}1246$	$.0^{6}1182$	$.0^{6}1122$	$.0^{6}1065$	$.0^{6}1011$	$.0^{7}9588$
4.9	$.0^{7}9096$	$.0^{7}8629$	$.0^{7}8185$	$.0^{7}7763$	$.0^{7}7362$	$.0^{7}6982$	$.0^{7}6620$	$.0^{7}6276$	$.0^{7}5950$	$.0^{7}5640$

The notation $.0^{n}$ signifies n zeroes following the decimal point. Examples: $.0^{3}3822$ is $.0003822$. $.0^{5}5468$ is $.000005468$.

Appendix C
Cumulative Binomial Distribution
$$P(R \geq r|n,p)$$
$$n = 1$$

p	01	02	03	04	05	06	07	08	09	10
r 1	0100	0200	0300	0400	0500	0600	0700	0800	0900	1000
p	11	12	13	14	15	16	17	18	19	20
r 1	1100	1200	1300	1400	1500	1600	1700	1800	1900	2000
p	21	22	23	24	25	26	27	28	29	30
r 1	2100	2200	2300	2400	2500	2600	2700	2800	2900	3000
p	31	32	33	34	35	36	37	38	39	40
r 1	3100	3200	3300	3400	3500	3600	3700	3800	3900	4000
p	41	42	43	44	45	46	47	48	49	50
r 1	4100	4200	4300	4400	4500	4600	4700	4800	4900	5000

$$n = 2$$

p	01	02	03	04	05	06	07	08	09	10
r 1	0199	0396	0591	0784	0975	1164	1351	1536	1719	1900
2	0001	0004	0009	0016	0025	0036	0049	0064	0081	0100
p	11	12	13	14	15	16	17	18	19	20
r 1	2079	2256	2431	2604	2775	2944	3111	3276	3439	3600
2	0121	0144	0169	0196	0225	0256	0289	0324	0361	0400
p	21	22	23	24	25	26	27	28	29	30
r 1	3759	3916	4071	4224	4375	4524	4671	4816	4959	5100
2	0441	0484	0529	0576	0625	0676	0729	0784	0841	0900
p	31	32	33	34	35	36	37	38	39	40
r 1	5239	5376	5511	5644	5775	5904	6031	6156	6279	6400
2	0961	1024	1089	1156	1225	1296	1369	1444	1521	1600
p	41	42	43	44	45	46	47	48	49	50
r 1	6519	6636	6751	6864	6975	7084	7191	7296	7399	7500
2	1681	1764	1849	1936	2025	2116	2209	2304	2401	2500

$$n = 3$$

p	01	02	03	04	05	06	07	08	09	10
r 1	0297	0588	0873	1153	1426	1694	1956	2213	2464	2710
2	0003	0012	0026	0047	0073	0104	0140	0182	0228	0280
3				0001	0001	0002	0003	0005	0007	0010
p	11	12	13	14	15	16	17	18	19	20
r 1	2950	3185	3415	3639	3859	4073	4282	4486	4686	4880
2	0336	0397	0463	0533	0608	0686	0769	0855	0946	1040
3	0013	0017	0022	0027	0034	0041	0049	0058	0069	0080
p	21	22	23	24	25	26	27	28	29	30
r 1	5070	5254	5435	5610	5781	5948	6110	6268	6421	6570
2	1138	1239	1344	1452	1563	1676	1793	1913	2035	2160
3	0093	0106	0122	0138	0156	0176	0197	0220	0244	0270
p	31	32	33	34	35	36	37	38	39	40
r 1	6715	6856	6992	7125	7254	7379	7500	7617	7730	7840
2	2287	2417	2548	2682	2818	2955	3094	3235	3377	3520
3	0298	0328	0359	0393	0429	0467	0507	0549	0593	0640

Williams S. Peters and George W. Summers, *Statistical Analysis for Business Decisions* 1968. By permission of Prentice-Hall, Inc., Englewood Cliffs, New Jersey.

$n = 3$

$$P(R \geq r \mid n, p)$$

p	41	42	43	44	45	46	47	48	49	50
r 1	7946	8049	8148	8244	8336	8425	8511	8594	8673	8750
2	3665	3810	3957	4104	4253	4401	4551	4700	4850	5000
3	0689	0741	0795	0852	0911	0973	1038	1106	1176	1250

$n = 4$

p	01	02	03	04	05	06	07	08	09	10
r 1	0394	0776	1147	1507	1855	2193	2519	2836	3143	3439
2	0006	0023	0052	0091	0140	0199	0267	0344	0430	0523
3			0001	0002	0005	0008	0013	0019	0027	0037
4									0001	0001

p	11	12	13	14	15	16	17	18	19	20
r 1	3726	4003	4271	4530	4780	5021	5254	5479	5695	5904
2	0624	0732	0847	0968	1095	1228	1366	1509	1656	1808
3	0049	0063	0079	0098	0120	0144	0171	0202	0235	0272
4	0001	0002	0003	0004	0005	0007	0008	0010	0013	0016

p	21	22	23	24	25	26	27	28	29	30
r 1	6105	6298	6485	6664	6836	7001	7160	7313	7459	7599
2	1963	2122	2285	2450	2617	2787	2959	3132	3307	3483
3	0312	0356	0403	0453	0508	0566	0628	0694	0763	0837
4	0019	0023	0028	0033	0039	0046	0053	0061	0071	0081

p	31	32	33	34	35	36	37	38	39	40
r 1	7733	7862	7985	8103	8215	8322	8425	8522	8615	8704
2	3660	3837	4015	4193	4370	4547	4724	4900	5075	5248
3	0915	0996	1082	1171	1265	1362	1464	1569	1679	1792
4	0092	0105	0119	0134	0150	0168	0187	0209	0231	0256

p	41	42	43	44	45	46	47	48	49	50
r 1	8788	8868	8944	9017	9085	9150	9211	9269	9323	9375
2	5420	5590	5759	5926	6090	6252	6412	6569	6724	6875
3	1909	2030	2155	2283	2415	2550	2689	2831	2977	3125
4	0283	0311	0342	0375	0410	0448	0488	0531	0576	0625

$n = 5$

p	01	02	03	04	05	06	07	08	09	10
r 1	0490	0961	1413	1846	2262	2661	3043	3409	3760	4095
2	0010	0038	0085	0148	0226	0319	0425	0544	0674	0815
3		0001	0003	0006	0012	0020	0031	0045	0063	0086
4						0001	0001	0002	0003	0005

p	11	12	13	14	15	16	17	18	19	20
r 1	4416	4723	5016	5296	5563	5818	6061	6293	6513	6723
2	0965	1125	1292	1467	1648	1835	2027	2224	2424	2627
3	0112	0143	0179	0220	0266	0318	0375	0437	0505	0579
4	0007	0009	0013	0017	0022	0029	0036	0045	0055	0067
5				0001	0001	0001	0001	0002	0002	0003

p	21	22	23	24	25	26	27	28	29	30
r 1	6923	7113	7293	7464	7627	7781	7927	8065	8196	8319
2	2833	3041	3251	3461	3672	3883	4093	4303	4511	4718
3	0659	0744	0836	0933	1035	1143	1257	1376	1501	1631
4	0081	0097	0114	0134	0156	0181	0208	0238	0272	0308
5	0004	0005	0006	0008	0010	0012	0014	0017	0021	0024

Cumulative Binomial Distribution

$$P(R \geq r | n,p)$$

n = 5

p	31	32	33	34	35	36	37	38	39	40
r 1	8436	8546	8650	8748	8840	8926	9008	9084	9155	9222
2	4923	5125	5325	5522	5716	5906	6093	6276	6455	6630
3	1766	1905	2050	2199	2352	2509	2670	2835	3003	3174
4	0347	0390	0436	0486	0540	0598	0660	0726	0796	0870
5	0029	0034	0039	0045	0053	0060	0069	0079	0090	0102

p	41	42	43	44	45	46	47	48	49	50
r 1	9285	9344	9398	9449	9497	9541	9582	9620	9655	9688
2	6801	6967	7129	7286	7438	7585	7728	7865	7998	8125
3	3349	3525	3705	3886	4069	4253	4439	4625	4813	5000
4	0949	1033	1121	1214	1312	1415	1522	1635	1753	1875
5	0116	0131	0147	0165	0185	0206	0229	0255	0282	0313

n = 6

p	01	02	03	04	05	06	07	08	09	10
r 1	0585	1142	1670	2172	2649	3101	3530	3936	4321	4686
2	0015	0057	0125	0216	0328	0459	0608	0773	0952	1143
3		0002	0005	0012	0022	0038	0058	0085	0118	0159
4					0001	0002	0003	0005	0008	0013
5										0001

p	11	12	13	14	15	16	17	18	19	20
r 1	5030	5356	5664	5954	6229	6487	6731	6960	7176	7379
2	1345	1556	1776	2003	2235	2472	2713	2956	3201	3446
3	0206	0261	0324	0395	0473	0560	0655	0759	0870	0989
4	0018	0025	0034	0045	0059	0075	0094	0116	0141	0170
5	0001	0001	0002	0003	0004	0005	0007	0010	0013	0016
6										0001

p	21	22	23	24	25	26	27	28	29	30
r 1	7569	7748	7916	8073	8220	8358	8487	8607	8719	8824
2	3692	3937	4180	4422	4661	4896	5128	5356	5580	5798
3	1115	1250	1391	1539	1694	1856	2023	2196	2374	2557
4	0202	0239	0280	0326	0376	0431	0492	0557	0628	0705
5	0020	0025	0031	0038	0046	0056	0067	0079	0093	0109
6	0001	0001	0001	0002	0002	0003	0004	0005	0006	0007

p	31	32	33	34	35	36	37	38	39	40
r 1	8921	9011	9095	9173	9246	9313	9375	9432	9485	9533
2	6012	6220	6422	6619	6809	6994	7172	7343	7508	7667
3	2744	2936	3130	3328	3529	3732	3937	4143	4350	4557
4	0787	0875	0969	1069	1174	1286	1404	1527	1657	1792
5	0127	0148	0170	0195	0223	0254	0288	0325	0365	0410
6	0009	0011	0013	0015	0018	0022	0026	0030	0035	0041

p	41	42	43	44	45	46	47	48	49	50
r 1	9578	9619	9657	9692	9723	9752	9778	9802	9824	9844
2	7819	7965	8105	8238	8364	8485	8599	8707	8810	8906
3	4764	4971	5177	5382	5585	5786	5985	6180	6373	6563
4	1933	2080	2232	2390	2553	2721	2893	3070	3252	3438
5	0458	0510	0566	0627	0692	0762	0837	0917	1003	1094
6	0048	0055	0063	0073	0083	0095	0108	0122	0138	0156

Appendix C [cont.]
Cumulative Binomial Distribution

$n = 7$

$$P(R \geq r \mid n,p)$$

$$n = 7$$

p / r	01	02	03	04	05	06	07	08	09	10
1	0679	1319	1920	2486	3017	3515	3983	4422	4832	5217
2	0020	0079	0171	0294	0444	0618	0813	1026	1255	1497
3		0003	0009	0020	0038	0063	0097	0140	0193	0257
4				0001	0002	0004	0007	0012	0018	0027
5								0001	0001	0002

p / r	11	12	13	14	15	16	17	18	19	20
1	5577	5913	6227	6521	6794	7049	7286	7507	7712	7903
2	1750	2012	2281	2556	2834	3115	3396	3677	3956	4233
3	0331	0416	0513	0620	0738	0866	1005	1154	1313	1480
4	0039	0054	0072	0094	0121	0153	0189	0231	0279	0333
5	0003	0004	0006	0009	0012	0017	0022	0029	0037	0047
6						0001	0001	0002	0003	0004

p / r	21	22	23	24	25	26	27	28	29	30
1	8080	8243	8395	8535	8665	8785	8895	8997	9090	9176
2	4506	4775	5040	5298	5551	5796	6035	6266	6490	6706
3	1657	1841	2033	2231	2436	2646	2861	3081	3304	3529
4	0394	0461	0536	0617	0706	0802	0905	1016	1134	1260
5	0058	0072	0088	0107	0129	0153	0181	0213	0248	0288
6	0005	0006	0008	0011	0013	0017	0021	0026	0031	0038
7					0001	0001	0001	0001	0002	0002

p / r	31	32	33	34	35	36	37	38	39	40
1	9255	9328	9394	9454	9510	9560	9606	9648	9686	9720
2	6914	7113	7304	7487	7662	7828	7987	8137	8279	8414
3	3757	3987	4217	4447	4677	4906	5134	5359	5581	5801
4	1394	1534	1682	1837	1998	2167	2341	2521	2707	2898
5	0332	0380	0434	0492	0556	0625	0701	0782	0869	0963
6	0046	0055	0065	0077	0090	0105	0123	0142	0164	0188
7	0003	0003	0004	0005	0006	0008	0009	0011	0014	0016

p / r	41	42	43	44	45	46	47	48	49	50
1	9751	9779	9805	9827	9848	9866	9883	9897	9910	9922
2	8541	8660	8772	8877	8976	9068	9153	9233	9307	9375
3	6017	6229	6436	6638	6836	7027	7213	7393	7567	7734
4	3094	3294	3498	3706	3917	4131	4346	4563	4781	5000
5	1063	1169	1282	1402	1529	1663	1803	1951	2105	2266
6	0216	0246	0279	0316	0357	0402	0451	0504	0562	0625
7	0019	0023	0027	0032	0037	0044	0051	0059	0068	0078

$$n = 8$$

p / r	01	02	03	04	05	06	07	08	09	10
1	0773	1492	2163	2786	3366	3904	4404	4868	5297	5695
2	0027	0103	0223	0381	0572	0792	1035	1298	1577	1869
3	0001	0004	0013	0031	0058	0096	0147	0211	0289	0381
4			0001	0002	0004	0007	0013	0022	0034	0050
5							0001	0001	0003	0004

Cumulative Binomial Distribution

$$P(R \geq r|n,p)$$

$n = 8$

	p	11	12	13	14	15	16	17	18	19	20
r	1	6063	6404	6718	7008	7275	7521	7748	7956	8147	8322
	2	2171	2480	2794	3111	3428	3744	4057	4366	4670	4967
	3	0487	0608	0743	0891	1052	1226	1412	1608	1815	2031
	4	0071	0097	0129	0168	0214	0267	0328	0397	0476	0563
	5	0007	0010	0015	0021	0029	0038	0050	0065	0083	0104
	6		0001	0001	0002	0002	0003	0005	0007	0009	0012
	7									0001	0001

	p	21	22	23	24	25	26	27	28	29	30
r	1	8483	8630	8764	8887	8999	9101	9194	9278	9354	9424
	2	5257	5538	5811	6075	6329	6573	6807	7031	7244	7447
	3	2255	2486	2724	2967	3215	3465	3718	3973	4228	4482
	4	0659	0765	0880	1004	1138	1281	1433	1594	1763	1941
	5	0129	0158	0191	0230	0273	0322	0377	0438	0505	0580
	6	0016	0021	0027	0034	0042	0052	0064	0078	0094	0113
	7	0001	0002	0002	0003	0004	0005	0006	0008	0010	0013
	8									0001	0001

	p	31	32	33	34	35	36	37	38	39	40
r	1	9486	9543	9594	9640	9681	9719	9752	9782	9808	9832
	2	7640	7822	7994	8156	8309	8452	8586	8711	8828	8936
	3	4736	4987	5236	5481	5722	5958	6189	6415	6634	6846
	4	2126	2319	2519	2724	2936	3153	3374	3599	3828	4059
	5	0661	0750	0846	0949	1061	1180	1307	1443	1586	1737
	6	0134	0159	0187	0218	0253	0293	0336	0385	0439	0498
	7	0016	0020	0024	0030	0036	0043	0051	0061	0072	0085
	8	0001	0001	0001	0002	0002	0003	0004	0004	0005	0007

	p	41	42	43	44	45	46	47	48	49	50
r	1	9853	9872	9889	9903	9916	9928	9938	9947	9954	9961
	2	9037	9130	9216	9295	9368	9435	9496	9552	9602	9648
	3	7052	7250	7440	7624	7799	7966	8125	8276	8419	8555
	4	4292	4527	4762	4996	5230	5463	5694	5922	6146	6367
	5	1895	2062	2235	2416	2604	2798	2999	3205	3416	3633
	6	0563	0634	0711	0794	0885	0982	1086	1198	1318	1445
	7	0100	0117	0136	0157	0181	0208	0239	0272	0310	0352
	8	0008	0010	0012	0014	0017	0020	0024	0028	0033	0039

$n = 9$

	p	01	02	03	04	05	06	07	08	09	10
r	1	0865	1663	2398	3075	3698	4270	4796	5278	5721	6126
	2	0034	0131	0282	0478	0712	0978	1271	1583	1912	2252
	3	0001	0006	0020	0045	0084	0138	0209	0298	0405	0530
	4			0001	0003	0006	0013	0023	0037	0057	0083
	5						0001	0002	0003	0005	0009
	6										0001

Cumulative Binomial Distribution

$n = 9$

$$P(R \geq r \mid n,p)$$

p / r	11	12	13	14	15	16	17	18	19	20
1	6496	6835	7145	7427	7684	7918	8131	8324	8499	8658
2	2599	2951	3304	3657	4005	4348	4685	5012	5330	5638
3	0672	0833	1009	1202	1409	1629	1861	2105	2357	2618
4	0117	0158	0209	0269	0339	0420	0512	0615	0730	0856
5	0014	0021	0030	0041	0056	0075	0098	0125	0158	0196
6	0001	0002	0003	0004	0006	0009	0013	0017	0023	0031
7						0001	0001	0002	0002	0003

p / r	21	22	23	24	25	26	27	28	29	30
1	8801	8931	9048	9154	9249	9335	9411	9480	9542	9596
2	5934	6218	6491	6750	6997	7230	7452	7660	7856	8040
3	2885	3158	3434	3713	3993	4273	4552	4829	5102	5372
4	0994	1144	1304	1475	1657	1849	2050	2260	2478	2703
5	0240	0291	0350	0416	0489	0571	0662	0762	0870	0988
6	0040	0051	0065	0081	0100	0122	0149	0179	0213	0253
7	0004	0006	0008	0010	0013	0017	0022	0028	0035	0043
8			0001	0001	0001	0001	0002	0003	0003	0004

p / r	31	32	33	34	35	36	37	38	39	40
1	9645	9689	9728	9762	9793	9820	9844	9865	9883	9899
2	8212	8372	8522	8661	8789	8908	9017	9118	9210	9295
3	5636	5894	6146	6390	6627	6856	7076	7287	7489	7682
4	2935	3173	3415	3662	3911	4163	4416	4669	4922	5174
5	1115	1252	1398	1553	1717	1890	2072	2262	2460	2666
6	0298	0348	0404	0467	0536	0612	0696	0787	0886	0994
7	0053	0064	0078	0094	0112	0133	0157	0184	0215	0250
8	0006	0007	0009	0011	0014	0017	0021	0026	0031	0038
9				0001	0001	0001	0001	0002	0002	0003

p / r	41	42	43	44	45	46	47	48	49	50
1	9913	9926	9936	9946	9954	9961	9967	9972	9977	9980
2	9372	9442	9505	9563	9615	9662	9704	9741	9775	9805
3	7866	8039	8204	8359	8505	8642	8769	8889	8999	9102
4	5424	5670	5913	6152	6386	6614	6836	7052	7260	7461
5	2878	3097	3322	3551	3786	4024	4265	4509	4754	5000
6	1109	1233	1366	1508	1658	1817	1985	2161	2346	2539
7	0290	0334	0383	0437	0498	0564	0637	0717	0804	0898
8	0046	0055	0065	0077	0091	0107	0125	0145	0169	0195
9	0003	0004	0005	0006	0008	0009	0011	0014	0016	0020

$n = 10$

p / r	01	02	03	04	05	06	07	08	09	10
1	0956	1829	2626	3352	4013	4614	5160	5656	6106	6513
2	0043	0162	0345	0582	0861	1176	1517	1879	2254	2639
3	0001	0009	0028	0062	0115	0188	0283	0401	0540	0702
4			0001	0004	0010	0020	0036	0058	0088	0128
5					0001	0002	0003	0006	0010	0016
6									0001	0001

Cumulative Binomial Distribution

$$P(R \geq r|n,p)$$

$n = 10$

p	11	12	13	14	15	16	17	18	19	20
r 1	6882	7215	7516	7787	8031	8251	8448	8626	8784	8926
2	3028	3417	3804	4184	4557	4920	5270	5608	5932	6242
3	0884	1087	1308	1545	1798	2064	2341	2628	2922	3222
4	0178	0239	0313	0400	0500	0614	0741	0883	1039	1209
5	0025	0037	0053	0073	0099	0130	0168	0213	0266	0328
6	0003	0004	0006	0010	0014	0020	0027	0037	0049	0064
7			0001	0001	0001	0002	0003	0004	0006	0009
8									0001	0001

p	21	22	23	24	25	26	27	28	29	30
r 1	9053	9166	9267	9357	9437	9508	9570	9626	9674	9718
2	6536	6815	7079	7327	7560	7778	7981	8170	8345	8507
3	3526	3831	4137	4442	4744	5042	5335	5622	5901	6172
4	1391	1587	1794	2012	2241	2479	2726	2979	3239	3504
5	0399	0479	0569	0670	0781	0904	1037	1181	1337	1503
6	0082	0104	0130	0161	0197	0239	0287	0342	0404	0473
7	0012	0016	0021	0027	0035	0045	0056	0070	0087	0106
8	0001	0002	0002	0003	0004	0006	0007	0010	0012	0016
9							0001	0001	0001	0001

p	31	32	33	34	35	36	37	38	39	40
r 1	9755	9789	9818	9843	9865	9885	9902	9916	9929	9940
2	8656	8794	8920	9035	9140	9236	9323	9402	9473	9536
3	6434	6687	6930	7162	7384	7595	7794	7983	8160	8327
4	3772	4044	4316	4589	4862	5132	5400	5664	5923	6177
5	1679	1867	2064	2270	2485	2708	2939	3177	3420	3669
6	0551	0637	0732	0836	0949	1072	1205	1348	1500	1662
7	0129	0155	0185	0220	0260	0305	0356	0413	0477	0548
8	0020	0025	0032	0039	0048	0059	0071	0086	0103	0123
9	0002	0003	0003	0004	0005	0007	0009	0011	0014	0017
10								0001	0001	0001

p	41	42	43	44	45	46	47	48	49	50
r 1	9949	9957	9964	9970	9975	9979	9983	9986	9988	9990
2	9594	9645	9691	9731	9767	9799	9827	9852	9874	9893
3	8483	8628	8764	8889	9004	9111	9209	9298	9379	9453
4	6425	6665	6898	7123	7340	7547	7745	7933	8112	8281
5	3922	4178	4436	4696	4956	5216	5474	5730	5982	6230
6	1834	2016	2207	2407	2616	2832	3057	3288	3526	3770
7	0626	0712	0806	0908	1020	1141	1271	1410	1560	1719
8	0146	0172	0202	0236	0274	0317	0366	0420	0480	0547
9	0021	0025	0031	0037	0045	0054	0065	0077	0091	0107
10	0001	0002	0002	0003	0003	0004	0005	0006	0008	0010

Cumulative Binomial Distribution

$n = 11$

$$P(R \geq r | n, p)$$

$n = 11$

p r	01	02	03	04	05	06	07	08	09	10
1	1047	1993	2847	3618	4312	4937	5499	6004	6456	6862
2	0052	0195	0413	0692	1019	1382	1772	2181	2601	3026
3	0002	0012	0037	0083	0152	0248	0370	0519	0695	0896
4			0002	0007	0016	0030	0053	0085	0129	0185
5					0001	0003	0005	0010	0017	0028
6								0001	0002	0003

p r	11	12	13	14	15	16	17	18	19	20
1	7225	7549	7839	8097	8327	8531	8712	8873	9015	9141
2	3452	3873	4286	4689	5078	5453	5811	6151	6474	6779
3	1120	1366	1632	1915	2212	2521	2839	3164	3494	3826
4	0256	0341	0442	0560	0694	0846	1013	1197	1397	1611
5	0042	0061	0087	0119	0159	0207	0266	0334	0413	0504
6	0005	0008	0012	0018	0027	0037	0051	0068	0090	0117
7		0001	0001	0002	0003	0005	0007	0010	0014	0020
8							0001	0001	0002	0002

p r	21	22	23	24	25	26	27	28	29	30
1	9252	9350	9436	9511	9578	9636	9686	9730	9769	9802
2	7065	7333	7582	7814	8029	8227	8410	8577	8730	8870
3	4158	4488	4814	5134	5448	5753	6049	6335	6610	6873
4	1840	2081	2333	2596	2867	3146	3430	3719	4011	4304
5	0607	0723	0851	0992	1146	1313	1493	1685	1888	2103
6	0148	0186	0231	0283	0343	0412	0490	0577	0674	0782
7	0027	0035	0046	0059	0076	0095	0119	0146	0179	0216
8	0003	0005	0007	0009	0012	0016	0021	0027	0034	0043
9			0001	0001	0001	0002	0002	0003	0004	0006

p r	31	32	33	34	35	36	37	38	39	40
1	9831	9856	9878	9896	9912	9926	9938	9948	9956	9964
2	8997	9112	9216	9310	9394	9470	9537	9597	9650	9698
3	7123	7361	7587	7799	7999	8186	8360	8522	8672	8811
4	4598	4890	5179	5464	5744	6019	6286	6545	6796	7037
5	2328	2563	2807	3059	3317	3581	3850	4122	4397	4672
6	0901	1031	1171	1324	1487	1661	1847	2043	2249	2465
7	0260	0309	0366	0430	0501	0581	0670	0768	0876	0994
8	0054	0067	0082	0101	0122	0148	0177	0210	0249	0293
9	0008	0010	0013	0016	0020	0026	0032	0039	0048	0059
10	0001	0001	0001	0002	0002	0003	0004	0005	0006	0007

Cumulative Binomial Distribution
$$P(R \geq r|n,p)$$

p \ r	41	42	43	44	45	46	47	48	49	50
1	9970	9975	9979	9983	9986	9989	9991	9992	9994	9995
2	9739	9776	9808	9836	9861	9882	9900	9916	9930	9941
3	8938	9055	9162	9260	9348	9428	9499	9564	9622	9673
4	7269	7490	7700	7900	8089	8266	8433	8588	8733	8867
5	4948	5223	5495	5764	6029	6288	6541	6787	7026	7256
6	2690	2924	3166	3414	3669	3929	4193	4460	4729	5000
7	1121	1260	1408	1568	1738	1919	2110	2312	2523	2744
8	0343	0399	0461	0532	0610	0696	0791	0895	1009	1133
9	0072	0087	0104	0125	0148	0175	0206	0241	0282	0327
10	0009	0012	0014	0018	0022	0027	0033	0040	0049	0059
11	0001	0001	0001	0001	0002	0002	0002	0003	0004	0005

$n = 12$

p \ r	01	02	03	04	05	06	07	08	09	10
1	1136	2153	3062	3873	4596	5241	5814	6323	6775	7176
2	0062	0231	0486	0809	1184	1595	2033	2487	2948	3410
3	0002	0015	0048	0107	0196	0316	0468	0652	0866	1109
4		0001	0003	0010	0022	0043	0075	0120	0180	0256
5				0001	0002	0004	0009	0016	0027	0043
6							0001	0002	0003	0005
7										0001

p \ r	11	12	13	14	15	16	17	18	19	20
1	7530	7843	8120	8363	8578	8766	8931	9076	9202	9313
2	3867	4314	4748	5166	5565	5945	6304	6641	6957	7251
3	1377	1667	1977	2303	2642	2990	3344	3702	4060	4417
4	0351	0464	0597	0750	0922	1114	1324	1552	1795	2054
5	0065	0095	0133	0181	0239	0310	0393	0489	0600	0726
6	0009	0014	0022	0033	0046	0065	0088	0116	0151	0194
7	0001	0002	0003	0004	0007	0010	0015	0021	0029	0039
8					0001	0001	0002	0003	0004	0006
9										0001

p \ r	21	22	23	24	25	26	27	28	29	30
1	9409	9493	9566	9629	9683	9730	9771	9806	9836	9862
2	7524	7776	8009	8222	8416	8594	8755	8900	9032	9150
3	4768	5114	5450	5778	6093	6397	6687	6963	7225	7472
4	2326	2610	2904	3205	3512	3824	4137	4452	4765	5075
5	0866	1021	1192	1377	1576	1790	2016	2254	2504	2763
6	0245	0304	0374	0453	0544	0646	0760	0887	1026	1178
7	0052	0068	0089	0113	0143	0178	0219	0267	0322	0386
8	0008	0011	0016	0021	0028	0036	0047	0060	0076	0095
9	0001	0001	0002	0003	0004	0005	0007	0010	0013	0017
10						0001	0001	0001	0002	0002

Cumulative Binomial Distribution

$n = 12$ $\qquad\qquad P(R \geq r|n,p)$

p	31	32	33	34	35	36	37	38	39	40
r 1	9884	9902	9918	9932	9943	9953	9961	9968	9973	9978
2	9256	9350	9435	9509	9576	9634	9685	9730	9770	9804
3	7704	7922	8124	8313	8487	8648	8795	8931	9054	9166
4	5381	5681	5973	6258	6533	6799	7053	7296	7528	7747
5	3032	3308	3590	3876	4167	4459	4751	5043	5332	5618
6	1343	1521	1711	1913	2127	2352	2588	2833	3087	3348
7	0458	0540	0632	0734	0846	0970	1106	1253	1411	1582
8	0118	0144	0176	0213	0255	0304	0359	0422	0493	0573
9	0022	0028	0036	0045	0056	0070	0086	0104	0127	0153
10	0003	0004	0005	0007	0008	0011	0014	0018	0022	0028
11				0001	0001	0001	0001	0002	0002	0003

p	41	42	43	44	45	46	47	48	49	50
r 1	9982	9986	9988	9990	9992	9994	9995	9996	9997	9998
2	9834	9860	9882	9901	9917	9931	9943	9953	9961	9968
3	9267	9358	9440	9513	9579	9637	9688	9733	9773	9807
4	7953	8147	8329	8498	8655	8801	8934	9057	9168	9270
5	5899	6175	6443	6704	6956	7198	7430	7652	7862	8062
6	3616	3889	4167	4448	4731	5014	5297	5577	5855	6128
7	1765	1959	2164	2380	2607	2843	3089	3343	3604	3872
8	0662	0760	0869	0988	1117	1258	1411	1575	1751	1938
9	0183	0218	0258	0304	0356	0415	0481	0555	0638	0730
10	0035	0043	0053	0065	0079	0095	0114	0137	0163	0193
11	0004	0005	0007	0009	0011	0014	0017	0021	0026	0032
12				0001	0001	0001	0001	0001	0002	0002

$n = 13$

p	01	02	03	04	05	06	07	08	09	10
r 1	1225	2310	3270	4118	4867	5526	6107	6617	7065	7458
2	0072	0270	0564	0932	1354	1814	2298	2794	3293	3787
3	0003	0020	0062	0135	0245	0392	0578	0799	1054	1339
4		0001	0005	0014	0031	0060	0103	0163	0242	0342
5				0001	0003	0007	0013	0024	0041	0065
6						0001	0001	0003	0005	0009
7									0001	0001

p	11	12	13	14	15	16	17	18	19	20
r 1	7802	8102	8364	8592	8791	8963	9113	9242	9354	9450
2	4270	4738	5186	5614	6017	6396	6751	7080	7384	7664
3	1651	1985	2337	2704	3080	3463	3848	4231	4611	4983
4	0464	0609	0776	0967	1180	1414	1667	1939	2226	2527
5	0097	0139	0193	0260	0342	0438	0551	0681	0827	0991
6	0015	0024	0036	0053	0075	0104	0139	0183	0237	0300
7	0002	0003	0005	0008	0013	0019	0027	0038	0052	0070
8			0001	0001	0002	0003	0004	0006	0009	0012
9								0001	0001	0002

Cumulative Binomial Distribution

$$P(R \geq r|n,p)$$

$n = 13$

p	21	22	23	24	25	26	27	28	29	30
r 1	9533	9604	9666	9718	9762	9800	9833	9860	9883	9903
2	7920	8154	8367	8559	8733	8889	9029	9154	9265	9363
3	5347	5699	6039	6364	6674	6968	7245	7505	7749	7975
4	2839	3161	3489	3822	4157	4493	4826	5155	5478	5794
5	1173	1371	1585	1816	2060	2319	2589	2870	3160	3457
6	0375	0462	0562	0675	0802	0944	1099	1270	1455	1654
7	0093	0120	0154	0195	0243	0299	0365	0440	0527	0624
8	0017	0024	0032	0043	0056	0073	0093	0118	0147	0182
9	0002	0004	0005	0007	0010	0013	0018	0024	0031	0040
10			0001	0001	0001	0002	0003	0004	0005	0007
11									0001	0001

p	31	32	33	34	35	36	37	38	39	40
r 1	9920	9934	9945	9955	9963	9970	9975	9980	9984	9987
2	9450	9527	9594	9653	9704	9749	9787	9821	9849	9874
3	8185	8379	8557	8720	8868	9003	9125	9235	9333	9421
4	6101	6398	6683	6957	7217	7464	7698	7917	8123	8314
5	3760	4067	4376	4686	4995	5301	5603	5899	6188	6470
6	1867	2093	2331	2581	2841	3111	3388	3673	3962	4256
7	0733	0854	0988	1135	1295	1468	1654	1853	2065	2288
8	0223	0271	0326	0390	0462	0544	0635	0738	0851	0977
9	0052	0065	0082	0102	0126	0154	0187	0225	0270	0321
10	0009	0012	0015	0020	0025	0032	0040	0051	0063	0078
11	0001	0001	0002	0003	0003	0005	0006	0008	0010	0013
12							0001	0001	0001	0001

p	41	42	43	44	45	46	47	48	49	50
r 1	9990	9992	9993	9995	9996	9997	9997	9998	9998	9999
2	9895	9912	9928	9940	9951	9960	9967	9974	9979	9983
3	9499	9569	9630	9684	9731	9772	9808	9838	9865	9888
4	8492	8656	8807	8945	9071	9185	9288	9381	9464	9539
5	6742	7003	7254	7493	7721	7935	8137	8326	8502	8666
6	4552	4849	5146	5441	5732	6019	6299	6573	6838	7095
7	2524	2770	3025	3290	3563	3842	4127	4415	4707	5000
8	1114	1264	1426	1600	1788	1988	2200	2424	2659	2905
9	0379	0446	0520	0605	0698	0803	0918	1045	1183	1334
10	0096	0117	0141	0170	0203	0242	0287	0338	0396	0461
11	0017	0021	0027	0033	0041	0051	0063	0077	0093	0112
12	0002	0002	0003	0004	0005	0007	0009	0011	0014	0017
13							0001	0001	0001	0001

$n = 14$

p	01	02	03	04	05	06	07	08	09	10
r 1	1313	2464	3472	4353	5123	5795	6380	6888	7330	7712
2	0084	0310	0645	1059	1530	2037	2564	3100	3632	4154
3	0003	0025	0077	0167	0301	0478	0698	0958	1255	1584
4		0001	0006	0019	0042	0080	0136	0214	0315	0441
5				0002	0004	0010	0020	0035	0059	0092
6						0001	0002	0004	0008	0015
7									0001	0002

Cumulative Binomial Distribution

$n = 14$ $P(R \geq r|n,p)$

p r	11	12	13	14	15	16	17	18	19	20
1	8044	8330	8577	8789	8972	9129	9264	9379	9477	9560
2	4658	5141	5599	6031	6433	6807	7152	7469	7758	8021
3	1939	2315	2708	3111	3521	3932	4341	4744	5138	5519
4	0594	0774	0979	1210	1465	1742	2038	2351	2679	3018
5	0137	0196	0269	0359	0467	0594	0741	0907	1093	1298
6	0024	0038	0057	0082	0115	0157	0209	0273	0349	0439
7	0003	0006	0009	0015	0022	0032	0046	0064	0087	0116
8		0001	0001	0002	0003	0005	0008	0012	0017	0024
9						0001	0001	0002	0003	0004

p r	21	22	23	24	25	26	27	28	29	30
1	9631	9691	9742	9786	9822	9852	9878	9899	9917	9932
2	8259	8473	8665	8837	8990	9126	9246	9352	9444	9525
3	5887	6239	6574	6891	7189	7467	7727	7967	8188	8392
4	3366	3719	4076	4432	4787	5136	5479	5813	6137	6448
5	1523	1765	2023	2297	2585	2884	3193	3509	3832	4158
6	0543	0662	0797	0949	1117	1301	1502	1718	1949	2195
7	0152	0196	0248	0310	0383	0467	0563	0673	0796	0933
8	0033	0045	0060	0079	0103	0132	0167	0208	0257	0315
9	0006	0008	0011	0016	0022	0029	0038	0050	0065	0083
10	0001	0001	0002	0002	0003	0005	0007	0009	0012	0017
11						0001	0001	0001	0002	0002

p r	31	32	33	34	35	36	37	38	39	40
1	9945	9955	9963	9970	9976	9981	9984	9988	9990	9992
2	9596	9657	9710	9756	9795	9828	9857	9881	9902	9919
3	8577	8746	8899	9037	9161	9271	9370	9457	9534	9602
4	6747	7032	7301	7556	7795	8018	8226	8418	8595	8757
5	4486	4813	5138	5458	5773	6080	6378	6666	6943	7207
6	2454	2724	3006	3297	3595	3899	4208	4519	4831	5141
7	1084	1250	1431	1626	1836	2059	2296	2545	2805	3075
8	0381	0458	0545	0643	0753	0876	1012	1162	1325	1501
9	0105	0131	0163	0200	0243	0294	0353	0420	0497	0583
10	0022	0029	0037	0048	0060	0076	0095	0117	0144	0175
11	0003	0005	0006	0008	0011	0014	0019	0024	0031	0039
12		0001	0001	0001	0001	0002	0003	0003	0005	0006
13										0001

p r	41	42	43	44	45	46	47	48	49	50
1	9994	9995	9996	9997	9998	9998	9999	9999	9999	9999
2	9934	9946	9956	9964	9971	9977	9981	9985	9988	9991
3	9661	9713	9758	9797	9830	9858	9883	9903	9921	9935
4	8905	9039	9161	9270	9368	9455	9532	9601	9661	9713
5	7459	7697	7922	8132	8328	8510	8678	8833	8974	9102
6	5450	5754	6052	6344	6627	6900	7163	7415	7654	7880
7	3355	3643	3937	4236	4539	4843	5148	5451	5751	6047
8	1692	1896	2113	2344	2586	2840	3105	3380	3663	3953
9	0680	0789	0910	1043	1189	1348	1520	1707	1906	2120
10	0212	0255	0304	0361	0426	0500	0583	0677	0782	0898
11	0049	0061	0076	0093	0114	0139	0168	0202	0241	0287
12	0008	0010	0013	0017	0022	0027	0034	0042	0053	0065
13	0001	0001	0001	0002	0003	0003	0004	0006	0007	0009
14										0001

$$P(R \geq r | n, p)$$

$n = 15$

p	01	02	03	04	05	06	07	08	09	10
r 1	1399	2614	3667	4579	5367	6047	6633	7137	7570	7941
2	0096	0353	0730	1191	1710	2262	2832	3403	3965	4510
3	0004	0030	0094	0203	0362	0571	0829	1130	1469	1841
4		0002	0008	0024	0055	0104	0175	0273	0399	0556
5			0001	0002	0006	0014	0028	0050	0082	0127
6					0001	0001	0003	0007	0013	0022
7							0001	0002	0003

p	11	12	13	14	15	16	17	18	19	20
r 1	8259	8530	8762	8959	9126	9269	9389	9490	9576	9648
2	5031	5524	5987	6417	6814	7179	7511	7813	8085	8329
3	2238	2654	3084	3520	3958	4392	4819	5234	5635	6020
4	0742	0959	1204	1476	1773	2092	2429	2782	3146	3518
5	0187	0265	0361	0478	0617	0778	0961	1167	1394	1642
6	0037	0057	0084	0121	0168	0227	0300	0387	0490	0611
7	0006	0010	0015	0024	0036	0052	0074	0102	0137	0181
8	0001	0001	0002	0004	0006	0010	0014	0021	0030	0042
9					0001	0001	0002	0003	0005	0008
10									0001	0001

p	21	22	23	24	25	26	27	28	29	30
r 1	9709	9759	9802	9837	9866	9891	9911	9928	9941	9953
2	8547	8741	8913	9065	9198	9315	9417	9505	9581	9647
3	6385	6731	7055	7358	7639	7899	8137	8355	8553	8732
4	3895	4274	4650	5022	5387	5742	6086	6416	6732	7031
5	1910	2195	2495	2810	3135	3469	3810	4154	4500	4845
6	0748	0905	1079	1272	1484	1713	1958	2220	2495	2784
7	0234	0298	0374	0463	0566	0684	0817	0965	1130	1311
8	0058	0078	0104	0135	0173	0219	0274	0338	0413	0500
9	0011	0016	0023	0031	0042	0056	0073	0094	0121	0152
10	0002	0003	0004	0006	0008	0011	0015	0021	0028	0037
11			0001	0001	0001	0002	0002	0003	0005	0007
12									0001	0001

p	31	32	33	34	35	36	37	38	39	40
r 1	9962	9969	9975	9980	9984	9988	9990	9992	9994	9995
2	9704	9752	9794	9829	9858	9883	9904	9922	9936	9948
3	8893	9038	9167	9281	9383	9472	9550	9618	9678	9729
4	7314	7580	7829	8060	8273	8469	8649	8813	8961	9095
5	5187	5523	5852	6171	6481	6778	7062	7332	7587	7827
6	3084	3393	3709	4032	4357	4684	5011	5335	5654	5968
7	1509	1722	1951	2194	2452	2722	3003	3295	3595	3902
8	0599	0711	0837	0977	1132	1302	1487	1687	1902	2131
9	0190	0236	0289	0351	0422	0504	0597	0702	0820	0950
10	0048	0062	0079	0099	0124	0154	0190	0232	0281	0338
11	0009	0012	0016	0022	0028	0037	0047	0059	0075	0093
12	0001	0002	0003	0004	0005	0006	0009	0011	0015	0019
13					0001	0001	0001	0002	0002	0003

Cumulative Binomial Distribution

$n = 15$ $\qquad P(R \geq r|n,p)$

p	41	42	43	44	45	46	47	48	49	50
r 1	9996	9997	9998	9998	9999	9999	9999	9999	10000	10000
2	9958	9966	9973	9979	9983	9987	9990	9992	9994	9995
3	9773	9811	9843	9870	9893	9913	9929	9943	9954	9963
4	9215	9322	9417	9502	9576	9641	9697	9746	9788	9824
5	8052	8261	8454	8633	8796	8945	9080	9201	9310	9408
6	6274	6570	6856	7131	7392	7641	7875	8095	8301	8491
7	4214	4530	4847	5164	5478	5789	6095	6394	6684	6964
8	2374	2630	2898	3176	3465	3762	4065	4374	4686	5000
9	1095	1254	1427	1615	1818	2034	2265	2510	2767	3036
10	0404	0479	0565	0661	0769	0890	1024	1171	1333	1509
11	0116	0143	0174	0211	0255	0305	0363	0430	0506	0592
12	0025	0032	0040	0051	0063	0079	0097	0119	0145	0176
13	0004	0005	0007	0009	0011	0014	0018	0023	0029	0037
14			0001	0001	0001	0002	0002	0003	0004	0005

$n = 16$

p	01	02	03	04	05	06	07	08	09	10
r 1	1485	2762	3857	4796	5599	6284	6869	7366	7789	8147
2	0109	0399	0818	1327	1892	2489	3098	3701	4289	4853
3	0005	0037	0113	0242	0429	0673	0969	1311	1694	2108
4		0002	0011	0032	0070	0132	0221	0342	0496	0684
5			0001	0003	0009	0019	0038	0068	0111	0170
6					0001	0002	0005	0010	0019	0033
7							0001	0001	0003	0005
8										0001

p	11	12	13	14	15	16	17	18	19	20
r 1	8450	8707	8923	9105	9257	9386	9493	9582	9657	9719
2	5386	5885	6347	6773	7161	7513	7830	8115	8368	8593
3	2545	2999	3461	3926	4386	4838	5277	5698	6101	6482
4	0907	1162	1448	1763	2101	2460	2836	3223	3619	4019
5	0248	0348	0471	0618	0791	0988	1211	1458	1727	2018
6	0053	0082	0120	0171	0235	0315	0412	0527	0662	0817
7	0009	0015	0024	0038	0056	0080	0112	0153	0204	0267
8	0001	0002	0004	0007	0011	0016	0024	0036	0051	0070
9			0001	0001	0002	0003	0004	0007	0010	0015
10							0001	0001	0002	0002

p	21	22	23	24	25	26	27	28	29	30
r 1	9770	9812	9847	9876	9900	9919	9935	9948	9958	9967
2	8791	8965	9117	9250	9365	9465	9550	9623	9686	9739
3	6839	7173	7483	7768	8029	8267	8482	8677	8851	9006
4	4418	4814	5203	5583	5950	6303	6640	6959	7260	7541
5	2327	2652	2991	3341	3698	4060	4425	4788	5147	5501
6	0992	1188	1405	1641	1897	2169	2458	2761	3077	3402
7	0342	0432	0536	0657	0796	0951	1125	1317	1526	1753
8	0095	0127	0166	0214	0271	0340	0420	0514	0621	0744
9	0021	0030	0041	0056	0075	0098	0127	0163	0206	0257
10	0004	0006	0008	0012	0016	0023	0031	0041	0055	0071
11	0001	0001	0001	0002	0003	0004	0006	0008	0011	0016
12						0001	0001	0001	0002	0003

Appendix C [cont.]

Cumulative Binomial Distribution

$$P(R \geq r \mid n,p)$$

$n = 16$

p	31	32	33	34	35	36	37	38	39	40
r 1	9974	9979	9984	9987	9990	9992	9994	9995	9996	9997
2	9784	9822	9854	9880	9902	9921	9936	9948	9959	9967
3	9144	9266	9374	9467	9549	9620	9681	9734	9778	9817
4	7804	8047	8270	8475	8661	8830	8982	9119	9241	9349
5	5846	6181	6504	6813	7108	7387	7649	7895	8123	8334
6	3736	4074	4416	4759	5100	5438	5770	6094	6408	6712
7	1997	2257	2531	2819	3119	3428	3746	4070	4398	4728
8	0881	1035	1205	1391	1594	1813	2048	2298	2562	2839
9	0317	0388	0470	0564	0671	0791	0926	1076	1242	1423
10	0092	0117	0148	0185	0229	0280	0341	0411	0491	0583
11	0021	0028	0037	0048	0062	0079	0100	0125	0155	0191
12	0004	0005	0007	0010	0013	0017	0023	0030	0038	0049
13		0001	0001	0001	0002	0003	0004	0005	0007	0009
14								0001	0001	0001

p	41	42	43	44	45	46	47	48	49	50
r 1	9998	9998	9999	9999	9999	9999	10000	10000	10000	10000
2	9974	9979	9984	9987	9990	9992	9994	9995	9997	9997
3	9849	9876	9899	9918	9934	9947	9958	9966	9973	9979
4	9444	9527	9600	9664	9719	9766	9806	9840	9869	9894
5	8529	8707	8869	9015	9147	9265	9370	9463	9544	9616
6	7003	7280	7543	7792	8024	8241	8441	8626	8795	8949
7	5058	5387	5711	6029	6340	6641	6932	7210	7476	7728
8	3128	3428	3736	4051	4371	4694	5019	5343	5665	5982
9	1619	1832	2060	2302	2559	2829	3111	3405	3707	4018
10	0687	0805	0936	1081	1241	1416	1607	1814	2036	2272
11	0234	0284	0342	0409	0486	0574	0674	0786	0911	1051
12	0062	0078	0098	0121	0149	0183	0222	0268	0322	0384
13	0012	0016	0021	0027	0035	0044	0055	0069	0086	0106
14	0002	0002	0003	0004	0006	0007	0010	0013	0016	0021
15					0001	0001	0001	0001	0002	0003

$n = 17$

p	01	02	03	04	05	06	07	08	09	10
r 1	1571	2907	4042	5004	5819	6507	7088	7577	7988	8332
2	0123	0446	0909	1465	2078	2717	3362	3995	4604	5182
3	0006	0044	0134	0286	0503	0782	1118	1503	1927	2382
4		0003	0014	0040	0088	0164	0273	0419	0603	0826
5			0001	0004	0012	0026	0051	0089	0145	0221
6					0001	0003	0007	0015	0027	0047
7							0001	0002	0004	0008
8										0001

p	11	12	13	14	15	16	17	18	19	20
r 1	8621	8862	9063	9230	9369	9484	9579	9657	9722	9775
2	5723	6223	6682	7099	7475	7813	8113	8379	8613	8818
3	2858	3345	3836	4324	4802	5266	5711	6133	6532	6904
4	1087	1383	1710	2065	2444	2841	3251	3669	4091	4511
5	0321	0446	0598	0778	0987	1224	1487	1775	2087	2418

$n = 17$ $P(R \geq r|n,p)$

p	11	12	13	14	15	16	17	18	19	20
r 6	0075	0114	0166	0234	0319	0423	0548	0695	0864	1057
7	0014	0023	0037	0056	0083	0118	0163	0220	0291	0377
8	0002	0004	0007	0011	0017	0027	0039	0057	0080	0109
9		0001	0001	0002	0003	0005	0008	0012	0018	0026
10						0001	0001	0002	0003	0005
11										0001

p	21	22	23	24	25	26	27	28	29	30
r 1	9818	9854	9882	9906	9925	9940	9953	9962	9970	9977
2	8996	9152	9285	9400	9499	9583	9654	9714	9765	9807
3	7249	7567	7859	8123	8363	8578	8771	8942	9093	9226
4	4927	5333	5728	6107	6470	6814	7137	7440	7721	7981
5	2766	3128	3500	3879	4261	4643	5023	5396	5760	6113
6	1273	1510	1770	2049	2347	2661	2989	3329	3677	4032
7	0479	0598	0736	0894	1071	1268	1485	1721	1976	2248
8	0147	0194	0251	0320	0402	0499	0611	0739	0884	1046
9	0037	0051	0070	0094	0124	0161	0206	0261	0326	0403
10	0007	0011	0016	0022	0031	0042	0057	0075	0098	0127
11	0001	0002	0003	0004	0006	0009	0013	0018	0024	0032
12				0001	0001	0002	0002	0003	0005	0007
13									0001	0001

p	31	32	33	34	35	36	37	38	39	40
r 1	9982	9986	9989	9991	9993	9995	9996	9997	9998	9998
2	9843	9872	9896	9917	9933	9946	9957	9966	9973	9979
3	9343	9444	9532	9608	9673	9728	9775	9815	9849	9877
4	8219	8437	8634	8812	8972	9115	9241	9353	9450	9536
5	6453	6778	7087	7378	7652	7906	8142	8360	8559	8740
6	4390	4749	5105	5458	5803	6139	6465	6778	7077	7361
7	2536	2838	3153	3479	3812	4152	4495	4839	5182	5522
8	1227	1426	1642	1877	2128	2395	2676	2971	3278	3595
9	0492	0595	0712	0845	0994	1159	1341	1541	1757	1989
10	0162	0204	0254	0314	0383	0464	0557	0664	0784	0919
11	0043	0057	0074	0095	0120	0151	0189	0234	0286	0348
12	0009	0013	0017	0023	0030	0040	0051	0066	0084	0106
13	0002	0002	0003	0004	0006	0008	0011	0015	0019	0025
14				0001	0001	0001	0002	0002	0003	0005
15										0001

p	41	42	43	44	45	46	47	48	49	50
r 1	9999	9999	9999	9999	10000	10000	10000	10000	10000	10000
2	9984	9987	9990	9992	9994	9996	9997	9998	9998	9999
3	9900	9920	9935	9948	9959	9968	9975	9980	9985	9988
4	9610	9674	9729	9776	9816	9849	9877	9901	9920	9936
5	8904	9051	9183	9301	9404	9495	9575	9644	9704	9755
6	7628	7879	8113	8330	8529	8712	8878	9028	9162	9283
7	5856	6182	6499	6805	7098	7377	7641	7890	8122	8338
8	3920	4250	4585	4921	5257	5590	5918	6239	6552	6855

Cumulative Binomial Distribution
$$P(R \geq r | n,p)$$

p	41	42	43	44	45	46	47	48	49	50
r 9	2238	2502	2780	3072	3374	3687	4008	4335	4667	5000
10	1070	1236	1419	1618	1834	2066	2314	2577	2855	3145
11	0420	0503	0597	0705	0826	0962	1112	1279	1462	1662
12	0133	0165	0203	0248	0301	0363	0434	0517	0611	0717
13	0033	0042	0054	0069	0086	0108	0134	0165	0202	0245
14	0006	0008	0011	0014	0019	0024	0031	0040	0050	0064
15	0001	0001	0002	0002	0003	0004	0005	0007	0009	0012
16							0001	0001	0001	0001

$n = 18$

p	01	02	03	04	05	06	07	08	09	10
r 1	1655	3049	4220	5204	6028	6717	7292	7771	8169	8499
2	0138	0495	1003	1607	2265	2945	3622	4281	4909	5497
3	0007	0052	0157	0333	0581	0898	1275	1702	2168	2662
4		0004	0018	0050	0109	0201	0333	0506	0723	0982
5			0002	0006	0015	0034	0067	0116	0186	0282
6				0001	0002	0005	0010	0021	0038	0064
7							0001	0003	0006	0012
8									0001	0002

p	11	12	13	14	15	16	17	18	19	20
r 1	8773	8998	9185	9338	9464	9566	9651	9719	9775	9820
2	6042	6540	6992	7398	7759	8080	8362	8609	8824	9009
3	3173	3690	4206	4713	5203	5673	6119	6538	6927	7287
4	1282	1618	1986	2382	2798	3229	3669	4112	4554	4990
5	0405	0558	0743	0959	1206	1482	1787	2116	2467	2836
6	0102	0154	0222	0310	0419	0551	0708	0889	1097	1329
7	0021	0034	0054	0081	0118	0167	0229	0306	0400	0513
8	0003	0006	0011	0017	0027	0041	0060	0086	0120	0163
9		0001	0002	0003	0005	0008	0013	0020	0029	0043
10					0001	0001	0002	0004	0006	0009
11								0001	0001	0002

p	21	22	23	24	25	26	27	28	29	30
r 1	9856	9886	9909	9928	9944	9956	9965	9973	9979	9984
2	9169	9306	9423	9522	9605	9676	9735	9784	9824	9858
3	7616	7916	8187	8430	8647	8839	9009	9158	9288	9400
4	5414	5825	6218	6591	6943	7272	7578	7860	8119	8354
5	3220	3613	4012	4414	4813	5208	5594	5968	6329	6673
6	1586	1866	2168	2488	2825	3176	3538	3907	4281	4656
7	0645	0799	0974	1171	1390	1630	1891	2171	2469	2783
8	0217	0283	0363	0458	0569	0699	0847	1014	1200	1407
9	0060	0083	0112	0148	0193	0249	0316	0395	0488	0596
10	0014	0020	0028	0039	0054	0073	0097	0127	0164	0210
11	0003	0004	0006	0009	0012	0018	0025	0034	0046	0061
12		0001	0001	0002	0002	0003	0005	0007	0010	0014
13						0001	0001	0001	0002	0003

Cumulative Binomial Distribution

$n = 18$

$$P(R \geq r \mid n,p)$$

p \ r	31	32	33	34	35	36	37	38	39	40
1	9987	9990	9993	9994	9996	9997	9998	9998	9999	9999
2	9886	9908	9927	9942	9954	9964	9972	9978	9983	9987
3	9498	9581	9652	9713	9764	9807	9843	9873	9897	9918
4	8568	8759	8931	9083	9217	9335	9439	9528	9606	9672
5	7001	7309	7598	7866	8114	8341	8549	8737	8907	9058
6	5029	5398	5759	6111	6450	6776	7086	7379	7655	7912
7	3111	3450	3797	4151	4509	4867	5224	5576	5921	6257
8	1633	1878	2141	2421	2717	3027	3349	3681	4021	4366
9	0720	0861	1019	1196	1391	1604	1835	2084	2350	2632
10	0264	0329	0405	0494	0597	0714	0847	0997	1163	1347
11	0080	0104	0133	0169	0212	0264	0325	0397	0480	0576
12	0020	0027	0036	0047	0062	0080	0102	0130	0163	0203
13	0004	0005	0008	0011	0014	0019	0026	0034	0044	0058
14	0001	0001	0001	0002	0003	0004	0005	0007	0010	0013
15						0001	0001	0001	0002	0002

p \ r	41	42	43	44	45	46	47	48	49	50
1	9999	9999	10000	10000	10000	10000	10000	10000	10000	10000
2	9990	9992	9994	9996	9997	9998	9998	9999	9999	9999
3	9934	9948	9959	9968	9975	9981	9985	9989	9991	9993
4	9729	9777	9818	9852	9880	9904	9923	9939	9952	9962
5	9193	9313	9418	9510	9589	9658	9717	9767	9810	9846
6	8151	8372	8573	8757	8923	9072	9205	9324	9428	9519
7	6582	6895	7193	7476	7742	7991	8222	8436	8632	8811
8	4713	5062	5408	5750	6085	6412	6728	7032	7322	7597
9	2928	3236	3556	3885	4222	4562	4906	5249	5591	5927
10	1549	1768	2004	2258	2527	2812	3110	3421	3742	4073
11	0686	0811	0951	1107	1280	1470	1677	1902	2144	2403
12	0250	0307	0372	0449	0537	0638	0753	0883	1028	1189
13	0074	0094	0118	0147	0183	0225	0275	0334	0402	0481
14	0017	0022	0029	0038	0049	0063	0079	0100	0125	0154
15	0003	0004	0006	0007	0010	0013	0017	0023	0029	0038
16		0001	0001	0001	0001	0002	0003	0004	0005	0007
17									0001	0001

$n = 19$

p \ r	01	02	03	04	05	06	07	08	09	10
1	1738	3188	4394	5396	6226	6914	7481	7949	8334	8649
2	0153	0546	1100	1751	2453	3171	3879	4560	5202	5797
3	0009	0061	0183	0384	0665	1021	1439	1908	2415	2946
4		0005	0022	0061	0132	0243	0398	0602	0853	1150
5			0002	0007	0020	0044	0085	0147	0235	0352
6				0001	0002	0006	0014	0029	0051	0086
7						0001	0002	0004	0009	0017
8								0001	0001	0003

Cumulative Binomial Distribution

$$P(R \geq r | n,p)$$

$n = 19$

p	11	12	13	14	15	16	17	18	19	20
r 1	8908	9119	9291	9431	9544	9636	9710	9770	9818	9856
2	6342	6835	7277	7669	8015	8318	8581	8809	9004	9171
3	3488	4032	4568	5089	5587	6059	6500	6910	7287	7631
4	1490	1867	2275	2708	3159	3620	4085	4549	5005	5449
5	0502	0685	0904	1158	1444	1762	2107	2476	2864	3267
6	0135	0202	0290	0401	0537	0700	0891	1110	1357	1631
7	0030	0048	0076	0113	0163	0228	0310	0411	0532	0676
8	0005	0009	0016	0026	0041	0061	0089	0126	0173	0233
9	0001	0002	0003	0005	0008	0014	0021	0032	0047	0067
10				0001	0001	0002	0004	0007	0010	0016
11							0001	0001	0002	0003

p	21	22	23	24	25	26	27	28	29	30
r 1	9887	9911	9930	9946	9958	9967	9975	9981	9985	9989
2	9313	9434	9535	9619	9690	9749	9797	9837	9869	9896
3	7942	8222	8471	8692	8887	9057	9205	9333	9443	9538
4	5877	6285	6671	7032	7369	7680	7965	8224	8458	8668
5	3681	4100	4520	4936	5346	5744	6129	6498	6848	7178
6	1929	2251	2592	2950	3322	3705	4093	4484	4875	5261
7	0843	1034	1248	1487	1749	2032	2336	2657	2995	3345
8	0307	0396	0503	0629	0775	0941	1129	1338	1568	1820
9	0093	0127	0169	0222	0287	0366	0459	0568	0694	0839
10	0023	0034	0047	0066	0089	0119	0156	0202	0258	0326
11	0005	0007	0011	0016	0023	0032	0044	0060	0080	0105
12	0001	0001	0002	0003	0005	0007	0010	0015	0021	0028
13				0001	0001	0001	0002	0003	0004	0006
14									0001	0001

p	31	32	33	34	35	36	37	38	39	40
r 1	9991	9993	9995	9996	9997	9998	9998	9999	9999	9999
2	9917	9935	9949	9960	9969	9976	9981	9986	9989	9992
3	9618	9686	9743	9791	9830	9863	9890	9913	9931	9945
4	8856	9022	9169	9297	9409	9505	9588	9659	9719	9770
5	7486	7773	8037	8280	8500	8699	8878	9038	9179	9304
6	5641	6010	6366	6707	7032	7339	7627	7895	8143	8371
7	3705	4073	4445	4818	5188	5554	5913	6261	6597	6919
8	2091	2381	2688	3010	3344	3690	4043	4401	4762	5122
9	1003	1186	1389	1612	1855	2116	2395	2691	3002	3325
10	0405	0499	0608	0733	0875	1035	1213	1410	1626	1861
11	0137	0176	0223	0280	0347	0426	0518	0625	0747	0885
12	0038	0051	0068	0089	0114	0146	0185	0231	0287	0352
13	0009	0012	0017	0023	0031	0041	0054	0070	0091	0116
14	0002	0002	0003	0005	0007	0009	0013	0017	0023	0031
15			0001	0001	0001	0002	0002	0003	0005	0006
16									0001	0001

Cumulative Binomial Distribution

$n = 19$ $P(R \geq r | n, p)$

p	41	42	43	44	45	46	47	48	49	50
r 1	10000	10000	10000	10000	10000	10000	10000	10000	10000	10000
2	9994	9995	9996	9997	9998	9999	9999	9999	9999	10000
3	9957	9967	9974	9980	9985	9988	9991	9993	9995	9996
4	9813	9849	9878	9903	9923	9939	9952	9963	9971	9978
5	9413	9508	9590	9660	9720	9771	9814	9850	9879	9904
6	8579	8767	8937	9088	9223	9342	9446	9537	9615	9682
7	7226	7515	7787	8039	8273	8488	8684	8862	9022	9165
8	5480	5832	6176	6509	6831	7138	7430	7706	7964	8204
9	3660	4003	4353	4706	5060	5413	5762	6105	6439	6762
10	2114	2385	2672	2974	3290	3617	3954	4299	4648	5000
11	1040	1213	1404	1613	1841	2087	2351	2631	2928	3238
12	0429	0518	0621	0738	0871	1021	1187	1372	1575	1796
13	0146	0183	0227	0280	0342	0415	0500	0597	0709	0835
14	0040	0052	0067	0086	0109	0137	0171	0212	0261	0318
15	0009	0012	0016	0021	0028	0036	0046	0060	0076	0096
16	0001	0002	0003	0004	0005	0007	0010	0013	0017	0022
17				0001	0001	0001	0001	0002	0003	0004

$n = 20$

p	01	02	03	04	05	06	07	08	09	10
r 1	1821	3324	4562	5580	6415	7099	7658	8113	8484	8784
2	0169	0599	1198	1897	2642	3395	4131	4831	5484	6083
3	0010	0071	0210	0439	0755	1150	1610	2121	2666	3231
4		0006	0027	0074	0159	0290	0471	0706	0993	1330
5			0003	0010	0026	0056	0107	0183	0290	0432
6				0001	0003	0009	0019	0038	0068	0113
7						0001	0003	0006	0013	0024
8								0001	0002	0004
9										0001

p	11	12	13	14	15	16	17	18	19	20
r 1	9028	9224	9383	9510	9612	9694	9759	9811	9852	9885
2	6624	7109	7539	7916	8244	8529	8773	8982	9159	9308
3	3802	4369	4920	5450	5951	6420	6854	7252	7614	7939
4	1710	2127	2573	3041	3523	4010	4496	4974	5439	5886
5	0610	0827	1083	1375	1702	2059	2443	2849	3271	3704
6	0175	0260	0370	0507	0673	0870	1098	1356	1643	1958
7	0041	0067	0103	0153	0219	0304	0409	0537	0689	0867
8	0008	0014	0024	0038	0059	0088	0127	0177	0241	0321
9	0001	0002	0005	0008	0013	0021	0033	0049	0071	0100
10			0001	0001	0002	0004	0007	0011	0017	0026
11						0001	0001	0002	0004	0006
12									0001	0001

p	21	22	23	24	25	26	27	28	29	30
r 1	9910	9931	9946	9959	9968	9976	9982	9986	9989	9992
2	9434	9539	9626	9698	9757	9805	9845	9877	9903	9924
3	8230	8488	8716	8915	9087	9237	9365	9474	9567	9645
4	6310	6711	7085	7431	7748	8038	8300	8534	8744	8929
5	4142	4580	5014	5439	5852	6248	6625	6981	7315	7625

Cumulative Binomial Distribution

$$P(R \geq r \,|\, n,p)$$

$n = 20$

p	21	22	23	24	25	26	27	28	29	30
r 6	2297	2657	3035	3427	3828	4235	4643	5048	5447	5836
7	1071	1301	1557	1838	2142	2467	2810	3169	3540	3920
8	0419	0536	0675	0835	1018	1225	1455	1707	1982	2277
9	0138	0186	0246	0320	0409	0515	0640	0784	0948	1133
10	0038	0054	0075	0103	0139	0183	0238	0305	0385	0480
11	0009	0013	0019	0028	0039	0055	0074	0100	0132	0171
12	0002	0003	0004	0006	0009	0014	0019	0027	0038	0051
13			0001	0001	0002	0003	0004	0006	0009	0013
14							0001	0001	0002	0003

p	31	32	33	34	35	36	37	38	39	40
r 1	9994	9996	9997	9998	9998	9999	9999	9999	9999	10000
2	9940	9953	9964	9972	9979	9984	9988	9991	9993	9995
3	9711	9765	9811	9848	9879	9904	9924	9940	9953	9964
4	9092	9235	9358	9465	9556	9634	9700	9755	9802	9840
5	7911	8173	8411	8626	8818	8989	9141	9274	9390	9490
6	6213	6574	6917	7242	7546	7829	8090	8329	8547	8744
7	4305	4693	5079	5460	5834	6197	6547	6882	7200	7500
8	2591	2922	3268	3624	3990	4361	4735	5108	5478	5841
9	1340	1568	1818	2087	2376	2683	3005	3341	3688	4044
10	0591	0719	0866	1032	1218	1424	1650	1897	2163	2447
11	0220	0279	0350	0434	0532	0645	0775	0923	1090	1275
12	0069	0091	0119	0154	0196	0247	0308	0381	0466	0565
13	0018	0025	0034	0045	0060	0079	0102	0132	0167	0210
14	0004	0006	0008	0011	0015	0021	0028	0037	0049	0065
15	0001	0001	0001	0002	0003	0004	0006	0009	0012	0016
16						0001	0001	0002	0002	0003

p	41	42	43	44	45	46	47	48	49	50
r 1	10000	10000	10000	10000	10000	10000	10000	10000	10000	10000
2	9996	9997	9998	9998	9999	9999	9999	10000	10000	10000
3	9972	9979	9984	9988	9991	9993	9995	9996	9997	9998
4	9872	9898	9920	9937	9951	9962	9971	9977	9983	9987
5	9577	9651	9714	9767	9811	9848	9879	9904	9924	9941
6	8921	9078	9217	9340	9447	9539	9619	9687	9745	9793
7	7780	8041	8281	8501	8701	8881	9042	9186	9312	9423
8	6196	6539	6868	7183	7480	7759	8020	8261	8482	8684
9	4406	4771	5136	5499	5857	6207	6546	6873	7186	7483
10	2748	3064	3394	3736	4086	4443	4804	5166	5525	5881
11	1480	1705	1949	2212	2493	2791	3104	3432	3771	4119
12	0679	0810	0958	1123	1308	1511	1734	1977	2238	2517
13	0262	0324	0397	0482	0580	0694	0823	0969	1133	1316
14	0084	0107	0136	0172	0214	0265	0326	0397	0480	0577
15	0022	0029	0038	0050	0064	0083	0105	0133	0166	0207
16	0004	0006	0008	0011	0015	0020	0027	0035	0046	0059
17	0001	0001	0001	0002	0003	0004	0005	0007	0010	0013
18						0001	0001	0001	0001	0002

Cumulative Binomial Distribution

$n = 50$

$$P(R \geq r | n,p)$$

$n = 50$

p	01	02	03	04	05	06	07	08	09	10
r 1	3950	6358	7819	8701	9231	9547	9734	9845	9910	9948
2	0894	2642	4447	5995	7206	8100	8735	9173	9468	9662
3	0138	0784	1892	3233	4595	5838	6892	7740	8395	8883
4	0016	0178	0628	1391	2396	3527	4673	5747	6697	7497
5	0001	0032	0168	0490	1036	1794	2710	3710	4723	5688
6		0005	0037	0144	0378	0776	1350	2081	2928	3839
7		0001	0007	0036	0118	0289	0583	1019	1596	2298
8			0001	0008	0032	0094	0220	0438	0768	1221
9				0001	0008	0027	0073	0167	0328	0579
10					0002	0007	0022	0056	0125	0245
11						0002	0006	0017	0043	0094
12							0001	0005	0013	0032
13								0001	0004	0010
14									0001	0003
15										0001

p	11	12	13	14	15	16	17	18	19	20
r 1	9971	9983	9991	9995	9997	9998	9999	10000	10000	10000
2	9788	9869	9920	9951	9971	9983	9990	9994	9997	9998
3	9237	9487	9661	9779	9858	9910	9944	9965	9979	9987
4	8146	8655	9042	9330	9540	9688	9792	9863	9912	9943
5	6562	7320	7956	8472	8879	9192	9428	9601	9726	9815
6	4760	5647	6463	7186	7806	8323	8741	9071	9327	9520
7	3091	3935	4789	5616	6387	7081	7686	8199	8624	8966
8	1793	2467	3217	4010	4812	5594	6328	6996	7587	8096
9	0932	1392	1955	2605	3319	4071	4832	5576	6280	6927
10	0435	0708	1074	1537	2089	2718	3403	4122	4849	5563
11	0183	0325	0535	0824	1199	1661	2203	2813	3473	4164
12	0069	0135	0242	0402	0628	0929	1309	1768	2300	2893
13	0024	0051	0100	0179	0301	0475	0714	1022	1405	1861
14	0008	0018	0037	0073	0132	0223	0357	0544	0791	1106
15	0002	0006	0013	0027	0053	0096	0164	0266	0411	0607
16	0001	0002	0004	0009	0019	0038	0070	0120	0197	0308
17			0001	0003	0007	0014	0027	0050	0087	0144
18				0001	0002	0005	0010	0019	0036	0063
19					0001	0001	0003	0007	0013	0025
20							0001	0002	0005	0009
21								0001	0002	0003
22										0001

p	21	22	23	24	25	26	27	28	29	30
r 1	10000	10000	10000	10000	10000	10000	10000	10000	10000	10000
2	9999	9999	10000	10000	10000	10000	10000	10000	10000	10000
3	9992	9995	9997	9998	9999	10000	10000	10000	10000	10000
4	9964	9978	9986	9992	9995	9997	9998	9999	9999	10000
5	9877	9919	9948	9967	9979	9987	9992	9995	9997	9998

$$P(R \geq r \mid n,p)$$

$n = 50$

p	21	22	23	24	25	26	27	28	29	30
r 6	9663	9767	9841	9893	9930	9954	9970	9981	9988	9993
7	9236	9445	9603	9720	9806	9868	9911	9941	9961	9975
8	8523	8874	9156	9377	9547	9676	9772	9842	9892	9927
9	7505	8009	8437	8794	9084	9316	9497	9635	9740	9817
10	6241	6870	7436	7934	8363	8724	9021	9260	9450	9598
11	4864	5552	6210	6822	7378	7871	8299	8663	8965	9211
12	3533	4201	4878	5544	6184	6782	7329	7817	8244	8610
13	2383	2963	3585	4233	4890	5539	6163	6749	7287	7771
14	1490	1942	2456	3023	3630	4261	4901	5534	6145	6721
15	0862	1181	1565	2013	2519	3075	3669	4286	4912	5532
16	0462	0665	0926	1247	1631	2075	2575	3121	3703	4308
17	0229	0347	0508	0718	0983	1306	1689	2130	2623	3161
18	0105	0168	0259	0384	0551	0766	1034	1359	1741	2178
19	0045	0075	0122	0191	0287	0418	0590	0809	1080	1406
20	0018	0031	0054	0088	0139	0212	0314	0449	0626	0848
21	0006	0012	0022	0038	0063	0100	0155	0232	0338	0478
22	0002	0004	0008	0015	0026	0044	0071	0112	0170	0251
23	0001	0001	0003	0006	0010	0018	0031	0050	0080	0123
24			0001	0002	0004	0007	0012	0021	0035	0056
25				0001	0001	0002	0004	0008	0014	0024
26						0001	0002	0003	0005	0009
27								0001	0002	0003
28									0001	0001

p	31	32	33	34	35	36	37	38	39	40
r 1	10000	10000	10000	10000	10000	10000	10000	10000	10000	10000
2	10000	10000	10000	10000	10000	10000	10000	10000	10000	10000
3	10000	10000	10000	10000	10000	10000	10000	10000	10000	10000
4	10000	10000	10000	10000	10000	10000	10000	10000	10000	10000
5	9999	9999	10000	10000	10000	10000	10000	10000	10000	10000
6	9996	9997	9998	9999	9999	10000	10000	10000	10000	10000
7	9984	9990	9994	9996	9998	9999	9999	10000	10000	10000
8	9952	9969	9980	9987	9992	9995	9997	9998	9999	9999
9	9874	9914	9942	9962	9975	9984	9990	9994	9996	9998
10	9710	9794	9856	9901	9933	9955	9971	9981	9988	9992
11	9409	9563	9683	9773	9840	9889	9924	9949	9966	9978
12	8916	9168	9371	9533	9658	9753	9825	9878	9916	9943
13	8197	8564	8873	9130	9339	9505	9635	9736	9811	9867
14	7253	7732	8157	8524	8837	9097	9310	9481	9616	9720
15	6131	6698	7223	7699	8122	8491	8805	9069	9286	9460
16	4922	5530	6120	6679	7199	7672	8094	8462	8779	9045
17	3734	4328	4931	5530	6111	6664	7179	7649	8070	8439
18	2666	3197	3760	4346	4940	5531	6105	6653	7164	7631
19	1786	2220	2703	3227	3784	4362	4949	5533	6101	6644
20	1121	1447	1826	2257	2736	3255	3805	4376	4957	5535
21	0657	0882	1156	1482	1861	2289	2764	3278	3824	4390
22	0360	0503	0685	0912	1187	1513	1890	2317	2788	3299
23	0184	0267	0379	0525	0710	0938	1214	1540	1916	2340
24	0087	0133	0196	0282	0396	0544	0730	0960	1236	1562

Appendix C [cont.]
Cumulative Binomial Distribution
$$P(R \geq r \mid n,p)$$

n = 50

p r	31	32	33	34	35	36	37	38	39	40
25	0039	0061	0094	0141	0207	0295	0411	0560	0748	0978
26	0016	0026	0042	0066	0100	0149	0216	0305	0423	0573
27	0006	0011	0018	0029	0045	0070	0106	0155	0223	0314
28	0002	0004	0007	0012	0019	0031	0048	0074	0110	0160
29	0001	0001	0002	0004	0007	0012	0020	0032	0050	0076
30			0001	0002	0003	0005	0008	0013	0021	0034
31					0001	0002	0003	0005	0008	0014
32						0001	0001	0002	0003	0005
33								0001	0001	0002
34										0001

p r	41	42	43	44	45	46	47	48	49	50
1	10000	10000	10000	10000	10000	10000	10000	10000	10000	10000
2	10000	10000	10000	10000	10000	10000	10000	10000	10000	10000
3	10000	10000	10000	10000	10000	10000	10000	10000	10000	10000
4	10000	10000	10000	10000	10000	10000	10000	10000	10000	10000
5	10000	10000	10000	10000	10000	10000	10000	10000	10000	10000
6	10000	10000	10000	10000	10000	10000	10000	10000	10000	10000
7	10000	10000	10000	10000	10000	10000	10000	10000	10000	10000
8	10000	10000	10000	10000	10000	10000	10000	10000	10000	10000
9	9999	9999	10000	10000	10000	10000	10000	10000	10000	10000
10	9995	9997	9998	9999	9999	10000	10000	10000	10000	10000
11	9986	9991	9994	9997	9998	9999	9999	10000	10000	10000
12	9962	9975	9984	9990	9994	9996	9998	9999	9999	10000
13	9908	9938	9958	9973	9982	9989	9993	9996	9997	9998
14	9799	9858	9902	9933	9955	9970	9981	9988	9992	9995
15	9599	9707	9789	9851	9896	9929	9952	9968	9980	9987
16	9265	9443	9585	9696	9780	9844	9892	9926	9950	9967
17	8757	9025	9248	9429	9573	9687	9774	9839	9888	9923
18	8051	8421	8740	9010	9235	9418	9565	9680	9769	9836
19	7152	7617	8037	8406	8727	8998	9225	9410	9559	9675
20	6099	6638	7143	7608	8026	8396	8718	8991	9219	9405
21	4965	5539	6099	6635	7138	7602	8020	8391	8713	8987
22	3840	4402	4973	5543	6100	6634	7137	7599	8018	8389
23	2809	3316	3854	4412	4981	5548	6104	6636	7138	7601
24	1936	2359	2826	3331	3866	4422	4989	5554	6109	6641
25	1255	1580	1953	2375	2840	3343	3876	4431	4996	5561
26	0762	0992	1269	1593	1966	2386	2850	3352	3885	4439
27	0432	0584	0772	1003	1279	1603	1975	2395	2858	3359
28	0229	0320	0439	0591	0780	1010	1286	1609	1981	2399
29	0113	0164	0233	0325	0444	0595	0784	1013	1289	1611
30	0052	0078	0115	0166	0235	0327	0446	0596	0784	1013
31	0022	0034	0053	0079	0116	0167	0236	0327	0445	0595
32	0009	0014	0022	0035	0053	0079	0116	0166	0234	0325
33	0003	0005	0009	0014	0022	0035	0053	0078	0114	0164
34	0001	0002	0003	0005	0009	0014	0022	0034	0052	0077
35		0001	0001	0002	0003	0005	0008	0014	0021	0033
36				0001	0001	0002	0003	0005	0008	0013

Cumulative Binomial Distribution
$$P(R \geq r|n,p)$$
$n = 50$

p r	41	42	43	44	45	46	47	48	49	50
37						0001	0001	0002	0003	0005
38								0001	0001	0002

$n = 100$

p r	01	02	03	04	05	06	07	08	09	10
1	6340	8674	9524	9831	9941	9979	9993	9998	9999	10000
2	2642	5967	8054	9128	9629	9848	9940	9977	9991	9997
3	0794	3233	5802	7679	8817	9434	9742	9887	9952	9981
4	0184	1410	3528	5705	7422	8570	9256	9633	9827	9922
5	0034	0508	1821	3711	5640	7232	8368	9097	9526	9763
6	0005	0155	0808	2116	3840	5593	7086	8201	8955	9424
7	0001	0041	0312	1064	2340	3936	5557	6968	8060	8828
8		0009	0106	0475	1280	2517	4012	5529	6872	7939
9		0002	0032	0190	0631	1463	2660	4074	5506	6791
10			0009	0068	0282	0775	1620	2780	4125	5487
11			0002	0022	0115	0376	0908	1757	2882	4168
12				0007	0043	0168	0469	1028	1876	2970
13				0002	0015	0069	0224	0559	1138	1982
14					0005	0026	0099	0282	0645	1239
15					0001	0009	0041	0133	0341	0726
16						0003	0016	0058	0169	0399
17						0001	0006	0024	0078	0206
18							0002	0009	0034	0100
19							0001	0003	0014	0046
20								0001	0005	0020
21									0002	0008
22									0001	0003
23										0001

p r	11	12	13	14	15	16	17	18	19	20
1	10000	10000	10000	10000	10000	10000	10000	10000	10000	10000
2	9999	10000	10000	10000	10000	10000	10000	10000	10000	10000
3	9992	9997	9999	10000	10000	10000	10000	10000	10000	10000
4	9966	9985	9994	9998	9999	10000	10000	10000	10000	10000
5	9886	9947	9977	9990	9996	9998	9999	10000	10000	10000
6	9698	9848	9926	9966	9984	9993	9997	9999	10000	10000
7	9328	9633	9808	9903	9953	9978	9990	9996	9998	9999
8	8715	9239	9569	9766	9878	9939	9970	9986	9994	9997
9	7835	8614	9155	9508	9725	9853	9924	9962	9982	9991
10	6722	7743	8523	9078	9449	9684	9826	9908	9953	9977
11	5471	6663	7663	8440	9006	9393	9644	9800	9891	9943
12	4206	5458	6611	7591	8365	8939	9340	9605	9773	9874
13	3046	4239	5446	6566	7527	8297	8876	9289	9567	9747
14	2076	3114	4268	5436	6526	7469	8234	8819	9241	9531
15	1330	2160	3173	4294	5428	6490	7417	8177	8765	9196
16	0802	1414	2236	3227	4317	5420	6458	7370	8125	8715
17	0456	0874	1492	2305	3275	4338	5414	6429	7327	8077
18	0244	0511	0942	1563	2367	3319	4357	5408	6403	7288

Cumulative Binomial Distribution

$$P(R \geq r | n, p)$$

$n = 100$

p	11	12	13	14	15	16	17	18	19	20
r 19	0123	0282	0564	1006	1628	2424	3359	4374	5403	6379
20	0059	0147	0319	0614	1065	1689	2477	3395	4391	5398
21	0026	0073	0172	0356	0663	1121	1745	2525	3429	4405
22	0011	0034	0088	0196	0393	0710	1174	1797	2570	3460
23	0005	0015	0042	0103	0221	0428	0754	1223	1846	2611
24	0002	0006	0020	0051	0119	0246	0462	0796	1270	1891
25	0001	0003	0009	0024	0061	0135	0271	0496	0837	1314
26		0001	0004	0011	0030	0071	0151	0295	0528	0875
27			0001	0005	0014	0035	0081	0168	0318	0558
28			0001	0002	0006	0017	0041	0091	0184	0342
29				0001	0003	0008	0020	0048	0102	0200
30					0001	0003	0009	0024	0054	0112
31						0001	0004	0011	0027	0061
32						0001	0002	0005	0013	0031
33							0001	0002	0006	0016
34								0001	0003	0007
35									0001	0003
36										0001
37										0001

p	21	22	23	24	25	26	27	28	29	30
r 1	10000	10000	10000	10000	10000	10000	10000	10000	10000	10000
2	10000	10000	10000	10000	10000	10000	10000	10000	10000	10000
3	10000	10000	10000	10000	10000	10000	10000	10000	10000	10000
4	10000	10000	10000	10000	10000	10000	10000	10000	10000	10000
5	10000	10000	10000	10000	10000	10000	10000	10000	10000	10000
6	10000	10000	10000	10000	10000	10000	10000	10000	10000	10000
7	10000	10000	10000	10000	10000	10000	10000	10000	10000	10000
8	9999	10000	10000	10000	10000	10000	10000	10000	10000	10000
9	9996	9998	9999	10000	10000	10000	10000	10000	10000	10000
10	9989	9995	9998	9999	10000	10000	10000	10000	10000	10000
11	9971	9986	9993	9997	9999	9999	10000	10000	10000	10000
12	9933	9965	9983	9992	9996	9998	9999	10000	10000	10000
13	9857	9922	9959	9979	9990	9995	9998	9999	10000	10000
14	9721	9840	9911	9953	9975	9988	9994	9997	9999	9999
15	9496	9695	9823	9900	9946	9972	9986	9993	9997	9998
16	9153	9462	9671	9806	9889	9939	9967	9983	9992	9996
17	8668	9112	9430	9647	9789	9878	9932	9963	9981	9990
18	8032	8625	9074	9399	9624	9773	9867	9925	9959	9978
19	7252	7991	8585	9038	9370	9601	9757	9856	9918	9955
20	6358	7220	7953	8547	9005	9342	9580	9741	9846	9911
21	5394	6338	7189	7918	8512	8973	9316	9560	9726	9835
22	4419	5391	6320	7162	7886	8479	8943	9291	9540	9712
23	3488	4432	5388	6304	7136	7856	8448	8915	9267	9521
24	2649	3514	4444	5386	6289	7113	7828	8420	8889	9245
25	1933	2684	3539	4455	5383	6276	7091	7802	8393	8864
26	1355	1972	2717	3561	4465	5381	6263	7071	7778	8369
27	0911	1393	2009	2748	3583	4475	5380	6252	7053	7756
28	0588	0945	1429	2043	2776	3602	4484	5378	6242	7036

683

$$P(R \geq r \mid n,p)$$

n = 100

p \ r	21	22	23	24	25	26	27	28	29	30
29	0364	0616	0978	1463	2075	2803	3621	4493	5377	6232
30	0216	0386	0643	1009	1495	2105	2828	3638	4501	5377
31	0123	0232	0406	0669	1038	1526	2134	2851	3654	4509
32	0067	0134	0247	0427	0693	1065	1554	2160	2873	3669
33	0035	0074	0144	0262	0446	0717	1091	1580	2184	2893
34	0018	0039	0081	0154	0276	0465	0739	1116	1605	2207
35	0009	0020	0044	0087	0164	0290	0482	0760	1139	1629
36	0004	0010	0023	0048	0094	0174	0303	0499	0780	1161
37	0002	0005	0011	0025	0052	0101	0183	0316	0515	0799
38	0001	0002	0005	0013	0027	0056	0107	0193	0328	0530
39		0001	0002	0006	0014	0030	0060	0113	0201	0340
40			0001	0003	0007	0015	0032	0064	0119	0210
41				0001	0003	0008	0017	0035	0068	0125
42				0001	0001	0004	0008	0018	0037	0072
43					0001	0002	0004	0009	0020	0040
44						0001	0002	0005	0010	0021
45							0001	0002	0005	0011
46								0001	0002	0005
47									0001	0003
48										0001
49										0001

p \ r	31	32	33	34	35	36	37	38	39	40
1	10000	10000	10000	10000	10000	10000	10000	10000	10000	10000
2	10000	10000	10000	10000	10000	10000	10000	10000	10000	10000
3	10000	10000	10000	10000	10000	10000	10000	10000	10000	10000
4	10000	10000	10000	10000	10000	10000	10000	10000	10000	10000
5	10000	10000	10000	10000	10000	10000	10000	10000	10000	10000
6	10000	10000	10000	10000	10000	10000	10000	10000	10000	10000
7	10000	10000	10000	10000	10000	10000	10000	10000	10000	10000
8	10000	10000	10000	10000	10000	10000	10000	10000	10000	10000
9	10000	10000	10000	10000	10000	10000	10000	10000	10000	10000
10	10000	10000	10000	10000	10000	10000	10000	10000	10000	10000
11	10000	10000	10000	10000	10000	10000	10000	10000	10000	10000
12	10000	10000	10000	10000	10000	10000	10000	10000	10000	10000
13	10000	10000	10000	10000	10000	10000	10000	10000	10000	10000
14	10000	10000	10000	10000	10000	10000	10000	10000	10000	10000
15	9999	10000	10000	10000	10000	10000	10000	10000	10000	10000
16	9998	9999	10000	10000	10000	10000	10000	10000	10000	10000
17	9995	9998	9999	10000	10000	10000	10000	10000	10000	10000
18	9989	9995	9997	9999	9999	10000	10000	10000	10000	10000
19	9976	9988	9994	9997	9999	9999	10000	10000	10000	10000
20	9950	9973	9986	9993	9997	9998	9999	10000	10000	10000
21	9904	9946	9971	9985	9992	9996	9998	9999	10000	10000
22	9825	9898	9942	9968	9983	9991	9996	9998	9999	10000
23	9698	9816	9891	9938	9966	9982	9991	9995	9998	9999
24	9504	9685	9806	9885	9934	9963	9980	9990	9995	9997
25	9224	9487	9672	9797	9879	9930	9961	9979	9989	9994
26	8841	9204	9471	9660	9789	9873	9926	9958	9977	9988

Appendix C [cont.]
Cumulative Binomial Distribution

$n = 100$

$$P(R \geq r \mid n,p)$$

p / r	31	32	33	34	35	36	37	38	39	40
27	8346	8820	9185	9456	9649	9780	9867	9922	9956	9976
28	7736	8325	8800	9168	9442	9638	9773	9862	9919	9954
29	7021	7717	8305	8781	9152	9429	9628	9765	9857	9916
30	6224	7007	7699	8287	8764	9137	9417	9618	9759	9852
31	5376	6216	6994	7684	8270	8748	9123	9405	9610	9752
32	4516	5376	6209	6982	7669	8254	8733	9110	9395	9602
33	3683	4523	5375	6203	6971	7656	8240	8720	9098	9385
34	2912	3696	4530	5375	6197	6961	7643	8227	8708	9087
35	2229	2929	3708	4536	5376	6192	6953	7632	8216	8697
36	1650	2249	2946	3720	4542	5376	6188	6945	7623	8205
37	1181	1671	2268	2961	3731	4547	5377	6184	6938	7614
38	0816	1200	1690	2285	2976	3741	4553	5377	6181	6932
39	0545	0833	1218	1708	2301	2989	3750	4558	5378	6178
40	0351	0558	0849	1235	1724	2316	3001	3759	4562	5379
41	0218	0361	0571	0863	1250	1739	2330	3012	3767	4567
42	0131	0226	0371	0583	0877	1265	1753	2343	3023	3755
43	0075	0136	0233	0380	0594	0889	1278	1766	2355	3033
44	0042	0079	0141	0240	0389	0605	0901	1290	1778	2365
45	0023	0044	0082	0146	0246	0397	0614	0911	1301	1789
46	0012	0024	0046	0085	0150	0252	0405	0623	0921	1311
47	0006	0012	0025	0048	0088	0154	0257	0411	0631	0930
48	0003	0006	0013	0026	0050	0091	0158	0262	0417	0638
49	0001	0003	0007	0014	0027	0052	0094	0162	0267	0423
50	0001	0001	0003	0007	0015	0029	0054	0096	0165	0271
51		0001	0002	0003	0007	0015	0030	0055	0098	0168
52			0001	0002	0004	0008	0016	0030	0056	0100
53				0001	0002	0004	0008	0016	0031	0058
54					0001	0002	0004	0008	0017	0032
55						0001	0002	0004	0009	0017
56							0001	0002	0004	0009
57								0002	0004	0004
58									0001	0002
59										0001

p / r	41	42	43	44	45	46	47	48	49	50
1	10000	10000	10000	10000	10000	10000	10000	10000	10000	10000
2	10000	10000	10000	10000	10000	10000	10000	10000	10000	10000
3	10000	10000	10000	10000	10000	10000	10000	10000	10000	10000
4	10000	10000	10000	10000	10000	10000	10000	10000	10000	10000
5	10000	10000	10000	10000	10000	10000	10000	10000	10000	10000
6	10000	10000	10000	10000	10000	10000	10000	10000	10000	10000
7	10000	10000	10000	10000	10000	10000	10000	10000	10000	10000
8	10000	10000	10000	10000	10000	10000	10000	10000	10000	10000
9	10000	10000	10000	10000	10000	10000	10000	10000	10000	10000
10	10000	10000	10000	10000	10000	10000	10000	10000	10000	10000
11	10000	10000	10000	10000	10000	10000	10000	10000	10000	10000
12	10000	10000	10000	10000	10000	10000	10000	10000	10000	10000
13	10000	10000	10000	10000	10000	10000	10000	10000	10000	10000
14	10000	10000	10000	10000	10000	10000	10000	10000	10000	10000

P r	41	42	43	44	45	46	47	48	49	50
15	10000	10000	10000	10000	10000	10000	10000	10000	10000	10000
16	10000	10000	10000	10000	10000	10000	10000	10000	10000	10000
17	10000	10000	10000	10000	10000	10000	10000	10000	10000	10000
18	10000	10000	10000	10000	10000	10000	10000	10000	10000	10000
19	10000	10000	10000	10000	10000	10000	10000	10000	10000	10000
20	10000	10000	10000	10000	10000	10000	10000	10000	10000	10000
21	10000	10000	10000	10000	10000	10000	10000	10000	10000	10000
22	10000	10000	10000	10000	10000	10000	10000	10000	10000	10000
23	10000	10000	10000	10000	10000	10000	10000	10000	10000	10000
24	9999	9999	10000	10000	10000	10000	10000	10000	10000	10000
25	9997	9999	9999	10000	10000	10000	10000	10000	10000	10000
26	9994	9997	9999	9999	10000	10000	10000	10000	10000	10000
27	9987	9994	9997	9998	9999	10000	10000	10000	10000	10000
28	9975	9987	9993	9997	9998	9999	10000	10000	10000	10000
29	9952	9974	9986	9993	9996	9998	9999	10000	10000	10000
30	9913	9950	9972	9985	9992	9996	9998	9999	10000	10000
31	9848	9910	9948	9971	9985	9992	9996	9998	9999	10000
32	9746	9844	9907	9947	9970	9984	9992	9996	9998	9999
33	9594	9741	9840	9905	9945	9969	9984	9991	9996	9998
34	9376	9587	9736	9837	9902	9944	9969	9983	9991	9996
35	9078	9368	9581	9732	9834	9900	9942	9968	9983	9991
36	8687	9069	9361	9576	9728	9831	9899	9941	9967	9982
37	8196	8678	9061	9355	9571	9724	9829	9897	9941	9967
38	7606	8188	8670	9054	9349	9567	9721	9827	9896	9940
39	6927	7599	8181	8663	9049	9345	9563	9719	9825	9895
40	6176	6922	7594	8174	8657	9044	9341	9561	9717	9824
41	5380	6174	6919	7589	8169	8653	9040	9338	9558	9716
42	4571	5382	6173	6916	7585	8165	8649	9037	9335	9557
43	3782	4576	5383	6173	6913	7582	8162	8646	9035	9334
44	3041	3788	4580	5385	6172	6912	7580	8160	8645	9033
45	2375	3049	3794	4583	5387	6173	6911	7579	8159	8644
46	1799	2384	3057	3799	4587	5389	6173	6911	7579	8159
47	1320	1807	2391	3063	3804	4590	5391	6174	6912	7579
48	0938	1328	1815	2398	3069	3809	4593	5393	6176	6914
49	0644	0944	1335	1822	2404	3074	3813	4596	5395	6178
50	0428	0650	0950	1341	1827	2409	3078	3816	4599	5398
51	0275	0432	0655	0955	1346	1832	2413	3082	3819	4602
52	0170	0278	0436	0659	0960	1350	1836	2417	3084	3822
53	0102	0172	0280	0439	0662	0963	1353	1838	2419	3086
54	0059	0103	0174	0282	0441	0664	0965	1355	1840	2421
55	0033	0059	0104	0175	0284	0443	0666	0967	1356	1841
56	0017	0033	0060	0105	0176	0285	0444	0667	0967	1356
57	0009	0018	0034	0061	0106	0177	0286	0444	0667	0967
58	0004	0009	0018	0034	0061	0106	0177	0286	0444	0666
59	0002	0005	0009	0018	0034	0061	0106	0177	0285	0443
60	0001	0002	0005	0009	0018	0034	0061	0106	0177	0284
61		0001	0002	0005	0009	0018	0034	0061	0106	0176
62			0001	0002	0005	0009	0018	0034	0061	0105
63				0001	0002	0005	0009	0018	0034	0060

Cumulative Binomial Distribution

$n = 100$ $P(R \geq r | n, p)$

r	p	41	42	43	44	45	46	47	48	49	50
	64					0001	0002	0005	0009	0018	0033
	65						0001	0002	0005	0009	0018
	66							0001	0002	0004	0009
	67								0001	0002	0004
	68									0001	0002
	69										0001

Cumulative Poisson Distribution Function

$$\sum_{x=x'}^{x=\infty} e^{-m} m^x / x!$$

Entries in the table are values of $\sum_{x=x'}^{x=\infty} e^{-m} m^x / x!$ for the indicated values of x' and m.

x'	0.1	0.2	0.3	0.4	0.5	0.6	0.7	0.8	0.9	1.0
0	1.0000	1.0000	1.0000	1.0000	1.0000	1.0000	1.0000	1.0000	1.0000	1.0000
1	.0952	.1813	.2592	.3297	.3935	.4512	.5034	.5507	.5934	.6321
2	.0047	.0175	.0369	.0616	.0902	.1219	.1558	.1912	.2275	.2642
3	.0002	.0011	.0036	.0079	.0144	.0231	.0341	.0474	.0629	.0803
4	.0000	.0001	.0003	.0008	.0018	.0034	.0058	.0091	.0135	.0190
5	.0000	.0000	.0000	.0001	.0002	.0004	.0008	.0014	.0023	.0037
6	.0000	.0000	.0000	.0000	.0000	.0000	.0001	.0002	.0003	.0006
7	.0000	.0000	.0000	.0000	.0000	.0000	.0000	.0000	.0000	.0001

x'	1.1	1.2	1.3	1.4	1.5	1.6	1.7	1.8	1.9	2.0
0	1.0000	1.0000	1.0000	1.0000	1.0000	1.0000	1.0000	1.0000	1.0000	1.0000
1	.6671	.6988	.7275	.7534	.7769	.7981	.8173	.8347	.8504	.8647
2	.3010	.3374	.3732	.4082	.4422	.4751	.5068	.5372	.5663	.5940
3	.0996	.1205	.1429	.1665	.1912	.2166	.2428	.2694	.2963	.3233
4	.0257	.0338	.0431	.0537	.0656	.0788	.0932	.1087	.1253	.1429
5	.0054	.0077	.0107	.0143	.0186	.0237	.0296	.0364	.0441	.0527
6	.0010	.0015	.0022	.0032	.0045	.0060	.0080	.0104	.0132	.0166
7	.0001	.0003	.0004	.0006	.0009	.0013	.0019	.0026	.0034	.0045
8	.0000	.0000	.0001	.0001	.0002	.0003	.0004	.0006	.0008	.0011
9	.0000	.0000	.0000	.0000	.0000	.0000	.0001	.0001	.0002	.0002

x'	2.1	2.2	2.3	2.4	2.5	2.6	2.7	2.8	2.9	3.0
0	1.0000	1.0000	1.0000	1.0000	1.0000	1.0000	1.0000	1.0000	1.0000	1.0000
1	.8775	.8892	.8997	.9093	.9179	.9257	.9328	.9392	.9450	.9502
2	.6204	.6454	.6691	.6916	.7127	.7326	.7513	.7689	.7854	.8009
3	.3504	.3773	.4040	.4303	.4562	.4816	.5064	.5305	.5540	.5768
4	.1614	.1806	.2007	.2213	.2424	.2640	.2859	.3081	.3304	.3528
5	.0621	.0725	.0838	.0959	.1088	.1226	.1371	.1523	.1682	.1847
6	.0204	.0249	.0300	.0357	.0420	.0490	.0567	.0651	.0742	.0839
7	.0059	.0075	.0094	.0116	.0142	.0172	.0206	.0244	.0287	.0335
8	.0015	.0020	.0026	.0033	.0042	.0053	.0066	.0081	.0099	.0119
9	.0003	.0005	.0006	.0009	.0011	.0015	.0019	.0024	.0031	.0038
10	.0001	.0001	.0001	.0002	.0003	.0004	.0005	.0007	.0009	.0011
11	.0000	.0000	.0000	.0000	.0001	.0001	.0001	.0002	.0002	.0003
12	.0000	.0000	.0000	.0000	.0000	.0000	.0000	.0000	.0001	.0001

x'	3.1	3.2	3.3	3.4	3.5	3.6	3.7	3.8	3.9	4.0
0	1.0000	1.0000	1.0000	1.0000	1.0000	1.0000	1.0000	1.0000	1.0000	1.0000
1	.9550	.9592	.9631	.9666	.9698	.9727	.9753	.9776	.9798	.9817
2	.8153	.8288	.8414	.8532	.8641	.8743	.8838	.8926	.9008	.9084
3	.5988	.6201	.6406	.6603	.6792	.6973	.7146	.7311	.7469	.7619
4	.3752	.3975	.4197	.4416	.4634	.4848	.5058	.5265	.5468	.5665
5	.2018	.2194	.2374	.2558	.2746	.2936	.3128	.3322	.3516	.3712
6	.0943	.1054	.1171	.1295	.1424	.1559	.1699	.1844	.1994	.2149
7	.0388	.0446	.0510	.0579	.0653	.0733	.0818	.0909	.1005	.1107
8	.0142	.0168	.0198	.0231	.0267	.0308	.0352	.0401	.0454	.0511
9	.0047	.0057	.0069	.0083	.0099	.0117	.0137	.0160	.0185	.0214
10	.0014	.0018	.0022	.0027	.0033	.0040	.0048	.0058	.0069	.0081
11	.0004	.0005	.0006	.0008	.0010	.0013	.0016	.0019	.0023	.0028
12	.0001	.0001	.0002	.0002	.0003	.0004	.0005	.0006	.0007	.0009
13	.0000	.0000	.0000	.0001	.0001	.0001	.0001	.0002	.0002	.0003
14	.0000	.0000	.0000	.0000	.0000	.0000	.0000	.0000	.0001	.0001

From *Handbook of Probability and Statistics* by Burlington and May. Second Edition. Copyright © 1970 by McGraw-Hill, Inc. Used with permission of McGraw-Hill Book Company.

Cumulative Poisson Distribution Function

$$\sum_{x=x'}^{x=\infty} e^{-m}m^x/x!$$

x'	4.1	4.2	4.3	4.4	4.5	4.6	4.7	4.8	4.9	5.0
0	1.0000	1.0000	1.0000	1.0000	1.0000	1.0000	1.0000	1.0000	1.0000	1.0000
1	.9834	.9850	.9864	.9877	.9889	.9899	.9909	.9918	.9926	.9933
2	.9155	.9220	.9281	.9337	.9389	.9437	.9482	.9523	.9561	.9596
3	.7762	.7898	.8026	.8149	.8264	.8374	.8477	.8575	.8667	.8753
4	.5858	.6046	.6228	.6406	.6577	.6743	.6903	.7058	.7207	.7350
5	.3907	.4102	.4296	.4488	.4679	.4868	.5054	.5237	.5418	.5595
6	.2307	.2469	.2633	.2801	.2971	.3142	.3316	.3490	.3665	.3840
7	.1214	.1325	.1442	.1564	.1689	.1820	.1954	.2092	.2233	.2378
8	.0573	.0639	.0710	.0786	.0866	.0951	.1040	.1133	.1231	.1334
9	.0245	.0279	.0317	.0358	.0403	.0451	.0503	.0558	.0618	.0681
10	.0095	.0111	.0129	.0149	.0171	.0195	.0222	.0251	.0282	.0318
11	.0034	.0041	.0048	.0057	.0067	.0078	.0090	.0104	.0120	.0137
12	.0011	.0014	.0017	.0020	.0024	.0029	.0034	.0040	.0047	.0055
13	.0003	.0004	.0005	.0007	.0008	.0010	.0012	.0014	.0017	.0020
14	.0001	.0001	.0002	.0002	.0003	.0003	.0004	.0005	.0006	.0007
15	.0000	.0000	.0000	.0001	.0001	.0001	.0001	.0001	.0002	.0002
16	.0000	.0000	.0000	.0000	.0000	.0000	.0000	.0000	.0001	.0001

x'	5.1	5.2	5.3	5.4	5.5	5.6	5.7	5.8	5.9	6.0
0	1.0000	1.0000	1.0000	1.0000	1.0000	1.0000	1.0000	1.0000	1.0000	1.0000
1	.9939	.9945	.9950	.9955	.9959	.9963	.9967	.9970	.9973	.9975
2	.9628	.9658	.9686	.9711	.9734	.9756	.9776	.9794	.9811	.9826
3	.8835	.8912	.8984	.9052	.9116	.9176	.9232	.9285	.9334	.9380
4	.7487	.7619	.7746	.7867	.7983	.8094	.8200	.8300	.8396	.8488
5	.5769	.5939	.6105	.6267	.6425	.6579	.6728	.6873	.7013	.7149
6	.4016	.4191	.4365	.4539	.4711	.4881	.5050	.5217	.5381	.5543
7	.2526	.2676	.2829	.2983	.3140	.3297	.3456	.3616	.3776	.3937
8	.1440	.1551	.1665	.1783	.1905	.2030	.2159	.2290	.2424	.2560
9	.0748	.0819	.0894	.0974	.1056	.1143	.1234	.1328	.1426	.1528
10	.0356	.0397	.0441	.0488	.0538	.0591	.0648	.0708	.0772	.0839
11	.0156	.0177	.0200	.0225	.0253	.0282	.0314	.0349	.0386	.0426
12	.0063	.0073	.0084	.0096	.0110	.0125	.0141	.0160	.0179	.0201
13	.0024	.0028	.0033	.0038	.0045	.0051	.0059	.0068	.0078	.0088
14	.0008	.0010	.0012	.0014	.0017	.0020	.0023	.0027	.0031	.0036
15	.0003	.0003	.0004	.0005	.0006	.0007	.0009	.0010	.0012	.0014
16	.0001	.0001	.0001	.0002	.0002	.0002	.0003	.0004	.0004	.0005
17	.0000	.0000	.0000	.0001	.0001	.0001	.0001	.0001	.0001	.0002
18	.0000	.0000	.0000	.0000	.0000	.0000	.0000	.0000	.0000	.0001

x'	6.1	6.2	6.3	6.4	6.5	6.6	6.7	6.8	6.9	7.0
0	1.0000	1.0000	1.0000	1.0000	1.0000	1.0000	1.0000	1.0000	1.0000	1.0000
1	.9978	.9980	.9982	.9983	.9985	.9986	.9988	.9989	.9990	.9991
2	.9841	.9854	.9866	.9877	.9887	.9897	.9905	.9913	.9920	.9927
3	.9423	.9464	.9502	.9537	.9570	.9600	.9629	.9656	.9680	.9704
4	.8575	.8658	.8736	.8811	.8882	.8948	.9012	.9072	.9129	.9182
5	.7281	.7408	.7531	.7649	.7763	.7873	.7978	.8080	.8177	.8270
6	.5702	.5859	.6012	.6163	.6310	.6453	.6594	.6730	.6863	.6993
7	.4098	.4258	.4418	.4577	.4735	.4892	.5047	.5201	.5353	.5503
8	.2699	.2840	.2983	.3127	.3272	.3419	.3567	.3715	.3864	.4013
9	.1633	.1741	.1852	.1967	.2084	.2204	.2327	.2452	.2580	.2709
10	.0910	.0984	.1061	.1142	.1226	.1314	.1404	.1498	.1505	.1695
11	.0469	.0514	.0563	.0614	.0668	.0726	.0786	.0849	.0916	.0985
12	.0224	.0250	.0277	.0307	.0339	.0373	.0409	.0448	.0490	.0534
13	.0100	.0113	.0127	.0143	.0160	.0179	.0199	.0221	.0245	.0270
14	.0042	.0048	.0055	.0063	.0071	.0080	.0091	.0102	.0115	.0128
15	.0016	.0019	.0022	.0026	.0030	.0034	.0039	.0044	.0050	.0057
16	.0006	.0007	.0008	.0010	.0012	.0014	.0016	.0018	.0021	.0024
17	.0002	.0003	.0003	.0004	.0004	.0005	.0006	.0006	.0008	.0010
18	.0001	.0001	.0001	.0001	.0002	.0002	.0002	.0003	.0003	.0004
19	.0000	.0000	.0000	.0000	.0001	.0001	.0001	.0001	.0001	.0001

Cumulative Poisson Distribution Function

$$\sum_{x=x'}^{x=\infty} e^{-m} m^x / x!$$

x'	7.1	7.2	7.3	7.4	7.5	7.6	7.7	7.8	7.9	8.0
0	1.0000	1.0000	1.0000	1.0000	1.0000	1.0000	1.0000	1.0000	1.0000	1.0000
1	.9992	.9993	.9993	.9994	.9994	.9995	.9995	.9996	.9996	.9997
2	.9933	.9939	.9944	.9949	.9953	.9957	.9961	.9964	.9967	.9970
3	.9725	.9745	.9764	.9781	.9797	.9812	.9826	.9839	.9851	.9862
4	.9233	.9281	.9326	.9368	.9409	.9446	.9482	.9515	.9547	.9576
5	.8359	.8445	.8527	.8605	.8679	.8751	.8819	.8883	.8945	.9004
6	.7119	.7241	.7360	.7474	.7586	.7693	.7797	.7897	.7994	.8088
7	.5651	.5796	.5940	.6080	.6218	.6354	.6486	.6616	.6743	.6866
8	.4162	.4311	.4459	.4607	.4754	.4900	.5044	.5188	.5330	.5470
9	.2840	.2973	.3108	.3243	.3380	.3518	.3657	.3796	.3935	.4075
10	.1798	.1904	.2012	.2123	.2236	.2351	.2469	.2589	.2710	.2834
11	.1058	.1133	.1212	.1293	.1378	.1465	.1555	.1648	.1743	.1841
12	.0580	.0629	.0681	.0735	.0792	.0852	.0915	.0980	.1048	.1119
13	.0297	.0327	.0358	.0391	.0427	.0464	.0504	.0546	.0591	.0638
14	.0143	.0159	.0176	.0195	.0216	.0238	.0261	.0286	.0313	.0342
15	.0065	.0073	.0082	.0092	.0103	.0114	.0127	.0141	.0156	.0173
16	.0028	.0031	.0036	.0041	.0046	.0052	.0059	.0066	.0074	.0082
17	.0011	.0013	.0015	.0017	.0020	.0022	.0026	.0029	.0033	.0037
18	.0004	.0005	.0006	.0007	.0008	.0009	.0011	.0012	.0014	.0016
19	.0002	.0002	.0002	.0003	.0003	.0004	.0004	.0005	.0006	.0006
20	.0001	.0001	.0001	.0001	.0001	.0001	.0002	.0002	.0002	.0003
21	.0000	.0000	.0000	.0000	.0000	.0000	.0001	.0001	.0001	.0001

x'	8.1	8.2	8.3	8.4	8.5	8.6	8.7	8.8	8.9	9.0
0	1.0000	1.0000	1.0000	1.0000	1.0000	1.0000	1.0000	1.0000	1.0000	1.0000
1	.9997	.9997	.9998	.9998	.9998	.9998	.9998	.9998	.9999	.9999
2	.9972	.9975	.9977	.9979	.9981	.9982	.9984	.9985	.9987	.9988
3	.9873	.9882	.9891	.9900	.9907	.9914	.9921	.9927	.9932	.9938
4	.9604	.9630	.9654	.9677	.9699	.9719	.9738	.9756	.9772	.9788
5	.9060	.9113	.9163	.9211	.9256	.9299	.9340	.9379	.9416	.9450
6	.8178	.8264	.8347	.8427	.8504	.8578	.8648	.8716	.8781	.8843
7	.6987	.7104	.7219	.7330	.7438	.7543	.7645	.7744	.7840	.7932
8	.5609	.5746	.5881	.6013	.6144	.6272	.6398	.6522	.6643	.6761
9	.4214	.4353	.4493	.4631	.4769	.4906	.5042	.5177	.5311	.5443
10	.2959	.3085	.3212	.3341	.3470	.3600	.3731	.3863	.3994	.4126
11	.1942	.2045	.2150	.2257	.2366	.2478	.2591	.2706	.2822	.2940
12	.1193	.1269	.1348	.1429	.1513	.1600	.1689	.1780	.1874	.1970
13	.0687	.0739	.0793	.0850	.0909	.0971	.1035	.1102	.1171	.1242
14	.0372	.0405	.0439	.0476	.0514	.0555	.0597	.0642	.0689	.0739
15	.0190	.0209	.0229	.0251	.0274	.0299	.0325	.0353	.0383	.0415
16	.0092	.0102	.0113	.0125	.0138	.0152	.0168	.0184	.0202	.0220
17	.0042	.0047	.0053	.0059	.0066	.0074	.0082	.0091	.0101	.0111
18	.0018	.0021	.0023	.0027	.0030	.0034	.0038	.0043	.0048	.0053
19	.0008	.0009	.0010	.0011	.0013	.0015	.0017	.0019	.0022	.0024
20	.0003	.0003	.0004	.0005	.0005	.0006	.0007	.0008	.0009	.0011
21	.0001	.0001	.0002	.0002	.0002	.0002	.0003	.0003	.0004	.0004
22	.0000	.0000	.0001	.0001	.0001	.0001	.0001	.0001	.0002	.0002
23	.0000	.0000	.0000	.0000	.0000	.0000	.0000	.0000	.0001	.0001

x'	9.1	9.2	9.3	9.4	9.5	9.6	9.7	9.8	9.9	10
0	1.0000	1.0000	1.0000	1.0000	1.0000	1.0000	1.0000	1.0000	1.0000	1.0000
1	.9999	.9999	.9999	.9999	.9999	.9999	.9999	.9999	1.0000	1.0000
2	.9989	.9990	.9991	.9991	.9992	.9993	.9993	.9994	.9995	.9995
3	.9942	.9947	.9951	.9955	.9958	.9962	.9965	.9967	.9970	.9972
4	.9802	.9816	.9828	.9840	.9851	.9862	.9871	.9880	.9889	.9897
5	.9483	.9514	.9544	.9571	.9597	.9622	.9645	.9667	.9688	.9707
6	.8902	.8959	.9014	.9065	.9115	.9162	.9207	.9250	.9290	.9329
7	.8022	.8108	.8192	.8273	.8351	.8426	.8498	.8567	.8634	.8699
8	.6877	.6990	.7101	.7208	.7313	.7416	.7515	.7612	.7706	.7798
9	.5574	.5704	.5832	.5958	.6082	.6204	.6324	.6442	.6558	.6672

Cumulative Poisson Distribution Function

$$\sum_{x=x'}^{x=\infty} e^{-m}m^x/x!$$

x'	9.1	9.2	9.3	9.4	9.5	9.6	9.7	9.8	9.9	10
10	.4258	.4389	.4521	.4651	.4782	.4911	.5040	.5168	.5295	.5421
11	.3059	.3180	.3301	.3424	.3547	.3671	.3795	.3920	.4045	.4170
12	.2068	.2168	.2270	.2374	.2480	.2588	.2697	.2807	.2919	.3032
13	.1316	.1393	.1471	.1552	.1636	.1721	.1809	.1899	.1991	.2084
14	.0790	.0844	.0900	.0958	.1019	.1081	.1147	.1214	.1284	.1355
15	.0448	.0483	.0520	.0559	.0600	.0643	.0688	.0735	.0784	.0835
16	.0240	.0262	.0285	.0309	.0335	.0362	.0391	.0421	.0454	.0487
17	.0122	.0135	.0148	.0162	.0177	.0194	.0211	.0230	.0249	.0270
18	.0059	.0066	.0073	.0081	.0089	.0098	.0108	.0119	.0130	.0143
19	.0027	.0031	.0034	.0038	.0043	.0048	.0053	.0059	.0065	.0072
20	.0012	.0014	.0015	.0017	.0020	.0022	.0025	.0028	.0031	.0035
21	.0005	.0006	.0007	.0008	.0009	.0010	.0011	.0013	.0014	.0016
22	.0002	.0002	.0003	.0003	.0004	.0004	.0005	.0005	.0006	.0007
23	.0001	.0001	.0001	.0001	.0001	.0002	.0002	.0002	.0003	.0003
24	.0000	.0000	.0000	.0000	.0001	.0001	.0001	.0001	.0001	.0001

x'	11	12	13	14	15	16	17	18	19	20
0	1.0000	1.0000	1.0000	1.0000	1.0000	1.0000	1.0000	1.0000	1.0000	1.0000
1	1.0000	1.0000	1.0000	1.0000	1.0000	1.0000	1.0000	1.0000	1.0000	1.0000
2	.9998	.9999	1.0000	1.0000	1.0000	1.0000	1.0000	1.0000	1.0000	1.0000
3	.9988	.9995	.9998	.9999	1.0000	1.0000	1.0000	1.0000	1.0000	1.0000
4	.9951	.9977	.9990	.9995	.9998	.9999	1.0000	1.0000	1.0000	1.0000
5	.9849	.9924	.9963	.9982	.9991	.9996	.9998	.9999	1.0000	1.0000
6	.9625	.9797	.9893	.9945	.9972	.9986	.9993	.9997	.9998	.9999
7	.9214	.9542	.9741	.9858	.9924	.9960	.9979	.9990	.9995	.9997
8	.8568	.9105	.9460	.9684	.9820	.9900	.9946	.9971	.9985	.9992
9	.7680	.8450	.9002	.9379	.9626	.9780	.9874	.9929	.9961	.9979
10	.6595	.7576	.8342	.8906	.9301	.9567	.9739	.9846	.9911	.9950
11	.5401	.6528	.7483	.8243	.8815	.9226	.9509	.9696	.9817	.9892
12	.4207	.5384	.6468	.7400	.8152	.8730	.9153	.9451	.9653	.9786
13	.3113	.4240	.5369	.6415	.7324	.8069	.8650	.9083	.9394	.9610
14	.2187	.3185	.4270	.5356	.6368	.7255	.7991	.8574	.9016	.9339
15	.1460	.2280	.3249	.4296	.5343	.6325	.7192	.7919	.8503	.8951
16	.0926	.1556	.2364	.3306	.4319	.5333	.6285	.7133	.7852	.8435
17	.0559	.1013	.1645	.2441	.3359	.4340	.5323	.6250	.7080	.7789
18	.0322	.0630	.1095	.1728	.2511	.3407	.4360	.5314	.6216	.7030
19	.0177	.0374	.0698	.1174	.1805	.2577	.3450	.4378	.5305	.6186
20	.0093	.0213	.0427	.0765	.1248	.1878	.2637	.3491	.4394	.5297
21	.0047	.0116	.0250	.0479	.0830	.1318	.1945	.2693	.3528	.4409
22	.0023	.0061	.0141	.0288	.0531	.0892	.1385	.2009	.2745	.3563
23	.0010	.0030	.0076	.0167	.0327	.0582	.0953	.1449	.2069	.2794
24	.0005	.0015	.0040	.0093	.0195	.0367	.0633	.1011	.1510	.2125
25	.0002	.0007	.0020	.0050	.0112	.0223	.0406	.0683	.1067	.1568
26	.0001	.0003	.0010	.0026	.0062	.0131	.0252	.0446	.0731	.1122
27	.0000	.0001	.0005	.0013	.0033	.0075	.0152	.0282	.0486	.0779
28	.0000	.0001	.0002	.0006	.0017	.0041	.0088	.0173	.0313	.0525
29	.0000	.0000	.0001	.0003	.0009	.0022	.0050	.0103	.0195	.0343
30	.0000	.0000	.0000	.0001	.0004	.0011	.0027	.0059	.0118	.0218
31	.0000	.0000	.0000	.0001	.0002	.0006	.0014	.0033	.0070	.0135
32	.0000	.0000	.0000	.0000	.0001	.0003	.0007	.0018	.0040	.0081
33	.0000	.0000	.0000	.0000	.0000	.0001	.0004	.0010	.0022	.0047
34	.0000	.0000	.0000	.0000	.0000	.0001	.0002	.0005	.0012	.0027
35	.0000	.0000	.0000	.0000	.0000	.0000	.0001	.0002	.0006	.0015
36	.0000	.0000	.0000	.0000	.0000	.0000	.0000	.0001	.0003	.0008
37	.0000	.0000	.0000	.0000	.0000	.0000	.0000	.0001	.0002	.0004
38	.0000	.0000	.0000	.0000	.0000	.0000	.0000	.0000	.0001	.0002
39	.0000	.0000	.0000	.0000	.0000	.0000	.0000	.0000	.0000	.0001
40	.0000	.0000	.0000	.0000	.0000	.0000	.0000	.0000	.0000	.0001

Appendix E

Uniform random variates between 0 and 1

0.339	0.027	0.911	0.851	0.204	0.712	0.818	0.794	0.968	0.965
0.908	0.740	0.082	0.534	0.081	0.189	0.746	0.424	0.425	0.539
0.500	0.887	0.448	0.822	0.941	0.182	0.104	0.861	0.562	0.303
0.710	0.809	0.697	0.985	0.192	0.742	0.847	0.698	0.090	0.731
0.903	0.203	0.153	0.779	0.922	0.218	0.155	0.290	0.422	0.662
0.028	0.035	0.328	0.872	0.276	0.594	0.034	0.305	0.776	0.919
0.166	0.257	0.629	0.002	0.467	0.602	0.087	0.110	0.046	0.160
0.215	0.952	0.981	0.595	0.842	0.179	0.437	0.002	0.525	0.360
0.556	0.210	0.691	0.391	0.859	0.862	0.340	0.453	0.512	0.520
0.288	0.024	0.564	0.313	0.330	0.229	0.646	0.375	0.187	0.599
0.719	0.834	0.444	0.128	0.068	0.625	0.643	0.185	0.440	0.091
0.852	0.638	0.686	0.002	0.057	0.200	0.738	0.453	0.717	0.608
0.008	0.706	0.538	0.801	0.957	0.146	0.240	0.842	0.929	0.284
0.106	0.102	0.907	0.610	0.082	0.071	0.703	0.147	0.556	0.311
0.317	0.717	0.805	0.596	0.191	0.708	0.092	0.726	0.375	0.604
0.717	0.282	0.043	0.226	0.203	0.959	0.816	0.628	0.141	0.421
0.129	0.661	0.126	0.715	0.362	0.611	0.784	0.013	0.862	0.618
0.469	0.178	0.374	0.062	0.430	0.740	0.853	0.556	0.468	0.383
0.132	0.034	0.399	0.767	0.706	0.958	0.957	0.378	0.244	0.122
0.837	0.060	0.056	0.755	0.785	0.093	0.372	0.305	0.760	0.923

Appendix F

Normally distributed random variates with mean 0 and standard deviation 1

−0.530	0.907	0.122	−0.584	1.384	−0.984	−0.353	−0.547	1.006	2.000
0.932	−1.317	0.552	−1.784	−0.133	−0.450	1.505	−0.497	−0.900	−0.378
−0.867	−0.409	0.932	1.196	−0.044	0.357	−0.044	1.461	2.209	0.074
−0.136	0.595	0.626	1.416	−1.049	0.357	−0.653	1.178	−1.336	−0.369
1.049	1.123	−1.943	−0.511	0.863	−0.787	−1.104	−0.710	−0.955	−0.739
0.598	1.307	0.520	2.201	0.432	−1.289	0.373	2.102	−1.612	−0.929
0.114	2.352	−1.186	0.188	−0.301	−0.845	−1.263	1.171	−0.534	0.738
−0.976	1.454	−1.467	0.722	0.579	−0.086	−1.160	−0.815	2.355	−0.290
−0.007	0.309	0.627	0.560	0.999	−1.587	0.871	0.721	1.232	0.396
0.943	−0.656	−0.379	0.527	0.627	−0.067	−0.743	−0.913	0.347	−0.420
1.691	0.121	0.787	−0.521	0.081	−1.188	0.480	−0.408	0.695	0.420
−0.256	0.413	−0.623	−0.088	−0.363	−0.457	0.288	0.519	0.354	0.287
0.465	−0.374	0.784	0.527	−1.127	1.071	−1.592	0.916	−0.113	−0.075
0.690	0.264	−1.479	−0.685	−0.601	−0.387	1.533	0.078	0.357	−0.520
2.151	1.786	−0.128	−0.786	0.580	0.113	0.167	0.867	−0.689	1.066
−0.615	−0.438	0.093	−0.199	−0.134	0.136	−1.377	−0.832	−0.438	0.325
−1.248	−0.148	1.422	−0.031	0.961	0.828	0.590	−0.413	−0.055	0.860
−1.344	−1.664	−0.700	0.045	1.757	0.320	−1.800	1.851	−0.103	0.452
−0.553	−0.186	−0.459	1.607	−0.862	−0.547	−0.152	−1.280	0.083	0.403
−0.412	−0.468	−0.074	−1.194	0.148	0.629	−1.210	0.748	−0.905	−0.091

Appendix G

Exponentially Distributed Random Numbers
with Mean 0

1.017	1.856	0.553	0.357	0.770	2.977	0.645	0.584	0.414	0.396
0.614	1.096	0.133	1.445	0.742	2.470	0.110	0.182	1.736	0.809
1.025	1.485	0.490	1.565	1.314	0.245	3.189	0.671	1.814	1.090
1.019	0.099	0.071	0.546	0.090	2.319	1.383	5.535	0.545	0.583
0.305	0.296	0.002	0.611	1.646	1.072	1.351	0.262	0.559	1.126
0.763	1.754	0.365	1.466	0.537	0.852	0.083	0.134	0.577	0.165
1.450	0.015	0.212	0.143	0.283	1.318	0.108	0.377	1.449	1.077
2.445	0.214	3.588	0.718	2.769	2.507	0.153	1.552	0.222	4.111
0.486	1.065	0.280	0.040	2.344	1.330	0.129	0.265	0.031	2.433
0.443	2.782	3.204	0.708	0.389	0.062	0.235	0.834	3.541	0.264
0.872	0.800	0.008	0.676	3.589	0.223	0.719	1.346	2.367	1.312
0.406	0.945	0.738	1.316	0.856	1.396	0.323	0.005	0.920	0.217
2.449	0.087	0.751	1.599	0.200	3.002	0.408	2.350	1.369	0.531
0.369	0.056	0.900	1.356	1.051	0.095	2.358	0.488	0.292	0.185
0.068	0.684	1.743	2.595	2.940	0.949	0.171	1.246	0.378	0.292
1.448	0.051	0.684	0.208	4.542	0.493	0.558	2.005	1.157	0.600
0.539	0.153	0.226	2.692	1.439	1.085	1.488	0.266	1.839	0.800
3.532	0.439	1.000	0.026	0.163	0.167	0.130	0.054	0.054	0.143
0.274	0.364	0.089	0.555	0.931	0.250	2.096	0.571	0.350	0.920
0.357	0.642	0.736	0.036	0.440	2.203	0.753	1.669	0.873	0.136
0.214	0.046	1.781	0.634	0.588	2.107	0.350	0.887	2.596	0.535
1.002	0.567	0.192	0.084	0.347	0.254	0.617	1.005	1.488	0.077
0.301	1.113	0.354	0.455	0.179	1.060	0.739	0.011	0.026	0.046
0.041	1.255	0.444	0.317	2.501	0.476	0.730	0.550	2.461	0.120
0.905	0.632	0.182	1.067	0.349	0.050	0.204	0.742	1.402	0.068
0.628	0.195	1.063	1.400	0.311	0.727	0.122	1.803	1.229	1.172
3.390	0.215	0.104	0.590	2.422	1.368	3.466	0.741	0.750	1.486
0.748	0.474	0.778	0.405	0.608	1.592	4.209	0.819	1.350	0.109
0.808	1.035	1.495	1.666	2.111	0.041	0.238	4.305	0.110	0.626
1.688	0.226	1.742	0.641	0.028	0.238	0.091	3.935	0.315	1.043
1.917	0.288	1.165	0.837	0.445	0.731	3.092	3.532	2.659	0.575
0.291	0.013	1.713	0.511	1.474	0.409	0.834	1.080	0.603	0.972
0.252	0.141	0.323	0.081	0.060	1.286	1.312	0.428	1.068	4.364
0.044	1.367	0.741	0.167	1.770	0.102	0.114	2.043	1.136	0.388
0.483	0.749	0.886	0.067	0.186	1.343	1.111	0.720	3.046	0.530
1.201	0.656	1.931	0.474	1.016	0.723	0.705	0.167	0.077	0.045
1.199	1.199	0.104	0.704	0.344	0.962	1.377	1.265	1.694	0.007
0.456	3.667	1.029	0.643	1.202	0.053	1.237	0.625	0.649	0.091
0.900	0.972	1.065	1.402	1.689	0.694	0.046	0.606	0.803	0.074
0.401	0.584	0.858	0.629	1.033	1.705	1.857	2.217	0.495	1.371

ANSWERS TO SELECTED EXERCISES

CHAPTER 2

2.12 (b) 0.067
2.16 (b) 0.18
2.17 (a) 0.4 (b) 0.467 (c) 0.2 (d) 0.267
2.18 (a) 0.3 (b) 0.35 (c) 0.45 (d) 0.5 (e) 0.333 (f) 0.70
2.19 (a) 0.067 (b) 0.733 (c) 0.2
2.20 (a) 0.7 (b) 0.24 (c) 0.6 (d) 0.40 and 0.88
2.23 (b) 0.31 (c) 0.06 (d) 0.087
2.25 (b) 0.73
2.26 (a) 0.126 (b) 0.18
2.27 (a) 0.4 (b) 0.15 (c) Yes
2.28 (a) 0.8 (b) 0.15
2.29 (a) 0.0296 (b) 0.9998
2.30 (b) 0.05 (c) 0.5 (d) No
2.31 (a) 0.20 (b) 0.15 (c) 0.5 (d) 0.333
2.32 (a) 0.025 (b) 0.9 (c) 0.075 (d) 0.975 (e) 0.325
2.33 (a) 0.13 (b) 0.462
2.34 (a) 0.19 (b) 0.632
2.35 (a) 0.703 (b) 0.569
2.36 (a) 0.02 (b) 0.231
2.37 (a) 0.765 (b) 0.19
2.38 (a) 0.015 (b) 0.333 (c) 0.198
2.39 (a) $P(\text{fair}) = 0.1333$, $P(\text{good}) = 0.6667$, $P(\text{excellent}) = 0.2$

CHAPTER 3

3.5 (b) 22.36 (c) 1.26
3.6 (b) 0.25 (c) 0.95 (d) 0.30 (e) 0.40 (f) 19.6 yr (g) 1.46 yr
3.7 (b) 9.94 days, 1.08 days
3.8 (b) -0.1, 1.29
3.10 (a) 3.60 (b) 0.88
3.13 (a) 0.6177 (b) 0.2508 (c) 0.6331
3.14 (a) 0.2322 (b) 0.1941 (c) 0.9915
3.15 (a) 0.6517 (b) 0.2401 (c) 6
3.16 (a) 0.9961 (b) 0.0913 (c) 0.1686 (d) 0.3789
3.17 (b) 0.2639 (c) 0.5443 (d) 0.6513, 0.1969
3.19 (a) 0.5333 (b) 0.4667
3.20 (a) 0.1414 (b) 0.4525 (c) 0.0020
3.23 (a) 0.0256 (b) 0.1556 (c) 0.3472 (d) 0.7437
3.24 (b) 0.8187 (c) 0.9989 (d) 0.1802
3.28 (a) 0.25 (b) 0.333 (c) 0.667

3.29 (a) 0.3 (b) 0.125 (c) 0.25
3.35 (a) 0.0475 (b) 0.1587 (c) 0.7935 (d) 0.4706
3.36 (a) 0.9772 (b) 0.8185 (c) 0.1587 (d) $55,200 (e) $41,800
3.37 (a) 0.9918 (b) 0.1587 (c) 0.0401 (d) 0.9940 (e) 7.44
3.38 (a) Yes (b) 0.5328 (c) 0.0668 (d) 46.33
3.39 (a) 0.8854 (b) 0.199 (c) 0.0196 decrease
3.40 (a) 41,600 gal (b) 62,800 gal (c) 43,300 and 55,200 gal
3.42 (b) 1. ~ 0.90 2. ~0.62 3. ~0.39
3.44 (a) 0.6065 (b) 0.3679 (c) 0.2231
3.45 (a) 0.3085 (b) 0.4325 (c) 0.1350
3.46 (a) 0.0036 (b) 0.5027 (c) 3875
3.48 (a) 0.9332 (b) 0.8644 (c) 0.0201
3.49 (a) $P(Z > 5) \cong 0$ (b) 0.0228
3.50 (a) 0.1056
3.51 (b) 95.0

CHAPTER 4

4.3 $2880
4.4 (a) $180,000, $20,000
4.5 (a) EMV = $750,000
4.7 (c) $21, 2
4.9 (b) EMV(spend $1 million) = $250,000, EMV(spend $2 million) = $0 (c) Spend $1 million (d) $1,000,000 (e) $750,000 (f) $750,000
4.10 Indifference values:
    (a) 0.571 (b) $2,500,000
4.11 (a) Conduct raid (b) $300
4.12 Indifference values:
    (a) 75 points (b) 0.333
4.13 (a) Partial, $28,000 (b) $8000, Partial (c) $8000 (d) Yes (by $1000)
4.14 (a) A or B, $86,000 (b) $19,000 (c) $105,000, $19,000
4.15 (a) 9, $0.73 (b) 9, $0.08 (c) $0.08, $0.81
4.17 (b) 8, $0.755
4.18 (b) 8, $0.775
4.19 $250 (expected additional cost = $25)
4.20 Indifference values:
    (a) $13.89 (b) 0.833
4.21 (b) small stockpile, $30,000, −$11,000 (d) $19,000
4.22 (a) 0 (b) $650
4.23 (b) Plan 2, $320/wk (c) Plan 3, $245/wk
4.24 (a) Don't test, $0.05 (b) $0.05
4.25 (a) 0.86 (b) Don't test, $0.05 (c) $0.036
4.26 (b) Test, $70,000 (c) $230,000
4.27 (b) $25,400
4.28 (a) 0.566
4.29 (c) $0 \le p \le 0.27$, Minimum; $0.27 \le p \le 0.50$, Partial; $0.50 \le p \le 0.80$, Full (d) Partial, $6000 (at $p = 0.80$)
4.30 (a) $x > $57,500, $x < $120,000 (b) $120,000
4.33 (a) 2000 units

4.34 (a) 5000 units (d) Yes
4.35 (b) 100,000
4.37 $125
4.38 (a) $791 (b) $1596 (c) $2791 (d) $4290
4.39 (b) $99.72 (c) $199.45 (d) $20.83 (e) $98.90
4.40 (c) Yes (d) $4047
4.41 (b) Issue card, $4104
4.42 (c) Plan 1, $225

CHAPTER 5

5.3 $400
5.6 (b) No
5.7 0.5
5.8 (a) 0.9 (b) −$400,000 (d) 0.83
5.9 (b) Minimum product line, 16.0 utiles, $23,000
5.12 (b) Don't fund project (d) >0.8
5.13 (b) $p > 0.52$
5.16 (b) ~0.35 utiles (d) Would invest
5.17 (b) $50 deductible
5.18 (b) Yes (c) No
5.20 Use low study contract effort. If prototype contract won, use high prototype contract effort
5.21 (a) Act 3 (b) Act 1 (c) Act 1 (d) Act 2
5.22 (a) Act 3 (b) Act 2 (c) Acts 2 or 3 (d) Act 3
5.23 (a) Full (b) Minimal (c) Full or Partial (d) Partial
5.24 (a) No stockpile (b) Large stockpile (c) Large stockpile (d) Large stockpile

CHAPTER 6

6.4 (b) Prob. percent defective is $0 = 0.228$; is $1 = 0.372$; is $2 = 0.299$; is $3 = 0.101$
6.5 (a) $P(20 \text{ cust./hr}) = 0.268$, $P(30 \text{ cust./hr}) = 0.501$
6.13 (d) EVSI = $24,300
6.14 (a) Make test (b) $250
6.15 $168.8
6.16 (a) Take new position (b) EVSI = $190; Yes, pay
6.17 (a) Don't use mechanic (b) Sample of 1 worthwhile
6.18 (a) Partial product line, $8000 (b) Not worthwhile
6.19 (a) Small stockpile, $19,000 (b) Up to $9500
6.22 CVSI (0 def.) = $0, CVSI (5 def.) = $54
6.23 3
6.24 (b) EOL(1) = $4000, EOL(2) = $2000; no (c) EOL(1) = $3220, EOL(2) = $2530; don't manufacture

CHAPTER 7

7.1 (b) Produce 1 unit of product 1, 3 units of product 2. Profit = $13.8 (d) Profit of product 1 > (3) × Profit of product 2

7.9 (a) 66.7 lb of ingredient 1, 33.3 lb of ingredient 2. Cost = $26.67 (b) When these costs are equal (c) No feasible solution (d) 40 lb of ingredient 1, 50 lb of ingredient 2. Cost = $25

7.18 $x_1 = 10$, $x_2 = 0$

7.19 $x_1 = 4$, $x_2 = 0$, $x_3 = 0$; or $x_1 = 0$, $x_2 = 6$, $x_3 = 0$

7.20 $x_1 = 0$, $x_2 = 2$, $x_3 = x_4 = 0$

7.22 $x_1 = 0$, $x_2 = 2$, $x_3 = 0$

7.23 $y_1 = 0$, $y_2 = 0.5$

7.24 (a) 150 standard, 60 deluxe. Profit = $3300.
   (b) Layout department has 210 hr; others have none.
   (d) Product mix same as (a); profit = $3600.
   (e) Product mix same as (a), or 300 standard only, or any solution between. Profit = $3000.

7.25 (b) 400 lb of wood shingles, 600 lb of slate shingles. $260
   (c) 800 lb of wood shingles, 400 lb of slate shingles. $280
   (d) 1200 lb.

7.26 (b) $x_1 = 10$, $x_3 = 24$, $x_4 = 19$, $x_5 = 3$, profit = $160

7.27 (d) 10 units (f) Yes

7.28 (i) 61 lb of material A, 39 lb of material C. $130.5

7.31 (b) $y_1 = 1.5$, $y_2 = 0.25$, $w = 212.5$ (c) $x_1 = 75$, $x_3 = 12.5$, $z = 212.5$

7.32 (c) $y_1 = 1$, $y_3 = -2$, $w = 10$

7.38 (b) 0 (c) 121⅓ (e) 21⅔

7.39 (b) 7 to 10 hr, 800 to 1200 lb
   (c) 300 lb of wood shingles, 700 lb of slate shingles. $270
   (d) Decrease $4 (e) Wood — $0.15 to $0.30/lb; slate — $0.2 to $0.4/lb
   (f) $290

7.40 (b) Wiring and Assembly Departments
   (d) Layout: ≥800 hr; Wiring: 1200 to 1575 hr
      Assembly: 1125 to 1400 hr
   (f) Standard: 125 units, deluxe: 70 units. $3350
   (g) Standard: 105 units, deluxe: 72 units. $3210
   (h) $25 to $37.5

7.41 (c) 25 to 36.25 lb
   (d) Ingredient 1: 86.67 lb, ingredient 2: 13.33 lb, $25.67
   (e) Ingredient 1: ≥ $0.20, ingredient 2: ≤ $0.35 (f) $25.33

CHAPTER 8

8.6 (a)

From	A	A	B	B	C	C	C
To	3	4	1	3	1	2	5
Units	50	350	150	450	150	200	350

Surcharge = $1.215/hr

(b)

From	A	A	B	B	C	C	C
To	3	4	1	3	1	2	5
Units	50	350	150	450	150	200	350

Surcharge = $1.165/hr

8.7 Optimal solution: total surcharge = $1.075/hr

From	A	A	B	B	C	C	C
To	3	4	1	3	2	4	5
Units	200	200	300	300	200	150	350

8.8 Optimal solution (non-unique): total profit = $988,000

From	A	B	B	C	D	D
To	T	S	T	S	R	T
1000s bbl	150	100	80	220	100	140

8.10 (a) VAM solution: cost = $1904

From	Denver	Denver	Detroit	Houston	Houston	Houston
To	Portland	Newark	Newark	Portland	Atlanta	Waco
Units	9	8	20	1	14	15

Mutually preferred flows solution: cost = $1925

From	Denver	Denver	Detroit	Houston	Houston	Houston
To	Portland	Newark	Newark	Atlanta	Waco	Newark
Units	10	7	20	14	15	1

(b) Optimal solution: cost = $1904 (VAM initial solution)

8.11 For optimal solution, see Exercise 8.13: cost = $98

(a) VAM solution: cost = $99

From	1	1	2	3	3	3
To	4	6	6	5	6	7
Units	1	1	5	3	1	2

(b) Mutually preferred flows solution: cost = $108

From	1	1	2	2	2	3
To	4	7	5	6	7	6
Units	1	1	3	1	1	6

8.13 (a) $9/unit. 3 cars (b) $2 increase, unlimited decrease. 3 cars (c) $4 increase, route (2, 7); $1 decrease, route (1, 6)

8.14 (a) More than $500 per 1000 bbl. Ship 80 units, drop route (B, T)
(b) Increase by $200 per 1000 bbl, route (B, dummy); no decrease, route (A, R)
(c) Increase by $500 per 1000 bbl, route (C, T);
decrease by $400 per 1000 bbl, route (A, S)

8.15 Initial solution: cost = $3900

From	A	B	C	C	C
To	D	F	E	F	G
Units	100	200	150	50	150

Optimal solution: cost = $3200

From	A	B	B	C	C	C
To	E	E	F	D	F	G
Units	100	50	150	100	100	150

8.18 Optimal solution: cost = $25,150

From	A	A	B	B	A(overtime)	B(overtime)
To	3	4	1	3	4	2
Units	150	250	200	200	50	250

8.19 Optimal solution: cost = $2271

From	1	1	2	2
To	1	2	2	3
Units	120	40	40	100

8.20 (a) Optimal solution: cost = $2151

From	1	2	2
To	1	2	3
Units	120	40	100

(b) Optimal solution: cost = $2157

From	1	2	2
To	1	2	3
Units	120	80	60

8.21 Optimal solution: cost = $203,000

Shift	1	2	1	1	2	2	1	2
Produce in quarter	1	1	2	3	3	3	4	4
For use in quarter	1	1	2	3	3	4	4	4
1000s of pounds	600	100	500	600	200	100	600	500

8.22 Optimal solution: cost = $4000

Produce in month*	0	0	0	1	2	3	3	4
For use in month	1	2	4	1	2	3	4	4
Units		200	400	400	3000	3000	2800	200	3000

*0 represents initial inventory

8.26 Optimal solution: profit = $16,800

Plant	1	1	2	2	3	3
Warehouse	1	2	1	4	1	3
Units	600	1000	300	900	400	1000

8.27 Optimal solution: profit = $1420

Plant	1	1	2	2
Customer	Jones	Smith	Smith	Young
Units	40	40	30	50

8.28 (b) Optimal solution: cost = $97

From location	1	1	2	3	3	3
To location	3	4	6	5	6	7
Number of cars	1	1	5	3	2	2

8.29 (c) Optimal solution: cost = $3050

From	A	B	C	C	C	D
To	E	F	D	F	G	E
Units	100	200	150	50	150	50

8.32 (a) Optimal solution: cost = $52,600

Company	A	B	C	D
Program	3	2	1	4

(b) Reduce bid by $400.

Company	A	B	C	D
Program	3	4	1	2

8.34 (a) Optimal solution: cost = $51,400

Company	A	B	C	E
Program	2	4	1	3

8.35 (a)

Inspector	U	V	W	X	Y
Product	P	Q	S	R	T
or Product	S	T	Q	P	R

There are additional optimal solutions also, since there are at least two zeroes in every row and column.

(b) Mean fraction defective = 0.5 percent

8.36 (a)

Student	Jones	Green	Smith	Adams
Major	D	A	C	B

Overall grade point average = 3.5

(b) Overall grade point average = 3.525

8.37

Operator	A	B	C	D
Task	IV	III	II	I
or Task	III	IV	II	I

There are also additional optimal solutions, all with an estimated total time of 21 hours.

8.38 (a) Optimal solution: cost = $3860

Team	1	2	3
Job	B	C	A

(b) Optimal solution: profit = $2040

8.39 Optimal solution: total layover time = 34 hr

Based in	Los Angeles			Houston		
Flights	2, 24	3, 25	6, 21	26, 1	22, 4	23, 5
Layover time, hr	4	6	4	9	4	7

CHAPTER 9

9.2

From city B to city:	A	C	D	E	F	G
Shortest distance, mi	270	260	440	500	690	930

9.3

From city G to city:	A	B	C	D	E	F
Shortest travel time, hr	17	12	9	13	7	5

9.4

From plant A to plant:	B	C	D	E	F	G	H	I
Relative cost	4	7	6	7	9	15	18	22

9.5 Islands to connect: AB,   AC,   CD,   DE,   EF

Total length of cable = 240 miles

9.6 (a) Villages to connect: AB,   AC,   AE,   CD

Road network length = 23.8 km

(b) $370,000

9.8 Maximal flow = 60,000 gallons/hr

Flows: A to B — 10,000 gal/hr, A to C — 35,000 gal/hr,
    A to D — 15,000 gal/hr, B to C — 15,000 gal/hr,
    D to B — 5,000 gal/hr, D to C — 10,000 gal/hr

9.9 (a) Optimal solution is non-unique. 65,000 bbl

Flows: X to A — 20,000 bbl, X to B — 20,000 bbl, X to C — 25,000 bbl
    A to B — 8,000 bbl, A to D — 12,000 bbl, B to D — 30,000 bbl,
    B to E — 8,000 bbl, C to B — 10,000 bbl, C to E — 15,000 bbl,
    D to E — 2,000 bbl, D to Y — 40,000 bbl, E to Y — 25,000 bbl

(b) 10,000 bbl

Route: X-B-E-Y — 5,000 bbl, X-C-B-E-Y — 5,000 bbl or X-B-D-E-Y — 5,000 bbl,
    X-C-B-D-E-Y — 5,000 bbl

9.10 22 paths. There are a number of optimal solutions.

From center	5	5	5	5	3	4	4	6	6
To center	2	3	4	6	2	2	3	2	4
Paths	6	4	2	10	6	7	2	3	7

or

From center	5	5	5	5	3	1	4	4	6	6
To center	2	3	4	6	2	2	1	2	2	4
Paths	6	4	2	10	4	2	2	7	3	7

9.11 (a) 6000 gallons/hr

(b) There are a number of optimal solutions.

From location	A	A	A	B	C	C	C	D	D	E	F	G
To location	B	C	D	E	D	E	F	F	G	H	H	H
100s of gal/hr	16	28	16	16	6	9	13	6	16	25	19	16

9.15

From reservoir	A	A	A	B	B	C
To reservoir	B	C	D	C	D	D
1000s of gal/hr	55	60	50	55	50	50

9.16 (a)

From refinery	1	1	1	2	2	3
To refinery	2	3	4	3	4	4
Daily flow, bbl	650	760	760	650	650	830

(b) 110 bbl/day

9.17 (a)

From refinery	1	1	1	2	2	3
To refinery	2	3	4	3	4	4
Daily flow, bbl	340	760	520	340	340	520

(c) Many possible solutions, such as:

From refinery	1	1	3
To refinery	3	4	4
Daily flow, bbl	280	240	280

9.19 (b) Project completion time = 11.5 weeks. Critical path: D-E-F-G-I

Task	A	B	C	H
Slack, days	2	2	3	3

(c) No. There are now two critical paths.

9.20 (b) Project completion time = 16 months. Critical path: C-D-G-H

Task	A	B	E	F
Slack, months	1	3	1	2

9.24 (a) Expected completion time = 36.7 days. Critical path: A-B-C-D-H-I-J

(b) April 6

9.25 (a) Expected completion time = 23.4 months
Critical path: A-B-C-D-F-H-K

Activity	E	G	I	J
Slack, months	8.4	8.4	11.2	11.2

(b)

Completion time, mo	21	24	27
Probability	0.097	0.626	0.974

9.26 $8800. Activities shortened: A, E, F, H

9.27 (a)

Activity	A	C	D	G
Months shortened	1	1	1	0.3

Completion time = 13.7 months

(b)

Activity	A	C	D	G	H
Months shortened	1	1	1	1	0.1

Completion time = 12.9 months

9.28   Task   B   D   F or G
        Additional man-days   2   5   2
        Project completion time = 8 weeks

CHAPTER 10

10.5   Parlor   1   2   3   4
        Staff size   3   3   3   3
        Profit = $510/day

10.6   Product   1   2   3   1   2   3
                                            or
        Allocation, $1000s 4   7   4   5   6   4
        Profit = $1520

10.7   Month   1   2   3
        Units to be ordered   5   0   4
        Cost = $51

10.8   Item   1   2   3   1   2   3
                                   or
        Units   1   1   1   3   0   0
        Optimal solutions yield a profit of $15 for a weight of 9 lb.

10.9 (b) Component 1   2   3
          Units   3   1   3
          Reliability = 0.8687

10.11 (b) District   1   2   3   4
           Legislators   2   3   4   1

10.12 (b) Replace once, either after 4 years or after 5 years.
          Total cost = $1940

10.18 (b) Assign 12 in period 2 and 13 in period 3.
          If number available in period 3 is: 13   12
          Assign in period 4:   12   11
          Expected cost = $476

10.19 Choose flight 1A; if Salt Lake City reached, choose flight 2B; if Denver reached, choose flight 3A. No other choices exist. Probability of reaching Miami = 0.859.

10.20 $25,400

10.21 (a) Keep if prize $\geqslant$\$1000. EMV = \$1451.
      (b) Keep if initial prize $\geqslant$\$2000. If trade made, keep if prize $\geqslant$\$1000. EMV = \$1860.8.
      (c) Keep if initial prize $\geqslant$\$2000. If trade made, keep if prize $\geqslant$\$2000. If second trade made, keep if prize $\geqslant$\$1000. EMV = \$2188.64.
      (d) Keep if initial prize = \$5000. If trade made, keep if prize $\geqslant$\$2000. If second trade made, keep if prize $\geqslant$\$2000. If third trade made, keep if prize $\geqslant$\$1000. EMV = \$2469.78.

CHAPTER 11

11.3 (a) 1000 gal (b) Every 3 mo (c) $8200
11.4 (a) 310 units; every 9 days (b) $1550 (c) 8 percent (d) $1551
11.7 (a) 5000 (b) 50 days between runs; 25 days (c) $1000
11.9 1155 gal, $8173

11.10 (a) 10 days (b) 400 (c) $1200 (d) $3000 (e) $8.89/yr
11.11 (a) 15 percent (b) $600; 1335 units
11.12 (a) 15 units; $1200 (b) 20 units; 4.2 percent (c) Both up 20 percent (d) Up 22 percent
11.14 4000 gal; $8005
11.15 (a) 500 units; $7863
11.18 (a)

Quarter	4th	1st	2nd	3rd
1000s of gal	160	0	0	70

   (b) Total cost = $133,100; savings = $700
11.19

Week	2	5	7
Units produced	78	89	68

   Cost = $12,168
11.20

Week	2	4
Units produced	46	189

   Cost = $11,862
11.21 (a) <$1.25 (b) >$5
11.24 (a) 80 (b) 58 (c) $286.5 per set of 4 tires (d) $88.5 per set of 4 tires
11.25 (a) 1 (b) $28.8 (c) ⩽$114.7
11.26 (a) 3 (b) 2

(c) Max. salvage value, $	0.0152	0.0467	0.0565	0.0593	0.06
Optimal no. of papers	2	3	4	5	6

11.27 (a) $1400 (b) 0 spares; $900
11.28

Optimal no. of spares	0	1	2
Value of e, $1000s	⩽5	5 to 20	⩾20

11.29 (a) 9 (b) 8 (c) 8 (d) If $f ⩽ 0.734$, stock 9. If not, stock 8.
11.30 (a) 28 dozen (b) 38 dozen
11.31 (a) 104 (b) 1. $58.5 2. $28.6
11.32 (a) 1243 (c) 1175
11.36 883
11.37 110, reorder level = 22
11.38 0.985
11.39 Indifference points are as follows:

Optimal order point	15	16	17	18	19	20	21	22	23	24	25	26	27	28
Penalty cost, $		1.03	1.27	1.64	2.19	3.06	4.4	6.6	10.4	16.7	28	50	92	183	275

11.40 (a) 67 units (b) 0.92

CHAPTER 12

12.3 (a) 0.40 (b) 0.216 (c) 1.5 (d) 22.5 min
12.4 (a) 24 min (b) 30 min (c) 3.2 (d) 4.0 (e) 0.2
12.5 (a) 4.5 min (b) 6.75 min (c) 0.9
12.6 (a) 2.6 min (b) 0.533 (c) 4.6 min
12.7 (a) 1.23 (b) 1.37 hr (c) 25 percent (d) 1.25 hr
12.8 (a) 0.75 min (c) 1.6 customers/min (d) 2.57 customers/min
12.9 Don't merge (W = 2.0 hr if merged, 1.67 hr if not)
12.10 (a) 0.46 (b) 0.099 (c) 0.9 (d) 10.0 min
12.11 (a) 0.102 (b) 9.6 min (c) 0.084

12.14 (a) 1.06 hr (individual W values must be weighted) (b) 0.91 hr, Yes
12.15 38.3/hr
12.16 (a) 4 (b) 5.4 min (c) 1.3 min
12.17 (a) 4 (b) 0.19 min (c) 0.76 (d) 0.059 (e) 0.124
12.18 (a) 0.092 (b) 0.150; 12.75/hr (c) 2.13
12.19 (a) 0.206 (b) 2.38 (c) 0.60 (d) 0.346
12.20 (a) 24.3/hr (b) 0.47 min (c) 0.189
12.21 (a) 0.011 (b) 1.265 (c) 0.84 min (d) 0.505
12.23 (a) 3600 (b) 4050
12.24 3940
12.25 (a) $55.8 (b) $43.2
12.26 (a) $30 (b) $35.7
12.27 (a) 4 (b) 5.4 min (c) $37.0 (d) $40.1
12.28 (a) 4 (b) 0.7
12.29 Either one. Both cost $200/day.
12.30 (a) $641/mo (b) $164
12.31 3 (expected cost = $89.84)
12.32 4 (expected cost = $93.07)
12.33 Self-service operation (incremental profit of $42.4/hr vs. $38.8/hr for current operation)
12.34 Type B (total relevant cost: A — $27.5/hr, B — $25.63/hr, C — $30/hr)
12.36 $15.75 to $65/hr
12.37 21.5 to 30.2 min
12.38 (a) $0 to $0.68/hr (b) $0.68 to $6.8/hr (c) $6.8 to $29.6/hr
12.39 (a) 1.86 to 2.96/min (b) 2.96 to 4.11/min (c) 4.11 to 5.28/min
12.40 (a) $0 to $2/hr (b) $2 to $6/hr (c) $6 to $12/hr (d) $12 to $20/hr (e) $20 to $30/hr

CHAPTER 13

13.6 (b) 2nd qtr — 46 percent, 3rd qtr. — 39.2 percent, 1st qtr — 37.84 percent
13.7 (b) Magazine A: 1 yr — 0.70, 2 yr — 0.55, 3 yr — 0.475
     (c) Magazine A: 1 yr — 0.20, 2 yr — 0.30, 3 yr — 0.35
13.8 (a) 1 yr: Asst. — 0.375, Assoc. — 0.28, Full — 0.345   2 yr: Asst. — 0.35475,
     Assoc. — 0.2615, Full — 0.38375
     (b) $18,200 (c) $20,819 (d) 0.288 ($753)
13.9 (c) $\begin{bmatrix} 0.3632 & 0.1664 & 0.1344 & 0.3360 \\ 0.2760 & 0.1136 & 0.0896 & 0.5208 \\ 0.2296 & 0.0864 & 0.0560 & 0.6280 \\ 0.2063 & 0.0732 & 0.0420 & 0.6785 \end{bmatrix}$
13.11 (a) Older text — 0.375
13.12 Asst. — 0.286, Assoc. — 0.143, Full — 0.571
13.13 City A — 0.257, city B — 0.143, city C — 0.600
13.17 (a) 3.33 (b) 3.89
13.18 (a) 10 (b) 15 (c) 5
13.19 (a) 6.67 (b) 7.78 (c) 0.60
13.20 (a) 3.0 (b) 1.7
13.21 (a) 1.82 (b) 0.55

13.22 (b) 1.22 wk (c) 0.167 (d) $75
13.23 (b) 13.3 mo (c) 0.67
13.25 (b) 5.0 (c) 3.33 (d) $120 ($1000 every 8.33 mo) (e) Yes. $11.22/mo (cost is $1450 every 13.33 mo)
13.26 (a, Asst. — 0.4, Assoc. — 0.2, Full — 0.4 (b) Yes. Annual savings = $686 per faculty member (c) $3715
13.27 Expected profit for new prospect = $3.71; expected profit for interested prospect = $11.41. Selling aids not worthwhile.

CHAPTER 14

14.6 (c) Expected value = 4.2
14.8 Expected time for activity A = 7.0 days
14.12 (b) Theoretical probability = 0.813
14.15 (d) Expected time = 29.32 min
14.17 (a) $94,300

SELECTED REFERENCES

QUANTITATIVE METHODS IN BUSINESS—*GENERAL*

Bierman, H., C. P. Bonini, and *W. H. Hausman,* **Quantitative Analysis for Business Decisions,** 4th Ed. Homewood, Ill.: Richard D. Irwin, Inc., 1973.

Horowitz, I., **An Introduction to Quantitative Business Analysis,** 2nd Ed. New York: McGraw-Hill Book Company, 1972.

Lapin, L., **Quantitative Methods for Business Decisions.** New York: Harcourt Brace Jovanovich, Inc., 1976.

Levin, R. and *C. Kirkpatrick,* **Quantitative Approaches to Management,** 3rd Ed. New York: McGraw-Hill Book Company, 1975.

PROBABILITY AND DECISION MAKING *(CHAPTERS 2–6)*

Chou, Y., **Probability and Statistics for Decision Making.** New York: Holt, Rinehart and Winston, Inc., 1972.

Dyckman, T. R., S. Smidt, and *A. K. McAdams,* **Management Decision Making under Uncertainty.** New York: The Macmillan Company, 1969.

Hamburg, M., **Statistical Analysis for Decision Making.** New York: Harcourt, Brace and World, Inc., 1970.

Hays, W. L. and *R. L. Winkler,* **Statistics: Probability, Inference and Decision,** 2nd Ed. New York: Holt, Rinehart and Winston, Inc., 1975.

Schlaifer, R., **Analysis of Decisions under Uncertainty.** New York: McGraw-Hill Book Company, 1969.

Willis, R. E. and *N. L. Chervany,* **Statistical Analysis and Modeling for Management Decision-making.** Belmont, Calif.: Wadsworth Publishing Company, Inc., 1974.

OPERATIONS RESEARCH—*GENERAL (CHAPTERS 7–14)*

Eck, R. D., **Operations Research for Business.** Belmont, Calif.: Wadsworth Publishing Company, Inc., 1976.

Hartley, R. V., **Operations Research: A Managerial Emphasis.** Pacific Palisades, Calif.: Goodyear Publishing Company, Inc., 1976.

Hillier, F. S. and *G. J. Lieberman,* **Introduction to Operations Research,** 2nd Ed. San Francisco: Holden-Day, Inc., 1974.

Shamblin, J. E., and *G. T. Stevens, Jr.,* **Operations Research—A Fundamental Approach.** New York: McGraw-Hill Book Company, 1974.

Taha, H. A. **Operations Research: An Introduction.** New York: The Macmillan Company, 1971.

Wagner, H. B., **Principles of Operations Research with Applications to Managerial Decisions,** 2nd Ed. Englewood Cliffs, N.J.: Prentice-Hall, Inc., 1975. (Contains a very extensive bibliography on topical areas in operations research)

LINEAR PROGRAMMING MODELS *(CHAPTERS 7 AND 8)*

Daellenbach, H. G. and *E. J. Bell,* **User's Guide to Linear Programming.** Englewood Cliffs, N.J.: Prentice-Hall, Inc., 1970.

Dantzig, G. B., **Linear Programming and Extensions.** Princeton, N.J.: Princeton University Press, 1963.

Driebeek, N. J., **Applied Linear Programming.** Reading, Mass.: Addison-Wesley Publishing Company, 1969.

Kim, C., **Introduction to Linear Programming.** New York: Holt, Rinehart and Winston, Inc., 1972.

Kwak, N. K., **Mathematical Programming with Business Applications.** New York: McGraw-Hill Book Company, 1973.

Simmons, D. M., **Linear Programming for Operations Research.** San Francisco: Holden-Day, Inc., 1972.

Strum, J. E., **Introduction to Linear Programming.** San Francisco: Holden-Day, Inc., 1972.

NETWORK MODELS *(CHAPTER 9)*

Ford, L. R., Jr. and *D. R. Fulkerson,* **Flows in Networks.** Princeton, N.J.: Princeton University Press, 1962.

Hu, T. C., **Integer Programming and Network Flows.** Reading, Mass.: Addison-Wesley Publishing Company, 1969.

Plane, D. R. and *C. McMillan, Jr.,* **Discrete Optimization: Integer Programming and Network Analysis for Management Decisions.** Englewood Cliffs, N.J.: Prentice-Hall, Inc., 1971.

DYNAMIC PROGRAMMING *(CHAPTER 10)*

Bellman, R. E., **Dynamic Programming.** Princeton, N.J.: Princeton University Press, 1957.

Bellman, R. E. and *S. E. Dreyfus,* **Applied Dynamic Programming.** Princeton, N.J.: Princeton University Press, 1962.

Denardo, E. V., **Dynamic Programming: Theory and Application.** Englewood Cliffs, N.J.: Prentice-Hall, Inc., 1975.

Nemhauser, G. L., **Introduction to Dynamic Programming.** New York: John Wiley and Sons, Inc., 1966.

White, D. J., **Dynamic Programming.** San Francisco: Holden-Day, Inc., 1969.

INVENTORY MODELS *(CHAPTER 11)*

Buchan, J. and *E. Koenigsberg,* **Scientific Inventory Management.** Englewood Cliffs, N.J.: Prentice-Hall, Inc., 1963.

Hadley, G. and *T. M. Whitin,* **Analysis of Inventory Systems.** Englewood Cliffs, N.J.: Prentice-Hall, Inc., 1963.

Naddor, E., **Inventory Systems.** New York: John Wiley and Sons, Inc., 1966.

Prichard, J. W. and *R. H. Eagle,* **Modern Inventory Management.** New York: John Wiley and Sons, Inc., 1965.

QUEUEING MODELS *(CHAPTER 12)*

Cox, D. R. and *W. L. Smith,* **Queues.** New York: John Wiley and Sons, Inc., 1961.

Gross D. and *C. M. Harris,* **Fundamentals of Queueing Theory.** New York: John Wiley and Sons, 1974.

Lee, A., **Applied Queueing Theory.** New York: St. Martin's Press, 1966.

Riordan, J., **Stochastic Service Systems.** New York: John Wiley and Sons, Inc., 1962.

Saaty, T. L. **Elements of Queueing Theory with Applications.** New York: McGraw-Hill Book Company, 1961.

SIMULATION MODELS *(CHAPTER 14)*

Emshoff, J. R. and *R. L. Sisson,* **Design and Use of Computer Simulation Models.** New York: The Macmillan Company, 1970.

Fishman, G. S., **Concepts and Methods in Discrete Event Digital Simulation.** New York: John Wiley and Sons, 1973.

Maisel, H. and *G. Gnugnoli,* **Simulation of Discrete Stochastic Systems.** Chicago: Science Research Associates, Inc., 1972.

Reitman, J., **Computer Simulation Applications.** New York: John Wiley and Sons, Inc., 1971.

Schmidt, J. W. and *R. E. Taylor,* **Simulation and Analysis of Industrial Systems.** Homewood, Ill.: Richard D. Irwin, Inc., 1970.

MARKOV ANALYSIS *(CHAPTER 13)*

Howard, R. A., **Dynamic Probabilistic Systems,** Volume I: **Markov Models;** Volume II: **Semi-Markov and Decision Processes.** New York: John Wiley and Sons, 1971.

Howard, R. A., **Dynamic Programming and Markov Processes.** Cambridge, Mass.: The Massachusetts Institute of Technology Press, 1960.

INDEX